Authors' acknowledgments

Many people contributed to the development of *Four Corners*. The authors and publisher would like to particularly thank the following **reviewers**:

Nele Noe, **Academy for Educational Development, Qatar Independent Secondary School for Girls**, Doha, Qatar; Yuan-hsun Chuang, **Soo Chow University**, Taipei, Taiwan; Celso Frade and Sonia Maria Baccari de Godoy, **Associaçao Alumni**, São Paulo, Brazil; Pablo Stucchi, **Antonio Raimondi School** and **Instituto San Ignacio de Loyola**, Lima, Peru; Kari Miller, **Binational Center**, Quito, Ecuador; Alex K. Oliveira, **Boston University**, Boston, MA, USA; Elisabeth Blom, **Casa Thomas Jefferson**, Brasilia, Brazil; Henry Grant, **CCBEU – Campinas**, Campinas, Brazil; Maria do Rosário, **CCBEU – Franca**, Franca, Brazil; Ane Cibele Palma, **CCBEU Inter Americano**, Curitiba, Brazil; Elen Flavia Penques da Costa, **Centro de Cultura Idiomas – Taubate**, Taubate, Brazil; Inara Lúcia Castillo Couto, **CEL LEP – São Paulo**, São Paulo, Brazil; Geysa de Azevedo Moreira, **Centro Cultural Brasil Estados Unidos (CCBEU Belém)**, Belém, Brazil; Sonia Patricia Cardoso, **Centro de Idiomas Universidad Manuela Beltrán**, Barrio Cedritos, Colombia; Geraldine Itiago Losada, **Centro Universitario Grupo Sol (Musali)**, Mexico City, Mexico; Nick Hilmers, **DePaul University**, Chicago, IL, USA; Monica L. Montemayor Menchaca, **EDIMSA**, Metepec, Mexico; Angela Whitby, **Edu-Idiomas Language School**, Cholula, Puebla, Mexico; Mary Segovia, **El Monte Rosemead Adult School**, Rosemead, CA, USA; Dr. Deborah Aldred, **ELS Language Centers, Middle East Region**, Abu Dhabi, United Arab Emirates; Leslie Lott, **Embassy CES**, Ft. Lauderdale, FL, USA; M. Martha Lengeling, **Escuela de Idiomas**, Guanajuato, Mexico; Pablo Frias, **Escuela de Idiomas UNAPEC**, Santo Domingo, Dominican Republic; Tracy Vanderhoek, **ESL Language Center**, Toronto, Canada; Kris Vicca and Michael McCollister, **Feng Chia University**, Taichung, Taiwan; Flávia Patricia do Nascimento Martins, **First Idiomas**, Sorocaba, Brazil; Andrea Taylor, **Florida State University in Panama**, Panamá, Panama; Carlos Lizárraga González, **Grupo Educativo Angloamericano**, Mexico City, Mexico; Dr. Martin Endley, **Hanyang University**, Seoul, Korea; Mauro Luiz Pinheiro, **IBEU Ceará**, Ceará, Brazil; Ana Lúcia da Costa Maia de Almeida, **IBEU Copacabana**, Copacabana, Brazil; Ana Lucia Almeida, Elisa Borges, **IBEU Rio**, Rio de Janeiro, Brazil; Maristela Silva, **ICBEU Manaus**, Manaus, Brazil; Magaly Mendes Lemos, **ICBEU São José dos Campos**, São José dos Campos, Brazil; Augusto Pelligrini Filho, **ICBEU São Luis**, São Luis, Brazil; Leonardo Mercado, **ICPNA**, Lima, Peru; Lucia Rangel Lugo, **Instituto Tecnológico de San Luis Potosí**, San Luis Potosí, Mexico; Maria Guadalupe Hernández Lozada, **Instituto Tecnológico de Tlalnepantla**, Tlalnepantla de Baz, Mexico; Greg Jankunis, **International Education Service**, Tokyo, Japan; Karen Stewart, **International House Veracruz**, Veracruz, Mexico; George Truscott, **Kinki University**, Osaka, Japan; Bo-Kyung Lee, **Hankuk University of Foreign Studies**, Seoul, Korea; Andy Burki, **Korea University, International Foreign Language School**, Seoul, Korea; Jinseo Noh, **Kwangwoon University**, Seoul, Korea; Nadezhda Nazarenko, **Lone Star College**, Houston, TX, USA; Carolyn Ho, **Lone Star College-Cy-Fair**, Cypress, TX, USA; Alice Ya-fen Chou, **National Taiwan University of Science and Technology**, Taipei, Taiwan; Gregory Hadley, **Niigata University of International and Information Studies, Department of Information Culture**, Niigata-shi, Japan; Raymond Dreyer, **Northern Essex Community College**, Lawrence, MA, USA; Mary Keter Terzian Megale, **One Way Línguas-Suzano**, São Paulo, Brazil; Jason Moser, **Osaka Shoin Joshi University**, Kashiba-shi, Japan; Bonnie Cheeseman, **Pasadena Community College** and **UCLA American Language Center**, Los Angeles, CA, USA; Simon Banha, **Phil Young's English School**, Curitiba, Brazil; Oh Jun Il, **Pukyong National University**, Busan, Korea; Carmen Gehrke, **Quatrum English Schools**, Porto Alegre, Brazil; Atsuko K. Yamazaki, **Shibaura Institute of Technology**, Saitama, Japan; Wen hsiang Su, **Shi Chien University, Kaohsiung Campus**, Kaohsiung, Taiwan; Richmond Stroupe, **Soka University, World Language Center**, Hachioji, Tokyo, Japan; Lynne Kim, **Sun Moon University (Institute for Language Education)**, Cheon An City, Chung Nam, Korea; Hiroko Nishikage, **Taisho University**, Tokyo, Japan; Diâna Peña Munoz and Zaira Kuri, **The Anglo**, Mexico City, Mexico; Alistair Campbell, **Tokyo University of Technology**, Tokyo, Japan; Song-won Kim, **TTI (Teacher's Training Institute)**, Seoul, Korea; Nancy Alarcón, **UNAM FES Zaragoza Language Center**, Mexico City, Mexico; Laura Emilia Fierro López, **Universidad Autónoma de Baja California**, Mexicali, Mexico; María del Rocío Domíngeuz Gaona, **Universidad Autónoma de Baja California**, Tijuana, Mexico; Saul Santos Garcia, **Universidad Autónoma de Nayarit**, Nayarit, Mexico; Christian Meléndez, **Universidad Católica de El Salvador**, San Salvador, El Salvador; Irasema Mora Pablo, **Universidad de Guanajuato**, Guanajuato, Mexico; Alberto Peto, **Universidad de Oxaca**, Tehuantepec, Mexico; Carolina Rodriguez Beltan, **Universidad Manuela Beltrán, Centro Colombo Americano**, and **Universidad Jorge Tadeo Lozano**, Bogotá, Colombia; Nidia Milena Molina Rodriguez, **Universidad Manuela Beltrán** and **Universidad Militar Nueva Granada**, Bogotá, Colombia; Yolima Perez Arias, **Universidad Nacional de Colombia**, Bogota, Colombia; Héctor Vázquez García, **Universidad Nacional Autónoma de Mexico**, Mexico City, Mexico; Pilar Barrera, **Universidad Técnica de Ambato**, Ambato, Ecuador; Deborah Hulston, **University of Regina**, Regina, Canada; Rebecca J. Shelton, **Valparaiso University, Interlink Language Center**, Valparaiso, IN, USA; Tae Lee, **Yonsei University**, Seodaemun-gu, Seoul, Korea; Claudia Thereza Nascimento Mendes, **York Language Institute**, Rio de Janeiro, Brazil; Jamila Jenny Hakam, **ELT Consultant**, Muscat, Oman; Stephanie Smith, **ELT Consultant**, Austin, TX, USA.

The authors would also like to thank the Four Corners editorial, production, and new media teams, as well as the Cambridge University Press staff and advisors around the world for their contributions and tireless commitment to quality.

Scope and sequence

LEVEL 3B	Learning outcomes	Grammar	Vocabulary
Unit 7 Pages 63–72			
Personalities **A** *You're extremely curious.* **B** *In my opinion, . . .* **C** *We've been friends for six years.* **D** *What is your personality?*	Students can . . . ☑ talk about personality traits ☑ give an opinion ☑ ask for agreement ☑ describe people's personalities ☑ talk about their personality	Adverbs modifying adjectives and verbs Present perfect with *for* and *since*	Personality traits More personality traits
Unit 8 Pages 73–82			
The environment **A** *Going green* **B** *I'd rather not say.* **C** *What will happen?* **D** *Finding solutions*	Students can . . . ☑ discuss environmental problems ☑ give an approximate answer ☑ avoid answering ☑ talk about future possibilities ☑ discuss solutions to problems	Quantifiers First conditional	Environmental impacts Tips to help the environment
Unit 9 Pages 83–92			
Relationships **A** *Healthy relationships* **B** *I'm really sorry.* **C** *That can't be the problem.* **D** *Getting advice*	Students can . . . ☑ discuss what's important in relationships ☑ apologize and give excuses ☑ accept an apology ☑ speculate about people ☑ give advice about relationships	*It's . . .* expressions Expressions with infinitives Modals for speculating	Relationship behaviors Inseparable phrasal verbs
Unit 10 Pages 93–102			
Living your life **A** *He taught himself.* **B** *I'll give it some thought.* **C** *What would you do?* **D** *What an accomplishment!*	Students can . . . ☑ talk about themselves and their experiences ☑ advise against something ☑ consider advice ☑ talk about imaginary situations ☑ ask and talk about accomplishments	Reflexive pronouns Second conditional	Qualities for success Separable phrasal verbs
Unit 11 Pages 103–112			
Music **A** *Music trivia* **B** *The first thing you do is . . .* **C** *Music and me* **D** *Thoughts on music*	Students can . . . ☑ talk about music ☑ give instructions ☑ talk about things they've done recently ☑ talk about memorable songs	Past passive Present perfect with *yet* and *already*	Compound adjectives Verb and noun formation
Unit 12 Pages 113–122			
On vacation **A** *Travel preferences* **B** *Don't forget to . . .* **C** *Rules and recommendations* **D** *Seeing the sights*	Students can . . . ☑ discuss travel preferences ☑ ask about preferences ☑ remind someone of something ☑ talk about rules and recommendations ☑ describe their dream trip	Gerunds Modals for necessity and recommendations	Vacation activities Extreme sports

Functional language	Listening and Pronunciation	Reading and Writing	Speaking
Interactions: Giving an opinion Asking for agreement	**Listening:** Common proverbs A personality quiz **Pronunciation:** Reduction of *don't you*	**Reading:** "The Signs of the Zodiac" Descriptions **Writing:** My personality	• Interview about personality traits • *Keep talking:* Left-brain versus right-brain quiz • Discussion about personality assumptions • Information exchange about friends and their personalities • *Keep talking:* Interviews about special people and things • Guessing game to match people and their personality descriptions
Interactions: Giving an approximate answer Avoiding answering	**Listening:** A survey on grocery shopping habits Award winners for environmental work **Pronunciation:** Stress in compound nouns	**Reading:** "One-of-a-Kind Homes" An article **Writing:** A letter about an environmental issue	• Discussion about community environmental problems • *Keep talking:* "Green" quiz • Survey about water usage • Cause and effect • *Keep talking:* Possible outcomes in different situations • Solutions to environmental issues
Interactions: Apologizing Accepting an apology	**Listening:** Apologetic phone calls A radio call-in show **Pronunciation:** Sentence stress	**Reading:** "Addy's Advice" Emails **Writing:** A piece of advice	• Tips for healthy relationships • *Keep talking:* Advice for relationship problems • Role play to apologize and make excuses • Speculations about classmates • *Keep talking:* Speculations about people • Discussion about relationship problems
Interactions: Advising against something Considering advice	**Listening:** Three problems Interviews about accomplishments **Pronunciation:** Stress shifts	**Reading:** "A Walk Across Japan" An interview **Writing:** An accomplishment	• Interview about personal experiences • *Keep talking:* "Find someone who" activity about personal experiences • Role play to give and consider advice • Discussion about hypothetical situations • *Keep talking:* Interview about hypothetical situations • "Find someone who" activity about accomplishments
Interactions: Beginning instructions Continuing instructions Ending instructions	**Listening:** How things work Song dedications **Pronunciation:** Syllable stress	**Reading:** "Richie Starr" A fan site **Writing:** A music review	• Guessing game about music • *Keep talking:* Discussion about music • Information exchange with instructions • "Find someone who" activity about recent actions • *Keep talking:* "Find the differences" activity about two friends • Information exchange about songs and memories
Interactions: Asking about preferences Reminding someone of something	**Listening:** Hostel check-in A white-water rafting trip **Pronunciation:** Reduction of verbs	**Reading:** "A Taste of Cairo" A food blog **Writing:** A walking tour	• Interview about vacation activities • *Keep talking:* Comparison of travel preferences • Role play about checking into a hotel • Discussion about extreme sports • *Keep talking:* Plan for a backpacking trip • Information exchange about dream trips

Classroom language

A 🔊 Complete the conversations with the correct sentences. Then listen and check your answers.

What page are we on?	✓Excuse me. I'm very sorry I'm late.
Can you repeat that, please?	May I go to the restroom, please?
What's our homework?	Which role do you want to play?

A: _Excuse me. I'm very sorry I'm late._

B: That's OK. Next time try to arrive on time.

A: _____

B: Thirteen. We're doing the Warm-up for Unit 2.

A: _____

B: Yes. I said, "Please work with a partner."

A: _____

B: I'll be Student A. You can be Student B.

A: _____

B: No problem. Please try to be quick.

A: _____

B: Please complete the activities for Unit 2 in your workbook.

B **Pair work** Practice the conversations.

Four Corners

Jack C. Richards · David Bohlke

3B

Student's Book

CAMBRIDGE
UNIVERSITY PRESS

CAMBRIDGE
UNIVERSITY PRESS

University Printing House, Cambridge CB2 8BS, United Kingdom

One Liberty Plaza, 20th Floor, New York, NY 10006, USA

477 Williamstown Road, Port Melbourne, VIC 3207, Australia

4843/24, 2nd Floor, Ansari Road, Daryaganj, Delhi – 110002, India

79 Anson Road, #06–04/06, Singapore 079906

Cambridge University Press is part of the University of Cambridge.

It furthers the University's mission by disseminating knowledge in the pursuit of education, learning and research at the highest international levels of excellence.

www.cambridge.org
Information on this title: www.cambridge.org/9780521127547

© Cambridge University Press 2011

First published 2011
20 19 18 17 16 15 14 13 12

Printed in Spain by GraphyCems

A catalog record for this publication is available from the British Library.

ISBN 978-0-521-12753-0 Student's Book 3A with Self-study CD-ROM
ISBN 978-0-521-12754-7 Student's Book 3B with Self-study CD-ROM
ISBN 978-0-521-12748-6 Workbook 3A
ISBN 978-0-521-12750-9 Workbook 3B
ISBN 978-0-521-12747-9 Teacher's Edition 3 with Assessment Audio CD / CD-ROM
ISBN 978-0-521-12743-1 Class Audio CDs 3
ISBN 978-0-521-12712-7 Classware 3
ISBN 978-0-521-12740-0 DVD 3

For a full list of components, visit www.cambridge.org/fourcorners

Art direction, book design, photo research, and layout services: Adventure House, NYC
Audio production: CityVox, NYC
Video production: Steadman Productions

Personalities

Warm-up

A Describe the people in the picture. Where are they? What are they doing?

B What do you think each person is like? Why?

1 Vocabulary Personality traits

A Match the adjectives and the sentences. Then listen and check your answers.

모험적인
모험성이 강한 1. adventurous __h__   a. I'm interested in learning about people and things around me.
야성있는   2. ambitious __c__   b. I'm friendly, and I like people.
             3. careful __e__   c. I set high goals for myself.
궁금한, 호기심이 4. curious __a__   d. I look on the bright side of things.
      많은   5. easygoing __g__ 태평한 e. I do things slowly and with attention to detail.
낙천적인 — 6. optimistic __d__   f. I don't like to change my mind.
사교적인 외향적인 7. outgoing __b__   g. I am relaxed, and I don't worry about little things.
완고한 고집스러운 8. stubborn __f__   h. I love trying new, exciting activities.

B **Pair work** Describe people you know with each personality trait. 특성
Tell your partner.   성격적 특성

"My baby brother is very curious about the world. He wants to touch everything."

2 Language in context Are you a believer?

A Read the personality descriptions. Underline the positive personality traits, and circle the negative ones.

Are you adventurous?

Answer ten questions in this quick personality test to find out just how adventurous you are!

Click here to begin. ▶

Year of the Monkey
Born in years 1968, 1980, 1992, and 2004
You're extremely curious and outgoing. You solve problems well, but you can be stubborn about some things.

Personality Test Results
Your score: **13**
You're very adventurous, but you're not a very careful person. Try not to make decisions quickly. Take time to consider your options seriously.

Your Birth Order
As the first-born child in your family, you are a natural leader. You're pretty ambitious and like to work hard. However, you don't work well without direction.

B What about you? Do you believe the things in Part A can tell you about your personality? Why or why not?

수정하다 부사 형용사

3 Grammar 🔊 Adverbs modifying adjectives and verbs

부사 Adverbs that modify adjectives come before the adjectives.

very

You're **pretty** ambitious.

You're **extremely** curious and outgoing.

Adverbs that modify verbs go after the verb or the verb and its object.

You don't work **well** without direction.

Try not to make decisions **quickly**.

Turn to page 152 for a list of adjective and adverb formations.

A Add the adverbs to the sentences. Then compare with a partner.

slowly
1. I move ˄ in the morning. (slowly)

2. I'm serious about my studies. (really)

3. I choose my words. (carefully)

4. I arrive at important meetings. (early)

5. My friends are important to me. (extremely)

6. I work in large groups. (well)

adjective
7. I'm optimistic about the future. (very)

8. It's easy for me to share my feelings. (fairly)

B Pair work Which sentences in Part A are true for you? Tell your partner.

4 Speaking My true self

찾아 보기

www.eslflow.com/Adjective

A Pair work Interview your partner and ask questions for more information. Take notes.

MD → Nevraska

	Name: Valentin	Yes	No	Extra information
1.	Are you very adventurous?	☑	☐	long drive travel.
2.	Do you make new friends easily?	☑	☐	nice Smate
3.	Do you make decisions quickly?	☐	☑	He need take a tzme.
4.	Are you really stubborn about anything?	☐	☑	
5.	Do you work and study hard?	☑	☐	60 Hours a Week. 11 Hours a Week.
6.	Do you get to class early?	☐	☑	because at the work
7.	Are you completely honest all the time?	☑	☐	Do Best.

A: *Are you very adventurous?*
B: *Yes, I think so.*
A: *What's the most adventurous thing you've ever done?*

You tube / ZORf5dVu6MA

B Pair work Share the most interesting information with another partner.

bad
badly

5 Keep talking!

Go to page 137 for more practice.

I can talk about personality traits. ☑

B *In my opinion, . . .* ~~apron~~

1 Interactions   Opinions

A Do you always tell people exactly what you think? Do you sometimes keep your opinions to yourself?

B 🔊 Listen to the conversation. Whose opinion do you agree with more? Then practice the conversation.

Fei: Have you seen Adam's new painting?

Ralph: Yes. I saw it last weekend.

Fei: It's not very good.

Ralph: No, it's not. He asked me what I thought of it. I said I didn't think it was his best painting.

Fei: You're kidding! How did he react?

Ralph: He didn't seem very happy to hear that. But he did ask.

Fei: In my opinion, it's better to say something positive, even if you don't really mean it. Don't you agree?

Ralph: I don't know. Why do you say that?

Fei: Well, it's not always easy to hear the truth.

Ralph: I'm not so sure. I find that honesty is always the best policy.

C 🔊 Read the expressions below. Complete each box with a similar expression from the conversation. Then listen and check your answers.

Giving an opinion
In my opinion
If you ask me, . . .
Maybe it's just me, but I think . . .

Asking for agreement
_____
Don't you think so?
Don't you think that's true?

D **Pair work** Check (✓) the opinions you agree with. Then ask your partner for agreement.

1. ☐ Women are more stubborn than men.
   ☑ Men are more stubborn than women.
2. ☐ It's never OK to lie.
   ☐ It's sometimes OK to lie.
3. ☑ A small group of friends is better than a large group of friends.
   ☐ A large group of friends is better than a small group of friends.

2 Pronunciation Reduction of *don't you*

A 🔊 Listen and repeat. Notice how *don't you* is pronounced /downtʃə/.

Don't you agree?   Don't you think so?   Don't you think that's true?

B Pair work Say the opinions in Exercise 1D again. Ask your partner for agreement. Reduce *don't you* to /downtʃə/.

(handwritten margin notes) Sound A / Cat / father / Cake / I / red / gree

3 Listening A book of proverbs

A 🔊 Listen to Tina and Cal talk about proverbs. Number the proverbs from 1 to 4 in the order you hear them.

Proverbs	Does Tina agree?	Does Cal agree?
3 Practice makes perfect.	yes / no	yes / no
2 Better late than never.	yes / no	yes / no
1 Beauty is only skin deep.	yes / no	yes / no
4 Two heads are better than one.	yes / no	yes / no

B 🔊 Listen again. Do Tina and Cal agree with the proverbs in Part A? Circle *yes* or *no*.

C Pair work Do you agree with each proverb? Why or why not? Do you know any similar proverbs in your own language? Tell your partner.

(handwritten margin notes) Sound I / it ice / sit nice / Pizza

4 Speaking Don't you think so?

A What's your opinion? Circle the words.

1. People are **more** / **less** ambitious these days.
2. Young people are **more** / **less** optimistic than older people.
3. **First-born** / **Last-born** children are usually very easygoing.
4. It's **possible** / **impossible** to change your personality.

B Group work Discuss your opinions from Part A.

A: *If you ask me, people are less ambitious these days. Don't you think so?*
B: *I'm not so sure. Why do you say that?*
C: *Well, maybe it's just me, but I feel no one wants to work hard these days.*
D: *I'm not sure I really agree. In my opinion, . . .*

C Group work Think of three other topics. Share your opinions about them. Does anyone agree with you?

"In my opinion, people worry about their appearance too much. Don't you agree?"

| I can **give an opinion**. | ☑ |
| I can **ask for agreement**. | ☑ |

C We've been friends for six years.

1 Vocabulary More personality traits

A 🔊 Match the adjectives and the definitions. Then listen and check your answers.

기분좋은 →
선뜻 동의하는

서러린는
배려하는

결정적인

결단력있는

어른스러운
분별력있는

믿을수있는

1. agreeable	_c_	a. thinking of the needs of others
2. considerate	_a_	b. treating people equally or right
3. decisive	_d_	c. friendly and pleasing
4. fair	_b_	d. making decisions quickly

5. honest	_g_	e. waiting without getting annoyed
6. mature	_h_	f. doing what is expected or promised
7. patient	_e_	g. truthful
8. reliable	_f_	h. behaving in a responsible way

짜증이나 약이오른

약속

B 🔊 Complete the chart with the opposites of the words in Part A. Then listen and check your answers.

dis-	im-	in-	un-
disagreeable	impatient	immature	unfair
dislike		inconsiderate	unreliable
dishonest		indecisive	

C Pair work What are the three best personality traits to have in a friend? What are the three worst? Discuss your ideas.

2 Conversation Time to say you're sorry

반응

A 🔊 Listen to the conversation. How does Lance describe Jill's reaction?

Lance: I don't know what to do about my friend Jill. I haven't spoken to her since last weekend, and she won't answer my text messages.
Emily: Did something happen?
Lance: Yeah. I said something about her to another friend. She found out, and now I feel terrible. To be honest, it wasn't anything serious, though. I think she's being unfair and a little immature.
Emily: Well, put yourself in her shoes. Imagine a friend saying something about you behind your back.
Lance: You're probably right.
Emily: Have you been friends for a long time?
Lance: Yes. We've been friends for six years, and we used to talk all the time.
Emily: Then I think you should do the considerate thing and call to say you're sorry.

B 🔊 Listen to Lance and Jill's phone conversation. What word does Lance use to describe himself?

have + verb + 3thd faim

starting point

3 Grammar 🔊   Present perfect with *for* and *since*

Use the present perfect to describe an action that began in the past and continues to now. Use for *to specify the amount of time. Use* since *to specify the starting point.*

How long have you been friends?
We've been friends **for six years**.
We've been friends **since middle school**.
She's been upset **for several days**.
I haven't spoken to her **since last weekend**.

for	since
ten minutes	3:00
two hours	last night
several days	Monday
a month	October
six years	2009
a long time	high school
quite a while	I was a kid

A Complete the sentences with *for* or *since*. Then compare with a partner.

1. Rod has become more considerate _____Since_____ he got married.
2. Mr. and Mrs. Kim haven't had an argument _____Since_____ 1981.
3. Pete and Lisa have been on the phone _____for_____ six hours.
4. Tim hasn't spoken with his brother _____for_____ a long time.
5. Jay's been totally unreliable _____Since_____ he started his new job.
6. Inez has been in her new job _____for_____ three months.
7. Annie has become less immature _____Since_____ high school.
8. Jessica and Hector have been married _____for_____ 25 years.

B Pair work Ask and answer the questions.

1. How long have you been in this class? *I have been for 2...*
2. What haven't you done since you were a kid? *I haven't done*
3. What have you wanted to do for a long time?

4 Speaking   Three friends

A Think of three friends. Complete the chart.

	Names	How long we've been friends	Their personality traits
1.			
2.			
3.			

B Group work Tell your group about your friends. Use your information from Part A.
Ask and answer questions for more information.

A: *I've known my friend Jesse since middle school.*
B: *What's he like?*
A: *He's very honest and reliable.*

5 Keep talking!

Go to page 138 for more practice.

I can describe people's personalities. ☑

D What is your personality?

1 Reading 🔊

A When were you born? Read the description of your zodiac sign.
Does it describe you well?

cambridge.org/thesignsofthezodiac

THE SIGNS OF THE ZODIAC

CAPRICORN Dec. 22 – Jan. 20
You're ambitious and good at business, but you sometimes worry about things too much.

AQUARIUS Jan. 21 – Feb. 19
You're creative and care about other people's feelings, but you can sometimes be difficult to work with.

PISCES Feb. 20 – March 20
You're considerate, but sometimes you don't help yourself enough. You decide things quickly and rarely change your mind.

ARIES March 21 – April 20
You're optimistic and creative. You know what you want, but you sometimes have difficulty sharing your feelings.

TAURUS April 21 – May 21
You're talkative and always say exactly what you think. You work hard, but you can get angry quickly.

GEMINI May 22 – June 21
You like adventure. You love to try new things and can be very creative. You can sometimes be unreliable.

CANCER June 22 – July 22
You're very patient and want everyone to get along, but you can have difficulty showing your feelings.

LEO July 23 – Aug. 23
You're a leader. You like to give, but you don't like to ask for things. You're not very patient.

VIRGO Aug. 24 – Sept. 22
You're ambitious and want things done with no mistakes. You are not always open to new ideas.

LIBRA Sept. 23 – Oct. 22
You get along with everyone and are curious about many things. You're always looking for something better.

SCORPIO Oct. 23 – Nov. 21
You're a reliable friend, but you can have difficulty sharing your feelings. You know exactly what you want.

SAGITTARIUS Nov. 22 – Dec. 21
You're honest – sometimes *too* honest. You don't always learn from your mistakes.

B Read the chart. Complete the sentences with the correct zodiac signs.

1. A ___Leo___ hates asking for things.
2. A ___Taurus___ talks a lot.
3. A ___Capricorn___ is good at business.
4. A ___Scorpio___ wants everything perfect.
5. A ___Gemini___ is adventurous.
6. A ___Pisces___ is decisive.
7. A ___Sagittarius___ always tells the truth.
8. A ___Aquarius___ is difficult to work with.

C Group work Think of three people you know. What is each person's zodiac sign? Does it describe their personalities well? Tell your group.

2 Listening Imagine you're in a forest . . .

A 🔊 Listen to the personality test. Number the questions from 1 to 7
in the order you hear them.

☐ What's it made of? _____

☐ Who are you with? _____

☐ What do you do with it? _____

☐ How big is it? _____

☐ What kind do you see? _____

☐ What's on the table? _____

☐ Is it open or closed? _____

B 🔊 Listen again. Now take the personality test. Answer
the questions with your own ideas.

C Pair work Compare your answers. Then turn to page 153 to see
what your answers mean.

3 Writing and speaking My personality

A Think about your personality. Answer the questions.

• What are your positive personality traits? _Ambitious, friendly, creative._

• Are there any traits you'd like to change? _____

• Has your personality changed through the years? If so, how? _I was very shy since_ _high school. I changed talkative and outgoing._

B Write a paragraph about your personality, but do not write your name!
Use the model and your answers in Part A to help you.

What Am I Like?

*I'm a pretty easygoing and outgoing
person. I'm also very optimistic about
the future. I think people like to be
around me. However, I can be stubborn
sometimes. . . .*

C Group work Put your papers facedown on the table. Take one paper and read
the description. Your group guesses who it is and agrees or disagrees with the
description. Take turns.

A: *I think that paragraph describes Dana.*
B: *Yes, that's right. I wrote that one.*
C: *I agree you're easygoing, Dana, but I don't really think you're stubborn.*
B: *Yes, I am!*

I can talk about my personality. ✓

Wrap-up

1 Quick pair review

Lesson A **Test your partner!** Say an adjective. Can your partner write the adverb form correctly? Take turns. You have two minutes.

"Careful."

1. _carefully_   3. _____   5. _____
2. _____   4. _____   6. _____

Lesson B **Give your opinion!** Look at the two pieces of art. What do you think of them? Give two opinions about each one. You have two minutes.

A: *If you ask me, I think the sculpture is weird. Don't you think so?*
B: *In my opinion, it's very interesting.*

Lesson C **Brainstorm!** Make a list of positive and negative personality traits. How many do you know? You have two minutes.

Lesson D **Find out!** Who are two people that you and your partner know with the same personality traits? You have two minutes.

A: *My friend John is really stubborn. Do you know a stubborn person?*
B: *Yes. My little sister!*

2 In the real world

What's your zodiac sign? Find your horoscope from yesterday or last week in an English-language newspaper, magazine, or website. Was it true? Write about it.

> *My Horoscope*
> *I'm a Pisces. My horoscope last week said, "You are going to have a difficult day at work." It was true. I was very busy and nervous because I had to give a presentation. Luckily, it went very well!*

The environment

Warm-up

A Look at the "before" and "after" pictures. What do you see? What has changed?

B Which was the biggest improvement? Which was the easiest to do? Which was the most difficult?

A Going green

(handwritten annotations) 환경(주변의 자연) — 영향을 주다 영향 / natural biological living / 오염 / 전자 폐기물 electronic waste / 핵에너지 / 효율

1 Vocabulary Environmental impacts

A 🔊 Label the pictures with the correct words. Then listen and check your answers.

e-waste	hybrid car	organic food	pollution	solar energy
global warming	nuclear energy	plastic bags	recycling bin	wind farm

1. global warming 2. e-waste 3. solar energy 4. plastic bags 5. nuclear energy

6. wind farm 7. organic food 8. pollution 9. recycling bin 10. hybrid car

B Pair work How do the things in Part A impact the environment?

2 Language in context Green products

A 🔊 Read the ads. What makes each product "green"?

GET GREEN GOODS!   HOME **PRODUCTS** SERVICES CONTACT

Compact fluorescent lightbulbs
Regular bulbs waste too much energy, so why not use compact fluorescent lightbulbs (CFLs)? They use less energy, and you save more money in the long term.
$20 for a pack of 3

Cloth shopping bag
Who needs paper or plastic? Bring your own cloth bag to the grocery store or mall. This bag makes an important statement and is made of 100% organic cotton.
$5

Recycled toothbrush
Made from 100% recyclable plastic, each toothbrush comes with a reusable travel case. Junior toothbrushes feature endangered animals.
$20 for a pack of 6, or $18 for a pack of 6 Junior toothbrushes

Steel water bottle
Why should we use fewer plastic water bottles? Because too many of them end up in landfills and cause pollution. It's cool to carry your own reusable bottle.
$15

B What about you? Do you own any green products? Would you buy these?

구량사 (all. both 처럼 양을 나타내는 한정사)

3 Grammar ◄)) Quantifiers

Quantifiers with count nouns
We need **more** wind farms.
There are**n't enough** recycling bins.
There are **too many** bottles in landfills.
People should buy **fewer** plastic bottles.

Quantifiers with noncount nouns
You save **more** money with CFLs.
People do**n't** buy **enough** organic food.
Regular lightbulbs use **too much** energy.
People should try to use **less** plastic.

Record
incineration
소각

A Complete the opinions with quantifiers. Then compare with a partner.

1. "I think it's good that ___more___ people are buying hybrid cars. They help reduce global warming."

2. "In my opinion, there's _____ e-waste in our landfills. We need better and safer ways to recycle electronics."

쓰레기 매립지 , 쓰레기 매립

문장하게도
유감스럽게도

3. "Farmers should grow _____ organic food. I prefer food without chemicals."

4. "Unfortunately, not _____ people use solar power. Is it because it's expensive?"

5. "I feel people should use _____ nuclear energy. Isn't it dangerous?"

6. "Some people say they don't have ___enough___ time to recycle. That's crazy!"

7. "Maybe it's just me, but I think shoppers should take _____ plastic and paper bags from the supermarket. I always bring my own bags."

8. "_____ people throw plastic bottles in garbage cans. They should use recycling bins."

B Pair work Do you agree with the opinions in Part A? Why or why not? Tell your partner.

4 Pronunciation Stress in compound nouns 합성어

A ◄)) Listen and repeat. Notice how the first noun in compound nouns often receives stronger stress.

landfill   **light**bulb   **travel** case   **water** bottle

B Pair work Practice the compound nouns. Stress the first noun.

toothbrush   garbage can   recycling bin   wind farm

5 Speaking Our community

A Pair work What environmental problems does your community have? Complete the sentences.

1. There's too much _____ .
2. There isn't enough _____ .
3. We should have fewer _____ .
4. There are too many _____ .
5. There aren't enough _____ .
6. We should use less _____ .

B Group work Share your ideas with another pair. Did you identify the same problems? Which are the most important?

6 Keep talking!

Go to page **139** for more practice.

I can discuss environmental problems. ☑

B I'd rather not say.

1 Interactions · Answering and avoiding answering

A Imagine these people are asking you questions. Are there any questions they might ask you that you think are too personal and that you would not answer?

| a doctor | a friend | a neighbor | a parent | a stranger | a teacher |

B 🔊 Listen to the conversation. What question doesn't Jim answer? Then practice the conversation.

Carl: So, Jim, how's the new car?

Jim: Hey, Carl. It's great. I'm really happy with it.

Carl: It's a hybrid, isn't it?

Jim: Yeah. It causes less pollution. I'm trying to do my part to help the environment, you know?

Carl: That's great. How long have you had it?

Jim: I've only had it for a week.

Carl: Really? How many kilometers have you driven?

Jim: I'd say about 150.

Carl: So, how does it run?

Jim: Oh, it runs very well. I'll give you a ride later if you want.

Carl: OK, thanks. How much did it cost, exactly?

Jim: Actually, I'd rather not say. But I know I made a good purchase.

C 🔊 Read the expressions below. Complete each box with a similar expression from the conversation. Then listen and check your answers.

Giving an approximate answer

_____

I'd say maybe . . .
Probably . . .

Avoiding answering

_____

I'd prefer not to say.
I'd rather not answer that.

D Match the questions and the responses. Then practice with a partner.

1. How often do you drive? _____
2. How much do you drive every day? _____
3. How many people have you given rides to? _____
4. How much did you sell your old car for? _____

a. I'd say about ten.
b. Probably five or six times a week.
c. I'd rather not answer that.
d. I'd say about 30 minutes.

2 Listening Consumer research

A 🔊 Listen to a man answer survey questions in a grocery store. Number the questions from 1 to 9 in the order you hear them.

☐ Have your buying habits changed in the last year? _____

1 How often do you walk to the grocery store? *All the time.* _____

☐ Do you usually ask for paper or plastic bags? _____

☐ How much do you spend on groceries every month? _____

☐ How many people are there in your household? _2_ _____

☐ What is the highest level of education you've completed? ___Collage_____

☐ What do you do for a living? _____

☐ Do you ever shop for groceries online? ___No_____

☐ How often do you buy environmentally friendly products? _____

B 🔊 Listen again. Write the man's answers.

C Pair work Ask and answer the questions in Part A. Answer with your own information, or avoid answering.

3 Speaking Do you waste water?

A Read the survey. Are there any questions you would avoid answering, or is there any information you wouldn't share?

WATER USE SURVEY

Name: _____   Phone number: _____

Address: _____   Email: _____

Age: _____   Education: _____

How many showers do you take in a week? ___Every day_____

How long do you spend in the shower? ___5 min._____

Do you ever leave the water running when you brush your teeth? ___Yes_____

Do you wash dishes by hand or use a dishwasher? ___hand_____

When you wash dishes, do you leave the water running? _____

When you wash clothes, is the washing machine always completely full? _____

Do you flush the toilet after every use? _____

B Pair work Interview your partner. Complete the survey with his or her answers. Mark an ✗ if he or she avoids answering.

C Pair work Compare your answers. Who uses more water? How could you use less water?

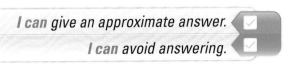

I can give an approximate answer. ☑

I can avoid answering. ☑

C What will happen?

1 Vocabulary Tips to help the environment

A 🔊 Match the tips and the pictures. Then listen and check your answers.

a. Buy local food.　　　d. Pay bills online.　　　　　　g. Use cloth shopping bags.
b. Fix leaky faucets.　　e. Take public transportation.　h. Use rechargeable batteries.
c. Grow your own food.　f. Use a clothesline.

 1. a

 2. d

 3. e

 4. g

 5. c

 6. b

 7. h

 8. f

B Pair work Which things in Part A do you do now? Which don't you do?
Tell your partner.

2 Conversation This is awful!

A 🔊 Listen to the conversation. When does Kendra want to start taking
public transportation?

Ina: This is awful! It's taking forever to get
to work.

Kendra: I know. There are just too many cars
these days! The traffic seems to get
worse and worse.

Ina: Maybe we should start taking public
transportation. If we take the subway,
we won't have to sit in traffic.

Kendra: And we might save money if we take
the subway.

Ina: I think you're right. Also, if we take
public transportation, we won't get
stressed out before work. So, when
do we start?

Kendra: How about tomorrow?

B 🔊 Listen to their conversation the next day.
What are they unhappy about?

3 Grammar 🔊 **First conditional**

*First conditional sentences describe real possibilities. Use the present
tense in the* if *clause (the condition). Use* will *in the main clause.*

If we **take** public transportation, we'**ll save** money.

If we **take** public transportation, we **won't get** stressed out.

Air pollution **will get** worse if we **don't reduce** the number of cars.

Use modals such as may, might, *or* could *in the main clause when you're
less certain about the results.*

If air pollution **gets** worse, more people **may get** sick.

If you **don't fix** your leaky faucet, you **might get** a high water bill.

You **could spend** money on other things if you **grow** your own food.

A Write first conditional sentences with the two clauses. Then compare
with a partner.

1. you'll use 60 percent less energy / you replace your regular lightbulbs with CFLs

   You'll use 60 percent less energy if you replace your regular lightbulbs with CFLs.

2. you pay your bills online / you'll use less paper

   _____

3. we fix our leaky faucets / we'll save water

   _____

4. there won't be much air pollution / everyone uses hybrid cars

   _____

5. you use a clothesline / other people may start to do the same

   _____

6. we use rechargeable batteries / we could save a lot of money

   _____

B Pair work What else will or may happen for each condition in Part A?
Discuss your ideas.

    A: *What else will happen if you replace your regular lightbulbs with CFLs?*
    B: *If I replace my regular lightbulbs with CFLs, I'll have cheaper electric bills.*

4 Speaking Around the circle

A Write a sentence about what will happen if you change a habit to become greener.

If I grow my own food, I will eat better.

B Group work Sit in a circle. Go around the circle and share your ideas. Repeat
your classmates' main clauses as conditions, and add new ideas.

    A: *If I grow my own food, I will eat better.*
    B: *If you eat better, you will feel healthier.*
    C: *If you feel healthier, you won't need to go to the doctor very often.*

5 Keep talking!

Go to page **140** for more practice.

    I can talk about future possibilities. ☑

D Finding solutions

1 Reading 🔊

A Look at the pictures. Which home would you prefer to live in? Why?

B Read the article. Write the captions under the correct pictures.

> The Recycled-Tire House   The Found-Object House   The Greenhouse

One-of-a-Kind HOMES

Shoichi wanted to live in an environmentally friendly home, and he always liked the greenhouses in his neighborhood in Tokyo, Japan. So he decided to create his own greenhouse-style home. Sunlight warms his new home, and a plastic cover around the house helps to keep the heat inside. There aren't any walls or rooms. The "rooms" are actually large boxes on wheels. He can move them anywhere he likes, even outside. He loves his home, but sometimes he would like to be able to move the whole house.

Ruth is an artist who lives in the Rocky Mountains in the U.S. state of Colorado. Over the years, she found and collected a lot of old objects for her art. When she decided she wanted to live in a more unusual home, she had a creative idea. She would use many of the old materials that she collected in the home's design. For example, she used old car parts in the front door and tire rubber as the roof. She also used the door of an old car as part of a wall, so she can still lower the window!

Wayne and Cate are a couple from the U.S. state of Montana. They wanted a new home that wasn't too expensive. Their solution was simple – they built their own home. They recycled and used 250 old tires as the base of the house and old glass for the windows. They even used 13,000 empty soda cans in the house. Their home also has large windows and lots of plants and flowers. Solar energy keeps the house warm, even on cold days.

C Read the article again. Answer the questions.

1. What warms the inside of Shoichi's home? _____
2. What would Shoichi like to be able to do? _____
3. What creative idea did Ruth have? _____
4. Where are there car parts in Ruth's home? _____
5. Why did Wayne and Cate build their own home? _____
6. What did Wayne and Cate use to build their home? _____

D Pair work Have you heard of or seen any unique homes or buildings? Were they environmentally friendly? Tell your partner.

2 Listening Award winners

A 🔊 Listen to the conversations about two award winners, Gabriela McCall and Tayler McGillis. Who do the phrases below describe? Write T (Tayler) or G (Gabriela).

1. __T__ raised money for local charities.
2. _____ is a student in Puerto Rico.
3. _____ won an award at age 12.
4. _____ collects and recycles cans.
5. _____ helps birds.
6. _____ teaches children.
7. _____ speaks at schools about recycling.
8. _____ took photos to start a project.

Tayler McGillis   Gabriela McCall

B 🔊 Listen again. Correct the false sentences.

1. Tayler raised more than ~~$900~~ for local charities.   ___$9,000___
2. Tayler's new goal is to collect 175,000 bottles every year.   _____
3. Gabriela's project helps protect the ocean for birds in Puerto Rico.   _____
4. Gabriela teaches children about recycling so that they respect the environment.   _____

3 Writing and speaking Local concerns

A Write a letter to a local official about an environmental problem in your community. Use the questions and the model to help you.

- What is the problem?
- Who or what does the problem affect?
- Who or what is causing it?
- What's a solution to the problem?

Dear City Councilman,
   I am a student. I am writing to tell you about the amount of noise near our school. There is a lot of construction work and traffic near our school. It is very difficult for us to study and learn during the day.
   I have an idea for a possible solution to this problem. If . . .

B Group work Share your letters. Do you think the solutions will solve the problems? Can you offer other solutions?

C Class activity What are the most important concerns in your community? Who else can you write to or talk to about your concerns?

I can discuss solutions to problems. ✓

Wrap-up

1 Quick pair review

Lesson A **Brainstorm!** Make a list of environmentally friendly products. How many do you know? You have two minutes.

Lesson B **Do you remember?** Is the sentence giving an approximate answer, or is it avoiding answering? Write AP (approximate answer) or AV (avoiding answering). You have one minute.

How much did your car cost?

I'd say about $3,000. _____

I'd prefer not to say. _____

I'd say maybe $6,000. _____

How much trash do you throw away a week?

I'd rather not answer that. _____

I'd rather not say. _____

Probably about five bags. _____

Lesson C **Give your opinion!** What do you think? Complete the sentences together. You have three minutes.

1. Our city will get cleaner if _____ .
2. If our school uses solar energy, _____ .
3. If we eat organic food, _____ .
4. We could recycle more if _____ .

Lesson D **Find out!** Who is one person you know who does each thing? You have two minutes.

• Who uses environmentally friendly products at home?
• Who takes public transportation to work?
• Who has taught you about an environmental issue?

A: *My aunt has solar panels on the roof of her house.*
B: *My father uses compact fluorescent lightbulbs.*

2 In the real world

How can we solve this? Go online and find information in English that gives solutions to one of these problems. Then write about them.

pollution from cars	pollution from factories
global warming	too much garbage

Our Pollution Problem
  If more people have hybrid cars, there will be less pollution. People can also carpool. If we share rides, there will be fewer cars on the road. Also, if we . . .

Relationships

LESSON **A**	LESSON **B**	LESSON **C**	LESSON **D**
• Relationship behaviors • Expressions with infinitives	• Apologizing • Accepting an apology	• Inseparable phrasal verbs • Modals for speculating	• Reading: "Addy's Advice" • Writing: A piece of advice

Warm-up

A What is the relationship between the people? Number the pictures.

1. brother and sister   2. neighbors   3. co-workers   4. friends

B What do you think is happening in each picture? Do they all have good relationships?

A *Healthy relationships*

1 **Vocabulary** Relationship behaviors

A 🔊 Match the words and the sentences. Then listen and check your answers.

1. apologize _____	a. No! I'm not listening to you.
2. argue _____	b. I think we really need to talk about it.
3. communicate _____	c. I'm really sorry. I didn't mean to hurt your feelings.

4. compromise _____	d. I know you're sorry. It's OK.
5. criticize _____	e. Why don't I wash the dishes and you do the laundry?
6. forgive _____	f. You're being unfair. It's your turn to take out the garbage.

7. gossip _____	g. I told her I liked her new dress, but I didn't.
8. judge _____	h. Others may disagree, but I think what you said was awful.
9. lie _____	i. Did you hear about Wendy? You'll never guess what I heard.

B Pair work Which actions from Part A should people do to have healthy relationships? Which shouldn't they do? Discuss your ideas.

2 **Language in context** Relationship tips

A 🔊 Read the relationship tips. Why is it a bad idea to criticize someone in front of others?

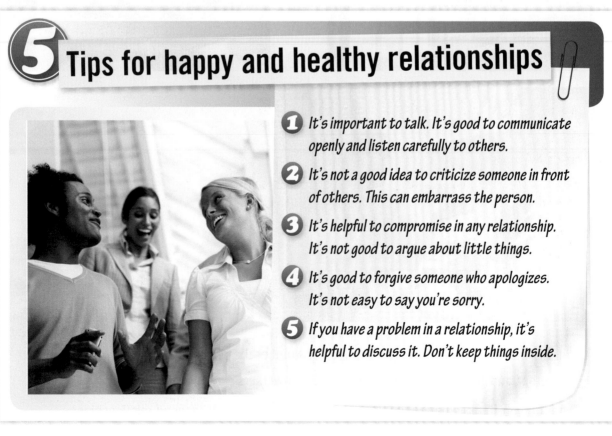

5 Tips for happy and healthy relationships

1 It's important to talk. It's good to communicate openly and listen carefully to others.

2 It's not a good idea to criticize someone in front of others. This can embarrass the person.

3 It's helpful to compromise in any relationship. It's not good to argue about little things.

4 It's good to forgive someone who apologizes. It's not easy to say you're sorry.

5 If you have a problem in a relationship, it's helpful to discuss it. Don't keep things inside.

B What about you? Do you agree with all the tips? Why or why not?

3 Grammar 🔊   Expressions with infinitives

Use infinitives after It's + *an adjective.*

It's good **to forgive** someone.   It's not good **to argue**.

It's important **to talk**.   It's never helpful **to judge** someone.

You can also use infinitives after It's + *a noun phrase.*

It's a good idea **to accept** an apology.   It's not a good idea **to criticize** someone.

A Circle the infinitives for the best relationship advice. Then compare with a partner.

1. It's important **to lie** / **to communicate** in a relationship.
2. It's helpful **to share** / **to forget** your feelings when you have a problem.
3. It's nice **to gossip** / **to think** about other people before making decisions.
4. It's a good idea **to judge** / **to meet** new people.
5. It's useful **to discuss** / **to accept** problems.
6. It's not a good idea **to argue** / **to compromise** with your friends a lot.

B Pair work Complete the sentences with your own ideas. Use *It's* expressions. Then discuss them.

1. _____ to be a reliable friend.
2. _____ to be honest with your parents.
3. _____ to apologize to someone but not really mean it.
4. _____ to say something if a friend is gossiping about you.

4 Pronunciation   Sentence stress

A 🔊 Listen and repeat. Notice the stress on the important words in the sentences.

It's **important** to **talk**.   It's **not good** to **argue** about **little things**.

B 🔊 Listen to the sentences. Underline the stressed words.

It's helpful to compromise.   It's not easy to say you're sorry.

5 Speaking   Good advice?

A Pair work Choose a relationship from the list below. Then make a list of the five most important tips to make the relationship happy and healthy. Discuss your ideas.

best friends	co-workers
a brother and sister	a married couple
a child and parent	a teacher and student

B Group work Share your tips with another pair. What's the best piece of advice you heard?

6 Keep talking!

Go to page 141 for more practice.

I can discuss what's important in relationships. ✓

B I'm really sorry.

1 Interactions — Apologizing

A Is it difficult for you to say you're sorry? Can you remember the last thing you apologized for?

B 🔊 Listen to the conversation. What excuse does Susan give Gina? Then practice the conversation.

Gina: Hello?
Susan: Gina?
Gina: Yeah.
Susan: Hi. It's Susan.
Gina: Hi, Susan.
Susan: Listen, I know I missed your party last night. I'm sorry.
Gina: Oh, that's OK. Is everything OK?
Susan: Yeah, but you'll never believe what happened. It's kind of embarrassing. I mixed up the date.
Gina: What do you mean?
Susan: I thought the party was on the 31st, not the 30th.
Gina: Oh, I see.
Susan: So, how was the party?
Gina: It was great. But we missed you!

C 🔊 Read the expressions below. Complete each box with a similar expression from the conversation. Then listen and check your answers.

Apologizing	Accepting an apology
_____	_____
I'm really sorry.	Don't worry about it.
My apologies.	There's no need to apologize.

D Number the sentences from 1 to 7. Then practice with a partner.

_____ **A:** I'm really sorry I didn't meet you at the café yesterday.

_____ **A:** Hi. It's Greg.

_____ **A:** Well, the repairs will be very expensive.

_____ **A:** My car broke down, and I forgot my phone.

_____ **B:** Is your car OK?

_____ **B:** Don't worry about it.

_____ **B:** Oh. Hi, Greg.

2 Listening What happened?

A 🔊 Listen to four people apologize over the phone. What happened?
Where did they *not* go? Number the pictures from 1 to 4.

B 🔊 Listen again. Complete the excuses with the correct information.

1. I was at the _____ and completely forgot the _____ .
2. I washed my _____ last night, and the _____ was in my pocket.
3. I was out of _____ . My grandmother was in the _____ .
4. I'm in a _____ at work. I can't _____ right now.

C Pair work Are all the excuses good ones? Would you accept each person's apology? Discuss your ideas.

3 Speaking Explain yourself!

A Read the situations. Write an excuse for each one. Be creative!

Situations	Excuses
You are 30 minutes late for your own wedding.	
You missed your dentist appointment.	
You didn't bring your résumé to a job interview.	
You forgot to pick up your friend.	
You didn't do your English homework.	
You broke your classmate's cell phone.	

B Pair work Role-play the situations. Then change roles.

Student A: Apologize to Student B for each situation in Part A.
Then make an excuse.

Student B: Ask Student A to explain each situation.
Then accept the apology.

I can apologize and give excuses. ✓
I can accept an apology. ✓

C   *That can't be the problem.*

1 Vocabulary   Inseparable phrasal verbs

A 🔊 Match the sentences. Then listen and check your answers.

1. It's awful when people **break up**. _____	a. They should call before they visit.
2. I need friends that I can **count on**. _____	b. It's always better to stay together.
3. It's not nice when friends just **drop by**. _____	c. My best friends are all reliable.

4. My family and I **get along** well. _____	d. They can be so immature.
5. My friends and I love to **get together**. _____	e. We meet every Saturday.
6. Most teenagers need to **grow up**. _____	f. We hardly ever argue.

7. People used to **pick on** me in class. _____	g. I sometimes see them at the coffee shop.
8. I love to **run into** old friends. _____	h. I'm just like her.
9. I **take after** my mother. _____	i. They were mean to me.

B Pair work Which sentences do you agree with or are true for you?
Tell your partner.

A: *I agree that it's awful when people break up, but I disagree that it's always better to stay together.*

B: *I agree with you. Some people shouldn't stay together when they argue a lot.*

2 Conversation   He must be really busy.

A 🔊 Listen to the conversation. What is Evan probably doing right now?

Ryan: My friend Evan never seems to have time for me these days. I just can't count on him anymore.

Katie: Well, he started a new job, right? He must be really busy.

Ryan: Yeah, I'm sure he is. But he used to drop by or call me all the time.

Katie: He might be feeling stressed out from the job. Or he could be upset with you about something.

Ryan: No, that can't be the problem. I haven't done anything wrong. I think I'd better call him.

Katie: Yeah, I think you should.

Ryan: OK. . . . Well, there's no answer.

Katie: He must still be sleeping. It's only 6:30!

B 🔊 Listen to Ryan call Evan later in the day. What was the real problem with Evan?

3 Grammar 🔊 Modals for speculating

Speculating with more certainty

He **must be** really busy. He started a new job.

He **must not leave** his house very often. He always seems to be busy.

He **can't be** upset with me. I haven't done anything to him.

Speculating with less certainty

He **could be** upset about something. Maybe you did something to him.

He **may not like** his new job. I haven't heard how he likes it.

He **might be feeling** stressed out. His new job may be a lot of work.

A Circle the correct words. Then compare with a partner.

1. I don't know his weekend plans. He **must** / **could** drop by on Saturday.
2. She didn't say much on the phone to him. They **must not** / **might** be getting along.
3. They **must** / **may not** come to the party. They're going out to dinner that night.
4. She **can't** / **could** take after her father. She's really tall, but he's pretty short.
5. You're coughing and sneezing so much. You **must** / **must not** be getting sick.
6. They **can't** / **might** be tired. Maybe they stayed up late to study for the test.

B Read the situations. Complete the sentences with your own ideas.
Then compare with a partner.

1. Pamela and Miguel don't get along anymore. She doesn't want to talk about it.
   Pamela must _____ .
2. Jeff just ran into his college friend Mary. He hasn't seen her for 20 years.
   Jeff could _____ .
3. Luis and Teresa arranged to get together at a restaurant, but she never came.
   Teresa may not _____ .
4. Brian dropped by and asked to copy your homework. You're not going to
   give it to him. Brian might _____ .

4 Speaking Look around!

A Pair work Look around the classroom. Speculate about your classmates.

A: *I think Tom must be playing tennis later. He has his tennis racket with him today.*
B: *And Carmen might be happy about something. She's smiling a lot.*

B Class activity Were your speculations correct? Ask your classmates.

A: *Tom, I see you have your tennis racket. Are you playing tennis later?*
B: *Actually, no. I played before class.*

5 Keep talking!

Go to pages 142–143 for more practice.

I can *speculate about people.* ☑

D Getting advice

1 Reading

A Do you ever listen to talk shows on the radio or watch them on TV? What kind of problems do they usually discuss? Do people give good advice on the shows?

B Read the first few sentences of each email sent to the radio show *Addy's Advice*. Who does each person have a problem with?

○ ○ ○

ADDY'S ADVICE

1. I have a big problem. It's my best friend. She doesn't really have any time for me these days. I call her, and she can't talk. I text her, and she doesn't answer right away. I think it's because of her cat, Peaches. She got this little cat for her 30th birthday, and now she takes it everywhere. She even dresses it in little sweaters and hats. I don't know what to do. Is it possible to be jealous of a cat? – **T. J.**

2. There's this new person at work. She works next to me and we get along, but she's always asking me to do things for her. For example, she asks me to get her coffee when I get some for myself. Or she drops by and asks me to copy things for her when she's "busy." She's not my boss! Should I just refuse to do things for her? I want to be nice, but I have to do my own work. Can you help me, please? – **Marcy**

3. My little brother is driving me crazy. I'm 15, and he's 10. He has his own friends, but he won't leave me and my friends alone. They come over a lot to study or just watch TV. He bothers me and sometimes tells my friends things that are personal about me. Maybe he just wants attention, but it's very annoying. He should just grow up! Anyway, I told my mom and dad, but they say I need to solve the problem. – **Kathy**

4. I'm a neat person, and I used to live alone. I got a roommate a few months ago to help with the rent. The problem is, my roommate is not like me at all. He never does any chores around the house. He just sits around playing video games and watching TV. The apartment is always a mess, and I'm the one who has to clean it up. I can't count on him for anything. Should I just clean the apartment myself? This is a big problem for me. – **Daniel**

C Read the emails again. Who is each question about? Check (✓) the correct answers.

Who . . . ?	T. J.	Marcy	Kathy	Daniel
lives with a messy person				
is a teenager				
is jealous of an animal				
is doing someone else's work				
lived alone last year				
mentions parents in the letter				

D Pair work Have you ever had similar problems? What did you do about them? Tell your partner.

2 **Listening** On the air

A 🔊 Listen to the radio show *Addy's Advice*. What advice does Addy give to each person from Exercise 1? Check (✓) the correct answers.

1. ☐ Show interest in the cat.
   ☐ Get a cat of your own.
2. ☐ Write your co-worker a note.
   ☐ Ask your co-worker to do things.
3. ☐ Go to someone else's house.
   ☐ Remind your parents of the situation.
4. ☐ Throw the roommate out.
   ☐ Communicate.

B 🔊 Listen again. Which statements does Addy probably agree or disagree with? Write A (agree) or D (disagree).

1. People never lose interest in things over time. _____
2. Most people have problems with co-workers at some time. _____
3. Parents don't always need to solve their children's problems. _____
4. Look for a new roommate if you have a problem. _____

3 **Writing** A piece of advice

A Choose an email from Exercise 1. Think of three pieces of advice.

B Write an email giving advice. Use the model and your ideas from Part A to help you.

C Group work Share your emails. Do you agree with the advice? What other advice can you give? Discuss your ideas.

> Dear T. J.,
> I read your email, and I understand your problem. It <u>is</u> possible to be jealous of a cat! I think it's important to find things that you can do with your friend and Peaches. It's a good idea to . . .

4 **Speaking** Take it or leave it.

A Imagine you have two relationship problems. Write two sentences about each one. Be creative!

B Group work Share your imaginary problems. Your group gives advice. Take turns.

1. My friends never remember my birthday. I always remember theirs!
2. My parents don't trust me. I need to call them every three hours.

A: *I have a problem. My friends never remember my birthday. I always remember theirs!*
B: *It's a good idea to help them remember. Why not send them reminders?*

C Group work Whose advice do you think you'd follow? Why? Tell your group.

I can **give advice about relationships.** ☑

Wrap-up

1 Quick pair review

Lesson A **Brainstorm!** Make a list of tips for healthy family relationships. How many can you think of? You have five minutes.

Lesson B **Test your partner!** Apologize to your partner for three different things. Can your partner accept your apologies in three different ways? Take turns. You have two minutes.

Lesson C **Guess!** Speculate about a celebrity, but don't say his or her name! Can your partner guess who it is? Take turns. You have two minutes.

A: *This person might win an award for his new movie.*
B: *Is it . . . ?*

Lesson D **Find out!** What is the best relationship advice your partner has ever received? Who gave the advice? You have two minutes.

2 In the real world

What advice do the experts give? Go online and find advice in English about one of these topics. Then write about it.

a jealous friend	a neighbor's noisy dog
a friend who talks too much	an annoying boss
a lazy husband or wife	an inconsiderate neighbor

Dealing with Jealous Friends
I found a website that gives advice about jealous friends. If you have a jealous friend, try to find out why the friend is jealous. Try to understand how your friend feels. It's a good idea to tell your friend about a time when you felt jealous, too. That way she will not feel alone or embarrassed. Tell your friend what you did to feel better. Another piece of advice on the website is . . .

Living your life

Warm-up

A Look at the pictures. What have the people accomplished?

B What are some of your accomplishments? What other things would you like to accomplish in your life?

A *He taught himself.*

1 **Vocabulary** Qualities for success

A 🔊 Match the words and their meanings. Then listen and check your answers.

1. bravery _____	a. the ability to develop original ideas
2. confidence _____	b. the belief that you can succeed
3. creativity _____	c. a commitment to something
4. dedication _____	d. the quality of showing no fear

5. enthusiasm _____	e. the ability to change easily
6. flexibility _____	f. a strong interest in something
7. talent _____	g. the ability to make good decisions
8. wisdom _____	h. the natural ability to do things well

B 🔊 Complete the chart with the correct adjective forms for the nouns. Then listen and check your answers.

Noun	Adjective	Noun	Adjective
bravery	*brave*	enthusiasm	
confidence		flexibility	
creativity		talent	
dedication		wisdom	

C Pair work Which qualities in Part A do you think people are born with? Which do they develop from experience or by watching others? Discuss your ideas.

2 **Language in context** A success story

A 🔊 Read the story of Yong-eun Yang. What did he do in 2009?

WEB ENCYCLOPEDIA

Yong-eun Yang

In his late teens, South Korea's Yong-eun Yang, or "Y. E.," enjoyed lifting weights and hoped to own his own gym someday. But that dream died when he hurt himself in the gym. So at age 19, he took a part-time job at a golf course. He picked up golf balls and began to observe other players. He started to practice the game by himself late at night, and he even forced himself to get up early to be at the course by 5:00 a.m. for more practice. This is how Y. E. taught himself to play golf. His dedication and patience paid off. He became a professional golfer in 1995, and, in 2009, this talented man won his first championship, beating Tiger Woods.

B What other qualities for success do you think Y. E. has?

3 Grammar 🔊 **Reflexive pronouns**

Use reflexive pronouns when the subject and object of a sentence refer to the same person or thing.

I hurt **myself** at work.

He taught **himself** to play golf.

They consider **themselves** brave.

By with a reflexive pronoun means "alone."

She traveled **by herself** to the United States.

Do you like to practice with another person or **by yourself**?

Personal pronouns	Reflexive pronouns
I	myself
you	yourself
he	himself
she	herself
it	itself
we	ourselves
you	yourselves
they	themselves

Complete the sentences with the correct reflexive pronouns.
Then compare with a partner.

1. I drew a picture of _____ in art class.
2. I like your new hairstyle. Did you cut it _____ ?
3. If you and Joe have problems, you need to help _____ .
4. They had a great time. They really enjoyed _____ .
5. My brother doesn't consider _____ brave, but he is.
6. Heather wrote that by _____ . Nobody helped her.
7. We taught _____ Spanish before we moved to Peru.
8. I hurt _____ at the gym last week. My arm still hurts.
9. I took a trip by _____ . It helped me be more confident.

4 Pronunciation Stress shifts

🔊 Listen and repeat. Notice the stress shifts when some words change from nouns to adjectives.

crea**ti**vity	dedi**ca**tion	enthu**si**asm	flexi**bi**lity
cre**a**tive	**de**dicated	enthusi**a**stic	**flex**ible

5 Speaking Self talk

A Pair work Interview your partner. Ask questions for more information.
Take notes.

- Have you ever hurt yourself?
- Do you consider yourself brave?
- Have you ever traveled by yourself?
- Have you ever taught yourself something?
- Are you enjoying yourself in this class?
- Do you consider yourself a flexible person?

B Pair work Tell another classmate about your partner.

"William hurt himself once. He broke his foot."

6 Keep talking!

Go to page 144 for more practice.

I **can** talk about myself and my experiences. ☑

B I'll give it some thought.

1 Interactions | Giving and considering advice

A What do you do if you have too much work or studying to do? Do you talk to anyone?

B 🔊 Listen to the conversation. What is Bryan thinking about doing? Then practice the conversation.

Marta: What's wrong, Bryan?
Bryan: Well, my job is just really stressful right now. My boss just seems to give me more and more work. It's not fair.
Marta: That's not good.
Bryan: Actually, I'm thinking about quitting and looking for another job.
Marta: Really? I wouldn't recommend that.
Bryan: Why not?
Marta: Well, because you may not find something better. And that would just give you more stress. Have you thought about talking to your boss?
Bryan: Not really.
Marta: Why don't you try that? Maybe there is something he can do.
Bryan: I'll see.

C 🔊 Read the expressions below. Complete each box with a similar expression from the conversation. Then listen and check your answers.

Advising against something
_____ I don't think you should do that. I'm not sure that's the best idea.

Considering advice
_____ I'll think about it. I'll give it some thought.

D How would you respond? Write A (advise against it) or C (consider it). Then practice with a partner.

1. I think you should call the doctor. ____
2. I plan to study all night before my test. ____
3. I recommend that you stay home tomorrow if you don't feel well. ____
4. I think you should visit your grandmother this weekend. ____
5. I'm going to paint my house bright pink. ____
6. I'm not going to class tomorrow because I want to watch a soccer game. ____

2 Listening Maybe I'll do that.

A 🔊 Listen to Tim give advice to three friends. What is each friend's problem?
Check (✓) the correct answers.

Problems	Recommendations
1. ☐ She needs to get a full-time job. ☐ She wants to take more classes. ☐ She's thinking about quitting her job. ☐ She's not going to graduate.	
2. ☐ He doesn't have the money. ☐ He doesn't have a credit card. ☐ The leather jacket doesn't fit. ☐ His friend won't lend him any money.	
3. ☐ She takes too many breaks. ☐ She can't do a math problem. ☐ She drank too much coffee. ☐ Tim is driving her crazy.	

B 🔊 Listen again. What does Tim tell each friend to do? Complete the chart with
his recommendations.

3 Speaking Think about it!

A Imagine your friend wants to do the things below. What advice would you give?
Write notes.

- Your friend wants to buy a new, expensive
  car. He doesn't have the money, and he
  doesn't know how to drive!

- Your friend wants to take two more
  classes. He's already taking five classes,
  and he has a part-time job!

- Your friend wants to go camping in the
  mountains by himself for a week. He's
  never gone camping before!

B Pair work Role-play the situations in Part A. Then change roles.

Student A: Imagine you want to do the things in Part A. Tell Student B what you want
to do and why. Consider his or her advice.

Student B: Advise Student A against doing the things in Part A and explain why.
Recommend something else. Use your ideas from Part A.

A: *I saw this really awesome car yesterday! I think I'm going to buy it.*
B: *I'm not sure that's the best idea.*
A: *Why not?*

I can advise against something. ☑
I can consider advice. ☑

C What would you do?

1 Vocabulary Separable phrasal verbs

A 🔊 Match the phrasal verbs and their meanings. Then listen and check your answers.

1. He won't talk about his job, so don't **bring** it **up**. _____	a. donate
2. I got a bad grade on this essay. I need to **do** it **over**. _____	b. return money
3. I don't need these books. I might **give** them **away**. _____	c. mention
4. This is Lynn's camera. I need to **give** it **back**. _____	d. do again
5. Paul lent me some money. I need to **pay** him **back**. _____	e. return

6. Which one is Susan? Can you **point** her **out**? _____	f. do later
7. We can't have this meeting now. Let's **put** it **off**. _____	g. identify
8. This is serious. We need to **talk** it **over**. _____	h. not accept
9. I may buy that car, but I want to **try** it **out** first. _____	i. use
10. I have a job offer, but I plan to **turn** it **down**. _____	j. discuss

B Pair work What have you done over, talked over, paid back, tried out, or put off recently? Tell your partner.

A: *Have you done anything over recently?*
B: *Yes, I have. I did my English homework over last night. I made a lot of mistakes the first time!*

2 Conversation I'm kind of broke.

A 🔊 Listen to the conversation. What is Neil thinking about doing?

Dana: I really like your camcorder.
 Neil: Actually, it's my friend Ben's. I'm just trying it out this week. I need to give it back to him tomorrow.
Dana: It looks really expensive.
 Neil: It is. I'm thinking about buying one, but I can't right now.
Dana: Why not?
 Neil: Well, I'm kind of broke. If I had more money, I'd buy it.
Dana: It would be nice to be rich, wouldn't it?
 Neil: Tell me about it. What would you do if you were rich?
Dana: Hmm. . . . If I were rich, I'd travel. I'd give some money away, too.
 Neil: That's nice.

B 🔊 Listen to the rest of the conversation. Why does Neil want a camcorder?

98

3 Grammar 🔊 Second conditional

Second conditional sentences describe "unreal" or imaginary situations. Use a past tense verb in the if *clause (the condition). Use* would *in the main clause.*

What **would** you **do** if you **had** more money?

    If I **had** more money, I **would buy** a camcorder.

Use were *for the past tense of* be *in the condition.*

Would you **travel** if you **were** rich?

    Yes, I **would**.   No, I **wouldn't**.

    Yes. If I **were** rich, I**'d travel** a lot.   No. I **wouldn't travel** a lot if I **were** rich.

A Complete the conversations with the correct words. Then compare with a partner.

1. **A:** What _____ you _____ (do) if you suddenly _____ (become) rich?

   B: I _____ (quit) my job. Then I _____ (travel) for a few months.

2. **A:** If a teacher _____ (give) you a good grade by mistake, what _____ you _____ (do)?

   B: I _____ (not / feel) right about it. I _____ (point) out the mistake.

3. **A:** How _____ you _____ (feel) if a friend _____ (call) you late at night?

   B: I _____ (be) surprised, but I _____ (not / feel) angry.

4. **A:** If you _____ (have) a relationship problem, who _____ you _____ (talk) to?

   B: I _____ (talk) about the problem with my best friend.

B Pair work Ask and answer the questions in Part A. Answer with your own information.

4 Speaking What would you do?

A Pair work Discuss the questions. Take notes.

- Where would you go if you had a lot of money?
- What would you give away if you were rich?
- What would you do if you saw your teacher or your boss at the supermarket?
- When would you turn down a job offer?
- Would you point out a mistake if a classmate made one? Why or why not?
- What would you do over if you had the chance?

B Group work Share your ideas with another pair. Are your ideas similar or different?

5 Keep talking!

Go to page **145** for more practice.

I can talk about imaginary situations. ☑

D What an accomplishment!

1 Reading

A What do you think it would be like to walk across your country? Why?

B Read the interview. Why did Mary and Etsuko often have to walk between 30 and 40 kilometers a day?

A Walk Across Japan

 Mary King and Etsuko Shimabukuro completed a 7,974-kilometer walk across Japan. Mary takes our questions about their incredible accomplishment.

Why did you walk across Japan?
The mapmaker Ino Tadataka *inspired* me. He spent 17 years *on and off* walking through Japan. He drew the country's first real maps.

How long did it take?
A year and a half. We walked from the island of Hokkaido, in the north, down to Okinawa. In Hokkaido, we walked about 40 kilometers a day, and on the other islands, about 30. We often had no choice about the distance because we had to find a place to sleep.

Describe a typical day.
There really wasn't one, but we tried to start by 7:00 a.m. and walk for 10 to 12 hours. Sometimes we had breakfast on the road. We had to be careful in Hokkaido because the bears there could smell our food. We saw bears twice, which was terrifying!

Did you walk every day?
No. We needed to do our laundry, check our email, and rest. Also, I wanted to interview people for my blog.

What were some of the best parts?
There were many! We stayed in a *haunted* guesthouse, walked on fire at a festival, and visited many wonderful hot springs.

Any low points?
You know, overall, we really enjoyed ourselves, but there were a lot of aches and pains along the way. The traffic could be scary because there weren't always sidewalks for *pedestrians*.

Did you ever think about *giving up*?
No, we never wanted to stop. Actually, I was sad when it ended. I wanted to walk from Okinawa back to Tokyo, but Etsuko said we had to accept that we accomplished our goal. It was time to go home.

Would you do it over again?
Definitely. I'd love to *retrace* our steps when I'm 80. But I've also set myself the goal of walking across the U.K. or India someday.

Source: http://japanonfoot.blogspot.com

C Find the words in *italics* in the article. What do they mean? Write the words next to the correct definitions.

1. inhabited by ghosts   ___*haunted*___
2. quitting _____
3. people who walk _____
4. go back over a route again _____
5. with breaks _____
6. gave someone an idea _____

D Pair work   How would you describe Mary's personality? Do you know anyone like her?

2 Listening Can I ask you . . . ?

A  Listen to four people talk about their biggest accomplishments this year. Write the accomplishments in the chart.

	Accomplishments	Qualities for success
1.		
2.		
3.		
4.		

B Listen again. What quality led to each person's success? Complete the chart.

C Pair work Who do you think had the biggest accomplishment? Why? Discuss your ideas.

3 Writing An accomplishment

A Write a paragraph about something you accomplished in your lifetime. Use the questions and the model to help you.

- What did you accomplish?
- Why did you decide to do it?
- How did you accomplish it?
- What was challenging about it?
- Why was it important?

A Healthy Change
I decided that I wanted to change something at our school. A lot of the vending machines had very unhealthy food, like chocolate, candy, and potato chips. Students wanted healthier food like fruits and yogurt. So I asked students and teachers to sign a petition to get healthier food. It was difficult at first . . .

B Group work Share your paragraphs. How are your accomplishments similar or different?

4 Speaking What have you done?

Class activity Find people who have done these things. Write their names and ask questions for more information.

Find someone who has . . .	Name	Extra information
helped someone with a challenging task		
won an award for doing something		
learned a new skill outside of school		
solved a problem at school, home, or work		
used technology to improve his or her English		

I can ask and talk about accomplishments. ☑

Wrap-up

1 Quick pair review

Lesson A **Test your partner!** Say three personal pronouns. Can your partner use the correct reflexive pronouns in sentences? Take turns. You have two minutes.

A: *He.*
B: *Himself. My neighbor introduced himself to me yesterday.*

Lesson B **Do you remember?** Which sentences are advising against something? Check (✓) the correct answers. You have one minute.

☐ I don't think you should do that.   ☐ I'll give it some thought.
☐ Please don't worry about it.   ☐ I'd rather not answer that.
☐ I'm not sure that's the best idea.   ☐ I wouldn't recommend that.

Lesson C **Find out!** What is one thing both you and your partner would do in each situation? You have three minutes.

• Where would you go if you won a free vacation?
• What would you buy if you received money for your birthday?
• What would you do if you lost your cell phone?

Lesson D **Brainstorm!** Make a list of accomplishments. How many can you think of? You have two minutes.

2 In the real world

Which country would you like to travel across? Go online and find information in English about one of these trips or your own idea. Then answer the questions and write about it.

| a car trip across the United States | a train trip across Canada |
| a bike trip across France | a walking trip across England |

• How far is it?
• How long would it take?
• How much would it cost?
• What would you need to take?
• Where would you stay?

> *A Road Trip in the U.S.A.*
> *I'd take a car trip across the United States. I'd start in Ocean City, Maryland, and drive to San Francisco, California. The trip is about 3,000 miles. The first place I would stop is . . .*

Music

Warm-up

Music Sales in the U.S.A.

other* 16%
jazz 1%
classical 2%
gospel 7%
pop 9%
R & B 10%
hip-hop 11%
rock 32%
country 12%
* Includes new age, soundtracks, electronic, ethnic, folk, etc.

Source: The Recording Industry Association of America, 2008

A Label the pictures with the correct types of music from the chart.

B What do you think are the most popular kinds of music where you live? What's your favorite kind of music? What's your least favorite? Why?

A Music trivia

1 Vocabulary Compound adjectives

A 🔊 Complete the compound adjectives with the correct participles.
Then listen and check your answers.

Compound adjective		Present participle
award- _winning_	video	selling
best-_____	artist	winning ✓
nice-_____	voice	breaking
record-_____	hit	sounding

Compound adjective		Past participle
high-_____	ticket	downloaded
oddly _____	group	priced
often-_____	performer	named
well-_____	singer	known

B Pair work Ask and answer questions with each phrase in Part A.
Answer with your own ideas.

A: *Can you name an award-winning video?*
B: *Yes. Michael Jackson's video for "Thriller" won a lot of awards.*

2 Language in context Musical firsts

A 🔊 Read about these musical firsts. Which were downloaded?

Milestones in Music History

The first rap recording was made by the Sugarhill Gang. In 1979, the band's song "Rapper's Delight" became the first rap song to make the U.S. pop charts.

The song "Crazy" by Gnarls Barkley was leaked in 2005, months before its release. When it was finally released in March 2006, it became the first song to reach number one from downloaded sales.

The band Radiohead was the first to sell their album online for whatever people wanted to pay. Over a million albums were downloaded before the CD was released in December 2007.

The well-known band Aerosmith was the first to have a video game created around their music. People can play the guitar and sing along to 41 of their songs. The game was released in June 2008.

B What else do you know about these musical firsts? Do you know of any others?

"The band Run-DMC also recorded the song 'Rapper's Delight.'"

104

3 Grammar 🔊 Past passive

The passive voice places the focus of a sentence on the receiver of an action instead of the doer of the action.

Active voice (simple past)
Fans **downloaded** <u>over a million albums</u>.

Passive voice (past of be *+ past participle)*
<u>Over a million albums</u> **were downloaded**.

Use the passive voice when the doer of the action is not known or not important.
The game **was released** in 2008.

When the doer of the action is important to know, use the passive voice with by.
The first rap recording **was made** <u>by</u> the Sugarhill Gang.

A Complete the sentences with the past passive forms of the verbs.
Then compare with a partner.

1. All of the high-priced tickets to the concert _____ (sell) online.
2. The best-selling artists of the year _____ (give) a special award.
3. The singer's record-breaking hit _____ (write) by her mother.
4. The performer's biggest hit song _____ (use) in a TV commercial.
5. The band's award-winning video _____ (see) by millions of people.
6. The songs on her album _____ (play) with traditional instruments.

B Pair work Say the trivia about the music group the Beatles.
Your partner changes the sentences to use the past passive. Take turns.

1. In 1960, John Lennon suggested the name "the Beatles."
2. Ringo Starr replaced the original drummer, Peter Best, in 1962.
3. Paul McCartney wrote "Hey Jude" for John Lennon's son Julian.
4. Many people called George Harrison "the quiet Beatle."
5. *Rolling Stone* magazine chose the Beatles as the best artists of all time.

A: *In 1960, John Lennon suggested the name "the Beatles."*
B: *In 1960, the name "the Beatles" was suggested by John Lennon.*

4 Speaking Name it!

A Write three sentences in the past passive about the same song, singer, musician, band, or album, but don't use the name!

B Group work Share your sentences. Your group guesses the name of the song, singer, musician, band, or album. Take turns.

1. *This singer's first album was called* **The Fame.**
2. *She was born in New York City.*
3. *She was made famous by her music and fashion statements.*
(*answer: Lady Gaga*)

5 Keep talking!

Go to page 146 for more practice.

I can talk about music. ✓

B The first thing you do is . . .

1 Interactions   Giving instructions

A What kinds of things do you use a computer for? How did you learn to do those things?

B ◀)) Listen to the conversation. What steps does Roger follow to download and play a song? Then practice the conversation.

Roger: This is so frustrating!
Dena: What are you doing, Dad?
Roger: I'm trying to download a song, but I'm not having much luck. What am I doing wrong?
Dena: It's not that hard. Here, let me show you.
Roger: Thanks.
Dena: First, type in the name of the artist or the title of the song in this search box and hit "search."
Roger: OK. Ah, here we go.
Dena: Next, choose the song you want and click "download."
Roger: Oh, look at that. It's so fast! Is that it?
Dena: Well, no. Finally, click "play."

C ◀)) Read the expressions below. Complete each box with a similar expression from the conversation. Then listen and check your answers.

Beginning instructions	**Continuing instructions**	**Ending instructions**
_____	_____	_____
To start, . . .	Then . . .	To finish, . . .
The first thing you do is . . .	After that, . . .	The last thing you do is . . .

D Pair work Number the instructions from 1 to 5. Then have a conversation like the one in Part B.

How to download a ringtone:

_____ Select the ringtone that you want.

_____ Register with the site that you chose.

_____ Send the ringtone to your phone by text.

_____ Listen to the ringtones that are available.

_____ Find websites that offer ringtones.

2 Listening How does it work?

A 🔊 Listen to people give instructions on how to use three different machines. Number the machines from 1 to 3. There is one extra machine.

B 🔊 Listen again. Each person makes one mistake when giving instructions. Write the mistakes.

1. She said _____ instead of _____ .

2. He said _____ instead of _____ .

3. She said _____ instead of _____ .

C Pair work Choose one of the machines above, and give instructions on how to use it. Add any additional instructions.

"To use a record player, first plug it in. Then . . ."

3 Speaking Step-by-step

A Pair work Choose a topic from the list below or your own idea. Make a list of instructions about how to do it.

| attach a file to an email |
| burn a CD or DVD |
| create a playlist |
| download a podcast |
| make an international call |
| send a text message |
| upload a video |

How to _____

1.

2.

3.

4.

5.

B Pair work Give your instructions to another classmate. Answer any questions.

A: *To attach a file to an email, first open your email account. After that, click "compose." Next, . . .*

I can give instructions. ✓

1 **Vocabulary** Verb and noun formation

A 🔊 Match the phrases and the pictures. Then listen and check your answers.

a. **announce** a tour	c. **compose** music	e. **perform** a song	g. **record** a song
b. **appreciate** music	d. **entertain** an audience	f. **produce** a song	h. **release** a new album

1.

2.

3.

4.

5.

6.

7.

8.

B 🔊 Write the noun forms of the verbs in Part A. Then listen and check your answers.

a. _announcement_   c. _____   e. _____   g. _____

b. _____   d. _____   f. _____   h. _____

C Pair work Do you know any friends, artists, or other people who do or have done the things in Part A? Tell your partner.

2 **Conversation** I'm his biggest fan!

A 🔊 Listen to the conversation. What does Andy tell Miranda to listen to?

Andy: Oh, look! Richie Starr is going to perform here.
Miranda: Yeah, I know. I'm planning to go.
Andy: Really? Have you gotten a ticket yet?
Miranda: Not yet. But I think you can still get them. I didn't know you were a fan.
Andy: Are you kidding? I'm his biggest fan!
Miranda: Have you heard his new album?
Andy: He hasn't released it yet. But I've already downloaded his new single. Here, listen.
Miranda: Nice! I hear he has a cool online fan club.
Andy: He does. It gives information about new album releases and announces all upcoming performances.

B 🔊 Listen to the rest of the conversation. Why didn't Andy know about the concert?

3 Grammar 🔊 Present perfect with *yet* and *already*

In questions, use yet when you expect the action to have happened.	In responses, already means the action has happened earlier.	In responses, yet means the action hasn't happened, but you expect it to.
Have you **gotten** a ticket **yet**? **Has** he **released** his album **yet**?	Yes, I**'ve already gotten** a ticket. Yes, he**'s already released** it.	No, I **haven't gotten** a ticket **yet**. No, **not yet**. He **hasn't released** it **yet**.

A Write sentences in the present perfect with *already* and *yet* about Richie Starr's goals. Then compare with a partner.

1. *Richie has already written four new songs.*
2. _____
3. _____
4. _____
5. _____
6. _____

Richie Starr's Goals
✓ write four new songs
   record two songs for his album
   release his new album
✓ entertain children at the hospital
✓ give a free performance in the park
   announce his retirement

B Pair work Look at Richie's list in Part A. Ask questions with *yet* and answer them.

4 Pronunciation Syllable stress

A 🔊 Listen and repeat. Notice how the stress stays on the same syllable when these verbs become nouns.

an**nounce**	enter**tain**	per**form**	pro**duce**
an**nounce**ment	enter**tain**ment	per**for**mance	pro**duc**tion

B 🔊 Listen. Circle the verb-noun pairs if the stress stays the same.

appreciate	compose	record	release
appreciation	composition	recording	release

5 Speaking The latest

A Class activity Complete the questions with your own ideas. Then find someone who has already done each thing, and ask questions for more information.

- Have you heard _____ (a new album or song) yet?
- Have you played _____ (a new video game) yet?
- Have you seen _____ (a new TV show or movie) yet?
- _____ ?

B Group work Share your information.

6 Keep talking!

Student A go to page 147 and
Student B go to page 148 for more practice.

I can talk about things I've done recently. ☑

D Thoughts on music

1 Reading

A What are "fan sites"? Who usually has them? What kind of information do the websites usually include?

B Look at the fan site. What things can fans do on this site?

RICHIE STARR ♪ ROCK / ALTERNATIVE

UPCOMING SHOWS

Jan 19	Rio de Janeiro	SOLD OUT
Jan 21	São Paulo	
Jan 24	Mexico City	SOLD OUT
Jan 25	Guadalajara	
Feb 1	Austin	SOLD OUT

View my
pics / albums / videos

Fans	15,339
Fans online	2,810
Profile views	46,027

PLAY	SONG TITLE	PRICE	DOWNLOAD
▶	*SPEAK TO ME*	$1.49	BUY
▶	*FOREVER*	$0.99	BUY

VIEW ALL

Paige Richie, I love your page here. I have all your music. When are you going to release something new? Have you written anything yet? Don't keep your fans waiting! :)

Richie Hi, Paige. To answer your question – yes, I've already written some new stuff, but I haven't recorded anything yet. I'm going into the studio next month to record a few tracks. Check back on this page. I'll post a sample!

Caroline Richie, your music has gotten me through some of the worst days of my life. Please add "Never Alone" to the music player sometime. It's my favorite. Looking forward to a new album!

Yoshi Some friends and I started our own band last year, and we've already played a few shows. We were reviewed in the local paper, but we need advice on how to get a recording contract. Can you post how you got started?

Ashley I tried to get a ticket to your show in Austin, but they were sold out! Can you stay in Austin for another night and do a second show? Please! By the way, your song "Forever" was sung at my wedding!

Danny I downloaded your song "Speak to Me" the other day, and I was pretty disappointed. It doesn't "speak to me," if you know what I mean. How do I get my money back?

Ines Hey! I know all of your songs! I've been a huge fan since high school. I can't wait to see you in Mexico City. I have front row seats! Thank you for the music. I'm a musician myself!

C Read the fan site. Answer the questions.

1. Who has concert tickets? _____
2. Who can't get concert tickets? _____
3. Who wants advice? _____
4. Who is unhappy with a song? _____
5. Who has Richie's music helped? _____
6. Who has all of Richie's music? _____

D Pair work Do you ever look at fan sites of musicians, actors, or athletes? Why or why not? Tell your partner.

2 **Writing** A music review

A Write a review of an album (or a song) you'd recommend. Use the questions and the model to help you.

- What's the name of the album / song?
- When was it released?
- What do you like about the album / song?
- Is there anything you don't like about it?
- Why would you recommend it?

B Class activity Post your reviews around the room. Read your classmates' reviews. Which songs or albums have you heard?

Momento

Bebel Gilberto's album Momento *was released in 2007. All of the songs are good, but the title song is excellent. On the album, she blends Brazilian bossa nova with electronica and has a beautiful-sounding voice. The only thing I don't like about it is that there aren't enough songs! I'd recommend it because it was recorded with Japanese guitarist Masa Shimizu and . . .*

3 **Listening** Song dedications

A 🔊 Listen to five people call a radio show to dedicate songs to their friends and family members. Who do they dedicate songs to? Write the people in the chart.

	People	Song titles
1.	*friend*	
2.		
3.		
4.		
5.		

B 🔊 Listen again. What are the song titles? Complete the chart.

C Pair work Imagine you can dedicate a song to someone. What song would you dedicate and to whom? Why? Tell your partner.

4 **Speaking** Soundtrack of my life

A Make a list of three songs that remind you of particular times or events in your life.

	Song titles	Memories
1.		
2.		
3.		

B Group work Discuss your songs and memories. Ask and answer questions for more information.

A: *The song . . . reminds me of middle school. It was my favorite song when I was 14.*
B: *I know that song! How do you feel now when you hear it?*
A: *Oh, I feel totally embarrassed. I can't stand it now!*

I can talk about memorable songs. ☑

Wrap-up

1 Quick pair review

Lesson A Brainstorm! Make a list of words and phrases related to music. How many do you know? You have two minutes.

Lesson B Do you remember? Complete the sentences with words or phrases to give instructions. You have one minute.

How to install software:

_____ turn on your computer.

_____ insert the CD and click "install."

_____ to do is restart your computer.

How to get money out of an ATM:

_____ put your ATM card in the machine.

_____ type in your code.

_____ select how much money you want.

Lesson C Find out! What are two things both you and your partner have already done today? What are two things you both haven't done yet? You have three minutes.

Lesson D Test your partner! Say (or sing) the words to a song you know in English. Can your partner guess the title and singer? You have two minutes.

2 In the real world

Who is your favorite singer? Go to the singer's website, and find information about his or her albums. Then write about them.

- What was the singer's first album? When was it released?
- When was the singer's last album released? Did it have any hit songs?
- What's your favorite song by this singer? What's it about?

> *Taylor Swift*
>
> *My favorite singer is Taylor Swift. Her first album was called* Taylor Swift. *It was released in 2006. I love it. My favorite song on the album is called "Tim McGraw", who is a famous country music singer himself. Taylor was only sixteen years old when the song was released. The song is about how one of Tim McGraw's songs always reminds her of . . .*

On vacation

Warm-up

A great day trip!

O.K. Bus

Origen: Ciudad de México, TAPO
Destino: Puebla, Pue.
Fecha: 29/05/2010
Hora de salida: 10:30 a.m.
Precio: $130.00

NATIONAL MUSEUM OF ANTHROPOLOGY

Mexico City

The best!

Café del Sol

Yum!

HC

Hotel de la Ciudad
Avenida de la Reforma 42
06040 México, D.F.
(55) 005 02 003

This was useful!

My favorite places

What a bargain!

A Look at Julie's scrapbook. Where did she go on her vacation? What do you think she did there?

B What do you like to do on vacation? What kinds of things do you usually bring back with you?

A Travel preferences

1 Vocabulary Vacation activities

A 🔊 Match the phrases and the pictures. Then listen and check your answers.

a. buy handicrafts	c. listen to live music	e. speak a foreign language	g. visit landmarks
b. go to clubs	d. see wildlife	f. try local food	h. volunteer

1.

2.

3.

4.

5.

6.

7.

8.

B Pair work Which things in Part A have you *never* done on vacation? Tell your partner.

2 Language in context Three types of tours

A 🔊 Read the ads for three tours. Which tour is best for someone who likes volunteering? someone who likes eating? someone who dislikes planning?

Cuisine Adventures

Trying local foods is a great way to learn about a culture. Call today if you are interested in joining our "Eat and Learn" tour.

ENVIRONMENTAL EXPERIENCES

Are you concerned about protecting the environment? Volunteering is a rewarding way to spend a vacation. Choose from over 20 tours.

No Worries Tours

Do you enjoy traveling by bus but dislike planning the details? We specialize in organizing tours with no stress.

B What about you? Which tour interests you? Why?

3 Grammar 🔊 Gerunds

A gerund is an -ing word that acts like a noun. Gerunds may be the subject of a sentence, or they may appear after some verbs or prepositions.

As subjects:	**Trying** local foods is a great way to learn about a culture.
	Volunteering is a rewarding way to spend a vacation.
After some verbs:	I **enjoy traveling** by bus.
	I **dislike planning** the travel details.
After prepositions:	I'm interested **in joining** the "Eat and Learn" tour.
	I'm concerned **about protecting** the environment.

A Complete the conversations with the gerund forms of the verbs. Then compare with a partner.

be	buy	get	go	help	lose	meet	✓travel	try	volunteer

1. **A:** Do you enjoy ___*traveling*___ alone or in a group?

   B: I prefer _____ in a large group. It's more fun.

2. **A:** Are you interested in _____ handicrafts when you travel?

   B: Not really. I like _____ to markets, but just to look.

3. **A:** _____ local food is the best way to learn about a culture. Don't you agree?

   B: I'm not really sure. _____ local people is also good.

4. **A:** Are you worried about _____ sick when you travel abroad?

   B: Not really. I'm more concerned about _____ my passport!

5. **A:** Do you think _____ on vacation would be fun?

   B: I do. _____ other people is a great thing to do.

B Pair work Ask and answer the questions in Part A. Answer with your own information.

4 Speaking Travel talk

A Complete the questions with your own ideas. Use gerunds.

- Do you enjoy _____ when you're on vacation?
- Are you interested in _____ on vacation?
- Which is more interesting on vacation, _____ or _____ ?
- Are you ever concerned about _____ when you travel?
- As a tourist, is _____ important to you?
- _____ ?
- _____ ?

B Group work Discuss your questions. Ask and answer questions to get more information.

5 Keep talking!

Go to page 149 for more practice.

I can discuss travel preferences. ☑

Don't forget to . . .

1 Interactions — Preferences and reminders

A Where do you usually stay when you travel? A hotel? A youth hostel?

B 🔊 Listen to the conversation. What doesn't the guest need help with? Then practice the conversation.

Clerk: Can I help you?
Guest: Yes. I'm looking for a room for two nights.
Clerk: Do you have a reservation?
Guest: No, I don't.
Clerk: Let me see what we have. Would you like a single room or a double room?
Guest: A single is fine. I only need one bed.
Clerk: I can give you room 13A. Please sign here. And there's a free breakfast from 7:00 to 9:00.
Guest: Oh, great. Thank you very much.
Clerk: Here's your key. Do you need help with your bag?
Guest: No, that's all right.
Clerk: OK. Remember to leave your key at the front desk when you go out.
Guest: No problem.
Clerk: Enjoy your stay.

C 🔊 Read the expressions below. Complete each box with a similar expression from the conversation. Then listen and check your answers.

Asking about preferences
_____
Would you prefer . . . or . . . ?
Would you rather have . . . or . . . ?

Reminding someone of something
_____
Don't forget to . . .
Let me remind you to . . .

D Match the sentences and the responses. Then practice with a partner.

1. May I help you? _____
2. Would you like a single room? _____
3. Would you prefer a garden or an ocean view? _____
4. Please remember to lock your door at night. _____
5. Don't forget to check out by 11:00. _____

a. I don't know. Which one is cheaper?
b. Eleven? I thought it was by noon.
c. Actually, we need a double.
d. Yes. I have a reservation for one night.
e. I will. Thanks for the reminder.

2 Listening At a hostel

A 🔊 Listen to a backpacker check into a hostel. Complete the form with the correct information.

Sydney Backpackers

Type of room:

☐ single ☐ double ☐ triple ☐ dorm

Number of nights? _____

Bathroom? ☐ yes ☐ no **Breakfast?** ☐ yes ☐ no

Method of payment:

☐ cash ☐ credit card

Room number: _____

B 🔊 Listen again. Answer the questions.

1. Why doesn't she get a single room? _____
2. What time is breakfast? _____
3. What floor is her room on? _____
4. What does the receptionist remind her to do? _____

3 Speaking Role play

Pair work Role-play the situation. Then change roles.

Student A: You want a room at a hotel. Student B is the clerk at the front desk. Circle your preferences. Then check in.

- You want a **single / double** room.
- You want to stay for **two / three / four** nights.
- You **want / don't want** your own bathroom.
- You **want / don't want** breakfast.

Student B: You are the clerk at the front desk of a hotel. Check Student A in. At the end, remind him or her of something.

B: *Can I help you?*
A: *Yes, thank you. I'd like a room, please.*
B: *All right. Would you prefer a single or a double?*
A: *I'd prefer . . .*
B: *How many nights would you like to stay?*
A: *. . .*
B: *. . . And please don't forget . . .*

| I can *ask about preferences.* | ☑ |
| I can *remind someone of something.* | ☑ |

1 Vocabulary Extreme sports

A 🔊 Label the pictures with the correct words. Then listen and check your answers.

bungee jumping	paragliding	skydiving	waterskiing
kite surfing	rock climbing	snowboarding	white-water rafting

1. _____   2. _____   3. _____   4. _____

5. _____   6. _____   7. _____   8. _____

B Pair work Which sports would you consider trying? Which wouldn't you do? Why not? Tell your partner.

2 Conversation First-time snowboarder

A 🔊 Listen to the conversation. Why does Sarah tell Kyle to stay in the beginners' section?

Kyle: Hi. I'd like to rent a snowboard, please.

Sarah: OK. Have you ever been snowboarding?

Kyle: Um, no. But I've skied before.

Sarah: Well, we offer lessons. You don't have to take them, but it's a good idea. You'll learn the basics.

Kyle: All right. When is your next lesson?

Sarah: At 11:00. You've got to complete this form here to sign up.

Kyle: No problem. What else do I need to know?

Sarah: After your lesson, you should stay in the beginners' section for a while. It's safer for the other snowboarders.

Kyle: OK. Anything else?

Sarah: Yes. You must wear a helmet. Oh, and you ought to wear sunscreen. The sun can be very strong.

B 🔊 Listen to the conversation between Kyle and his instructor. Why is Kyle uncomfortable?

3 Grammar 🔊 Modals for necessity and recommendations

Necessity

You **must** wear a helmet.

You**'ve got to** complete this form.

You **have to** listen to your instructor.

Lack of necessity

You **don't have to** take a lesson.

Recommendations

You**'d better** be back before dark.

You **ought to** wear sunscreen.

You **should** stay in the beginners' section.

You **shouldn't** go in the advanced section.

A Circle the best travel advice. Then compare with a partner.

1. You **should / must** get a passport before you go abroad. Everybody needs one.
2. You **don't have to / 've got to** visit every landmark. Choose just a few instead.
3. You **should / don't have to** book a hotel online. It's often cheaper that way.
4. You **ought to / shouldn't** get to your hotel too early. You can't check in until 2:00.
5. You **shouldn't / 'd better** keep your money in a safe place. Losing it would be awful.
6. You **have to / should** pay for some things in cash. Many places don't take credit cards.
7. You **must / don't have to** show your student ID to get a discount. Don't forget it!
8. You **ought to / shouldn't** try some local food. It can be full of nice surprises!

B Pair work What advice would you give? Complete the sentences with modals for necessity or recommendations. Then compare answers.

1. You _____ go paragliding on a very windy day.
2. You _____ have experience to go waterskiing.
3. You _____ have special equipment to go bungee jumping.
4. You _____ be in good shape to go kite surfing.

4 Pronunciation Reduction of verbs

A 🔊 Listen and repeat. Notice the reduction of the modal verbs.

You've **got to**	You **have to**	You **ought to**
pay in cash.	check out by noon.	try the food.

B Pair work Practice the sentences in Exercise 3. Reduce the modal verbs.

5 Speaking Rules of the game

A Group work Choose an extreme sport from Exercise 1. What rules do you think there are? What recommendations would you give to someone who wanted to try it?

> **A:** *You must sign a form before you go bungee jumping.*
> **B:** *Yeah. And you should wear a helmet.*
> **C:** *Oh, and you shouldn't be afraid.*

B Class activity Share your ideas.

6 Keep talking!

Go to page 150 for more practice.

I can talk about rules and recommendations. ☑

D Seeing the sights

1 Reading ◀))

A Do you ever read food or travel blogs? Do you ever watch food or travel TV shows?

B Read the blog. Write the headings above the correct paragraphs.

> A Delicious Dinner   Juice Break   The Market   Sweet Shop

Home | About Arlen | **My Blog** | Q&A | Messages | Video | Recipes

A Taste of Cairo

Cookbook author Arlen Gargagliano is always looking for new travel experiences. Join her on her blog as she takes a food tour of Cairo, Egypt.

_____ 1:45 p.m.
Today I walked through the narrow streets of a famous Cairo market. There were many areas to explore, but my favorite was the spice market. Each shop had huge containers of colorful spices. I bought a bag of mixed spices for a friend and some dark henna to dye my hair red!

_____ 3:15 p.m.
I stopped for one of my favorite drinks – sugar cane juice! A man took pieces of sugar cane, put them in a machine, and made juice. He gave me a glass of the juice, and I drank it quickly. It was sweet and delicious! It gave me lots of energy.

_____ 6:30 p.m.
I ate dinner at the Abou el Sid restaurant. I tried several appetizers. My two favorites were a creamy bean dish in a spicy sauce and fried eggplant with garlic. I had them with fresh flatbread. I also tried a famous Egyptian dish made with a green vegetable. I want to live in this place!

_____ 8:00 p.m.
Before walking back to the hotel, I made one last stop at a place that sells wonderful Egyptian sweets in el Hussein Square. It was busy, but I sat down and ordered a cup of tea and *basbousa*, a kind of cake made with semolina and sugar syrup. It was out of this world!

C Read the blog again. Write the initials of the blog headings (D, J, M, or S) in which Arlen did the activities below. (More than one answer is possible.)

1. ate a meal _____
2. bought a gift _____
3. drank something _____
4. had something sweet _____
5. saw spices _____
6. tried vegetables _____

D Pair work Would you enjoy a tour like this? Why or why not? Discuss your ideas.

2 **Writing** A walking tour

A Pair work Choose a topic for an interesting walking tour in your town or city. Use one of the topics below or your own idea.

architecture and design	historical sights	parks and nature
food and drink	nightlife	shopping

B Pair work Write a description of your walking tour.

Historic Old San Juan

To really learn about the history of Puerto Rico, you have to walk through Old San Juan. You should start your walking tour at the city walls. Follow these walls along the sea to San Juan Gate, which was built around 1635. Go through the gate, turn right, and walk uphill. At the end of the street you can see La Fortaleza. . . .

C Group work Present your tour to another pair. Did you include any of the same places?

La Fortaleza
Old San Juan, Puerto Rico

3 **Listening** An adventure tour

A 🔊 Listen to a guide talk to some tourists before a Grand Canyon rafting trip. What does the guide tell the tourists to do? Check (✓) the correct answers.

- ☐ wear a safety vest
- ☐ drink a lot of water
- ☐ bring water
- ☐ bring food

- ☐ wear sunscreen
- ☐ wear a hat
- ☐ leave your camera
- ☐ bring plastic bags

- ☐ bring your cell phone
- ☐ wear a swimsuit
- ☐ wear tennis shoes
- ☐ listen to your guide

B 🔊 Listen again. Are the statements true or false? Write T (true) or F (false).

1. The most important thing to remember is to have fun. _____

2. The tourists need to wear safety vests at all times on the raft. _____

3. There is no eating or drinking allowed. _____

4. The tourists shouldn't leave their phones on the bus. _____

4 **Speaking** Dream trip

A Imagine you can go anywhere in the world for three weeks. Answer the questions.

- What kind of trip are you interested in taking?
- What places would you like to visit? Why?
- What would you like to do in each place?
- How long do you plan to spend in each place?
- How can you get from place to place?

B Pair work Tell your partner about your dream trip. Ask and answer questions for more information.

I can describe my dream trip. ☑

Wrap-up

1 Quick pair review

Lesson A **Test your partner!** Say four vacation activities. Can your partner use the gerund form of the phrase in a sentence correctly? You have three minutes.

A: *See wildlife.*
B: *I'm not interested in seeing wildlife on vacation.*

Lesson B **Give your opinion!** Ask your partner which vacation he or she prefers from each pair of pictures. Then remind your partner to do or take something on the trip. Take turns. You have two minutes.

A: *Would you prefer going to an island or to the mountains?*
B: *I'd prefer going to an island.*
A: *OK. Remember to take sunscreen.*

Lesson C **Brainstorm!** Make a list of extreme sports people do in the water, in the air, and on land. How many do you know? You have one minute.

Lesson D **Guess!** Describe your dream trip to your partner, but don't say where it is. Can your partner guess where it is? Take turns. You have two minutes.

2 In the real world

Would you like to try a new sport? Go online and find recommendations in English for people who want to try a new sport. Use one of the sports below or your own idea. Then write about it.

| sandboarding | downhill mountain biking | base jumping | bodyboarding |

> *Sandboarding*
> Sandboarding is like snowboarding, but you do it on sand, not snow. You must have a sandboard for this sport. You should wear glasses so that you don't get sand in your eyes.

122

Left brain / right brain

A Pair work Interview your partner. Check (✓) his or her answers.

Left Brain vs. Right Brain

Do you use your right or left brain more often? Try this fun quiz and find out.

1. How do you remember things?
   - a. with words
   - b. with pictures
   - c. both

2. Which can you remember easily?
   - a. names
   - b. faces
   - c. both

3. Which math subject do you like?
   - a. algebra
   - b. geometry
   - c. both

4. How do you like to work in class?
   - a. alone
   - b. in groups
   - c. both

5. How do you like to study alone?
   - a. quietly
   - b. with music playing
   - c. both

6. Which activity do you enjoy?
   - a. writing
   - b. drawing
   - c. both

7. What kinds of tests do you like?
   - a. multiple choice
   - b. essay
   - c. both

8. How do you like things explained to you?
   - a. with words
   - b. with actions
   - c. both

9. What do you use to make decisions?
   - a. the facts
   - b. my experience
   - c. both

10. How do you like to solve problems?
    - a. one at a time
    - b. at the same time
    - c. both

11. How do you manage your time?
    - a. very carefully
    - b. not very carefully
    - c. both

12. Which animals do you like?
    - a. dogs
    - b. cats
    - c. both

Source: library.thinkquest.org

B Pair work Score your partner's answers. Is he or she left-brained or right-brained? (More *c* answers or the same number of *a* and *b* answers means your partner has traits for both.)

More *a* answers: Left-brained	More *b* answers: Right-brained
More verbal than visual	More visual than verbal
Likes to do things step by step	Likes to do things at the same time
Very organized	Not always organized
Follows rules without questioning	Often asks why
Strong sense of time	Little sense of time
Learns by seeing	Learns by doing
Uses few gestures when talking	Talks with hands
Listens to what is said	Listens to how something is said

C Group work Do your results in Part B describe you well? What do you think your results say about your personality?

People on my mind

A Write the name of someone you know for each description. Then think about answers to the questions.

Someone I miss very much:

_____mom_____

- How long have you known this person? 68
- When did you last see him or her?
- When will you see each other again?

Someone who gave me a special gift:

_____Kwon_____

- What was the gift?
- How long have you had it?
- What made the gift special?

Someone I'd like to know better:

_____Book_____

- How long have you known this person?
- When was the last time you spoke?
- What's he or she like?

Someone I've admired since I was a child: _respect_

_____I was_____

- When did you first meet this person?
- What do you admire about him or her?
- Do you share any of the same qualities?

B **Pair work** Interview your partner about each person. Ask questions for more information.

A: *Who is someone you miss very much?*
B: *I miss my grandmother very much.*
A: *How long have you known her?*
B: *I've known her since I was born! But I haven't seen her since April.*

A green quiz

A **Pair work** Interview your partner. Circle his or her answers.

HOW GREEN ARE YOU?
Try this quiz to find out.

1. You're leaving for the weekend, but you're not taking your computer. What do you do?
   a. Put it to "sleep."
   b. Shut it down.
   c. Turn it off and unplug it.

2. You're planning to go to a movie with several friends. What do you do?
   a. Go in separate cars.
   b. Meet and go in one car.
   c. Take public transportation.

3. You're walking and see some empty bottles on the sidewalk. What do you do?
   a. Leave the bottles there.
   b. Put them in a garbage can.
   c. Put them in a recycling bin.

4. Your office has a watercooler with plastic cups for people to use. What do you do?
   a. Use a different plastic cup each time.
   b. Use the same plastic cup all day.
   c. Use your own regular cup.

5. You're buying a magazine, and the cashier starts to put it in a bag. What do you do?
   a. Take the bag and throw it away later.
   b. Take the bag, but reuse it.
   c. Just take the magazine.

6. You have some old, unused medicine that you don't need. What do you do?
   a. Flush it down the toilet.
   b. Throw it in the garbage.
   c. Return it to a pharmacy.

7. You're making a salad and realize you don't have enough lettuce. What do you do?
   a. Get any lettuce at the nearest store.
   b. Buy organic lettuce at a farmer's market.
   c. Pick some lettuce from your own garden.

8. A company in your neighborhood is harming the environment. What do you do?
   a. Nothing.
   b. Tell your friends.
   c. Write a letter to the local newspaper about it.

B **Pair work** Score your partner's answers. How green is he or she? Are the results accurate?

a answers = 0 points
b answers = 1 point
c answers = 2 points

11–16 Congratulations! You lead a very green life.
6–10 You're green in some ways, but not in others.
0–5 You're not very green. It's not too late to change!

C **Pair work** What other things do you do to help the environment? Tell your partner.

Be an optimist!

A **Pair work** Add two situations to the chart. Then discuss what will, could, or might happen in each situation. Take notes.

If we . . . ,	we will . . .	we might . . .
eat too much fast food		
spend all day at the beach		
use cell phones in class		
read the news every day		
never study English		
watch too much TV		
don't get enough sleep		
spend too much time online		

A: *What do you think will happen if we eat too much fast food?*
B: *If we eat too much fast food, we'll gain weight.*

B **Group work** Share your ideas with another pair. Which ideas are the best? Do you have any other ideas?

What to do?

A Group work Imagine you have one of the relationship problems below. Your group gives you advice. Take turns.

My friend texts me constantly and then gets angry if I don't answer right away. Is it important to answer every text? I'm not sure what to do about this. I prefer to communicate by phone.

My sister has a new hairstyle, and I think it looks pretty awful. I don't really want to criticize her, but I think it's a good idea to say something to her. But what exactly do I say?

My co-worker won't talk to me. She says I gossiped about her. I guess I did, but it wasn't anything serious. It feels like she's judging me. I hope she can forgive me. After all, we need to work together.

My classmate always tries to copy my answers when we are taking tests or working on our own. It makes me angry. I don't want the teacher to think I'm cheating, too. Should I tell my teacher?

A: *My friend texts me constantly and then . . .*
B: *It's not important to answer every text. Just ignore them.*
C: *But it's not good to ignore them. Say something to your friend about it.*
D: *That's good advice. It's also a good idea to . . .*

B Group work Which advice was the best? Why? Tell your group.

"Maria gave the best advice. It's important to tell the truth."

C Group work Have you ever given relationship advice to someone? Who? What was the advice? Tell your group.

What do you think?

A Pair work Look at the picture. Make one speculation about each person. Use *must, could, can't, may,* or *might*.

A: *Diego is buying a dress, but it can't be for his wife. It's too small.*
B: *Right. He might be buying it for his daughter.*
A: *Yeah. And he must be rich. The store looks very expensive.*

B **Group work** Compare your speculations with another pair. Did you make any of the same ones?

Reflections

A Class activity Find classmates who answer "yes" to each question. Write their names and ask questions for more information.

Questions	Name	Extra information
1. Have you ever eaten an entire pizza by yourself?		
2. Do you learn better by studying in a group than by yourself?		
3. Did you teach yourself how to cook?		
4. Do you see yourself living in another country in five years?		
5. Have you ever traveled anywhere by yourself?		
6. Would you like to change something about yourself?		
7. Have you ever lived by yourself?		
8. Do you know someone who taught himself or herself a foreign language?		

A: *Have you ever eaten an entire pizza by yourself?*
B: *Yes, I have!*
A: *Wow! That's a lot of pizza. What kind of pizza was it?*
B: *It had cheese, pepperoni, onions, and peppers on it.*

B Share your information. What's the most interesting thing you learned? Who else in the class answered "yes" to each question?

Imagine that!

A Guess your partner's answers to the questions. Write your guesses in the chart.

Questions	My guesses	My partner's answers
1. What would you do if you saw your favorite celebrity?		
2. What would you do if your best friend moved to another country?		
3. How would you feel if someone brought up something embarrassing about you at a party?		
4. What would you do if you broke something expensive in a store?		
5. Where would you go if you had one week to travel anywhere in the world?		
6. What would you do if a friend borrowed some money from you and then didn't pay you back?		
7. What would you do if your grades in this class suddenly dropped?		

B **Pair work** Interview your partner. Complete the chart with his or her answers. How many of your partner's answers did you guess correctly?

C **Class activity** Do any of your partner's answers surprise you? Would you and your partner do any similar things? Tell the class.

Facts and opinions

A **Group work** Add two sets of questions about music to the list. Then discuss the questions. Ask follow-up questions to get more information.

1. What bands were formed in the 1960s? '70s? '80s? '90s? What was their music like?
2. What male singer do you think has a nice-sounding voice? What female singer?
3. What well-known singers or bands do you not like very much? Why not?
4. Were any record-breaking hits released last year? What did you think of the songs?
5. Was any truly awful music released in the past few years? What made it so terrible?
6. What was the last music awards show you saw on TV? Who was on it?
7. Who are the best-selling singers from your country? Do you enjoy their music?
8. What are some easily learned songs in your native language? Do you know all the words?
9. _____ ? _____ ?
10. _____ ? _____ ?

The Rolling Stones, 1960s

ABBA, 1970s

R.E.M., 1980s

The Spice Girls, 1990s

A: *The Rolling Stones were formed in the 1960s.*
B: *How was their music?*
A: *Their music was fantastic. It still is.*
C: *Can you name the band members?*

B **Class activity** Share any interesting information.

Find the differences

Student A

You and your partner have pictures of Monica and Victor, but they aren't exactly the same. Ask questions with *yet* to find the differences. Circle the items that are different.

see a movie

get a new stereo

download a song

send a text

buy a CD

sing a song

A: *Have Monica and Victor seen a movie yet?*
B: *No, they haven't. In my picture, they haven't seen it yet. They're going inside.*
A: *So that's different. In my picture, they're leaving the movie theater.*

Find the differences

Student B

You and your partner have pictures of Monica and Victor, but they aren't exactly the same. Ask questions with *yet* to find the differences. Circle the items that are different.

see a movie

get a new stereo

download a song

send a text

buy a CD

sing a song

A: *Have Monica and Victor seen a movie yet?*
B: *No, they haven't. In my picture, they haven't seen it yet. They're going inside.*
A: *So that's different. In my picture, they're leaving the movie theater.*

Travel partners

A Add three questions about travel preferences to the chart. Then check (✓) your answers.

When you travel, . . .	Me Yes	Me No	Name: _____ Yes	No
1. do you like being in a large group?	☐	☐	☐	☐
2. are you interested in meeting new people?	☐	☐	☐	☐
3. is saving money important to you?	☐	☐	☐	☐
4. do you like trying new foods?	☐	☐	☐	☐
5. is asking directions embarrassing to you?	☐	☐	☐	☐
6. do you like knowing your schedule in advance?	☐	☐	☐	☐
7. is camping more fun than staying in hotels?	☐	☐	☐	☐
8. do you enjoy shopping for souvenirs?	☐	☐	☐	☐
9. do you like big cities?	☐	☐	☐	☐
10. do you like going to clubs?	☐	☐	☐	☐
11. is seeing everything possible important to you?	☐	☐	☐	☐
12.	☐	☐	☐	☐
13.	☐	☐	☐	☐
14.	☐	☐	☐	☐

B Pair work Interview your partner. Complete the chart with his or her answers.

C Pair work Compare your answers. Would you make good travel partners? Why or why not?

A: *We wouldn't make good travel partners. You like being in a large group. I don't.*
B: *Yes, but we're both interested in meeting new people.*
A: *Well, that's true. And saving money is important to us.*

A backpacking trip

A **Pair work** Imagine someone is planning a two-week backpacking trip to your country. What rules and recommendations would you give for each category? Take notes.

Packing	Communication
Health and safety	**Places to stay**
Transportation	**Money**
Food	**Other**

B **Group work** Share your ideas with another pair. Did you have any of the same rules or recommendations? Can you think of any other rules or recommendations?

A: *You shouldn't pack too many clothes.*
B: *Yes, but you have to have enough clothes!*
C: *Also, you ought to bring your cell phone.*

Irregular verbs

Base form	Simple past	Past participle
be	was, were	been
become	became	become
break	broke	broken
build	built	built
buy	bought	bought
choose	chose	chosen
come	came	come
do	did	done
draw	drew	drawn
drink	drank	drunk
drive	drove	driven
eat	ate	eaten
fall	fell	fallen
feel	felt	felt
fly	flew	flown
forget	forgot	forgotten
get	got	gotten
give	gave	given
go	went	gone
hang	hung	hung
have	had	had
hear	heard	heard
hold	held	held
know	knew	known
leave	left	left

Base form	Simple past	Past participle
lose	lost	lost
make	made	made
meet	met	met
pay	paid	paid
put	put	put
read	read	read
ride	rode	ridden
run	ran	run
say	said	said
see	saw	seen
sell	sold	sold
send	sent	sent
sing	sang	sung
sit	sat	sat
sleep	slept	slept
speak	spoke	spoken
spend	spent	spent
stand	stood	stood
swim	swam	swum
take	took	taken
teach	taught	taught
think	thought	thought
wear	wore	worn
win	won	won
write	wrote	written

Adjective and adverb formations

Adjectives	Adverbs
agreeable	agreeably
amazing	amazingly
ambitious	ambitiously
angry	angrily
brave	bravely
careful	carefully
confident	confidently
considerate	considerately
creative	creatively
curious	curiously
decisive	decisively
disagreeable	disagreeably
dishonest	dishonestly
early	early
easy	easily
enthusiastic	enthusiastically
extreme	extremely
fair	fairly
fashionable	fashionably
fast	fast
fortunate	fortunately
glamorous	glamorously
good	well
hard	hard
honest	honestly

Adjectives	Adverbs
immature	immaturely
impatient	impatiently
inconsiderate	inconsiderately
indecisive	indecisively
interesting	interestingly
late	late
lucky	luckily
mature	maturely
nervous	nervously
optimistic	optimistically
patient	patiently
quick	quickly
rare	rarely
reliable	reliably
sad	sadly
serious	seriously
similar	similarly
strange	strangely
stubborn	stubbornly
sudden	suddenly
surprising	surprisingly
unfair	unfairly
unfortunate	unfortunately
unreliable	unreliably
wise	wisely

Answer key

Unit 7 Lesson D (page 71)
Listening

This personality test is just for fun. Don't take the answers *too* seriously!

1. This person is the most important person in your life.

2. If you see a big animal, you think you have big problems.

3. If you have a big house, you are very ambitious.

4. If the door is open, you're happy for people to visit anytime. If it's closed, you prefer people to call first.

5. If there is food or flowers on the table, you are very optimistic.

6. If the material is strong (like metal or plastic), you have a strong relationship with the person in number 1.

7. If you keep the cup, you want to keep a good relationship with the person in number 1.

Credits

CONTENTS

FROMMER'S

COMPREHENSIVE TRAVEL GUIDE

NEW YORK '93

by Faye Hammel
Assisted by Michael Kaminer

PRENTICE HALL TRAVEL

NEW YORK • LONDON • TORONTO • SYDNEY • TOKYO • SINGAPORE

The Walking Tour on page 226 is from *Frommer's New York State
'92–'93* by John Foreman.

FROMMER BOOKS

Published by Prentice Hall General Reference
A division of Simon & Schuster Inc.
15 Columbus Circle
New York, NY 10023

ISBN 0-671-84682-5
ISSN 0899-7675

Design by Robert Bull Design
Maps by Geografix Inc.

FROMMER'S NEW YORK '93
Editorial Director: Marilyn Wood
Senior Editors: Judith de Rubini, Alice Fellows, Lisa Renaud
Editors: Thomas F. Hirsch, Peter Katucki, Sara Hinsey Raveret, Theodore
    Stavrou
Assistant Editors: Margaret Bowen, Lee Gray, Ian Wilker
Managing Editor: Leanne Coupe

Special Sales

Bulk purchases of Frommer's Travel Guides are available at special discounts. The publishers are happy to custom-make publications for corporate clients who wish to use them as premiums or sales promotions. We
can excerpt the contents, provide covers with corporate imprints, or create
books to meet specific needs. For more information write to Special Sales,
Prentice Hall Travel, Paramount Communications Building, 15 Columbus
Circle, New York, NY 10023

Manufactured in the United States of America

LIST OF MAPS

WALKING TOURS

INVITATION TO THE READERS

In researching this book, I have come across many fine establishments, the best of which I have included here. I am sure that many of you will also come across appealing hotels, inns, restaurants, guesthouses, shops, and attractions. Please don't keep them to yourself. Share your experiences, especially if you want to comment on places that have been included in this edition that have changed for the worse. You can address your letters to:

Faye Hammel
Frommer's New York
Prentice Hall Travel
15 Columbus Circle
New York, NY 10023

A DISCLAIMER

Readers are advised that prices fluctuate in the course of time, and travel information changes under the impact of the varied and volatile factors that affect the travel industry. Neither the author nor the publisher can be held responsible for the experiences of readers while traveling. Readers are invited to write to the publisher with ideas, comments, and suggestions for future editions.

INFLATION ALERT

Inflation affects New York as it does everyplace else. I have spent laborious hours attempting to ensure the accuracy of prices appearing in this guide. As the book goes to press, I believe I have obtained the most reliable data possible. Nonetheless, in the lifetime of this edition, the wise traveler might add 10% to 15% to the prices quoted throughout these pages.

SAFETY ADVISORY

Whenever you're traveling in an unfamiliar city or country, stay alert. Be aware of your immediate surroundings. Wear a moneybelt and keep a close eye on your possessions. Be particularly careful with cameras, purses, and wallets—all favorite targets of thieves and pickpockets.

CHAPTER 1

INTRODUCING NEW YORK

New York—it's a great place to visit, as the saying goes, but it's not an easy city to know. Because there is so much happening here, such a wealth of things that bombard the visitor, it's easy to come to New York and leave it without having experienced the best of it. And when it comes to spending your dollar wisely, here in one of the most expensive cities on earth, it takes some special knowhow. Here, then, is the inside dope, the special tips that can make all the difference between feeling like a native or a newcomer. Read on to find which hotels offer the best values for the dollar, from the Waldorf to the "Y"; which restaurants are worth declaring bankruptcy for and which will feed you well for a pittance; and how to get tickets for a top Broadway musical without paying scalper's rates or having an uncle who works for the producer. You'll discover how to enjoy the city's sights in the most efficient, relaxed manner possible; how to discover the shopping secrets of New York's out-of-the-way bargain meccas; and how to find the coziest pub, the latest disco, or the newest supper club. A series of walking tours will help you explore the city's rich architectural history. Hopefully, this catalog of the best New York has to offer will be useful to you, whether it's your first trip to the city or your 110th. First, though, a word of warning to newcomers.

There is one dangerous aspect of coming to New York for the first time: not of getting lost, mugged, or caught in a blackout, but of falling so desperately in love with the city that you may not want to go home again. Or, if you do, it may be just to pack your bags. With most visitors to New York, it's usually love or hate at first sight. Either you are so enthralled by the dazzle, the tempo, the sense of adventure that only a great city can give, that you immediately make it your own . . . or you may find the noise, the smog, the traffic, the poverty evidenced in the streets by the homeless, the seeming callousness of the natives, all just too much. But New York is still the magic town, and the younger you are, the more potent is its spell. *Caveat emptor.*

WHAT MAKES NEW YORK TICK To describe New York fully would take volumes—and besides, it's indescribable. New York simply must be experienced, in all its incredible variety, to be comprehended. It is unlike any other city in America—more like a small (or not-so-small) country of its own. New York is a lot more like London than it is like Chicago or Los Angeles, but it is really an entity only to itself.

It is noted for its size (with a population of around eight million, it is the nation's largest city); its diversity (more different kinds of people do their thing here than just about anywhere else); and perhaps most

✓ WHAT'S SPECIAL ABOUT NEW YORK

World-Class Attractions
- ☐ The Statue of Liberty, restored and shining brighter than ever.
- ☐ Ellis Island, the portal through which 12 million immigrants entered the United States from 1892 to 1954, now welcoming tourists.
- ☐ The United Nations, international enclave on the East River.

Architectural Highlights
- ☐ City Hall (1811), a formal Federal-style building.
- ☐ The Federal Hall National Memorial (1842–62), a prime example of Greek Revival style.
- ☐ The New York Public Library (1898–1911), a superb example of Beaux Arts design, with those famous lions.
- ☐ The Flatiron Building (1902), shaped like a flatiron.
- ☐ Grand Central Terminal (1903–13), one of the great interior spaces of the city.
- ☐ The Empire State Building (1931), at 102 stories high the symbol of the city.
- ☐ The Seagram Building (1958), which heralded the arrival of the modern office tower in New York.

Museums
- ☐ The Metropolitan Museum of Art, one of the major art palaces of the world.
- ☐ The Museum of Modern Art, for the best of modern art.
- ☐ The Whitney Museum, with an outstanding collection of 20th-century American art.
- ☐ The Guggenheim Museum, designed by Frank Lloyd Wright, an unconventional setting for modern art.

Shopping
- ☐ Macy's, the world's largest store, and other major department and specialty stores.
- ☐ Madison Avenue and SoHo for elegant boutiques.
- ☐ The Lower East Side for incredible bargains.

Zoos
- ☐ The Bronx Zoo, one of the best in the world.
- ☐ Central Park Zoo, small and enchanting, a delight for kids.

Public Gardens
- ☐ Central Park, the city's great rural playground.
- ☐ New York Botanical Garden in the Bronx, with an acre of gardens under glass.
- ☐ Brooklyn Botanic Garden, 52 glorious acres of flowers, trees, exotic plants, and Japanese cherry trees that blossom in the spring.

After Dark
- ☐ World-class theater, music, dance, and films, plus an exciting club scene.

For the Kids
- ☐ The *Intrepid* Sea-Air-Space Museum, a floating museum of naval history and technology.
- ☐ The American Museum of Natural History, with exhibitions, giant-screen films, and the Discovery Center.
- ☐ The Children's Museum of Manhattan, a mind-boggling place for kids 3 to 15.
- ☐ The AT&T InfoQuest Center, with interactive exhibits for older children: robotics, holograms, microelectronics, and more.

important of all, the magnetism that attracts the brightest, most creative, most ambitious, most determined people from everywhere. For this is the central city, the megalopolis, the nerve center of the world's finance and trade; of advertising, publishing, and fashion; of theater, ballet, and music; and, with the United Nations here, of world diplomacy as well. It is the vortex that pulls into its center a lot of the best (and worst) people and projects and theories and schemes from everywhere. New York is the eye of the hurricane. This is what gives the city its special feeling of intensity, the high-powered vibration that is felt immediately by even the most casual visitor. It is what makes New York one of the most exciting places on the planet.

1. GEOGRAPHY, HISTORY & POLITICS

GEOGRAPHY New York City is the southernmost point in New York State, comprising over 300 square miles just east of the state of New Jersey, on the northeast coast of the United States. Of the five boroughs that constitute the city, the Bronx is the only one that is part of the mainland. The island of Manhattan is bounded by the Hudson River to the west, the Harlem River to the north, the East River to the east, and Upper New York Bay to the south. Staten Island is surrounded by the Arthur Kill Channel and Upper and Lower New York Bays. Queens and Brooklyn are on the westernmost point of Long Island.

Manhattan is, of course, an island, and a rather small one at that (12 miles long, 2½ miles across at its widest point). You probably already know that New York City is divided into five boroughs: Manhattan, the most important; the Bronx, to the north; Brooklyn, to the south; Queens (where Kennedy and LaGuardia airports and Shea Stadium are), to the east; and Staten Island, southeast of New York harbor. Since you'll probably be spending most of your time in Manhattan, there's no need to concern yourself with the details of getting around the other boroughs. If you do visit them, be sure to get specific directions and pick up some good maps in advance.

HISTORY & POLITICS New York is a city always in transition, the unofficial capital of the world. It is the world's center for the arts; commerce; and, most of all, industry. It has always been a trading post, founded as such as Nieuw Amsterdam in 1623 by the Dutch West India Company. Ever since Peter Minuit landed with his small group of Dutch settlers in 1626 and drove a shrewd bargain with the Indians for the purchase of Manhattan for $24 (60 guilders) worth of trinkets, trade has been the chief occupation. There had been earlier discoveries: In 1524, Italian explorer Giovanni da Verrazano had found New York harbor to be "an agreeable situation . . . in the midst of which flowed . . . a very great

DATELINE

- **1524** Giovanni da Verrazano is first to explore the bay of New York.
- **1609** Henry Hudson sails as far as Albany in search of a passage to the Orient.
- **1614** Adriaen Block charts the waters around Manhattan, naming the area "New Netherland."

(continues)

4 • INTRODUCING NEW YORK

river." The Narrows he sailed through, and the bridge that now spans it, bear his name. In 1609, Henry Hudson, an Englishman searching for a northwest passage to the Orient, sailed his *Half Moon* as far north as Albany up the river later named for him.

From the beginning, Nieuw Amsterdam was run as a business. To attract new settlers, the Dutch offered land inducements to merchants willing to come and set up shop. As the population increased, new settlements were established: Staten Island in 1630; Queens a year later; and, finally, in 1639, the Bronx. A fur trade flourished; in 1635 alone, $53,000 worth of pelts were exported. The town early earned a reputation for dissolution and lawlessness. Liquor stores lined the streets, drunkenness was rampant; there was blatant disregard for rules and ordinances, much to the chagrin of Gov. Peter Stuyvesant, who was constantly at odds with his unruly subjects.

Although rigidly autocratic, Stuyvesant was well regarded. Under his administration Nieuw Amsterdam acquired its first City Hall (a converted tavern) along with its first city government; its first building and fire codes; its first ferry service; the first ordinances against fast driving, excessive drinking, and fighting in the streets; and its first city police. A fortified wall was built along what is now Wall Street to keep out the Indians and the British; and a canal on Broad Street was designed to give the city more of a Dutch appeal.

When the British suddenly attacked in 1664, Stuyvesant was in no position to fight, since Fort Amsterdam was in a state of disrepair because the home government had not allocated funds for its defense. So Nieuw Amsterdam became New York, and though it was recaptured by the Dutch in 1673 (and held for over a year), it was returned to the British in exchange for Java, considered a more valuable asset. In 1683 the city received its first British Charter and Official Seal. New York had its first pre-Revolutionary civil liberties battle in 1734, when John Peter Zenger, editor of the *New York Weekly Journal*, was prosecuted for libel for articles he had written criticizing British rule. Public opinion led to his acquittal, and freedom of the press was born. For most of the Revolution, the British were headquartered in New York, but when it was all over, a victorious George Washington rode into town to cheering crowds and bade farewell to his troops at historic Fraunces Tavern "with a heart full of love and gratitude. . . ."

For a short time (1789–91) New York was the capital of the New United States, and in its first year George Washington was inaugurated at Federal Hall. New York's economic development continued with the beginning of the stock exchange and the founding of the Bank of New York by Alexander Hamilton. As a result of the population so rapidly expanding, the city water supply became a serious problem. Yellow fever and cholera killed thousands; survivors fled in droves to the "country" north of 14th Street. By 1799, the first public utility was established to supply the city with fresh water.

New York boomed after 1812, largely due to the opening of the Erie Canal, which gave the city a virtual monopoly on transportation to the west. The City Planning Commission, organized in 1811, designed Manhattan's present-day grid system of streets. In 1858, Frederick Law Olmsted, a landscape architect, and Calvert Vaux, an architect, won the competition and $2,000 prize to design Central Park, a swampland then inhabited by squatters.

During the Civil War—although the well-to-do could buy their way out of the army for $300, and the poor, resentful of this injustice, rioted in the streets—many of New York's 750,000 went to war. Afterward, economic recovery was rapid, and corruption commonplace; it existed in both the business and the public sectors. The money stolen from the city during William "Boss" Tweed's administration of Tammany Hall, the political organization that ran the city in the 1860s and '70s, has been estimated as high as $200 million.

Tremendous waves of immigration (between 1892 and 1894, 12 million people arrived) produced the manpower for building the elevated railway, the Brooklyn Bridge, and the first skyscrapers.

The late 19th and 20th centuries have seen stupendous expansion only temporarily interrupted by economic depressions and two world wars. In 1898, Brooklyn and Queens were annexed into Greater New York (the Bronx already had been annexed). Following the Tammany Hall regime, Mayor Fiorello La Guardia, "The Little Flower,"

DATELINE

lumbia University— is chartered.

- **1761** Oil lamps on posts are Manhattan's first street lights.
- **1765** Stamp Act enforced; Congress convenes in New York to protest taxes.
- **1774** English ship loaded with tea turned back in New York's own "tea party."
- **1776** The American Revolutionary War begins.
- **1783** British forces leave New York. George Washington delivers his farewell address at Fraunces Tavern.
- **1789** George Washington is sworn in as first President of the United States, at Federal Hall.
- **1790** The first census counts almost 100,000.
- **1791** Stock Exchange started.
- **1797** Capital of New York State moved to Albany.
- **1807** The *Clermont*, Robert Fulton's steamboat, voyages up the Hudson to Albany.
- **1817** New York State decrees that all slaves be freed by 1827.
- **1820** Population reaches 120,000.
- **1825** Erie Canal completed.
- **1831** New York University founded.

(continues)

DATELINE

- **1840** Population reaches 312,710.
- **1848** Ireland's potato famine and Germany's political uprisings cause an influx of immigrants.
- **1850** Population soars to 696,115.
- **1851** The *New York Times* is founded.
- **1853** Crystal Palace houses the World's Fair on the site of Bryant Park.
- **1858** Calvert Vaux and Frederick Law Olmsted win the competition to design Central Park.
- **1863** Less affluent New Yorkers stage "Draft Riots" when a law allows individuals to avoid conscription for the Civil War by paying $300.
- **1870** Population reaches nearly a million.
- **1871** "Boss" Tweed and his political cronies are jailed for stealing millions from the city while in power.
- **1880** Metropolitan Museum of Art opens.
- **1882** Electric power plant built by Thomas Edison provides city with electricity.
- **1883** Brooklyn Bridge opens to traffic.
- **1885** United States receives the Statue of Liberty as *(continues)*

restored color, character, and optimism to an office lacking all three. La Guardia saw his city through the Depression years, creating jobs, improving buildings and parks, and securing federal aid for the poor.

In 1952, the United Nations moved to Manhattan, making it more than ever a political sounding board to the world. Today New York glitters as a bastion of capitalism, its mighty skyscrapers dominating the skyline with a zeal that out-of-towners find overwhelming, even terrifying. Yet New York is a beautiful city, beautiful of line, color, and dramatic impetus. There are incomparable museums, theaters, art galleries, and concert halls and every kind of antique shop, bookseller, clock dealer, and jade carver. By common consent, New York restaurants are among the finest in the world. A seamless ritual of rejuvenation and hope still prevails, perhaps a carryover from the days of immigration, when America was the haven for all the world's oppressed. New York is America at its bold best, the noblest of symbols, the most exciting city on earth.

2. ARCHITECTURE & THE ARTS

ARCHITECTURE New York is a polyglot city, a rich warren of architectural styles that reflect the diversity of its culture and its historical heritage.

The Great Fires of 1776 and 1835 ravaged New York and destroyed many of the Georgian and early Federal buildings. Those that remain are largely neglected and scattered throughout the city. Some examples of buildings in these styles still to be found are St. Paul's Chapel (1766), the earliest surviving pre-Revolutionary nonresidential building in New York, and the Morris-Jumel Mansion (1768), an excellent example of Georgian Colonial, although it was remodeled in the Federal style in 1810.

In the first half of the 19th century, Greek and Gothic Revival emerged. The Federal Hall National Memorial (1842–62) recalls an Athenian temple, and many attached town houses have facades decorated in the Greek style. Richard Upjohn's Trinity Church (1846) at the end of Wall Street is a classic example of Gothic Revivalism, while Stanford White's Washington Arch, along with the town houses along Washington Square North (c. 1832) reflect a passion for Greek Revivalism.

After the Civil War, a resurgence of international travel and trade brought to New York a renewed interest in European architecture. Examples of Tudor, Romanesque, Italian Renaissance, and French Second Empire can all be found—not infrequently in the same structure. Villard House (1886), for example, was clearly inspired by the Palazzo della Cancelleria in Rome. Despite revolutionary technology, such as steel pile foundations and steel frames, there was very little change in architectural styles at first, as well as a seeming unawareness of the possibilities this technology offered in terms of design. The invention of the hydraulic lift allowed for the erection of skyscrapers, but their steel frames were disguised with facades from other periods. The rusticated stone facade and the Florentine Renaissance cornices of the Flatiron Building (1902) are typical examples of the continued use of earlier architectural styles. Another building constructed in a similar vein is the Woolworth Building (1913), with its adaptation of a Gothic cathedral—complete with gargoyles—to skyscraper form.

In residential architecture, brownstone row houses reminiscent of those in Paris persisted, though available technology also produced such luxury high-rise apartment buildings as the Chelsea and the Dakota (both 1884). The neoclassical decoration of the Metropolitan Museum of Art (1902) exhibited the strong interest in the beaux arts movement prevalent as the 20th century began.

Modernist architecture began to develop through the form-follows-function model of Louis Sullivan, who was the first to break from the idea that older architectural styles were necessary to the facades of skyscrapers. Art deco was the next major innovation. The Chrysler Building (1930), the Empire State Building (1931), and the 1932 RCA Building (now called the GE Building) are stunning examples of the heights to which skyscraper architecture rose.

Economic recovery after the depression saw the development of glass-walled buildings, where the weight-bearing function

DATELINE

a gift from the French people.

- **1887** Electric street cars run on elevated railways.
- **1889** Arch at Washington Square commemorates Centennial of George Washington's Inauguration.
- **1892** An immigration center is established on Ellis Island.
- **1898** Greater New York City is formed by incorporation of all five boroughs.
- **1899** Bronx Zoo opens.
- **1900** Construction of subways begins.
- **1901** Macy's department store opens for business.
- **1904** IRT subway line opens, running from City Hall to 145th Street.
- **1911** New York Public Library at 42nd Street opens.
- **1917** United States enters WWI. New York City is chief port of embarkation for troops.
- **1920** Population is 5,620,048.
- **1923** Yankee Stadium becomes home to New York Yankees.
- **1929** Stock market crash precipitates onset of the Great Depression.
- **1930** Population is 6,930,446. Chrysler Building completed.

(continues)

DATELINE

- **1931** George Washington Bridge and Empire State Building open.
- **1932** Radio City Music Hall raises its curtain to mixed reviews.
- **1934** Rainbow Room restaurant and bar opens on top of one-year-old RCA Building.
- **1939** LaGuardia Airport opens in time for second World's Fair.
- **1948** Idlewild Airport, renamed for John F. Kennedy in 1963, opens.
- **1951** United Nations complex finished.
- **1954** Ellis Island is closed.
- **1959** Construction begins on Lincoln Center for the Performing Arts.
- **1964** Original Pennsylvania Station demolished and Madison Square Garden Sports Arena built. World's Fair in Flushing Meadows, Queens, has 50 million visitors in two years.
- **1973** Twin towers of the World Trade Center completed.
- **1980** On December 10, former Beatle John Lennon is murdered outside the Dakota Apartments on Central Park West.
- **1981** Mayor Edward I. Koch, first politician to carry *(continues)*

rested on steel skeletons. Lever House (1952) and the Seagram Building (1958) are the first examples of the glass-and-steel-curtain walls of the new International Style.

In recent times, sculptural planes and masses have become prevalent and are in evidence in such buildings as the Whitney Museum (1966) and the Waterside Houses (1974). An interest in decorative facades is currently being exhibited, such as is seen in the Chippendale cornice of the AT&T Building (1978–82).

THE ARTS No sooner was New York City settled than its artistic citizens found an avenue for expression. Theaters became increasingly popular from the time the first one opened on Maiden Lane in 1732. Painters, however, were not to see New York as their venue for nearly two centuries. The city's lack of interest in art (commerce and trade were the chief foci) drove them to Europe, a pattern established by such artists as Benjamin West and John Singleton Copley.

However, with the growth of fascism in Europe in the 1930s, the trend reversed with the influx of a number of artist-teachers such as Hans Hoffman. After World War II, the New York School became prominent with artists such as Jackson Pollock, Robert Motherwell, Mark Rothko, Willem de Kooning, Philip Guston, and Franz Kline.

As New York became an international center for the arts, artists gained almost unlimited support, and buildings were erected to showcase their talents. The Guggenheim Museum (1959) was constructed as a repository for modern painting and sculpture, while Lincoln Center (1966) was built to house the Metropolitan Opera; the Philharmonic Orchestra; the city opera and ballet companies; a repertory theater; a concert hall for chamber music; and the Juilliard School for actors, musicians, and dancers. The Metropolitan Museum and the Museum of Modern Art were expanded as well, and the Whitney Museum of American Art was built.

In an earlier time, the simultaneous progression of vaudeville and the legitimate theater started at Crystal Palace, then gradually moved uptown, finally reaching Times Square around the turn of the century. In music, Carnegie Hall (1891) established

New York as a major venue for performing artists.

In recent years, experimentation in the visual arts has been high, with a variety of new techniques and media strongly in evidence. This is an unrestrained and provocative scene that encourages much growth and innovation.

3. RECOMMENDED BOOKS & FILMS

DATELINE

Democratic and Republican mayoral endorsements, wins second term with 75% of vote.
- **1990** Newly restored Immigration Museum opens to public on Ellis Island.
- **1992** Democratic National Convention held in New York's Madison Square Garden.

BOOKS

GENERAL

Cudahy, Brian J. *Over and Back* (Fordham University Press, 1989).

Dolkart, Andrew S. *The Texture of Tribeca* (Tribeca Community Association, 1989).

Dunlap, David W. *On Broadway* (Rizzoli International, 1990).

Furia, Philip. *The Poets of Tin Pan Alley* (Oxford University Press, 1990).

Kinkead, Eugene. *Central Park: The Birth, Decline, and Renewal of a National Treasure* (Norton, 1990).

Kisseloff, Jeff. *You Must Remember This* (Schocken Books, 1989).

Miller, Terry. *Greenwich Village and How It Got That Way* (Crown, 1990).

Morris, Jan. *Manhattan '45* (Oxford University Press, 1987).

Schermerhorn, Gene. *Letters to Phil* (New York Bound, 1982).

Snyder, Robert. *The Voice of the City: Vaudeville and Popular Culture in New York* (Oxford University Press, 1989).

Trager, James. *Park Avenue: Street of Dreams* (Atheneum, 1989).

Trager, James. *West of Fifth: The Rise and Fall of Manhattan's West Side* (Atheneum, 1987).

ECONOMIC, POLITICAL & SOCIAL HISTORY

Allen, Oliver E. *New York, New York: A History of the World's Most Exhilarating & Challenging City* (Macmillan, 1990).

Asbury, Herbert. *The Gangs of New York* (Capricorn Books, 1989).

Baldwin, James. *Notes of a Native Son* (Beacon Press, 1990).

Blackmar, Elizabeth. *Manhattan for Rent, Seventeen Eighty-five to Eighteen Fifty* (Cornell University Press, 1988).

Brandt, Nat. *The Man Who Tried to Burn New York* (Syracuse University Press, 1986).

Cohen, B., Heller, S., and Chwast, S. *New York Observed* (Harry N. Abrams, 1987).

Gambee, Robert. *Wall Street Christmas* (Norton, 1990).

Jacobs, William Jay. *Ellis Island* (Macmillan, 1990).

Kazin, Alfred. *Our New York* (Harper & Row, 1989).

Kessner, Thomas. *Fiorello H. La Guardia and The Making of Modern New York* (McGraw-Hill, 1989).

Kotker, Norman. *Ellis Island* (Aperture Foundation, 1989).

MacKay, Ernst A. *The Civil War & New York City* (Syracuse University Press, 1990).

Marshall, Richard. *Fifty New York Artists: A Critical Selection of Painters & Sculptors Working in New York* (Chronicle Books, 1986).

Patterson, Jerry E. *The Vanderbilts* (Harry N. Abrams, 1989).

Rink, Oliver A. *Holland on the Hudson* (New York State Historical Association, 1986).

Sharp, Robert M. *The Love and Legends of Wall Street* (Dow Jones–Irwin, 1989).

Whitman, Walt. *Walt Whitman's New York* (Macmillan, 1963).

ARCHITECTURE & THE ARTS

Bogart, Michele H. *Public Sculpture and the Civic Ideal in New York City 1890–1989* (University of Chicago Press, 1989).

Boyer, M. Christine. *Manhattan Manners: Architecture & Style 1850–1900* (Rizzoli International, 1985).

Goldberg, Paul. *Skyscraper* (Knopf, 1981).

Lieberman, Nathaniel. *Manhattan Lightscape* (Abbeville Press, 1990).

Mackay, Donald A. *The Building of Manhattan: How Manhattan Was Built Overground & Underground, from the Dutch Settlers to the Skyscrapers* (Harper & Row, 1987).

Orkin, Ruth. *More Pictures from My Window* (Rizzoli International, 1989).

Rajs, Jake. *Manhattan: An Island in Focus* (Rizzoli International, 1985).

Rosen, Laura. *Top of the City: New York's Hidden Rooftop World* (Thames & Hudson, 1990).

Silver, Nathan. *Lost New York* (American Legacy, 1982).

Stern, Robert A. M., Gilmartin, Gregory, and Massengale, John M. *New York 1900: Metropolitan Architecture and Urbanism 1890–1915* (Rizzoli International, 1983).

Valenzi, Kathleen D., ed. *Private Moments: Images of Manhattan* (Howell Press, 1989).

Watson, Edward B. *New York Then & Now: Eighty-three Manhattan Sites Photographed in the Past & Present* (Dover Publications, 1976).

Willensky, Elliot, and White, Norval. *AIA Guide to New York City* (Harcourt Brace Jovanovich, 1989).

FICTION   For Adults

Finney, Jack. *Time and Again* (Simon & Schuster, 1986).

Fitzgerald, F. Scott. *The Great Gatsby* (Macmillan, 1981).

James, Henry. *Washington Square* (G. K. Hall & Co., 1980).

Liebling, A. J. *The Telephone Booth Indian* (North Point Press, 1990).

Powell, Dawn. *The Locusts Have No King* (Yarrow Press, 1989).

Wharton, Edith. *The Age of Innocence* (Macmillan, 1983).

For Kids

Barracca, Sal. *The Adventures of Taxi Dog* (Halcyon Books, 1990).
Gangloff, Deborah. *Albert and Victoria* (Crown, 1989).
Jacobs, William Jay. *Ellis Island* (Macmillan, 1990).
Macaulay, David. *Underground* (Houghton Mifflin, 1976).
Selden, George. *The Cricket in Times Square* (Dell, 1970).
Swift, Hildegarde H. *The Little Red Lighthouse and The Great Gray Bridge* (Harcourt Brace Jovanovich, 1974).
Thomson, Kay. *Eloise* (Simon & Schuster, 1969).
Waber, Bernard. *Lyle, Lyle, Crocodile and The House on East 88th Street* (Houghton Mifflin, 1965).
White, E. B. *Stuart Little* (Harper & Row, 1973).

FILMS

Hundreds of movies have been made about New York and in New York—it's one of the most familiar movie sets in the world. Woody Allen's films, perhaps more than any other, catch the humor and *angst* of current-day New Yorkers, especially in *Annie Hall, Manhattan,* and *Hannah and Her Sisters.* Nobody tells about growing up in the city better than Neil Simon in *Brighton Beach Memoirs.* Italian family life in New York is portrayed in *Moonstruck. Godfather III, Prizzi's Honor,* and *Goodfellas* deal with the world of organized crime in New York. Several scenes in *Ghostbusters* were shot at Columbia University; *Ghost* took place in SoHo, Brooklyn, and downtown Manhattan. *Tootsie* deals with the television world in New York. *Crossing Delancey* shuttles between the old-world Jewish culture of the Lower East Side and Manhattan's uptown literary set. Spike Lee portrays the seamy streets of Brooklyn in *Do the Right Thing.* And then, of course, there's the all-time New York classic, *Breakfast at Tiffany's.* And the list goes on.

CHAPTER 2

PLANNING A TRIP TO NEW YORK

Here's some basic information to work with as you start to plan your trip to New York. After deciding where to go, most people have two basic questions: What will it cost? and How do I get there? This chapter will answer both these questions, as well as provide information about when to go, what to pack, where to obtain special services, and where to get more information about New York.

1. INFORMATION & MONEY

INFORMATION As soon as you know you're going to New York, contact the **New York Convention and Visitors Bureau,** 2 Columbus Circle, New York, NY 10019 (tel. 212/397-8222), and ask for their information packet. They'll send you information on hotels, restaurants, shopping, tour packages, timely events, and lots more.

MONEY New York, in general, is an expensive city, among the most expensive in the United States. But don't let that deter you: You can choose where to save and where you really want to spend. Save money on hotels by staying at a B&B and splurge on the best French restaurants; go all out at luxury hotels and eat picnics in the park; enjoy free poetry readings and concerts and have a shopping spree; or get two in the orchestra for a Broadway musical and buy bargains on the Lower East Side. In short, what you'll spend in New York pretty much depends on your own tastes: The city can accommodate every reasonable budget.

WHAT THINGS COST IN NEW YORK — U.S. $

Taxi from Kennedy Airport to Manhattan (plus tip)	$30.00–$35.00
Carey bus from Kennedy Airport to Manhattan	$11.00
Local telephone call	.25
Double at the Drake Swissotel (deluxe)	$240.00–$290.00

	U.S. $
Double at the Mayflower Hotel (moderate)	$180.00
Double at the Roger Williams Hotel (budget)	$60.00–$75.00
Lunch for one at Teachers Too (moderate)	$10.00–$12.00
Lunch for one at Living Springs (budget)	$5.00–$8.00
Dinner for one, without wine, at The Sign of the Dove (deluxe)	$60.00–$70.00
Dinner for one, with wine, at American Festival Café (moderate)	$25.00
Dinner for one, without wine, at Dallas BBQ (budget)	$10.00–$12.00
Bottle of beer (at a bar)	$3.00–$4.00
Coca-Cola	$1.50
Cup of coffee	$1.50
Roll of ASA 100 Kodacolor film, 36 exposures	$5.75
Admission to the Museum of Modern Art	$7.00
Movie ticket	$7.50
Theater ticket to *Jelly's Last Jam*	$40.00–$60.00

2. WHEN TO GO

CLIMATE   New York's weather is changing. We used to have very hot summers, very cold winters (often including snow), and several weeks of idyllic 70°F spring and fall days. In the last few years, winters have been mild with very little snow and followed by very short springs; summer, which is still hot and muggy, begins early and lasts late, often through September. But still, the city is great to visit at any time you can. Both central heating and air conditioning are practically universal, so the weather is never a problem. The winter is the height of the theater and entertainment season, but if you come in the summer you'll be ahead of the game, since most residents will be out at the beach, and you have the city practically to yourself. It's much easier then to pick up tickets for Broadway plays at the last minute as well as to get into the charming little restaurants, and you don't have to fight off the mobs in the big stores.

Average Monthly Temperatures [°F]

Jan	Feb	Mar	Apr	May	June	July	Aug	Sept	Oct	Nov	Dec
38	40	48	61	71	80	85	84	77	67	54	42

NEW YORK
CALENDAR OF EVENTS

JANUARY

☐ **Ice Capades** glides into Madison Square Garden. January 17–26. Tickets: Madison Square Garden Box Office (tel. 212/465-MSG1) or Ticketmaster (tel. 212/307-7171).

✪ *WINTER ANTIQUES SHOW   A prestigious event showcasing choice collectibles.*
   Where: Seventh Regiment Armory, 68th Street and Park Avenue. When: Jan 22–31. How: $10 admission at door.

FEBRUARY

☐ **Chinese New Year** celebrations to usher in the Year of the Chicken 4691. Celebrations all over the city, but especially in Chinatown. Feb 20–26.

MARCH

✪ *NEW YORK FLOWER SHOW   Annual harbinger of spring presented by the Horticultural Society of New York.*
   Where: Pier 92, 51st Street and Twelfth Avenue. When: March 13–21. How: $10 adults, $4 children—admission at door.

APRIL

✪ *OPENING OF THE NEW YORK METS BASEBALL SEASON*
   Where: Shea Stadium. When: April through September. How: Tickets from Ticketmaster (tel. 212/307-7171 or 506-0303).

✪ *OPENING OF THE NEW YORK YANKEES BASEBALL SEASON*
   Where: Yankee Stadium. When: April through September. How: Tickets from Ticketmaster (tel. 212/307-7171). For information, call 293-6000.

MAY

☐ **Memorial Day Parade,** 72nd Street and Broadway to Soldier's and Sailor's Monument, Riverside Drive at 90th Street.

JUNE

☐ **Shakespeare in the Park** at Delacorte Theater, through August. Free. For information, call 598-7100.
☐ **Metropolitan Opera,** free concerts in the parks.

JULY

✪ **SUMMERGARDEN CONCERTS OF CLASSICAL MUSIC**
 Where: *Museum of Modern Art sculpture garden.*
When: *Friday and Saturday evenings, from the first weekend in July through August.* **How:** *Free.*

☐ **July 4th weekend.** Harbor Festival '93, including Macy's Fireworks Celebrations on the East River.

AUGUST

✪ **23RD ANNUAL LINCOLN CENTER OUT-OF-DOORS FESTIVAL** *A free celebration of performing arts, held in all the outdoor spaces of Lincoln Center.*
 Where: *Lincoln Center.* **When:** *Month of August.* **How:** *For information, phone 212/875-5400.*

SEPTEMBER

☐ **Washington Square Outdoor Art Exhibit,** Greenwich Village. Re-run of a classic. Early September.

NOVEMBER

✪ **RADIO CITY MUSIC HALL CHRISTMAS SPECTACULAR** *A fitting climax to Radio City's 61st anniversary year.*
 When: *Mid-November to early January.* **Where:** *Radio City Music Hall, Sixth Avenue at 50th Street.* **How:** *In person at box office or via phone at Ticketmaster's Radio City Hotline: 212/307-1000.*

☐ **Macy's Thanksgiving Day Parade.** A New York tradition.

DECEMBER

☐ **Rockefeller Center Christmas Tree** is lit. Early December.
☐ **Giant Hanukkah Menorah** is lit at Grand Army Plaza, Fifth Avenue.
☐ **The Nutcracker,** New York City Ballet at Lincoln Center.
☐ **New Year's Eve** Fireworks and midnight run in Central Park; lighted ball drops from the top of One Times Square.

3. WHAT TO PACK

Because New York weather is so variable, you'll need to be flexible with your wardrobe. It's always best to dress in layers so you can quickly adjust to changing temperatures. In summer, try to wear very cool clothes—the city is hot and muggy. New Yorkers wear everything from very sporty clothes to very dressy ones, so it all depends on your life-style. Jackets and ties are necessary for men in the fancier restaurants; denim is always out in these places. People tend to get dressed up to go to theater and concerts, and in some nightclubs, especially the discos, the more outrageous the costume, the better. Basically, dress as you would in any American city: New Yorkers are amazingly tolerant when it comes to what other people are wearing.

Bring your umbrella and a raincoat—you never know.

4. TIPS FOR THE DISABLED, SENIORS, SINGLES, FAMILIES & STUDENTS

FOR THE DISABLED   New York has one of the most extensive services and programs for the disabled. For information about special events and programs, call the **New York Association for the Blind,** at the Communications Department of The Lighthouse, 111 E. 59th St., New York, NY 10021 (tel. 212/808-0077); or the **New York Society for the Deaf,** 817 Broadway, New York, NY 10003 (tel. 777-3900; for emergencies, 673-6500). Other helpful contacts: **Deafness Information and Referral Service,** 30th Avenue and 75th Street, Jackson Heights, NY 11370 (tel. 718/899-8800); **Disabled American Veterans,** 252 Seventh Ave., New York, NY (tel. 212/620-6644).

FOR SENIORS   Most hotels will give seniors a discount. Be sure to travel with your AARP card; it opens the doors to many discounts. Few restaurants offer senior discounts, but they are available in many stores (look for signs) and at movie theaters during certain weekday hours. Most museums and attractions offer special prices. With your Social Security Health Insurance card (for those over 65), you need pay only 65¢ on buses or subways.

FOR SINGLES   Unfortunately, the price of single and double hotel rooms are almost the same; singles save only a few dollars. Savings for singles are somewhat better in B&Bs.

FOR FAMILIES   Children (usually under 17) can stay free in their parents' hotel room, when using existing bedding, in many of the hotels listed in this book. Hilton Hotels have a unique deal: Children of *any age* can stay free with their parents in the same room. A few hotels offer a second room for children at a lower price.

FOR STUDENTS   High-school and college students with valid I.D.s are often eligible for discounts at theaters, concert halls, museums, and other places (look for signs).

5. GETTING THERE

BY PLANE

The major domestic carriers flying into New York are **American, America West, Continental, Delta, TWA, USAir,** and **United.** Most of the major international carriers also fly into New York.

The airports serving New York City are John F. Kennedy International Airport and LaGuardia Airport, both in Queens, and Newark International Airport in New Jersey. (See Chapter 4, Section 1, "Orientation," for details on arriving in the New York area.)

GETTING THE BEST PRICES To get the best price on your airline ticket to New York, be prepared to do a little shopping around and always ask for the lowest fare. Fares are volatile; they vary from airline to airline and even from the same airline from day to day. Try to schedule your traveling for weekdays during the busy summer season and avoid major holiday periods, when fares go up. In general, the lowest fares are **Economy** or **APEX** fares—the former has no restrictions, while the latter (an Advance Purchase Excursion fare) requires you to reserve and pay for the ticket 7, 14, 21, or 30 days in advance and to stay for a minimum number of days; it also may have other restrictions, like flying before a specific date. APEX fares are usually nonrefundable, and there is a charge for changing dates; however, the savings are considerable. For example, on a recent day last summer, Continental's first-class Los Angeles–New York round-trip fully refundable fare was $1,420; its cheapest, nonrefundable APEX fare was $380 round trip. From Chicago to New York, the first-class, fully refundable fare was $1,120 round trip; the cheapest, nonrefundable APEX fare was $255 round trip. There are a variety of prices in-between these extremes, depending on how much of the payment is refundable, what days you travel, availability, and so on.

 FROMMER'S SMART TRAVELER: AIRFARES

1. Use a travel agent only if you know he or she will really put in time and effort to get you the cheapest fare; otherwise, do your own homework or use a discount travel agency (see below). It pays off!
2. Shop all the airlines that fly to New York.
3. Ask for the lowest fare, not just a discounted fare.
4. Keep calling: Airlines sometimes open up additional low-cost seats as a departure date nears.
5. Plan to travel during the week—avoid weekends and holiday periods.
6. Make sure to purchase your tickets at least 21 days in advance to take advantage of the very cheapest APEX (advance purchase) fares; next cheapest are 14-day, then 7-day advance-purchase fares.

Knowing all this, get on the phone, call your travel agent or a number of airlines, and work out a deal.

Another possibility is to call a discount travel agency like **Travel Avenue** in Chicago (tel. toll free 800/333-3335). Unlike most travel agencies, this one does not offer advice or itinerary planning; it does, however, offer good discounts on fares from major airlines. For example, on a recent day last summer, their lowest round-trip ticket from Los Angeles to New York was $385, with a 14-day advance purchase. From Chicago to New York, it was $198 round trip, with a 14-day advance purchase.

BY TRAIN

Amtrak (tel. toll free 800/USA-RAIL) runs frequent service to New York City. Here are sample fares (subject to change) and travel times from four major cities. Boston: $50 unreserved, $55 reserved one way, $89 round trip; 4 hours, 30 minutes to 5 hours, 40 minutes. Chicago: $124 one way, $156–$199 round trip; 18 hours, 25 minutes to 26 hours, 49 minutes. Washington, D.C.: $64 one way, $129 round-trip excursion; 3 hours, 20 minutes. Philadelphia: $31 one way, $47 round trip; one hour, 20 minutes.

BY BUS

Here are sample fares (subject to change) and travel times via **Greyhound Bus Lines** (tel. 212/971-6363, or check your local telephone book). Boston: $32 one way, $60 round trip; 4 to 5 hours. Chicago: $119.50 one way, $135 round trip; 16 to 24 hours. Philadelphia: $16 one way, $24 to $26 round trip; 2 to 3 hours. Washington, D.C.: one way $31.50 weekdays and $34 weekends, and $63 and $67.50 round trip; 4 to 6 hours. *Note:* Ask about advance-purchase tickets to realize extra savings.

BY CAR

From the south, the New Jersey Turnpike (I-95) leads to the Holland Tunnel, the Lincoln Tunnel, and the George Washington Bridge. From the north, the New York Thruway (Rtes. 287 and 87) leads to Manhattan's East and West Sides; the New England Thruway (I-95) leads via connecting roads to Manhattan and the other boroughs. From the west, the Bergen-Passaic Expressway (I-80) leads to Manhattan and the other boroughs. Driving times should be about the same as bus times (see above). *Note:* Having a car in Manhattan is not an asset. Hotels charge very high parking rates, usually with no in-and-out privileges; parking spaces on city streets are very difficult to come by; garage rates are exorbitant. Drive only if you must.

CHAPTER 3

FOR FOREIGN VISITORS

1. **PREPARING FOR YOUR TRIP**
2. **GETTING TO THE UNITED STATES**
- **FAST FACTS: FOR THE FOREIGN TRAVELER**

Although American fads and fashions have spread across Europe and other parts of the world so that America may seem like familiar territory before your arrival, there are still many peculiarities and uniquely American situations that any foreign visitor will encounter.

1. PREPARING FOR YOUR TRIP

ENTRY REQUIREMENTS

DOCUMENTS Canadian nationals need only proof of Canadian residence to visit the United States. Citizens of Great Britain and Japan need only a current passport. Citizens of other countries, including Australia and New Zealand, usually need two documents: a valid **passport** with an expiration date at least six months later than the scheduled end of their visit to the United States and a **tourist visa** available at no charge from a U.S. embassy or consulate.

To get a tourist or business visa to enter the United States, contact the nearest American embassy or consulate in your country; if there is none, you will have to apply in person in a country where there is a U.S. embassy or consulate. Present your passport; a passport-size photo of yourself; and a completed application, which is available through the embassy or consulate. You may be asked to provide information about how you plan to finance your trip or show a letter of invitation from a friend with whom you plan to stay. Those applying for a business visa may be asked to show evidence that they will not receive a salary in the United States. Be sure to check the length of stay on your visa; usually it is six months. If you want to stay longer, you may file for an extension with the Immigration and Naturalization Service once you are in the country. If permission to stay is granted, a new visa is not required unless you leave the United States and want to reenter.

MEDICAL REQUIREMENTS No inoculations are needed to enter the United States unless you are coming from, or have stopped over in, areas known to be suffering from epidemics, especially of cholera or yellow fever.

If you have a disease requiring treatment with medications containing narcotics or drugs requiring a syringe, carry a valid signed prescription from your physician to allay any suspicions that you are smuggling drugs.

CUSTOMS REQUIREMENTS   Every adult visitor may bring in the following, free of duty: one liter of wine or hard liquor; 200 cigarettes or 100 cigars (but no cigars from Cuba) or three pounds of smoking tobacco; $400 worth of gifts. These exemptions are offered to travelers who spend at least 72 hours in the United States and who have not claimed them within the preceding six months. It is altogether forbidden to bring into the country foodstuffs (particularly cheese, fruit, cooked meats, and canned goods) and plants (vegetables, seeds, tropical plants, and so on). Foreign tourists may bring in or take out up to $10,000 in U.S. or foreign currency with no formalities; larger sums must be declared to Customs on entering or leaving.

INSURANCE

Unlike in most other countries, there is no national health system in the United States. Because the cost of medical care is extremely high, I strongly advise every traveler to secure health coverage before setting out. Therefore, you may want to take out a comprehensive travel policy that covers (for a relatively low premium) sickness or injury cost (medical, surgical, and hospital); loss or theft of your baggage; trip-cancellation costs; guarantee of bail in case you are sued; and costs of accident, repatriation, or death. Such packages (for example, "Europe Assistance" in Europe) are sold by automobile clubs at attractive rates, as well as by insurance companies and travel agencies.

2. GETTING TO THE UNITED STATES

Travelers from overseas can take advantage of the **APEX (Advance Purchase Excursion) fares** offered by all the major U.S. and European carriers. Aside from these, attractive values are offered by **Icelandair** on flights from Luxembourg to New York and by **Virgin Atlantic** from London to New York/Newark.

Some large American airlines (for example, TWA, American Airlines, Northwest, United, and Delta) offer travelers—on their transatlantic or transpacific flights—special discount tickets under the name **Visit USA,** allowing travel between any U.S. destinations at minimum rates. They are not on sale in the United States, and must, therefore, be purchased before you leave your foreign point of departure. This system is the best, easiest, and fastest way to see America at low cost. You should obtain information well in advance from your travel agent or the office of the airline concerned, since the conditions attached to these discount tickets can be changed without advance notice.

The visitor arriving by air, no matter what the port of entry, should cultivate patience and resignation before setting foot on U.S.

soil. Getting through Immigration control may take as long as two hours on some days, especially summer weekends. Add the time it takes to clear Customs and you will see that you should make very generous allowance for delay in planning connections between international and domestic flights—an average of two to three hours at least.

In contrast, for the traveler arriving by car or by rail from Canada, the border-crossing formalities have been streamlined to the vanishing point. And for the traveler by air from Canada, Bermuda, and some points in the Caribbean, you can sometimes go through Customs and Immigration at the point of departure, which is much quicker and less painful.

For further information about travel to and arriving in New York see "Getting There" in Chapter 2 and "Arriving" in Chapter 4, Section 1.

FAST FACTS FOR THE FOREIGN TRAVELER

Business Hours **Banks** open weekdays from 9am to 3pm; however, there's 24-hour access to the automatic tellers at most banks and other outlets. Generally, **offices** are open weekdays from 9am to 5pm. **Stores** are open six days a week with many open on Sunday, too; department stores usually stay open until 9pm on Thursday.

Climate See Chapter 2, Section 2.

Currency/Exchange The U.S. monetary system has a decimal base: One American **dollar** ($1) = 100 **cents** (100¢).

Dollar **bills** commonly come in $1 ("a buck"), $5, $10, $20, $50, and $100 denominations (the last two are not welcome when paying for small purchases and are not accepted in taxis or at subway ticket booths).

There are six denominations of **coins:** 1¢ (one cent or "penny"); 5¢ (five cents or "nickel"); 10¢ (ten cents or "dime"); 25¢ (twenty-five cents or "quarter"); 50¢ (fifty cents or "half dollar"); and the rare—and prized by collectors—$1 piece (both the older, large silver dollars and the newer, small Susan B. Anthony coin).

Traveler's checks denominated in dollars are accepted without demur at most hotels, motels, restaurants, and large stores. But as any experienced traveler knows, the best place to change traveler's checks is at a bank.

Credit cards are the method of payment most widely used: VISA (BarclayCard in Britain), MasterCard (EuroCard in Europe, Access in Britain, Diamond in Japan), American Express, Diners Club, and Carte Blanche, in descending order of acceptance. You can save yourself trouble by using "plastic money," rather than cash or traveler's checks, in 95% of all hotels, motels, restaurants, and retail stores. A credit card can also serve as a deposit for renting a car; as proof of identity (often carrying more weight than a passport); or as a "cash card," enabling you to draw money from banks that accept them.

For **currency exchange** in New York city, go to **Thomas Cook Currency Services** (formerly Deak International, which offers a wide variety of services, over 100 currencies, commission-free traveler's checks, drafts and wire transfers, check collections, and precious metal coins and bars. The rates are competitive, and the service is excellent. They are located at the JFK Airport International Arrivals Building (tel. 718/656-8444), daily from 8am to 9:30pm; at Rockefeller Center at 630 Fifth Ave. (between 50th and 51st streets) (tel. 757-6915), Monday to Friday from 9am to 5pm and Saturday from 10am to 3pm; at Grand Central Terminal, 41 E. 42nd St. (tel. 212/883-0400), Monday to Friday from 9am to 5pm, and Saturday from 10am to 3pm; at Herald Center Shopping Mall at 1 Herald Square (between 33rd and 34th streets on Sixth Avenue) (tel. 212/736-9790), Monday to Friday from 9:30am to 5:30pm and Saturday from 10am to 3pm; and downtown at 29 Broadway (tel. 212/363-6207), Monday to Friday from 9am to 5pm.

Many midtown hotels will exchange currency if you are a registered guest.

Note: The "foreign-exchange bureaus" so common in Europe are rare even at airports in the United States and nonexistent outside major cities. Try to avoid having to change foreign money, or traveler's checks denominated other than in U.S. dollars, at a small-town bank or even at a branch in a big city; in fact, leave any currency other than U.S. dollars at home—it may prove more nuisance to you than it's worth.

Drinking Laws   See "Fast Facts: New York" in Chapter 4.

Electric Current   The United States uses 110–120 volts, 60 cycles, compared to 220–240 volts, 50 cycles, as in most of Europe. Besides a 100-volt converter, small appliances of non-American manufacture, such as hairdryers or shavers, will require a plug adapter with two flat, parallel pins.

Embassies/Consulates   All embassies are located in the national capital, Washington, D.C.; some consulates are located in major cities, and most nations have a mission to the United Nations in New York City.

Listed here are the embassies and New York consulates of the major English-speaking countries—Australia, Canada, Ireland, New Zealand, and Britain. If you are from another country, you can get the telephone number of your embassy by calling "Information" in Washington, D.C. (tel. 202/555-1212).

The **Australian embassy** is at 1601 Massachusetts Ave. NW, Washington, DC 20036 (tel. 202/797-3000). The **consulate** is located at the International Building, 636 Fifth Ave., New York, NY 10111 (tel. 212/245-4000).

The **Canadian embassy** is at 501 Pennsylvania Ave. NW, Washington, DC 20001 (tel. 202/682-1740). The **consulate** is located at 1251 Ave. of the Americas, NY 10020 (tel. 212/586-2400).

The **Irish embassy** is at 2234 Massachusetts Ave. NW, Washington, DC 20008 (tel. 202/462-3939). The **consulate** is located at 515 Madison Ave., New York, NY 10022 (tel. 212/319-2555).

The **New Zealand embassy** is at 37 Observatory Circle NW, Washington, DC 20008 (tel. 202/328-4800). There is no **consulate** in New York.

The **British embassy** is at 3100 Massachusetts Ave. NW, Washington, DC 20008 (tel. 202/462-1340). The **consulate** is located at 845 Third Ave., New York, NY 10022 (tel. 212/752-8400).

Emergencies   Call **911** for fire, police, and ambulance. If you encounter such travelers' problems as sickness, accident, and lost or stolen baggage, call **Traveler's Aid,** an organization that specializes in helping distressed travelers, whether American or foreign. Call 944-0013 in Manhattan or 718/656-4870 at Kennedy International Airport. See Chapter 4, Section 1, for more details.

Holidays   On the following legal national holidays, banks, government offices, post offices, and many stores, restaurants, and museums are closed: January 1 (New Year's Day), third Monday in January (Martin Luther King, Jr. Day), third Monday in February (President's Day, Washington's Birthday), last Monday in May (Memorial Day), July 4 (Independence day), first Monday in September (Labor Day), second Monday in October (Columbus Day), November 11 (Veteran's Day/Armistice Day), last Thursday in November (Thanksgiving Day), and December 25 (Christmas Day).

The Tuesday following the first Monday in November is Election Day; it is a legal holiday in presidential-election years.

Information   See Chapter 2, Section 1.

Legal Aid   If you are stopped for a minor infraction (for example, of the highway code, such as speeding), never attempt to pay the fine directly to a police officer; you may be arrested on the much more serious charge of attempted bribery. Pay fines by mail or directly into the hands of the clerk of the court. If you're accused of a more serious offense, it is wise to say and do nothing before consulting a lawyer. Under U.S. law, an arrested person is allowed one telephone call to a party of his or her choice. Call your embassy or consulate.

Mail   If you aren't sure of your address, your mail can be sent to you, in your name, **c/o General Delivery** at the main post office at Eighth Avenue and 33rd Street. The addressee must pick it up in person and must produce proof of identity (driver's license, credit card, passport, and so on).

Mailboxes are blue with a red-and-white logo and carry the inscription "U.S. MAIL." A first-class **stamp** is 29¢.

Newspapers/Magazines   See "Fast Facts: New York" in Chapter 4.

Post Office   The main Post Office is at Eighth Avenue and 33rd Street (tel. 212/967-8585).

Radio/Television   There are dozens of radio stations (both AM and FM), each broadcasting talk shows; continuous news; or a particular kind of music—classical, country, jazz, pop, gospel—punctuated by frequent commercials. Television, with four coast-to-coast networks—ABC, CBS, NBC and Fox—joined in recent years by the Public Broadcasting System (PBS) and a growing network of cable channels, plays a major part in American life. New York has 7 network and local channels transmitting 24 hours a day, plus a large number of cable channels and a few pay-TV channels showing recent movies or sports events.

Safety   Whenever you're traveling in an unfamiliar city or country, stay alert. Be aware of your immediate surroundings. Wear a moneybelt and don't flash expensive jewelry and cameras in public. This will minimize the possibility of your becoming a crime victim. Be alert even in heavily touristed areas. New York City has a reputation for violent crime and you should observe proper precautions. Avoid Central Park and other deserted areas at night. If you ride the subway at night, stand in the area of the platform marked for off-hours waiting. (Also see "Fast Facts: New York" in Chapter 4.)

Taxes   In the United States there is no VAT (Value-Added Tax) or other indirect tax at a national level. Every state, and each city in it, is allowed to levy its own local tax on all purchases, including hotel and restaurant checks, airline tickets, and so on. In New York City the **sales tax rate** is 8¼%.

Telephone/Telegraph/Telex/Fax Pay phones and (less frequently) credit-card phones can be found on street corners, as well as in bars, restaurants, public buildings, stores, and service stations. Local calls cost 25¢.

For **long-distance or international calls,** stock up with a supply of quarters; the pay phone will instruct you when you should put them into the slot. For long-distance calls in the United States, dial 1 followed by the area code and number you want. For direct overseas calls, first dial 011, followed by the country code (Australia, 61; Republic of Ireland, 353; New Zealand, 64; United Kingdom, 44; and so on), and then by the city code (for example, 71 or 81 for London, 21 for Birmingham) and the number of the person you wish to call.

Before calling from a hotel room, always ask the hotel phone operator if there are any telephone surcharges. These are best avoided by using a public phone, calling collect, or using a telephone charge card.

For **reversed-charge or collect calls,** and for **person-to-person calls,** dial 0 (zero, not the letter "O") followed by the area code and number you want; an operator will then come on the line and you should specify that you are calling collect, or person-to-person, or both. If your operator-assisted call is international, ask for the overseas operator.

For local directory assistance ("Information"), dial 411; for long-distance information dial 1, then the appropriate area code and 555-1212.

Like the telephone system, **telegraph** and **telex** services are provided by private corporations like ITT, MCI, and above all, Western Union. You can bring your telegram to the nearest Western Union office (there are hundreds across the country) or dictate it over the phone (a toll-free call, 800/325-6000). You can also telegraph money or have it telegraphed to you very quickly over the Western Union system.

Most hotels have **fax** machines available to their customers (ask if there is a charge to use it). You will also see signs for public faxes in the windows of small shops.

Time The United States is divided into six time zones. From east to west, these are: Eastern Standard Time (EST), Central Standard Time (CST), Mountain Standard Time (MST), Pacific Standard Time (PST), Alaska Standard Time (AST), and Hawaii Standard Time (HST). Always keep the changing time zones in mind if you are traveling (or even telephoning) long distances. For example, noon in New York City (EST) is 11am in Chicago (CST), 10am in Denver (MST), 9am in Los Angeles (PST), 8am in Anchorage (AST), and 7am in Honolulu (HST). When it is noon in London (GMT, or Greenwich Mean Time), it is 7am in New York.

Daylight Saving Time is in effect from 1am on the first Sunday in April until 2am on the last Sunday in October, except in Arizona, Hawaii, part of Indiana, and Puerto Rico.

Tipping See Chapter 4, "Fast Facts: New York."

Toilets Often euphemistically referred to as restrooms, public toilets are virtually nonexistent on the streets of New York City. They can be found, though, in bars, restaurants, hotel lobbies, museums, department stores, and service stations—and will probably be clean (although the last-mentioned sometimes leave much to be desired). Note, however, that some restaurants and bars display a notice that "Toilets are for use of patrons only." You can ignore this sign, or better yet, avoid arguments by paying for a cup of coffee or soft drink, which will qualify you as a patron. The cleanliness of toilets at railroad stations and bus depots may be questionable; some public places are equipped with pay toilets that require you to insert one or two dimes (10¢) or a quarter (25¢) into a slot on the door before it will open. In restrooms with attendants, leaving at least a 25¢ tip is customary.

Yellow Pages The local phone company provides two kinds of telephone directory. The general directory, called the "white pages," lists subscribers (business and personal residences) in alphabetical order. The inside front cover lists emergency numbers for police, fire, and ambulance, and other vital numbers (like the Coast Guard, poison control center, crime-victims hotline, and so on). The first few pages are devoted to community-service numbers, including a guide to long-distance and international calling, complete with country codes and area codes.

The second directory, the "yellow pages," lists all local services, businesses, and industries by type, with an index at the back. The listings cover not only such obvious items as automobile repairs by make of car, or drugstores (pharmacies), often by geographical location, but also restaurants by type of cuisine and geographical location, bookstores by special subject and/or language, places of worship by religious denomination, and other information that the tourist might otherwise not readily find. The Yellow Pages also include city plans or detailed area maps, often showing postal ZIP codes and public transportation.

CHAPTER 4

GETTING TO KNOW NEW YORK

This chapter will answer a number of questions you might have upon your arrival and during your stay in New York—from how to find your way around New York to numbers to call for information during your stay.

1. ORIENTATION

ARRIVING

BY PLANE There are three major airports serving New York: **John F. Kennedy International Airport (JFK),** which is about 15 miles (or one hour's driving time) from midtown Manhattan; **LaGuardia Airport,** 8 miles (or 30 minutes) from midtown; and New Jersey's **Newark International Airport,** 16 miles (or 45 minutes) from New York.

For information on getting to and from the airports, call 800/AIR-RIDE.

Carey Transportation (tel. 718/632-0509) provides bus service between both JFK and LaGuardia airports. Buses leave from JFK every 30 minutes with midtown stops at 125 Park Avenue, near Grand Central Terminal between 41st and 42nd streets; or at the Air TransCenter at the Port Authority Bus Terminal at 42nd Street between Eighth and Ninth avenues ($11 one way). Buses leave from LaGuardia every 15 minutes for the Park Avenue and Port Authority terminals ($8.50).

New Jersey Transit (tel. 212/564-8484 or 201/460-8444) provides Airport Express service from Newark Airport to the Port Authority Bus Terminal's Airport Bus Center at 42nd Street and Eighth Avenue. **Olympia Trails** (tel. 212/964-6233) provides service to the Port Authority at 42nd Street and Eighth Avenue, to Grand Central Terminal at 41st Street and Park Avenue, and to One World Trade Center at the tip of Manhattan. Both bus services cost $7 one way. Buses leave every 20 minutes.

The **Gray Line Air Shuttle** (tel. 212/397-2620 or toll free 800/669-0051) provides airport-to-hotel service for all Manhattan hotels between 23rd and 63rd streets as well as to its terminal at Eighth Avenue between 53rd and 54th streets. The shuttle's fleet of

11-seat vans and 21-seat buses operates between 7am and 10pm from JFK, LaGuardia, and Newark airports. One-way fares, payable on arrival at your hotel, are $14 from JFK, $11 from LaGuardia, and $16 from Newark. For pick-ups at the airports, consult the ground transportation desk or use the courtesy phones located in the baggage claim areas. For pick-up at hotels, passengers must have tickets, which may be purchased at the transportation desk at their hotels or at the Gray Line Air Terminal.

Taxis are available at designated taxi stands at all three New York area airports. At JFK and LaGuardia, yellow taxis with the fares printed on the front doors are the only ones that are licensed by the New York Taxi and Limousine Commission. New Jersey cabs available from curbside dispatchers at Newark can be different colors. Fares between JFK, LaGuardia, and Newark airports are metered, costing approximately $30 to $35, $20 to $25, and $30 plus tolls, respectively. (Going to Newark in New Jersey from New York, a trip that crosses state lines, the fare in a yellow cab is the amount on the meter plus $10.) There is a 50¢ surcharge between 8pm and 6am on all taxis. Metered fares include everyone in the taxi and are not per person.

One final tip: On the cab ride from the airports to the city, out-of-town and foreign visitors should be wary of cab drivers demanding huge sums; take only a metered cab and pay only *exactly* what the meter reads, plus a tip and toll charges. At the airports, take only the taxis at curbside or those available from official dispatchers, not from hustlers in the terminal halls themselves.

BY TRAIN   If you come to New York by train, you will arrive at either **Pennsylvania Station** (34th Street and Seventh Avenue) or **Grand Central Terminal** (42nd Street and Park Avenue). Both are located in mid-Manhattan, minutes from your hotel, and you'll be able to make subway connections or hail a cab easily from both stations.

BY BUS   If you come by bus, you will arrive at the **Port of New York Authority Bus Terminal** (41st Street and Eighth Avenue). It's a seedy neighborhood and not particularly safe at night, so try to schedule your arrival during daylight hours.

TOURIST INFORMATION

The **New York Convention and Visitors Bureau,** 2 Columbus Circle at 59th Street (212/397-8222), has a wealth of information about the city, including pamphlets and brochures on sightseeing, hotels, restaurants, shopping, and current activities, as well as city subway and bus maps and free tickets to TV shows and discount tickets to theaters. The offices are open Monday to Friday from 9am to 5pm. A recorded message also gives information on all free events (tel. 212/360-1333).

The **Visitors Center** at A&S Plaza, 32nd Street and Herald Square, 7th floor (tel. 212/465-0600), also offers free information and services.

Traveler's Aid can provide many kinds of help for visitors and stranded travelers in New York City. Their offices are at 158–160 W. 42nd St., near Broadway (tel. 212/944-0013); and in the lobby of the International Arrivals Building at JFK Airport (tel. 718/656-4870).

CITY LAYOUT
MAIN ARTERIES & STREETS

If you can count and you know your east from your west, you can find your way around Manhattan. All you have to remember is that streets run east and west and are numbered consecutively; avenues run north and south and most have numbers, although a few have names; and streets and avenues usually bisect one another at right angles. (Unfortunately, this does not apply to Lower Manhattan—Wall Street, Chinatown, SoHo, and Greenwich Village—since these neighborhoods grew before the engineers came up with this brilliant scheme; take a map when you explore these areas.)

As for the east and west street designations, the key to the mystery is **Fifth Avenue,** the big dividing line between the East and West Sides of town (below Washington Square, **Broadway** is the dividing line). So, for example, to get to 20 East 57th Street, you would walk about one block east of Fifth; to get to 20 West 57th Street, you'd walk about one block west. To get uptown of a certain point, simply walk north of, or to a higher-numbered street than, where you are; downtown is south of (or a lower-numbered street than) your current location. Got that? All that's left to learn are the names of the major avenues. Starting at Fifth Avenue and going east (toward the East River), they are **Madison; Park** (Park Avenue South below 34th Street), **Lexington; Third; Second; First; York** (from East 60th Street to East 92nd Street), which becomes **Sutton Place** (from East 51st Street to East 59th Street); and **East End** (from East 79th Street to East 90th Street). On the Lower East Side, First Avenue gives way to **avenues A, B, C, and D.** Starting again at Fifth Avenue and working west, we have **Avenue of the Americas** (everybody calls it **Sixth Avenue**); **Seventh Avenue; Broadway; Eighth Avenue** (which continues as **Central Park West** at 59th Street); **Ninth Avenue** (continues as **Columbus Avenue** at 59th Street); **Tenth Avenue** (called **Amsterdam Avenue** after 59th Street); **Eleventh Avenue** (becomes **West End Avenue** from 59th to 107th streets); and **Riverside Drive,** beginning at 72nd Street.

FINDING AN ADDRESS
Avenue Addresses

New Yorkers have the following system for finding the cross street on an avenue address: Drop the last digit of the number of the address and divide the remaining number by two. Then add or subtract the following appropriate number:

Avenue A, B, C, or D	add 3
First Avenue	add 3
Second Avenue	add 3
Third Avenue	add 10
Fourth Avenue (Park Avenue South)	add 8
Fifth Avenue	
1 to 200	add 13
201 to 400	add 16
401 to 600	add 18
601 to 775	add 20
From 776 to 1286 cancel last figure and subtract 18	

Sixth Avenue (Avenue of the Americas)	subtract 12
Seventh Avenue below Central Park	add 12
Eighth Avenue below Central Park	add 10
Ninth Avenue	add 13
Tenth Avenue	add 14
Eleventh Avenue	add 15
Amsterdam Avenue	add 60
Broadway	
1 to 754	below 8th Street
755 to 858	subtract 29
859 to 958	subtract 25
Above 1000	subtract 31
Columbus Avenue	add 60
Lexington Avenue	add 22
Madison Avenue	add 26
Park Avenue	add 35
Riverside Drive	divide number by 10 and add 72
West End Avenue	add 60

For example, if you were trying to locate 645 Fifth Avenue, you would drop the 5, leaving 64. Then you would divide 64 by 2, leaving 32. According to the chart, you would then add 20. Thus 645 Fifth Avenue stands at about 52nd Street.

Street Addresses

BETWEEN 14TH & 59TH STREETS Here is a chart to help you locate street addresses between 14th Street and 59th Street:

East Side
1 at Fifth Avenue
100 at Park Avenue
200 at Third Avenue
300 at Second Avenue
400 at First Avenue

West Side
1 at Fifth Avenue
100 at Sixth Avenue
200 at Seventh Avenue
300 at Eighth Avenue
400 at Ninth Avenue
500 at Tenth Avenue
600 at Eleventh Avenue

59TH TO 110TH STREETS Above 59th Street and all the way to 110th Street, things are different on the *Upper West Side only.* This is the region west of Central Park, where numbers on the streets start at Central Park West and continue upward all the way to West End Avenue, as outlined below:

1 at Central Park West (Eighth Avenue)
100 at Columbus Avenue (Ninth Avenue)
200 at Amsterdam Avenue (Tenth Avenue)
300 at West End Avenue (Eleventh Avenue)

NEIGHBORHOODS IN BRIEF
Lower Manhattan/Financial District This is the oldest part of New York, containing among other sights the Brooklyn Bridge, the City Hall and the courthouse area, the South Street Seaport, Wall Street, the New York Stock Exchange, the World Trade Center, and the World Financial Center in Battery Park City.

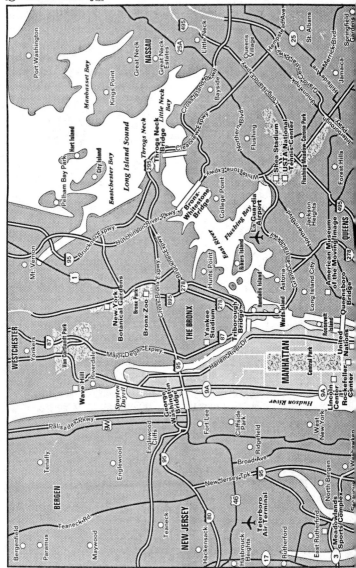

TriBeCa Just south of SoHo in the triangle below Canal Street and west of Broadway, this is a newer artists' colony.

Chinatown Located south of Canal Street, this Chinese community centers on Mott and Pell streets.

Little Italy The heart of this ethnic enclave, just east of Broadway between Houston and Canal streets, is Mulberry Street.

SoHo Centered around West Broadway and Spring and Greene streets between Houston and Canal streets (just west of Little Italy),

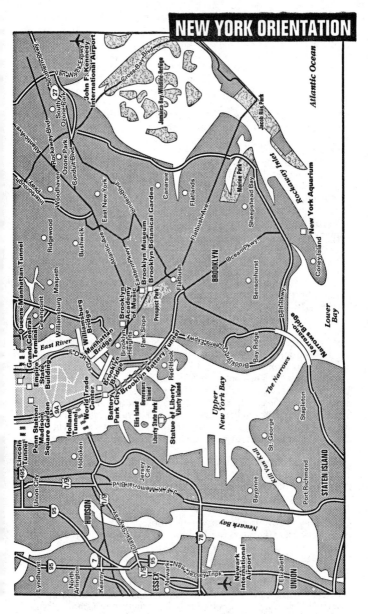

SoHo is home to the world's largest collection of cast-iron commercial architecture and is one of New York's most vital artists' colony.

The Lower East Side This area, also south of Houston Street but east of Little Italy, is where thousands of immigrants settled into the New World in the early 1900s—some to struggle and be engulfed, some to conquer. Most of the Jews, Irish, and Italians have fled uptown from the ghettos or to the suburbs, but little colonies still remain, although most of the population is now

Hispanic. Around Grand and Orchard streets there is still a Jewish neighborhood, known mostly for incredible bargain shopping.

Greenwich Village From 14th Street to Houston on the West Side this is the heart of New York's Bohemia. It begins on the West Side at the Hudson River and extends all the way across town to Broadway.

The East Village The one-time home of the hippies and the flower children (now home to many young artists), this area extends from Broadway to First Avenue and beyond to avenues A, B, and C. The northern border is 14th Street and the southern is Houston.

Chelsea In the West 20s, Chelsea houses the Flower Market (if you get up early in the morning, you can pick and choose with the city's retail florists).

Gramercy Park/Murray Hill Flanked on the west by Fifth Avenue and on the East by First Avenue, on the south by 14th Street and on the north by 42nd Street, this is a mixed residential/commercial area housing some of Manhattan's finest old buildings.

The Garment and Fur District From the upper 20s to 40th Street along Seventh Avenue, the streets become crowded with trucks and throngs of people pushing minks and other garments on racks along the sidewalks. This is Manhattan's (and the nation's) vibrant, hectic, and legendary fashion capital.

Herald Square The area around 34th Street and Broadway is home to Macy's, the world's largest department store. To the east are the shops of 34th Street and Fifth Avenue; to the west and south, A&S and A&S Plaza at 33rd Street and Sixth Avenue, and Madison Square Garden Center rising above Pennsylvania Station between Seventh and Eighth avenues and 31st and 33rd streets.

Midtown The center of things and the heart of the city, this area runs, roughly, from the East River to the Hudson and from 33rd Street to 59th Street. In this neighborhood you'll find the Empire State Building, Rockefeller Center, the Broadway theaters, the great shipping piers, the major department stores, many business offices—and, of course, most of the hotels and restaurants that cater to visitors.

Central Park Starting north of 59th Street, this magnificent sweep of greensward, running between Fifth Avenue and Central Park West, is the great divide between the Upper East and West Sides.

Lincoln Center At 65th Street and Broadway, the Lincoln Center for the Performing Arts is a veritable fortress of culture (containing the Metropolitan Opera House, Avery Fisher Hall, the New York State Theater, the Juilliard School of Music, the Vivian Beaumont Theater, and Alice Tully Hall).

Upper West Side A mainly residential district, with the lovely buildings of Central Park West on one boundary and Riverside Drive on the other, it starts north of 59th Street. At 116th Street and Broadway is the campus of Columbia University, and as you go up Riverside Drive, you will see the massive structure of Grant's Tomb and the great Gothic spires of Riverside Church.

Upper East Side This neighborhood, starting north of 59th Street, is the home of the Beautiful People, many of the fashionable schools and shops, and the prestigious Metropolitan Museum of Art. Included in this area is the once German and Central European section called Yorkville that centers on 86th Street between Park and First avenues.

Harlem This area begins at 125th Street on the West Side and

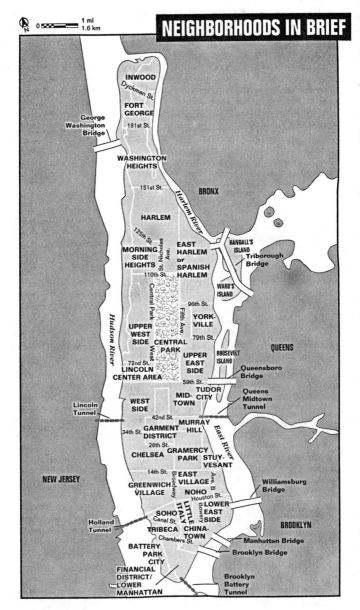

NEIGHBORHOODS IN BRIEF

0 ____ 1 mi
1.6 km

INWOOD
Dyckman St.
FORT
GEORGE
George
Washington
Bridge
181st St.

WASHINGTON
HEIGHTS

151st St.

BRONX

Harlem River

HARLEM

125th St.

MORNING
SIDE
HEIGHTS

St. Nicholas Ave.

EAST
HARLEM
or
SPANISH
HARLEM

RANDALL'S
ISLAND
Triborough
Bridge

110th St.

WARD'S
ISLAND

Central Park West

96th St.

Fifth Ave.

YORK-
VILLE

Hudson River

UPPER
WEST
SIDE

CENTRAL
PARK

79th St.

QUEENS

72nd St.

Central Park West

LINCOLN
CENTER AREA

UPPER
EAST
SIDE

ROOSEVELT
ISLAND

Queensboro
Bridge

59th St.

Lincoln
Tunnel

WEST
SIDE

MID-
TOWN

TUDOR
CITY

Queens
Midtown
Tunnel

East River

42nd St.

MURRAY
HILL

34th St.

GARMENT
DISTRICT

28th St.

CHELSEA

GRAMERCY
PARK

STUY-
VESANT

NEW JERSEY

14th St.

GREENWICH
VILLAGE

Broadway

EAST
VILLAGE

Ave. B

NOHO
Houston St.

Williamsburg
Bridge

SOHO

LITTLE
ITALY

Bowery

LOWER
EAST
SIDE

Holland
Tunnel

Canal St.

TRIBECA

CHINA-
TOWN

Chambers St.

BROOKLYN

BATTERY
PARK
CITY

Manhattan Bridge

Brooklyn Bridge

FINANCIAL
DISTRICT/
LOWER
MANHATTAN

Brooklyn
Battery
Tunnel

96th Street on the East, and around East 110th Street is the center of the sprawling Hispanic neighborhood of New York: **Spanish Harlem,** or **El Barrio.**

   Washington Heights   This mixed residential neighborhood, near the northern tip of the island, embraces Fort Tryon Park and the beautiful Cloisters of the Metropolitan Museum of Art, a serene vantage point from which to contemplate the incredible diversity of incredible New York.

STREET MAPS

The **New York Visitor's Guide and Map** is available (in six languages) at the offices of the New York Convention and Visitors Bureau at 2 Columbus Circle (tel. 212/397-8222). A map of the New York City subway system is also available at the visitors bureau, or you can pick one up at subway token booths. See also the subway maps in this book.

2. GETTING AROUND

New York is one of the few cities left in this country where walking not only is encouraged but also is altogether feasible, since everything is so close together. Walking, in fact, is often the quickest way to get somewhere, especially during the midday lunch crush and the evening rush hour (5 to 6pm), when surface traffic seems to move at the rate of 2 miles per hour.

BY SUBWAY Everyone should ride the New York subway at least once—just for the experience. If you manage to survive a rush-hour crush (8 to 9:30 in the morning, 5 to 6 in the evening on weekdays), you'll have something to tell the folks back home. The rest of the time, the subway is relatively uncrowded and will take you where you want to go quickly (no traffic!), fairly efficiently, and at a cost of $1.25 per token. *Note:* Senior citizens (over 65) can show their Social Security Health Insurance Card and ride buses and subways for 55¢.

Use our maps or pick up a free color-coded one at many token booths. East Side trains (numbers 4, 5, and 6) run along Lexington Avenue; the line is known as the Lexington Avenue Subway. On the West Side, the trains (numbers 1, 2, 3, and 9), go along Broadway and Seventh Avenue (the 1 and 9 go north to Columbia University and Washington Heights and wind up in the Bronx at Van Cortlandt Park; the 2 and 3 branch eastward north of 96th Street to Seventh Avenue and up Lenox Avenue through Harlem). The east and west branches are connected by the Grand Central/Times Square Shuttle (the S train) and the 14th Street–Canarsie Line (the L). The Flushing line (number 7) runs beneath the shuttle from Times Square to Grand Central and then east into Queens. The Sixth and Eighth avenue lines (B, D, F, and Q, and A, C, and E trains, respectively) have major stops in Greenwich Village at West 4th Street, at the Port of New York Authority Bus Terminal area at 41st Street, and at Columbus Circle (59th Street).

For information on how to get from one place to another by subway, call 718/330-1234.

BY BUS Slower than subways but cheaper than taxis, the buses solve a lot of transportation problems. Almost every major avenue has its own bus (they run either north or south: downtown on Fifth, uptown on Madison, downtown on Lexington, uptown on Third, and so on). There are crosstown buses at strategic locations all around town: 8th Street (eastbound), 9th (westbound), 14th, 23rd, 34th, and 42nd (east- and westbound), 49th (eastbound), 50th (westbound), 57th (east- and westbound), 65th (eastbound across the West Side, through the park, then north on Madison, continuing east on 68th to York Avenue), 67th (eastbound on the East Side to Fifth Avenue, then south on Fifth, continuing west on 66th Street through the park and across the West Side to West End Avenue), 79th, 86th, 96th, 116th, and 125th (east- and westbound). Some of the buses, however, are erratic: The M104, for example, starts at the East River, then turns at Eighth Avenue and goes up Broadway. The buses of the Fifth Avenue line go up Madison or Sixth and follow various routes around the city. Check the maps on the bus signs, or ask the driver, to be sure.

Note: Since bus drivers are no longer allowed to make change, you must have your exact fare ready: a subway token or $1.25 (in change, not bills), which includes a transfer ticket to an intersecting bus line (ask the driver for one when you board the bus).

For information on how to get from one place to another by bus, call 718/330-1234.

BY TAXI   The most convenient way to get around town, of course, is by cab, which can be hailed on any street. Official New York taxis are yellow, have the rates painted on the front doors, and have lights on the roof (when the light is on, the taxi is available). Other cabs are best avoided.

However, taxis are expensive. As soon as you step into the cab, the meter clicks to $1.50; the charge is then 25¢ for each one-fifth of a mile and 25¢ for each minute of waiting time in traffic. There is also a 50¢ surcharge between 8pm and 6am. You are, of course, expected to tip about 20% to 25%.

If you wish to have a cab come directly to your door (often helpful during rush hour), simply check the Yellow Pages under "Taxicab Service." If you wish to call a car service to take you directly to the airport, call, among others, **Carmel** (tel. 662-2222) or **Tel Aviv** (tel. 777-7777).

Note: It's best to give a cab driver an intersection rather than a numbered address so you'll sound like a local who can't be taken on the scenic route.

BY CAR   It is really not feasible to drive a car around Manhattan. Traffic is horrendous; parking in garages is exorbitant (between $18 and $25 per day), especially in the business and entertainment areas; and street parking is very difficult to find, except after 7pm, and then it usually involves moving the car in the morning when alternate-side-of-the-street parking rules go into effect. Not recommended for visitors.

The main office of the **American Automobile Association** in Manhattan is at Broadway and 62nd Street (tel. 757-2000 or 586-1166).

The major national **car-rental companies**—Avis, Budget, Dollar, Hertz, and so on—all have agencies in Manhattan. Consult the Yellow Pages of the phone book for offices close to your hotel. Rates are high. A one-day rate at Avis last summer for an automatic compact was around $87. Prices come down on longer rentals.

For discount rentals, try two local companies: **A A M Car,** 303 W. 96th St. (tel. 222-8500) and **USA Rent A Car,** 30 W. 60th St. (tel. 427-1800).

map continues on next page

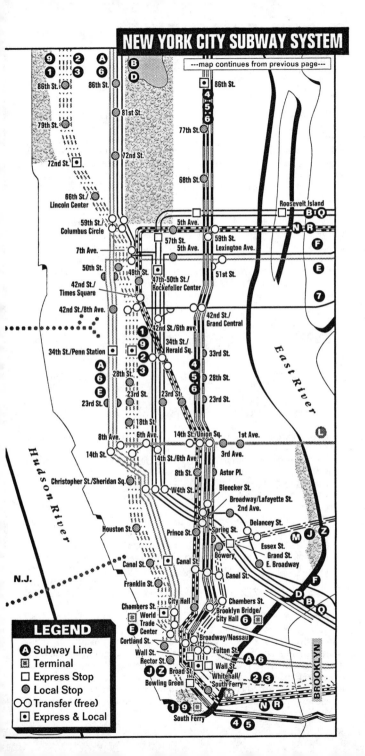

NEW YORK CITY SUBWAY SYSTEM

---map continues from previous page---

BY BICYCLE Many New Yorkers ride their bikes through heavily trafficked areas, but, again, this is not recommended for visitors. Riding a bike through the parks, however, can be fun. **Gene's,** 242 E. 79th St. (tel. 249-9218), charges $3 per hour, $10.50 per day, $50 per week.

TRAINS TO THE SUBURBS The **PATH** (Port Authority Trans-Hudson) rail transit system (tel. toll free 800/234-7284) is the primary transit link between Manhattan and neighboring New Jersey urban communities, as well as with New Jersey's suburban commuter railroad (New Jersey Transit, with which it has connections at Newark and Hoboken). PATH operates four lines: Newark–World Trade Center; Journal Square–33rd Street; Hoboken–WTC, and Hoboken–33rd Street. PATH service, all air-conditioned, runs 24 hours a day, 7 days a week. The fare is $1.15.

    Metro North (tel. 532-4900) provides service from Grand Central Station at 42nd Street between Vanderbilt and Lexington avenues to Westchester County and other northern suburbs. The **Long Island Rail Road** (tel. 718/217-5477) serves all of Long Island from Pennsylvania Station on Seventh Avenue between 31st and 33rd streets. **Amtrak** (tel. toll free 800/USA-RAIL) serves destinations farther afield.

FAST NEW YORK

    Area Codes All telephone numbers in Manhattan have the 212 area code. In Brooklyn, Queens, the Bronx, and Staten Island, the area code is 718. To dial outside the 212 area code, you must dial "1" before the area code. For instance, to call Information in Brooklyn, dial 1/718/555-1212.

    Babysitters Most hotel concierges can recommend babysitters.

    Business Hours Standard business hours are weekdays from 9am to 5pm.

    Car Rentals See "Getting Around" in this chapter.

    Climate See "When to Go" in Chapter 2.

    Crime See "Safety," below.

    Currency Exchange See "Fast Facts: For the Foreign Traveler" in Chapter 3.

    Dentists Preventive Dental Associates, which has five Manhattan offices, is open Monday from 7am to 7pm; Tuesday, Wednesday, and Thursday from 9am to 8pm; Friday from 9am to 6pm; and Saturday from 9am to 5pm. It also has a 24-hour answering service. Call 683-2722 and a dentist will return your call and give you professional advice.

    Doctors Should you need a doctor when you're in New York, do not go to a hospital emergency room unless you are in a potentially serious or life-threatening situation. Waits in over-crowded, understaffed hospital emergency rooms can be agonizingly long. Nonemergency situations can be better handled at a place like **Manhattan Medical Care,** 152 W. 72nd St. (tel. 496-9620), where Dr. Richard Shepard and his staff provide expert care, without the necessity of an appointment. They are open weekdays from 8am to 8pm and Saturday from 10am to 6pm. A basic office visit is $75. If you are in doubt as to whether you should go to a hospital or can be taken care of here, phone and discuss your situation with the nurse.

Downtown, **Beth Israel Medical Center** runs Doctors Walk-In at 57 E. 34th St. (tel. 683-1000), which charges $65 for an office visit and is open weekdays from 8am to 6pm and Saturday from 10am to 2pm. No lab or X-ray work can be done after 4pm.

House calls are available from **Doctors on Call** (tel. 718/238-2100) 24 hours a day, 7 days a week, for a charge of between $70 and $85 a visit, depending on the time of day or night. Minimum waiting time is 1½ hours. If the situation sounds serious, you will be advised to go to a hospital emergency room (see "Hospitals," below).

Drugstores **Kaufman Pharmacy,** Lexington Avenue at 50th Street (tel. 755-2266), is open 24 hours a day, 7 days a week, and will make emergency deliveries (you pay the cab fare).

Emergencies Dial **911** to reach the police or the fire department or to summon an ambulance. Call the **Poison Control Center** at 764-7667. (Also see "Hotlines," below.)

Eyeglasses **Lenscrafters,** with two offices in Manhattan, at 901 Sixth Avenue at 33rd Street and 2040 Broadway at 70th Street, can replace a pair of glasses in one hour.

Hospitals Excellent emergency care is provided at **St. Luke's–Roosevelt Hospital Center,** corner of 58th Street and Ninth Avenue (tel. 523-4000); at **New York University Medical Center,** 550 First Avenue at 33rd Street (tel. 263-7300); and at **New York Hospital's** Emergency Pavilion at 510 E. 70th St. (tel. 746-5050).

Hotlines Crime Victims Hotline (tel. 577-7777); Suicide Prevention Hotline (tel. 718/389-9608); Suicide Hotline Samaritans of New York (tel. 673-3000); and Youth Hotline (tel. 683-4388).

Information See "Tourist Information" in Section 1 of this chapter.

Laundry/Dry Cleaning Usually your hotel can take care of this for you. Or try the closest cleaner at hand; there is at least one on most blocks.

Libraries The main branch of the **New York Public Library** is at 42nd Street and Fifth Avenue.

Liquor Laws Liquor is sold only in licensed package stores. It cannot be sold to anyone under 21 in stores, bars, or restaurants. Liquor stores are closed on Sunday.

Newspapers/Magazines New York has four daily papers: The *New York Times,* the *Daily News,* the *New York Post,* and *New York Newsday.* They all have information about what's going on about town. Several New York City–based weekly newspapers and magazines also provide comprehensive coverage: *The New Yorker, New York* magazine, the *Village Voice,* and the *New York Observer.* These are all available at newsstands throughout the city.

Hotaling's, 142 W. 42nd St., between Sixth Avenue and Broadway (tel. 840-1868), carries hundreds of newspapers from out of town and around the world.

Photographic Needs **Willoughby Peerless Camera Store,** 110 W. 32nd St., near Herald Square (tel. 564-1600) can provide any kind of photographic service. Film can be purchased at any drugstore.

Police Call 911 for emergency calls to the police.

Post Office   The **General Post Office** is at Eighth Avenue and 33rd Street (tel. 966-8585); a convenient East Side station is the FDR, Third Avenue at 53rd Street (tel. 826-4878).

Religious Services   Saturday's *New York Times* runs a listing of Sunday services.

Restrooms   The best ones are in hotels, department stores, and public buildings. Restaurants try to limit the use of their restrooms to customers, but if you are well dressed and ask nicely, they may allow you to use them. Never use the restrooms in the subway stations.

Safety   Let's look at the facts. New York does have a high incidence of crime, but so does every other major U.S. city; because it's in New York, it gets more publicity. Second, considering that some 8 million people live in the city, and that all go about their business freely, the out-of-towner's frequent impression that New York is a dangerous place just doesn't make sense. However, take certain precautions. Try not to look like a tourist, flashing a big camera and a big wallet. Keep your camera inconspicuous, put your money in traveler's checks, and leave your valuables in the hotel safe or at home. (Never, of course, leave your valuables in a hotel room unless there is an in-room safe.) Whenever you're traveling in an unfamiliar city or country, stay alert and be aware of your immediate surroundings. Wear a moneybelt and keep a close eye on your possessions. Be particularly careful with cameras, purses, and wallets—all favorite targets of thieves and pickpockets.

There are certain areas to avoid at night: One is the East Village, where there is drug traffic on the far eastern streets; the second is Amsterdam Avenue and its cross streets above 96th Street on the West Side; and third is the area around Times Square, particularly between Seventh and Eighth avenues, now lined with lurid pornographic theaters and bookstores. The parks are taboo after sundown, unless you're going to a festival or theatrical performance in Central Park, in which case the access routes will be well lighted. And it's safer to take a cab home late at night than a subway. (Stay well back from the edge of subway platforms at all times.) Unfortunately, what you've heard about the homeless and people begging on the streets is true; there's at least one per block. However—and this is important—these people are generally not dangerous.

Taxes   New York City taxes are high—8¼% on many goods and services, including restaurant meals. For hotel taxes, see Chapter 5.

Taxis   See "Getting Around" in this chapter.

Telegrams/Telex   For **Western Union,** dial toll free 800/325-6000.

Television   See local papers for listings.

Tipping   In restaurants, waiters are tipped about 15%, 20% in case of extraordinary service; taxi drivers are tipped 20% to 25%, never less than 25¢. Bellhops should be tipped $1 to carry a few bags to your room; airport porters should be tipped 50¢ for a small bag, $1 for a larger one.

Transit Information   Call the **MTA** at 718/330-1234 (24 hours a day, 7 days a week) for schedules and routes. Bus and subway maps are available at Grand Central Terminal, Pennsylvania Station, and the Port Authority Bus Terminal. For information on getting to and from the area's three major airports, John F. Kennedy International, Newark International, and LaGuardia, see "Arriving" in Section 1 of this chapter or call toll free 800/AIR-RIDE.

Useful Telephone Numbers   For the correct **time,** dial 976-1616. For a **weather** report, dial 976-1212.

3. NETWORKS & RESOURCES

FOR STUDENTS   Visiting students might check the bulletin boards at Columbia University and New York University; many events will be open to them.

FOR GAY MEN & LESBIANS   These organizations offer information and special help: the **Gay and Lesbian Switchboard of New York** (tel. 777-1800); and the **Lesbian and Gay Community Services Center,** 208 W. 13th St. (tel. 620-7310), which sponsors dances on the second and fourth Saturday of the month (except in summer).

FOR WOMEN   A variety of information and help is available from **Woman's Counseling Service of New York** (tel. 439-0106); **Women's Psychotherapy Referral Service** (tel. 242-8597); **Women's Roommate Referrals** (tel. 972-9899); and the **National Organization for Women** (tel. 807-0721).

FOR SENIORS   For information, call the **Gray Panthers** (tel. 799-7572).

CHAPTER 5

NEW YORK ACCOMMODATIONS

- **FROMMER'S SMART TRAVELER: HOTELS**
1. **LOWER MANHATTAN/ FINANCIAL DISTRICT**
2. **GREENWICH VILLAGE**
3. **PENN STATION/HERALD SQUARE**
4. **GRAMERCY PARK/MURRAY HILL**
- **FROMMER'S COOL FOR KIDS: HOTELS**
5. **MIDTOWN WEST**
6. **MIDTOWN EAST/UPPER EAST SIDE**
7. **LINCOLN CENTER/UPPER WEST SIDE**

New York City has more hotel rooms than some small countries have people. In a city where at least a handful of establishments can each accommodate 2,000 guests, where a "small hotel" is one with fewer than 1,000 rooms, you won't spend your nights sleeping in Central Park.

But—and it's a rather big but—getting exactly the kind of hotel room you want, in the location you want, at the price you want to pay, is another cup of tea.

In general, the price picture breaks down like this. To stay in one of the top elegant hotels of the city, those geared to international business travelers and other members of the expense-account set, you can expect to pay $200 and up for a double room. To stay in one of the city's first-class, efficiently run, and comfortable hotels, expect to spend around $175 and up for a double; to stay in a still comfortable but more modest establishment, prepare to part with around $125. You can also still find some respectable establishments where you can get a double for $80 or less a night. Therefore, I have divided the hotels into four categories and, allowing for some inevitable overlapping, they break down like this: **very expensive:** $200 and up per night; **expensive:** $175 and up per night; **moderate:** around $125 per night; and **budget:** $80 and under per night.

I have described here some 63 hotels—which, in my opinion, offer excellent values in each price category and are representative of what you will find everywhere in New York.

I have made every effort to be absolutely accurate about prices, but the hotel business presents a highly competitive, changing situation, and prices may go up or down (usually up) a bit, depending on the season and the demand for rooms. Since new labor contracts are usually settled around the middle of the year, some of the hotels may raise their prices in June.

All of the rates listed, unless otherwise stated, are for European Plan only, which means that no food is included. The rates given are "transient rates"; for those who stay in some hotels on a weekly or monthly basis, lower rates are usually available. All rooms in the listings have private baths unless otherwise specified. Reservations in advance are always a good idea, especially during the busy summer

**FROMMER'S SMART TRAVELER:
HOTELS**

1. Make a deal. It's almost never necessary to pay full "rack rates," the rates that hotels quote. When you make reservations, always ask for any special discounts that might apply: corporate rates; family rates; package deals; senior-citizen rates (almost all hotels have these); or rates for students, military and government employees, clergy, airline employees, or whatever is appropriate.
2. When dealing with a national chain, if you call a hotel directly rather than phoning an 800 number, you have a better chance of negotiating a discount rate.
3. Remember that a hotel room is a perishable commodity. If it's not sold, the revenue is lost forever. Therefore, it is a fact that rates are linked to the hotel's occupancy level. If it's 90% occupied, the price goes up; if it's 50% occupied, the price goes down. So always try negotiating by stating your price.
4. Consider a bed-and-breakfast accommodation; their rates are about half of those in hotels.
5. Try to schedule your trip for a weekend. Weekend package deals, even at some of New York's best hotels, are incredible bargains.
6. If you're staying for a week or longer, you can usually get a cheaper rate.
7. Book your room through a discount service: See information on Accommodations Express and Express Hotel Reservations, below.
8. Watch that phone! Phone calls can take an enormous toll on your bill, since charges for long-distance calls from hotel rooms are no longer regulated by law. Inquire about phone charges, and, if you're not satisfied, use the public phones in the lobby. Keep a record of all calls you make from your room, in case there are any problems on your bill.

months: From Easter to October is high season in New York. If you haven't planned in advance, you will almost always be able to get some sort of room, but perhaps not just the one you would like.

Finally, I'm sorry to have to break it to you, but New York City's **hotel taxes** are among the highest in the world. All rates quoted here are subject to a 16¼% New York City room tax, plus an additional $2 per night bed tax for hotels charging under $100. For hotels charging over $100, it's even worse: 21¼% plus $2 per room per night.

WEEKEND PACKAGES If you're coming to New York for just the weekend, you're in luck. That's when business travelers clear out and expensive hotel rooms go empty. Rather than let this happen, some of the loveliest hotels in town woo the vacationer with attractive weekend package rates, which often include some meals, sightseeing, theater tickets, and many extras. Because these packages vary greatly and change frequently, your best deal is to call the hotel you're interested in, and/or write the **New York Convention and Visitors Bureau,** 2 Columbus Circle, New York, NY 10019, requesting their brochure "New York City Tour Package Directory." Also note that many weekend packages are advertised in the travel section of the Sunday *New York Times,* available in most major cities.

RESERVATION SERVICES   Need to make a last-minute reservation? Need advice on what hotel best suits your particular needs? Hope to save a few dollars on your bill? A reservation service can help. **Accommodations Express** works with 80% of all hotels in New York, in every price category from budget to luxury. Not only can they offer you immediate confirmation, but they can often help you realize a nice savings off rack rates—at least 10% and sometimes much more. The service is free, and their toll-free 800 number is answered seven days a week from 8am to 9pm. They can also help if you're going to continue your travels farther south, to Atlantic City, Philadelphia, Washington, D.C.—or out west to Las Vegas. For New York City reservations, call toll free 800/444-7666, ext. 114.

Large firms have always secured "corporate rates" for their employees. A Colorado-based firm, ✪ **Express Hotel Reservations,** does the same for individual travelers to New York and Los Angeles. They can save you from $20 to $70 per night at some 26 major New York establishments in every price category—and customer service is outstanding. To contact the free service, call toll free 800/356-1123 between 10am and 7pm Eastern Time, Monday to Friday.

BED-&-BREAKFAST   If you'd like to get away from the glitzy atmosphere of New York hotels, you might want to consider using a Bed & Breakfast service. Staying in a B&B is a good way to get a firsthand sense of what it's like to actually live in New York City. Lodgings can be either hosted or unhosted. Hosts can range from struggling actors to doctors to various New York yuppies. Who knows—you might find yourself in a huge SoHo loft filled with Andy Warhol paintings, or perhaps an Upper East Side *pied-à-terre* steps from Central Park.

City Lights Bed & Breakfast, Ltd., P.O. Box 20355 Cherokee Station, New York, NY 10028 (tel. 212/737-7049 or 737-8251; fax 212/535-2755), is a well-established and highly praised B&B service; they are moving into the moderate-to-luxurious price range as the city becomes more gentrified. In addition to accommodations, they also offer settings for small business meetings and conferences, a personalized shopping service for B&B clients, and individualized tours for art lovers and architecture buffs. Accommodations are available in Manhattan and parts of Brooklyn, on Long Island, and in Westchester. Rates for single occupancy range from $60 to $75, and doubles go for $70 to $90, depending on the length of stay, location, and "opulence." They also rent unhosted apartments from $95 to $250 and up, and some of these—like a garden apartment in a posh East Side town house—can be magnificent. They also book B&B accommodations in the major capitals of Europe.

Another popular agency, **New World Bed & Breakfast,** 150 Fifth Ave., Suite 711, New York, NY 10011 (tel. 212/675-5600), has fewer listings, but an important difference: It is the only B&B agency in New York to have a toll-free number for reservations and inquiries: 800/443-3800 in the United States and Canada. They also have toll-free numbers from the United Kingdom (0/800/89-1696) and Australia (0014/800/125-496), as well as other countries. Their local numbers are 212/675-5600 and fax 212/675-6366. Rooms, in Manhattan only, go from $50 to $75 for a single and $60 to $90 for a double; unhosted apartments range from $70 to $200 a night single or double, plus $10 to $20 for each additional person.

Sasha Karas, a licensed real estate broker, runs one of the newer B&B agencies in town, **Bed & Breakfast Bureau,** 330 W. 42nd St., New York, NY 10036 (tel. 212/957-9786; fax 212/957-7000). She can arrange anything from a stay of a few nights to a stay of a few months or even more. The rooms and unhosted apartments are located all over Manhattan, and their prices can be very competitive, especially if you ask for "seasonal discounts." Moderately priced rooms begin at $50 for a single and $60 for a double; unhosted apartments start at $75 for a single and $85 for a double; deluxe accommodations, some in fashionable East Side condos, can cost from $150 to $200, or more for glorious penthouses.

1. LOWER MANHATTAN/ FINANCIAL DISTRICT

EXPENSIVE

THE HOTEL MILLENIUM, 55 Church St., New York, NY 10017. Tel. 212/693-2001, or toll free 800/835-2220. Fax 212/571-2317. 561 rms and suites. A/C MINIBAR TV TEL

$ Rates: $225–$245 single; $245–$265 double; $305 Millenium rooms (junior suites); $295–$2500 suites. Weekend; $150 single or double, $195 single or double. Millenium rooms and suites. Extra person $20. **Parking:** On premises $24 weekdays, $9 weekends. AE, CB, DC, DISC, JCB, MC, V.

There's no need to wait until the millennium—the good life is already here for travelers who pick this handsome hotel, the newest in the downtown area. Built at an estimated cost of $150,000,000, the 58-story Millenium is a sleek tower directly across from the World Trade Center. It's within walking distance, and offers superb views, of downtown's major attractions, including the Statue of Liberty, Ellis Island, and the South Street Seaport. Every effort is being made to provide the traveler with every amenity and service on a 'round-the-clock basis, in a setting of great warmth, comfort, and charm.

From the gracefully understated lobby, done in rosewood and Minnesota granite, rosewood-lined elevators lead the way to the guest floors. The rooms, of generous size, are quiet and comfortably elegant, with excellent city views (rooms from the higher floors offer splendid views of the Brooklyn Bridge and the Statue of Liberty). Rooms are decorated in soft tones of taupe, peach, and platinum, with either teak or curly-maple furnishings. Each features ample workspace, with two-line phones in the bedroom and bathroom, plus

dataports for fax and personal computers. The closets are stocked with bathrobes, slippers, a shopping bag (there's great shopping in the neighborhood!), and even an umbrella. The rooms also have in-room safes and remote-control cable TVs.

Because the hotel welcomes many guests for "weekend escapes," there is a weekend planning service (tours, sightseeing, restaurant and shopping recommendations, and much more). Many themed weekends are also held throughout the year.

Dining/Entertainment: The premier dining room, Taliesin,

LOWER MANHATTAN & FINANCIAL DISTRICT ACCOMMODATIONS

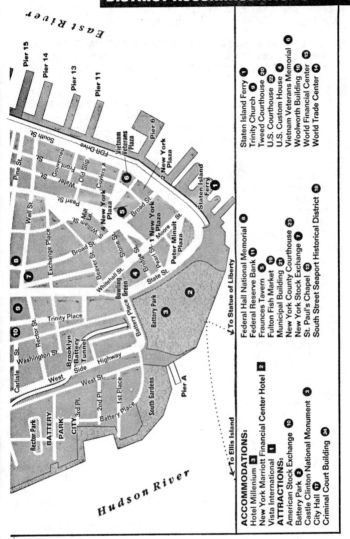

East River

Pier 15
Pier 14
Pier 13
Pier 11

South St.
Front St.
Water St.
Governeur
Pine St.
Old Slip
Coenties
FDR Drive
Vietnam Veterans Plaza
Pier 6
2 New York Plaza

Wall St.
Exchange Place
William St.
Mill St.
Stone St.
Pearl St.
Broad St.
Beaver St.
Whitehall St.
State St.
Bridge St.
Pearl St.
Peter Minuit Plaza
Staten Island Ferry
4 New York Plaza
5
1 New York Plaza
4 Moore St.

Bowling Green
Battery Park

Trinity Place
Rector St.
Washington St.
Carlisle St.
Brooklyn Battery Tunnel
West Side Highway
West St.

Battery Park City
Rector Park
3rd Pl.
2nd Pl.
1st Place
Battery Place
South Gardens
Pier A

To Statue of Liberty

To Ellis Island

Hudson River

Staten Island Ferry	1
Trinity Church	9
Tweed Courthouse	20
U.S. Courthouse	22
U.S. Custom House	4
Vietnam Veterans Memorial	6
Woolworth Building	16
World Financial Center	15
World Trade Center	14

Federal Hall National Memorial	8
Federal Reserve Bank	11
Fraunces Tavern	5
Fulton Fish Market	19
Municipal Building	21
New York County Courthouse	23
New York Stock Exchange	7
St. Paul's Chapel	13
South Street Seaport Historical District	18

ACCOMMODATIONS:
Hotel Millenium 3
New York Marriott Financial Center Hotel 2
Vista International 1

ATTRACTIONS:
American Stock Exchange 10
Battery Park 2
Castle Clinton National Monument 3
City Hall 17
Criminal Court Building 26

offers American cuisine with Mediterranean and Asian accents. Frank Lloyd Wright's architectural style is recalled in the decor. The Grille offers casual American food and ambiance; the Connoisseur Bar, a popular downtown watering hole, serves breakfast and light fare and snacks, as well as classic drinks and bottles from an impressive wine list.

Services: Multilingual staff, concierge, valet parking, 24-hour room service, free video checkout, valet parking, complimentary limo service.

Facilities: Fitness center with swimming pool in greenhouselike setting overlooking St. Paul's Chapel; Business Center with secretarial, messenger, courier, phone, fax, and telex services, plus rental of fax machines, PCs, VCRs, and mobile telephones.

NEW YORK MARRIOTT FINANCIAL CENTER HOTEL, 85 West St., New York, NY, 10006. Tel. 212/385-4900, or toll free 800/242-8685. Fax 212/227-8136. 504 rms and suites. A/C MINIBAR TV TEL

$ Rates: $229 single; $249 double; $495 Executive Suite; $329 Hospitality Suite. Extra person free. Children 18 and under free in parents' room. Weekend packages available, including a "Two for Breakfast" deal at $119 per night, single or double. **Parking:** $20 Mon–Thurs; $15 Fri–Sat. AE, CB, DC, DISC, EURO, JCB, MC, V.

The newest of Marriott's megahotels, this 38-story property just a block south of the World Trade Center affords spectacular views. Besides being convenient to Wall Street, it's in a key location for the sightseeing attractions of Lower Manhattan, as well as the ferries to the Statue of Liberty and Ellis Island.

The hotel's spiffy, almost brand-new rooms and suites are large, comfortable, and nicely appointed in shades of peach and pearl gray, with the expected hotel furniture (here polished walnut armoires substitute for closets) and writing desks. Standard amenities are clock-radios; two phones with a dataport for computer and fax access; and remote-control color cable TVs equipped not only for in-room movies but also with an extra feature that enables guests to receive phone messages, order room service, review their bills, and check out of their rooms. A Concierge Level has its own lounge and business center.

Dining/Entertainment: JWs at the Financial Center is a good option for informal meals, served all day and evening. An all-you-can-eat lunch buffet (soup, an assortment of salads, a carvery item, and fresh fruit) runs about $12. Wines are available by the glass or bottle. Also on the premises is the Liberty Lounge for a light lunch, cocktails, and evening snacks.

Services: Room service 6:30am–midnight, concierge, laundry/valet, express video checkout, babysitting referral.

Facilities: Indoor lap pool, health club, gift shop.

VISTA INTERNATIONAL, 3 World Trade Center, New York, NY 10048. Tel. 212/938-9100, or toll free 800/258-2505. Fax 212/321-2237. 821 rms, 21 suites. A/C TV TEL

$ Rates: $215–$265 single; $240–$290 double. Executive Floor, $280 single, $305 double; $410–$880 suite. Extra person $25. Weekend packages $139–$199 per room per night. **Parking:** $24. AE, MC, V.

The $70-million, 23-story flagship of Hilton International in the continental United States, the Vista is gaining a reputation as a superbly efficient home base for business travelers during the week and as a resort destination in the heart of New York's most historic neighborhood on the weekends. Throughout the hotel—from the dramatic gold mylar sculpture of "sails" that sweeps upward between the first two levels to the rooftop swimming pool—an aura of understated elegance makes its presence known.

The elegant guest rooms, which have some of the most striking views in the city, are done in soft earth tones of dusty peach, beige, and muted greens, with blond oak and rattan furniture. They feature cable color TVs and in-room movies, an electronic keyless lock system, and handsome bathrooms with toiletries. Vista Executive Floor rooms on the 20th and 21st floors have even more special amenities, like a private lounge that serves complimentary continental breakfast, cocktails, and canapes.

Dining/Entertainment: The American Harvest Restaurant has a traditional American menu that changes with the seasons and the harvests. The Greenhouse Restaurant, glass enclosed and brilliant with trees and flowers, offers buffets and a wine bar. The Tall Ships Bar offers cocktails and luncheon.

Services: Shuttle bus to shopping and historic areas of Lower Manhattan or to Broadway theaters, nightly turndown service with chocolates, 24-hour room service.

Facilities: Business travelers can use the services of the Executive Business Center. All visitors have use of the Penthouse Fitness Center with racquetball courts, a jogging track, and a glorious heated indoor pool on the rooftop.

2. GREENWICH VILLAGE

MODERATE

THE WASHINGTON SQUARE HOTEL, 103 Waverly Place, New York, NY 10011. Tel. 212/777-9515, or toll free 800/222-0418. Fax 212/979-8373. Telex 12-6909. 180 rms. A/C TV TEL

$ Rates: Unrefurbished, $52 single; $74–$95 double standard. Refurbished, $60 single; $83–$105 deluxe. **Parking:** Nearby, $9. AE, MC, JCB, V.

Just a few steps away from famed Washington Square is a gem of a hotel in a perfect Village location. It's on a quiet street yet a short stroll from the Off-Broadway theaters, clubs, and restaurants that have made the area famous. The hotel was built in 1902, but it has been thoroughly renovated, and work on the rooms steadily continues. The management strives to make every detail perfect, even down to the handpainted walls with muted floral design, the well-coordinated colors, and other tasteful decorations. All rooms have cable color TVs, individually controlled air conditioning, and baths with shower or tub. All are compact and pretty, but the renovated "deluxe" rooms are much nicer and cost a bit more.

The hotel's exterior is plain, but a brass–and–wrought-iron gate leads to a small lobby with a marble floor and a winding staircase, in the style of turn-of-the-century hotels. The canopy at the entrance was painstakingly carved to revive the 1902 features. CIII, an affordable contemporary American restaurant, serves all three meals; guests receive a 10% discount at breakfast. Practical details include a room with storage lockers, an ice and vending machine, and public phones. Guests may use the telex and fax machines in the office. And Sonny Christopher, the manager, takes delight in briefing guests on where to go in the Village and even helping them secure tickets to special attractions and clubs. The hotel, the only one in Greenwich Village, is owned by the same family that transformed the Herald Square and Portland Square Hotels farther uptown.

---

3. PENN STATION/ HERALD SQUARE

MODERATE

HOTEL STANFORD, 42 West 33rd St., New York, NY 10001. Tel. 212/563-1480. Fax 212/629-0043. 135 rms. A/C TV TEL

$ Rates: $80 single, $90 double, $100 twin; $120 larger double with extra bed; $130 larger twin; $180 and up suite for four to six persons. Children under 12 free in parents' room, extra person $15. AE, DC, JCB, MC, V.

The somewhat Asian Hotel Stanford is a tasteful and inexpensive place to stay, especially for families. Korean-owned, the hotel caters to an international trade and maintains high standards. The rooms were completely renovated a few years back, and now the Stanford offers many of the amenities of a larger hotel while maintaining the friendliness and security of a small one. The lobby is bright and compact, featuring a small Japanese garden. Also available are a travel agency that sells local sightseeing tours; a limo and shopping haulage service to the airport; and the Garden coffee shop, which offers three meals a day. Sorabol, a Korean restaurant, offers authentic specialties for under $10. On the second floor is Maxim's, a very cozy piano bar with quite low prices.

The tastefully decorated rooms have cable color TVs, individually controlled air conditioning, and small refrigerators. All the bathrooms are new. Suites, some with lovely Asian-style partitions dividing the space, are available. The Stanford is practically next door to Macy's and A&S.

RAMADA HOTEL AT MADISON SQUARE GARDEN, 401 Seventh Ave., at 33rd St., New York, NY 10001. Tel. 212/736-5000, or toll free 800/223-8585. Fax 212/502-8712. 1,705 rms and suites. A/C TV TEL

$ Rates: $99–$115 single; $109–$135 double; $200–$1,000 suite. Children 18 and under free in parents' room. Weekend and other special packages available. **Parking:** $26 daily. AE, DC, DISC, ER, JCB, MC, V.

This 21-story hotel is one of the largest in the city, and one of its prime convention and exhibit hotels. Designed by McKim, Mead, and White, it began life as the Hotel Pennsylvania in 1919 and became famous as the setting for lavish parties during the "Roaring" 1920s and for Big Band concerts 1930s and '40s. Subsequent changes

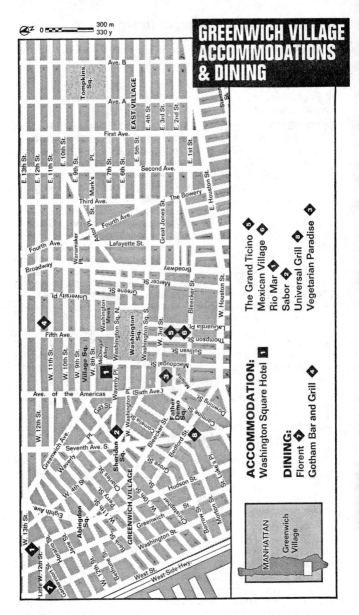

GREENWICH VILLAGE ACCOMMODATIONS & DINING

ACCOMMODATION:
Washington Square Hotel 1

DINING:
Florent 7
Gotham Bar and Grill 4
The Grand Ticino 5
Mexican Village 6
Rio Mar 1
Sabor 2
Universal Grill 8
Vegetarian Paradise 3

in ownership gave it a new identity—as the Penta in 1983—and a total renovation. It became a Ramada hotel in August 1991.

The guest rooms are done in soft colors with custom-designed traditional and contemporary furnishings. The rooms are not large, but they are designed to give a feeling of comfort. Larger suites are accented with special features, including bars, living and dining areas, and kitchenettes. Conveniences include color TVs with in-room movies and individually controlled air conditioning.

Dining/Entertainment: There are three distinctly different on-premises restaurants: Cassini's, the Time Out Café, and the Penn Bar.

Services: Electronic security system, multilingual staff.

Facilities: Business center and meeting rooms; use of the Vertical Club, a health club a block away.

SOUTHGATE TOWER SUITE HOTEL, 371 Seventh Ave., at 31st St., New York, NY 10001. Tel. 212/563-1800, or toll free 800/637-8483. Fax 212/643-8028. Telex 220939. 522 apts. A/C TV TEL

$ Rates: $90–$125 guest room single; $139–$174 studio suite single; $170–$210 one-bedroom suite single; $110–$145 guest room double; $159–$194 studio suite double; $190–$230 one-bedroom double; $395–$495 two-bedroom double. Each extra person $20, up to four for one-bedroom suite. **Parking:** $19. AE, DC, DISC, MC, V.

Just across the street from all the excitement at Madison Square Garden and the new Paramount Theater is a hotel with the ambiance of a quiet, gracious home. At the Southgate, New York's largest all-suite hotel, every suite accommodation—even a studio—has a fully equipped modern kitchen including an automatic coffeemaker and a microwave oven. It's so comfortable that many relocating executives stay here for extended periods of time.

The spacious suites, some with terraces, are beautifully furnished, all containing cable color TVs with in-room movies, VCRs, and kitchens with coffeemakers and microwave ovens. The housekeeping is tops. Southgate Mall, the main lobby, is like a European street with fountains and plants, and shops and services lining each side of the plaza. Considering all you get here, and the savings of eating in, this has to be among the better values in town. Southgate Tower is part of Manhattan East Suite Hotels, which means that you can often realize substantial savings (as much as 50% on weekends); summer and holiday rates are also often significantly lower. Write or call the hotel for information.

Dining/Entertainment: Niles serves continental cuisine; the Penn Garden Coffee Shop provides all three meals; and Goldberg's Famous Delicatessen provides deli favorites.

Services: Room service from all three restaurants, concierge service, secretarial and other business services.

Facilities: Fitness center.

BUDGET

HERALD SQUARE HOTEL, 19 West 31st St., New York, NY 10001. Tel. 212/279-4017, or toll free 800/727-1888. 112 rms (most with private bath). A/C (in summer) TV TEL

$ Rates: $40 single with shared bathroom; $50–$55 small single or double with private bath with shower; $65 standard single with bathroom with shower and tub; $70–$75 standard double with bathroom with shower and tub; $85 large double; $90 large double with three beds; $95 large double for four with two doubles or four twins; all large doubles with private bathroom. AE, DISC, JCB, MC, V.

Located near the Empire State Building and a block from Macy's and A&S, this beautifully renovated hotel is a real find for budgeteers. The once-rundown hotel has been lovingly transformed by the Puchall family, also in charge at the Portland Square Hotel (see below) and the Washington Square Hotel (see above). Back in 1937, the building housed the offices of *Life* magazine. Focusing on this theme, the hotel now has a restored statue of *Winged Life* over the entrance, and tasteful reproductions of old *Life* covers adorn the small lobby, halls, and rooms. Rose gardens bloom in front of the building and in all interior courtyards. The rooms are small but comfortable and well decorated in pastels and wainscoting. Each has a cable color TV and an AM/FM radio.

The hotel is small enough so that guests can get plenty of attention from the multilingual staff. Since 31st Street is relatively quiet at night, the street is monitored by the hotel's own video surveillance unit. Manager Abraham Puchall can often be found in the lobby advising guests on where to sightsee and shop.

---

4. GRAMERCY PARK/ MURRAY HILL

VERY EXPENSIVE

MORGANS, 237 Madison Ave., between 37th and 38th Sts., New York, NY 10016. Tel. 212/686-0300, or toll free 800/334-3408. Fax 212/779-8352. Telex 288908 (MORG-UR). 83 rms, 30 suites. A/C TV TEL

$ Rates: $180–$210 single; $205–$235 double; $275–$400 suite; $1,000 Penthouse. Extra person $25. Weekend packages available. AE, DC, ER, JCB, MC, V. **Parking:** $27 overnight.

Although not for everyone, Morgans' ultramodern, unabashedly eccentric chic attracts an arty international set that includes the likes of Mick Jagger and Billy Joel. This "boutique hotel" without a sign to identify it, or a real lobby, or even the word "hotel" in its name, is as unconventional as you can get in its high-tech design concept. The 20-story building, dating from 1929, has undergone a complete transformation by French interior designer Andrée Putnam, who masterminded the entire multimillion-dollar refurbishment, right down to the custom-designed furniture. The color scheme is gray, black, and white throughout, with touches of melon and green to soften the drama. A bold geometric carpet and milky-glass–and–bronze wall panels dominate the minimalist lobby area. The guest rooms have walls and built-in storage units of warm gray-laminated bird's-eye maple imported from France and dotted with specially commissioned black-and-white photographs in a limited edition by the controversial Robert Mapplethorpe. Low-to-the-floor beds are covered with gray-pinstriped oxford-cloth sheets and duvets, down pillows, and black-and-white plaid blankets—very French, very attractive. Chrome blinds and beige Roman shades decorate the windows; bud vases hold exotic fresh flowers. Every room has a stocked refrigerator (no alcoholic beverages), a gift box of freshly baked gourmet cookies, a color cable TV with in-room movies, a VCR (videos can be rented inexpensively from the management's library of 200), a two-line telephone, and a stereo cassette deck. The bathrooms feature deep-soaking tubs and a separate shower area. Morgans' youthful, exuberant staff provides first-rate attention to guests' needs and requests. Incidentally, the hotel is named for 19th-century industrialist J. P. Morgan, whose former residence, now an important museum and library, is only a block away.

Dining/Entertainment: There's no restaurant, but complimentary breakfast is offered from 7 to 10:30am on Monday to Friday and from 8am to noon on weekends in the 4th-floor breakfast room. Afternoon tea, though not complimentary, is available daily from 4 to 7pm.

Services: 24-hour room service, laundry/valet, seamstress, nightly turn-down, complimentary shoeshine, free newspaper.

MODERATE

GRAMERCY PARK HOTEL, 2 Lexington Ave., at 21st St., New York, NY 10010. Tel. 212/475-4320, or toll free 800/221-4083. Fax 212/305-0535. 200 rms, 160 suites. A/C TV TEL

$ Rates: $125–$135 single; $130–$140 double; from $160 one-bedroom family suite. Extra person $10. Children 12 and under free in parents' room. Weekend packages available. AE, CB, DC, EURO, JCB, MC, V.

Slightly off the beaten track, the 18-story Gramercy Park Hotel is an especially good bet during peak times when rooms in the midtown area are hard to come by. Besides, the place has real

---

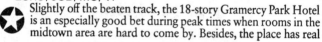

FROMMER'S COOL FOR KIDS: HOTELS

Omni Park Central (see p. 69). Omni's Concierge for Kids service can help with suggestions on places parents and children can go together. A babysitting service is available. Family units, consisting of one large room with a king-sized bed and an adjacent room with two double beds, and shared bathroom, can be requested; depending on availability, they run between $139 and $250.

Paramount (see p. 70). Here kids have a wonderful play room filled with plush stuffed animals (parental supervision necessary).

Travel Inn Motor Hotel (see p. 73). An Olympic-size swimming pool, a large recreation area, and plenty of space in which the kids can let off a little steam make this a family favorite.

Days Inn—New York (see p. 71). Kids adore the open-to-the-sky rooftop swimming pool at this hotel. They may not want to go anywhere else!

Ramada Hotel (see p. 73) also has an open-air rooftop pool. There are indoor pools the kids will like at **Holiday Inn Crowne Plaza** (see p. 58), **Parker Meridien** (see p. 63), and **Sheraton Manhattan Hotel** (see p. 66).

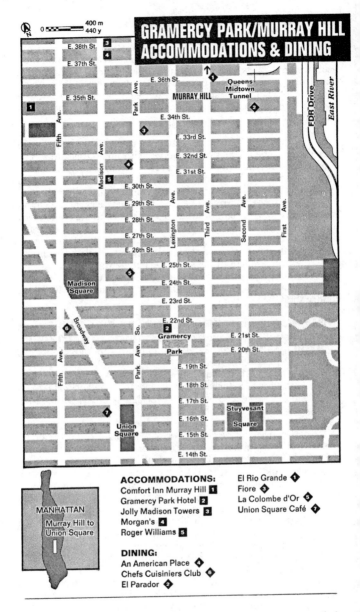

GRAMERCY PARK/MURRAY HILL ACCOMMODATIONS & DINING

ACCOMMODATIONS:
Comfort Inn Murray Hill **1**
Gramercy Park Hotel **2**
Jolly Madison Towers **3**
Morgan's **4**
Roger Williams **5**

DINING:
An American Place ◆
Chefs Cuisiniers Club ◆
El Parador ◆

El Rio Grande ◆
Fiore ◆
La Colombe d'Or ◆
Union Square Café ◆

character and history. It opened in 1924 (retaining some of the marble fireplaces from the Stanford White brownstones it replaced) and has since hosted such celebrities as Humphrey Bogart; James Cagney; Irish actress Siobhan McKenna, to whose memory a plaque hangs in the lobby; and, more recently, actor Matt Dillon.

This is a gem of a property, a charming European-style hotel whose multilingual staff really seems to care. The building overlooks

New York's only private residential park (guests have access), so you can request a room with a view. The wraparound lobby has recently been restored to its original burnished pine-paneled walls, crystal chandeliers, and dramatic potted plants—very evocative, sensual, and romantic. The guest rooms, although undistinguished, are spacious enough, their typical vintage hotel furniture brightened by pastel-printed bedspreads and matching drapes.

Accommodations vary in size from a standard double-bedded room to the family suite, consisting of two double beds and a queen-size sofabed. Suites are equipped with minirefrigerators. The Gramercy Park is also one of only a few New York hotels that offer monthly rates for long-term residential guests, either in studio apartments or in suites, both of which come with small kitchens.

Dining/Entertainment: Le Parc, the hotel's elegant restaurant, is popular with the neighborhood cognoscenti, who are attracted by the combination of gorgeous ambiance—grape velvet furniture, deep-green carpet, stunning flower arrangements, exquisite service—and better-than-average food at moderate prices. Hours are continuous daily from 7:30am to 10:30pm. Definitely worthwhile.

Services: Room service 7:30am–10:30pm, laundry/valet.

Facilities: Newsstand (complimentary city guides are available), sundry shop, beauty salon.

JOLLY MADISON TOWERS HOTEL, 22 East 38th St., at Madison Ave., New York, NY 10016. Tel. 212/685-3700, or toll free 800/225-4340 (outside New York State). Fax 212/447-0747. 246 rms, 10 suites. A/C TV TEL

$ Rates: $130–$150 single; $150–$170 double. Special for readers of this book: $99 single and double; $250 and up suite. Extra person $20. Weekend packages available. AE, DC, EURO, MC, V. **Parking:** At nearby garage $18.

Clean; cheerful; well priced; and located in a charming, safe, and convenient neighborhood—what more could the price-conscious traveler ask for in a hotel? That's what you'll find at the Jolly Madison Towers, the happy result of a $5-million renovation of a 60-year-old hotel. It sparkles from its small, pretty lobby with leather sofas, marble floors, and mirrored ceilings, to the 18 stories of guest rooms above. The rooms are irregularly shaped, which makes them interesting; most are twin-bedded and pleasantly decorated in tones of green, blue, and peach. They're fully carpeted and furnished with reproductions of American antiques. The bathrooms have marblelike sinks, full tubs and showers, and an extra phone.

Many of the guests are involved with the fashion industry (the Garment District is just across town), and you can often find them having a drink or entertaining clients in front of the baronial wood-burning fireplace at the Whaler Bar, a stunning re-creation of a popular New York cocktail lounge of the 1940s and 1950s. The Tower Restaurant serves dinner every night.

Facilities: Asian-style health spa offering Shiatsu massage, beauty salon.

JOURNEY'S END HOTEL, 3 East 40th St., New York, NY 10016. Tel. 212/447-1500, or toll free 800/668-4200. Fax 212/213-0972. 189 rms. A/C TV TEL

$ Rates: $131.88 single; $141.88 double (the 88¢ is a company tradition). Extra person $10. Children under 12 free in parents' room. AE, DC, MC, V. **Parking:** Nearby, $30.

Ⓢ The opening of the first Journey's End hotel in New York is cause for celebration for the value-minded traveler. Journey's End is a 13-year-old Canadian corporation that has achieved phenomenal success by offering "limited service lodging." They have no meeting rooms, swimming pools, or room service—what they do have are handsome new buildings; clean, comfortable rooms; and plenty of friendly and personal service. Considering its moderate rates and superb location—just off Fifth Avenue across the street from the New York Public Library, around the corner from Grand Central Terminal, and within walking distance of Broadway theaters—this hotel is a very good deal indeed.

Perfect for both families and business travelers, the 29-story high-rise has a small, attractive lobby and a mezzanine where guests can have complimentary coffee and read the local newspapers in the morning. The rooms are of average size and attractively furnished, most with queen-size beds and a sofa that can convert to a small bed; some have two double beds. A nice touch is that each room has a large desk where a businessperson can spread out. Rooms also have wheelchair access.

BUDGET

THE ROGER WILLIAMS HOTEL, 28 East 31st St., New York, NY 10016. Tel. 212/684-7500, or toll free 800/637-9773. Fax 212/576-4343. 211 rms. A/C TV TEL

$ **Rates:** $55–$65 single; $60–$70 double; $65–$75 twin; $75–$80 triple; $80–$90 quad. Children under 12 free in parents' room; weekly rates sometimes available. AE, MC, V. **Parking:** At nearby garages, $17.70.

Ⓢ There's a one-of-a-kind find in this neighborhood: the Roger Williams. The Roger Williams is an old building in a quiet, safe, and central location, and all of its rooms have kitchenettes (two-burner gas stoves, sink, refrigerator, cabinet space). They also have large bathrooms with tub and shower, simple but new furnishings, color cable TVs, individually controlled air conditioning, and direct-dial phones. Staying here is like having your own studio apartment in this pleasant Murray Hill area. Across the street is the American Academy of Dramatic Arts, as well as a 24-hour deli salad bar, which solves the problem of what to eat in that kitchenette.

Why is this place so cheap? For years, the hotel had housed mostly long-term residents, some from the United Nations and some temporary American Red Cross disaster victims. Now, with the resurgence of Murray Hill, the Roger Williams began redoing its interior and upgrading its service, as did many of the older hotels in the area. The lobby was redone in art deco style, all the rooms were renovated, and they began accepting many more transient guests.

The rooms vary in size, but most are large and all are comfortable. Some even have terraces. As for the kitchenettes, a "Kitchen Kit" sets you up with a kettle; paper plates; cups; plastic cutlery; and tea, coffee, sugar, and salt (you're on your own for pots and pans, if you need them).

Genial manager Peter Arest and his staff, mainly old-timers here, are very friendly and informal and like to help guests. If possible, they will give you a room with a terrace, advise you where to shop, or suggest what to eat in the Chinese restaurant in the lobby. Flanked by churches, this is exactly the kind of hotel that budget tourists pray for.

5. MIDTOWN WEST

If you've come to New York to go to the theater, to see the sights, to conduct business, or just to be in the heart of everything, you can't pick a more convenient location than Midtown West. Bounded on the north by the West 50s, passing through the Broadway theater district in the 40s, and bordered on the south by Madison Square Garden Center, you'll be within walking distance of just about everywhere you want to be, including Rockefeller Center, Carnegie Hall, Lincoln Center, not far north; and the art galleries and elegant shops of 57th Street and Fifth Avenue.

VERY EXPENSIVE

HOLIDAY INN CROWNE PLAZA, 1605 Broadway, at 49th St., New York, NY 10019. Tel. 212/977-4000, or toll free 800/243-NYNY. Fax 212/333-7393. 746 rms, 24 suites. A/C MINIBAR TV TEL

$ Rates: $185–$210 single or double; $220–$240 Crowne Plaza Club single or double; $350–$1,100 suite. $159 per night Stress Reduction Weekend, including continental breakfast in bed, use of health club, parking. AE, DC, MC, V. **Parking:** $25.

With a 100-foot granite archway that recalls the proscenium arch of Broadway theaters and 12 stories of dazzling lights and signage, this $300-million hotel is perhaps the most architecturally lavish new building in New York. Whether one thinks it's gorgeous or garish or would fit in better in Las Vegas is a matter of opinion, but everyone does agree that it's a major boost to the revitalization of the tawdry Times Square area. They would also agree that this flagship hotel of the Holiday Inn Crowne Plaza's worldwide system is a splendid full-service environment for tourists and business travelers alike.

As for the guest rooms, all are of good size and tastefully decorated, with marble baths; remote-control color cable TVs; direct dial, two-line phones; and many nice touches. Families will like the convenience of two double beds. Four floors are devoted to Concierge Rooms, where guests receive complimentary continental breakfast, evening hors d'oeuvres, and many other amenities. No-smoking and handicapped-accessible rooms are available.

Dining/Entertainment: The Balcony Café offers breakfast and lunch buffets daily in a greenhouse setting. The opulent Broadway Grill, created by David Liederman (of David's Cookie's fame), offers fresh grilled meats, seafood, thin-crust pizzas, and a premier wine selection. Samplings Bar, a multitiered room with a splendid panorama of Broadway, offers entertaining light food and a lavish Sunday brunch buffet, New York's best buy at only $15.95. The Lobby Bar is an intimate lounge.

Services: Valet parking, same-day cleaning service, 24-hour room service, concierge service, babysitting arrangements.

Facilities: A spectacular 50-foot glass-domed swimming pool, perfect for swimming under a starry sky, is the centerpiece of the

New York Sports Club, a state-of-the-art fitness center, complete with exercise physiologists who can give guests personal fitness evaluations and design individual workout programs. A comprehensive business center offers fax service, personal computers, and secretarial services.

THE HOTEL MACKLOWE, 145 West 44th St., between Broadway and Sixth Ave., New York, NY 10036. Tel. 212/768-4400, or toll free 800/622-5569. Fax 212/768-0847. 628 rms, 10 suites. A/C MINIBAR TV TEL

$ Rates: $210 single; $230 double; $425 suite. Extra person $20. Weekend packages available. AE, CB, DC, DISC, JCB, MC, V.
Parking: At garage across street, $28.

The Macklowe is something altogether new on the New York scene: the city's first and only self-contained hotel, conference center, and theater complex, a haven for the business traveler and weekender alike, offering an extraordinary degree of attention to the travelers' needs. In the midst of what is becoming Manhattan's new corporate center, the bustling Times Square area, this 52-story skyscraper manages to offer the feeling of quiet retreat. Eight types of delicately veined black marble mined to the hotel's specifications, the grand staircase, the rich African mahogany paneling, classical architectural details, and Renaissance-style murals in the lobby set the mood of elegant comfort. The upper floors contain the good-sized guest rooms, strikingly appointed in tones of black and gray, and very quiet thanks to insulated windows and their height above the street noise. Special features include chairs designed to support the lower back, two dual-line phones, a message service in four languages, windows that really open, all-cotton sheets and 100% down pillows, digital clock radios, baths with oversize tub and glass-enclosed showers and double marble vanities.

Next door to the hotel itself is the landmark Hudson Theater, a Broadway legend dating back to 1903, restored to its original turn-of-the-century grandeur and now being used as a full-service auditorium and screening facility for fashion, industry, science, and educational presentations.

Dining/Entertainment: Restaurant Charlotte, a bastion of subdued elegance, serving contemporary American cuisine, offers all three meals daily, with a prix-fixe pretheater dinner at $23.95, daily from 5–8pm.

Services: Old-fashioned, guest-pampering services are very much in evidence here. Tailors will sew on buttons or mend a tear; laundry and dry-cleaning can be done and delivered the same day; and personal trainers are available to help you work out or even jog with you through Central Park. Massage therapists will treat guests at the fitness center or in their rooms or even provide seated massage during "stress breaks" from conferences. And you can even leave a complete change of clothing with the hotel from one visit to the next: They'll clean it, store it, and have it waiting in your room when you return. The hotel attracts many female travelers who are especially appreciative of such services—and of the superb security, among the finest in New York. The multilingual concierge service is ready to attend to any needs.

Facilities: The lower floors are given over to commercial offices and a state-of-the-art conference center, complete with secretarial and word-processing services, fax machines, photocopiers, and

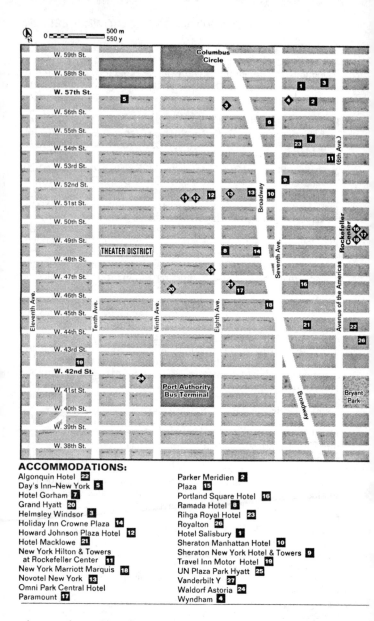

ACCOMMODATIONS:

Algonquin Hotel **22**
Day's Inn–New York **5**
Hotel Gorham **7**
Grand Hyatt **20**
Helmsley Windsor **3**
Holiday Inn Crowne Plaza **14**
Howard Johnson Plaza Hotel **12**
Hotel Macklowe **21**
New York Hilton & Towers at Rockefeller Center **11**
New York Marriott Marquis **18**
Novotel New York **13**
Omni Park Central Hotel
Paramount **17**

Parker Meridien **2**
Plaza **15**
Portland Square Hotel **16**
Ramada Hotel **8**
Rihga Royal Hotel **23**
Royalton **26**
Hotel Salisbury **1**
Sheraton Manhattan Hotel **10**
Sheraton New York Hotel & Towers **9**
Travel Inn Motor Hotel **19**
UN Plaza Park Hyatt **25**
Vanderbilt Y **27**
Waldorf Astoria **24**
Wyndham **4**

photography and graphics studios. There's also a state-of-the-art fitness center.

THE NEW YORK HILTON AND TOWERS AT ROCKEFELLER CENTER, 1335 Avenue of the Americas, between 53rd and 54th Sts., New York, NY 10019. Tel. 212/586-7000, or toll free 800/HILTONS. Fax 212/315-1374. Telex NYHUR 238492. 2,042 rms and suites. A/C MINIBAR TV TEL

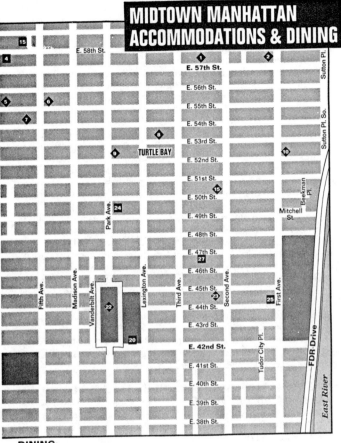

MIDTOWN MANHATTAN ACCOMMODATIONS & DINING

DINING:

American Festival Café ⬥16	Le Perigord ⬥10
Aquavit ⬥7	Lutéce ⬥15
Averginos ⬥8	Palm ⬥23
B. Smith's ⬥19	Pierre Au Tunnel ⬥21
Chez Josephine ⬥24	Rainbow Room ⬥17
Felidia ⬥1	René Pujol ⬥11
Four Seasons ⬥9	Rosa Mexicano ⬥2
Gallagher's Steak House ⬥13	Russian Tea Room ⬥4
La Côte Basque ⬥6	Sea Grill ⬥18
La Fondue ⬥5	Symphony Café ⬥3
La Vieille Auberge ⬥20	Tout Va Bien ⬥12
Le Bernardin ⬥14	Tropical Bar & Seafood House ⬥22

$ Rates: $189–$229 single; $209–$249 double or twin. Extra person $30. No charge for children occupying same room as parent. Executive Tower: $249 single; $269 double; $375–$600 suite. Weekend packages available. AE, CB, DC, DISC, ER, HIL, JCB, MC, V. **Parking:** $27.

This is one of New York's major hotels, an international center with a huge array of services and facilities for both business and pleasure travelers within its soaring glass-sided column. Its Grand Ballroom is big enough for small armies to parade in (up to 3,300 people). A $120-million renovation, completed in 1991, has made the hotel, with its extensive art collection in public areas and guest accommodations, more handsome than ever.

The wall-to-wall blue-tinted windows in the guest rooms provide dramatic vistas of New York's skyline. The rooms, nicely decorated with a modern touch, have color cable TVs with in-house movies at a nominal charge, refreshment centers, voice mall, and computer dataports. Special rooms are available for the handicapped, and 564 rooms on 10 floors are reserved for nonsmokers. The Executive Tower, a hotel within a hotel on the 39th through 44th floors, features its own registration desk, a private lounge and boardroom, concierge service, and many special amenities. Continental breakfast, afternoon tea, and hors d'oeuvres are served here.

Dining/Entertainment: There's plenty of wining and dining excitement here, including Grill 53 for prime beef, fresh seafood, and pasta at lunch and dinner; Café New York, a popular-price restaurant with counter and table service, as well as American and Japanese buffet breakfasts every morning; Mirage, a lobby cocktail lounge; and the International Promenade, great fun for cocktails, express breakfast, and people-watching through floor-to-ceiling windows.

Services: The Hilton's staff is multilingual (some 25 languages are spoken); there is an International Visitors Information Service, and guest information and menus are in several languages. Foreign currency exchange is available 24 hours a day. Room service is available from 5am to 1am.

Facilities: The Fitness Center, a state-of-the-art exercise facility, offers extensive equipment, dry saunas, massage. The Business Center provides secretarial and other services.

NEW YORK MARRIOTT MARQUIS, 1535 Broadway, between 45th and 46th Sts., New York, NY 10036. Tel. 212/398-1900, 212/704-8700 (reservations), or toll free 800/ 228-9290. Fax 212/704-8930. 1,874 rms, 147 suites. A/C MINIBAR TV TEL

$ Rates: Sun–Thurs, $260 single; $295 double. Fri–Sat, usually $199 single or double. Concierge rooms, $265 single; $300 double; $425–$3,500 suite. Other special packages and rates sometimes available. AE, CB, DISC, JCB, MC, V. **Parking:** $29.

The 1985 opening of the Marriott Marquis signaled the glamorous rebirth of Times Square. Located in the heart of the theater district, this is Marriott's flagship and one of New York's largest hotels, with the world's tallest atrium (half the size of the Empire State Building). Architect/developer John Portman's 50-story, $450-million colossus is a dazzling city-within-a-city where one could sleep in comfort, dine in style, attend a business convention, take in a Broadway show, work out in the fitness center, and shop in a wealth of specialty stores, with no need ever to venture out-of-doors.

Although the hotel does cater to many business and convention travelers with its state-of-the-art facilities, it also provides a world of excitement and glamour for the vacationer. Glass-enclosed elevators rise eight stories to the spectacular atrium lobby, which suggests a wondrous indoor park with giant trees, abundant plantings, and fountains—all creating a feeling of tropical, rather than urban, splendor. The guest rooms are oversize by New York standards, each with two views (an exterior one overlooking the city, an interior one overlooking the atrium lobby). All with two telephones, love seats, armchairs, and desks, they are done in traditional walnut woods and deep-purple and green color schemes. The bathrooms have many luxurious amenities. Rooms for the handicapped are available. If you need to conduct a small business meeting in your room, get one of the 24 parlors that feature Murphy-type sleeping units and double as small meeting rooms. Concierge Rooms offer even more amenities and services.

Dining/Entertainment: Lining the atrium are a variety of restaurants, lounges, and people-watching spots: the revolving Broadway Lounge; the Encore sidewalk-like café for casual dining (and New York's largest lunchtime salad buffet); the sunken Atrium Café with built-in deli; and the elegantly understated JW's Steakhouse. It's become a New York tradition to meet friends "under the clock"— the 3½-story centerpiece of the dramatic Clock Lounge, an intimate seating area amid the trees. On the top of the hotel is The View, a three-story rooftop revolving restaurant and lounge, offering excellent food and some of the grandest views in New York (see the review in Chapter 6, Section 13, "Specialty Dining").

Services: Video express checkout, 24-hour room service, newspaper delivered every morning.

Facilities: A full-service business center offers secretarial service, translation service, computer use, and more. Guests have free use of the hotel's health club, with Universal equipment, whirlpool, and sauna.

THE PARKER MERIDIEN, 118 West 57th St., New York, NY 10019. Tel. 212/245-5000, or toll free 800/543-4300. Fax 212/708-7477. Telex 680-1134. 700 rms, 200 suites. A/C MINIBAR TV TEL

$ Rates: $200–$225 single; $225–$250 double; $250–$275 junior suite; $300–$650 one- and two-bedroom suite. Weekend packages available. AE, DC, EURO, JCB, MC, V. **Parking:** At neighboring garage, $28.

If you love Paris in the springtime, then you're surely going to love the Parker Meridien, for that's the feeling one gets anytime of the year at New York's first French hotel. This $75-million, 41-story beauty is the North American flagship of Meridien Hotels, a division of Air France. From its splendid entrance promenade with 65-foot-high gold-leaf ceiling and marble arch, to the lobby and balconied atrium alive with trees and plantings, to the elegant restaurants, guest rooms, and rooftop swimming pool, there's a special ambiance here: the good life, à la française.

The rooms and suites are beautifully done, with built-in blond oak furniture, blond marble tops, accents of brass, and art imported from Paris. There's usually a king-size or two double beds, and bathrooms have floor-to-ceiling marble and include a telephone. The state-of-the-art telephone system is equipped with voice mail, an electronic messaging system. An in-room video aerobic exercise program airs continuously.

Dining/Entertainment: A splendid Asian carpet adorns the hotel's premier restaurant, Maurice, a highly praised "haute brasserie" serving French and American cooking. Eighteenth- and 19th-century French tapestries lead the way to Le Patio, a smart but casual rendezvous for buffet breakfasts, light lunches, and afternoon and evening hors d'oeuvres. A Jazz Brunch is served on Sunday. Works by the French impressionists are reproduced in lighted, chiseled glass in Bar Montparnasse, a Parisian piano bar, where live jazz trios perform each night.

Services: Multilingual staff, Japanese Assistance Network, business services, concierge service, laundry and dry cleaning, 24-hour room service, in-room massages available from health club staff.

Facilities: Guests can make use of the hotel's Club La Racquette, complete with regulation racquetball, squash, and handball courts; aerobics classes, and fitness equipment. On the roof is a splendid glass-enclosed pool, with a beautiful view of both a Bernard LaMotte mural and Central Park far below. There are indoor and outdoor sun decks and a jogging path as well.

RAMADA RENAISSANCE TIMES SQUARE, Two Times Square (Broadway between 47th and 48th Sts.), New York, NY 10036. Tel. 212/765-7676, or toll free 800/228-9898. Fax 212/765-1962. 25 rms, 10 suites. A/C MINIBAR TV TEL

$ Rates: $195–$215 single, $235 butler single; $220–$240 double, $260 butler double; $155 single or double weekends, $205 butler weekends; $425 suite, $425 butler suite. AE, DC, DISC, ER, EU, JCB, MC, V. **Parking:** $26.

White-coated butlers on Times Square? They are only part of the sometimes surprising amenities that await the visitor at this new four-star luxury hotel. Celebrating a renaissance of the glamour that was Times Square, with its art deco Manhattan-of-the-'30's look, the Ramada boasts a marble-and-mahogany lobby with Atlaslike sculptures; the Renaissance Club overlooking the lights of Times Square; and superbly furnished, all-mahogany guest rooms. Designed for the demanding international and domestic business traveler, the hotel provides an extraordinary level of personal service and comfort.

The guest rooms are oversized and decorated in mahogany and dark pastels, with down quilts on the bed, in-room safes, large desks, three dual-line phones (suites have four), and a fax machine available at no extra charge (50 rooms have permanent fax machines). Should you avail yourself of the butler services, your clothes will be unpacked for you and tucked away in a five-foot-wide European armoire instead of in the usual closet.

Dining/Entertainment: At the third-floor Renaissance Club, guests are greeted by a multilingual concierge, then escorted to either the Renaissance Lounge, with a full menu from 11am to 7pm and desserts and cordials after 10pm; or to the pièce de résistance, the "2 Times Square" Restaurant and Bar, which commands a spectacular view and offers Italian-Mediterranean cuisine, including pre- and after-theater dining.

Services: Butler service (including anything from having temporary business cards printed to securing theater tickets to drawing the bath), concierge.

Facilities: Business services center, cardiovascular weight-training room.

RIHGA ROYAL HOTEL, 151 West 54th St., New York, NY 10019. Tel. 212/307-5000, or toll free 800/937-5454. Fax 212/765-6530. Telex 212/245-0170. 500 suites. A/C TV TEL

$ Rates: $260–$390 one-bedroom suite; $450–$700 two-bedroom suite; $1,500–$1,800 Grand Royal Suite. Weekend rates available. AE, DC, DISC, JCB, MC, V. **Parking:** At nearby garages, $28.

New York's tallest hotel, the 54-story RIHGA Royal opened in 1990 and was immediately hailed as one of the most architecturally splendid of the new hotels of New York. With its facade of rose-beige brick and granite and a horizontal array of bay windows creating a set-back effect and offering panoramic views of the Manhattan skyline and the rivers, the hotel is a classic form reminiscent of the skyscrapers of the 1920s and '30s. The small, exquisite lobby is in the style of Park Avenue apartment house lobbies built in that period. This hotel contains only deluxe suites with full service. Security is excellent throughout the hotel; a computer-controlled, timed key system is used.

The suites themselves are custom-designed, done in peach or teal color schemes, the latter with an especially cool, restful effect. They are very quiet, since six inches of wall space between the units blocks out the noise from one's neighbors and double-pane windows eliminate street noise. Each suite has an octagonal-shaped living room, good for a small gathering, and one or two luxurious bedrooms. They all contain VCRs, under-the-counter refrigerators and icemakers with soft drinks and snacks, three telephones with two separate lines, computer and fax lines, and in-room safes. The rose-beige marble bathrooms, with separate tubs, shower stalls, and dressing areas with vanity, are surely among the most luxurious in New York. The six Royal Suites are each uniquely designed and furnished as if they were exquisite private apartments.

Opulence and elegance extend to every area of the RIHGA Royal, with marble, mahogany, and brass touches and glorious flowers everywhere. The hotel represents the entry into the United States of a Japan-based luxury hotel chain, the Royal Hotel, Ltd.

Dining/Entertainment: The award-winning Halcyon Restaurant, serves contemporary American cuisine, with pre- and post-theatre menus; the Halcyon Lounge offers music, cocktails, and light meals.

Services: 24-hour in-suite dining service, served butler style on the finest china and crystal; a multinational staff; free shoeshine; valet and laundry service; shuttle to Wall Street.

Facilities: Banquet and meeting rooms on the top floors; fully equipped business center; fitness center with sauna, exercise machines, and massage service.

THE ROYALTON, 44 West 44th St., between Fifth and Sixth aves., New York, NY 10036. Tel. 212/869-4400, or toll free 800/635-9013. Fax 212/869-8965; telex 213875. 167 rms, 24 suites. A/C MINIBAR TV TEL

$ Rates: $210–$290 single; $235–$315 double; $325–$370 suite. DC, ER, MC, V. **Parking:** $25.

A small hotel that makes a large design statement, the Royalton is one of the most talked-about new hotels in New York City. The $40-million makeover of the cozy old theatrical residential hotel has made the new Royalton like something out of a futuristic stage set, with an almost surreal, dreamlike quality; it could be of the next century or something out of antiquity, a hotel in which the cutting edge meets the classic.

Former nightclub impresarios Steve Rubell and Ian Schrager enlisted the services of Philippe Starck, the self-designated "rock star" of the international design world, to flesh out their concept of "hotel as theater." The results are extraordinary: a long, low lobby with a wall of seemingly endless mahogany doors, a cobalt-blue carpet forming a runway-style path, club chairs covered with white slipcovers as in a deserted house, light fixtures that look like projecting rhino horns, and a sunken library table; and with all the standard hotel fixtures—guest registration, porters, elevators—tactfully concealed. There is no name on the door outside, and "doormen" are black-clad youths who dare not smile.

Upstairs, dark, mysterious hallways, with deep-blue walls and carpeting, lead to the guest rooms, which also make a design statement: Huge, luxurious beds are surrounded by wraparound mahogany headboards and nightstands shaped like portholes. There are velvet banquettes; working fireplaces in many rooms, with wood supplied by room service; arched mantelpieces with a single candleholder and lighted taper set atop a strange wall sculpture. Above it, just one small frame holds an art postcard that is changed daily—the only picture in the room. Custom furnishings, down comforters and pillows, and colors are on the stark side—again, that strange combination of minimalism and luxury. Among the most spacious in New York (they average 400 square feet), all rooms and suites have separate areas for entertaining and working, as well as sleeping. Each room has a writing desk; a dining table; a queen- or king-size bed; a cushioned window seat; a refrigerator; a 13-inch Sony Triniton TV set atop a specially designed stand containing a remote-control stereo "boom box" and VCR; a cassette deck player; and two-line telephones, at bedside and in the bathroom. And the bathrooms! They are the pièce de résistance. Many have five-foot custom bathtubs, usually circular, built in a concave slate wall; others have a slate-and-glass enclosed shower. There are mirrored dressing rooms, Italian cut-glass vanities, and luxurious amenities.

Dining/Entertainment: At the end of the fantastical lobby is "44," a critically acclaimed restaurant serving New American cuisine, a haven for smart celebrities and theater folk, the 1990s answer to the Round Table of the Algonquin Hotel across the street. The Round Bar in the lobby, inspired by Ernest Hemingway's favorite bar at the Ritz in Paris, is the setting for "lobby socializing." Food and beverage service is available throughout the lobby from 5pm.

Services: Impeccable service, with the entire staff fulfilling the role of "concierge." An example of the niceties: a film ordered from the 500-film tape library (no charge) arrives with warm popcorn. Also, 24-hour room service, valet parking, turndown service, valet/laundry service, and in-room delivery of the *New York Times*.

Facilities: LifeCycle equipment in rooms.

SHERATON MANHATTAN HOTEL, Seventh Ave. at 52nd St., New York, NY 10019. Tel. 212/581-3300, or toll free 800/325-3535. Fax 212/541-9219. Telex 640-458. 650 rms, 7 suites. A/C TV TEL

$ Rates: $179–$219 single; $199–$239 double; $400–$600 suite. AE, CB, DC, ER, JCB, MC, V. **Parking:** $18.75.

A $47-million renovation has turned the former Sheraton City Squire Hotel into a stunning boutique hotel, tailored for the needs of business travelers, with well-thought-out business amenities in each room—everything from a generous desk with phone to a dataport hookup for portable PCs and fax machines to such office "necessities" as a dictionary, stapler, note pads, highlighting pens, and more. Handsome new rooms feature oversized beds, brightly lit bathrooms, a sofa or lounge chairs, coffeemakers, and TV viewing from both bed and sitting areas. Executive Rooms, with pullout sofas in the sitting areas, are designed for business travelers accompanied by their families. Solicitous attention is paid to each guest, with the aim of providing the facilities of a large hotel and the personal touch of a small one. No-smoking rooms and handicapped facilities are available.

Dining/Entertainment: Adjoining the lobby is Bistro 790, a popular American/Mediterranean restaurant with a lively bar and a show kitchen.

Services: Automated self-checkout system in lobby; in-room video account review and checkout; voice-mail messaging; concierge service—including in-depth itinerary and activity planning; and morning newspaper.

Facilities: Glass-enclosed swimming pool, Fitness Center with state-of-the-art exercise equipment, sauna, and locker rooms with handicap facilities; business center with photocopiers, fax machines, personal computers, and full range of support services. Fax machines and PCs available for in-room rental.

SHERATON NEW YORK HOTEL & TOWERS, Seventh Ave. at 53rd St., New York, NY 10019. Tel. 212/581-1000, or toll free 800/325-3535. Fax 212/581-1000. Telex 421130. 1,758 rooms, 31 suites. A/C MINIBAR TV TEL

$ Rates: $179–$219 single; $199–$239 double; $550–$700 suites. Towers, $229 single; $255 double; $750–$1,500 suites. Weekend packages sometimes available. AE, CB, DC, MC, V.

Parking: $24.

This 50-story hostelry has recently completed a $142.6-million construction and renovation program that assures its stature as one of New York's premier convention and business travelers' hotels, with state-of-the-art facilities and superior service. The guest rooms and suites, all completely renovated and re-outfitted, are handsomely furnished and boast king- and queen-sized beds, well-defined work and relaxation areas with a full-size writing desk, comfortable sofas or lounge chairs, in-room safes, and individually controlled heating and cooling units. All rooms now have double-glazed tinted windows to muffle sound. Handicapped and no-smoking rooms are available. Rooms in the Sheraton Towers, a luxury hotel within the main hotel, boast English Regency–style furnishings and such touches as fresh flowers and plush bed and bath linens. Sheraton Towers has its own express elevators and a grand expanded lounge on the 46th floor.

Dining/Entertainment: The large glass-enclosed Streeter's New York Café on the lobby level offers three American-style meals a day. Hudson's Bar and Grill features intimate booths and video screens. The Lobby Court is the place for continental breakfast, evening cocktails, and nightly entertainment.

Services: Multilingual staff, room service 6am–1am, concierge service. For Towers guests: bar and breakfast buffet, pantry, butler service, cocktail hour, and more.

Facilities: Free use of the swimming pool, exercise room, and sauna at the Sheraton Manhattan Hotel, across the street.

EXPENSIVE

ALGONQUIN HOTEL, 59 West 44th St. (between Fifth and Sixth Aves.), New York, NY 10036. Tel. 212/840-6800, or toll free 800/548-0345. Fax 212/944-1419. 142 rms, 23 suites. A/C TV TEL

$ Rates: $160–$180 single or double, $120–$150 weekend; $250–$300 suite at all times during week. Extra person $25. Children 12 and under free in parents' room. Weekend packages available. AE, CB, DC, DISC, EURO, ER, JCB, MC, V. **Parking:** $25.

I know of no other hotel lobby in New York that is so full of fascinating ghosts as the Algonquin's. Every time I sit down at one of the plush little sofas in the oak-paneled lobby-lounge and ring the bell for a drink—or a spot of tea—I am reminded of the generations of actors and writers and celebrated wits who have held forth here since 1902. Although Robert Benchley, James Thurber, H. L. Mencken, and Dorothy Parker are part of the Algonquin's storied past, the Algonquin is still as much a literary and artistic club as it is a hotel. But it is a hotel, very much in the manner of an inn, where you needn't be a celebrity to feel at home.

The newly updated guest rooms—the entire hotel has undergone a $20-million complete renovation—welcome with Chippendale-style mahogany antique and reproduction furniture; Chinese porcelain lamps; and, in many rooms, upholstered window seats with colorful throw pillows. The effect is homey and cozy, a refreshing change from the modern megahotel chains. Theatrical drawings and caricatures by Algonquin habitués James Thurber and Al Hirshfeld decorate rooms and halls. Guests are pampered with free in-room movies through remote-control TV, electronic key cards, personal safes, complimentary copies of *The New Yorker* magazine (said to have been conceived at the hotel's Round Table), the *New York Times,* and nightly chocolates on the pillow.

Dining/Entertainment: The Rose Room serves lunch, dinner, pre- and post-theater supper, and Saturday and Sunday brunch in posh Louis XVI surroundings. At night the Oak Room turns into a cabaret showcasing some of the best talent in the country. Drinks and light meals and snacks are available at the Blue Bar from noon to 1am. But the Algonquin's highlight remains the lobby, alive all day and evening, for drinks, conversation, and even afternoon tea.

Services: Room service 7am–11pm, concierge, theater tickets, laundry/valet, babysitting, multilingual staff.

Facilities: Newsstand.

THE HELMSLEY WINDSOR, 100 West 58th St., New York, NY 10019. Tel. 212/265-2100, or toll free 800/221-4982. Fax 212/315-0371. 208 rms, 36 suites. A/C TV TEL

$ Rates: Sun–Thurs, $135–$145 single; $145–$155 double or twin; $215–$225 one-bedroom suite; from $325 two-bedroom suite. Fri–Sat, $114 single or double; $144 one-bedroom suite; $258 two-bedroom suite. AE, CB, DC, MC, V. **Parking:** Nearby garage, $21.

This is the kind of gracious, small hotel that people tell their friends about. A favorite for almost half a century, the Windsor is close to Central Park and has a beautiful old-world lobby with mirrored ceiling, fireplace, and chandeliers. The old-world theme is carried out in the generously sized rooms (even the singles have king-size beds!) with traditional furniture, wall-to-wall carpeting, and good closets (most rooms have two). Computerized no-key locks assure absolute protection. You'll find performing artists (the hotel is near the major music and theater centers), corporate types, and international visitors enjoying the peacefulness of a stay here.

NOVOTEL NEW YORK, 226 West 52nd St., at Broadway, New York, NY 10019. Tel. 212/315-0100, or toll free 800/221-3185. Fax 212/765-5369. Telex 220352. 474 rms. A/C MINIBAR TV TEL

$ Rates: Sun–Thurs, $159–$190 single; $169–$199 double. Fri–Sat, $135 single or double. AE, CB, DC, JCB, MC, V. **Parking:** At neighboring garage, $10.

Novotel New York caters to a sophisticated traveler who appreciates comfort, security, a Gallic flair, and a realistic tariff. The tiny street-level entrance hardly suggests what awaits above (the Novotel was built over an already existing four-story building), but in the seventh-floor Sky Lobby, a whole new world opens up—a world of soaring glass windows, rose-colored sofas, beautiful plantings, and chic style.

The guest rooms are unpretentious but very comfortable. They are of decent size with king-size or two double beds, soft pastel color schemes, French posters on the walls, and cable TV systems with built-in radios and alarm clocks. Each room also has an in-room safe, a two-line phone system, a comfortable workspace for the business traveler, and—very welcome for New York—soundproof rooms with double-paneled windows, which perhaps accounts for the hotel's great popularity among musicians (the Houston, Cleveland, Vienna, and Baltimore symphonies have all been guests here). Security is excellent, with two levels of checkpoints. The efficiency and courtesy of the multilingual staff (who are all given European training and who rotate their assignments) have been given high marks by its many repeat visitors. Room service is available from 6am to midnight.

Dining/Entertainment: You can visit the handsome, glass-sided, two-tiered Café Nicole during the day or before and after the theater to see the lights and stars (celestial and celebrity—Jerry Ohrbach or Tony Randall might also be dining here). American and European specials are offered at lunch and dinner, with "Le Grand Bonjour" buffet at breakfast.

OMNI PARK CENTRAL HOTEL, 870 Seventh Ave., at 56th St., New York, NY 10019. Tel. 212/247-8000, or toll free 800/THE-OMNI. Fax 212/541-8506. Telex 424434. 1,269 rms, 179 suites. A/C TV TEL

$ Rates: $175 single; $195 double; $225 and up suite; $130–$259 two-room family units, subject to availability. Extra person $20. Children under 17 stay free in parents' room. AE, DC, DISC, JCB, MC, V. **Parking:** $26.

Located across the street and around the corner from Carnegie Hall and within walking distance of Lincoln Center, Rockefeller Center, and Broadway theaters, the Omni is very popular with knowledgeable travelers. Its management offers guests all sorts of special incentives to lure them here—call the hotel at the local number listed above and ask if they are offering any weekend or midweek promotional packages or rates.

All rooms are spacious and comfortable, with color TVs and in-house movies, Thermopane windows for insulation and noise control, custom-made furniture and appointments, and individually controlled air conditioning and heating units.

Dining/Entertainment: Restaurants abound near the hotel, but right at hand is the charming Café Nicole, a Parisian-style brasserie with a menu of French country fare from the Alsace-Lorraine region, serving all three meals. Notes is a stylish bar and lounge with nightly entertainment, a relaxing place to unwind.

Services: Multilingual staff; multilingual computerized telephones. Select Guest Service offers special services for businesspeople, like complimentary van service to Wall Street and market areas. Concierge for Kids provides children's programs.

Facilities: Access to the Vertical Club for $20 per day.

PARAMOUNT, 235 West 46th St. (between Broadway and Eighth Ave.), New York, NY 10036. Tel. 212/764-5500, or toll free 800/225-7474. Fax 212/354-5237. 610 rms, 12 suites. A/C TV TEL

$ Rates: $99–$180 single; $155–$200 double; $320–$430 suite. Children 12 and under free in parents' room. Weekend packages, some including parking, available. AE, DC, MC, V. **Parking:** At garage across street, $16.

This intriguing hotel, witty, even slightly zany in decor, is the newest in a trio that includes the Royalton and Morgans (see above). Entertainment entrepreneurs Steve Rubell and Ian Schrager bought it in 1986; French interior designer Philippe Starck (he did the Beauborg Museum in Paris) has turned it into hotel-as-theater, a striking, high-style ocean liner in the middle of Manhattan.

There's no sign outside, so look for the fresh-faced young doormen in white T-shirts and black jackets (now *there's* a clue to the hotel's image.) The focal point of the lobby is a "floating" marble staircase right out of Hollywood circa 1930 (remember "I'll Build a Stairway to Paradise"?). This is not so much a lobby as an environment, with a dark color palette, high ceilings, recessed lighting, eclectic custom-designed furniture, and spectacular flower arrangements. The guest rooms, like ships' staterooms, are small but compact. Walls, most furniture (the swivel cyclops-eye armoire is a showstopper), and beds are white; gray-and-black carpets cover the floors; offbeat, curvy green chairs add to the whimsy. But the real surprise here (single rooms only) are the headboards: oversize silkscreen reproductions of Vermeer's famous 17th-century painting *The Lacemaker,* framed in gilt and glowing above the pristine white beds. Fresh flowers grace every room, and even the smallest accommodations have color cable TVs, two-line phones with computer capability, and VCRs (tapes can be rented from the desk).

Occupying an ornate 1927 building, formerly the Century Paramount Hotel, the property is located in the heart of the Theater District.

Dining/Entertainment: The Paramount's "very in" dining spots include the stylish Mezzanine, the soon-to-open Brasserie du Theatre, the Dean & Delucca Café, and the Whiskey Bar. All are great for before- or after-theater dining and mingling.

Services: Room service 6am–midnight, concierge, laundry/valet, babysitting and limo services arranged.

Facilities: Children's playroom, business center, fully equipped sports room, meeting room, newsstand.

MODERATE

COMFORT INN MURRAY HILL, 42 West 35th St., New York, NY 10001. Tel. 212/947-0200, or toll free 800/228-5150. Fax 212/594-3047. 120 rms. A/C TV TEL

$ Rates: $94 room with double bed; $99 room with double bed and pullout sofa; $99, room with queen-size bed; $120 room with king-size bed; all for one or two people. Extra person $12. Weekend packages available. AE, CB, DC, DISC, ER, JCB, MC, V. **Parking:** At nearby garage, $20.

Small luxury hotels abound in New York—at rates of $200 a night and over! What a treat, then, to find an "affordable luxury hotel" like the Comfort Inn, which boasts European charm, personal service, and moderate rates. Located just around the corner from Fifth Avenue department stores, near Seventh Avenue's Garment District and the Jacob Javits Convention Center, it's considered an "in" find among fashion buyers and other smart business and vacation travelers. Most of its rooms are sold out every night, and over 60% of its guests are repeat customers.

Built over 70 years ago (meaning thick walls and relative quiet), the building was treated to a $4.5-million renovation and opened as a hotel in the summer of 1986. Complimentary coffee and Danish are served every morning in the charming small lobby with its winding marble staircase, Greek columns, and plush furnishings. Manager Shirley Solomon can often be found there; she likes to get to know her guests, and she and her front desk staff are concerned that guests have a good time during their stay. (She prefers individual travelers and will not take large groups.) The 12-story hotel has no more than 12 rooms per floor, which makes for a cozy feeling (women traveling alone seem to feel especially safe), and these rooms are very pleasantly decorated in soothing pastels; all have individually controlled air conditioning and newly tiled baths. A floor for nonsmokers is available. *Note:* Ms. Solomon advises that you call the hotel directly (rather than the 800 number); you may qualify for AARP, AAA, senior-citizen, corporate, fashion industry, or other discounts.

DAYS INN—NEW YORK, 440 West 57th St., between Ninth and Tenth Aves., New York, NY 10019. Tel. 212/581-8100, or toll free 800/325-2525. Fax 212/581-8719. 591 rms, 5 suites. A/C TV TEL

$ Rates: $149 single; $164 double; $325 suite. Discounts of 15% for senior citizens who are members of "September Days Club" ($12 membership fee; phone toll free 800/241-5050). AE, DC, DISC, MC, V. **Parking:** $7.

One of New York's best hotel swimming pools opens to the sun on the roof of the Days Inn, and that's just the beginning of the good life that awaits at this New York City version of the popular suburban chain. Days Inn has long been known for comfortable rooms at comfortable prices, a combination sorely needed in overpriced New York. Well located, within minutes of Carnegie Hall, Lincoln Center, the Jacob Javits Convention Center, Fifth Avenue shops, and Rockefeller Center, Days Inn is on a lively residential street, so guests can feel safe about going out at night—perhaps to the Hard Rock Café, just a few blocks away. Security is excellent; the card locks are changed every time a guest leaves. There's a multilingual staff at the front desk. The rooms and suites, quite large by New York standards, are done in soft pastel and earth tones, and each has a desk. Most rooms have two double beds, a few have king-size ones; King Leisure or Deluxe rooms all have sofas, and a few of these even have a balcony. Facilities are available for the handicapped.

The Greenery Restaurant, offers dinner specials from $7.95 for a complete meal; the rooftop café, opposite the pool, also offers moderately priced specials daily (summer only). The Apples Lounge has daily drink specials and a large-screen TV.

HOTEL GORHAM, 136 West 55th St., New York, NY 10019. Tel. and fax 212/245-1800. 70 rms, 50 suites. A/C TV TEL

$ Rates: $150–$185 single; $160–$195 double; $195–$210 suite. Extra person or child $20. Weekend packages available. AE, CB, DC, DISC, EURO, MC, V. **Parking:** $25 daily.

The Gorham has just completed a multimillion-dollar overhaul that includes everything from new windows to custom-designed furniture. Its rooms and suites (this is a small property styled for easy living) are freshly painted and decorated in either pale gray and white or lavender and white. Custom-built armoires in burgundy lacquer conceal the TVs and provide extra drawers to supplement the already ample closets. Other built-ins include desks and luggage storage units. The rooms are spacious, large enough for either one king or two queen-size beds; suites have separate living areas with pullout couches accommodating as many as five.

Besides the expected features, the Gorham offers two-line phones (three per room) with call waiting and computer/fax access, custom-designed wet bars with refrigerators and microwaves, and in-room safes (security is tight here). Brand-new, sleek beige marble-and-glass bathrooms provide such luxuries as deep oval tubs (with whirlpools in many rooms and all of the suites), hairdryers, digital water-temperature control valves, and telephone extensions.

Dining/Entertainment: The on-premises Castellano's is an attractive upscale restaurant that serves lunch (it can get crowded, so be forewarned) and dinner. Also in the building is a convenience-store/deli where you can buy a sandwich and picnic in the charming vest-pocket park just east of the hotel.

Services: Nightly turndown, concierge, laundry/valet.

HOTEL SALISBURY, 123 West 57th St., New York, NY 10010. Tel. 212/246-1300, or toll free 800/223-0680 in the U.S., 800/228-0822 in Canada. Fax 212/977-7752. Telex 668366. 320 rms, 86 suites. A/C TV TEL

$ Rates (including continental breakfast): $129–$139 single; $139–$149 double; $149–$179 one-bedroom suite; $200 two-bedroom suite. Extra person $15. **Parking:** Garage a block away, $15.

Just about the closest hotel to Carnegie Hall is the Salisbury, across the street from the venerable concert hall; since 1931, it's been attracting not only musical folks, but businesspeople, politicians, internationals, and sophisticated travelers who appreciate its old-fashioned courtesy and competitive rates (a one-bedroom suite here compares to the cost of a bedroom in other midtown hotels).

Because it was once largely a residential hotel, its rooms are quite large, with generous closet space (16 rooms on the top floor have serving pantries, with small refrigerators, coffeemakers, and microwave ovens; these cost $5 more per day), traditional American furnishings, and in-room safes. A junior suite—a living room with a queen-size sofabed and a bedroom with two double beds—is an excellent buy. Two-bedroom suites, with living and dining rooms, are spacious enough to sleep six and hold a small business meeting. A free newspaper is delivered each day, and guests have access to the hotel's fax services. Complimentary continental breakfast is served daily. The lobby looks a bit dowdy, but it houses a small restaurant, the Terrace Café, which provides room service.

HOWARD JOHNSON PLAZA HOTEL, 851 Eighth Ave., between 51st and 52nd Sts., New York, NY 10019. Tel. 212/581-4100, or toll free 800/654-2000. Fax 212/974-7502. 300 rms, 3 suites. A/C TV TEL

$ Rates: $101–$142 single; $113–$154 double or twin; $180 and up suite. Extra person $20. Children under 18 free in parents' room. AE, CB, DC, DISC, JCB, MC, V. **Parking:** $7.50.

We're accustomed to seeing Howard Johnsons on highways, but here in New York you'll find one right in the midtown area within walking distance of Broadway theaters and all the cultural attractions of the West 50s. The rooms here are very attractive, with modern decor, wall-to-wall carpets, large bathrooms, and color TVs that also show first-run in-house movies (for a few extra dollars). On the premises is the Café 52 Restaurant and Piano Bar.

RAMADA HOTEL, 790 Eighth Ave., between 48th and 49th Sts., New York, NY 10019. Tel. 212/581-7000, or toll free 800/2-RAMADA. Fax 212/974-0291. Telex 147182. 366 rms. A/C TV TEL

$ Rates: $108–$128 single; $120–$150 double; $185–$205 one-bedroom suite; $235–$255 two-bedroom suite. Extra person $20. Children under 18 free in parents' room. AE, DC, DISC, MC, V. **Parking:** $7.75.

A good place to stay with children is the Ramada Hotel. There's no fancy formality here, and kids will love the open-air pool up on the roof with its cozy cabana deck and snack bar for poolside lounging. The rooms are nicely furnished, with picture windows, color TVs featuring in-room first-run movies, oversize beds, and good-size closets. Jerry's Metro Restaurant and Bar, an informal American deli, provides three meals a day.

TRAVEL INN MOTOR HOTEL, 515 West 42nd St., New York, NY 10036. Tel. 212/695-7171, or toll free 800/869-4630. Fax 212/967-5025. Telex 205633, 160 rms. A/C TV TEL

$ Rates: From $90 single; $105 double; $115 three people; $135 four people. AE, DC, MC, V. **Parking:** Free.

You'd hardly know you were in the heart of New York once you step inside the Travel Inn—it's very much the typical American motor hotel, with an Olympic-size outdoor swimming pool and recreation areas, lots of family groups, and free self-parking that allows you to use your car as often as you like with no extra charge. (At most New York hotels there are in-and-out charges.) Just 3½ short blocks from the Jacob Javits Convention Center, Travel Inn is situated in the Off-Off-Broadway theater area of New York, several blocks (or a short bus ride) west of Times Square. All the rooms have been done in first-class fashion, with custom draperies, imported furnishings, and new bathrooms. Many face a courtyard overlooking the pool and sunning area, which are surrounded by a lovely garden and outdoor furniture. The Stage Restaurant is on the premises, and there are many others within a one-block radius.

THE WYNDHAM, 42 West 58th St., between Fifth and Sixth Aves., New York, NY 10019. Tel. 212/753-3500. 152 rms, 60 suites. A/C TV TEL

$ Rates: $115–$125 single; $130–$140 double; $175–$205 one-bedroom suite; $290–$340 two-bedroom suite. AE, DC, MC, V. Monthly rentals available. **Parking:** At garage next door, $28.

The rooms are usually booked far in advance at the Wyndham, because word-of-mouth and an appreciative press have made this homey hotel into a favorite address for visiting film, theater, and literary people. Sir Laurence Olivier used to stay here when he was appearing on Broadway. Eva Marie Saint, Sir Alec Guinness, Peter O'Toole, Philip Roth, Eva Gabor, and Peter Ustinov are among the celebrated names on the guest list. Famous people flock here despite its relatively low prices and limited services, because of resident owners John and Suzanne Mados and their staff, who provide their guests with old-fashioned hospitality, warmth, and friendship; staying here is akin to being a guest in a private club where everybody knows your name. And the Madoses have created a world of charm, from the plush lobby that looks like the living room of a European country inn, to the rooms and suites, each with a distinctive personality. All the rooms are European in feeling, with a tasteful mixture of antiques and one-of-a-kind pieces, good paintings on the walls, good-size baths, and graceful touches throughout. But the suites are the real glory of this hotel, and it's well worth a splurge for these graceful dwellings, each with a pantry (refrigerator, sink, and cabinet). Sir Laurence's favorite was Suite 1401, handsome with its chandeliers, huge bed, gilt-edged mirrors, and Persian carpets.

The Wyndham has its own restaurant, Jonathan's, which serves three reasonably priced meals a day. The Plaza Hotel is just across the street. Security is excellent: The front door is always locked and guests are buzzed in. The two elevators are manned. With Mr. and Mrs. Mados usually on duty, this tasteful "Mom-and-Pop" hotel offers one of the best values in New York in its price range.

BUDGET

THE PORTLAND SQUARE HOTEL, 132 West 47th St., New York, NY 10036. Tel. 212/382-0600, or toll free 800/388-8988. Fax 212/382-0684. 104 rms (most with bath). A/C TV TEL

$ Rates: $40 single with shared bath, $60 single with private bath; $75 double with one bed and private bath, $85 double with two beds and private bath; $90 double for three persons with private bath; $95 double for four persons with private bath. AE, MC, V. **Parking:** At nearby garages, from $20.

The Portland Square was formerly called the Rio. Both the hotel, built in 1904, and the block had declined from the early days of the century, when the area attracted famous theatrical names. But the block and the hotel are a Cinderella story, for they are both now highly desirable. The area, well-lit and with new buildings, is a short stroll from the Broadway theaters, the diamond district, and Radio City. The hotel has been completely renovated, and its rooms, although tiny, are tidy and among the best budget buys in New York. The lobby is simple, the photos adorning the walls showing how New York looked earlier in this century. This motif is carried into the halls, which pictorially re-create old New York. Certainly the prices re-create it, especially the four small single rooms with sink (bathroom down the hall) on each floor for an incredible rate of $40. The rooms are tastefully furnished and spanking clean; all have color cable TVs with remote control, direct-dial phones, individually controlled air conditioning, and comforters on the beds.

The building is owned by the Puchall family, who operate similar "Cinderella" hotels, the Herald Square Hotel on West 31st Street and the Washington Square Hotel in Greenwich Village (see above). They make every effort to service their guests in the old-fashioned way. They provide lockers, where guests may store luggage after they've checked out, and a comfortable sitting area, a rarity in budget hotels. The Portland Square describes itself as a "classic limited-service budget hotel." There's no room service.

6. MIDTOWN EAST/UPPER EAST SIDE

New York's East Side is traditionally known for being a bit more peaceful, a bit less frenzied than the West Side. Some—especially women—feel it's safer at night. The location couldn't be better. You're near Grand Central Terminal, the United Nations, and the Fifth Avenue department stores. Plus all posh specialty shops of Madison Avenue and the swinging boutiques of Lexington and Third avenues are nearby.

VERY EXPENSIVE

THE DRAKE SWISSOTEL, 440 Park Ave., at 56th St., New York, NY 10022. Tel. 212/421-0900, or toll free 800/DRAKE-NY. Fax 212/421-0900. Telex 14178. 552 rms, 65 suites. A/C TV TEL

$ Rates: $215–$265 single; $240–$290 double; $425–$500 one-bedroom suite. AE, CB, DC, DISC, ER, JCB, MC, V. **Parking:** $20.

This premier North American hotel for Swissotel, the prestigious Swiss chain, is the result of a $52-million renovation of one of New York's landmark hotels, and its handsome lobby sets the scene for luxury living.

Because the Drake was once a residential hotel, its rooms are bigger—and nicer—than many elsewhere. Subtle ivory-toned rooms boasting soft coral, celadon green, and ivory prints; fruitwood furniture; desks; full-length mirrors; and plants all give the feeling of guest bedrooms in a country home. Special extras include foolproof locks, peepholes, individual safes, three telephones with call-waiting, jacks for computers and fax machines, ice buckets, digital AM/FM clock radios in addition to color TV (complimentary HBO plus pay movies) concealed in the cabinetry, along with small refrigerators and beautiful marble bathrooms with hairdryers and bathroom scales. No-smoking and handicapped-accessible rooms are available. Several Park Avenue suites feature spacious terraces overlooking Manhattan (one even has a wood-burning fireplace). Rooms with a Murphy bed are available.

Dining/Entertainment: The handsome European-style Café Suisse is an informal continental cuisine restaurant serving all three meals. The Drake Bar, which overlooks Park Avenue like a sidewalk café, has nightly piano entertainment and is ideal for either a romantic evening or an informal business meeting. The pièce de résistance is Restaurant Lafayette, with its elegant French/American cuisine; it serves lunch and dinner on Tuesday to Saturday.

Services: Complimentary limousine service to Wall Street weekday mornings, multilingual concierge staff, 24-hour room service.

Facilities: Guests may use (for $25 per day) the nearby New York Health & Racquet Club, a state-of-the-art fitness center.

THE GRAND HYATT NEW YORK, Park Ave. at Grand Central Terminal, New York, NY 10017. Tel. 212/883-1234, or toll free 800/233-1234. Fax 212/692-3772. Telex 645601. 1,407 rms, 87 suites. A/C TV TEL

$ Rates: $220 single; $225 double. Regency Club, $255 single; $285 double. Weekend package (including parking), $145 single or double. AE, CB, DC, DISC, JCB, MC, V. **Parking:** $34.

The striking hotel that heralded the renaissance of 42nd Street, the Grand Hyatt is perhaps the most dramatically modern of New York hotels, a 34-story building that has been hailed as a triumph of modern architectural design. From the silver-mirrored facade that reflects such neighborhood landmarks as the Chrysler Building and Grand Central Terminal to the four-story plant-filled atrium with its cascading waterfall and 100-foot bronze abstract sculpture, the effect is one of dazzle and glitter.

In contrast, the guest rooms are quiet and subdued, done in soft pastel and decorated with handsome prints. All rooms have color TVs with in-room movies, clock-radios, plush carpeting, skirt hangers in the closets, and luxurious bathrooms with amenity baskets of toiletries. Deluxe king rooms have separate seating areas, desks, and chairs. Even more luxurious are the 110 rooms in the Hyatt Regency Club, which occupies the entire 31st and 32nd floors and offers a special concierge and a hospitality lounge.

Dining/Entertainment: Dining rooms and lounges continue the glamour theme of the lobby, especially the Sun Garden Lounge, a sidewalk café and cocktail spot cantilevered spectacularly right over busy 42nd Street. The Crystal Fountain, the hotel's full-service restaurant, is handsome, with a reflecting pool and a mirrored ceiling that reflects the busy goings-on of the street. Sunday brunch is a lavish treat here. The decor at Trumpets, an elegant haven of nouvelle cuisine, is more traditional and subdued.

Services: Concierge, Hyatt Passport Service for preregistration and express checkout, 24-hour room service, complimentary weekday morning paper, same-day valet/laundry service, Japanese welcome service, multilingual staff.

Facilities: State-of-the-art business center, with personal computers, fax and copy machines, secretarial and translation services, and more. Guest privileges can be arranged at nearby health clubs.

THE HELMSLEY PALACE, 455 Madison Ave., at 50th St., New York, NY 10022. Tel. 212/888-7000, or toll free 800/221-4982. Fax 212/303-6000. Telex 640543. 887 rms, 86 suites. A/C TV TEL

$ Rates: $240–$300 single; $265–$325 double; $400–$3,000 suite. Weekend packages available. AE, CB, DC, JCB, MC, V. **Parking:** $46.

Perhaps the grandest of the city's newer hotels is the Helmsley Palace. Above the landmark turn-of-the-century Villard house, a Neo-Renaissance Italian palazzo built in American brownstone for railroad tycoon and journalist Henry Villard, rises a 51-story bronzed glass tower. While the painstakingly and magnificently restored public rooms have won nothing but praise from the critics, the new tower has been dubbed, in contrast, a "mediocrity." The rooms inside are lovely, and the public rooms are perhaps the finest in New York. Guests enter through the Villard cobblestone courtyard and proceed up the grand marble staircase to view the red Verona marble fireplace of Augustus Saint-Gaudens. And they are surrounded by the works of such noted artists as Louis Comfort Tiffany, John La Farge, and George Breck.

Amid all this splendor are all the conveniences of modern hotel living. Some of the oversized guest rooms have king-size beds with gilded headboards, and others have two doubles. Interior colors are soft pastels, with velvet chairs and carpeting. Rooms have remote-control color TVs and in-house movies, digital clock-radios, dual telephone lines with fax and PC hookups, VCRs on request, and minirefrigerators, a welcome extra. Electric blankets are available, and the bathrooms are sumptuous. The suites include one-bedroom apartments and fairy-tale triplexes with roof gardens and solariums.

Dining/Entertainment: Le Trianon is the elegant fine dining room; Harry's New York Bar and the Hunt Bar are popular watering holes; the lovely Gold Room is the setting for high tea in the afternoon.

Services: Multilingual staff, 24-hour concierge service, 24-hour room service.

Facilities: Guest passes available for New York Health & Racquet Club. Portable telephones and fax machines available.

THE KIMBERLY, a Suite Hotel, 145 East 50th St., between Lexington and Third Aves., New York, NY 10022. Tel. 212/755-0400, or toll free 800/683-0400. Fax 212/486-6915. 34 rms. 158 suites. A/C TV TEL

$ Rates: $170 single or double; $205 studio suites; $265 one-bedroom suites; $370 two-bedroom suites. Extra person $20. Children under 12 free in parents' room. **Weekend rates:** $135 single or double; $159 one-bedroom suites; $295 two-bedroom suites. Weekly and monthly rates available. Summer Specials (June, July, Aug), $100 less on all suites. AE, DC, MC, V. **Parking:** At nearby garage, discounted rate of $25.

⭐ Here's a charming way to have a pied-à-terre in New York: Stay at the Kimberly. Although this is mostly a suite hotel, even the regular guest rooms give you that feeling of being able to settle in for a long, comfortable stay. All accommodations are handsomely decorated in rich classical furnishings of brocade, velvet, and warm woods. The beds are mostly double doubles, with some king-size; the stunning bathrooms are done all in marble and have deep soaking tubs. The regular guest rooms have minirefrigerators; the suites have fully equipped kitchens, complete with utensils, silverware, and china. Each suite also has a rare luxury for New York—a private balcony affording stunning views. Everything about the hotel, beginning with its small lobby, done in rich Italian marble with fine Oriental carpetings, is calm, quiet, and elegant. No wonder it's a big hit with people from the United Nations and with visiting Europeans and South Americans. When the special summer rates are in force (see above), a suite here is often less than a bedroom alone in many other New York hotels.

Dining/Entertainment: Adjoining the hotel is the exquisite Paradis Barcelona, a restaurant in the classical Spanish tradition, which provides extraordinary room service. At night, it features a popular tapas bar. Tatou offers American cuisine with cabaret, blues music, and nightclub dancing.

Services: Concierge, free newspapers, 24-hour room service, same-day valet service, secretarial and business services on request.

Facilities: Guests have complimentary privileges at the nearby New York Health & Racquet Club, which boasts an excellent swimming pool, and at 5 other NYHRC locations as well.

THE MARK, 25 East 77 St., between Fifth and Madison Aves. New York, NY 10021. Tel. 212/744-4300, or toll free 800/THE MARK; in Canada, 800/223-1588. Fax 212/744-2749. 120 rms, 60 suites. A/C TV TEL

$ Rates: $265–$295 single or double; from $450 suite. Extra person $20. Children 15 and under free in parents' room. AE, DC, JCB, MC, V.

⭐ One of the prettiest and most deliciously elegant of the city's circle of small luxury hotels, The Mark is a worthy rival of that grande dame of the genre just across the street, the Carlyle. Elegant maybe, but its definitely not stuffy. Pop star Madonna stayed here. Art and antiques dealers favor it, as do museum buffs (the Metropolitan, Whitney, and Frick are within a very few blocks) and anyone who comes to town for serious shopping in the swanky boutiques of Madison Avenue. The original hotel was built in 1929 (the copper tower and black vitro glass marquee, spectacularly floodlit at night, are very art deco), later became the Madison Avenue Hotel, and in 1989 it was acquired by the Rafael Group, which spent $30 million transforming the property down to the most minute detail. Now its rooms and suites (in 10 configurations of size and layout) pamper with king-sized beds, custom-designed furniture (Queen Anne style), museum-quality Piranesi architectural drawings decorating the walls (and corridors), all-wool Gundolt carpets, remote-control Sony Trinitron TVs (with in-room movies) in custom-designed cabinets, clock-radios, and two double-line direct-dial phones with fax capability. There's even an umbrella in every room, compliments of the management. Most top-floor suites come with pantries and small refrigerators; all suites are equipped with Braun

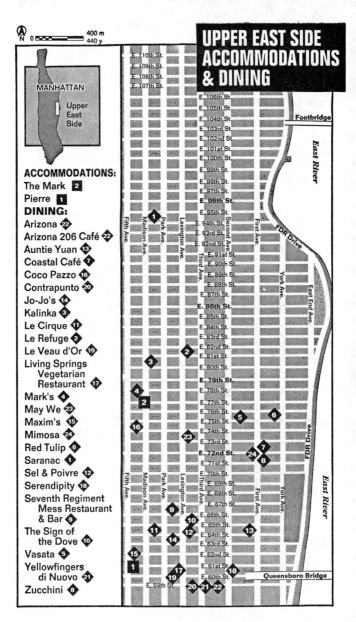

UPPER EAST SIDE ACCOMMODATIONS & DINING

MANHATTAN

Upper East Side

ACCOMMODATIONS:
The Mark **2**
Pierre **1**
DINING:
Arizona **22**
Arizona 206 Café **22**
Auntie Yuan **13**
Coastal Café **7**
Coco Pazzo **16**
Contrapunto **20**
Jo-Jo's **14**
Kalinka **3**
Le Cirque **11**
Le Refuge **2**
Le Veau d'Or **19**
Living Springs Vegetarian Restaurant **17**
Mark's **4**
May We **23**
Maxim's **15**
Mimosa **24**
Red Tulip **6**
Saranac **1**
Sel & Poivre **12**
Serendipity **18**
Seventh Regiment Mess Restaurant & Bar **9**
The Sign of the Dove **10**
Vasata **5**
Yellowfingers di Nuovo **21**
Zucchini **8**

coffeemakers. The large and luxurious bathrooms have telephones, deep-soak tubs, separate stall showers, heating lamps, hairdryers, scales, and crystal boxes that contain the finest toiletries.

Dining/Entertainment: Mark's restaurant serves French/American cuisine in an exquisite setting for breakfast, lunch, afternoon tea, and dinner. Mark's Bar, with a separate entrance on 77th St., offers pre- and post-theater hors d'oeuvres and cocktails from 5pm to midnight.

Services: 24-hour room service, concierge, laundry/valet, limousine.

Facilities: Meeting and banquet rooms. There's no health club, but management will arrange entrée at one nearby.

THE NEW YORK HELMSLEY, 212 East 42nd St., New York, NY 10017. Tel. 212/490-8900, or toll free 800/221-4982. Fax 212/986-4792. Telex 127724. 800 rms, 10 suites. A/C TV TEL

$ Rates: Sun–Thurs, $180 single; $205 double; $390 suite. Fri–Sat, usually $140 or less single or double. AE, DC, MC, V.
Parking: $33.

Not quite as grandiose as the Helmsley Palace but handsome in its own right, this 41-story brick–and–bronzed-glass tower is a model of grace in both its luxurious appointments and its efficiency, the kind that top-level business executives demand. The beautifully appointed guest rooms have 25-inch color TVs with cable and remote controls, digital alarm clock–radios, and such amenities as oversize down pillows and skirt hangers in the closet. The bathrooms are luxurious, with both phones and scales, full-length mirrors, sheet-size bath towels, and the usual package of toiletries found in luxury hotels. All the suites are situated on corners on the top five floors.

Dining/Entertainment: Breakfast, lunch, and dinner are served at Mindy's, the hotel's full-service restaurant, which offers fine French cuisine in a glorious multilevel setting with many trees and plantings and an entire glass wall overlooking an open-air landscaped plaza. Harry's New York Bar is a popular gathering spot for lunch and cocktails—plus free hors d'oeuvres.

Services: Concierge, fast checkin and checkout service, currency exchange, multilingual secretarial and business services.

Facilities: Nearby health club facilities.

NEW YORK MARRIOTT EAST SIDE, 525 Lexington Ave., at 49th St., New York, NY 10017. Tel. 212/755-4000, or toll free 800/242-8684. Fax 212/751-3440. 665 rms, 12 suites. A/C MINIBAR TV TEL

$ Rates: $205–$240 single; $220–$260 double; from $450 suite. Extra person $20. Children 18 and under free in parents' room. Weekend packages available. AE, CB, DC, DISC, EURO, MC, V.
Parking: $25.

Add to the ever-widening list of recently refurbished Manhattan hotels the Marriott East Side, formerly Halloran House, and before that, the Shelton Towers Hotel, put up during the 1920s as a "residence for men accustomed to the finer things in life." The lively and well-established hostelry now wears oak-paneled walls, a black-and-white marble floor, and traditional print furniture in its lobby. Because the building itself dates from an era in architecture when lower costs allowed for larger room dimensions, the guest accommodations here are extra-spacious, all newly redone with gracious Queen Anne–style furniture in shades of camel or blue-gray. Happily, the old-world refinement is combined with such up-to-the-minute amenities as alarm clock–radios, color cable TVs (with remote control and equipped for in-room movies), safety-deposit boxes, and bathroom phone extensions. The suites, some with small refrigerators and wraparound terraces, can be spectacular. Floors 26 to 33 are premium-tab; up there in the 32nd-floor Concierge Lounge guests get complimentary breakfast; cocktails and hors d'oeuvres, albeit not free of charge (they use an honor system); and all-evening sweets from a grab bag that changes each day.

Dining/Entertainment: The hotel's Shelton Grille offers classic continental cuisine (three meals daily) in a European bistro setting. Champions, the American Sports Bar Restaurant, serves lunch and dinner. For quiet cocktails before the theater (or any time during the evening), the Crest Lounge is a congenial spot.

Services: Room service 6:30am–11pm, concierge, laundry/valet, nightly turndown.

THE PIERRE, Fifth Ave. at 61st St., New York, NY 10021-8402. Tel. 212/838-8000, or toll free 800/332-3442. Fax 212/940-8109. 205 rms, 50 suites. A/C TV TEL

$ Rates: $280–$410 single; $310–$440 double; from $600 suite. Extra person $25. Children 18 and under free in parents' room. Holiday, summer, and weekend packages available. **Parking:** $30. AE, CB, DC, ER, EURO, JCB, MC, V.

The Pierre, like the Plaza, the Waldorf, and the St. Regis, is a reminder of the city's more gracious and dignified past. Its chronology is fascinating: In 1930 Charles Pierre, a chef with loftier aspirations, opened his new European-style hotel that set out "to create the atmosphere of a private club or residence, catering to only those of refined tastes who can afford the best in the way of hotel luxury." He succeeded admirably until the Depression hit, forcing Charles Pierre into bankruptcy in 1933. But the hotel survived. By 1960 more than half its rooms and suites had been sold to individual residents. In 1981 the estimable Canadian Four Seasons chain took over, updating its image to attract a more diverse clientele. You can still rub elbows with the haute monde and occasional member of royalty (after all, the Pierre *is* a world-class hotel) but for all its elegance and grandeur, its lovely European lobby and Italianate rotunda, the Pierre is warm and hospitable.

There are 28 types of accommodations interspersed with privately owned apartments on 42 floors. Rooms and suites vary in size, configuration, and views, and decor runs the gamut from English country cottage to splendid baronial mansion. A typical single room, very charming, might have walls papered in palest blue and trimmed in white, blue-gray carpet, and a romantic floral chintz bedskirt (with drapes to match) under a white heirloom coverlet. Suites have fully furnished living rooms, many with fireplaces, with lovely mahogany antique furniture and reproductions, mirrors, and paintings. In-room amenities include digital clock-radios, direct-dial two-line phones, remote-control color cable TVs with in-room movies, and individual safes. Bathrooms, while not lavish (they retain the stream-lined simplicity of their art deco origins) provide many nice touches.

Dining/Entertainment: Like a room in a French château, with its ceiling and wall murals, ornate mirrors, and gray-and-gold color scheme, the intimate (and very swanky) 54-seat Café Pierre is open for breakfast, lunch, dinner, pre- and post-theater supper (prix-fixe $37.50 and $55, respectively), and Sunday brunch. The Café Lounge offers nightly piano music to sip champagne by, and the Rotunda is a stunner for afternoon tea, light meals, and snacks.

Services: 24-hour room service, twice-daily chamber service, multilingual concierge, laundry/valet service, one-hour pressing, theater desk, complimentary shoeshine, unpacking service (on request), currency exchange, notary public, secretarial services.

Facilities: Sundries shop, barber, hair salon.

THE PLAZA, 768 Fifth Ave., between 58th and 59th Sts., New York, NY 10019. Tel. 212/759-3000, or toll free 800/228-3000. Fax 212/759-3167. Telex 23698. 815 rms, 96 suites. A/C MINIBAR TV TEL

$ Rates: $235–$550 single; $260–$585 double; $500–$15,000 suites. Weekend packages sometimes available. AE, DC, DISC, JCB, MC, V. **Parking:** $35.

⭐ Synonymous with New York elegance, the Plaza has been attracting the cognoscenti since early in the century. Built in 1907, it has officially been designated as a "landmark of New York." Frank Lloyd Wright called it his home-away-from-home; Eloise grew up there; Donald Trump took it over; and it is a favorite choice of visiting royalty. Looking incongruously like a European château on the New York skyline, the French Renaissance structure is full of splendid touches, inside and out. Some of the rooms have 14-foot ceilings, crystal chandeliers, ornamental plaster moldings, and thick mahogany doors, while some parlors also have carved marble fireplaces. Many of the rooms afford spectacular views of Central Park and Fifth Avenue.

Dining/Entertainment: The Plaza's dining rooms include the romantic, gardenlike Palm Court, especially popular for Sunday brunch and afternoon tea; the classic Edwardian and Oak rooms (the Oak Bar is the place to celebrity-watch and be seen); and the casual Oyster Bar, a cross between an English pub and a fish house.

Services: Concierge service, laundry/valet service, 24-hour room service, shoeshine, money exchange.

THE ST. REGIS, Two East 55th St., at Fifth Ave., New York, NY 10022. Tel. 212/753-4500, or toll free 800/759-7550. Fax 212/787-3447. 227 rms, 90 suites. A/C MINIBAR TV TEL

$ Rates: $350 superior; $395 deluxe; $450 grand luxe; from $550–$3,000 suite. Weekend rates available. Children 17 and under free in parents' room. AE, CB, DC, ER, EURO, JCB, MC, V, and more. **Parking:** $30.

⭐ The doyen of New York hotels has reopened after a three-year, $100-million restoration that has returned it to the opulence of its original and glorious past, its decor scrupulously restored down to the last detail. In 1904, when John Jacob Astor opened the St. Regis, it was the city's tallest hotel building—18 stories. The hotel was finished in marble (even in the walls of the boiler room) and furnished with Louis XV antiques, rare Flemish tapestries, crystal chandeliers, Oriental rugs, and a library fully stocked with gold-tooled books bound in leather. Such architectural details as the Astor Court with its vaulted ceiling, trompe-l'oeil cloud murals and faux marbre, ornate brass cashier's windows, and yard upon exquisite yard of real 22-karat gold leafing have either been preserved or restored.

The St. Regis is probably New York's most expensive hotel, the rationale being that stand-out luxuries usually costing extra are included in the tariff here, like tea brought to your room on arrival, butler service (each floor has its own pantry and butler), fresh flowers daily, complimentary local phone calls, and a different-each-day amenity in your room. All rooms also offer international direct-dial phones that can be programmed in six different languages. Suites come with fax machines. The guest rooms and suites (60 sizes) wear an elegant, essentially Louis XV decor, with crystal chandeliers, silk wallcoverings with matching drapes, contrasting printed bedspreads and upholstery, and accents of gleaming gilt. Colors are muted greens or blues with eggshell (suites are done in silver-blue and ruby). European deep soaking tubs, two sinks, and separate shower areas distinguish the all-marble bathrooms.

Dining/Entertainment: Afternoon tea is an art at the splendid Astor Court. The old King Cole mural has been restored and returned to the King Cole Bar and Lounge, where Fernand Petit invented the Bloody Mary almost 60 years ago. At Lespinasse, the hotel's formal restaurant, Swiss chef Gray Kunz adapts classical cuisine with flavors and textures from the Far East. The St. Regis Roof is New York's only rooftop ballroom.

Services: 24-hour room service, laundry/valet service, nightly turndown, butler service, concierge, secretarial and confidential office service, multilingual staff.

Facilities: Business center; barber shop; health club; florist; information library on local commerce; Bijan, Christian Dior, La Boutique, and Godiva boutiques.

UN PLAZA PARK HYATT HOTEL, One United Nations Plaza, on East 44th St. just west of First Ave., New York, NY 10017-3575. Tel. 212/355-3400, or toll free 800/233-1234. Fax 212/702-5051. 428 rms, 45 suites. A/C TV TEL

$ Rates: $240–$260 single; $260–$280 double; $150 weekend (including American breakfast and parking), $350–$660 suite; $200–$450 weekend suite. AE, CB, MC, JCB, V. **Parking:** $24.

This masterpiece of understated elegance perfectly befits the ambassadors, diplomats, and heads of state who choose it for the kind of serenity and security that few other New York hotels possess. Just across the street from the United Nations (although its rates are too steep for most U.N. personnel), the hotel was designed by Kevin Roche of Kevin Roche–John Dinkeloo and Associates, and his fine hand is seen everywhere. The guest rooms begin on the 28th floor (offices occupy the first 27 floors), so there's scarcely a whisper of traffic noise, and all have beautiful views, subtly modern decor, radios, and all the amenities. Many have kitchens. Rooms and halls are decorated with tapestries and textiles from around the world.

Dining/Entertainment: The stunning Ambassador Grill and Lounge has a ceiling of mirrored glass that refracts light in a series of prisms within prisms, making the 14-foot ceiling seem cathedral-high. Breakfast, lunch, and dinner are served, as well as an immensely popular Sunday Champagne Brunch, featuring lobster, smoked salmon, and omelettes made to order ($35 for adults and $17.50 for children under 12; reservations are necessary). The Ambassador Lounge serves a weekday pasta buffet and offers piano entertainment nightly; the Wisteria Room offers a breakfast buffet and lunch.

Services: The multilingual staff gives guests all sorts of personal services—even providing heating pads, hair rollers, plug adapters, voltage transformers, and a butler! Shoes are polished overnight and there's 24-hour room service, complimentary weekday limousine service to Wall Street and the Garment District, and complimentary transportation to the theater district. The *New York Times* is delivered to your door every day.

Facilities: Guests may swim in the glorious glass-enclosed swimming pool in the sky, enjoy the complimentary health club, and play tennis for a fee at the hotel's 39th floor regulation-size indoor court (the only one in a New York City hotel).

THE WALDORF-ASTORIA, 301 Park Ave., at 50th St. New York, NY 10022. Tel. 212/355-3000, or toll free 800/445-8667. Fax 212/758-9209. Telex WUI 666747-RCA275797. 1,210 rms, 200 suites. A/C MINIBAR TV TEL

$ **Rates:** Jan 1–Sept 13, $225–$300 single; $250–$325 double or twin; $375–$800 suite; $325 minisuite. Sept 14–Dec 31, $235–$310 single; $260–$335 double; $400–$850 suite; $350 minisuite. Waldorf Towers: Jan 1–Sept 13, $325–$350 single; $350–$375 double or twin; $500–$4,000 suite. Sept 14–Dec 31, $350–$375 single; $375–$400 double or twin; $550–$4,000 suite. AE, CB, DC, DISC, MC, V. **Parking:** $29.

Could there be anyone who has not heard of the Waldorf-Astoria? As much a part of the New York scene as the Empire State Building (the site of the original Waldorf-Astoria), it's legendary among New York's luxury hotels. Its lushly carpeted and beautifully furnished lobby, with meandering arcades and quiet little corners, is one of the few true hotel lobbies left in the city. Waldorf guests have always included the world famous: You might run into Frank Sinatra or Mrs. Douglas MacArthur.

Not content to rest on its laurels, however, the Waldorf, under the Hilton banner, has refurnished and redecorated all of its rooms and equipped them, of course, with all the necessities: color TVs (with first-run cinema service), direct-dial telephones, and old-world amenities. Champagne and room service breakfasts are offered at no extra charge to honeymooners.

Dining/Entertainment: Oscar's, the famous coffee shop at the Waldorf, is decorated as an indoor garden. The Bull & Bear has a giant Maltese-cross bar of African mahogany with a footrail and serves both British and American food. Sir Harry's Bar has an African safari setting; Inagiku serves Japan's finest food. And, of course, there's still Peacock Alley, which has always been one of the nicest *intime* spots in town. Featuring Cole Porter's own piano, it is the scene, every Sunday, of mind-boggling brunches that are among the most lavish in town ($35.50 for adults, $17.50 for children).

Services: International concierge service, 24-hour room service, theater desk, tour desk, beauty salon, barber shop, secretarial service, nightly turndown service.

Facilities: Guests may use the Plus One Fitness Center, with state-of-the-art equipment, six personal trainers, and two massage therapists.

EXPENSIVE

THE DORAL COURT, 130 East 39th St., New York, NY 10016. Tel. 212/685-1100, or toll free 800/624-0607. Fax 212/889-0287. Telex 679-9532. 248 rms, 50 suites. A/C TV TEL

$ **Rates:** $160–$185 single; $180–$205 double; $250–$450 single; $270–$470 double suite. AE, DC, MC, V. **Parking:** At nearby garage, $34.50.

The Doral Court is a quiet, personal hotel with attentive service. The rooms are spacious and sunny, with walk-in closets, king-size beds, writing desks, comfortable chairs, foyers, and separate dressing alcoves that also house refrigerators. Kitchenettes are available upon request, as is an exercise bicycle. For more serious fitness buffs, use of the Doral's fitness center, a block away, is complimentary. The suites are cozy enough to settle down in for a good stay; all have walk-in kitchens, and some have balconies. The Courtyard Café serves breakfast, lunch, dinner, and Sunday brunch; there's an intimate bar area and indoor-outdoor seating.

LOEW'S NEW YORK, 569 Lexington Ave., at 51st St., New York, NY 10022. Tel. 212/752-7000, or toll free 800/23-LOEWS. Fax 212/758-6311. Telex 147181. 688 rms, 38 suites. A/C TV TEL

$ Rates: $185 single, $199 double; Concierge Floor, $205 single, $239 double; $225–$239 junior suites; $295 one-bedroom suite; $375 two-bedroom suite. Extra person $25. Children under 14 free in parents' room. AE, CB, DC, DISC, MC, V. **Parking:** Next door, $19.

Casual, comfortable, and exciting—all these are good words to describe this three-star hotel, a popular gathering place for sports teams and sports fans alike. Loew's New York is the official hotel of the U.S. Open; the Denver Broncos, the Washington Capitals, the Harlem Globetrotters, and many other teams stay here. The nine big-screen TVs in the handsome circular bar are often tuned in to a game. A $26-million renovation has transformed the old Summit Hotel, giving it a new art deco lobby and beautifully equipped rooms of good size. Each room has its own refrigerator, desk area, in-room safe, custom furnishings, remote-control TV with in-house movies, and two phones in every room (three in the handsome suites).

Dining/Entertainment: The Lexington Avenue Grill has become one of the city's "hot" new restaurants for breakfast, lunch, and dinner. Adjoining it is the lively Lexington Avenue Lounge.

Services: Concierge Floor for Extra Special Patrons (ESP) has its own lounge serving continental breakfast and snacks and cordials in the evening. Children can get games from the concierge and special menus and games in the restaurant. Room service is from 7am to 1am.

Facilities: The health center is state-of-the-art, with personal trainers and a sauna and Jacuzzi. The full-service business center features secretarial services, personal computers, and more.

ROGER SMITH, 501 Lexington Ave., at 47th St., New York, NY 10017. Tel. 212/755-1400, or toll free 800/445-0277. Fax 212/319-9130. 108 rms, 28 suites. A/C TV TEL

$ Rates (including continental breakfast): $170–$195 single; $190–$215 double; $225–$285 suite. $130 single or double weekend, summer, and holidays. Extra person $20. AE, CB, DC, MC, V. **Parking:** Adjacent to hotel, $23.

If what you cherish in a hotel is a feeling of space, comfort, and quiet relaxation, you're going to love the Roger Smith. A multimillion-dollar, top-to-bottom renovation has made this comfortable, 17-story old-timer better than ever; values here are among the best on the East Side. The lobby is small but attractive, with a stunning display of mahogany, bronze, and polished granite.

The real story is up in the rooms: very large, by New York

standards, and elegantly redesigned in a classic continental style. Design schemes make use of deep fruitwood furniture; dusty-rose chairs and sofas; thick carpeting; and two-poster or four-poster (sometimes canopied) queen-size, king-size, twin or double/double beds. Soundproof windows make this one of the quieter hotels on the East Side. The spacious rooms are furnished with original artworks, antiques, and quality 18th-century reproductions. All rooms have automatic coffeemakers, minirefrigerators, renovated bathrooms, and color TVs with radio and cable—also, pets can be accommodated. The two- and three-room suites, some boasting fireplaces and terraces, all have butler's pantry. Many guests from Europe and Asia, as well as diplomats and United Nations personnel, frequent the Roger Smith. Continental fare is available at Lily's Restaurant and Bar.

Services: Weekday newspaper delivery, movie rentals with VCR.

MODERATE

DORAL INN, 541 Lexington Ave., at 49th St., New York, NY 10022. Tel. 212/755-1200, or toll free 800/22-DORAL. Fax 212/319-8344. Telex 236641. 652 rms, 55 suites. A/C TV TEL

$ Rates: $155–$170 single; $170–$190 double; $200 and up suites. Executive Club Level, $160 single; $175 double. AE, DC, ER, JCB, MC. **Parking:** $23.

The location for this East Side favorite couldn't be more convenient, since it's smack in the midtown shopping area, across the street, in fact, from the Waldorf-Astoria. It's a busy, with-it hotel, the first in New York to have indoor squash courts available at a nominal fee. When you're not chasing the ball around the court, you can enjoy the feeling of quiet comfort in the well-appointed rooms, decorated in smart beige motifs. Small refrigerators are available on request. Two- and three-room suites are perfect for family living; some of the newer suites contain their own saunas, and the penthouse floor has executive rooms and suites, subdivided by terraces. The new Executive Club Level on the 6th and 8th floors provides many special amenities, including express checkin and checkout, complimentary continental breakfasts, complimentary personal computers, fax machines, newspapers, and more. A laundry room and ice machines are available. Downstairs, the Equinox Café, serving American cuisine, is open 24 hours a day; and the lovely Mormandos Restaurant offers Italian cuisine until 1am.

The same Doral management is also in charge at two smaller hotels in the Murray Hill area: **Doral Park Avenue Hotel,** 70 Park Ave., at 38th St. (tel. 212/949-5924, or toll free 800/847-4135), and the **Doral Tuscany Hotel,** 120 E. 39th St. (tel. 212/686-1600, or toll free 800/847-4078).

THE HELMSLEY MIDDLETOWNE HOTEL, 148 East 48th St., New York, NY 10017. Tel. 212/755-3000, or toll free 800/221-4982. Fax 212/832-0261. 147 rms, 47 suites. A/C MINIBAR TV TEL

$ Rates: $135–$145 single; $145–$155 double; $175 executive; $195 junior suite; $225–$380 larger suite. AE, CB, DC, JCB, MC, V. **Parking:** $23.

The Helmsley Middletowne is one of the real finds in the New York hotel scene. Since it was converted from an apartment building, its rooms still have apartment amenities; they're spacious, each with two large closets; best of all, the larger suites boast fully equipped walk-in kitchens, wonderfully handy for those who must entertain, as well as for visitors who wish to save on the high cost of always eating out. The rooms are prettily furnished with bright colors and have two-line direct-dial phones with fax and computer hookups, as well as bathroom phones. Twelfth-floor rooms have tiny terraces.

Dining/Entertainment: Bukhara, an Indian restaurant located off the lobby, serves lunch and dinner daily.

Services: Multilingual staff, in-house movies, fax service at front desk, laundry/valet service.

HOTEL BEVERLY, 125 East 50th St., at Lexington Ave., New York, NY 10022. Tel. 212/753-2700, or toll free 800/223-0945 outside New York State, including Canada. Fax 212/753-2700, ext. 48. Telex 66579. 175 suites, 25 rms. A/C TV TEL

$ Rates: $129–$149 single; $149–$159 double. Junior suite, $139–$159 single; $149–$169 double; one-bedroom suite $170–$190 single; $180–$200 double. Weekend packages available. AE, CB, DC, JCB, MC, V. **Parking:** Across street, $23.

The European-style Hotel Beverly is a longtime favorite on the East Side. There's a quiet, calm feeling about this family-owned hotel, refreshingly unusual in the hubbub of the city. Also unusual is the fact that this is largely a suite hotel. For the cost of a bedroom in other hotels, you can have all the comforts of a private apartment—living room; bedroom; bath; and full kitchenette, complete with refrigerator, cooking unit, dinnerware, and utensils. And even the regular rooms, without kitchenettes, all have refrigerators. The rooms are individually decorated in fine taste, and although the decor varies from traditional to contemporary, all are spacious and lovely. Some of the junior suites have sofas and desk areas. The hotel is especially proud of its security (you have the only key) walk-in closets. Many corporations keep permanent rooms here for their executives; it seems they find the location and ambience congenial. So, too, do international tourists, U.N. people, and visiting families (all groups of three or more must take suites).

The Beverly's lobby has warm fruitwood-paneled walls, an Oriental-pattern carpet, and traditional furnishings that create the feeling of an 18th-century English living room. A concierge is at the ready; there are valet parking and room service; and Kenny's Steak & Seafood and a 24-hour pharmacy are off the lobby.

BUDGET

VANDERBILT YMCA, 224 East 47th St., New York, NY 10017. Tel. 212/755-2410. Fax 212/752-0210. 429 rms (none with bath). A/C TV TEL

$ Rates: $40–$45 single; $50–$60 double; $66 triple; $88 quad. AE, MC, V. **Parking:** At nearby garages, $20–$30 per day.

The fully coed Vanderbilt Y boasts an excellent East Side location not far from the United Nations, and a popular health club free to guests: You might find yourself sharing the two swimming pools, sauna, and gym with U.N. personnel and businesspeople who work in the area. Beginning this year, rooms will be completely renovated. At present, none has a private bath; showers are down the hall. On the premises are a brand-new, full-service restaurant and a cafeteria, both open daily and featuring an extensive yet inexpensive menu. International telephone and fax service is available for guests; there are safety deposit boxes at the front desk and a self-service laundry. Reservations can also be made here for YMCAs in major cities around the world.

7. LINCOLN CENTER/ UPPER WEST SIDE

EXPENSIVE

THE MAYFLOWER HOTEL, 15 Central Park West, New York, NY 10023. Tel. 212/265-0060, or toll free 800/223-4164 (U.S. & Canada), 0-800-891-256 (U.K.). Fax 212/265-5098. Telex 4972657 MAYFLOW. 377 rms, 200 suites. A/C TV TEL
$ Rates: $145 single; $160 double; $235 suite. Parkview, $165 single; $180 double; $275 suite; $300–$500 penthouse terrace suite. **Weekend rates:** $138 single; $145 double; $167 triple (including continental breakfast and complimentary parking); suites $171 single, $190 double, $224 triple (including welcome cocktail, full American breakfast, Sunday brunch, and complimentary parking). AE, DC, DISC, JCB, MC, V. **Parking:** At nearby garage, $15.

Music makers and music lovers alike sing the praises of this venerable hotel, the only one on Central Park West, about a five-minute walk from Lincoln Center and Carnegie Hall. Built in 1925 as a residential hotel, it has spacious rooms, thick walls, a sense of peace and quiet, and the kind of dedicated service that can come only from a loyal staff who have been here for many years and know the large number of returning guests by name. Celebrity guests abound: At a recent visit, the Bolshoi Opera Company had just left and the Royal Ballet had just arrived. Liza Minnelli and Cher have been guests, and so has Robert de Niro, who lived at the hotel for a year and a half.

Since the Mayflower has so many suites, it's quite possible that your room may be upgraded. All of the rooms are nicely decorated—large enough for king-size, queen-size, or two double beds—and have individually controlled air conditioning, radio alarms, and voice-mail messaging. There are two to three enormous walk-in closets in every room, and most rooms have pantries with small refrigerators (coffeemakers on request). Suites are gracious, and some have terraces overlooking the city skyline. If you're planning a small wedding reception or other function, request one of the 17th-floor suites, where you have a choice of terraces overlooking Central Park or the Hudson River.

Dining/Entertainment: The Conservatory Café, facing Central Park, is a sunny spot for breakfast, lunch, and dinner, with a popular Sunday brunch and four-course pretheater dinner for $16.95.

Services: Room service 7am–12:30am, concierge service via the bellman, international telephone translation service.

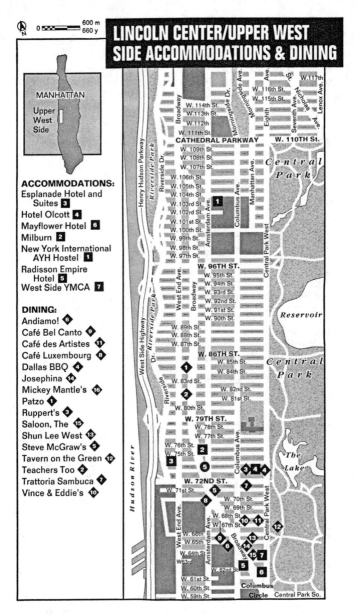

LINCOLN CENTER/UPPER WEST SIDE ACCOMMODATIONS & DINING

0 — 600 m / 660 y

MANHATTAN
Upper West Side

ACCOMMODATIONS:
Esplanade Hotel and Suites **3**
Hotel Olcott **4**
Mayflower Hotel **6**
Milburn **2**
New York International AYH Hostel **1**
Radisson Empire Hotel **5**
West Side YMCA **7**

DINING:
Andiamo! **6**
Café Bel Canto **9**
Café des Artistes **11**
Café Luxembourg **8**
Dallas BBQ **4**
Josephina **14**
Mickey Mantle's **16**
Patzo **1**
Ruppert's **3**
Saloon, The **15**
Shun Lee West **13**
Steve McGraw's **5**
Tavern on the Green **12**
Teachers Too **2**
Trattoria Sambuca **7**
Vince & Eddie's **10**

Facilities: Fitness center with state-of-the-art equipment and two 58-inch TVs.

RADISSON EMPIRE HOTEL, 44 West 63rd St., New York, NY 10023. Tel. 212/265-7400, or toll free 800/333-3333. Fax 212/765-6125. 375 rms, 25 suites. A/C MINIBAR TV TEL
$ Rates: $120–$210 single; $120–$230 double; from $220 suite. Extra person $20. Children 13 and under free in parents' room.

Weekend packages available. AE, CB, DC, DISC, JCB, MC, V.
Parking: $20.50 daily.

You can't get much closer to all the excitement of Lincoln Center than the Radisson Empire Hotel. The Empire is, in fact, the "official" Lincoln Center hotel, and it has emerged after a $25-million renovation as one of the better hotel values in the city for comfort, service, quality, and rates. Music and dance groups (the Bolshoi Ballet has stayed here), international types, and visitors who enjoy being away from the midtown madness all favor this place.

The small lobby, with its dioramas in the hallway and magnificent fresh flowers, has a gracious quality about it; so, too, do the guest rooms, which look as though they belong in a lovely country home. Traditional furnishings, two-poster beds, floral chintz bedspreads and drapes, and down comforters set a homey scene, yet every high-tech convenience is at hand, including Nakamini CD and cassette stereo systems, NEC VCRs and color TVs (you can order your favorite CDs and videos from the front desk), two-line telephones with dataports for computer link-up, voice-mail messaging, and bathroom phones. The bathrooms are especially lovely, with deep soaking tubs. The rooms, although not large, are adequate in size; most have queen-size beds, and some of the smaller rooms have twins or a double bed.

Dining/Entertainment: The stylish Empire Grill serves moderately priced cuisine and a special pretheater supper for $24.95. The Guest Lounge is the place for evening cocktails, billiards, and entertainment.

Services: 24-hour room service, laundry/valet, concierge.

Facilities: Adjacent health club. Planned for the future: a complete business center offering secretarial services, computers, fax machines, and private office suites.

MODERATE

HOTEL OLCOTT, 27 West 72nd St., New York, NY 10023. Tel. 212/877-4200. Fax 212/580-0511. 45 studios, 55 suites. A/C TV TEL

$ Rates: $80 daily, $475 weekly studio for one person; $90 daily, $535 weekly studio for two persons; $110 daily, $650 weekly one-bedroom suite for one or two persons. Extra person $15 daily, $70 weekly. No credit cards. **Parking:** At nearby garage, $20.

One of the best choices in the Lincoln Center area is an undiscovered hotel right off Central Park West. Most out-of-towners don't know about this place because it's largely a residential hotel—most guests are longtime residents or entertainers, diplomats, U.N. people, and the like, in New York for a few months. But there are studios and suites available to transients, and as anyone who's discovered the Olcott will tell you, they are among the top buys in the city for the money. These are full one-bedroom apartments, comfortable enough to live in for a long time, and their size ranges from large to enormous. Each has a living room; a twin-bedded bedroom; a private tile bath and shower; and that great money-saver, a kitchenette, complete with dishes and cooking utensils. Additional rollaway beds can be added, for a small charge, to comfortably accommodate up to four people. Single and double bedrooms are also available. All rooms have pantries, cable color TVs, and direct-dial phones. Furnishings are attractive and comfortable, and service is excellent. There's a fantastic budget restaurant off the lobby, Dallas BBQ (see Chapter 6 for a review). In addition to all this, 72nd Street abounds with coffee shops, restaurants, and gift boutiques, and it's in the very heart of the bustling Columbus Avenue scene. A short bus or subway ride will take you to midtown and the theater district; a short walk, to Lincoln Center.

The management states that weekly rentals, reserved in advance, are given preference; however, with luck, you may get a room or suite for a night or two on short notice.

THE MILBURN, 242 West 76th St., New York, NY 10023, Tel. 212/362-1006, or toll free 800/833-9622. Fax 212/721-5476. 52 studios, 38 suites. A/C TV

$ Rates: $89–$99 studios single or double; $112–$180 suites. Children under 12 free in parents' room. Extra person $10. AE, CB, DC, MC, V. **Parking:** One block away, $14.

While midtown hotel prices soar out of sight, rates at Upper West Side hotels stay realistic. More and more visitors are thrilled to discover places like the Milburn, actually a fine West Side apartment building that recently spent some $4 million converting half of its 120 apartments into attractive hotel accommodations. Both studios and suites are available, and all of them have fully equipped kitchenettes with microwave ovens and in-room coffee service. The rooms are large, fully carpeted, and cheerfully decorated with modern furniture and attractive posters. There's a choice of twin-, queen-, and king-size beds; and all units sport new baths. Each suite consists of a living room (the sofa opens up into a queen-size bed) plus a bedroom.

Many extras make a stay at the Milburn especially pleasant. Room phones have speed-dialing to nearby takeout/delivery restaurants; press a button and you can order Chinese food, pizza, or meals round the clock from a nearby deli. Milburn Dining offers discounts at many neighborhood restaurants. For $10 per day, guests have privileges at the nearby Equinox Club. VCRs are available, and tapes can be rented nearby.

BUDGET

ESPLANADE HOTEL AND SUITES, 305 West End Ave., at 74th St., New York, NY 10023. Tel. 212/874-5000, or toll free 800/367-1763 from U.S., Canada, & Mexico. Fax 212/496-0367. 50 rms, 150 suites. A/C TV TEL

$ Rates: $65–$80 single or double; $75–$99 one-bedroom suite; $145–$200 two-bedroom suite. Additional person $10, up to four in one-bedroom, up to six in two-bedroom. Special promotions and rates available on long-term stays. AE, CB, DC, DISC, JCB, MC, V. **Parking:** At nearby garage, $10.

One of the best values in the Lincoln Center/Upper West Side area, the Esplanade is known for an especially helpful and friendly staff and for the size and comfort of its rooms. Artists performing at nearby Lincoln Center (the Royal Winnipeg Dance Company recently stayed here), students at the prestigious nearby dance companies, people who are having their apartments redone, as well as many guests from Europe enjoy staying at this spacious hotel on a lovely, tree-lined residential street, just a block from Broadway and major bus and subway lines.

All the rooms are nicely furnished, and many have walk-in closets. All feature refrigerators, plus hot plates, tea kettles, and plastic paperware on request, which makes it easy to fix light meals with food from the nearby gourmet emporiums. But the suites are the real glory of this place: Each has a huge living room with a sofa bed, one or two bedrooms with double beds, plus a kitchenette with an oven.

This is one of the few places in town that welcomes pets. On the premises are a Nautilus-equipped exercise room and a laundry room. A cheerful and spacious moderately priced Chinese restaurant and bar, right off the lobby, provides room service.

NEW YORK INTERNATIONAL AYH HOSTEL, 891 Amsterdam Ave., at 103rd St., New York, NY 10025. Tel. 212/932-2300. Fax 212/932-2574. 480 beds. A/C

$ Rates: $20 AYH members; $23 nonmembers. Nonmembers may purchase a welcome stamp for $3 a night, which can be applied to the purchase of an AYH membership (around $25). Stays usually limited to 7 days. MC, V.

Surely, the best news for budget travelers in many a New York moon was the 1990 opening of this youth hostel. In a city where one is lucky to find a room for $100 a night, its rates do not top $23. This facility is the first American Youth Hostel in New York, the largest in the nation, and the most ambitious hostel project in the world. It is housed in a century-old, neoclassical landmark structure, transformed with a $15-million renovation from a sad state of disrepair into a gracious building with almost an acre of gardens in back for sunning and sitting. The building is just a block from a subway station, in a multiethnic neighborhood that will most certainly improve as a result of the presence of the hostel.

As in all AYH hostels, there are common rooms, self-service kitchens, a cafeteria, and a friendly atmosphere designed to foster cross-cultural exchange between visiting foreigners and Americans. NYIYH is different from most other hostels in several ways: It has no curfew and no closing time and operates on a full, 24-hour schedule. No chores are required. And although most of the sleeping rooms, with bunk beds, will be for four, six, and eight people, there are some rooms for couples, even a few with queen- or king-size beds. Family rooms are sometimes available at around $60. Hostelers should bring a sheet sleeping sack with them, or they can rent bedsheets for $3 and purchase towels for $2. There are no private bathrooms, but there is in-room storage space, bicycle storage rooms, and telephones on each floor. The hostel is fully accessible to the handicapped. And, of course, it is open to people of all ages and nationalities. The building also contains conference rooms for nonprofit groups, and a full-service travel agency.

WEST SIDE YMCA, 5 West 63rd St., New York, NY 10023. Tel. 212/787-4400. Fax 212/580-0441. 525 rms (some with private bath). A/C TV

$ Rates: $36–$42 single; $48–$52 double. AE, MC, V. **Parking:** On side streets or at nearby garages, $10–$20.

Close to Lincoln Center, the American Museum of Natural History, and the Hayden Planetarium, this attractive building right off Central Park is also steps away from the trendy restaurants and shops of the Upper West Side and close to major bus and subway lines. A multimillion-dollar renovation, to be completed early this year, has modernized and upgraded all the public areas and guest rooms, which are now bright and attractive, all with new furniture, lighting, air-conditioners, and TVs. There are both single and double rooms, some with bath, some without. The place is perfect for sports and fitness enthusiasts: It has no fewer than two swimming pools, four handball courts, two squash courts, gyms, two weight rooms, a new strength-training room, and a running track (so the joggers can run either indoors here or outdoors in Central Park). Rooms are available on a transient basis for both men and women.

CHAPTER 6

NEW YORK DINING

New York is the restaurant capital of the country, but unless you have time on your hands and money to burn, you will have to be very selective. To help you make your way through the perplexing maze of the New York restaurant world, I have set forth some very simple guidelines. I have chosen those restaurants that, in my opinion, offer the best buys in dining in New York, regardless of how much you spend. (Some other New Yorker might come up with a very different selection; but no matter—getting two New Yorkers to agree on the favorite restaurants is like getting Yankees fans and Mets fans to agree on the favorite players. That's part of the fun.) And because the price range in New York restaurants is enormous, I have grouped these selections first by neighborhood and then by price category. You should first know, however, that thanks to inflation, the cost of dining in New York is at an all-time high. New Yorkers expect to pay at least $25 to $30 for a good dinner, and that's before cocktails, wine, tax, and tip; if they get by with less, they consider themselves lucky. Thankfully, restaurants have recently lowered prices a bit. Still, there seems to be no limit to how much restaurants will charge or people will spend; at a very posh restaurant a $125 meal is not uncommon, especially with a good bottle of wine. My price categories, then, allowing for inevitable overlapping, since prices for à la carte items vary considerably within the same establishment, are set forth for dinner for one person as follows: **expensive:** $50 and up; **moderate:** $25 to $50; and **budget:** less than $25. (For easy reference, the restaurants in this book are organized by cuisine in the Index.)

LUNCH A good way to stretch your food budget is to eat your main meals at lunch, when the values are always best—usually 15% to 20% less than dinner. Even some of the most expensive restaurants offer reasonable prix-fixe lunches.

BEVERAGES Cocktails will cost about $6 or more per drink. Be careful when you order wine: A prize-year vintage in a luxury restaurant could skyrocket your bill to the tune of $50 to $100 or more. If you are not familiar with the subtleties of wines, put yourself in the hands of the waiter or wine steward and ask him to suggest the proper wine in your price range to accompany your dinner. For four people, order a full bottle; for two or three, a half bottle will do nicely. To save on the tab, order the "vin de maison," or house wine, which is good and less expensive than bottled wines; it can be bought by the glass or in a carafe.

TIPPING   Leave your slide rule at home and relax. At most places, the rule is to give the waiter 15% of your check (just double New York's 8¼% tax added to all meal tabs). At a very posh establishment, consider 18% to 20%. If a captain is involved, he should receive 5% more.

HOURS   The dinner hour stretches rather late in New York, and many restaurants also serve after-theater suppers. Many are closed on Sunday and, during summer, some take rather long vacations. So it's always best to check before you go.

CALL AHEAD   New York restaurants have a very high rate of mortality, all due to the craziness that makes one place "hot" and "trendy" for a few months, then causes it to fall out of favor while the restless crowds move on to still another venue. As a result, closings are frequent. Always call in advance.

1. FINANCIAL DISTRICT/ TRIBECA

FINANCIAL DISTRICT
EXPENSIVE

THE HUDSON RIVER CLUB, 4 World Financial Center, 250 Vesey St., at the West Side Hwy. Tel. 786-1500, or 945-0505 for more information on the World Financial Center.
  Cuisine: AMERICAN. **Reservations:** Recommended, especially at lunch.
$ **Prices:** Appetizers $7.25–$17.50; main courses $24.50–$27. Hudson Valley Dinner $62; Sun brunch $19.50; Sun dinner $29.50. AE, MC, V.
  Open: Lunch, Mon–Fri 11:30am–2:30pm. Dinner, Mon–Sat 5–9:30pm, Sun noon–6pm. Brunch, Sun noon–3pm. **Subway:** 1, 2, 3, 9, C, E, R or Path to World Trade Center. Follow signs to World Financial Center.

The premier dining room of the World Financial Center (just below the World Trade Center) is a very clubby place, an "in" spot for the Wall Street crowd. Weekdays at lunchtime, the bankers, brokers, and assorted CEO's from capitalism-central pack the long, sleek dining room. It's a handsome setting, with light oak paneling, brass accents, and glass-walled wine caves; and it's triple-tiered so that all 40 tables face south and every diner has a waterfront view. At dinnertime the place is much quieter, so that's a good time to come and gaze at the Statue of Liberty and the excellent menu, which focuses on the foods and wines of the Hudson River Valley. (Appropriately, art from the Hudson River Valley School lines the walls.) Chef Waldy Malouf buys from boutique farms and vineyards whose standards are the highest, and he varies his menus to reflect the finest in available produce.

You might begin with the New York foie gras, sautéed with gratin potatoes; or the incredibly good blue crab, potato, and almond fritter with spiced tomato sauce; or the heady scallop-and-crab bisque. Follow this with a main course of perfectly done soft-shell crabs, roast squab with fresh fava beans, or Catskills mountain rainbow brook trout with black-olive vinaigrette. The six-course Hudson Valley menu might feature New York foie gras, followed by roasted oysters with leeks, venison chop with morels and chestnuts, Maine coast halibut, Hudson Valley farmhouse cheese and wild greens, and apple tart with candied walnut ice cream. The desserts are quite wonderful, especially the "tear-of-the-clouds" poached pear with apricot sorbet and sabayon and the Tower of Chocolate—a brownie, mousse, and meringue. The wine list focuses on American vintages at fair prices. At lunch, you can dine a bit more lightly, with perhaps a lobster, potato, and onion omelet or a salad of grilled quail and warm goat cheese for your main course.

WINDOWS ON THE WORLD, 107th floor, One World Trade Center, at Trinity Place between Vesey and Liberty Sts. Tel. 938-1111.
Cuisine: CONTINENTAL. **Reservations:** Required in The Restaurant and Cellar in the Sky; not accepted at the Hors d'Oeuvrerie, except for Sun brunch.
$ Prices: The Restaurant: Appetizers $5–$18; main courses $25–$38; prix-fixe dinner $36; Grand Buffet $25.50; Sunset Supper

---

 FROMMER'S SMART TRAVELER: RESTAURANTS

1. Eat your main meal at lunch when prices are as much as 15% to 20% lower. At some of the most fancy restaurants, prix-fixe lunches are quite affordable.
2. Look for "Pretheater" menus. Comparable to "Early Bird" specials in other cities, they offer considerable savings.
3. Eat ethnic: Chinese, Indian, and Thai restaurants abound. Look for Japanese noodle shops as opposed to fancier Japanese places.
4. Eat where the students do, near the campuses of New York University or Columbia University.
5. Get picnic fare at numerous take-out places or at the salad bars found in almost every grocery shop—then head for the parks.
6. Make reservations. At any of the better restaurants (and this includes even moderately priced ones that have heavy neighborhood trade or have caught on with the cognoscenti), reservations are a must. For the hotter ones, even calling a week in advance will not be enough. New Yorkers consider 7:30 to 9:30pm prime dining hours, so last-minute reservations at those times can be hard to come by. But you may be in luck if you want to dine earlier or later (in fact, you may find a hot restaurant totally empty at 6pm), or if you're here in August when New Yorkers flee the city.

from $27. Cellar in the Sky: Prix-fixe dinner, with wines, $90. The Hors d'Oeuvrerie: Appetizer menu $5.50–$14. Sun brunch $9–$15. AE, DC, DISC, JCB, MC.

Open: The Restaurant: Lunch, Mon–Fri noon–2:30pm. Dinner, Mon–Sat 5–10pm. Grand Buffet Brunch, Sat–Sun noon–3pm. Special Sunset Supper, Mon–Sat 5–6:30pm. Cellar in the Sky: One seating at 7:30pm Mon–Sat. The Hors d'Oeuvrerie: Mon–Sat 3pm–1am; Sun brunch noon–3pm, full service 4–9pm. **Subway:** and PATH stations inside building. **Bus:** No. 6 to Cortlandt St.

The quintessential New York restaurant experience? It's that dazzling showplace in the sky, 107 floors up, up, up above the city. Windows on the World is one of those magic, mind-blowing places that leaves even jaded city sophisticates gasping, a place that reaffirms the greatness and glamour of New York. Encompassing a veritable acre of glass, the various dining rooms, cocktail lounges, and private rooms afford 360-degree views of the city, the bridges lacing the rivers, the busy traffic of sea and sky; on a clear day, you can see 50 miles. The decor within is almost as stunning. Using muted tones of gold and beige and pale rose; lavish touches of mirror, brass, and wood; and abundant exquisite plants and fresh flowers, architect Warren Platner has created an ambiance that is futuristic yet warm, a brilliant tour-de-force of almost science-fiction–like splendor. Walking along the mirrored reception chamber lined by huge semiprecious rocks, being greeted by waiters in white uniforms with flashing gold epaulets, then being seated in a multitiered dining room where the ingenious use of mirrors affords full views to every diner, you get the feeling of floating in a gigantic luxury liner, suspended in a sea of sky.

Actually, there are three distinct dining areas that must be considered separately. The first is **The Restaurant,** which serves both a prix-fixe and an à la carte menu. Grilled baby red snapper over buttered leaf spinach is excellent, as is the rack of lamb James Beard with tomatoes and cured black olives. Wild mushroom ravioli with tomato and romano cheese makes a succulent beginning to the meal. And the desserts—especially the golden lemon tart and the raspberry tart with bitter-chocolate mousse—are wonderful. Those same desserts make a smashing finale to the weekend brunchtime Grand Buffet, a veritable taste trip around the world: bulghur wheat salad with cumin, marinated shrimp with huge peppercorns, Japanese noodle salad with mushrooms, smoked chicken, and hot curries suggest the lavish fare. A Sunset Supper offers excellent value: three elegant courses from $27.

At the very center of Windows on the World is a jewel-box dining room called **Cellar in the Sky:** Surrounded by thousands of colorful wine bottles, guests are treated to a spectacular dinner fashioned around five choice wines, with careful attention to the balance of wine and food usually done only at food and wine societies' dinners. Cost of this spectacular experience, limited to 35 guests every night (except Sunday) at 7:30pm is $90 prix-fixe, including wines.

Another part of Windows on the World that's both charming and popular is the **Hors d'Oeuvrerie,** which contains the City Lights Bar. It's a romantic cocktail lounge and grill, where you can sample "little dishes" from the International Cook's table—perhaps coconut fried shrimp with curried chutney, sushi and sashimi, Chinese dim sum, or spicy lamb kebobs. Piano music starts at 4pm; a trio playing soft, swinging jazz for dancing takes over at 7:30pm and plays until 1am on Monday to Saturday. When the sun goes down and the lights wink on over the city, there's no doubt that this is one of the most idyllic spots in town for dreaming and dancing.

Parking in the basement of the World Trade Center is free for Windows on the World patrons.

MODERATE

BRIDGE CAFÉ, 279 Water St., at the corner of Dover St. Tel. 227-3344.
   Cuisine: CONTEMPORARY AMERICAN. **Reservations:** Recommended, especially at lunch.
$ **Prices:** Appetizers $4.95–$7.95; main courses $11.95–$18.50; Sun brunch $11.95. AE, DC, MC, V.
   Open: Lunch, Mon–Fri 11:45am–5pm. Dinner, Tues–Sat 5pm–midnight; Sun–Mon 5–10pm. Brunch, Sun 11:45am–5pm. **Subway:** 6 to Fulton St. or Brooklyn Bridge.

Perfect for a meal after you've toured the South Street Seaport or other downtown attractions is the Bridge Café, just under the Brooklyn Bridge and just north of the Seaport. It's on the first floor of an old clapboard house, now painted a deep red, but a coat of paint is about the only visible sign of remodeling that's been done in many a year, and this is all part of the charm. A long, dark bar; red-checkered tablecloths; clay pots filled with flowering plants sitting in the windows; and wainscoting on the walls—all add to the decor of this waterfront bistro/restaurant.

The congenial group that works here makes you feel at home, and the prices make you relax. The menu changes every two weeks. Typical appetizers might include chilled fennel-and-cucumber soup, cold salmon mousse with watercress purée, and herb-breaded calamari with spicy tomato mayonnaise. Popular entrees include grilled marinated chicken with Reisling and roasted garlic; spinach linguine putanesca; pan-seared mahimahi and citrus-marinated sliced beef with endive and watercress. Brunch also features imaginative dishes and desserts, such as blueberry cobbler, chocolate indulgence cake, and fresh fruit cheesecake—all created on the premises. The Bar Menu, served after 2pm, features half a chilled lobster for $3.25.

SLOPPY LOUIE'S, 92 South St., in the Fulton Fish Market, Tel. 509-9694.
   Cuisine: SEAFOOD. **Reservations:** Recommended for 10 or more.
$ **Prices:** Appetizers $2.15–$6.25; main courses $10.45–$20.95. AE, DC, MC, V.
   Open: Mon–Sat 11am–9pm; Sun noon–7pm. **Subway:** 2, 3, or A to Fulton St. Walk east toward the river.

Another good choice if you're touring the financial district downtown or visiting the South Street Seaport, Sloppy Louie's is practically a New York institution, like the Brooklyn Bridge or the Staten Island Ferry. Its prices are cheap and its seafood is wonderful, but perhaps best of all it is still as unadorned and unpretentious as it was over 60 years ago when Louie took over (there has been a restaurant in this building since 1811). The restoration done in this block by the South Street Seaport has made Louie's a little more comfortable but hasn't changed the style very much: Everyone still has a grand time, sitting at long wooden tables, feasting on succulent plates of hot fish, and brushing shoulders with the Wall Street executives, fish market truck drivers, and others who throng the place. The main attraction is, of course, the fish. Everything is à la carte, but the entrees come with potatoes and vegetables, so they are almost a meal in themselves. Ask the waiter what's in season before you order. The shad roe, when they have it, is delicate and lovely, and also good are the Florida red snapper, the oyster fry, and the shrimp Creole. I'm especially partial to Louie's famous bouillabaisse, a huge, steaming concoction, just as good as the last time you tried it in Marseilles ($17.95). The big, hearty bowls of fish soup, like Maine lobster soup and Long Island clam chowder, are also a treat. Everything at Louie's is, in fact, good and absolutely fresh, since the fish comes right from the market and only the choicest selections are bought. The freshest of lobsters are served at very fair prices. Liquor is available, along with beer and wine.

STEAMER'S LANDING, 375 South End Ave., in Battery Park City. Tel. 432-1451.

Cuisine: SEAFOOD. **Reservations:** Recommended.

$ Prices: Appetizers $3.50–$10.50; main courses $9.75–$21.50.
Open: Lunch, Mon–Fri noon–3pm. Dinner, Tues–Sat 5–11pm; Sun–Mon 5–10pm. Brunch, Sat and Sun noon–4pm. **Subway:** 1, 2, 3, 9, C, E, R, or PATH to World Trade Center, follow signs to World Financial Center.

Walk a few blocks along the Esplanade from the World Financial Center and you'll come on this charming café with an outdoor terrace that's just perfect for waterfront dining in good weather. Indoors, huge windows overlook the harbor. Maryland crab cakes with a red-pepper rémoulade and fried calamari are perky appetizers; for a main course, go with the fresh fish of the day, the New York sirloin steak au poivre, or the grilled chicken breast with wild mushrooms. Tiramisu and bourbon bread pudding are the favorite desserts. For brunch, have eggs Benedict, a frittata, or a crab-cake sandwich with salad while you gaze at the Statue of Liberty.

BUDGET

PIPELINE, 2 World Financial Center. Tel. 945-2755.

Cuisine: AMERICAN/MEXICAN/ITALIAN. **Reservations:** Recommended for parties of six or more.

$ Prices: Appetizers $4.95–$6.95; main courses $11.95–$14.50; brunch $10.95.
Open: Daily 11am–11pm. Brunch, Sat and Sun 11am–5pm.
Subway: 1, 2, 3, 9, C, E, R, or PATH trains to World Trade Center; follow signs to World Financial Center.

Remember this place on a fine summer day when you want to sit outdoors on the plaza of the World Financial Center overlooking the marina. The deep-fried burrito, nachos, and buffalo chicken wings are popular appetizers. Sandwiches; burgers; salads; pastas; and a few entrees such as grilled fish of the day, omelet of the day, grilled chicken enchiladas, and a steamed vegetable platter provide something for every taste. The desserts—including cappuccino cheesecake, challah-bread pudding, and a brownie ice-cream sundae topped with fresh strawberries and macadamia nuts—are extravagantly good. Sunday brunch includes a cocktail, an entree, and unlimited beverages.

TRIBECA

EXPENSIVE

BOULEY, 165 Duane St., between Hudson and Greenwich Sts. Tel. 608-3852.
Cuisine: FRENCH/AMERICAN. **Reservations:** Essential, as far in advance as possible.
$ Prices: Appetizers $7–$22; main courses $23–$27; prix-fixe tasting menu $65.
Open: Lunch, Mon–Fri noon–3pm. Dinner, Mon–Sat 6–11pm.
Subway: 1, 2, or 3 to Chambers St. Walk two blocks north to Hudson St.

Fans and food critics call Bouley the best restaurant in America; I certainly rank it one of New York City's finest. Chef/owner Pierre Bouley trained with such superstars as Paul Bocuse and Roger Verge before opening the chic Montrachet (see below) in 1985, and he struck out on his own again two years later. He redefines French cooking here, harmonizing organically grown ingredients from hand-picked produce into exquisite combinations that are virtually free of cream or butter. The results are smashing. Although the menu changes constantly, recent offerings included such appetizers as Cape Cod squid roasted with a sauce of tomatoes and bay leaves, Maine day-boat lobster with glazed endive and watercress, and yellowtail tuna with garlic and chives in an aromatic ginger sauce. Among the entrees were organic guinea hen with fresh Italian parsley, fettucine, and hen-of-the-wood mushrooms; Casco Bay wolf fish with New England Cherrystone clams; and Provincetown codfish with early leeks in black-olive sauce. The desserts are marvelous—such as the hot raspberry soufflé and the tart of glazed shredded apples. You'll enjoy it all on Limoges china in a flower-filled room that transports you to a gentler, more romantic place and time. To savor the full spectrum of Bouley's wizardry, we recommend the dinner tasting menu at $65 or the five-course prix-fixe lunch at $32 (appetizers and main courses are slightly lower at lunch than at dinner). But be warned: After dining here, it may take you a while to return to earth.

MONTRACHET, 239 W. Broadway. Tel. 219-2777.
Cuisine: FRENCH. **Reservations:** Recommended.
$ Prices: Appetizers $9–$18; main courses $19–$29; prix-fixe dinners $25, $32, $45.
Open: Lunch, Fri noon–2:30pm. Dinner Mon–Thurs 6–10:30pm; Fri–Sat 6–11pm. **Subway:** 1 to Franklin St. Walk one block to W. Broadway.

In April 1985, Montrachet opened in Tribeca to well-deserved raves, including a three-star rating from the *New York Times*. Since then, they've managed to keep that rating and add more stars from *Forbes* magazine, as well as an award of excellence from *The Wine Spectator* for an outstanding (but not outrageously priced) list of fine French and California vintages. Stressing simplicity in decor and elegant modern French cuisine, they offer three prix-fixe dinners, as well as à la carte entrees. The $25 meal typically includes a

Roquefort, bacon, and endive salad as appetizer, a main course of pasta with wild mushrooms, and chocolate dacquoise for dessert. For $32, the appetizer will probably be pasta and a vegetable terrine with a hot tomato butter, the entree will be roast duck with ginger sauce, and the dessert will be crème brûlée. For $45, the appetizer might be a choice of braised black sea bass with saffron vinaigrette (a house specialty) or pigeon salad, and the entree may be venison in peppercorn sauce (game is often served in season), roast lobster, or loin of lamb with couscous. The dessert is a divine presentation of hot raspberry and chocolate soufflés. Lunch is served only on Friday and features salads, lighter foods, and fresh fish dishes on the order of Norwegian salmon.

TRIBECA GRILL, 375 Greenwich St., at the corner of Franklin St. Tel. 941-3900.

Cuisine: CONTEMPORARY AMERICAN. **Reservations:** Needed at least several days in advance for dinner, recommended at lunch.

$ Prices: Appetizers $7–$12; main courses $16–$26. AE, MC, V. **Open:** Lunch, Mon–Sat noon–2:30pm. Dinner, Mon–Thurs 6pm–10:45pm; Fri–Sat to 11:15. Brunch, Sun 11am–3pm. **Subway:** 1 to Franklin St.

For several years, this has been one of the hottest restaurant scenes in New York. With owners like Robert De Niro, Sean Penn, Bill Murray, Christopher Walken, and Mikhail Baryshnikov in the picture, it was inevitable that the place would become a celebrity hangout. Dustin Hoffman is a regular, so are Stephen Spielberg, Martin Scorsese, and Tom Selleck. People from nearby film studios and production companies make it their club (the top floors of the building house a screening room and Miramax Films). But star-gazing is not the only reason people flock to TriBeCa Grill: The atmosphere is warm and inviting, and the food just happens to be terrific.

TriBeCa Grill is the brainchild of Drew Nieporent, the managing partner, who is also responsible for the wonderful French restaurant Montrachet (see above). Although the food is simple, focusing mostly on grills, whatever chef Don Pintabona does is quite special. The heart of the dinner menu is very fresh fish—salmon, mahimahi, snapper, or whatever is best in the market. You get a choice of three preparations: grilled plain, with a sweet-corn succotash; sautéed with lemon and herbs; or roasted, with warm vinaigrette. Then there's a roasted chicken, veal with real old-fashioned whipped potatoes, breast of duck with wild-mushroom canneloni, and a nightly lobster special. Appetizers are also memorable, like the warm goat cheese salad, gazpacho, or arugula salad with bocconcini and basil oil. Desserts are ethereal, especially the warm Mascarpone blintz with fresh fruit and the chocolate torte, a tantalizing array of chocolate flavors and textures. Lunch starts off with similar salads ($7 to $8), features a fish special and a grilled chicken special and grilled focaccia salads ($10–$18). Desserts are the same as at dinner.

For the visitor, TriBeCa Grill makes good sense. You can tie it in with a trip to the World Financial Center and Battery Park City, the World Trade Center, or South Street Seaport.

MODERATE

TWO ELEVEN, 211 West Broadway. Tel. 925-7202.

Cuisine: CONTEMPORARY AMERICAN. **Reservations:** Recommended.

$ Prices: Appetizers $6.50–$9.25; main courses $8.50–$22.00. AE, MC, V.

Open: Lunch, Mon–Fri 11:30am–6pm. Dinner, Sun–Thurs 6pm–midnight. Brunch Sat and Sun 11:30am–4:30pm. **Subway:** 1 to Franklin St.

Walter Hinds brings imagination to the table that ranks him among New York's most intriguing young chefs. Drawing on his experience at Odeon, Sign of the Dove, and Gotham Bar and Grill, Hinds prepares his plates with equal parts flair and skill. Almost architectural, his dishes tower from the plate with such grace you almost regret eating them, but your compunction will pass once you take a taste. The grilled rabbit loin appetizer with spring greens, black-bean purée, and paprika-oil vinaigrette is heavenly, as is the pepper-seared tuna with Asian greens, cilantro oil, and rice noodles; even the humble breast of chicken, served with quinoa, mustard greens, and confit of garlic, tastes luxurious. Save room for the crème brûlée accented with lavender and chocolate or the mango tart. Featuring tablecloths with embroidered fleurs-de-lis and whitewashed walls, the cavernous, columned room is relaxing, if underwhelming; the service is indulgent but slow.

BUDGET

NOSMO KING, 54 Varick St. Tel. 966-1239.

Cuisine: AMERICAN. **Reservations:** Recommended.

$ Prices: Appetizers $4–$8; main courses $11–$17. AE, MC, V.

Open: Lunch, Mon–Fri noon–3pm. Dinner Mon–Fri 6–11pm; Sat and Sun 5:30–11pm. **Closed:** Sun in July and Aug. **Subway:** 1 to Canal St. Walk south across intersection of Varick and Canal Sts.

At Nosmo King (*no smoking*—get it?), your preconceptions of "health food" will melt away like so many inches off your waistline; dining here promises decadence with none of the morning-after regrets. Using mostly organic ingredients, chef Alan Harding composes dazzling dishes that taste as wonderful as they look. Best of all, they're good for you. Splendid samplings from a recent seasonal menu are sautéed morels with lentils and tangy asparagus vinaigrette as appetizers and cumin-flavored baby-goat ragoût and marvelous rare tuna on spinach with warm white beans as main courses. Don't miss the desserts here, especially the raspberry, chocolate, and peanut-butter pie and the toasted coconut cake with pineapple sorbet. A thoughtfully selected wine list boasts many organic labels; the restaurant even belongs to a cooperative organic farm on Long Island. Gracious service and an alluring, loftlike room have helped elevate this place from curiosity to major-player status on the downtown dining scene.

RIVERRUN, 176 Franklin St. Tel. 966-3894.

Cuisine: AMERICAN. **Reservations:** Recommended.

$ Prices: Appetizers $4–$7.95; main courses $8.25–$15.90. AE, CB, DC, MC, V.

Open: Lunch, daily 11:30am–5pm. Dinner daily 5pm–1am. **Closed:** Thanksgiving and Christmas. **Subway:** 1 to Franklin St.

⭐ Riverrun caters to a neighborhood crowd—but when that neighborhood is TriBeCa, near City Hall and home to lots of celebrities, that means you may find former mayor Ed Koch or actor Robert De Niro dining there frequently. Riverrun was one of TriBeCa's very first restaurants, and now the area and the restaurant are both "hot." It's no wonder—the food here is delicious and thankfully non-nouvelle, the service is friendly and attentive, and, wonder of wonders, the prices are modest. There's a very popular bar up front (it keeps winning all sorts of awards) and simple, semienclosed tables in the rear. Hanging on the walls are paintings and photographs of high quality (some are for sale) done by local artists.

The dinner menu provides everything from sandwiches (like blackened chicken on rye, with roasted red pepper and fries) and burgers to salad niçoise and caesar salad, and on to such main dishes as roast chicken tarragon with homemade mashed potatoes, Thai-style shrimp with garlic pepper, and steamed mussels Chardonnay with garlic and tomato. I started my meal here with yummy fried potato skins stuffed with cheese and bacon, dined on a special of broiled rainbow trout stuffed with crabmeat, and succumbed to the house's wickedly fattening chocolate mud cake for dessert. Key lime pie and carrot cake are also memorable. There's a full lunch menu at slightly lower prices, and Saturday and Sunday brunch specials run $6.25 to $7.95. The service is friendly yet professional, and there's an overall good feeling about this one. There's plenty of street parking (call for driving directions).

2. CHINATOWN

Manhattan is dotted with Chinese restaurants, and you can have an adequate Chinese meal almost anywhere in the city. But make the trek down to Chinatown, not only to combine a little sightseeing with your meal (see details in Chapter 7) but also because the city's best, most authentic Chinese kitchens are found here.

For a real experience in Chinese eating, choose a dim sum lunch at **Silver Palace,** 50 Bowery (tel. 964-1204); **Oriental Pearl,** 103 Mott St. (tel. 219-8388); or **Mandarin Court,** 61 Mott St. (tel. 608-3838)—the most "in" establishments at this moment. All are jammed on weekends, so come as early as you can for the best selections. Dim sum, in case you haven't heard, is the umbrella term for dumplings and other exotic morsels that are served early in the day, always accompanied by pots and pots of tea. The correct procedure for a tea lunch is to choose whatever appeals to you from the carts and trays that are constantly whisked by your table (dim sum never offers a menu). Your bill is tallied by counting the number of empty plates you've amassed. It's perfectly proper to linger over tea lunch and continue eating until you're thoroughly sated. You'll be seated communal style with lots of other diners, all happily eating away. Individual selections average about $1.80 to $5.95. At the Silver Palace, dumpling hours are 8am to 4pm; at Oriental Pearl, 8am to 4pm; at Mandarin Court, 7:30am to 3:30pm. To reach Chinatown, take the 6 to Canal Street.

MANHATTAN
SoHo, TriBeCa,
Little Italy &
Chinatown

Alison on
  Dominick Street ❶
Bouley ❸
Great Shanghai ⓫
Greene Street
  Restaurant ❻
Grotta Azzurra ❽
Hwa Yuan ⓬
L'Ecole ❾
Montrachet ❹
Nha Trang Vietnamese
  Restaurant ⓰
Nosmo King ⓯
Riverrun ❸
Soho Kitchen and Bar ❺
Spring Street Natural
  Restaurant ❼
Tribeca Grill ❷
Two Eleven ⓮
Vegetarian Paradise ❿

BUDGET

GREAT SHANGHAI, 27 Division St. Tel. 966-7663.
  Cuisine: CHINESE. **Reservations:** Only for parties of 10 or
  more.
$ Prices: Appetizers $2.60–$8.95; main courses $7.95–$14.45;
  weekday lunch special $4.95–$8.50. AE.
  Open: Sun–Thurs 11:30am–10pm; Fri–Sat 11:30am–11pm.

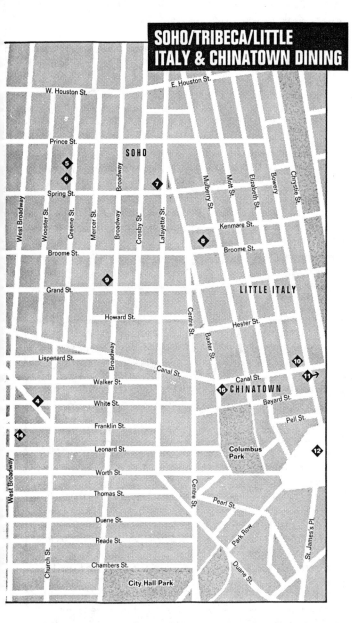

SOHO/TRIBECA/LITTLE ITALY & CHINATOWN DINING

E. Houston St.

W. Houston St.

Prince St.

SOHO

Spring St.

West Broadway

Wooster St.

Greene St.

Mercer St.

Broadway

Crosby St.

Lafayette St.

Mulberry St.

Mott St.

Elizabeth St.

Bowery

Chrystie St.

Kenmare St.

Broome St.

Broome St.

Grand St.

LITTLE ITALY

Howard St.

Centre St.

Hester St.

Baxter St.

Lispenard St.

Broadway

Canal St.

Canal St.

Walker St.

CHINATOWN

White St.

Bayard St.

Franklin St.

Pell St.

Leonard St.

Columbus Park

West Broadway

Worth St.

Thomas St.

Centre St.

Duane St.

Pearl St.

Reade St.

Park Row

Church St.

Chambers St.

Duane St.

St. James's Pl.

City Hall Park

Dim sum lunch, daily 11:30am–3pm. **Subway:** 6 to Canal St. Walk several blocks to Bowery; turn right on Bowery. Cross Bowery east of Division St.

S Great Shanghai is a large, crowded, modern restaurant specializing in Soo-hang food, one of the most delicate of the Chinese cuisines, which originated in the southern part of China along the Yangtze River. The innovation here, available only in winter, is the Chinese fondue, a cook-it-yourself affair. A simmering broth in a large pot is brought to your table and placed on a gas burner. You order a variety of small meat, fish, and vegetable dishes—the ones we like best are the fish balls, squid, and paper-thin chicken—which you cook yourself in the broth, dipping them into the steaming brew with a wire-mesh basket. The waitress brings a tray of condiments and mixes you a sauce—hot or mildly spicy, as you designate. We thought it was wonderful. (Depending on how many ingredients you choose, the price should be about $12 to $14 per person.)

Any time of the year, enjoy such dishes as sautéed prawns, sea bass, and classic Peking duck (a $28 duck should feed two to four hungry people). You'll want to order steamed dumplings and spring rolls as appetizers and maybe fried bananas for dessert. For dim sum, come at lunchtime.

You can also have the same Peking duck at another restaurant under the same management called **Peking Duck House Restaurant,** 22 Mott St. (tel. 227-1810).

NHA TRANG VIETNAMESE RESTAURANT, 87 Baxter St. Tel. 233-5984.
Cuisine: VIETNAMESE. **Reservations:** Recommended on weekends.

Ⓕ FROMMER'S COOL FOR KIDS: RESTAURANTS

Mickey Mantle's *(see p. 149)* The legendary New York Yankees hitter often drops by to soak up the atmosphere and autograph baseballs and the like for young fans.

Two Boots *(see p. 118)* Even the staff has fun at this playful East Village Cajun/Italian emporium, whose tasty offerings include dinner and brunch specials—and coloring books—for the little ones.

Dallas BBQ *(see p. 154)* Parents will enjoy the stylish setting, kids will love the barbecued chicken and ribs and the wonderful onion rings.

Saranac *(see p. 166)* It looks like summer camp in the Adirondacks and welcomes the stroller set, and those older, with a special children's menu.

Serendipity 3 *(see p. 166)* Little girls tend to favor the whimsical food here—Ftatateeta's toast, a foot-long chili hot dog, lemon ice-box pie, and unforgettable frozen hot chocolate.

Tavern on the Green *(see p. 149)* Like a trip to fairyland, all silver and glass and glitter, this is the kind of place of which childhood memories are made. Kids are given balloons to take home.

Chinatown *(see p. 103)* After marveling at the pagoda-style phone booths and the exotic shops, kids will find the restaurants here a treat.

$ Prices: Appetizers and main courses $3.50–$6.50.
Open: Daily 10am–10pm. **Subway:** 6 to Canal St.

This place has to be one of the best bargains in Chinatown, maybe in the whole city. It's hopping with tourists and locals alike who are drawn by delicious Vietnamese food so inexpensive it's hard to make dinner for two exceed $20. Dip the cool, light spring rolls with rice vermicelli in sweet peanut sauce to start; follow them with flavorful barbecued shrimp on real sugar cane, frog legs in chile-and-lemongrass sauce with rice, or—an incredible bargain—a big plate of seafood with vegetables and white rice for all of $3.50! Try some of the unusual beverages, like the green bean with coconut milk, sweet enough to be a dessert; and the French black coffee, good and strong. There's nothing fancy about this place—glass covers over white tablecloths, paper napkins, and plastic flowers—but the service is fast and friendly (often a rarity in Chinatown), and the value is just wonderful.

Right next door, **Pho Pasteur,** 85 Baxter St. (tel. 608-3656), also serves delicious Vietnamese food at low prices, but in a simpler setting. You can't go wrong at either place.

VEGETARIAN PARADISE, 48 Bowery. Tel. 571-1535.
Cuisine: CHINESE/VEGETARIAN **Reservations:** Recommended for four or more.
$ Prices: Appetizers $3–$5; main courses $5.95–$12.95. AE, MC, V.
Open: Sun–Thurs noon–10:30pm; Fri–Sat noon–11:30pm.
Subway: 6 to Canal St. walk east three blocks to Bowery; turn right ¼ block.

Vegetarians can usually find something to eat at any Chinese restaurant, but here the vegetarian is king. You may dine on "prawns" in black-bean sauce (really baby corn), sweet-and-pungent "pork" (tofu), or vegetarian "roast duck" (made of tofu skins). Best of all, the food is absolutely delicious and the prices are tiny. Buddha's lo mein is a winner, as is the lemon "chicken," and the large variety of soups—hot and sour, seaweed, snow cabbage with bean curd—are almost big enough for a meal. There are just a few plain tables, and you may have to wait to get in. There's another Vegetarian Paradise farther uptown in Greenwich Village (see Section 5, below, for details).

3. LITTLE ITALY

For those who love lusty, truly ethnic Italian food, the greatest neighborhood in the city has to be Little Italy, a subway stop or two below Greenwich Village. The streets are lined with homey, family-style restaurants where they make the fried mozzarella, lobster Fra Diablo, clams in garlic sauce, steak in hot peppers, and fried zucchini the way they did back in Naples or Sicily. Come for lunch after you've been touring downtown Manhattan and join the local politicians and legal eagles (City Hall and the courts are just a few blocks away) wheeling and dealing over the steaming pastas. If you come for dinner on a weekend, be prepared to join the hungry throngs standing in long lines, since most of these restaurants do not accept reservations.

Prices here are slightly lower than those uptown, and you can probably get a good meal for anywhere from $15 to $20. In addition to **Grotta Azzura** and **Adriana's** (detailed below), consider also **Paolucci's,** 149 Mulberry St., long a personal favorite. Other delicious choices are **Forlini's,** 93 Baxter St.; **Puglia,** 189 Hester St., which boasts live entertainment nightly; and **Vincent's Clam Bar,** 119 Mott St., for the best Italian fish dishes anywhere. It's nice to walk around the streets a little bit beforehand, poke your head into the grocery stores, and smell the marvelous cheese and sausages, perhaps listen to a strain of a Caruso record. Finish your evening with a heavenly pastry and espresso at any of the wonderful Italian coffeehouses that line the streets: Two of our favorites are **Café Roma,** 385 Broome St., and the oldest "pasticceria" in the country, **Ferrara's,** 195 Grand St., where, in summer, you can sit at the sidewalk café and pretend, perhaps, that you're on the Via Veneto.

MODERATE

ADRIANA'S RISTORANTE, 19 Cleveland Place (between Spring and Kenmare Sts). Tel. 941-8080.
    Cuisine: ITALIAN. **Reservations:** Recommended.
$ Prices: Appetizers $4.75–$8.50; main courses $9.95–$16.95.
    Open: Mon–Sat noon–11pm; Sun noon–10pm.
This is a sophisticated new dining spot in Little Italy. A cozy front bar, an open kitchen, exposed-brick walls, tables well-spaced for conversation, and Billie Holiday photos and music set the scene for imaginative renderings of classic cuisine. Sauces are kept on the light side, oils take precedence over butter, and herbs are used subtly. Start your meal with the lusty stuffed artichoke or the Portobello wild mushrooms, grilled and basted to taste like the most tender of steaks—a vegetarian's dream. Angel-hair pasta with fresh greens, pasta with sardines and fennel, and veal chops sautéed with a cognac-cream sauce are all favorites, as are the chicken sautéed with pistachio nuts in cream sauce and the red snapper with tomato, olives, and capers. Talented chef Douglas Tilyou also does all the pastries, and his tiramisu is one of the most subtly flavored in town. The wine list, mostly Italian, is distinctive and reasonably priced.
    Note: At press time, Adriana's was offering a remarkable airline travel discount to its guests: that offer may or may not be available by the time you read this, but be sure to ask.

GROTTA AZZURRA, 387 Broome St. Tel. 226-9283 or 925-8775
    Cuisine: ITALIAN. **Reservations:** Not accepted.
$ Prices: Appetizers $5.25–$13.95; main courses $10–$20.
    Open: Tues–Thurs noon–11pm; Friday noon–midnight; Sat noon–12:30pm; Sun noon–11pm. **Subway:** 6 to Canal St.; walk east several blocks, then turn left on Mulberry St.
This is the most popular restaurant in Little Italy, and the one where the lines are the longest. But you won't be disappointed: The place is attractive, the service professional, and the crowd lively. And the food is excellent, especially such old standbys as steamed mussels or clams and stuffed artichokes among the appetizers, veal scaloppine with mushrooms, chicken rollatini, and saltimbocca à la Florentina among the main courses. For dessert, the cold zabaglione with strawberries is a must.

4. SOHO

In this eclectic, electric neighborhood, it pays to choose carefully, so I've listed some of my favorites in addition to those below. For clever, clean American fare, gallery gawkers flock to **Jerry's,** 101 Prince St. (tel. 966-9464), where people-watching qualifies as an Olympic sport. A few doors east, **Fanelli,** 94 Prince St. (tel. 226-9412), serves homey, hearty pub fare in a memorabilia-packed saloon atmosphere. Lines form early at the bright, cheery **Elephant & Castle,** 183 Prince St. (tel. 260-3600), for Saturday and Sunday brunch; mammoth omelets make the wait worthwhile. For European ambiance (and attitude), light a Gauloise and head to **Lucky Strike,** 59 Grand St. (tel. 941-0479), or to its next-door rival, **La Jumelle,** 55 Grand St. (tel. 941-9651). Both turn out surprisingly serious French fare for the young, rich, and thin set through the wee hours. In an Italian mood? Within a three-block stretch, you'll find the warm **Amici Miei,** 475 W. Broadway (tel. 533-1933); hip **I Tre Merli,** 463 W. Broadway (tel. 254-8699); and convivial **Vucciria,** 422 W. Broadway (tel. 941-5811)—all of which have earned the loyalty of locals, no mean feat down here. Subway: Take the 6 to Spring Street or R to Prince Street.

EXPENSIVE

ALISON ON DOMINICK STREET, 38 Dominick St., one block south of Spring St., between Varick and Hudson Sts. Tel. 727-1188.
   Cuisine: FRENCH. **Reservations:** Required well in advance.
$ **Prices:** Appetizers $6–$15; main courses $19–$27. Sun prix-fixe dinner for two $49; pretheater dinner Mon–Sat, $29. AE, DC, MC, V.
   Open: Dinner only, Mon–Thurs 5:30–10:30pm; Fri–Sat 5:30–11pm; Sun 5:30–9:30pm. **Subway:** 1 to Canal St.; E or C to Spring St.

Why are all those limos double-parked on a nondescript street that nobody has ever heard of just north of the Holland Tunnel? Dominick Street is the home of a stylish bistro so good that people go out of their way to enjoy the soul-satisfying food of southwestern France that chef Tom Valenti creates here. Proprietor Alison Price Becker, an actress turned restaurateur, has created an old-fashioned restaurant—a cozy, candlelit spot with creamy white walls, midnight-blue banquettes, silvery black-and-white photos of France on the walls, and a long white taper on each table. Soft, unobtrusive jazz plays in the background. Waiters and waitresses are friendly and knowledgeable, and Alison herself is always on hand.

Against such a harmonious background, the food can really shine—and it does! Chef Valenti prefers to go light on the butter, heavy cream, and cheese sauces but still manages to turn out wonderful dishes from Gascogne, Languedoc, and the Basque country. Braised lamb shank with fava beans and wilted chicory, in a sauce of roast garlic and parsley, and roast guinea hen with a risotto of black olives, roasted tomatoes, and thyme, are his signature dishes, which are widely praised; also quite fine is the sautéed skate with braised cabbage. Appetizers are satisfying, too, especially the roasted quail salad with cracked wheat. The menu changes with the seasons; game in season is featured. Be prepared to linger and enjoy. Artists and theatrical folk come here at night, so you may spy a celebrity or two.

MODERATE

L'ECOLE, 462 Broadway, at Grand St. Tel. 219-8890.

Cuisine: FRENCH. **Reservations:** Recommended.

$ Prices: Prix-fixe lunch Mon–Fri, three courses $16, five courses $20; prix-fixe dinner Mon–Sat, three courses $26, five courses $32. Also à la carte: appetizers $3.50–$8; main courses $7–$15. AE, DC, MC, V.

Open: Lunch, Mon–Fri noon–1:30pm. Dinner, Tues–Sat 6–9:30pm; Mon 8–9:30pm. Closed Sun and major hols. **Subway:** 6 to Spring St. walk one block.

To enjoy the best in classic French cuisine, it pays to go to school. And the school we're talking about is L'Ecole, the student-operated restaurant of the French Culinary Institute of New York, in SoHo. Here, in a light and airy two-tiered dining room, with white-napped tables well-spaced for conversation and colorful artwork on the walls, you can enjoy the classic cuisine of France at a fraction of the price you would pay at one of the great restaurants of New York or Paris. Students get to hone their skills, patrons get to enjoy sumptuous food and save money: Everybody benefits.

The French Culinary Institute of New York is a sister school to prestigious Ferrandi in Paris. Students undergo a rigorous 600-hour curriculum under the guidance of Dean of Special Studies Jacques Pepin; Dean of Culinary Arts Alain Sailhac; and a team of instructors from some of the richest culinary regions of France—Lyons, Alsace, Ile de France, and Corsica. So well trained are the students that, upon graduation, many of them land jobs in some of New York's most prestigious kitchens—Lutèce, Le Bernardin, Le Cirque, and Montrachet among them. Here's a chance to catch them at the beginning of their careers.

The five-course lunch or dinner always includes an appetizer or soup, a fish course, a meat course, a green salad, and a dessert. The menu changes daily. You might start with Alsatian potato salad with garlic sausage, puréed fresh vegetable soup, or cod salad with red peppers. Fish and meat courses include pan-seared salmon on braised endive, country lamb shank with cassoulet beans, or steak frites. The desserts are as wonderful as the food. They could be chocolate sponge cake filled with chocolate mousse, poached pears with ice cream, crème brûlée, or perfect fresh fruit tarts. Various à la carte dishes are also available, from $3.95 to $12.95. L'Ecole's wine list has won the *Wine Spectator*'s Award of Excellence; each week, four bottled wines are offered at wine-shop prices.

GREENE STREET RESTAURANT, 101 Greene St. Tel. 925-2415.

Cuisine: INTERNATIONAL. **Reservations:** Recommended.

$ Prices: Appetizers $6–$11; main courses $17–$26; prix-fixe dinner $25. AE, DC, MC, V.

Open: Wed–Sat 6–11:30pm; Sun noon–9:30pm. **Subway:** 6 or E to Spring St., or R to Prince St. Walk west to Greene St.

This SoHo supper club boasts exemplary food and good jazz in a soaring multilevel space dotted with tall plants, tall windows, brick walls, and an abstract earth-tone mural splashed across the back wall; ample antique wicker chairs snuggle cozily around tables—not too close—and small brass lamps adorn each table. This is one of the most comfortable spots in New York to enjoy live jazz with dinner ($3 cover charge on weekdays, $5 on weekends). Chinese-born chef Shao Kwoan Pang presents an eclectic menu featuring French, Italian, and American dishes with some Asian accents. For openers try goat-cheese salad; lobster ravioli stuffed with wild mushrooms; or, when available, bluepoint oysters served warm with a lemon-butter sauce. Seafood is a house specialty, and every day there is a seasonal fresh fish selection, a vegetable plate, and a pasta dish. I recommend the filet of salmon with three caviars in a lemon-butter sauce and sautéed breast of chicken with roasted garlic. The desserts are rich and satisfying, especially the luscious chocolate truffle cake or gateau Marquis. A special Sunday menu features light entrees and a variety of omelets and other egg dishes. The wine list is enormous, with roughly 100 selections; there are always several available by the glass.

BUDGET

SOHO KITCHEN AND BAR, 103 Greene St. Tel. 925-1866.

Cuisine: INTERNATIONAL. **Reservations:** Only for large groups.

$ Prices: Appetizers $2.75–$7.25; main courses $6.75–$15.75. AE, DC, MC, V.

Open: Mon–Thurs 11:30am–2am (kitchen serves until midnight); Fri–Sat 11:30am–3am (kitchen serves until 12:30am), Sun noon–11pm (kitchen serves until 12:30am), Sun noon–11pm (kitchen serves until 10pm). **Subway:** 6 or E to Spring St., or R to Prince St. Walk west to Greene St.

Right next door to Greene Street and under the same management, SoHo Kitchen and Bar offers one of the finest and most extensive selections of wines by the glass anywhere in the world—a total of 110. Along with tasting the wines, dedicated oenophiles can munch on salads, omelets, pizzas, burgers, pastas, and sandwiches, plus weekend brunch specials and a few dinner grill items, all at pleasingly moderate prices.

SPRING STREET NATURAL RESTAURANT, 62 Spring St., at the corner of Lafayette. Tel. 966-0290.

Cuisine: NATURAL FOODS. **Reservations:** Not accepted.

$ Prices: Appetizers $3.75–$7; main courses $6.25–$14. AE, CB, DC, MC, V.

Open: Daily 11:30am–2am. Brunch Sun 11:30am–4pm. **Subway:** 6 to Spring St.

It would be difficult to improve on this SoHo favorite; it just keeps getting better. Spring Street Natural is a great big, airy place, with windows overlooking both sides of the two-level café; wooden tables, exposed-brick walls with paintings by local artists, tall plants, and overhanging fans set the mood for dining on wonderful food that is wholesome, unprocessed, beautifully prepared, and reasonably priced. Everything is home-made, superfresh, and prepared from all-natural ingredients. And the service is friendly and efficient. An excellent regular menu plus a long printed sheet of daily specials make it difficult to choose among the wide array of fish and seafood, pasta, and vegetarian and natural gourmet specials. At a recent meal, our party started with thick, chunky Tahitian chicken soup with fresh basil; sampled yummy appetizers like deep-fried plantains with lime chutney and smoked mozzarella with roasted red peppers; then moved on to a flavorful Caesar salad and spinach lasagne with tempeh, tofu, and ricotta. Our entrees were a wonderful sautéed shrimp with a tomato-cream sauce, a sautéed breast of chicken with miso jalapeño sauce, and a roasted acorn squash stuffed with scallions, apples, tofu, wild rice, and curried yogurt. The desserts ($3.50) were wondrous: sweet-potato Grand Marnier pie, a chocolate soufflé torte, and a pecan bourbon tart. With food so good and prices so low, you can see why this place is always packed. Sunday brunch is a special treat, with a large menu of soups, salads, appetizers, egg dishes, and great desserts, in addition to the regular menu. You can have drinks at the big, friendly bar up front, crowded with locals.

5. GREENWICH VILLAGE

The Village has, in addition to those highlighted below, a vast variety of places to eat or just sit over cappuccino and watch the sights go by. In a vein similar to The Grand Ticino (see below), you might want to try **Rocco's,** 181 Thompson St. (tel. 677-0590); **Villa Mosconi,** 69 MacDougal St. (tel. 673-0390); and **Cucina Stagionale,** 275 Bleecker St., off Seventh Avenue (tel. 924-2707), where there's always an eager line waiting to get in (no bar, so BYOB.) Have desserts at these restaurants, or, even better, visit one of the famous Italian caffès of the Village, ideal for a cappuccino on ice or a piping hot espresso; they are great places to sit, talk, play a game of chess, read the papers—or just watch the world whirl by. Our favorite caffès on MacDougal Street are **Caffè Dante** at no. 79 and **Caffè Reggio** at no. 119. Another pleasant place to linger is **The Peacock,** 24 Greenwich Ave. Take the A, B, C, D, E, F, or Q train to West 4th Street; walk south two blocks.

EXPENSIVE

GOTHAM BAR AND GRILL, 12 East 12th St. Tel. 620-4020.
   Cuisine: AMERICAN. **Reservations:** Strongly recommended.
$ **Prices:** Appetizers $8.50–$14; main courses $26.50–$30. AE, CB, DC, MC, V.
   Open: Lunch, Mon–Fri noon–2:30pm. Dinner, Mon–Thurs 5:30–10pm; Fri–Sat 5:30–11pm; Sun 5:30–9:45pm. **Bus:** Fifth Ave. No. 5. **Subway:** 6 to 14th St.

The beautiful, chic Gotham Bar and Grill celebrated its ninth anniversary recently, and the crowds, limos, and celebrities are still there. The hurrahs are for one of New York's best restaurants and the exquisite presentations of its young chef de cuisine, Alfred Portale, a veteran of Troisgros and other stellar restaurants in France. Diners are seated at small tables placed among huge, soaring columns, in an art deco postmodern atmosphere that is at once soothing and exciting. As a first course, the seafood salad comes highly recommended, as does the goat-cheese ravioli and the veal carpaccio. Among the main courses, steamed Atlantic salmon with boiled potatoes and smoked onions and the duck choucrôute are given top billing, along with the grilled swordfish in lemon-almond butter. For dessert, the pecan banana tart, served warm with caramel ice cream, is quite lovely—as is the summer strawberry tart, with lemon curd, mint, and Mascarpone sorbet.

EXPENSIVE TO MODERATE

K-PAUL'S NEW YORK, 622 Broadway, between Bleecker and Houston Sts. Tel. 460-9633.
   Cuisine: CAJUN. **Reservations:** Recommended for Fri–Sat.
$ Prices: Appetizers $4–$8; main courses $14–$26. AE, CB, DC, MC, V.
   Open: Dinner only, Tues–Sat 5:30–11pm. **Subway:** 6 to Bleecker St. or N or R to Prince St.

There's no need to head for New Orleans to sample real Cajun cooking any more: From its wrought-iron door to its glassed-in kitchen to its fiery menu, K-Paul's New York is a loving re-creation of its New Orleans counterpart. And chef Paul Prudhomme, the bearded, rotund, undisputed guru of Cajun cooking, is often here, too, supervising the works, testing the sauces, and giving out autographs to adoring fans. It's a show, an experience, and a great gastronomic adventure—as long as you like it "hot." The term *Cajun* refers to French-speaking emigrants from Nova Scotia (then called Acadia) who settled in southern Louisiana in the 1700s, when the French also settled there. Chef Paul has helped maintain their gastronomical heritage, and, although he probably won't cook your dinner himself, he's trained the cooks, who have mastered the unique blending of spices and peppers and the balancing of textures that make his food inimitable.

The waiters and waitresses have been trained to guide you through the K-Paul experience; follow the guidelines and you're promised "a natural, healthy emotional high in return." To get those tastebuds going, sample a "Cajun Martini"—vodka with hot peppers, chef Prudhomme's signature drink.

The menu changes daily, so you might start with one of the great soups, like classic gumbo or "totally hot" Cajun jambalaya. Don't miss Cajun popcorn—fried puffs of battered crayfish, with a sherry sauce. Then you can proceed to a main course like crayfish étouffé with rice and salad, pan-fried grouper with seafood Bienville buttercream, or eggplant pirogue. The desserts are as wonderful as you would expect—sweet-potato pecan pie, bread pudding with lemon sauce and Chantilly, or spiced pecan layer cake. The atmosphere is totally informal; cartoon menus adorn the walls and ceilings, and every now and then a "Dixieland conga line" breaks out. There's nothing else quite like this place—east of the Mississippi.

THE NEW DEAL RESTAURANT AND GARDEN, 133 West 13th St., between Sixth and Seventh Aves. Tel. 741-3663.
   Cuisine: CONTEMPORARY AMERICAN. **Reservations:** Recommended.
$ Prices: Appetizers $7.50–$8.50; main courses $15.75–$22.50; three-course prix-fixe dinner $18.75. AE, MC, V.

Open: Brunch, Sat and Sun 11:30am–3pm. Dinner, Sun–Thurs 5–10:30pm; Sat and Sun 5–11:15pm. **Subway:** 1, 2, 3, or 9 to 14th St.

In its previous incarnation in SoHo, WPA murals of the 1930s dominated the decor at The New Deal. There's no room for them in this new space in a Greenwich Village town house, but no matter: The narrow brick-walled room with its fireplace and grand piano (there's music to dine by Thursday, Friday, and Saturday night) is invitingly cozy, and the outdoor garden with its umbrellaed tables is one of the most relaxing al fresco dining spots around. Chef Jeffrey Nathan's seasonal menus, using fresh herbs from the garden, turn up some invigorating surprises. Among the appetizers are crab cakes served on a tomato-butter sauce with chives and aïoli and an unusual lasagne of layered lobster, potatoes, and cheese flavored with lobster au jus. Among the main courses are black buck antelope leg marinated in bourbon and sour cherries, coated with fresh lavender and thyme, pan roasted, and then served with a sauce of sour cherries sage; and also baked salmon coated with a finely ground garlic crust. The prix-fixe menu, which includes an appetizer, an entree from a varied list, coffee, and dessert, is one of New York's best buys. Fall brings their annual game festival. The desserts are special: homemade ice creams with fresh fruits and berries, sinfully rich chocolate decadence cake, and mud pie. Nothing beats an outdoor weekend brunch, especially if you can have zucchini-and-parmesan frittata or eggs Callet (Virginia ham, a chiffonade of spinach, and scrambled eggs atop a warm croissant). There are a full bar and a sensibly priced wine list.

BUDGET

FLORENT, 69 Gansevoort St. Tel. 989-5779.
Cuisine: FRENCH. **Reservations:** Not accepted.
$ Prices: Appetizers $3.50–$8.25; main courses $8.50–$16.75.
Open: Breakfast, daily 2:30–11am. Lunch, Mon–Fri 11am–3:30pm. Brunch, Sat and Sun 11am–4pm. Dinner, daily 6:30pm–midnight. Supper, daily midnight–2:30am. **Subway:** A to 14th St; walk two blocks west of Ninth Ave. and two blocks south of 14th St. (taxi advised).

Five in the morning at Florent feels like the dinner rush anywhere else. Club kids, models, artists, and downtown icons such as Laurie Anderson—spotted on a recent visit—retreat to this bright bistro-cum-coffee shop at all hours for straightforward Gallic cuisine; old favorites like homemade tripe, boudin noir, and steak au poivre share the menu with surprises like Thai bouillabaisse. Lunch is a bargain, with huge hamburgers, a delicious herbed half chicken, and sensational sandwiches like flank steak with horseradish cream. Breakfast in the wee hours, however, is the time to make a real entrance and enjoy generous omelets, pancakes, salads, and pâtés. You'll have to shout over the din, and the tables nearly sit atop one another, but you'll gawk so much that you'll hardly notice. And that's just at the model-quality staff.

THE GRAND TICINO, 228 Thompson St. between W. 3rd and Bleecker Sts. Tel. 777-5922.
Cuisine: ITALIAN. **Reservations:** Recommended.
$ Prices: Appetizers $4–$8; main courses $11–$19. AE, CB, DC, MC, V.

Open: Lunch, Mon–Fri noon–3pm. Dinner, Mon–Fri 5–11pm, Sat and Sun 3–11pm. Brunch, Sat and Sun noon–3pm. **Subway:** A, B, C, D, E, F, or Q to W. 4th St.; walk south two blocks, east one block.

This is your classic Greenwich Village Italian restaurant, typical of many where the prices are moderate and the food is rich and hearty in the grand old southern Italian tradition. This restaurant may look familiar if you've seen the movie *Moonstruck.* Try the assorted hot antipasto to begin, then maybe follow with a bowl of their famous minestrone or tortellini in brodo. Entrees include sweetbreads with capers, breast of chicken with prosciutto and fontina cheese, and an excellent veal chop. Saturday and Sunday brunch is festive, with pastas, soups, main courses, and hearty frittata del giorno (omelets of the day).

MEXICAN VILLAGE, 224 Thompson St. Tel. 475-9805.
   Cuisine: MEXICAN. **Reservations:** Not required.
$ Prices: Appetizers $2–$6.95, main courses $8.25–$11. AE, MC, V.
   Open: Daily noon–midnight. **Subway:** A, B, C, D, E, F, or Q to W. 4th St. Walk south two blocks, east one block.

Mexican Village is always busy, even on a cold winter weeknight when everyplace else is practically empty. Its popularity has continued for over 27 years, and with good reason. Not only is the atmosphere *muy simpático,* with lots of wood and brick, and Mexican glass lanterns, but also the food is authentic and reasonably priced. To the traditional Mexican favorites, they often add new dishes not done in New York before, like enchiladas Oaxaca; shredded beef chimichangas; chiles relleños poblanos (stuffed with cheese and sweet pork); and enchiladas de mer (flour tortillas stuffed with seafood). Be sure to ask about the daily specials. Vegetarians can enjoy meatless enchiladas supremas, as well as vegetarian tacos, enchiladas, and burritos. The chile sauces on the table are hot, so use them sparingly; to cool off, you can always order some iced mint tea or a bottle of Carta Blanca cerveza—the ideal accompaniment. It's pleasant to linger over your tequila while you're waiting for the delicacies to emerge from the hole-in-the-wall kitchen.

RIO MAR, 7 Ninth Ave., at Little West 12th St. Tel. 243-9015.
   Cuisine: SPANISH. **Reservations:** Recommended for large parties.
$ Prices: Appetizers $4.75–$5.50; main courses $8.50–$14.25. AE.
   Open: Lunch, Mon–Sun noon–3pm. Dinner Sun–Thurs 3pm–2am, Fri–Sat 3pm–3am. **Subway:** A to 14th St. Walk one block west and two blocks south (taxi advised).

Just one block east of the Hudson River in the meat-packing district, Rio Mar is a real find. The cuisine and ambiance are authentically Spanish, the service is attentively friendly, and the prices are modest. This cozy place seats just 14 diners on the main level, 13 at the bar, and about 45 on the second level. The juke box offers a Spanish hit parade, and on Saturday evenings at about 10, the entertainment goes live, as Roberto, one of the multitalented veteran waiters, plays Mexican flamenco and maybe sings a song or two.

Camarones en salsa verde (shrimps in green sauce); paella; and an assortment of appetizers (also available as tapas at the bar) like chorizos (Spanish sausages), mejillones (mussels), pulpo (octopus) enjoyed with a pitcher of sangría, easily feeds four. Mariscada Rio Mar (mussels, clams, shrimp, and lobster) has a sauce so delicious one could dip an entire loaf of bread into it so as not to miss a drop; the sauce of the camarones en salsa verde is also wonderful. The langosta (deep broiled lobster with clams, shrimp, and mussels) is another favorite. You can also order veal, chicken, and pork dishes; and veal, steak, or sausage sandwiches are available at dinner. If you fancy flan, do try it here.

At lunchtime the platters are a great buy—seafood, chicken, veal, and more—and you can enjoy them with french fries, boiled potato, or rice and salad.

The ambiance—cozy, earthy, and friendly—attracts a young artistic crowd, but all types are welcome and graciously served. Another restaurant owned by the same crew, natives of Galicia in northwest Spain, is **Café Riazor** at 245 W. 16th St. (tel. 727-2132). The menu is the same at that location, and the proprietor is also the chef.

SABOR, 20 Cornelia St. Tel. 243-9579.

Cuisine: CUBAN. **Reservations:** Recommended.
$ Prices: Appetizers $3.50–$7; main courses $11.75–$12.95. AE, MC, V.
Open: Dinner, Sun–Thurs 5:30–11pm; Fri–Sat 5:30pm–midnight. **Subway:** 1 to Christopher St.

Haute cuisine Cubano is the specialty at Sabor, a tiny, almost out-of-the-way restaurant you can tell your friends about. First, tell them where to find Cornelia Street: It's the small block that runs diagonally off Sixth Avenue at West Fourth Street and ends at Bleecker Street. Then, tell them to reserve, for this really is a small place, serving a maximum of 32 persons at 16 small tables. Then, tell them to expect classy, classic Cuban cuisine at refreshingly moderate prices. The room, rather plain with buttery-yellow walls, a deep-rose stamped tin ceiling, and ceiling fans, does not compete with the food for attention. But chef/owner Ronny Ginnever cooks up a Caribbean storm in her miniature kitchen. And when the mixer churns her superb fresh lime margaritas (don't miss!), conversation stops for a few seconds.

Tell the waiter how hot you like your food and follow his suggestions. Among the appetizers, frituras de malanga, Caribbean root vegetables puréed and then deep-fried, with a green hot sauce, are potent. A little less so are the calamares picantes, marinated cold squid (a frequent special), and the zarzuela de mejillones, steamed mussels in a piquant tomato sauce. Highlights among the entrées are camarones á la criolla (shrimps in a spicy tomato sauce), ropa vieja (shredded flank steak in a cloves-and-cinnamon tomato sauce), and a nicely done pollo con cumino (baked, boneless breast of chicken in a lime-juice marinade). And there are daily specials. Top off this literally mouth-watering repast with one of their sweet, cooling desserts, like a commendable Key lime pie or brazo gitano—that's a rolled sponge cake filled with custard and topped with Grand Marnier and fresh orange sauce. *Sabor* means "taste" or "flavor," and that's just what this place is all about.

UNIVERSAL GRILL, 44 Bedford St. Tel. 989-5621.

Cuisine: AMERICAN. **Reservations:** Not accepted.

$ Prices: Appetizers $3.75–$6.95; main courses $8.95–$14.50. AE.

Open: Lunch, Mon–Fri 11:30am–3:30pm. Dinner, daily 6pm–midnight. Brunch, Sat and Sun 11am–3:30pm. **Subway:** 1 or 9 to Christopher St. walk two blocks south.

As the sound system blares Abba's "Dancing Queen," tambourine-toting waiters serenade a shocked diner and gingerly deliver a birthday dessert. That's just another night at Universal Grill, a West Village newcomer so hot the waiting crowds could fill a subway station. For a "scene" restaurant, Universal delivers surprisingly solid comfort food: Southwestern duck chili, pan-roasted half chicken with gravy, and the Universal Club sandwich rank among the tastiest I've had anywhere. Downtown hipsters have already made brunch a neighborhood institution; reasonably priced, massive platters of French toast, pancakes, omelets, and heavenly biscuits keep them coming. The room isn't decorated as much as accumulated, with knick-knacks that could have come from a maiden aunt's attic; take it all in as you pass the inevitable moments in line.

VEGETARIAN PARADISE 2 [V P 2], 144 W. 4th St., between Fifth and Sixth aves. Tel. 260-7130.
Cuisine: CHINESE/VEGETARIAN. **Reservations:** Not required.
$ Prices: Appetizers $3–$4.95; main courses $6.75–$12.95. AE, CB, DC, MC, V.
Open: Sun–Thurs noon–11pm; Fri–Sat noon–midnight. **Subway:** 1 or 9 to Christopher St., or A, B, C, D, E, F, or Q to W. 4th St.

They began with a vegetarian restaurant in their native Hong Kong, moved on to Chinatown, and now they've opened their second restaurant, here in Greenwich Village. The Tang family, the people in charge at V P 2, are creative cooks whose vegetarian cuisine stems both from their Buddhist beliefs in nonviolence and their commitment to a healthful, low-cholesterol cuisine that uses no fish, animal, or dairy products; no white sugar; and no preservatives. Besides the usual Chinese vegetarian dishes, they also create mock "meat" entrees—lemon chicken (made with Chinese yams), sweet-and-pungent pork (based on eggplant), and deep-fried oysters (really baby corn). And the food is delicious. Their Paradise Hot Clay Pots are a special treat. The desserts are surprisingly good, especially the lemon tofu and banana-date puddings. The place is plain and narrow, with a minimum of decor, but pleasant enough. Two doors away, at **VP-2-GO** (tel. 260-7049), 140 W. 4th St., they make authentic vegetarian dim sum take-out—a special treat if you're planning a picnic.

6. EAST VILLAGE/LOWER EAST SIDE

EAST VILLAGE

It's not just a meal, it's an adventure. Dining in the East Village can take you from India to Poland to Jamaica—in one block. Since locals are mostly working-class folk, artists, and students, the restaurants down here offer wonderful fare that's cheaper than in almost any other neighborhood. In addition to those below, I suggest the following for a quick culinary trip around the world. In what feels like a loony Swiss cottage, **Roettele AG,** 126 E. 7th St. (tel. 674-4140), surrounds you with cuckoo clocks and kitsch and pampers you with Alpine soul food like goulash and Wienerschnitzel. For fine Indian fare, skip the strip on East Sixth Street and head for **Haveli,** 100 Second Ave. (tel. 982-0533), a standout for its snazzy decor and equally appealing food. Across the street, **103,** 103 Second Ave. (tel. 777-4120), may as well be across the globe. Come for clean American food, a hip crowd, and a great-looking staff; the softly lit space and lively bar make it a scene. With a Mexican accent, **Maryann's Distrito Federal,** 300 E. 5th St. (tel. 475-5939), dishes out delicious, inexpensive fare and terrific drinks to a youngish crowd. For authentic Polish and Ukrainian favorites like pierogi and kielbasa—and an even more authentic staff—check out **Kiev,** 117 Second Ave. (tel. 674-4040), or **Veselka** (tel. 228-9682), 144 Second Ave., both open 24 hours and such a bargain you'll think you're still in the old country. And at **Two Boots,** 37 Ave. A (tel. 505-2276), New York's (and maybe the world's) first Cajun pizza joint, calamari ravioli share the menu with pasta jambalaya and crayfish pizza. More traditionally Italian, **Cucina di Pesce,** 87 E. 4th St. (tel. 260-6800), and **Frutti Di Mare,** 84 E. 4th St. (tel. 979-1034), both under the same management, offer fresh pasta and seafood dishes that may be among the best bargains in New York; both have some sidewalk seating, friendly crowds, and free mussels at the bar to tide you over while waiting.

BUDGET

LA SPAGHETTERIA, 178 Second Ave., between 11th and 12th Sts. Tel. 995-0900.

Cuisine: ITALIAN REGIONAL. **Reservations:** Recommended especially on weekends.

$ Prices: Appetizers $3.50–$6.95; main courses at lunch $6.95–$9.50, at dinner $8.95–$13.95.

Open: Sun–Thurs noon–midnight; Fri–Sat noon–1am. **Bus:** Any Second Ave. bus.

Casually elegant, La Spaghetteria is a second home to neighborhood artists, writers, and actors playing at the Public and other local theaters. A beautiful flower arrangement, with desserts—including a big basket of fruit—temptingly displayed on a white-lineened table commands the center of the room; candlelight sets the mood and in summer, although there's no al fresco dining area, windows overlook a lovely garden.

The menu—supplemented by daily specials—changes seasonally. You might begin with an antipasto misto—a plate of scrumptious daily-changing items, such as white-bean salad vinaigrette, grilled eggplant, roasted cauliflower, strips of fennel studded with roasted garlic, and ricotta salata in mint-flavored extra-virgin olive oil. Ask for oil and vinegar and soak it all up with chunks of Spaghetteria's terrific Tuscan breads. Pasta courses include penne tossed with grilled fresh tuna, coarsely chopped tomatoes, and black olives in a light tomato sauce. At dinner there's always a gnocchi special—for example, pesto dumplings in a fresh tomato purée garnished with thin strips of roasted red and yellow peppers. Secondi piatti (main courses) include pollo arrosto—roasted half chicken marinated in garlic and rosemary-scented olive oil, then served with oven-roasted potatoes and the vegetable du jour (perhaps grilled broccoli fleurets). At lunch there are also frittatas and sandwiches. The Italian/Californian wine list highlights eight premium wines by the glass. And the dessert list usually offers a heavenly tiramisu and an assortment of delicious tortas, such as an orange tart with a thick chocolate crust.

THE MIRACLE GRILL, 112 First Ave., near 7th St. Tel. 254-2353.

Cuisine: SOUTHWESTERN. **Reservations:** Accepted only for six or more.

$ Prices: Appetizers $4.95–$7.95; main courses $7.95–$16.95. Brunch main courses $5.95–$8.95. AE, MC, V.

Open: Dinner, Mon–Thurs 5:30–11:30pm; Fri 6pm–midnight; Sat 11:30am–midnight; Sun 11:30am–11pm. Brunch, Sat and Sun 11:30am–3pm. **Subway:** 6 to Astor Place. Walk three blocks east, one block south.

It is indeed a miracle that the small kitchen at this East Village restaurant turns out such terrific food. The Miracle Grill is a great find for devotees of the chile pepper who like their food hot, their prices moderate, and their atmosphere cool and casual. It's great fun, especially in warm weather, when you can sit out in the rambling garden in back. The place is decorated in Southwestern minimal, and the kitchen is kept open, so that patrons can watch the chef work his magic. Miracle Grill presents the hearty foods of the Southwest in a style better suited to health-conscious New Yorkers: They go easy on the butter, cheese, and salt, giving the food a clean, sharp, lighter taste. The menu is changed every six months, but the basic dishes remain similar.

Dig right in and begin with the spicy black-bean soup; go for the equally delicious quesadilla with chiles, corn, zucchini, two cheeses, and guacamole; or try the enchiladas with chicken and goat cheese. While you're sipping a Mexican beer to go along with this, consider such entrees as grilled chicken breast in a soy-and-ginger marinade, served with crispy Southwestern fries; a grilled vegetable salad with herbed goat cheese and balsamic vinaigrette, a top choice for vegetarians; or a burrito with shrimp and black beans, served with salsa verde. Dessert might be a chocolate buñuelos, deep-fried cinnamon-and-sugar tortillas, served here with two scoops of vanilla Häagen Dazs ice cream and topped with chocolate sauce. Saturday and Sunday brunch feature a wonderfully varied and exotic menu.

SUGAR REEF, 93 Second Ave. (between 5th and 6th Sts.). Tel. 47-SUGAR (477-8427), or 477-8754 for reservations.

Cuisine: JAMAICAN. **Reservations:** Recommended.

$ Prices: Appetizers $3–$6.50; main courses $9.25–$14.50. AE.

Open: Dinner only, Mon–Thurs 5–11:45pm; Fri 5pm–1am; Sat 3pm–1am; Sun 3–11:45pm. **Subway:** 6 to Astor Place. Walk three blocks east, two blocks south.

The food and the mood both sizzle at Sugar Reef, which is as invigorating as a quick trip to Jamaica. Loud, lively, crowded, Sugar Reef sports a bar whose base is made of multicolored steel drums and lots of fake bananas and birds to accompany the vibrant island music. The food is wonderful for those who like it hot.

Corn fritters, coconut shrimp, and mango pepperpot are among the tasty appetizers. Favorite main dishes include curried chicken and coconut with pumpkin rice and smothered cabbage; shrimp-and-conch brochette; and classic ropa viega (a Latin-style pot roast stewed and then shredded, with tostones, black beans, and rice). Vegetarians might have the vegetable roti (curried vegetables wrapped in roti bread, with peas, rice, and cucumber salad). For an unusual side dish, try island yams, mashed with rum, butter, and coconut milk; for dessert, have the sweet plantain tart served warm with coconut ice cream. Jamaican ginger beer goes well with a meal like this, and café con leche would be a good finale.

TELEPHONE BAR & GRILL, 149 Second Ave., between 9th and 10th Sts. Tel. 529-5000.

Cuisine: ENGLISH. **Reservations:** Recommended for parties of six or more.

$ Prices: Appetizers $4–$7; main courses $7–$15; Sun brunch $6–$12. AE, MC, V.

Open: Sun–Thur 11:30am–2am; Fri–Sat 11:30am–4am. Brunch, Sun 11:30am–4pm. **Bus:** Any Second Ave. bus.

You'll recognize Telephone by the row of authentic shiny red British phone booths imported from Plymouth, England, out front. Within, there's an atmosphere of cozy elegance; exposed-brick walls adorned with whimsical murals, fleur-de-lis-topped columns, stained-glass windows, and a handsome marble-and-cherrywood bar. The back room features a bibliothèque decor, complete with fireplace. And in good weather you can also dine at café tables out front on Second Avenue.

Telephone is often the scene of publishing and celebrity parties, but it's more than just another chic party venue. The food is great, portions are enormous, and prices are extremely moderate—most items are under $10. In line with the English theme, items like shepherd's pie and fish and chips are featured—along with appetizers such as Scotch eggs and Stilton cheese fritters. However, there are also scrumptious salads (try the Waldorf goat-cheese salad with green-apple slices and walnuts), and hearty fare such as half roast chicken with challah-apple stuffing, served with freshly made mashed potatoes and sweet-and-sour red cabbage. You can get great soups and burgers here, too. Salads, sandwiches, and under-$6 entrees are featured at lunch. The desserts range from ultrarich chocolate cake topped with raspberry sauce to English trifle. And, on Sunday, a brunch menu proffers everything from a bagel/salmon/cream cheese platter to scrambled eggs with kippers, bacon, or bangers (sausages).

LOWER EAST SIDE

EXPENSIVE

SAMMY'S FAMOUS ROUMANIAN STEAK HOUSE, 157 Chrystie St., north of Delancey. Tel. 673-0330.

Cuisine: JEWISH/ROUMANIAN. **Reservations:** Recommended.

$ Prices: Appetizers $3.95–$9.95; main courses $10.95–$28.95. AE, DC, MC, V.

Open: Daily 4pm–midnight ("Jewish time"—maybe a little earlier, maybe a little later). **Closed:** Yom Kippur. **Subway:** D to Grand St. Walk two blocks north.

✪ You don't have to be Jewish to love Sammy's, but it sure helps. Who else could understand the zany humor of the emcee or appreciate the food fragrant with garlic and chicken fat or the *freiliche* atmosphere that reminds you of your cousin Irving's noisy, long-forgotten Bar Mitzvah? Surprisingly, however, many of Sammy's most devoted patrons are not Jewish. "Do you have to be Japanese to like Japanese food?" asks owner Stanley (there is no Sammy) Zimmerman. "People come because they love the food and the friendliness, and they know they can relax here."

Sammy's is a one-of-a-kind restaurant, a happening, a seven-nights-a-week show for which no tickets are required, as heartwarming as it is sometimes heartburning. Stanley knows everybody; many of New York's top politicians dine here regularly. The decor is wall-to-wall people, especially on weekends. Don't come to Sammy's for a quiet, sedate evening. Come for a party and bring all your relatives.

Oh, yes, the food. It's Jewish style without being kosher, and Roumanian—this refers mostly to such dishes as a very flavorful Roumanian tenderloin, mush steak (the eye of the rib), and a sausage called karnatzlack—for garlic eaters only. Sammy's eggplant salad with fresh green peppers is authentic and delicious. As soon as you sit down, a bottle of seltzer and huge bowls of sour pickles, sour tomatoes, and roasted peppers are brought to your table along with assorted breads, including challah. You could happily make a meal on the appetizers alone—chopped liver, grated radish and chopped onions with chicken fat, broiled chicken livers, and unborn eggs—all rich, greasy, and unforgettable. A bottle of chicken fat is put on the table, just in case you like it greasier.

Main dishes might include flanken with mushroom-barley gravy, stuffed cabbage, broiled veal chops (excellent!), or Roumanian tenderloins. Side dishes are memorable: mashed potatoes with grieven and schmalz, potato latkes with applesauce, and kasha varnishkes. What's for dessert? You really don't need it after all this. They'll replace your bottle of seltzer and bring out a bottle of Fox's U-Bet Chocolate Syrup, plus a container of milk; you mix your own egg creams at the table.

Now you can sit back and enjoy the entertainment. Tuvia Zimmer, a joke-cracking Israeli musician is at the piano on Wednesday to Sunday ("Your stomach isn't feeling so hot? Take two egg creams and call me in the morning"); on Friday, Saturday, and Sunday he is joined by a soprano and tenor from the New York City Opera. And on Monday and Tuesday, when the mood is much quieter, Reuben Levine plays the violin.

BUDGET

LUDLOW STREET CAFE, 165 Ludlow St., between E. Houston and Stanton Sts. Tel. 353-0536.
  Cuisine: AMERICAN. **Reservations:** Not required.
$ Prices: Appetizers, $1.50–$5.75; main courses $5.75–$8.75.
  Open: Mon–Fri 6pm–midnight, Fri–Sat 6pm–8am. Brunch, Fri–Sat 11am–4pm. **Subway:** F to Second Ave. Exit right, walk two blocks east and ½ block south.

A funky sanctuary from uptown stuffiness, this quintessential downtown fixture offers hearty pastas, chicken dishes, sandwiches, and burgers to a black-clad clientele in a warm, wood-paneled dining room/bar. Add live music from around 10pm each evening (regularly featuring local favorites The Niagaras) and you've got a very New York night on the town. One of the pioneers behind the recent Lower East Side revival, Ludlow Street Café also offers a $7.95 brunch that merits a special trip to this slightly outré block—choices include huevos rancheros, yapingachos (a traditional Ecuadoran breakfast of fried eggs, potatoes, and spicy peanut sauce), and frittatas (the best in town, says the *New York Times*). A mimosa or champagne costs an extra dollar.

RATNER'S, 138 Delancey St., between Norfolk and Suffolk Sts. Tel. 677-5588.
    Cuisine: JEWISH DAIRY. **Reservations:** Not required.
$ **Prices:** Appetizers $4–$6; main courses $8–$16. AE, MC, V.
    Open: Sun–Thurs 6am–midnight; Friday 6am–3pm; Sat nights after sundown. **Subway:** F to Delancey St.

Should you find yourself downtown, bargain hunting on the Lower East Side (an activity we heartily recommend), you can have a great dairy-vegetarian-fish meal at Ratner's. The prices are moderate— most items are $7 to $12—and the food is fresh and delicious. Don't miss the pastries!

7. CHELSEA

Once a staid industrial/commercial neighborhood, east Chelsea (otherwise known as the Flatiron District, 14th through 28th streets from Fifth to Seventh avenues) has evolved into a 1990s Restaurant Row, with some of the liveliest, loveliest spots in town. Many of the buildings used to house warehouses (and still do), so restaurants have taken advantage of loftlike, airy spaces to create one-of-a-kind rooms. In addition to those below, I recommend the bright, busy **Cal's,** 55 W. 21st St., (tel. 929-0740), perpetually packed with publishing, modeling, and ad folk; unlike most New York restaurants, there's actually breathing room between tables. From a late-1980s scene, **Le Madri,** 168 W. 18th St. (tel. 727-8022), has evolved into a full-fledged institution where the thin and rich crowd roosts for earthy Northern Italian cuisine. Tables here are a rare commodity, so reservations are recommended. The same is true at **Mesa Grill,** 102 Fifth Ave. (tel. 807-7400), which is still hot as a jalapeño for chef Bobby Flay's nouvelle Mexican creations and a whimsical Southwest/surrealist decor.

Farther west, Seventh, Eighth, and Ninth avenues boast a dazzling range of cuisines for a gamut of budgets. My favorites include **Cola's,** 148 Eighth Ave. (tel. 633-8020), a smart little trattoria beloved by locals for creative, inexpensive pasta dishes; **Eighteenth & Eighth,** 159 Eighth Ave. (tel. 242-5000), a sort of upscale coffee shop whose young regulars don't seem to mind waiting in line for fresh, inexpensive American food; **Meriken,** 189 Seventh Ave. (tel. 260-9684), arguably New York's hippest sushi joint, whose front door boasts a strobe-lit Statue of Liberty crown; **Artie's Warehouse,** 539 W. 21st St. (tel. 989-9500), a loud, lively steakhouse sequestered on an otherwise-desolate block near the West Side Highway; **Bright Food Shop,** 216 Eighth Ave. (tel. 243-4433), a kitschy converted diner that cross-breeds Chinese and Mexican cuisines on an imaginative, well-priced menu; and the stalwart **Man Ray,** 169 Eighth Ave. (tel. 627-4220), still trendy after all these years, whose deco-from-another-planet decor and French-accented food draw hipsters from all over the city.

EXPENSIVE

LOLA, 30 West 22nd St. Tel. 675-6700.

Cuisine: AMERICAN/CARIBBEAN. **Reservations:** Necessary two weeks in advance for Gospel Brunch; strongly recommended at all times.

$ Prices: Appetizers $7–$9.50; main courses $18.50–$24. Prix-fixe "Express Lunch" $10. AE, MC, V.

Open: Lunch, Mon–Fri noon–3pm. Dinner, Mon–Thurs 6pm–midnight. Sun Gospel Brunch, two performances: June, July, Aug at noon and 2pm; at all other times at 1 and 3pm, with seating ½ hour before the show. Sun Gospel Supper seatings at 6 and 7pm, show at 7:30pm. No Sat lunch. **Subway:** 1 to 23rd St.

This chic gathering spot is frequented by a smart young crowd who work or play nearby. The long, narrow room with a lively bar up front opens into a spacious, modernistic dining room with mirrors, huge vases of flowers, and tasteful prints of old New York gracing the walls. The menu is an eclectic wonder—a bit of the West Indies, a fillip of Asian, a swirl of Mexican, a helping of American, some European, a dash of Mediterranean, and Italian preparations as well; everything is imaginative. There's a different menu almost every day, plus daily specials of a featured wine (usually $4.50 a glass) and featured small and large plates.

Among chef Lynne Aronson's signature dishes are first courses such as fiery cayenne ribbon onion rings, luscious jumbo lump crab cake in lime oil, and warm wild-mushroom salad on baby greens with a lusty mushroom vinaigrette. Second courses include Lola's celebrated 100-spice Caribbean fried chicken, satisfying spicy short ribs, and elegant striped bass and sea scallops with leeks and roasted pepper rouille. Fasten your seatbelts for dessert; deep-chocolate-and–peanut-truffle cake with caramel buttercream and whipped cream is a descent into decadence.

If you visit Lola on Monday or Tuesday at around 7:30pm, and other evenings around 8:30, you may hear live jazz, calypso, Motown, and gospel trills. A frequent attraction is the Spirit Ensemble, an Afro-Caribbean band, complete with steel drums, other island instruments, and original compositions. Noted gospel singer Maryel Epps is usually on hand at the spirited Sunday Gospel Brunch.

PRIX FIXE, 18 West 18th St. Tel. 675-6777.

Cuisine: CONTINENTAL. **Reservations:** Suggested for parties of 5 or more.

$ Prices: Prix-fixe dinner $21 or $36; prix-fixe lunch $13.50 or $18.50; $15 for selections from the chef's table; Sun brunch $18.50. AE, DC, MC, V.

Open: Lunch, Mon–Fri 11:30–3:30. Dinner, Mon–Thurs 5:30–11:30; Fri–Sat 5pm–12:30am; Sun 5–10:30pm. Brunch, Sun 11:30am–5pm. No brunch July 1–Labor Day. **Subway:** 1 to 18th St.

It could be the sweeping lobby of a fin-de-siècle European hotel.

Glide into the cavernous interior through a mahogany-and-glass revolving door to behold a pair of dazzling, vintage 1920s chandeliers. Mosaic accents throughout call to mind an ancient Roman bath. Handsome faux marbre columns mingle with bits of neoclassical splendor sprinkled throughout—a Greek Revival bust and clamshell-ensconced cherubim draped in faux pearls. There's also a rotating exhibit of paintings by neighborhood artists, and at the bar, a seemingly ever-present assortment of fashionable, leggy young women accompanied by their pony-tailed escorts.

The price of your prix-fixe meal brings you an appetizer, an entree, and a dessert. Chef-partner Terance Brennan's fare, which changes with the seasons, is rich and imaginative, whether you choose the $21 or $36 meal. At the $21 level, you might start your dinner with warm terrine of goat cheese and artichoke, paired with a salad of new potatoes and asparagus, followed by an entree like tournedos of Atlantic salmon with salmon caviar in a horseradish sauce. At the $36 level, you could begin with appetizers such as New York State duck foie gras "au poivre" with cinnamon and sweet-and-sour rhubarb, and your main course could be the grilled loin of lamb with tarragon spaetzel, young spinach, and mustard broth; or a daily rotating soft-shell crab preparation. It's easy to succumb to such dessert treats as warm chocolate banana burst with candied pecan ice cream, risotto pudding with dried cherries and burnt sugar, and rhubarb consommé with Mascarpone mousse and strawberries.

Lunch offers similar selections, and Sunday Brunch is especially wonderful—apple griddle cakes with homemade sausage; French toast with stewed fruits, nuts, and ginger; and the seven-spice bourbon cake with fig–and–juniper-berry ice cream.

EXPENSIVE TO MODERATE

EMPIRE DINER, 210 Tenth Ave., at 22nd St. Tel. 243-2736.

  Cuisine: AMERICAN. **Reservations:** Not required.

$ Prices: Appetizers $2.95–$5.95; main courses $8.50–$14.95. Weekend brunch $9.50. AE, MC, V.

  Open: 24 hrs. **Subway:** E or C to 23rd St.; walk two blocks west, one block south.

This gleaming art deco diner is one of New York's liveliest after-hours scenes. From nearby nightclubs and bars, patrons stroll in wearing anything from black tie to black leather. In warm-weather months, the spectacle spills onto the sidewalk as well. If the crowd seems trendy, the food isn't, relying on basics like a generous home-roasted turkey platter, stir-fried vegetables, a vegetarian lentil burger, and overstuffed sandwiches. Brunch here includes fresh juice, one drink, and coffee, plus wonderful omelets, or bagels and lox, or French toast dipped in egg and vanilla ice cream. There's live piano every night, though it's sometimes inaudible over the din; when he first came to New York, a very young Harry Connick, Jr., found work as their piano player.

LUMA, 200 Ninth Ave., between 22nd and 23rd Sts. Tel. 633-8033.

  Cuisine: GOURMET NATURAL FOODS. **Reservations:** Recommended.

$ Prices: Appetizers $8–$11; main courses $13–$21. CB, DC, MC, V.

Open: Dinner only, Mon–Sat 5:30–11pm; Sun 5–10pm. **Subway:** A to 23rd St.

People come from all over to sample the "healthful elegant dining" here, including many celebrities. Luma uses organic ingredients whenever possible; avoids dairy, sugar, and eggs; and maintains a strict no-smoking policy. There is no bar, but wine and beer are served. Start with soup of the day or any one of their unusual salads for a first course: Tot soi (a Chinese vegetable somewhere in between bok choy and mustard greens), for example, is served with roasted wild forest mushrooms and white miso dressing. Grilled polenta with chargrilled tomato and pesto is a popular special among the appetizers, and so is the penne with sautéed wild mushrooms. For an entree, you might try grilled blackfish with quinoa-couscous tabouli, early summer vegetables and a toasted cumin-seed lime vinaigrette, or roasted free-range chicken with artichoke/sweet-potato hash. And for vegetarians, sautéed tempeh scallopine with mustard-lemon dill sauce is a nice choice. Desserts substitute organic maple syrup and rice syrup for sugar, and the improvement in taste is notable: Don't miss their Chocolate Devastation, a tender, dark-chocolate mousse cake with a puddle of bittersweet chocolate sauce. Blueberry/peach crumb pie with a maple-pecan crumb topping is excellent as well.

PERIYALI, 35 W. 20th St., between Fifth and Sixth Aves. Tel. 463-7890.

Cuisine: GREEK. **Reservations:** Recommended.

$ Prices: Appetizers $5–$10; main courses $15–$21. AE, DC, MC, V.

Open: Lunch, Mon–Fri noon–3pm. Dinner, Mon–Sat 5:30–11pm. **Subway:** B to 23rd St.

Here you can enjoy Greek "home-cooking" in a charming Mediterranean setting, with burnished red-oak floors, a billowed fabric ceiling (to help minimize noise), banquettes, and whitewashed walls hung with antique wooden cooking utensils. Exotic plants and cut flowers complete the soothing interior, and an outdoor garden is available in summer. Chef Charles Bowman, a graduate of the Culinary Institute of America, worked at La Côte Basque and the River Café before taking command of Periyali's kitchen in 1987.

For starters, try pikantikes salates, a tangy vegetable assortment. Also excellent are the white beans in garlicky vinaigrette and the rich broiled goat cheese garnished with arugula and tomato (very filling, so be prepared!). The simple roast shoulder of lamb with a sauce of egg yolk and lemon is a delicious entree, as is an exceptionally light moussaka. Daily specials always include one or two seafood choices not on the menu, so be sure to ask your waiter. (Service at Periyali is always cheerful and efficient.) The wine list, reasonably priced, features a full page of regional Greek wines as well as the usual international selections. The extraordinary desserts are baked on the premises: Classical baklava, here made with toasted almonds rather than walnuts, is a delight, as is an uncommonly moist lemon cake.

Periyali is dynamic and original—an altogether tasteful restaurant in the heart of Chelsea. A visit here is as refreshing as one to the seashore (the translation of *periyali*).

ROGERS & BARBERO, 149 Eighth Ave., between 17th and 18th Sts. Tel. 243-2020.

Cuisine: AMERICAN. **Reservations:** Recommended.

$ Prices: Appetizers $4.50–$7; main courses $9–$15.50; prix-fixe menu $13.95 dinner, $10.50 lunch. AE, MC, V.
Open: Lunch, Mon–Fri noon–5:30pm. Dinner, daily 5:30pm–midnight. Brunch, Sat–Sun noon–4pm. **Subway:** C or E to 23rd St.

Rogers & Barbero continues to win bravos from the food establishment as well as from neighborhood people and theater-goers en route to the nearby Joyce Theater. Tables are well spaced for conversation in the lovely pale-yellow art deco dining room. The menu changes seasonally, but most likely you'll be able to try such dishes as ravioli filled with spring vegetables among the pastas and roast chicken and chicken-leg confit with savoy cabbage or mahimahi with a salsa of black olives and tomato among the meat and fish selections. The grilled vegetables and the salami, white bean, and fennel salad are popular appetizers. The prix-fixe menu—appetizer, entree, dessert, and coffee—is a very good deal. For lunch, you can have anything from a chicken club sandwich to fresh fish from $6.45 to $10.50.

8. GRAMERCY PARK/ MURRAY HILL

EXPENSIVE

AN AMERICAN PLACE, 2 Park Ave., entrance on 32nd St. Tel. 684-2122.
Cuisine: AMERICAN. **Reservations:** Recommended.
$ Prices: Appetizers $7.50–$12.50; main courses $15–$25. AE, CB, DC, MC, V.
Open: Lunch, Mon–Fri 11:45am–3pm. Dinner, Mon–Sat 5:45–10pm. **Subway:** 6 to 33rd St.

An American Place is just that: a totally unusual, totally American, and quite extraordinary restaurant. The menu changes seasonally but always features traditional American recipes reinterpreted for lighter, more modern sensibilities.

The huge, high-ceilinged room, furnished in postmodern style, boasts Frank Stella paintings. But the decor has been kept purposely neutral to bring the focus onto the diners and the food. Unusual appetizers get dinner off to a lively start—perhaps grilled peanut barbecued Gulf shrimp or Maine lobster and wild-mushroom ravioli. Next come such entrees as charred Black Angus steak filet with Iowa blue cheese, potato gratin, and roast shallot sauce; crisp Adirondack free-range duck glazed with wildflower honey and accompanied by roast garlic-whipped potatoes; or cedar-planked Atlantic salmon served with a soft corn pudding, morels, and wild-leek vinaigrette. The desserts are heartwarming old favorites like fresh berry shortcake, homemade peanut-butter ice-cream sandwich; and warm bread pudding with bourbon sauce. Special lunch features are the old-fashioned Hollywood Brown Derby Cobb salad (diced chicken breast, avocado, egg, bacon, tomato, and more, all in a "derby dressing") and a crispy buffalo-style chicken salad with blue-cheese dressing.

CHEFS CUISINIERS CLUB, 36 East 22nd St. Tel. 228-4399.

Cuisine: AMERICAN. **Reservations:** Recommended.

$ Prices: Appetizers $6–$7; main dishes $15–$20. AE, MC, V. **Open:** Lunch, Mon–Fri noon–2:30. Dinner, Sun 5:30–10:30pm; Mon–Wed 5:30–midnight; Thurs–Sat 5:30pm–2am. **Subway:** 6 to 33rd St.

✪ Opened by four top New York chefs who conceived it as a place for their colleagues—and themselves—to hobnob after hours, the Chefs Cuisiniers Club (known in the trade as the "Triple C") bustles most of the time, as well it should. The ambiance is convivial, the service friendly and intelligent, and the food absolutely superb. If you dine late, you can discreetly ogle the celebrity chefs who really do stop by.

Civilian diners here are also truly knowledgeable about the fine points of cuisine, and there are often lively debates going on between the tables as guests try to identify the fresh herbs and spices combined with mastery by chef Peter Assue. Join in if you like—the friendly and casual atmosphere invites cross-talk, and you'll doubtless come away having learned something new.

Appetizers are expansive and well-priced; many are big enough for two or even more, like the plate of calamari with citrus mayonnaise and the generous tasting plate of baba ghanoush, hummus, and tabbouleh, with pita wedges. Main courses are sublime. Charcoal-grilled salmon, smothered in luscious preserved tomatoes and smooth-as-silk new potatoes mashed with olive oil is extraordinary. Lemon-grilled chicken with potato dumplings, sweet garlic, and tomato; pork tenderloin; and poached mussels marinière should please the most discriminating palates. Lunch offers similar entrees, plus some imaginative salads and sandwiches.

Although portions are so generous that it would be more than easy to pass up dessert, under no circumstances should you do that. Oversized double-chocolate walnut cookies (at $1 each the best bargain in New York City) are sinfully good. All other desserts are $5. Pear-and-almond tart with essence of raspberries and cream is indescribably delicious. Do not miss!

LA COLOMBE D'OR, 134 East 26th St. Tel. 689-0666.

Cuisine: FRENCH/PROVENÇAL. **Reservations:** Recommended.

$ Prices: Appetizers $5.75–$11.50; main courses $16.50–$22.50. AE, DC, MC, JCB, V. **Open:** Lunch, Mon–Fri noon–2:30pm. Dinner, Mon–Sat 6–11pm; Sun 5:30–9:30pm. **Subway:** N or R to 28th St.

Even a brief visit to Provence does wonders for the palate and spirit, and a trip to La Colombe d'Or is the next best thing. The handsome restaurant, rated two stars by the *New York Times,* which *Glamour* magazine has called "the most romantic restaurant in New York," is Provençal all the way—from the traditional print fabric used for chairs, banquettes, and waitresses' aprons to the ratatouille and soupe de poisson on the menu. The foods of southern France are marked by an imaginative use of garlic and tomatoes, and, of course, seafood is a highlight. Provence is the home of bouillabaisse, and La Colombe d'Or's version, available at both lunch and dinner, does not disappoint. You might start here with ratatouille or a green salad with roasted peppers and goat cheese. Soups are so filling that only the biggest eaters should start with one of these. Entrees include a hearty winter cassoulet, grilled breast of duck, monkfish sautéed with tomatoes and fresh herbs, and grilled spring lamb chops with rosemary potatoes. A tempting dessert cart offers a luscious array of homemade pastries. Lunch offers similar dishes in a slightly lower price range.

UNION SQUARE CAFE, 21 East 16th St. Tel. 243-4020.
   Cuisine: INTERNATIONAL. **Reservations:** Required at least a week in advance at dinner; accepted up to a month in advance. Parties of eight are the maximum.
$ Prices: Appetizers $5.95–$9.50; main courses $16.50–$24.
   Open: Lunch, Mon–Sat noon–2:30pm. Dinner, Mon–Thurs 6–10:30pm; Fri–Sat 6–11:30pm; Sun 5:30–10pm. **Subway:** 1, 2, 3, or 9 to 14th St.

Union Square Café is hot!—so much so that the house will accept your reservations up to a month in advance, and they keep a waiting list. For lunch, a day ahead is usually enough, so maybe that's when you'll come down to sample the exuberant French and mostly northern Italian fare that has won this place three coveted stars from the *New York Times*. In the six years since genial owner Danny Meyer opened his doors, nearby publishing and ad people, Village painters and writers, and a chic crowd have become regulars. Everyone gets a warm welcome, and the food just keeps getting better all the time.

The decor is warm, country-style, and not at all fancy. The attractive young staff in their button-down shirts and aprons have been thoroughly trained, so they can really be of assistance—and they move fast. Appetizers are the same at lunch and dinner: Try the grilled crostini with a mousse of sage and chicken livers, and the fried calamari to dip in anchovy mayonnaise. For a main dish at lunch, how about a hearty quail stew with cranberry beans? Or herb roasted chicken with tomato-mashed potatoes? You could happily make lunch just on some of the side dishes ($2.95 to $4.95), like the irresistible hot garlic potato chips, the mashed turnips with crispy shallots, or the bruschetta (garlic-rubbed grilled sourdough with tomatoes, basil, and olive oil). Dinner presents such main courses as sautéed salmon filet with black-peppercorn sauce; seared sea scallops with scallion three-grain rice, and crisp-roasted lemon-pepper duck with honey-baked pear and spinach flan. Daily specials change with the seasons: With luck, you might get to try the roast suckling pig on Wednesday or the lusty fisherman's mixed grill on Friday. Desserts are stellar, especially the homemade maha-caramel tartuffo and the warm banana tart topped with vanilla ice cream and macadamia-nut brittle. The wine list is one of the best in New York, with prices beginning at $17 per bottle.

Smoking is permitted only at the bar.

EXPENSIVE TO MODERATE

EL PARADOR, 325 East 34th St., between First and Second Aves. Tel. 679-6812.
   Cuisine: MEXICAN. **Reservations:** Not accepted.
$ Prices: Appetizers $3–$9; main courses $9.50–$20.75. AE, CB, DC, MC, V.
   Open: Daily noon–11pm. **Subway:** 6 to 33rd St.

There's no need to fly to Mexico City for a great meal—the

aficionados consider El Parador on a level with the best anywhere. It's done in a Mexican colonial motif, but it's so jammed with people that you probably won't notice the decor; be prepared to wait in line on weekends unless you arrive early—between 5 and 7pm. But you *will* notice the food: It's excellent. You'll find the old Mexican standbys, as well as fancier dishes, like the superb pollo Parador (one of the three Spanish dishes on the menu, steamed with onions and heady with garlic), mole poblano (chicken in a spicy chocolate sauce), chicken fajitas (marinated and charcoal-broiled strips), and camarónes en salsa tomatilla (shrimp in a mild green-tomato sauce). The appetizers are almost as good as the main dishes: You'll find it hard to choose between the guacamole, the ceviche (whitefish marinated in lime juice), and the nachos. The classic Mexican and Spanish desserts, flan and natilla, are here, as well as mango and guava shell preserves. And, of course, you'll want a cooling pitcher of sangría or some Carta Blanca, Negra Modelo, or Dos Equis, imported Mexican cervezas, to go with the hot and spicy delicacies.

EL RIO GRANDE, 160 East 38th St., at Third Ave. Tel. 867-0922.
   Cuisine: TEX-MEX. **Reservations:** Recommended.
$ Prices: Appetizers $4.25–$11.95; main courses $7.95–$19.95. AE, CB, DC, MC, V.
   Open: Sun–Thurs noon–midnight; Fri–Sat noon–1am. **Subway:** 6 to 33rd St.

To get from Texas to Mexico, simply cross the Rio Grande. That's accomplished very easily at this spot, where two separate restaurants sharing one kitchen have been ingeniously converted into a Tex-Mex eatery divided by the Rio Grande (otherwise known as the kitchen). And while both sides share the same menu, each reflects its own theme in decor.

   And the food! It's certainly some of the best and most original Tex-Mex in town. For a mouth-watering (and sinus-clearing) appetizer try the deep-fried jalapeño peppers, stuffed with jumbo shrimp and Monterey Jack cheese, then served with a much appreciated dollop of sour cream, or try the quesos fundidos, a melted cheese casserole with vegetables and chicken or seafood, served with a flour tortilla. The fajita asada, traditional Mexican steak charbroiled and topped with grilled onion, that I had was cooked to perfection, as was the grilled swordfish. Sopapillas, deep-fried pastry puffs dusted with powdered sugar and cinnamon, make a nice finish.

BUDGET

FIORE, 4 Park Ave., at 33rd St. Tel. 686-0226.
   Cuisine: ITALIAN. **Reservations:** Not accepted.
$ Prices: Appetizers $3.50–$6.50; main courses $8.50–$12.95. Early Bird special dinner (4–7pm), $13.95. AE, MC, V.
   Open: Mon–Fri 11:30am–11pm. **Subway:** 6 to 33rd St.

What a find Fiore is! The smart, stylish midtown watering hole is perfect when you're out shopping or sightseeing (it's two blocks from the Empire State Building), and it's near many midtown hotels. The large room, with its vaulted ceilings and wide columns, was once the rathskeller of the old Hotel Vanderbilt. It has a subterranean feeling—in fact, in an earlier incarnation, it was actually a subway station! Now it's an attractive restaurant with a large bar and tables nicely spaced for conversation and comfort. The modestly priced menu is the same at lunch and dinner.

Among the appetizers, popcorn shrimp and grilled sausage with roasted peppers are both very good. The delicious pizza with sun-dried tomatoes, smoked mozzarella, and fresh basil is easily a complete meal. Of the pastas, the most popular is the angel hair with shrimp in a pesto-cream sauce; another excellent one is penne with broccoli, sun-dried tomatoes, and pignola nuts. Recommended entrees include the fish of the day (I sampled a succulent grilled salmon) and the grilled boneless breast of chicken, coated with a marinade of cracked pepper and mustard. The desserts are marvelous: especially the Mississippi mud pie (triple-dense chocolate), gelato, and apple Brown Betty.

9. MIDTOWN WEST

EXPENSIVE

AQUAVIT, 13 West 54th St., just off Fifth Ave. Tel. 307-7311.

Cuisine: SCANDINAVIAN. **Reservations:** Not accepted in café at lunch; recommended for downstairs dining room.

$ Prices: Café: Appetizers $7–$16.50; main courses $13.50–$18.50; two-course pretheater dinner $19. Dining room: prix-fixe lunch $36; prix-fixe dinner $60; three-course pretheater dinner $39. AE, DC, MC, V.

Open: Dining room: Lunch, Mon–Fri noon–2:30pm. Dinner, Mon–Sat 5:30–10:30pm. Café: Lunch, Mon–Fri noon–3pm. Dinner, Mon–Sat 5:30–10:30pm. **Bus:** Any Fifth Ave. bus to 54th St.

Scandinavian restaurants are a rare commodity in New York, so a hardy *Skål!* or two is definitely in order for Aquavit, handsomely ensconced in the former town house of John D. Rockefeller. The ground floor houses a long, sleek bar and café where a huge cooler dispenses eight flavors of aquavit, that potent vodkalike distillate flavored with fruit or spices and served ice cold. The luxurious downstairs dining room is a marvel of contemporary Scandinavian decor—cool and serene, with a glassed-in atrium, birch trees, and a real waterfall.

In the upstairs café, a homecooked meal might include open-faced Danish sandwiches or peel-and-eat Scandinavian shrimp with lemon mayonnaise and caviar sauce. The sensational smörgåsbord plate includes several herrings treated to sauces of caviar, cream, or wine vinegar; home-cured gravlax; and liver pâté.

In the downstairs atrium dining room, menus are prix fixe, and a few dishes carry supplements. To start, consider the traditional gravlax in mustard sauce and dill and wash it down with a shot of mixed-berry aquavit (essential!). Try the blini: Swedish buckwheat pancakes garnished with trout roe, crème fraîche, and onions. Also sample the superb, thinly sliced loin of Arctic venison with diced apples, mushrooms, Swedish lingonberries, and carrot purée. At least three different salmon dishes are available each day, all of them imaginatively prepared and beautifully presented.

Leave room for dessert—a creamy chocolate cake with burnt-almond crust and raspberry sauce or homemade brambleberry sorbet in a baked almond shell shaped like a crown and dripping with fresh vanilla sauce. If the "Grand Dessert" is available, by all means order it for a divine sampling of most of the desserts on the menu. Wines are expensive: Most range from $30 to $60.

Aquavit's take-out counter also sells the restaurant's own seafood, caviar, salads, and sandwiches.

GALLAGHER'S STEAK HOUSE, 228 West 52nd St. Tel. 245-5336.
Cuisine: AMERICAN/STEAKS/SEAFOOD. **Reservations:** Recommended.
$ Prices: Appetizers $4.25–$10.95; main courses $14.95–$29.75. AE, DC, DISC, MC, JCB, V.
Open: Daily noon–midnight. **Subway:** 1 or 9 to 50th St.

Gallagher's is this country's first steak house. Opened on the same spot in 1927, it has been world famous ever since for great American food served in huge, old-fashioned portions. The wood-paneled walls are covered with pictures of sports and theatrical celebrities, and it's quite likely that you'll catch a glimpse of a few of them, since many of the stars of Broadway shows eat here. Shirley MacLaine, Warren Beatty, Dolly Parton, Jackie Mason, and Stephen Sondheim are all familiar customers. Gallagher's is in the heart of the theater district, and the dress code is formal *or* informal—comfortable.

Look right into the front window and see $75,000 worth of beef aging here in the cooler, resulting in steaks of outstanding flavor and texture.

Some people swear by the incredible roast beef or lamb chops, while others flock here for the freshest fish, shellfish, and giant Maine lobsters. For an appetizer, it's hard to choose between the unique oxtail soup, supreme oysters, or extraordinary spinach salad. But do save room for dessert: American hot apple pie with an enormous scoop of ice cream atop, the best rice pudding anywhere, or sinful chocolate-mousse cake. There are an excellent wine list and excellent service. No wonder Gallagher's has lasted since 1927.

LE BERNARDIN, 155 West 51st St., between Sixth and Seventh Aves. Tel. 489-1515.
Cuisine: FRENCH/SEAFOOD. **Reservations:** Required far in advance.
$ Prices: Prix-fixe lunch $42; prix-fixe dinner $68. AE, DC, MC, V.
Open: Lunch, Mon–Sat noon–2:15pm. Dinner, Mon–Thurs 6–10:15pm; Fri–Sat 5:30–11pm. **Closed:** No lunch June–Sept.
Subway: 1 or 9 to 50th St.

Some say it's the best seafood restaurant in the country. I agree that it's certainly among the best in New York. Since its opening six years back, Le Bernardin has won rhapsodic praise from critics and the sophisticated international set alike. This four-star brainchild of brother and sister Gilbert and Maguy Le Coze, who come from a long line of Breton restaurateurs, serves fish and seafood exclusively, all of it prepared with dazzling flair and presented with low-keyed but impeccable style. Posh, expensive, and very French but distinctly New York (waiters are bilingual, menus are in English), Le Bernardin is so popular that tables are booked months in advance—be forewarned.

Don't be fooled by the sterile facade of the Equitable Assurance Tower that houses the restaurant. Enter through the cozy cocktail lounge to the spacious dining room, where the decor is elegant but decidedly "clubby." Your prix-fixe meal automatically begins with a heavenly sampling of seafood canapés, accompanied by the crustiest French rolls this side of the Atlantic. Next, order an appetizer of sparkling carpaccio of tuna: thin, flat slices of the raw fish served in gingered mayonnaise. The Le Cozes have a mania for freshness, scavenging the markets at 3am to select their catch, so menu items vary slightly from day to day. By all means, try the famous fricassée of shellfish, lightly done in cream, white wine, and shallots, or the jumbo Louisiana shrimp rolled in pepper and sautéed in sherry vinegar, olive oil, and thyme. Sautéed red snapper is delicious in basil-perfumed olive oil, and roasted monkfish arrives layered onto Savoie cabbage. Among the desserts, the "Caramel Variation," which includes a floating island, caramel ice cream in a pastry shell, caramel mousse, and crème caramel, is pure inspiration. A tall stand of petit fours is offered to crown a truly royal meal.

RAINBOW ROOM, on the 65th floor of 30 Rockefeller Plaza. Tel. 632-5000.

Cuisine: CONTINENTAL. **Reservations:** Required.

$ Prices: Rainbow Room: Appetizers $5–$14; main courses $26–$32. Rainbow Promenade Bar: "Little meals" $9–$12; "feasts for sharing" $25. AE.

Open: Dinner, Tues–Sat 6:30–10pm. Pre-theater fixed-price dinner Tues–Sat, seatings at 5:30 and 6pm. Supper, Tues–Sat 10:30pm to midnight. Rainbow Promenade: Sun–Thurs 3pm–12:30am, Fri 3pm–1:30am, Sat noon–2am. Sun brunch 11:30am–2pm. **Bus:** Any Fifth Ave. bus to 50th St. **Subway:** B, D, F, or Q to 47–50 Sts.

Bring your pot of gold when you visit the newly restored Rainbow Room—an evening here will be at least $100 per person. But who's counting? Here's a chance to step back into the glamorous prewar world of New York's café society, when socialites, celebrities, and star-struck lovers wined and dined at one of New York's most romantic and sophisticated supper clubs. After a two-year hiatus and a $20-million restoration, the Rainbow Room is back, restored to its original luster, and the critics agree that "S'Wonderful."

Dining at the **Rainbow Room** is in every way a theatrical experience. Wraparound views of New York from the floor-to-ceiling windows, colored lights flickering across the domed ceiling, an enormous crystal chandelier over the revolving dance floor, waiters in pastel tails, cigarette girls in outfits from the Rockefeller Center past, and silver lamé tablecloths are all part of the background. Don't come here if you're in a hurry; dinner will take several hours, the meal deliberately paced so that the women in sequined gowns and the men in black tie (not required but very evident) can merengue and rhumba and fox-trot between courses.

Dinner might begin with lobster bisque with whiskey, cake of wild mushrooms with herb sauce, or—appropriately—oysters Rockefeller. Well recommended among the entrees are the lobster Thermidor, the roast rack of lamb for two, and the crispy roasted squab with pancetta and apples. For dessert, go all out and order the Baked Alaska—flamed at your table—if you can bear to pass up the frozen praline soufflé with its rich hot-chocolate sauce. The pretheater dinner offers good value at $38.50, and after 10:30pm, you can have a stylish supper for slightly less than dinner prices.

If you don't spend an evening at the Rainbow Room, at least visit the **Rainbow Promenade.** Just a few steps from the Rainbow Room, it's a "little meals" restaurant and bar. The views are front-row center on the Statue of Liberty, the Empire State Building, the World Trade Center, and the rivers and their bridges. While you're soaking in the view, you can sip a Stork Club Cocktail or a Manhattan (both $6.50)—and treat yourself to some "little meals." They feature appetizer-size portions of fried chicken Caesar salad or lime-chicken brochettes with guacamole and tortillas.

Rainbow and Stars, the complex's intimate nightclub, features its own menu and top cabaret performers on the order of Tony Bennett, Rosemary Clooney, and Jerry Herman. (For details, see Chapter 10.)

RUSSIAN TEA ROOM, 150 West 57th St. Tel. 265-0947.

Cuisine: RUSSIAN. **Reservations:** Recommended.

$ Prices: Appetizers $6.95–$65.50 (for beluga Malossol caviar); main courses $22.75–$34.50. AE, CB, DC, MC, V.

Open: Lunch, Mon–Fri 11:30am–4:30pm. Dinner, daily 4:30–11:30pm. Brunch, Sat–Sun 11am–4:30pm. **Subway:** B, D, or E to Seventh Ave., or B, N, R, or Q to 57th St.

New York's most celebrated artistic "salon" is the venerable Russian Tea Room, located "slightly to the left of Carnegie Hall" and as famous for its loyal following of musicians, dancers, and performers as it is for its borscht, caviar, and blinis. It's an incredibly warm and cozy place, always heady with excitement (could that have been Nureyev over in the corner?) and good talk and the aroma of those marvelous Russian favorites. Here's your chance to feast on steaming bowls of borscht (perfect on a cold New York winter day), delicate blinchiki (crêpes stuffed with cottage cheese and preserves and topped with sour cream), rich beef Stroganoff, shashlik Caucasian, luli kebab (Georgian lamb sausage), or salmon Pojarsky. Desserts are special, and I often have hot tea, served steaming in a glass, and some kissel (cranberry purée) or kasha à la Gourieff (warm farina with fruit baklava). There are two complete dinners, The Kiev and The Blini with Red Caviar, each $39.75; otherwise, the menu is all à la carte.

It's fun to arrive at the Russian Tea Room about 6 in the evening to see the people who make this place so special; or you can come after the performance and join them as they reminisce, over a glass of vodka or a bowl of borscht, about the high notes or the grand jetés. Sunday is cabaret night, with shows at 8 and 10pm.

THE SEA GRILL, 19 West 49th St., at Rockefeller Plaza. Tel. 246-9201.

Cuisine: AMERICAN/CONTINENTAL. **Reservations:** Required for lunch; recommended for dinner.

$ Prices: Appetizers $8.50–$12.50; main courses $22.50–$29.50; prix-fixe dinner $35. AE, DC, MC, V.

Open: Lunch, Mon–Fri 11:30am–3pm. Dinner, Mon–Sat 5–11pm. **Closed:** Sat lunch and Sun, except during the holiday season; call to check. **Subway:** B, D, F, or Q to 47–50 Sts., or N or R to 49th St.

A spectacular domed glass elevator takes guests down to the Sea Grill,

Rockefeller Center's elegantly understated luxury restaurant. Soft seashore colors are used in its furnishings; light is captured in glass-bottom pools on the ceiling; a second pair of pools bubbles at floor level; and an outdoor glass wall is screened by thousands of bottles of wine. The dramatic setting—with a view of the sunken outdoor terrace cooled by a waterfall cascade in summer and the ice-skating rink in winter—is a perfect foil for the magical cuisine of Swiss-trained chef Seppi Regli, formerly of The Four Seasons, who wins stars-a-plenty from the New York food establishment. Among the appetizers, the Maryland crabcake and the Sea Grill chowder with lobster, shrimp, and clams are outstanding. So, too, are such entrees as tuna mignon with zucchini and pancetta, swordfish steak with white beans and tomato, and breast of free-range chicken with chargrilled vegetables. Key lime pie is a signature dessert; the hazelnut praline cake is heavenly.

Free parking for up to 7 hours at the Rockefeller Center garage is included after 5pm, a true boon to theatergoers. And the Sea Grill's three-course prix-fixe dinner, served from 5 to 6:30pm Monday to Saturday, including the parking, for $35, is worth noting.

MODERATE

AMERICAN FESTIVAL CAFE, 20 West 50th St., at Rockefeller Center. Tel. 246-6699.
   Cuisine: AMERICAN. **Reservations:** Recommended.
$ **Prices:** Appetizers $6.95–$10.95; main courses $12.95–$24.95; prix-fixe dinner $24.95; prix-fixe brunch $18.95. AE, DC, MC, V.
   Open: Mon–Fri 7:30am–midnight; Sat–Sun 9am–midnight. Brunch, Sat–Sun 10am–3:30pm. **Subway:** B, D, F, or Q to 47–50 Sts., or N or R to 49th St.

The most popular dining place for Rockefeller Center visitors is the American Festival Café, an exuberant celebration of Americana, with changing exhibits of primitive and folk art from the American Museum of Folk Art always on display. It has the largest number of tables available in the garden. And you don't have to be going to the theater to take advantage of their pretheater dinner; it's served all the way from 4 to 10pm on Monday to Saturday, and since it includes complimentary parking at the Rockefeller Center Garage, it's one of the best buys in town. You have a choice of such appetizers as Texas Gulf shrimp cocktail or Pennsylvania mushroom-and-spinach salad, and such entrees as grilled breast of chicken over rosemary-braised white beans and tomato, certified Angus sirloin steak, or rib au jus. Desserts include Key lime pie, Mississippi mud pie, and New York cheesecake. You never know what special celebration you'll find going on here—it might be the cooking of California's missions, along with a gold-medal–winning California wine list, a Baltimore crab feast, or the cooking of Florida. Regional dishes, old American favorites, and lightly cooked entrees are all featured. Breakfasts are also intriguingly (and differently) themed and in summer, out in the garden, offer a wonderful way to begin a day in New York for under $10.

A special section of the restaurant is called the Bar-Carvery, where trenchermen can fill up on sandwiches or platters of handcarved meat.

B. SMITH'S, 771 Eighth Ave., at 47th St. Tel. 247-2222.

Cuisine: CARIBBEAN. **Reservations:** Recommended.
$ Prices: Appetizers $5.95–$9.95; main courses $11.95–$19.50; Sun brunch $8–$12.50. AE, CB, DC, DISC, MC, V.
Open: Daily noon–11:30pm. Brunch, Sun 11am–4pm. **Subway:** 1 or 9 to 50th St.

For pre- and after-theater dining, this dynamic, up-tempo restaurant offers good down-home Caribbean cooking adapted to northern tastes. The sleek and glossy art deco building houses a lively bar where a sleek, stylish, multiracial crowd of "regulars" unwinds nightly over drinks and conversation.

Begin your dinner here with a spicy "frico" whose crust of melted Gruyère cheese holds a mixture of diced onion, tomato, capers, olives, and Swiss chard under a lemon vinaigrette; or sample the garlicky Gulf shrimp steeped in Chardonnay. The best-bet entree is the popular lobster ravioli with tarragon shellfish bisque and warm Mascarpone cheese. Other items on the all à la carte menu include sandwiches, salads, and several Cajun specialties. There's a good selection of wines in the $25 range. Desserts are a joy like the sweet-potato pecan pie, spiced with nutmeg and topped with gobs of whipped cream, or the roast fresh pineapple, finished with a Caribbean coconut rum sauce and a tropical sorbet. Sunday brunch features a live jazz duo, with no extra music charge. B. Smith's Rooftop Café is a highly popular jazz and blues spot (see Chapter 10 for details).

CHEZ JOSEPHINE, 414 West 42nd St., between Ninth and Tenth Aves. Tel. 594-1925.
Cuisine: FRENCH. **Reservations:** Recommended.
$ Prices: Appetizers $5.50–$8; main courses $16.50–$21.50. AE, MC, V.
Open: Dinner only, Mon–Sat 5pm–midnight. **Subway:** A to 42nd St. **Bus:** M 106.

For a bit of Montmartre in New York, nothing beats Chez Josephine, a lively, theatrical French bistro run by Jean-Claude Baker, one of the many adopted children of legendary entertainer Josephine Baker. Risqué posters adorn the walls, and colorful balloons and gaudy pseudo-palm leaves dangle from the ceiling. The atmosphere is exotic, jazzy, and electric. At the far end of the smallish dining room, a mirrored wall spotlights the piano player improvising on Josephine Baker's own piano, the one she used before she left for Paris in 1925. This delightful restaurant specializes in before- and after-theater suppers. It's a popular hangout for theater folks. Mr. Baker himself, always on hand, is a "frustrated actor," and even the waiters are Broadway hopefuls.

Service will be prompt, friendly, and efficient. Start your meal with soup (try the gazpacho), the smooth pâté de la maison, or the typically French leeks in warm tomato vinaigrette. For a main course, I'm partial to the robust cassoulet of lobster, shrimp, scallops, and small black beans served in a soup bowl and garnished with fresh parsley. Also noteworthy is the delicious filet of roast monkfish over a bed of spinach, with diced tomatoes, snow peas, and julienne vegetables. The wine list is limited but relatively inexpensive. For dessert, try the sublime warm apple-and-rhubarb crêpe cake or opt for a creamy chocolate-mousse cake called la delice Josephine.

LA TOPIAIRE, 120 West 45th St. Tel. 819-1405.
Cuisine: FRENCH. **Reservations:** Recommended.

$ Prices: Appetizers $5–$9.50; main courses $17.50–$20.50. AE, MC, V.

Open: Mon–Sat 11:30am–11:30pm. **Bus:** M104 to 44th St.

La Topiaire's soaring, sunny space looks more like it belongs to SoHo rather than in Midtown. Lilac accents and floor-to-ceiling windows add an airy ambiance that makes for an exceptionally relaxing lunch or dinner. Chef Joel Benjamin, an alumnus of Lutèce and Tavern on the Green, offers light renditions of French classics, from translucent lobster ravioli to rare peppered-tuna salad to sweetbreads in Madeira sauce. He also does excellent renditions of grilled cod on a bed of roasted apples and peppers, striped bass with leek velouté, and caramelized roast rack of lamb. Don't miss the French chickory salad with Roquefort croutons and Caesar dressing, or the scrumptious desserts—Chocolate-mousse cake, served with a sabayon sauce (cream with vanilla and cloves) is out of this world. The friendly and efficient service deserves a special mention.

LA VIEILLE AUBERGE, 347 West 46th St., between Eighth and Ninth Aves. Tel. 247-4284.

Cuisine: FRENCH. **Reservations:** Recommended.

$ Prices: Prix-fixe dinner $22.50–$32; prix-fixe lunch $16; lunch main courses $13.75–$18.75.

Open: Lunch, Mon–Sat noon–2:30pm. Dinner, Mon–Thurs 5–9pm; Fri–Sat 5:30–10pm. **Bus:** M104 to 46th St.

With its aura of quiet charm, La Vielle Auberge gives one the feeling of dining in a private home, and the dessert display will make you anxious to be seated and begin feasting. For the price of your dinner entree, you can enjoy a complete meal, and that includes either appetizers like duck pâté, quiche Lorraine, and stuffed mussels, or the soup du jour, vichyssoise, or lobster bisque. And wonderful home-made desserts—like mousse au chocolat, lemon sorbet, and cheesecake—are included as well. Well recommended among the entrees are the salmon and scrod in lobster sauce, the veal scallopine with wild mushrooms, and the rack of lamb. Lunch offers similar value, with the entree including an appetizer or soup and a lovely dessert (coffee is extra).

LE BAR BAT, 309 West 57th St. Tel. 307-7228.

Cuisine: SOUTHEAST ASIAN. **Reservations:** Recommended.

$ Prices: Appetizers $4.50–$15; main courses $7.50–$26. AE, DC, MC, V.

Open: Lunch, Mon–Sat noon–3pm. Dinner, Mon–Sat 5pm–midnight. Late supper, Mon–Sat 11pm–3am. **Bus:** M104 to 57th St.

Avoid Le Bar Bat at all costs if you have any phobia to winged creatures. Surrealistic bats—in stainless steel, copper, and glowing cobalt glass—populate this fantastic "environment" carved out of a former church. Everything about Le Bar Bat crackles with the same irreverence. Drinks bear monikers like Confucius Colada, Echolation Libation, and Bora Borta Tomorrow; a monstrous con-coction called the Bat Bite, designed for two, spews a volcanolike geyser when it reaches your table. Chef Romeo Dorotan's food, however, is a serious amalgam of French and Vietnamese elements. Don't miss his steak au poivre with grilled pineapple, rare charred tuna with green-mango vinaigrette, and Vietnamese barbecued lamb.

After dinner, hang out with the masses who've made Le Bar Bat an all-night after-work singles haven.

MEZZANINE RESTAURANT, 235 West 46th St. Tel. 764-5500.

Cuisine: AMERICAN. **Reservations:** Not required.
$ Prices: Appetizers $4.75–$8; main courses $9.50–$24.50.
Open: Mon–Thurs 7am–1am; Fri 7am–2am; Sat 7:30am–2am; Sun 7:30am–1am. **Bus:** M104 to 46th St.

When the ultradramatic Paramount Hotel opened in 1990, it pioneered the "cheap chic" concept in hospitality. Its Mezzanine Restaurant brings the same sensibility to dining with uncommon, but uneven, results. The restaurant encircles the breathtaking lobby, designed by France's Philippe Starck to recall the sweeping public spaces of the grand old hotels. But that's about the only nod to tradition you'll find here. Instead of conventional chairs, you sit in overstuffed armchairs and on muslin-covered banquettes; a single plastic lamp illuminates each black table. You might recognize anything from Julee Cruise to Yaz over the speakers. The menu doesn't match the setting for imagination, but it delivers competent versions of satisfying standards. I usually stick with the salad of smoky grilled chicken breast and wild mushrooms atop a mountain of greens, black linguine brightened by fresh vegetables, and bulging burgers and sandwiches. A silky carrot soup makes regular appearances as a special appetizer. Depending on the night, the service can be accommodating and warm or dizzy and indifferent. If nothing else, dine here just to see it. Note: Dean & Deluca, a famous gourmet-food purveyor, operates off the Paramount's lobby a sparse, whitewashed coffee bar that has become a haunt for neighborhood publicists, theater people, and publishing types. The expensive-but-worth-it fare includes coffees, pastries, muffins, bagels, sandwiches, cakes, and pies. At press time, **Brasserie du Theatre,** a French restaurant, was also scheduled to open on the Paramount's ground floor. Maître d' Max Bernard promises a wide-concept French menu, from beer on tap to caviar, with old-fashioned service—such as tableside preparations.

PIERRE AU TUNNEL, 250 West 47th St. Tel. 575-1220.

Cuisine: FRENCH. **Reservations:** Recommended.
$ Prices: Prix-fixe dinner $26; surcharges $3–$7. AE, MC, V.
Open: Lunch, Mon–Sat noon–3pm. Dinner, Mon 5:30–10pm; Tues and Thurs–Fri 5:30–11:30pm; Wed and Sat 4:30–11:30pm.
Subway: 1 or 9 to 50th St. **Bus:** M104 to 50th St.

One of New York's oldest French bistros and still one of its most deservedly popular, Pierre au Tunnel charms everyone who passes through its doorway. So do Jacqueline and Jean-Claude Lincey, the daughter and son-in-law of Pierre and Jane Pujol, the original owners, who now run this family business. White napery, good wine, courteous waitresses, and flowers at the entrance set a convivial mood. You could begin with a plate of hors d'oeuvres variés, proceed to onion soup or a terrine de poisson, then move on to a favorite like red snapper à la croûte d'herbe or pan-broiled baby chicken. If it's Friday, don't miss the bouillabaisse à la Marseillaise. My favorite dessert here is the mousse au chocolat. Lunchtime prices are lower, from $10 to $16 (à la carte) for dishes like calves' liver sauté, tête de veau vinaigrette, and broiled lamb chops.

RENE PUJOL, 321 West 51st St., between Eighth and Ninth Aves. Tel. 246-3023.

Cuisine: FRENCH. **Reservations:** Recommended.

$ Prices: Appetizers $4–$12; main courses $18–$25; prix-fixe lunch $23; prix-fixe dinner $32. AE, DC, MC, V.

Open: Lunch, Mon–Fri noon–3pm. Dinner, Mon–Thurs 5–10:30pm; Fri–Sat 5–11:30pm. **Subway:** 1 or 9 to 50th St. **Bus:** M104 to 50th St.

Don't wait until you're going to the theater to have dinner here. But if you do want to make an 8 o'clock curtain, make an early reservation so you can leisurely enjoy the complete dinner. Two French country rooms, one with a working fireplace, provide comfortable and attractive surroundings in which to savor a first-class French meal. The complete dinner includes an appetizer—pâté, steamed crab dumpling, or lobster raviolis are all good—plus either onion soup, lobster consommé, or soup of the day. After these two courses, you're ready for pan-seared salmon with sorel sauce, steak with green peppercorns, veal scallops in cream sauce, chicken in Calvados cream sauce, or whatever you choose as an entree. And all of these delectable selections will be accompanied by vegetables and a salad. Now for coffee and dessert: Crème caramel and chocolate mousse are the usual fine choices, and at René Pujol, they are unusually good. (*Note:* Many of the appetizers and desserts cost extra.) A complete lunch is served with all the same trimmings; the only real difference is that the list of entrees is a bit shorter and a mushroom omelet has been added. Dinner is à la carte only after 8pm, and there's an extensive wine list, which has received an award of excellence from *Wine Spectator.*

SYMPHONY CAFE, 950 Eighth Ave., at 56th St. Tel. 397-9595.

Cuisine: NEW AMERICAN. **Reservations:** Recommended for pretheater dinner.

$ Prices: Appetizers $4.50–$9.50; main courses $13–$25; prix-fixe lunch $25; prix-fixe dinner $33; Sat and Sun brunch $15.95. AE, DC, DISC, MC, V.

Open: Lunch, Mon–Fri 11:30–4pm. Dinner, Mon–Fri 5pm–midnight; Sat 3pm–midnight; Sun 3–9pm. Brunch, Sat–Sun 11am–3pm. **Bus:** M104 to 57th St.

The Symphony Café, just around the corner from Carnegie Hall, opened to bravos a few years ago and is continuing to reap warm applause from the theater- and concert-going crowd. Spacious and handsome, with mahogany walls, large glass windows, and an eye-catching mural of Carnegie Hall, this is just the kind of place where you can relax after the show, discuss the performance, and maybe spot a few celebrities at the next table. Theatrical memorabilia are all about, and the menu is worth your attention, too, as Executive Chef James Lenzi is being praised for his interpretations of new American cuisine. At dinner, you might begin with coconut shrimp with orange horseradish dip, Maryland crabcakes, or cheese-and-spinach ravioli. For a main course, choose the commendable pan-seared salmon, the grilled filet mignon, or the roast chicken in its natural juices, with homemade mashed potatoes. Pastas, burgers, omelets, and several salads offer alternative light dining. The desserts are rich treats: pecan pie with whipped cream, a chocolate sundae, and a warm apple tart with ice cream.

BUDGET

LA FONDUE, 43 West 55th St., between Fifth and Sixth Aves. Tel. 581-0820.
Cuisine: FONDUE. **Reservations:** Not required.
$ Prices: Appetizers $3.45–$4.95; main courses at lunch $6.50–$12.95. at dinner $6.50–$17.95. No credit cards.
Open: Mon–Thurs noon–midnight; Fri–Sat noon–12:30am; Sun noon–11pm. Full dinners and snacks served until closing. **Bus:** M104 to 50th St.

It's a cheese-lover's idea of Paradise, and even if you don't know your Emmenthal from your Esrom, we think you'll still enjoy a visit here. Owned by one of the largest cheese importers and retailers in the city, La Fondue is a large, French Provincial–looking place that handles hungry cheese-loving hordes very well at the busier times of the day. But if you come a bit late for lunch, on a weekday for dinner, or after the theater or concert, you'll really have the time and comfort for enjoying the quality food. There are five kinds of fondues—the classic Swiss cheese fondue, the prime filet mignon fondue, a stuffed crab claws fondue, a prime filet mignon and stuffed crab claws fondue, and a heavenly Swiss chocolate fondue (cubed banana bread and assorted fruits are used for dunking). There is also a variety of cheese and sausage boards, excellent quiches and croques, even le cheeseburger, all modestly priced à la carte. Pasta primavera with pesto, and fish and meat dishes are available for noncheese eaters. Five-course dinners have plenty of cheese choices (from quiche Lorraine and cheddar-cheese soup to fondue and cheesecake), and most are well under $20. Lunch offers many à la carte choices, as well as several terrific complete lunches. Cider, beer, and wine, plus Swiss grape juice, are available, as well as cocktails.

PLANET HOLLYWOOD, 140 West 57th St. Tel. 333-STAR (333-7827).
Cuisine: AMERICAN. **Reservations:** Not accepted.
$ Prices: Appetizers $4.95–$6.95; main courses $6.95–$17.95. AE, MC, V.
Open: Daily 11am–2am. **Bus:** M104 to 57th St.

Part restaurant, part movie museum, and part merchandising machine, the $15-million Planet Hollywood keeps drawing curious hordes anxious for a glimpse of investors Arnold Schwarzenegger, Sylvester Stallone, and Bruce Willis. Alas, Arnold, Sly, and Bruce seem to hang out elsewhere, so Planet Hollywood diners have to settle for a look at the *Terminator 2* cyborg, James Dean's motorcycle from *Rebel Without a Cause,* and Judy Garland's dress from *The Wizard of Oz,* plus a host of other memorabilia. But those artifacts alone, and the late Anton Furst's stunning design, make it worth a visit (and an interminable wait in line on weekends). A kind of Gotham City meets Malibu, the interior should keep the kids wide-eyed and occupied throughout a rather average meal; the menu offers wide-ranging "Californian cuisine"—from Chinese chicken salad to fajitas to grilled sirloin steak. But the food, obviously, isn't the point here.

TOUT VA BIEN, 311 West 51st St. Tel. 974-9051.
Cuisine: FRENCH. **Reservations:** Not required.
$ Prices: Appetizers $3–$7; main courses $9–$18. AE, MC, V.
Open: Lunch, Mon–Sat noon–2:30pm. Dinner, Mon–Sat 5–

11:30pm; Sun 4–10pm. **Subway:** 1 or 9 to 50th St. **Bus:** M104 to 50th St.

A longtime French favorite, this small one-room French bistro, complete with red-checkered tablecloths, is a family affair, and its faithful clients have come here for years for good, solid home cooking—none of that fancy nouvelle stuff here. The entrees are reasonably priced and about $1 cheaper at lunch—the likes of coq au vin, boeuf bourguignon, frogs' legs, salade niçoise, and Cornish game hen. The hors d'oeuvres are excellent, especially the pâté maison and the haricots blancs avec oignons (white beans with onions). Bouillabaisse is available on Friday in winter for about $18. Desserts include spumoni and tortoni, as well as the most expected French offerings like pêche Melba and poire Helene.

ZEN PALATE, 663 Ninth Ave. at 46th St. Tel. 582-1669.
   Cuisine: VEGETARIAN/CHINESE/JAPANESE. **Reservations:** Recommended.
$ Prices: Appetizers $3–$7; main courses $9–$15; prix-fixe lunch $6.55–$9.55.
   Open: Lunch, Mon–Sat 11:30am–3pm; Sun noon–3pm. Dinner, Mon–Sat 3pm–10:45pm; Sun 3pm–10:30pm. **Subway:** A to 42nd St. **Bus:** 49th St. Crosstown.

Through Zen meditation, "one can attempt to enter the realm of a worry-free space from a chaotic environment," explains the menu. You might say the same about Zen Palate, a stylish oasis from frenzied Ninth Avenue. From its understated, angular entryway to its highly original vegetarian cuisine, this place leaves both belly and soul satisfied. The closest to nouvelle Chinese I've ever seen, the menu brings a light touch to familiar appetizers—like dumplings and hot-and-sour soup—and exotic entrees—like vegetarian ham with basil, black mushrooms, and bamboo shoots. Zen Palate's signature dish, deep-sea vegetables with black mushrooms, carrots, and baby cabbage, tastes altogether ethereal. Among the desserts, fried jelly rolls and tofu cheesecake stand out; the service is impeccable, too. At lunch, entrees include special rice, spring rolls, and dessert. At press time, Zen Palate had not yet obtained a liquor license, but you may bring your own.

10. MIDTOWN EAST

EXPENSIVE

ADRIENNE, at the Peninsula Hotel, 700 Fifth Ave., at 55th St. Tel. 903-3918.
   Cuisine: CONTEMPORARY AMERICAN. **Reservations:** Recommended.
$ Prices: Appetizers $7.50–$15.50; main courses $19.50–$29; two-course pre-theater dinner $32; three-course pre-theater dinner $38.
   Open: Lunch, Mon–Sat noon–2:30pm. Dinner, Tues.–Sat. 6–10pm. Pre-theater dinner 6–7:30pm. Sun brunch 11am–2:30pm.
   Bus: Any Fifth Ave. or Madison Ave. bus.

To maintain one's sense of balance in New York, it sometimes helps to retreat somewhere that lets you forget the outside world. In

Midtown, the place to escape is Adrienne, an art deco jewel featuring the globe-hopping cuisine of Dutch-born, Paris-trained chef Adam Odegard, one of the brightest stars in New York. A recent menu offered such appetizers as applewood-smoked salmon with honey-mustard Mascarpone and ginger chicken with spicy mango relish; the succulent entrees included roasted Montana lamb chops with eggplant compote, parsley jus, and tabouleh, as well as loin of ahi tuna with tangerine peel and mint oil served with polenta and fried leeks. Crown dinner in style with a dessert such as hot banana-walnut tart with luxurious nutmeg ice cream. The pre-theater dinner offer a good value. Solicitous service complements the superb cuisine.

FELIDIA, 243 East 58th St. Tel. 758-1479.

Cuisine: ITALIAN. **Reservations:** Recommended, several days in advance for prime time.

$ Prices: Appetizers $7–$12; main courses $25–$28. AE, CB, DC, DISC, MC, V.

Open: Lunch, Mon–Fri noon–3pm. Dinner, Mon–Sat 5pm–midnight. **Bus:** Any Third Ave. bus.

Felidia is one of the great Northern Italian restaurants of New York. The dining experience is exemplary and expensive, but it's well worth it. And the place is lovely, with brick and whitewashed walls, lush vegetation, skylights that create almost a greenhouse effect, brocade chairs, and terra-cotta floors. And the food can be awe-inspiring.

You might start a meal here with a superb appetizer such as a heady wild mushroom soup or a hearty minestrone. (Or you can have mussels in a sauce of garlic and white wine or grilled polenta with fonduta cheese and wild mushrooms.) Then proceed to poached salmon in mustard sauce or the Dover sole, both outstanding. The calves' liver balsamic here is fantasy-perfect, and several unusual pasta dishes are wonderful, too. Daily specials often include roasted breast of pheasant, or other game. Rare, fresh white truffles are often served with pastas. Desserts—fudge cake, raspberry tart, and blueberry cheesecake—are worth breaking any diet. Finish with some cappuccino and anisette, perhaps, and leave feeling totally content with the world.

Felidia's owner, Lydia Bastianich, shares her recipes and her life story in a highly praised book, *La Cucina di Lydia* (Doubleday, $24), which you can pick up on your way out of the restaurant.

THE FOUR SEASONS, 99 East 52nd St. Tel. 754-9494.

Cuisine: CONTINENTAL. **Reservations:** Essential.

$ Prices: Appetizers $8.50–$25; main courses $30–$45. Prix-fixe dinner served in Pool Room 5–6:15pm and 10–11:15pm, in Grill Room all evening, $41.50. AE, CB, DC, DISC, JCB, MC, V.

Open: Lunch, Mon–Fri noon–2:30pm. Dinner Mon–Sat 5–11:15pm. **Subway:** 6 to 51st St.

One of the great showplace restaurants of New York—and the only one ever to be designated a New York City Landmark—the Four Seasons is a place where the food, wine, decor, and service are artfully combined to catch the spirit of New York today. As seasons change, so do the menus and decor. The art collection is highlighted by the world's largest Picasso and a 24-foot-long James Rosenquist painting. The restaurant is really two-in-one. The Pool Room, with its marble reflecting pool and lavish use of space, offers elaborate, inventive fare and formal service. The Grill Room, where the space is just as lavish, does things on a simpler scale, but this is where the movers and shakers of New York congregate for lunch. The wine cellar is considered one of the most complete in America.

There are several menus at the Four Seasons. In the Pool Room, there's a special pre-theater dinner from 5 to 6:15pm and after-theater dinner from 10 to 11:15pm—these are your best bet. Entrees that appear frequently on the menu include soft-shell crabs with herbs, mustard, and fiddlehead ferns; or grilled loin of rabbit with lemongrass and peanut sauce. And you can also choose from the highly popular Spa Cuisine menu for the health-conscious, with appetizers like mussels in green chile sauce, and main courses like escalope of sturgeon with tomatillo sauce or breast of pigeon with grilled polenta and shiitake mushrooms. Desserts might include flamed strawberry crêpe or a guava-and-macadamia soufflé. In the Grill Room, lunch and dinner are offered, and from 10:30pm to midnight, desserts and a cheese tray are served. Jackets are required, ties requested. Dress up for the Pool Room: *Le tout* New York will be there.

LA COTE BASQUE, 5 East 55th St. Tel. 688-6525.

Cuisine: FRENCH. **Reservations:** Essential.

$ Prices: Prix-fixe dinner $55; prix-fixe lunch $28. AE, CB, DC, JCB, MC, V.

Open: Lunch, Mon–Sat noon–2:30pm. Dinner, Mon–Sat 6–10pm. **Bus:** Any Fifth Ave. or Madison Ave. bus.

La Côte Basque has long been one of the great dining places for the beautiful people, and beautiful it is. The Bernard Lamotte murals of St. Jean-de-Luz make you feel you're dining by the seaside in a French café; the service is gracious and courtly (especially if you're known to the management), and the company is top-drawer. For three decades now, La Côte Basque has been a favorite with a well-heeled crowd (they usually arrive by limo), who favor the traditional classics of French cooking, in generous portions. Among the appetizers on the prix-fixe menu are very light quenelles, a hearty vol au vent de St. Jacques or foie gras; entrees like noisettes de veau, steak au poivre, ragoût de homard, sweetbreads, and bay scallops de Long Island are always excellent. Game dishes are also well prepared. For dessert, there are heady temptations of sorbets and pâtisseries, and sinful delights like mousses au chocolat or Grand Marnier. Fruit tarts are memorable, and few desserts can compare with the frozen raspberry soufflé with fresh berries.

LE PERIGORD, 405 East 52nd St., east of First Ave. Tel. 755-6244.

Cuisine: CLASSIC FRENCH. **Reservations:** Recommended.

$ Prices: Prix-fixe lunch $29; prix-fixe dinner $49 (with selected dishes available at an additional $3–$15).

Open: Lunch, Mon–Fri noon–3pm. Dinner, Mon–Sat 5:15–10:30pm. Open Sun for private parties of 35–100 only. Ties and jackets required at all times. **Subway:** E or F to Lexington-Third aves.

One of New York's favorite French restaurants for 28 years, Le Perigord is named for the province in southwest France where, historically, luxuries like truffles and foie gras are as plentiful as the heather on the moors. And, indeed, stepping into Le Perigord is like traveling back in time. The tone in the dining room evokes that found in a typical French château restaurant, where dulcet tones seem fitting. A soft din is punctuated only by the occasional tinkling of goblets. The considerate service could be described as "en famille," if your warm yet slightly formal family happens to be landed gentry.

Chef Antoine Bouterin, born in Provence, creates food that is both earthy and sophisticated. The five-course prix-fixe lunch could include a light asparagus or artichoke in vinaigrette, a delicate crêpe of sweetbread, or a tasty vegetable tarte with lemon butter. A full-bodied lobster bisque, grilled salmon, and roast duck with seasonal fresh fruits are just a few of the specialties. The prix-fixe dinner will permit you such treats as melt-in-your-mouth marinated salmon, light but hearty smoked trout Napoleon, noodles bedecked with shrimp and smoked salmon, lush sautéed bay scallops, grilled Dover sole, or veal kidney with Burgundy sauce.

The array of desserts is dazzling—chocolate mousse, second-to-none chocolate cake, distinctive "floating islands" of meringue and caramel, unforgettable chocolate soufflé. All are perfect finales for your exquisite and leisurely meal at Le Perigord.

LUTECE, 249 East 50th St. Tel. 752-2225.

Cuisine: FRENCH. **Reservations:** Essential—accepted up to one month in advance.

$ Prices: Prix-fixe dinner $60; prix-fixe lunch $38. AE, CB, DC, MC, V.

Open: Lunch, Tues–Fri noon–2pm. Dinner, Mon–Sat 6–10pm. **Closed:** Sun and major hols, Sat in summer. **Bus:** Any Third Ave. bus. **Subway:** 6 to 51st St.

One of the ultimate French restaurants in New York must surely be Lutèce, where André Soltner serves what many consider the finest haute cuisine in the city. You can sit in a greenhouse setting where the city landscape is reflected hazily under a mylar dome or, in colder weather, upstairs in the elegant dining room typical of a private town house. The food can be as unreal as this gracious setting. The prix-fixe menus are good value for a New York restaurant of this caliber. Among the appetizers at lunch, the fish pâté and all the pâtés en croûte are superbly flavored. For your main course, ask what the chef has dreamed up for the day. Good lunch menu choices are poulet en croûte, escalopes de veau, and delicate filet of sole amandine. Everything is prepared in the grand manner and served with flair. For dessert, you can't surpass the rich mousse au chocolat au rhum or the light and lovely tarte tatin.

The dinner menu is much more extensive, with a variety of amazing appetizers (salmon, mousse of duckling with juniper berries, sauté of lobster); and entrees like the house specialty, the mignon de boeuf en feuilleté Lutèce (a variation of beef Wellington), filet of lamb with peppercorns, and sweetbreads with capers. Rabbit is often available and especially well prepared here. The desserts are classics: crêpes flambées Alsatian style, frozen raspberry soufflé, and a warm soufflé, which you must remember to order at the beginning of your meal.

MARCH, 408 East 58th St. Tel. 838-9393.

Cuisine: AMERICAN. **Reservations:** Recommended.

$ Prices: $50 prix-fixe dinner. AE, DC, MC, V.

Open: Dinner only, Mon–Sat 6–10pm. **Bus:** Any First Ave. bus.

A veteran of the venerable Quilted Giraffe and Le Colombe d'Or, chef Wayne Nish struck out on his own with this small, sumptuous spot in a swank Sutton Place town house. With "cosmopolitan" cuisine that combines seemingly discordant elements, Nish spins gold from strange bedfellows like squab with sesame sauce; crabmeat with sweet-corn–and–black-truffle vinaigrette; lake sturgeon with spaetzle and piperade; and Atlantic salmon with Middle Eastern spices and wild mushrooms. Nish's desserts boast equal artistry and attention to detail: Don't miss the crispy pancakes with vanilla ice cream, mango, and berries; warm chocolate cake with pistachio halvah; and March's signature dish, grapefruit sorbet and grapefruit sections in gin syrup with coriander seed. Host/co-owner Joseph Scalice has designed a room as inspired as the cooking, with a graceful Chinese tapestry on one wall; turn-of-the-century chandeliers; reproduction Biedermeier furnishings; and, in colder months, a roaring fireplace. For the price category, this is a wonderful value.

THE PALM, 837 Second Ave., between 44th and 45th Sts. Tel. 687-2953.

Cuisine: STEAK. **Reservations:** Recommended only at lunch.
$ **Prices:** Appetizers $5–$14; main courses $14.50–$27 (double steak $54; lobster $55 and up).
Open: Mon–Fri noon–11:30pm; Sat 5–11:30pm. **Bus:** Any Second or Third Ave. bus.

Those of you who have come to New York in quest of the perfect steak need search no further. For the New York Steak Experience, don't miss The Palm—it's noisy, it's crowded, there's sawdust all over the floors, and the waiters are rushed and can be curt. But the true trencherman overlooks all such indignities, for those thick grilled steaks, those succulent fried onion rings and hash brown potatoes, and those monstrous lobsters. Prices vary according to the market; recently, filet mignon was $26 and lobster was out of sight! (I find one order of 4-pounds-plus of lobster perfectly adequate for two—almost big enough for three.) Try the clams Casino (baked clams with bacon) for an appetizer and the terrific cheesecake for dessert (if you have room for anything else after those steaks!).

If there's no room at The Palm, you'll be just as happy at **Palm Too,** at 840 Second Ave., just across the street (tel. 697-5198)—with the same mood, same food, same hours, same madness.

TROPICA BAR AND SEAFOOD HOUSE, 200 Park Ave., at 44th St., in the concourse of the Pan Am Building. Tel. 867-6767.

Cuisine: SEAFOOD/CARIBBEAN. **Reservations:** Required, especially at lunch in dining room. Lounge: first come, first served.
$ **Prices:** Appetizers $7.50–$12.50; main courses $17–$27; prix-fixe dinner $27. AE, CB, DC, JCB, MC, V.
Open: Lunch, Mon–Fri 11:30am–3pm. Dinner, Mon–Fri 5–11pm. Lounge open 11:30am–midnight. **Closed:** Sat and Sun.
Subway: 4, 5, or 6 to 42nd St.

A tropical island of calm amid the rush and bustle of the Grand Central area is the Tropica, very popular with an upscale business-lunch crowd. This creation of savvy Restaurant Associates (American Festival Café, The Sea Grill) has the decor of a Bahamian Great House, with rattan and wicker chairs; Floridian decorations; and antique prints of tropical fruit, flowers, and birds.

The bar, with its large glass windows for watching the passing parade, and the handsome, spacious dining room with full views of the kitchen, both provide an engaging setting for the imaginative fresh fish, seafood, and other Caribbean specialties. At lunch, you might begin with one of the "Small Plates"—perhaps the savory crabcakes with mustard sauce or the lusty black bean soup with Andouille sausage. You could make a meal of the salad of stir-fried chicken with sesame-honey dressing. Or go for the lobster and shrimp risotto; the marinated barbequed shrimp; or one of the grilled fresh fish specialties, with exotic selections flown in from Hawaii. Desserts carry out the tropical theme, with a lovely Key lime pie and a delicious coconut crème brûlée. At dinner, the menu is similar, with prices higher by only a dollar or two.

Light food is served in the lounge continuously throughout the day: The specials are the same as in the main dining room, but soups, salads, and burgers are also available.

EXPENSIVE TO MODERATE

AVGERINOS, at the Market at Citicorp Center, Plaza Level, 153 East 53rd St., between Lexington and Third Aves. Tel. 688-8828.
   Cuisine: GREEK. **Reservations:** Recommended.
$ Prices: Appetizers $4.50–$9.95; main courses $11.25–$16.95. AE, CB, DC, MC, V.
   Open: Daily 11:30am–10pm. **Subway:** E or F to Lexington-Third Aves.

You could be in a little taverna in the isles of Greece: Avgerinos, our favorite spot at Citicorp, is that authentic. It features whitewashed arched walls, graceful artifacts, the wail of a bouzouki in the background—and food as good as you'd find back in the motherland. I often like to stop by here at lunchtime and feast on the Greek antipasto—a mixture of such wonderful tidbits as fish-roe dip, cucumber-yogurt dip, eggplant dip, feta cheese, and stuffed grape leaves. There's a similar platter of hot appetizers, mixed hot mezedakia, that allows you to try the spinach pie, the Greek meatballs, sautéed liver, and more. As for the entrees, I usually go with one of the tasty souvlakis—chicken or lamb or seafood, but equally good are the moussaka and the pastitsio. The menu is the same at lunch and dinner but prices vary. Of course you won't want to leave without sampling one of the house's homemade desserts: A personal favorite is the bougatsa, a lemon-scented warm custard wrapped in phyllo dough. And to go with it have thick and dark Greek coffee, of course.

ROSA MEXICANO, 1063 First Ave., at 58th St. Tel. 753-7407.
   Cuisine: MEXICAN. **Reservations:** Recommended.
$ Prices: Appetizers $5–$11; main courses $15–$24; Sun brunch $28. AE, CB, DC, MC, V.
   Open: Dinner only, daily 5pm–midnight. **Bus:** Any First Ave. bus.

Don't expect the usual Tex-Mex food and ambiance. Instead, join the delighted throngs who come here (and keep coming back) for the classic regional Mexican cuisine, served in a warm and inviting house-party atmosphere. My favorite Mexican restaurant in New York is the creation of Josefina Howard, who is credited for leading much of the current "Mexican Revolution" in the city. Rosa Mexicano is a study in pinks and mauves, with tall Mexican-colonial wooden chairs and tables flanking the long tile bar and an open grill, or *parilla*. Choose the first room for bustle and sparkle; opt for the back room for quiet conversation in a setting of tropical plantings.

Start your dinner with a margarita made tangy with fresh pomegranate juice, then sit back and study the menu. Someone in your party should have the knockout guacamole, prepared right at your table, and someone else should order the cold seafood platter, the better to sample the superb ceviche, shrimp, oysters, and more. The entrees offer delightful choices: unusual enchiladas filled with chicken and topped with a mole sauce that includes chocolate as well as 19 other spices; crêpes camarones, filled with chopped shrimp and served with a chile pasilla sauce; and pescado en cilantro, baked filet of fish with fresh coriander, tomato, and onion. Desserts, too, are wondrous: flan with a sauce of cactus pears or fresh pineapple sautéed with coconut and pecans. The service is gracious and friendly.

11. LINCOLN CENTER/UPPER WEST SIDE

A sophisticated dinner on the Upper West Side used to mean Szechuan Chinese. But over the last decade, gentrification and yuppification have altered the landscape. Today, this part of town boasts some of New York's quirkiest, coziest places—plus some of its best values. I recommend, in addition to those given full listings below, the capacious **Carmine's,** 2450 Broadway at 90th St. (tel. 362-2200), for gargantuan "family-style" portions of old-fashioned Italian food; dark, bustling **Docks,** 2427 Broadway at 90th St. (tel. 724-5588), which prides itself on impeccably fresh fish and seafood; and the chic, clubby **Poiret,** 474 Columbus Ave. at 83rd St. (tel. 724-6880), lauded by locals for fine French fare. For the health conscious, both **Mana,** 2444 Broadway at 90th St. (tel. 787-1110), and **Ozu,** 566 Amsterdam Ave. at 87th St. (tel. 787-8316), provide macrobiotic and natural Japanese cooking in simple, spare settings; **Pumpkin Eater,** 2452 Broadway at 91st St. (tel. 877-0132), provides a full range of tasty vegetarian dishes and fish entrees as well. Charming **BTI,** 250 W. 86th St., between Broadway and West End Ave. (tel. 875-0460), is a little bit of the Far East, with selections from Burmese, Indonesian, and Thai cuisines—all at low prices. **Coastal,** 300 Amsterdam Ave. at 74th St. (tel. 769-3988), packs in a neighborhood and Lincoln Center crowd for very fresh, superbly prepared seafood at very fair prices; and **Trattoria Sambuca** (tel. 787-5656), 20 W. 72nd St., just off Central Park West, dishes out tasty, old-fashioned Italian food on heaping platters.

On the homey front, join the neighbors at the warm, welcoming **Popover Café,** 551 Amsterdam Ave. at 87th St. (tel. 595-8555), for satisfying soups, sandwiches, and those luscious popovers. On weekends, neither rain nor snow nor sleet deters crowds from **Sarabeth's Kitchen,** 423 Amsterdam Ave. at 81st St. (tel. 496-6280), or its younger rival **Good Enough to Eat,** 483 Amsterdam Ave. at 83rd St. (tel. 496-0163); the sublime comfort food and hearty brunches make the long waits worthwhile. On Sunday, the masses also flock to **Barney Greengrass,** 541 Amsterdam Ave. at 86th St.

(tel. 724-4707)—a classic New York deli complete with grouchy waiters—where lox and bagels become high art. Even more down to earth—with prices to match—is **EJ's Luncheonette,** 433 Amsterdam Ave. at 81st St. (tel. 873-3444), which cleans up classic diner food in a whimsical 1950s setting. For dessert, the crowded **Café Lalo,** 201 W. 83rd St. (tel. 496-6031), a favorite for sinful sweets, is about as close as you'll get to Paris in New York.

EXPENSIVE

ANDIAMO!, 1991 Broadway, between 67th and 68th Sts. Tel. 362-3315.
  Cuisine: NORTHERN ITALIAN NUOVA CUCINA. **Reservations:** Recommended.
  $ Prices: Appetizers $6.50–$12; main courses $17–$26; pre-theater dinner $26–$32. Sun brunch $16.95.
  Open: Dinner, daily 5:30pm–midnight. Brunch, Sun 11:30am–3pm. **Bus:** M104 to 67th St. **Subway:** 1 or 9 to 66 St.

Imagine everybody's dream of an architecturally striking, soaring SoHo loft, filled with modern art and sculpture—then imagine that it's not in SoHo but close to Lincoln Center and that it serves some of the finest nuova cucina (contemporary Northern Italian cuisine) in New York. There you have Andiamo! A high note among the Lincoln Center clutch of restaurants, Andiamo! is fine for nourishment before the curtain and even better for a leisurely meal when the chef's inspirations are the main event of the evening. Tables are large and spaced to allow real conversation; critically acclaimed jazz groups perform Monday to Saturday—and top blues bands on Sunday—making this one of the few places to do some serious eating while listening to fine jazz.

"Italian cooking has always been infused with the influences of many cultures, from Marco Polo on," says proprietor Lewis Futterman, who collected the art and designed the space and food concepts. Certainly, this kind of eclecticism is well-handled here. Consider, for example, the angel-hair pasta with saffron-based sauce; the whole-wheat fettucine with veal sausage; arugula, and toasted fennel seeds; and the terrine of warm goat cheese and potato with arugula and Belgian endive. The menu changes seasonally, and there are daily specials; typical entrees are crabmeat ravioli with carrot-butter sauce, seared salmon with salmon pearls in citrus vinaigrette, and grilled lamb chops with warm white-bean salad au jus. Desserts are lavish: Try the warm lemon tart with raspberry coulis and fresh strawberries or layered chocolate and raspberry mousse wrapped in an intense dark Belgian chocolate—a personal favorite (all desserts are $7). Sunday brunch features a plentiful antipasti table plus main courses like smoked duck breast, frittatas, and peasant-bread French toast served with warm fruit compote.

Andiamo! is somewhat hidden from the street, sitting directly behind the modestly priced Café Bel Canto, owned by the same management (see below).

CAFE DES ARTISTES, 1 West 67th St. Tel. 877-3500.
  Cuisine: FRENCH. **Reservations:** Recommended a week or two in advance.
  $ Prices: Appetizers $6–$15; main courses $15–$29; three-course prix-fixe dinner $32.50; three-course prix-fixe lunch

$19.50; Great Dessert Plate $19.50; Sun brunch main courses $10–$23.

Open: Lunch, Mon–Sat noon–3pm. Dinner, Mon–Sat 5:30pm–midnight; Sun 5:30–11pm. Brunch, Sun 10am–3pm. **Bus:** M104 to 68th St. and Broadway. **Subway:** 1 or 9 to 66th St.

⭐ Many of its regular customers like to think of Café des Artistes as their neighborhood restaurant—and when the neighborhood happens to be Lincoln Center, this means that the regulars are apt to be celebrities: For example, James Levine of the Metropolitan Opera or Barbara Walters from ABC. But long before there was a Lincoln Center, artistic-minded New Yorkers were enjoying the fine art of eating good food in this stylish, European café atmosphere, and since famed restaurateur George Lang took over about 18 years ago, it's more renowned than ever. The restored Howard Chandler Christy murals of nude wood nymphs can provide a lively topic of conversation if you happen to sit up in the bustling front dining room (a quieter, less formal dining room near the bar in back offers no murals but more privacy for conversation).

The menu is huge and eclectic. You might start with a plate of cold salmon in four variations or a dish of sweetbread headcheese with cucumber from the charcuterie. At both lunch and dinner, you may order a prix-fixe meal consisting of an appetizer, a main course, a dessert, and coffee. The menu changes daily and may include lusty pot au feu, paillard of swordfish with mustard-and-butter sauce, and stuffed breast of veal. You might, however, wish to eat lightly here and save your strength: For the true glutton there is the "Great Dessert Plate"—a piece of every pie, cake, and pastry on the changing menu—and the hazelnut gianduia, toasted-orange pound cake, macadamia-nut pie, and homemade sherbets are worth the wait. Café des Artistes is also fine for Sunday brunch, which features cold buffet plates and an extensive choice of favorite egg dishes. Jackets are required for men after 5pm.

CAFE LUXEMBOURG, 200 West 70th St. Tel. 873-7411.

Cuisine: FRENCH/AMERICAN. **Reservations:** Required on weekends and for pre-theater dinner (5:30–6:30pm).

$ **Prices:** Appetizers $6.75–$12; main courses $16–$28; prix-fixe dinner $28; Sun brunch $8.50–$17.

Open: Dinner, Mon–Thurs 5:30pm–12:30am; Fri–Sat 5:30pm–1am; Sun 6–11:30pm. Brunch, Sun 11am–3pm. Prix-fixe dinner served nightly 5:30–6:30pm and after 11pm. **Subway:** 1, 2, or 3 to 72nd St.

Café Luxembourg has won itself a reputation as an oasis of outstanding cooking on New York's trendy Upper West Side and as a haven for local glitterati—Mick Jagger, Jackie O., and the entire cast of "Saturday Night Live" have been frequent patrons. Were it not for the high noise level, it would be just about perfect. The decor—yellow and blue tiles, mirrored center columns, tile floors, and colorful wicker chairs—is cheery and cozy. The wide-ranging à la carte menu is a masterful combination of French modern and American fresh; it changes seasonally. To start your meal, either the sautéed crab cakes or country salad come highly recommended. Follow these with grilled leg of lamb, cassoulet (in winter), grilled tuna, or crispy roast duckling. Pasta de jour is $16, and fish de jour is market priced. Desserts are uniformly delicious, with special kudos for the chocolate mousse, crème brûlée, and lemon tart.

MICKEY MANTLE'S RESTAURANT AND SPORTS BAR,
42 Central Park South, between Fifth and Sixth Aves. Tel. 688-7777.

Cuisine: CONTEMPORARY AMERICAN. **Reservations:** Recommended.

$ Prices: Appetizers $4.95–$7.25; main courses $11.95–$22.95; Little League Menu (children's portions) $7.25–$8.50. AE, CB, DC, JCB, MC, V.

Open: Mon–Sat noon–1am; Sun noon–midnight; same menu served continuously. **Bus:** M5, M6, or M7. **Subway:** N or R to Fifth Ave.

Here's a place that will please both you and the kids. Named for the legendary New York Yankees hitter, Mickey Mantle's gets top ratings for its display of museum-quality memorabilia as well as for its something-for-everyone menu. A commemorative plaque from Yankee Stadium's centerfield, on the restaurant's front door, shares billing with vintage photographs, paintings, and lithographs (many are for sale, along with souvenirs). Mick himself frequently stops by and is, I am told, very gracious about autographing baseballs and the like. Other pro athletes and celebrities also tend to hang out here, especially on Tuesday and Thursday from 10am to 2pm, when WFAN sports radio's live interview show is broadcast weekly from the restaurant. A sidewalk café facing Central Park across the street is a plus in summer.

The cuisine is Mickey Mantle's selection of "home-cooking" Oklahoma delights, starting with such appetizers as fried calamari with spicy tomato sauce, blue-corn nachos with guacamole and salsa and wild-mushroom ravioli with fresh thyme and tomato. The entrees are home-run caliber: sublime chef's salad prepared with grilled sirloin, roast chicken, and fresh mozzarella; angel-hair pasta with seared shrimp; and grilled chicken with charred broccoli, rosemary, and garlic new potatoes. As side dishes, try Texas onion rings; mashed potatoes with cream gravy; and fried waffle potatoes, a house specialty. "Spring Training Specials" include grilled and roasted summer vegetables and wild mushrooms with red-pepper marmalade, a vegetarian's delight. Non-calorie counters can indulge in such desserts as chocolate, banana, and coconut cream pies; fresh berry crumb cobbler à la mode; and hot-fudge–and–brownie sundae, to name a heavenly few.

TAVERN ON THE GREEN, in Central Park, at West 67th St. Tel. 873-3200.

Cuisine: CONTINENTAL. **Reservations:** Advised, well in advance.

$ Prices: Appetizers $5–$14.50; main courses $11.50–$28; three-course pre-theater dinner $19.50–$24.50; three-course late-night dinner $15–$24.50; three-course prix-fixe lunch $15.50–$19.50; Sat–Sun brunch entrees $12–$32.50. AE, DC, MC, V.

Open: Lunch, Mon–Fri noon–3:30pm. Dinner, Sun–Fri 5:30pm–11pm; Sat 5pm–1am. Brunch, Sat and Sun 10am–3:30pm. Pre-theater dinner served Mon–Fri 5:30–6:45pm; late-night dinner Mon–Fri 10pm–11pm. **Bus:** M10, Central Park West.

New York's venerable Tavern on the Green, right in Central Park, is a fantasyland come to life. Rooms of crystal and frosted mirrors, of glass and sparkling lights reflected from the trees in the park, of dazzling chandeliers and Tiffany-style lamps, create a kind of modern rococo setting. When you call for reservations, ask to be seated in the Crystal Room; with its three walls of glass and ornate chandeliers, you'll feel as if you're inside a huge, transparent wedding cake. And the mood is as festive as that of a wedding, too, with masses of flowers everywhere and all kinds of festivities and celebrations going on at neighboring tables. Of all the restaurants in New York, it seems that the Tavern is most perfectly suited for celebrations. Service is deft and professional, and you will be well taken care of by a friendly crew.

The food is first-rate: Chef Marc Poidevin, who won accolades for his work as executive chef at Maxim's and as executive sous chef at Le Cirque, has revamped the menu. His style is basically French, with Northern Italian accents. Mozzarella bocconcini with sautéed shiitake mushrooms and string beans and light asparagus soup are both good ways to start dinner. Two or three pastas are available (I especially like the fetuccine with spring vegetables), along with half a dozen seafood choices (chef Marc does an excellent grilled swordfish steak with lime sauce and vegetables). Other grills and entrees included roast rack of lamb with spring vegetables; flavorful sautéed quail with rosemary and polenta; and roasted half chicken with apricot-cumin sausage, mashed potatoes, and thyme sauce. Save room for a dessert like the "voluptuous chocolate top hat" with raspberries; classic crème brûlée; or the "red, sweet, cold and crisp" conconction of raspberries and strawberries in phyllo pastry with vanilla ice cream. Lunch and brunch have similar menus and are somewhat less expensive.

Tavern on the Green offers outdoor seating in a lovely garden in fair weather. There's dancing on summer evenings only, to both live and taped music. The mood is pure magic. Tuesday through Saturday, the Chestnut Room features live jazz.

VINCE & EDDIE'S, 70 West 68th St. Tel. 721-0068.

Cuisine: AMERICAN. **Reservations:** Recommended a week in advance; try for cancellations.

$ Prices: Appetizers $4.50–$12; main courses $13.95–$18.95.

Open: Lunch, Mon–Sat noon–3pm. Dinner, Mon–Sat 5pm–midnight; Sun 5–11pm. Brunch, Sun noon–3pm. **Bus:** M10 to Central Park West.

One is almost tempted to say, "Welcome Home to Vince and Eddie's." Ensconced in a cosy brownstone, with a lovely garden in back for warm-weather dining, this warm and tasteful yet unpretentious place serves the kind of food your grandmother used to make—and if your grandmother happened to be a simple yet superb cook with a light touch, you'll definitely feel at home. In cool weather, a fire roars in the hearth just opposite the bar.

Checkered table linens, handsome antiques, and warmly attentive service underscore the innlike ambiance. The selection of dishes includes melt-in-your-mouth charcoal-grilled salmon, which arrives resting atop a bed of tender young steamed asparagus au beurre and makes you wonder why anyone would even consider eating plain old meat and potatoes again—that is, until you taste Vince & Eddie's grilled shell steak with peppercorn sauce and french fries. Red snapper with pecans and pan-fried quail with sweet potato fries are slightly whimsical—and delicious—variations on a theme. The rather short menu rotates, so don't expect to find everything I've described, but whatever is on the menu will be excellent. Desserts, too, are winners.

NOTE: Vince and Eddie themselves—Vincent Orgera and Eddie Schoenfeld—recently opened **Fishin Eddie,** 73 W. 71st St. (tel. 874-3474), a fish house that serves terrific Italian-accented seafood, such as pasta in white-clam sauce, lobster, and Dungeness crab. You'll find the same friendly young professionals at Vince & Eddie's shuttling between the busy front bar and back tables.

MODERATE

JOSEPHINA, 1900 Broadway, between 63rd and 64th Sts. Tel. 799-1000.
   Cuisine: CONTEMPORARY ITALIAN/SEAFOOD. **Reservations:** Essential for pretheater dinner.
$ **Prices:** Appetizers $4.75–$6.75; main courses $9.75–$15.75; three-course pre-theater dinner $23. AE, MC, V.
   Open: Lunch, Tues–Fri noon–2:45pm. Dinner, daily 5:30–midnight. Pre-theater dinner daily 5:30–7:30pm. Brunch, Sat–Sun 11am–3pm. Bar open noon–1am, light food available in between lunch and dinner. **Bus:** M104.

Fifty years ago, people ate healthy without knowing it, claims Louis Lanza, owner/chef at this smashing new grand café directly across the street from Lincoln Center. High-ceilinged and with a casual-yet-sophisticated Mediterranean/Caribbean mood, Josephina boasts two outdoor dining areas, one on the sidewalk facing Lincoln Center, the other in a private garden out back. Lanza's grandmother, Josephina, for whom the restaurant is named and from whom he learned to cook, used olive oil instead of butter and plenty of mineral-filled greens like broccoli, rabe, and arugula. Louis has adapted her ideas and come up with a winning menu, emphasizing food that's high in taste but low in fat; all at good prices. Poached shrimp and sea scallops in a lemongrass vegetable broth with sweet-potato–and–cashew dumplings and julienne vegetables, pasta pesto, and horseradish-crusted salmon are among his signature main courses; Thai shrimp on cool Asian noodles and flavorful grilled portobello mushrooms are among the appetizers. Free-range chicken, organic greens when available, and organic quinoa grain underscore the kitchen's commitment. A pre-theater menu is offered nightly; come before 6:30pm and they guarantee to get you into your seat by curtain time. You can—and should—come back after for the dessert sampler ($5 per person); heavenly lemon-ribbon ice-cream pie, macadamia-and-oat apple crisp with vanilla-bean ice cream, and chocolate ovation bring the crowds to their feet.

PATZO, 2330 Broadway, corner of 85th St. Tel. 496-9240.
   Cuisine: NORTHERN ITALIAN. **Reservations:** Recommended.
$ **Prices:** Appetizers $2.95–$5.95; main courses $7.95–$15.95. AE, CB, DC, MC, V.
   Open: Daily 11:30am–1am. Bar open until 2 or 3am. **Bus:** M104.

This pleasant, casually stylish Upper West Side café emphasizes light Northern Italian cooking. Patzo is a two-story space with an atrium stairway and a huge bar on one side of the first floor. The other side of the ground floor has banquettes and tables, and upstairs is a large seating area, my favorite section, with large windows looking out on the bustling street life. The decor is understated, but the color is all there in the delicious food.

Their wonderful little pizzas and pastas make nice late-night suppers; baked lasagna and canneloni verdi, both served with a house salad, are especially good. For a regular dinner, you may want to start with a salad (maybe endive, radicchio, and watercress) or their hearty minestrone. Recommended among the main courses are fresh salmon steak, grilled to perfection and topped with basil and fresh plum tomatoes; penne primavera with vegetables, garlic, and light tomato-cream sauce; and tender pieces of chicken on the bone, sautéed with garlic, white wine, and sausage. Don't miss the desserts: The homemade tazzini di crema, rich with bittersweet chocolate and cream, served in an espresso cup, is divine; so, too, are the tiramisu and the chef's own cheesecake. You can enjoy Saturday or Sunday brunch to the tune of a live jazz combo.

THE SALOON, 1920 Broadway, at 64th St. Tel. 874-1500.
   Cuisine: AMERICAN/CONTINENTAL. **Reservations:** Recommended, especially for pre-theater dinner.
   $ Prices: Appetizers $4.25–$7.95; main courses $7.50–$18.95. AE, CB, DC, MC, V.
   Open: Sun–Thurs 11:30am–midnight for food, bar until 2am; Fri–Sat 11:30am–2am for food, bar until 3am. **Bus:** M104.

One of the most enjoyable restaurants at Lincoln Center is this bustling and attractive place, with an invitingly spacious sidewalk café open in nice weather. The menu has something for just about everyone—burgers, omelets, a hot salad of wild mushrooms and fresh salmon, and roast chicken with black olives. They'll see that you get to your Lincoln Center event promptly if you tell them you have a curtain to make. And after the curtain falls, plenty of luscious desserts; a variety of coffees, teas, and mineral waters; and an extensive wine list make this a perfect place for discussing the niceties of the performance. Yes, they do have roller-skating waiters.

SHUN LEE WEST, 43 West 65th St. Tel. 595-8895.
   Cuisine: CHINESE. **Reservations:** Recommended.
   $ Prices: Appetizers $4.50–$14.95; main courses $12.95–$35. AE, CB, DC, MC, V.
   Open: Daily noon–midnight. **Bus:** M104.

Long a darling of the food critics, Shun Lee West, a half block from Lincoln Center, is a large, sleek establishment where Chinese food takes on a new meaning. No chow mein or egg foo yung are served here. Rather, there is the delicate Neptune's Net, fresh-sliced shrimp, scallops, sea bass, and lobster sautéed in a wine sauce and served in a potato basket; chan-do-chicken, chicken nuggets marinated in spices and sautéed with ginger and hot pepper; and leg of lamb Hunan style. Peking duck is a specialty (a $35 order can serve about four), and it need not be ordered in advance.

The ambiance is as exciting as the food. The bar's white monkey and dragon sculptures, with their tiny, flashing eyes, lead the way to the boldly elegant dining area. Tall booths ring an open center eating area; high banquettes offer total privacy. Each table is set with pink table linen and black tableware. Down a couple of steps are the open tables, also laid with the dramatic pink-and-black settings. Surrounding the entire ceiling is a continuous white dragon. All in all, it's an impressive sight.

In addition, the newer **Shun Lee Café,** adjacent to Shun Lee but with its own 65th Street entrance, serves dim sum, the traditional Chinese tea lunch, and Chinese street foods from rolling carts. It is open weekdays from 5:30pm to midnight and Saturday and Sunday from noon to 2:30pm, with dim sum available at all times.

STEVE MCGRAW'S, 158 West 72nd St. Tel. 362-2590.

Cuisine: CONTINENTAL. **Reservations:** Recommended for restaurant, imperative for show.

$ Prices: Appetizers $4.25–$8; main courses $8–$20; Sun brunch $6.25–$8.75. AE, DC, MC, V.

Open: Dinner, Sun–Thurs 5pm–2am; Fri–Sat 5pm–4am. Brunch, Sun noon–4pm. **Bus:** M104.

Most New Yorkers know Steve McGraw's as a supper club with top-notch cabaret revues. (*Forever Plaid* is its current long-running hit—see Chapter 10.) But people may not know that Steve McGraw's is also an excellent restaurant; you can have a very good meal in the attractive little dining room downstairs whether or not you attend the upstairs entertainment afterward. Lots of Broadway casts come here after their own shows are finished. The food is continental, with leanings both Italian—like Cornish hen rusticana, chicken piccata, and fritto misto—and Finnish—like fresh fish smoked to order via a hickory-smoking process. For starters you could have roasted peppers and mozzarella with pesto sauce or tabouli salad. Then on to the main course, like brochette of shrimps and scallops enlivened with a honey, lime, and horseradish marinade; poached filet of snapper in white wine and ginger; or broiled porterhouse veal chop with escargot butter. All entrees are accompanied by vegetables and roasted potato. Desserts can be wonderful, like New Orleans mud cake, mocha cheesecake, or just fresh strawberries with whipped cream and cinnamon.

It's fun to come for Sunday brunch, too, and maybe catch a performance of *Forever Plaid* at the same time. Tickets for *Forever Plaid* are $30 on Sunday and Tuesday to Thursday and $35 on Friday and Saturday.

TEACHERS TOO, 2271 Broadway, between 81st and 82nd Sts. Tel. 362-4900.

Cuisine: CONTEMPORARY AMERICAN. **Reservations:** Recommended.

$ Prices: Appetizers $2.95–$7.95; main courses $6.50–$16.95; Sun brunch $4.95–$7.95. AE, DC, MC, V.

Open: Sun–Thurs 11am–1am; Fri–Sat 11am–2am. Brunch, Sun 11am–4pm. **Bus:** M104.

There's a very relaxed feeling at Teachers Too, a hangout for many of the city's artists, writers, and other members of the intelligentsia who live on the West Side. Since it's just about 15 blocks (a short bus ride) from Lincoln Center, it makes sense to enjoy a delicious, reasonably priced meal here before or after a Lincoln Center event. Walk past the big mahogany bar up front and you'll find a dining room with natural-wood walls, butcher-block tables, and an intimate yet lively atmosphere. All the paintings and photographs on the walls were done by customers or by the aspiring artists and performers who wait tables with good cheer and courteous attention.

The food is the work of its artistic Thai cook, who is known for his lightly spiced chicken gai yung and traditional pad thai, as well as other inspirations, like Santa Fe chicken fajitas, Indonesian chicken satay, and Roumanian steak smothered in caramelized onions. Blackboard specials always include at least five broiled fresh (never frozen) fish dishes every night. Teachers Too is also known for its tasty spinach-and-bacon salad (if you find sand in it, your meal is on the house!); great appetizers like fresh Maine mussels, fried Cajun rock shrimp, and a nacho platter with guacamole; and luscious desserts, of which the praline ice-cream cake and the orange pound cake are standouts.

Come on Sunday and indulge in one of the liveliest brunches in town—eggs Benedict, eggs rancheros, caviar and sour cream, and the like, with a cocktail thrown in for good measure. In warm weather, it's fun to sit at the sidewalk café.

BUDGET

CAFE BEL CANTO, 1991 Broadway, between 67th and 68th Sts. Tel. 362-4642.

Cuisine: ITALIAN. **Reservations:** Not required.
$ Prices: Main courses $7–$10. AE, MC, V.
Open: Daily 10am–11pm. **Bus:** M104.

I wish New York had many more places like Café Bel Canto, a few blocks from Lincoln Center. It's a charming, open-to-the-street café, which is also a public space: Users are not required to purchase food or drink, which means that, after the concert or the ballet at Lincoln Center, you can simply come and sit with friends, maybe have a meal, a cup of tea—or nothing at all! And if you get a table near the front, you can enjoy the great free show of the passing parade. If you do wish to eat, however, we can tell you that the food is delightful, and very modestly priced. Cold dishes include a flavorful bruschetta (grilled Italian bread topped with basil and olive oil, served with tomato salad and Italian salami); a tomato, avocado, and mozzarella plate with Italian peasant bread; several good salads and sandwiches Italian style; and a nice selection of fresh fruits and cheese. Frittata, calamari fritti, several pastas, pizzas, a zesty grilled chicken and zucchini sandwich with smoked mozzarella, and a grilled sirloin steak are among the hot dishes. Espresso, cappuccino, regular and herbal teas, beer, and juices, and attractive homemade Italian desserts are also available. Bravo Bel Canto!

DALLAS BBQ, 27 West 72nd St., just off Central Park West. Tel. 873-2004.

Cuisine: AMERICAN. **Reservations:** Not accepted.
$ Prices: Appetizers $2.95–$7.95; main courses $3.95–$8.95; Early Bird special $7.95 for two, Mon–Fri noon to 6pm.
Open: Sun–Thurs noon–midnight; Fri–Sat noon–1am. **Bus:** M10, Central Brk West.

One of the Upper West Side's busiest thoroughfares, West 72nd Street boasts one of the best bargains in town. If your taste runs to barbecued chicken and ribs, then Dallas is a must. Arrive early, or you'll have to wait in line. The crowds are drawn by the combination of the attractive room—a two-level space with modern art on the walls—and the incredibly reasonable prices on the chicken and ribs. Side orders of fresh vegetable tempura and a loaf of onion rings, huge enough for several famished eaters, should not be missed. Burgers, Texas-style chili, chicken salad, and fried Texas-style chicken wings are also crowd pleasers. The best buy of all is the Early Bird special, on Monday to Friday from noon to 6pm, which includes chicken-vegetable soup, half a barbecued chicken, corn bread, and potatoes. This place is crowded, noisy, and lots of fun. And their margaritas are first-rate.

Note: Dallas BBQ has spread its wings all over town, including two tremendously popular outlets in Greenwich Village: at 21 University Place (tel. 674-4450) and 132 Second Ave. at 8th Street (tel. 777-5574); on the Upper East Side (tel. 772-9393), a chrome-and-neon version is at 1265 Third Ave., between 72nd and 73rd Sts. All feature the same menus, and prices rarely vary by more than a dollar or two.

RUPPERT'S, 269 Columbus Ave., between 72nd and 73rd Sts. Tel. 873-9400.

Cuisine: AMERICAN. **Reservations:** Recommended.

$ Prices: Appetizers $.95–$2.95–$4.95; main courses $3.95–$11.50; Sat and Sun brunch $5.95–$10.95. AE, MC, V.

Open: Lunch, daily 11am–4pm. Dinner Sun–Thurs 5pm–12:45am; Fri–Sat 5pm–1:45am. Sat and Sun 10:30am–4pm.

Bus: M104.

Ruppert's is a big favorite just a short walk from Lincoln Center, and its 40-seat glassed-in sidewalk café allows you a prime vantage point from which to watch the people parade on Columbus Avenue. Indoors, you'll enjoy the delightful mood of an 1877 salon restored to its turn-of-the-century Victorian atmosphere, so pretty with its mirrors and big mahogany bar and forest-green leather banquettes. Ruppert's is a lively, with-it, sometimes noisy New York scene. The food is always satisfying, imaginatively seasoned, without being at all pretentious. You might start your meal with steamed mussels marinara or strips of fried chicken breasts with warm honey-mustard sauce. Pastas and salads are imaginative and, among the main courses, the grilled fresh salmon steak with chive butter and the sautéed calves' liver with caramelized onions and bacon are favorites. Lunch, similar but with the addition of a few interesting sandwiches (such as blackened breast of chicken), runs a few dollars less. And Saturday and Sunday brunch is always fun.

There's another Ruppert's, also refreshingly inexpensive, over on the Upper East Side, 1662 Third Ave. at 93rd St. (tel. 831-1900).

12. UPPER EAST SIDE

EXPENSIVE

LE CIRQUE, 58 East 65th St. Tel. 794-9292.

Cuisine: FRENCH. **Reservations:** Required one to two weeks in advance.

$ Prices: Appetizers $11–$31; main courses $28–$33; prix-fixe dinner $65 and $80; prix-fixe lunch $34. AE, DC, MC, V, and more.

Open: Lunch, Mon–Sat noon–3pm. Dinner, Mon–Sat 6–10:30pm. **Closed:** July. **Bus:** Any Fifth or Madison Ave. bus.

There's no other restaurant quite like Le Cirque for glamour, prestige, and the meal of a lifetime, served in elegant continental splendor. Awarded four stars by the *New York Times* and the only U.S. restaurant rated 19 out of 20 toques by Gault Millau, it is the place to see and be seen—unique, memorable, and expensive. Credit much of Le Cirque's success to dedicated owner Sirio Maccioni and chef Daniel Boulud, an astounding talent, who comes up with a menu of impressive scope and variety. Note the interior's soft French blue color scheme and the witty murals of costumed monkeys in chefs' toques. Cheerful lighting and bouquets of fresh flowers complement the romantic baroque interior.

A relatively "inexpensive" way to visit Le Cirque is to opt for the three-course prix-fixe luncheon at $34, not including wine. Start with chilled baby artichokes in basil dressing with assorted seed toasts or exquisite tuna tartar seasoned with curry, radishes, and fried celery root. Roasted saddle and braised leg of rabbit is an eminently worthwhile main course, as is the lobster risotto with shredded green cabbage and lobster sauce with rosemary. Desserts are irresistible—the heavenly brûlée "Le Cirque" is considered the best in town, and a crisp, thin disc of chocolate alternating with layers of raspberry mousse is superb.

Dinner, à la carte, usually runs about $85 to $95, excluding wine, tax, and tip (the exceptionally broad international wine list has won awards for excellence). Appetizers include a baked potato in sea salt stuffed with fresh black or white truffles. Among the entrees is black bass wrapped in red potatoes and treated to red-wine sauce. Yet another suggestion is roasted saddle of rabbit with garlic and with carrot purée. Dinner shares the same "cartes des desserts" as lunch, but an extra finishing touch is "l'inspiration du chef patissier," an offering of three or four of the day's pastries to round out your four-star meal.

MARK'S, at The Mark Hotel, 25 East 77th St. Tel. 879-1864.

Cuisine: FRENCH CUISINE BOURGEOISE/AMERICAN. **Reservations:** Recommended.

$ Prices: Appetizers $7.50–$14; main courses $18–$32, prix-fixe dinner $38–$50. Lunch main courses $14–$18; two-course prix-fixe lunch $24, three-course prix-fixe lunch $28. Sun brunch: three-course prix-fixe $30 (also à la carte). AE, CB, DC, MC, V. **Open:** Breakfast daily 6:30–10am. Lunch, Mon–Sat 11:30am–2:30pm. Dinner, daily 6:30pm–10:30pm. Afternoon tea, daily 2:30–5:30pm. Brunch, Sun 11:30am–2:30pm. **Subway:** 6 to 77th St.

Sublime food, an exquisite setting, and the air of a romantic retreat are winning high praise for Mark's, a perfect place for lunch or dinner if you're museum- or gallery-hopping uptown. Arranged in tiers and dimly lit, Mark's is an intimate, clublike oasis appointed in velvet, silk, and mahogany and dotted with potted orchids and palms, antique prints, marble columns, brocaded pillows, and tufted, heavily fringed, English-style banquettes. Mark's tables are set with Villeroy & Boch china and engraved silver—a perfect background for exquisite food.

Chef Philippe Boulot, who learned and refined his art in his native France, has been acclaimed by New York restaurant critics as one of the stars of the 1990s. Many selections change seasonally. At dinner, you might begin with ragout of snails and sweet garlic custard, New York goat-cheese parfait, or Napoleon of asparagus. Roasted free-range chicken for two, served with mashed potatoes, is a simple yet excellent entree, matched but not outdone by such selections as crisp roast breast of guinea fowl with calvados and baby turnip sauce, sautéed sweetbreads with ragoût of chanterelles, and grilled dry-aged sirloin steak with peppercorn sauce. A monthly rotating "Vinter's Dinner," available every evening ($38 without wine), pairs the personal selection of a notable winemaker with a three-course degustation menu created by chef Philippe Boulot. And desserts are lovely—perhaps the Gourmandise of chocolate, fruit soup flavored with lemongrass, or crème brûlée with nougatine crust.

Lunch is fun, too, with two-course and three-course prix-fixe meals, plus à la carte selections. Whether it be Louisiana prawns on lentil salad with parsley vinaigrette or Boulot's signature deli sandwich—turkey, ham, and Swiss cheese on farm rye—it will be executed to perfection. And many lunchtime salads are available as either an appetizer or a main course. Afternoon tea is à la carte or $15 prix-fixe. And brunch is a Sunday favorite.

THE SIGN OF THE DOVE, 1110 Third Ave., at 65th St. Tel. 861-8080.

Cuisine: CONTEMPORARY AMERICAN. **Reservations:** Recommended.

$ Prices: Appetizers $8–$16; main courses $19–$36; prix-fixe dinner $59. At the Café Bar, appetizers $8–$12; main courses $12–$18. AE, CB, DC, DISC, MC, V.

Open: Lunch, Tues–Fri noon–2:30pm. Dinner, Mon–Fri 6–11pm; Sat 5:30–11:30pm; Sun 6–10pm. Brunch, Sat and Sun 11:30am–2:30pm. Café Bar open until the "wee hours." **Bus:** Any Third Ave. bus. **Subway:** B or Q to Lexington Ave.

This is perhaps New York's most unabashedly romantic restaurant. For years people have been raving about the beauty of its old-world Mediterranean-style setting. Its dining areas are separated by brick walls with wrought-iron filigree; its skylight admits sunlight by day and soft lights by night; its decor features glorious flowers, antiques, and mirrors—and tables well spaced for privacy. But the cuisine seldom lived up to the splendor of the setting until a few years ago when a new chef, Andrew D'Amico, created a French-influenced contemporary American menu that has all the food critics raving; since then, the *New York Times* has twice given it a coveted three-star rating. Dinner choices are difficult, since almost all the dishes are exquisite. Among the appetizers, the pumpkin ravioli with parmesan and truffle oil and the delicate casserole of oysters and spring vegetables are well recommended. Main courses are similarly imaginative, with international accents: pan-seared yellowfin tuna is served with bok choy, napa, coriander, and a green curry broth; Indian spiced lentils, basmati rice, and cucumber raita accompany roast baby chicken. Grilled Muscovy duck is delicious, served with pumpkin pancakes, cranberry chutney, and roast pears. Portions are not large, but you'll probably be pleasantly full by the time they arrive, since the wine list is outstanding, and the bread basket—filled with double-walnut bread, pepper brioche, or dark sourdough—is one of the marvels of New York! (All breads are baked at their own bread shop, Ecce Panis, three doors away, and are also for sale at the shop.) Desserts, like the chocolate devil's-food cake with orange cream and the ricotta-and-lemon ice-cream cassata, dazzle.

To sample the fare for a less exalted bill, come for lunch, when entrees like the focaccia sandwich with roast marinated chicken and escarole and angel-hair pasta with lump crabmeat and roasted tomato broth are in a comfortable $12–$20 range. Brunch (most main dishes $12–$18) is splendid, or you can have your meal in the oh-so-cozy Café/Bar, a very "in," East Side scene. While the bass and piano purr in the background, couples sip and share the likes of fried platanos and avocado salsa, a Maine lobster salad sandwich, or grilled sourdough with roast chicken. Dress in this part of the restaurant can be anything from blue jeans to black tie—and often is. Tuesday to Friday there's a pianist/singer from 5 to 9pm and jazz from 9:30pm to 1:30am. On Saturday evening it's jazz from 10pm to 2am, and on Sunday and Monday there's jazz from 8:30pm to 12:30am.

MODERATE

ARIZONA 206, 206 E. 60th St. Tel. 838-0440.
　　Cuisine: NOUVELLE SOUTHWESTERN. **Reservations:** Recommended.
$ Prices: Appetizers $5–$10; main courses $16–$26. AE, DC, MC, V.
　　Open: Lunch, Tues–Sat noon–3pm. Dinner, Mon–Thurs 6–11pm; Fri 6–11:30pm; Sat 5–11:30pm; Sun 6–10:30pm. **Bus:** Any Third Ave. bus.

Some of the best nouvelle Southwestern cuisine anywhere can be found right here in New York at Arizona 206, one of the liveliest and most-talked-about restaurants in town. The setting is long, narrow, and cavelike, with adobe plaster walls, natural pine floors and tables, and a whimsical fireplace decorated with papier-mâché animals and hung with cowbells. The atmosphere is charged with animated conversation (if you're sensitive to noise, go at off-peak hours), and the menu is innovative and irresistible. The food is, quite simply, delicious. To guarantee the freshest ingredients and offer the widest possible diversity, menus change seasonally. Among the appetizers, the tequila-cured salmon quesadilla with basil crème fraîche and the herbed stuffed quail with a salsa of black-beans and corn and tarragon sauce are presented with the imaginative flair that characterizes everything here. Highly recommended entrees include grilled Muscovy duck with wild-rice corn fritters, seared salmon with jicama-and-tangerine salsa, and Pacific sturgeon with jalapeño pasta. The wine list, mostly Californian vintages with a few interesting choice from Texas and Oregon, is reasonably priced. For dessert, try the Ibarra truffle diablo cake, with fans of white and gianduja chocolate, or the Grand Marnier spice cake with jasmine-ginger ice cream.

COCO PAZZO, 23 East 74th St. Tel. 794-0205.
　　Cuisine: ITALIAN. **Reservations:** Necessary.
$ Prices: Appetizers, $6–$9.50; main courses $17–$29.00. AE, MC, V.
　　Open: Lunch, Mon–Fri noon–3pm. Dinner, Mon–Sat 6pm–midnight; Sun 5:30–11:30pm. Brunch, Sat and Sun noon–3pm. **Closed:** No brunch July 1–Labor Day. **Bus:** Any Madison Ave. bus.

The name means "crazy chef," but the cook here seems about as crazy as a fox. Raves—and crowds—have poured in since this white-hot Upper East Sider opened in 1991. The secret: simplicity, from the bright interior to the generous portions of solid

Italian fare. Roasting and grilling make familiar favorites fresh; start with a mouth-watering salad of mushrooms with olive oil, lemon, and celery on air-dried beef; light but satisfying grilled vegetables; or a tangy, tantalizing salad of fennel and blood oranges. Don't miss main courses like Spaghetti alle Vongole (baby clams sautéed in olive oil, garlic, crushed red pepper, and tomato) and Salmone con Lenticchie e Bietola (roasted salmon with rosemary, served with warm beets and lentils). On weekends, Coco Pazzo offers a "family-style" menu featuring huge, shareable portions; although not cheap, it's one of the neighborhood's better values.

CONTRAPUNTO, 200 E. 60th St. Tel. 751-8616.

Cuisine: NOUVELLE ITALIAN (mostly pasta). **Reservations:** Not accepted.

$ Prices: Appetizers $6.50–$9.50; main courses $13–$21.50. AE, DC, MC, V.

Open: Daily noon–midnight. **Bus:** Any Third Ave. bus.

Contrapunto has to be the best thing that's happened to Third Avenue since Bloomingdale's. Located on the corner right across the street from that famed shopping emporium, Contrapunto is also the best thing to happen to the noodle since Marco Polo came back from China. Two sides of this stylish, second-story trattoria are totally glass, so your view is of Third Avenue, just above Cinema Row. Everything in the room, which seats 60, is snow white—walls, napery (white tablecloths under glass)—and there is sparkling track lighting.

Contrapunto's theme is to serve as "counterpoint" to other restaurants serving pasta, and they carry it off with class. The menu lists 21 creations of either fresh or imported pasta; and since they're all so good, you might do best to come here with a group and try a little bit of several. I like the capelli bergino (angel-hair pasta enlivened with sun-dried tomatos and artichokes); the papparedelle boscaiola (a wide ribbon pasta with fresh mushrooms); and best of all, the tagliarini conga d'ora (a thin ribbon pasta with julienned vegetables). Other specialties include a very good broiled veal chop served with braised escarole, tomatoes, and garlic; and a whole Cornish hen, grilled and roasted with a white wine and bay leaves. Let your group also share some flavorful appetizers, like the grilled Portabello mushrooms with arugula. And when it comes to dessert, no one should have to choose between creamy homemade gelati of praline or white chocolate (the flavors change every day) or chocolate Mascarpone cake, so don't—share them all.

JO-JO'S, 160 East 64th St. Tel. 223-5656.

Cuisine: FRENCH LOW FAT. **Reservations:** Crucial; should be made two weeks in advance.

$ Prices: Appetizers $8–$12; main courses $15–$22. AE, DISC, MC, V.

Open: Lunch, Mon–Fri noon–2pm. Dinner Mon–Sat 6–11pm. **Bus:** Any Lexington or Third Ave. bus.

Jo-Jo is such a cute-as-a-button name that you might be tempted not to take this place seriously. That would be a mistake. Jo-Jo derives its name completely honorably. It is the nickname of owner/chef Jean-Georges Vongerichten, the young Frenchman whose culinary expertise catapulted Restaurant Lafayette at the Drake Hotel to stardom.

This intimate restaurant on two levels of a lovely East Side town house is noisy and cheery. On the main level, red banquettes, beveled gold-leaf mirrors, and pink Venetian glass sconces set the warmly elegant mood. Paper tablecloths and purple, yellow, and orange plastic napkin rings let you know things are a bit tongue-in-cheek. Upstairs, oil lamps, bold cartoonlike oil paintings, and mahogany bentwood chairs with black leather seats are a bit more serious. And there's an irresistible back room with a fireplace, a fringed Victorian lamp, regal Queen Anne chairs, and a large faux leopard divan. It looks good enough to move into. The food is even better.

The simple and deliberately clear menu offers just six choices for each course. Jean-Georges favors cooking with vegetable juices and flavored oils instead of rich sauces. You could start, for example, with terrine of goat cheese and potatoes with arugula juice, rabbit ravioli with Swiss chard and tomato oil, or shrimp in a spiced carrot juice with Thai lime leaves. Lobster with sautéed mushrooms is flavored with asparagus juice. Refreshing salmon with citrus vinaigrette is wrapped in rice paper. Lamb cutlet and shoulder confit with basil oil is served with eggplant pancake. Desserts, created by colleague Eric Hubert, include light and cool melon sorbet with chocolate seeds, crunchy almond crisp with raspberry cream and vanilla syrup, and aromatic brioche "perdu" topped with caramelized apples.

For food of this calibre, Jo-Jo's is not expensive. Even the wine list includes 10 wines under $20. Jean-Georges—Jo-Jo to his friends and fans—wanted to give people a sophisticated neighborhood place they would feel comfortable coming back to again and again.

KALINKA, 1067 Madison Ave., at 81st St. Tel. 472-9656.
Cuisine: RUSSIAN. **Reservations:** Recommended.
$ Prices: Appetizers $2.50–$17.50; main courses $13.50–$17.75; lunch main courses $9.80–$14.90. AE, CB, DC, MC, V. **Open:** Lunch, daily 11am–4pm. Dinner, daily 4–9:45pm. **Bus:** Any Madison Ave. bus.

A block from the Metropolitan Museum of Art is Kalinka, with its bright-red tile facade; burgundy canopy; and romantic, cozy, and hospitable ambiance. Stop in for moderately priced, home-cooked Russian cuisine in an old-world setting.

Start your dinner with the glorious zakuski supreme—a platter of red caviar, pâté, herring, diced and marinated eggplant, potato salad, and beets, all arranged with style and finesse. Kalinka's soups are also highly recommended: the hot borscht, thick with meat, cabbage, beets, and sour cream; and the classic cold borscht, very refreshing on a hot summer day. A wonderful seasonal specialty, available only on request, is ucha, a salmon broth with fresh dill, black olives, carrots, potatoes, and lemon. As for an entree, try a first-rate Kulibiaka (salmon in pastry, with kasha, mushrooms, and vegetable), or chicken Kiev, served as in old Russia, with mashed potatoes and green peas. It's hard to resist the blini, those versatile Russian pancakes, so satisfying for lunch, dinner, or a snack. For a touch of class, Kalinka accents them with red caviar and sour cream. Another special dish is pojarksi: well-seasoned ground chicken and veal sautéed in butter-and-mushroom sauce. If you passed up the blini earlier, order them for dessert, this time garnished with sour-cherry preserves and a dollop of sour cream—they're perfect for sharing. Equally good is lodochka—a boat-shaped cookie filled with chocolate butter cream and flavored with rum. Russian tea, served in a glass and accompanied by sour-cherry preserves, is a fitting finale to your meal. Wine is available by the glass or bottle.

Lunch at Kalinka offers similar appetizers and many of the same main courses, plus stuffed cabbage, garlic Cornish hen, and garnished herring with steamed potatoes.

LE REFUGE, 166 East 82nd St., between Lexington and Third Aves. Tel. 861-4505.

Cuisine: FRENCH. **Reservations:** Recommended.

$ Prices: Appetizers $5.50–$9.50; main courses $16.50–$23.50. No credit cards.

Open: Lunch, Mon–Sat noon–3pm. Dinner, Mon–Sat 5:30–11pm; Sun 5–9:30pm. Brunch, Sun noon–4pm. **Bus:** Any Third Ave. bus.

If it were in the French countryside instead of on Manhattan's East Side, Le Refuge would probably have a rating of three stars in the French guidebooks. And it wins several stars from me, too. Visiting this enchanting bistro, now in its 17th year, is the next best thing to being in France. The atmosphere is relaxed and romantic; the service by the young, friendly staff is impeccable; and the food is traditional French country fare of the highest order.

Of the several dining rooms, my favorites are in the rear: One, with a 17th-century French tapestry, overlooks a small garden; another has a fireplace, and there are beamed ceilings and brick walls all about. A meal could start with a mild, extremely tasty and creamy potato-leek soup; a carpaccio of tuna; or a commendable ravioli stuffed with langoustines and a warm goat-cheese salad. Of the main courses, the filet of beef with green peppers, loin of veal with wild mushrooms, Norwegian salmon garnished with caviar, and bouillabaisse are highly recommended. Desserts are not to be missed, especially the chocolate-soufflé cake. The extensive French wine list is personally overseen by chef/owner Pierre Saint-Denis and has several moderately priced selections.

Since Le Refuge is within walking distance of the Metropolitan Museum of Art and the rest of Fifth Avenue's Museum Mile, it's an excellent lunch stop for light fare like omelets and salads.

LE VEAU D'OR, 129 East 60th St., between Park and Lexington Aves. Tel. 838-8133.

Cuisine: FRENCH. **Reservations:** Recommended.

$ Prices: Prix-fixe dinner $24–$30; prix-fixe lunch $16–$22. AE, MC, V.

Open: Lunch, Mon–Sat noon–3pm. Dinner, Mon–Sat 5:30–10pm. **Closed:** Sat in July and Aug. **Bus:** Any Lexington or Third Ave. bus.

Le Veau d'Or has long been hailed as one of New York's best French bistros. Its robust, hearty, bourgeois fare is responsible for drawing almost unmanageable crowds night in, night out. And no wonder: The food and service are impeccable, and you can have a complete meal, from pâté to fromage, for the price of an entree. Rarely have I been disappointed in any of the house specials—and that includes the filet of sole amandine, veal kidneys with mustard sauce, roast duck with cherry sauce and wild rice, and grilled lamb chops with watercress garnish. You may begin with an appetizer like artichoke vinaigrette or pâté, have onion soup or soup of the day, and end with a lovely dessert like crème caramel or pêche Melba. This is not the place for a quiet, hand-holding dinner—it's too crowded and tends to get noisy. For more relaxation, come at lunchtime, when it's not quite as frantic.

MAY WE, 1022 Lexington Ave., at 73rd St. Tel. 249-0200.
Cuisine: SOUTHERN FRENCH/NORTHERN ITALIAN. **Reservations:** Recommended.
$ Prices: Appetizers $5.50–$12; main courses $16–$19.50. AE, DC, MC, V.
Open: Lunch, Tues–Fri noon–2:30pm. Dinner Tues–Fri 5:30–10:30pm; Sat–Sun 5:30–11pm. Brunch, Sat and Sun (except summer) noon–3pm. **Bus:** Any Lexington or Third Ave. bus.

After stints in Paris and at prestigious Le Colombe d'Or in New York, chef Mark May has opened his own little restaurant, and his combination of southern French and northern Italian cooking, with a bit of Moroccan spicing thrown in for good measure, has the posh neighborhood folks cheering. The two-story restaurant is a real, old-fashioned, Mom-and-Pop affair: host Nini May greets customers, seating them either downstairs at the bar (where they thoughtfully serve complete meals) or upstairs via a spiral staircase in an elongated dining room overlooking the street, its walls painted with a floral mural. Appetizers steal the show: On no account miss the ethereal bouillabaisse ravioli in saffron fumet or prickly shrimp with garlic flan and vegetable broth. The ragoût of pig's feet and sweetbreads with cèpes, morels, and creamy polenta is another marvel of the chef's art; and his socca roulade, a chickpea pancake fried and stuffed with warm ratatouille and goat cheese, is a unique creation. As for main courses, semicured cod with blended celery root and white beans, seared tuna with beet frites and orange-braised endive, and roasted monkfish with fettucine all suggest May's innovative way with fish; calf's liver with a pistachio-nut crust and sweet onion plus grilled breast and confit of duck with honey and lavender flowers are other stars of the dinner menu. Similar lunch entrees are modestly priced ($8.50–$14). At either meal desserts are wondrous, especially the signature apple tart topped with cinnamon ice cream and the extravagantly rich chocolate fondant. Brunch brings such treats as brioche French toast with fresh berries, buckwheat pancakes with caramelized apples, and duck confit with crisp risotto cake. The wine list is decently priced and well thought out. Do I like this place? *Mais oui.*

MIMOSA, 1354 First Ave., between 72nd and 73rd Sts. Tel. 988-0002.
Cuisine: MEDITERRANEAN. **Reservations:** Required.
$ Prices: Appetizers $4.75–$8; main courses $11–$20. AE, MC, V.
Open: Lunch, Mon–Fri noon–2:30pm. Dinner, Mon–Thurs 5:30–11pm; Fri–Sat 5:30pm–midnight; Sun 5–10pm. **Bus:** Any First Ave. bus.

From its rather nondescript room—cream walls, red-tiled floor, and white linen tablecloths—you'd never guess that Mimosa serves some of the Upper East Side's most delightful cuisine. Mediterranean flavors and colors infuse chef Marilyn Frobuccino's simple, intense appetizers, such as Caesar salad with anchovy-flavored polenta croutons or Greek saganaki cheese with fried okra and red onion rings; and her entrees, such as hake in lemon batter with almond sauce, black olives, and escarole, or rib-eye of lamb in mustard, parsley, and bread crumbs. A classic dessert like apple pie and strawberry napoleon will transport you back to familiar territory. In a neighborhood renowned for difficult service, Mimosa has proved a consistent pleasure; there's also an intelligently chosen, well-priced wine list.

RED TULIP, 439 East 75th St., between First and York Aves. Tel. 734-4893.

Cuisine: HUNGARIAN. **Reservations:** Necessary only for large parties.

$ Prices: Appetizers $3.75–$5; main courses $13.50–$16. AE, MC, V.

Open: Dinner only, Wed–Sat 6–11:30pm or midnight or later; Sun 5–11:30pm or midnight or later. **Bus:** Any First Ave. bus.

A visit here is like an instant trip to the Hungarian countryside, complete with charming folk art and delicious authentic food. All the furniture was handmade by Hungarian owners Kazmer and Marianne Kovacs. There are hand-embroidered pillows and woven table linens and cushions throughout; eyelet curtains; wooden floors; a tall beamed ceiling; handpainted hearts and tulips; Tyrolean doors; and the pièce de résistance, an entire Transylvanian gate, whose handsome doors are hinged open to reveal a large, romantically lit dining room lined along one side with wooden booths. There are tiny spinning wheels and native pottery, plus fresh flowers and a candle on every table, even a strolling musician.

If you can manage to come down to earth, do have dinner. The food is homey and lovely. As soon as you sit down, order a bottle of world-famous Egri Bikaver ($18), a lightly sweet (not at all syrupy) Hungarian wine commonly called "bull's blood." It will stand you in good stead all evening and is unforgettably good. You could make a meal of the appetizers alone: lesco (sliced sausage with onion, green pepper, and tomato); chicken liver Tulipan, with onions, mushrooms, and peppers; or breaded mushroom with tartar sauce and rice. The boiled beef with potatoes, veggies, and horseradish is home-cooking at its best. Paprikas, chicken or veal, comes with egg dumplings. Weiner schnitzel shows the German influence. If you care to go light, have the grilled trout or salmon or sole, broiled to a turn.

As for desserts, the Gundel-style palacsinta—crêpes flambéed in chocolate-rum sauce—are probably as good as those served in the days of the Austro-Hapsburg Empire. These, or rigo fancsi—creamy chocolate-mousse cake, alongside a cappuccino or Hungarian espresso with Hungarian apricot brandy—would make a perfect after-theater snack as well.

SEL & POIVRE, 853 Lexington Ave., between 64th and 65th Sts. Tel. 517-5780.

Cuisine: FRENCH. **Reservations:** Recommended.

$ Prices: Appetizers $5–$9.50; main courses $13.95–$22.95; prix-fixe pre-theater dinner 5–6:15pm $19.95; prix-fixe lunch $12.95; Sun brunch $12.95. AE, DC, MC, V.

Open: Lunch, Mon–Sat noon–5pm. Dinner, daily 5–11pm or later; Brunch, Sun noon–5pm. **Bus:** Any Lexington or Third Ave. bus.

Remember those good old days before prices for French food

skyrocketed? When it was still possible to get a good bistro-style meal for a reasonable sum? Sel & Poivre, a charming little restaurant, remembers, and that's good news for a smart crowd of neighborhood people, shoppers from nearby Bloomingdale's, and visitors who've discovered it. Owner Noma Dumich, who runs the restaurant with her two daughters, Pamela and Penny, has decorated the place with a splendid antique breakfront, charming photographs taken by the family in Paris, white tablecloths, and flowers on every table. The best savings can be had on the prix-fixe pre-theater menu, which includes a choice of soup du jour, salade du jour, or grilled eggplant with goat cheese. For an entree, you may choose from fish du jour, penne pasta with pink vodka sauce and caviar, and roasted chicken aux fines herbes. For dessert, you can feast on lovely lemon sorbet, fresh fruit, or chocolate-banana mousse. Chef Bernard Teissedre does a good job with everything. If you come a little later in the evening, the menu expands and the prices go up, but not that much. Among the appetizers, favorites are the clams Possillippo and the escargots. A commendable bouillabaisse can be had, or you can choose the likes of roasted quail with mushrooms in Madeira sauce, grilled salmon with pepper and ginger, or sliced steak with shallots and vinegar. Come on Friday or Saturday night and enjoy the chef's special couscous. There's always a good array of desserts. Prix-fixe lunch and Sunday brunch are also winners.

BUDGET

ARIZONA CAFE, 206 East 60th St. Tel. 838-0440.
   Cuisine: NOUVELLE SOUTHWESTERN. **Reservations:** Not accepted.
$ Prices: Appetizers $6–$10; main courses $12–$17. AE, DC, MC, V.
   Open: Mon–Sat noon–midnight; Sun 5–11pm. **Bus:** Any Third Ave. bus.

To sample the delicious—and expensive—nouvelle Southwestern cuisine of Arizona 206 (reviewed separately in this chapter) at budget prices, come right into the main restaurant at 206 E. 60th St. (tel. 838-0440) and walk through the archway to the right of the reservations desk to the Arizona Café, where scrumptious small-portioned goodies from the chef's brilliant menu await you. The beamed ceiling, natural wood tables and chairs, and handmade Mexican floor tiles suggest a Southwestern interior. At the center of it all is a fabulous white-tiled, open kitchen displaying a myriad of foodstuffs to stimulate the senses. The menu, which changes to accommodate market specials, offers a limited but exciting selection of the day's specialties priced by category; two diners would find four plates perfect for sharing. How about seared tuna rolls with ginger-wasabi aïoli, salmon Quesadilla with crème fraîche and salsa cruda, or a Southwestern Caesar salad with chile croutons? For dessert, there's lemon-pepperbread pudding with raspberry sauce or strawberry margarita mousse with cinnamon crisps. The café, like the main restaurant, tends to be noisy—all part of the fun!

COASTAL CAFE, 1557 First Ave., at 73rd St. Tel. 472-6204.
   Cuisine: SEAFOOD/PASTA. **Reservations:** Recommended for 4 or more.

$ Prices: Appetizers $4.75–$6.75; main courses $7.75–$14.75. MC, V.
Open: Dinner, Mon–Thurs 5:30–11pm; Fri–Sat 5:30–midnight; Sun 5:30–10pm. Brunch, Sat–Sun 11:30am–3pm. **Bus:** Any First Ave. bus.

Seafood lovers keep Coastal Café packed every night, and with good reason: This attractive restaurant with its spacious, modern feeling, murals on the walls, and a lively bar scene offers super-fresh, wonderful fish and seafood (flown directly from Hawaii, Louisiana, and other faraway ports), delicious pastas and Southwestern dishes, too, all at very moderate prices for the pricey East Side. And they've mastered the delicate art of preparing fish just about perfectly, with a choice of delicate sauces. The blackboard menu of fresh-grilled fish, seasonal specialties, and side dishes changes every night. On the regular menu, you can count on such appealing appetizers as ginger-glazed skewered chicken with warm sesame-peanut sauce; black-bean crabcakes with cilantro mayonnaise; and a plate of guacamole, salsa, and roasted eggplant dips. Angel-hair pasta and shrimp with stir-fry vegetables in a light basil stock is a popular pasta choice, and among the main courses, the Southwestern paella (with Gulf shrimp, smoked chicken, and Andouille sausage), chicken fajitas, and grilled poached salmon are always winners. For the health-conscious, dishes can be prepared to suit your individual dietary needs. They have even printed a supplement that gives a complete dietary breakdown of every item on the menu. For those unconcerned with such matters, they offer some of New York's most sublime desserts—chocolate-mousse cake, strawberry tulip, and warm blueberry pie. Best of all is lemon-ribbon ice-cream pie—a graham-cracker crust topped with vanilla ice cream interspersed with swirls of lemon curd and topped with a baked meringue. Five stars!

Note: The same menu is available at Coastal Café's sister restaurant, **Coastal,** 300 Amsterdam Ave. at 74th St. (tel. 769-3988).

LIVING SPRINGS VEGETARIAN RESTAURANT, 116 East 60th St. Tel. 319-7850.

Cuisine: NATURAL FOODS. **Reservations:** Not accepted.
$ Prices: All-you-can-eat, $10; average portions, by the pound, $5–$8. No credit cards.
Open: Lunch Mon–Thurs 11:30am–3pm; Fri 11:30am–2pm. Dinner, Sun–Thurs 5–8pm. Brunch, Sun 10:30am–3pm. **Bus:** Any Third Ave. bus.

If you'd like a wholesome, healthful vegetarian buffet lunch or dinner, stop in at Living Springs. It's run by Seventh Day Adventists who are dedicated to assisting people in living more healthfully. No animal products or dairy foods are used. Entrees are also low in sodium and oil. At dinner and lunch all-you-can-eat of salads, breads, a grain, a vegetarian entrée, steamed vegetables, and fruit salad can be had for a fixed price. If all-you-can-eat is not for you, pay just $4.29 per pound for any of the same offerings. Desserts and beverages are extra. Homemade desserts have neither sugar nor honey. Take your food to the large upstairs skylit dining room, decorated in attractive country decor, with classical music playing in the background. On the way out, you can get information on their Living Springs Health Retreat upstate and on the low-cost or free classes in cooking, quitting smoking, and so on, given upstairs.

SARANAC, 1350 Madison Ave., between 94th and 95th Sts. Tel. 289-9600.

Cuisine: CLASSIC AMERICAN. **Reservations:** Recommended for large parties.

$ Prices: Appetizers $4.50–$6.60; main courses $7.75–$14.75; sandwiches and burgers $6–$12.75. Kid's Corner (daily 4:30–6:30pm) $6.50, including beverage.

Open: Lunch, Mon–Fri noon–5:30pm. Dinner, Sun–Thurs 5:30–11:30pm; Fri–Sat 5:30–midnight. Brunch, Sat–Sun 11am–3:30pm. **Bus:** Any Madison Ave. bus.

Just the ticket for jaded city sophisticates, this restaurant makes you think you're up at Saranac, a picturesque lake in the Adirondacks. The dining room's focal point is a mural depicting a lakeshore vista, with a blue sky, a hound dog, a slice of summer cottage with the couple next door relaxing on the porch, and a patch of green lawn. Sit at one of the tables for two that flank this and you'll swear you're looking through a picture window.

The owners seem to have unearthed treasures from the family attic, and these fill every available cranny—old fishing nets, snowshoes, a pair of hand-carved cuckoo clocks, and vintage watercolors and photos. An entire Native American canoe is suspended from the ceiling, and an antlered chandelier is the room's centerpiece. The many artists and writers and other folks who live in this neighborhood find this setting a perfect retreat. The atmosphere is convivial yet low-key, and the food is very good indeed.

The menu is basically the same all day, with the addition of specials at lunch and dinner. Conjure up the waterfront with Point Jude fried calamari; Prince Edward Island mussels in white wine and garlic; or, in season, South Carolina steamers in beer broth. Try the Cobb salad or the Saranac salmon salad, with olives and capers and more. The Saranac burger is like none other: It shares bun space with Black Forest ham, Swiss cheese, grilled onions and mushrooms, and horseradish dressing. Perennial favorites are the chicken pot pie, the grilled wieners with brown-sugar baked beans, and the Kansas City fried chicken with onion mashers. There are also great steak sandwiches and grilled tuna and salmon. Bring the kids. There's a special menu for the pint-sized from 5:30–7:30pm, and the stroller set is welcome.

SERENDIPITY 3, 225 East 60th St. Tel. 838-3531.

Cuisine: CONTEMPORARY AMERICAN/NATURAL FOODS.
Reservations: Recommended.

$ Prices: Main courses and sandwiches $4.50–$14.95. AE, CB, DC, MC, V.

Open: Sun–Thurs 11:30am–12:30am; Fri 11:30am–1am; Sat 11:30am–2am. **Bus:** Any Third Ave. bus.

I doubt if there's another place in New York—or anywhere else for that matter—quite like Serendipity 3, a block east of Bloomingdale's. It's a way-out country store that has been selling Tiffany shades and cinnamon toast, Hebrew eye charts and Zen hash, frivolous hats and frozen hot-chocolate drinks, for 39 years now. The prettiest people lunch at marble-topped coffeetables and meet here for afternoon tea and after theater; and while the food is on the whimsical side, there are times when fantasy is more fun than meat and potatoes. Personally, I have long found Serendipity 3 to be one of the city's happier happenings. The "serious food" side of the menu features very good casseroles (curried chicken, burgundy beef, and shepherd's pie), omelets, a foot-long chili hot dog, hamburgers, and the enticing Ftatateeta's toast. Zen hash and a variety of open-faced vegetable sandwiches are there for those on natural-food trips. But don't dream of coming here without indulging in the desserts: perhaps the heavenly apricot smush, the frozen mochaccino, the lemon ice-box pie, or the dark-devil mousse . . . not to mention the glorious espressos and hot chocolates and spicy teas and chocolaccinos—but come and see for yourself.

SEVENTH REGIMENT MESS RESTAURANT & BAR, Seventh Regiment Armory, 643 Park Ave., at 67th St. Tel. 744-4107.
   Cuisine: AMERICAN. **Reservations:** Not required.
$ **Prices:** Appetizers $2.75–$5.50; complete dinners $7.75–$17. AE, MC, V.
   Open: Dinner only, Tues–Sat 5–9:30pm. **Closed:** July. **Subway:** 6 to 68th St.
   This is one of New York's best-kept restaurant secrets. Housed on the fourth floor of the Seventh Regiment Armory, a historic building completed in 1890 as headquarters for the volunteer militia unit of "gentlemen soldiers" that became a precursor of the National Guard, the dining room, with its superb windows and fine wrought iron, was designed by no less than Louis Comfort Tiffany. In this spacious Victorian setting you can dine on good food at some of the most amazing prices in New York. Where else can you sit down in such comfort, order a drink from the popular bar, and be served such main courses as fresh fish of the day, baked manicotti, lasagne, chicken cacciatore, fresh roast turkey, broiled lamb chops or roast prime rib of beef au jus, accompanied not only by soup and salad, but also by vegetables, potatoes, and coffee for prices that begin at $7? Should you feel the need of dessert, fresh pastries and cakes are also available, for another $3.50. The service is friendly and efficient. And happily, because this place is still much of a secret, the huge dining room is almost never crowded; it's a great place to come with friends when you want to really relax. There's a good wine list as well.
   Note: For those interested in architecture, tours of the building can be arranged upon request (tel. 744-2968 in advance). The remarkable collection of furnishings, objets d'art, and regimental memorabilia have caused the Armory to be designated as both a New York City and a National Historic Landmark.

VASATA, 339 East 75th St., between Second and First Aves. Tel. 988-7166.
   Cuisine: CZECHOSLOVAKIAN. **Reservations:** Recommended.
$ **Prices:** Appetizers $3.50–$5.75; main courses $11–$18.95. AE, MC, V.
   Open: Tues–Sat 5–10:45pm; Sun noon–9:45pm. **Closed:** Three weeks in July. **Bus:** Any First or Second Ave. bus.
   Although New York's Yorkville, once the home to thousands of Germans, Hungarians, Czechs, and Ukrainians, has changed, there are still plenty of Central European beer halls and cafés, intriguing butcher shops, and fragrant spice and cookery

emporiums (**Paprikas Weiss,** one of the best, at 81st Street and Second Avenue, stays open until 6pm for pre-dinner browsers). Almost all of the restaurants are good here, but Vasata is one of the best. The setting is very comfortable, something right out of the old country—and so are many of the guests—Vasata has been popular with a Central European crowd for many years. Whitewashed brick walls are decorated with ceramic plates, and crisp white cloths cover the tables.

The traditional Czech appetizers—marinated herring, homemade duck liver pâté with pistachios, and headcheese with onions—are all here. Entrees include the side dishes, like dumplings, potato salad, and sauerkraut, and might feature three kinds of veal schnitzel, pork chops, shish-kebab, fresh-breaded calves' brains, and, of course, the ever-popular roast duckling. During the winter you can feast on roast goose (no need to wait for Christmas!) and on winter Thursdays you can usually get some form of game. Now for the desserts! Chocolate-mousse cake, poppyseed cake, and those wonderful palacsintas (here stuffed with either apricot preserves or chocolate sauce) are hard to resist.

YELLOWFINGERS DI NUOVO, 200 East 60th St., corner of Third Ave. Tel. 751-8615.

Cuisine: CALIFORNIA/ITALIAN. **Reservations:** Not accepted.
$ Prices: Appetizers $3.50–$7.50; main courses $7.50–$17. AE, DC, MC, V.
Open: Sun–Wed 11:30am–11:45pm; Thurs–Sat 11:30am–12:45am. **Bus:** Any Third Ave. bus.

Take the freshest natural ingredients (produce, herbs, and spices), add a dash of daring, cook everything to order, and you have the latest California-style cuisine. Accent it with an Italian flair and you have Yellowfingers di Nuovo, a well-priced restaurant with an ingenious menu. The spacious dining area features a fascinating open kitchen, a stainless-steel ceiling and, at the far end, a bar that jumps with activity. Sometimes noisy (I like to request the quieter, glass-enclosed café), often crowded, but very New York, Yellowfingers is both casual and upbeat.

One diversified à la carte menu covers both lunch, dinner, and everything in between. A neat starter might be the seasonal field lettuces with balsamic vinegar and olive oil, or the basket of focaccia (yeast bread) sprinkled with slivers of roasted peppers and onion. Among the appealing entrees are the pepper-seared tuna, served rare, and the grilled cornish hen with sweet-potato streusel and cranberry chutney. By all means, try "fa'vecchia," a wonderful crusty pizza done with various toppings (my favorite is the melted mozzarella and sliced tomatoes) and the frittata, a fluffy mozzarella omelet with red and yellow peppers, afloat in a light tomato sauce. The wine list is moderately priced, if somewhat limited, with many selections available by the glass. Taking advantage of the best seasonal fruits, the pastry chef dreams up such scrumptious desserts as poached pear-and-berry tart and citrus cheesecake with chocolate-orange sauce.

ZUCCHINI, 1336 First Ave., at 72nd St. Tel. 249-0559.

Cuisine: NATURAL FOODS. **Reservations:** Recommended for three or more.
$ Prices: Appetizers $5.50–$8.95; main courses $10.95–$15.95; specials $17.95. Early Bird dinner Mon–Fri 4–7pm $9.95; lunch $6.95–$8.95. Sat–Sun brunch $9.95. AE, MC, V.

Open: Lunch, Mon–Fri 11am–4pm. Dinner, daily 5–10:30pm. Brunch, Sat–Sun 11am–4pm.

A gourmet natural-foods restaurant, a cut above the usual, this spot offers lots more than zucchini: Dinner in three attractively decorated little rooms with oak tables and antiques, plants, changing art exhibits, and (praise be) classical music in the background, is quite special. In addition to imaginative daily specials, there are a dozen organic salads everyday, giant bowls of pasta and sauce, tossed with steamed garden vegetables, an array of fresh fish daily from the mixed-wood grill, as well as any number of fresh fish and seafood specials, including a lusty bouillabaisse. There are many vegetarian entrees, plus whole-wheat crust, California-style pan pizza. Salad, bread, brown rice, veggies, and tofu or melted cheese accompany most entrees. Soups are homemade and fresh (cream of zucchini is excellent), and their double-chocolate velvet cake, with its subtle almond flavor and a slice of lemon on the side, is truly something to shout about. Lunch is a wonderful buy, with choices of pasta, fish, chicken, wood-grilled kebobs, soups, salads, pita pocket sandwiches, and more. There's also a delicious weekend brunch. In short, here's an ideal menu for health-conscious gourmets who are also watching the pocketbook. *Note:* At press time lunch prices were being discounted 10% if you paid cash.

13. SPECIALTY DINING

KOSHER GOURMET

There was a time when the typical kosher restaurant in New York served either blintzes and gefilte fish or chicken soup with matzoh balls and beef flanken—in other words, Jewish Eastern European-style food. These restaurants are still around, of course, but with large numbers of well-educated, affluent, and cosmopolitan New York Jews beginning to observe dietary laws, a whole new breed of kosher restaurants has risen on the scene. They're continental, Moroccan, Chinese, Israeli—even Indian. And they're very sophisticated. And you needn't be kosher—or even Jewish—to enjoy them. Herewith a sampling of the best of the new breed. *Note:* Hours vary, but most are closed on Friday; some reopen late on Saturday night, after the Sabbath. Call to confirm hours.

Glatt Yacht offers kosher dining at sea. Three nights a week, the company charters the splendid restaurant yachts of World Yacht Cruises and offers a three-hour sail around Lower Manhattan, with entertainment, and a continental dinner with hors d'oeuvres, a choice of three entrees, salads, and a dessert cart; cost is $59 or $68 per person. The yachts take off from Pier 62 on West 23rd Street Tuesday, Wednesday, and Sunday nights at 6pm. Call 212/869-5400 or 718/384-4954 for reservations. *Note:* All yachts are available for private parties.

As for kosher Chinese restaurants, they just keep proliferating. On the East Side, try **Hunan New York,** 1049 Second Ave., between 55th and 56th Sts. (tel. 888-2256); on the Upper West Side, go to **China Shalom,** 686 Columbus Ave., between 93rd and 94th Sts. (tel. 662-9676), and **Taam Hunan,** 212 W. 72nd St. (362-2101), a Glatt Kosher restaurant with a pleasant-enough menu, not far from

Lincoln Center; and downtown, try **Yoffee Chai,** 210 W. 14th St. (tel. 627-1923), between Seventh and Eighth Aves.

EXPENSIVE

LA KASBAH, 70 West 71st St. Tel. 769-1690.
Cuisine: KOSHER MOROCCAN/MEDITERRANEAN. **Reservations:** Recommended.
$ **Prices:** Appetizers $3.75–$6.50; main courses $13.50–$31.50. AE, CB, DC, MC, V.
Open: Mon–Thurs 5–11pm; Sat (Oct–May) sundown to 1am. Sun 2–11pm. **Closed:** Every Fri–Sat (June–Sept); call for exact dates. **Bus:** M104 or M10.

How about kosher Moroccan food? You can get outstanding couscous, with vegetables, chicken, or lamb, at this attractive restaurant serving Moroccan and Mediterranean cuisine. The available entrees are shish-kebab, Moroccan koufta, baby lamb chops, and salmon on the grill; appetizers include falafel, hummus, tahini, and other Middle Eastern standbys.

LEVANA, 141 West 69th St. Tel. 877-8457.
Cuisine: CONTINENTAL/GLATT KOSHER. **Reservations:** Recommended.
$ **Prices:** Appetizers $5–$18; main courses $17–$34 ($44 for buffalo venison); prix-fixe dinner $27.95 and $37.95. AE, MC, V.
Open: Lunch, Mon–Thurs 11:30am–2:30pm. Dinner, Sun–Thurs 5–11pm; Sat 7–11pm (fall and winter only). **Bus:** M104.

Levana is the innovative leader of the genre. Beautiful, romantic, very European, with a unique, mostly nouvelle menu—it's the only Glatt kosher restaurant in the world, they claim, to serve buffalo and venison! Lamb cannelloni with rosemary glace d'agneau is a unique appetizer; entrees include baby rack of lamb, prime meats (they're noted for their 12-ounce steaks and 2-inch-thick veal chops), fresh Dover sole and other fish, wonderful pastas, and extraordinary desserts, like chocolate truffle torte with mint crème anglaise.

MODERATE

DELI KASBAH, 251 West 85th St. Tel. 496-1500.
Cuisine: KOSHER ISRAELI. **Reservations:** Not accepted.
$ **Prices:** Appetizers $3–$9.50; main courses $6.50–$17.50; lunch main courses $4.95–$11.50. MC, V.
Open: Sun–Thurs 12:30–11:30pm; Sat sundown–1am (winter only). **Closed:** Every Fri, Sat in summer. **Bus:** M104.

Israeli grills abound, and Deli Kasbah is very popular on the Upper West Side, with a moderately priced menu featuring salads and deli sandwiches. A daily lunch special might be a fresh turkey sandwich barbecued on the grill, served with french fries and a salad.

MADRAS PALACE, 104 Lexington Ave., off 27th St. Tel. 532-3314.
Cuisine: KOSHER INDIAN. **Reservations:** Recommended for 3 or more.
$ **Prices:** Appetizers at dinner $1.25–$6.25; main courses at dinner $4.25–$18.95; lunch $4.25–$10.95. AE, DC, MC, V.

Open: Lunch, Mon–Fri noon–3pm. Dinner, Mon–Thurs 5:30–10pm; Sat 8–10pm; Sun noon–10pm. **Bus:** Any Lexington Ave. bus.

Kosher Indian food? Why not? Madras Palace offers the cuisine of North and South India, strictly vegetarian and strictly kosher (the decor is strictly Indian). Main courses include curries, pullaus, dosai, and uthappam; and lavish complete dinners are available. The food is delicious.

MADRAS WOODLANDS, 308 East 49th St., between Second and First Aves. Tel. 759-2440.

Cuisine: KOSHER/SOUTHERN INDIAN VEGETARIAN. **Reservations:** Recommended.

$ Prices: Appetizers $1.95–$6.95; main courses $4.75–$7.75, prix-fixe dinners $14.95, $15.95, $20.95; prix-fixe luncheon buffet $9.95. AE, CB, DC, MC.

Open: Daily noon–10:30pm. Buffet lunch Mon–Fri noon–2:45pm. **Bus:** Any First or Second Ave. bus.

This softly carpeted restaurant is quiet and peaceful, elegant in its understatement. Fine examples of Indian art and piped-in Indian music create a serene atmosphere for dining. Your best choices are the complete meals—South India Thali, Madras Special, or Woodland Special. All are served with wine, dessert, and coffee or tea, and all provide a broad overview of this delicious cuisine. Let your waiter be your guide: The tiny print on the menu is almost illegible, and most dishes are transliterated (not translated) from Hindi or Farsi, so you'll need assistance in deciphering what things are. Come with a group, order copiously, and pass dishes around for all to enjoy.

DELIS

New York has long been famous for its Jewish (but not kosher) delicatessens, but the genuine article is no longer so easy to find in Manhattan. True mavens advise that you avoid all imitations and head directly for any of these five places, where the traditions of succulent corned beef and spicy pastrami, greasy gribenes, and caloric chopped liver (with chicken fat) are still honored.

CARNEGIE DELICATESSEN, 854 Seventh Ave., near 55th St. Tel. 757-2245.

Cuisine: JEWISH DELI. **Reservations:** Not accepted.

$ Prices: Appetizers $6.45–$9.45; main courses and sandwiches $9.95–$14.95. No credit cards.

Open: Daily 6:30am–4am. **Bus:** M104.

On the West Side, the shrine for deli lovers is near the shrine for music lovers: The Carnegie Deli has practiced and practiced for years to turn out some of the juiciest and most flavorful corned beef on ryes in New York. Main courses are also tasty, and prices are affordable. Widely known as a celebrity hangout, Carnegie Delicatessen was used by Woody Allen for some of the scenes in *Broadway Danny Rose.*

GAIETY DELICATESSEN, 224 West 47th St. Tel. 921-5566.

Cuisine: JEWISH DELI. **Reservations:** Not required.

$ Prices: Appetizers $1–$6.25; main courses $4.75–$9.75; deli sandwiches $5.25–$7.75. No credit cards.

Open: Daily 7am–11pm. **Bus:** M104.

Closest deli to the theater district is the Gaiety, which serves stars and stargazers alike. Pastrami, corned beef and brisket, and all the usual favorites are available. This place is very popular for after-theater snacks and drinks.

KAPLAN'S AT THE DELMONICO, in the Delmonico Hotel, 59 East 59th St. Tel. 755-5959.

Cuisine: JEWISH DELI. **Reservations:** Not required.

$ Prices: Appetizers $3.95–$5.75; main courses $8.95–$14.95. AE, DC, MC, V.

Open: Mon–Sat 7am–10pm; Sun 8am–10pm; same menu all day. **Bus:** Any Madison Ave. bus.

On the East Side, this is the classiest of the lot. High marks go to the deli sandwiches, as well as to such old-time favorites as chicken or beef in the pot, Roumanian tenderloin, stuffed cabbage, and potato latkes.

SECOND AVENUE DELICATESSEN, 156 Second Ave., at the corner of 10th St. Tel. 677-0606.

Cuisine: JEWISH DELI. **Reservations:** Not required.

$ Prices: Appetizers $2.50–$5.50; main courses $10.95–$16.95.

Open: Sun–Thurs 7am–midnight; Fri–Sat 7am–2am. **Bus:** Any Second Ave. bus.

The best prices for this kind of food can be found downtown at the long-beloved spot where you may have to stand in line to sample the superlative chopped liver. A café room, named after Molly Picon and decorated with memorabilia from her career, adjoins the plain main dining room. The meat is kosher, with generous portions.

STAGE DELICATESSEN, 834 Seventh Ave., off 53rd St. Tel. 245-7850.

Cuisine: JEWISH DELI. **Reservations:** Not required.

$ Prices: Appetizers $5.75–$7.25; main courses and sandwiches $8.50–$16.75. No credit cards.

Open: Daily 6am–2am; same menu all day. **Bus:** M104.

Begun in 1937 by the almost legendary deli man, Max Asnas, this is probably the oldest continuous deli in New York. The Stage is bright and cheerful and adorned with photos of the many show-biz personalities who have had a knish or a kasha varnishka for an appetizer, then gone on to one of the famous Stage Specialty sandwiches, 29 at the last count (most around $12), all named after famous people. The Dolly Parton, for example, is corned beef and pastrami on twin rolls. They also now offer a menu in Japanese, since Japanese tour groups seem to revel in such exotica as pastrami and cream cheese with lox on bagels.

DINING WITH A VIEW

New York's waterways and skyscrapers afford some of the most extraordinary views in any city. A handful of restaurants show them to full advantage. In addition to those reviewed below, glorious views are also available at **The Hudson River Club** and **Windows on the World** in downtown Manhattan, and at the **Rainbow Room** in Midtown, all covered earlier in this chapter.

EXPENSIVE

THE RIVER CAFE, 1 Water St., Brooklyn. Tel. 718/522-5200.
Cuisine: AMERICAN NOUVELLE. **Reservations:** Recommended.
$ Prices: Prix-fixe dinner $58; Appetizers at lunch $8–$16; main courses at lunch $19–$24.
Open: Lunch, Mon–Sat noon–2:30pm. Dinner, daily 6–11pm, with seatings almost every half-hour. Brunch, Sun 11:30am–2pm. Bar open daily until 1am, outdoor deck Fri–Sat until 2am in summer. **Subway:** 2, 3, or A.

A bastion of American nouvelle cuisine exists in exotic Brooklyn, at the River Café. One of the city's see-and-be-seen restaurants, the Café is built on a barge underneath the Brooklyn Bridge and commands a truly spectacular view of lower Manhattan and New York Harbor. Perfect for a romantic night rendezvous, it has a special daytime appeal, too, as you watch the river busy with waterborne traffic. Beautifully appointed in pale tones, with each table sporting a tiny shaded lamp evocative of a 1930s supper club, the River Café is movie-star glamorous. But the food—a unique style of American cooking concentrating on seasonal changes and the finest, freshest products available—is not to be ignored. The prix-fixe dinner may include appetizers such as sea scallop en croûte with asparagus butter, sautéed salmon with grilled vegetarian lasagne, quesadillas, or Moroccan glazed and grilled prawns. Main courses such as grilled swordfish with bacon, potato cake, and shiitake hash, or mustard-crusted rack of lamb are impressive. Desserts are wickedly wonderful, on the order of chocolate marquis and caramel mousse tarte or peanut-butter crème caramel with banana ice cream.

THE WATER'S EDGE, 44th Drive at the East River, East River Yacht Club, Long Island City. Tel. 718/482-0033.
Cuisine: AMERICAN/CONTINENTAL. **Reservations:** Recommended.
$ Prices: Dinner: Appetizers $7.50–$15; main courses $20–$32. Appetizers at lunch $6–$12; main courses at lunch $9.50–$18. AE, DC, MC, V.
Open: Lunch, Mon–Fri noon–3pm. Dinner, Mon–Sat 6–11pm. **Subway:** E or F to 23rd St. & Ely; walk down 44th Dr. to river.

⭐ The restaurant with the best views of the Manhattan skyline is not in Manhattan at all—it's in Long Island City. Surely, there can be few more glamorous evenings in New York than one that begins at the restaurant's own Riverboat, which shuttles guests from 34th Street across the East River (champagne is available during the 10-minute crossing) to the glass-enclosed restaurant, where every table affords a view of sailboats, sunsets, and the fabled Manhattan skyline. The restaurant itself (whose upstairs dining room is one of the city's "in" spots for weddings), is attractive, with a sophisticated French country decor and a working fireplace. The menu has an international flair. Choice appetizers include smoked salmon with buckwheat waffles, crème fraîche, and a trio of caviars, and a warm goat-cheese, potato, and herb napoleon. For a main dish, try roasted medallions of salmon with lemongrass; grilled veal chops with morels, gnocchi, and asparagus, or roasted free-range baby chicken with couscous and preserved lemons. Seasonal specialties might include smoked foie gras or grilled sea scallops with polenta and

Swiss chard. Save room for dessert—maybe the chocolate truffle with white-chocolate mousse. Dinner guests may dance to a trio on Wednesday to Friday or be serenaded by a pianist on Tuesday to Saturday from 7 to 11pm.

In warm weather, sit outdoors on the garden deck and enjoy light fare on the café menu, which features such choices as warm oysters with champagne, leeks, cream, and caviar, and a salad of fresh tomatoes and mozzarella ($7–$12), along with rotating dessert selections, exotic coffees, and wines by the glass.

The Riverboat shuttle operates from 34th Street at the East River, weather permitting, between 6 and 11pm on Tuesday to Saturday, with return trips leaving the restaurant on the half-hour from 6 to 11:30pm. Reservations are required only for groups of six or more. If you plan to drive from Manhattan, phone the restaurant for directions; you go via the 59th Street Bridge or the Midtown Tunnel.

THE VIEW, at The New York Marriott Marquis, 1535 Broadway, between 45th and 46th Sts. Tel. 704-8900. Cuisine: AMERICAN/FRENCH/ITALIAN. **Reservations:** Recommended.

$ Prices: Appetizers $5.75–$13.95; main courses $22.95–$29.50; pre- and post-theater menu $36.95; Sun brunch $29.95. AE, CB, DC, DISC, JCB, MC, V.
Open: Dinner, Sun–Thurs 5:30–11pm; Fri and Sat 5–12pm. Brunch, Sun 10:30am–2:30pm. Theater dinners daily 5–7pm and 10:30–midnight. **Bus:** M104.

There's no chance you can get bored with the view here: It changes constantly. New York's only rooftop restaurant revolves slowly, moving a full 360 degrees in the space of an hour. It's a splendid way to see the major vistas of the city while dining on either a French, an Italian, or an American menu, or combinations thereof. You might start with a French appetizer of coquilles St.-Jacques or napoleon of escargots, then move on to an American main course like swordfish Louisiana or whole Maine lobster. Or begin with an American appetizer like New England crabcakes, then have minestrone soup and veal picatta from the Italian selections. There are many possibilities, and the food is nicely done. A dessert cart covers all bases.

After dinner, amble over to The View lounge, one of the most romantic spots in the city; there's live entertainment and dancing Friday and Saturday nights ($5 cover charge per person).

WORLD YACHT CRUISES, Pier 81, West 42nd St., at the Hudson River. Tel. 630-8100. Cuisine: CONTINENTAL. **Reservations:** Essential.

$ Prices: Sun–Thurs dinner cruise $62; Fri–Sat cruise $69.50; Liberty Luncheon cruise $27.50 adults, $16 children; Sun brunch cruise $39.95 adults, $25 children. AE, MC, V.
Open: Weeknight cruise 7–10pm. Liberty Luncheon cruise noon–2pm. Sunday brunch cruise 12:30–2:30pm. All cruises can be boarded 1 hour before sailing time. **Bus:** M106.

The whole of New York Harbor becomes your view when you dine aboard one of the five luxury restaurant yachts operated by World Yacht Cruises. Every night, some 2,000 people board the glamorous yachts to embark on an evening of gourmet dining, dancing to live music, and watching some of the most spectacular views New York has to offer. Between the appetizers and the coffee, the sun sets over the water, the boat steams around the tip of the island, cruises halfway up the East River, and then down again. By the time dessert is on the table, it's dark and the thousand lights of the city are ablaze.

The state-of-the-art ships sport glassed-in and climate-controlled dining rooms surrounded by large windows that provide panoramic views. Full restaurant galleys enable all food to be prepared on board by an executive chef and staff. Menu selections are not large but are choice. I began one meal with a complimentary "Amuse," a seasonal pre-appetizer. Among the appetizers, Concarneau Ravioli (artichoke-and-mushroom ravioli served with a porcini-cream sauce) was excellent; so was the Salad de Printemps topped with a creamy garlic vinaigrette and croutons. Main courses include rack of lamb, roasted Norwegian salmon with a dill beurre-blanc sauce, and filet mignon. Menus change with the season. The dessert course is unlimited pastries, fresh fruit, cheeses, and vanilla ice cream. There's an excellent wine list and a variety of champagnes for a celebration.

Beverages and gratuities are not included in the quoted prices. Inquire about special evening cruises and afternoon theme cruises. On-site parking is available at a nominal fee.

SUNDAY BRUNCH

Sunday brunch is a favorite New York institution. After sleeping late and reading the *Times,* many a New Yorker heads for a restaurant close to home or farther afield, to meet friends and relax over eggs Benedict or waffles or lox and bagels or. . . . The choice of brunch spots is enormous, everything from the grand hotel and restaurant buffets to more modest meals at neighborhood places where two courses plus champagne or a cocktail costs under $10.

I'll start with some of the most sumptuous buffets, particularly enjoyable for the visitor because each gives you a chance to dine in posh surroundings and sample wonderful food for much less than the cost of dinner. One of my all-time favorites is the enormous spread in **Peacock Alley** at the Waldorf-Astoria Hotel, where the cost is $38.50 for adults and $19.50 for children. The **Ambassador Grill** at the United Nations Plaza Hotel, 1 United Nations Plaza (tel. 355-3400), has a Sunday Champagne Brunch (lobster, smoked salmon, omelets made to order, boudin blanc with lentils, and unlimited bubbly) at $35 for adults and $17.50 for children. Its mirrored glass ceiling of prisms within prisms creates an extraordinary effect. The **Crystal Fountain** at the Grand Hyatt Hotel, Park Ave. at Grand Central Terminal (tel. 883-1234), offers a glorious à la carte menu from $11 to 27, including cocktails, seafood, steaks, omelets, and many desserts.

For brunch with a view, visit **Windows on the World,** 1 World Trade Center (tel. 938-1111), and enjoy either the scrumptious Grand Buffet in the main dining room for $25.50 or the more modest brunch in the **Hors d'Oeuvrerie** (à la carte for $8 to $17). Or, in Midtown, ascend to the 65th floor of Rockefeller Center for the posh, art deco **Rainbow Room,** 30 Rockefeller Plaza (tel. 632-5000), where an à la carte meal (approximately $35 to $40 per person) is enhanced by views of the skyscrapers of Manhattan and the rivers bordering them.

Reserve a table in the **Crystal Room** of Tavern on the Green in Central Park and enjoy a varied brunch menu in a sparkling crystal-and-glass room that's as pretty as a wedding cake and meant for celebrations. Brunch entrees cost between $12 and $32.50.

For sheer variety, venture over to Times Square and **Samplings Bar** at the Holiday Inn Crowne Plaza, 1605 Broadway (tel. 315-6000), before a matinee. Sunday from 11am to 3pm, the sweeping bar carries breakfast food from smoked salmon and whitefish to waffles, omelets, and pâtés for $15.95; Napua Davoy, a lovely singer/pianist, entertains.

Lola's presents a spirited Gospel Brunch every Sunday, with performances by gospel musicians free with the cost of the meal; these meals are so popular that reservations must be made at least two weeks in advance.

DINING COMPLEXES

SOUTH STREET SEAPORT & MARKETPLACE, between Fulton and South Sts. at the East River.

This "museum without walls" celebrates the days of the tall ships. The South Street Seaport is one of New York's top visitor attractions (see Chapter 7). It also has 16 bonafide restaurants, 20 quick-stop eateries, and 7 gourmet takeout stores—all of which makes it a good place to repair to for a meal when you're touring downtown Manhattan. Here are some of my favorites at the Seaport:

Roebling's, on the Mezzanine Level of the Fulton Market Building (tel. 608-3980), is a great place to sit and watch all the busy goings-on at the ground-level shops and stalls. The atmosphere is casual, and the 70-foot corner bar always attracts a lively crowd, especially on Friday afternoon when Wall Street folks quit for the week. The food is elegant and imaginative, with a daunting selection of fresh fish and seafood dishes. In addition, the menu, the same for lunch and dinner, boasts a wide variety of South American favorites, and lush, rich desserts on the order of Mississippi mud pie and Georgia pecan pie. Most main courses are below $14.95.

Gilmore's Deep Blue, in the Fulton Market Building (tel. 227-9328), serves sandwiches and steaks and churasco, a specially prepared Brazilian grilled chicken. Most dishes are below $15.

Gianni's, in the Cannon Walk block (tel. 698-7300), is a glass-enclosed, sophisticated, people-watching restaurant serving Northern Italian cuisine. Its active outdoor café overlooks the South Street Seaport's cobblestone walk. Featured are garlic bread with gorgonzola sauce, fresh fish, veal, pasta, individual pizzas, outstanding desserts, and an extensive wine list. Most checks run $25 and up per person.

Liberty Café and Oyster Bar, atop Pier 17 (tel. 406-1111), provides direct waterfront views from anywhere in its dining room or private outdoor terrace. The 100-foot bar contains a working replica of a cross-country train. Featured are seasonal seafood as well as a variety of pasta dishes, pizzas from the woodburning oven, steaks, and chops. Most main courses are below $18.95. Sunday brunch is especially enjoyable. The Oyster Bar features fresh clams and oysters served at a bar surrounding a unique shark aquarium.

Pedro O'Hara's, at Pier 17 (tel. 227-6735), has a 50-foot bar for those who would like to sip a margarita before indulging in Mexican specialties. Prices range from $15 to $25 per person.

To get a good meal for $5 or $6 or less at the Seaport, repair to the food court on the third floor of Pier 17 and help yourself to dishes from such places as **Pizza on the Pier, Salad Bowl, Seaport Fries, South Philly Steak & Fries,** and **Acropolis;** try to get a seat on the deck outside, where you can watch the busy harbor traffic on the river below. There's a similar food court (but without the sensational view and breezes) at the Fulton Market Building: **Burger Boys of Brooklyn, Bananas, Pastrami Factory,** and **Kam Man Foods** are some of the possibilities.

A&S PLAZA'S TASTE OF THE TOWN, Sixth Ave. at 33rd St.

Should you find yourself in the Herald Square area, perhaps shopping at Macy's or A&S or A&S Plaza and want a quick lunch or snack, a good choice is the Taste of the Town food court on the 7th level at A&S Plaza. A huge central dining area provides seating for a number of imaginative fast-food stands: Possibilities include **Sbarro** for pizzas and pastas, **Wok 'n Roll** for Chinese food, **Flamers** for chicken or burgers charbroiled over an open flame, **Amir's Kitchen** for Middle Eastern foods, and **The Salad Bowl** and the **Great Steak and Fry Company,** whose names say it all. Try to get a table near the windows and watch the crowds go by.

(*Note:* The 7th level also contains the A&S Plaza Visitors Center, with helpful information on attractions, transportation, restaurant and theater reservations, car services, and more.)

THE MARKET at Citicorp Center, 53rd St., between Lexington and Third Aves.

Midtown on the East Side, this handsome skylit atrium has three levels of shops and restaurants surrounding a graceful central café. One of my favorite Greek restaurants, **Avgerinos** (reviewed earlier), is there, and so are such attractive other sit-down restaurants as **Alfredo, The Original of Rome** (tel. 371-3367) serving Italian cuisine; **La Brochette** (tel. 223-0919), an upscale French bistro with an open rotisserie; and **Cinco de Mayo** (tel. 755-5033), a terrific Mexican restaurant with powerful margaritas. Or pick up a snack from **Nyborg & Nelson** (Swedish delicacies and deli food), **The Market Coffee Shop, Au Bon Pain,** or **Alfredo to Go,** and take it to one of the courtyard tables. You might be able to enjoy a free concert or show while you munch.

STREET FOOD & PIZZA

Many people don't realize that even New York executives often eat their lunch at one of the hundred or more hot-dog wagons seen on corners all over Midtown and at other high-traffic locations—near train stations, outside museums, and elsewhere. New Yorkers are people in a hurry, and when you're in a hurry, street food fills the bill. It's cheap and often surprisingly good.

Ice cream and hot dogs—stadium fare—are still the most abundant. **Haagen Däzs** and **Ben and Jerry's** wagons and **Good Humor** and **Mr. Softy** trucks are everywhere, and so are **Sabretts.** But ethnic food also finds its way into New York's thoroughfares. Italian sausages, Jewish knishes, Chinese dumplings, and Japanese tempura are appetizing more for their aroma than the way in which they are displayed, but people wolf them down anyway. Pita-wrapped falafel sandwiches, burritos, vegetarian food, and fried fish are all very popular.

Other roadside snacks include orange juice squeezed on the spot, honey-roasted peanuts, and Italian ices. Fruit vendors offer whatever's in season at bargain basement prices. In the winter, you can buy wonderful roasted chestnuts. Great New York–style soft pretzels, bagels, donuts, and coffee are dispensed from carts parked anywhere people seem to be hurrying to work.

Pizza is the only popular New York food that hasn't found its way onto the street, but you will see hole-in-the-wall outlets where you can grab a slice on the run as well as larger places. Most of New York's pizza parlors offer certainly passable, and rarely inedible slices and pies, but here are some favorites. **John's Pizzeria,** 278 Bleecker St. in Greenwich Village (tel. 243-1680), sells its outstanding pizza only by the pie and has sit-down service. The place is so packed in the evenings and on weekends with Village regulars, college kids, and visitors to the neighborhood, that it must be the only pizzeria in New York with a line longer than the one at the Palladium on Saturday night. They also have an outpost slightly north, at 344 E. 16th St. There, the pizza is equally great, and the place is not such a madhouse. **Arturo's,** 106 W. Houston (tel. 677-3820), boasts brick oven pizza that is quite good and also has live jazz. And **Goldberg's Pizzeria,** if you can believe it, has fantastic pies. There's one at 1443 York Ave., between 76th and 77th Sts. (tel. 570-6480), and another at 996 Second Ave., between 52nd and 53rd Sts. (tel. 593-2172). **Mimi's Pizza** at 1248 Lexington Ave., at the corner of 84th St., is practically an institution, having been in the same spot for 30 years. The pizza is very good, and if you want a real treat, order a hero on "homemade" bread, baked with pizza dough. This fantastic bread is also available by the loaf for $2.

TEA TIME

Although New York is surely not London, it does have its share of tearooms (some independent establishments, some in the more elegant hotels). These do a lovely job of celebrating the time-honored English tradition known as afternoon tea. Most places serve a multicourse tea featuring scones with jam and Devonshire cream (or a Devonshire cream taste-alike). Finger sandwiches and pastry are pretty much universal. And most, too, have a copious selection of traditional teas, herbals, and heady aromatics (fruit-infused teas). Many also serve tea dainties à la carte and make a glass of sherry, port, champagne or whatever available. Not all places below take reservations, but it's best to call ahead.

INDEPENDENT ESTABLISHMENTS

Anglers & Writers, 420 Hudson St., at St. Luke's Place (tel. 675-0810), serves a splendid tea with all the fixings each afternoon from 3 to 6pm for a modest $12.50 amid a decor of antiques and fishing paraphernalia.

Book Friends Café, 16 W. 18th St., between Fifth and Sixth Aves. (tel. 255-7407), serves tea from 3 to 5pm; a few times a year the café holds an actual tea dance on the premises from 7 to 10pm (otherwise they close at 7pm). An enthralling assortment of antique books (from the period 1840 to 1940–Victorians, old New York, Paris in the 1920's—) can be perused, but if you want to skim one as you sip, you'll have to purchase it before sitting down. Tea is $11.95. Call for a schedule of literary events, tea dances, and special theme dinners.

Danal, 90 E. 10th St., between Third and Fourth Aves. (tel. 982-6930), serves its tea, with aplomb, from 3:30 to 5:30pm. There are 40 teas to choose from, and all can be purchased loose for your home teapot for $5 to $7 the quarter pound; the meal is $12. You may sit at one of the antique tables or sink into a pair of lovingly worn chocolate-brown love seats. There's lots of bric-a-brac to look at (and some to buy—the front is an antique and gift shop), and there's also a garden with tables in back. Scones are baked on premises, and lemon tartelettes and meringue often comprise dessert. *Note:* Closed on Monday, Tuesday, and Wednesday; reservations are required.

Little Nell's Tea Room, 343 E. 85th St., between Second and First Aves. (tel. 772-2046), named for Dickens' Little Nell of *The Old Curiosity Shop,* distinguishes, don't you know, between afternoon tea, yours for the asking for $12.95 from 2 to 5pm, and high tea, brought on with a bit more pomp (and food) at $16.95 from 5 to 6pm. The first features sandwiches, Nell's own scones, and her homemade lemon pound cake, as well as other goodies. The more elevated version, really an early supper, consists of soup, salad, chicken, delicious assorted desserts, and tea or coffee. Classical music wafts through the air, and special touches include an English settee, exposed-brick walls, tastefully threadbare Oriental rugs, antique lace curtains, and cabbage-rose chintz drapes, as well as an old-fashioned miniature Christmas tree on display all year.

You'd be hard-pressed to find a more authentic tea than the daily service at **Tea & Sympathy,** 108 Greenwich Ave. (tel. 807-8329), a whimsical West Village salon. Owner Nikki Perry, a London native, loads a three-tiered cake stand with tea sandwiches, cakes, scones with clotted cream, and jam; her unusual tea selections, strained and served "the proper way," range from Ty-Phoo (a rare British variety) to Mango to Licorice. Tea, offered from noon to 6pm, is $10.50 per person. For lunch and dinner, Tea & Sympathy also serves such British treats as bangers and mash (sausages and mashed potatoes), Welsh rarebit, and ploughman's lunch.

HOTEL TEAROOMS

The **Carlyle,** 35 E. 76th St. (tel. 744-1600), serves tea in its intimate Gallery. The decor, modeled on that found in Istanbul's famed Topkapi Palace, is similar to the "Turkish room" found in many 18th- and 19th-century European country homes. Italian hand-painted paper has been painstakingly applied to screens and walls in an intricate mosaic pattern, and the burgundy velvet sofas have been appliquéd with antique kilims. A soft paisley carpet completes the effect. Tea, served from 3 to 5:30pm, is $16 for three ample courses.

The Helmsley Palace, 455 Madison Ave. (tel. 888-7000), offers tea in the aptly named Gold Room each afternoon from 2 to 5pm. The atmosphere is regal-rococo: frescoes and gilding everywhere, silk brocade Louis XIV chairs, and a harpist playing in the gallery above. The tea is up to snuff, and the atmosphere, rather formal, is geared to aristocrats, would-be aristocrats, and those who simply appreciate elegant service. The price is $30.

The Lowell, 28 E. 63rd St. (tel. 838-1400), pours its tea from a samovar and features silver service. Ladylike charm and manners reign supreme in the small, second-floor Pembroke Room, where English chintz abounds. F. Scott and Zelda Fitzgerald, Noël Coward, Dorothy Parker, and other literary lights all roamed these premises at one time. All this history and tea, too, for just $15.50, from 3:30 to 6:30pm.

The Mayfair Hotel, 610 Park Ave., at 65th St. (tel. 288-0800), serves tea in its engaging balconied lobby lounge every day from 3 to 5:30pm. There are settees as far as the eye can see. Sconces and chandeliers light the room, and columns are interspersed with flowers and palms. People-watching is recommended and eavesdropping advised, if at all possible. The waitresses dress English-style in long skirts for the occasion. The staff is courteously warm and the mood contagiously celebratory. The tea is $15.50.

The Omni Berkshire Place, 21 E. 52nd St. (tel. 753-5800), serves afternoon tea from 3 to 5:30pm in its sunlit, skylit Atrium. The room's centerpiece is a 15-foot-high Chinese lacquered cabinet, which anchors a grouping of Kelly-green sofas and is set against walls of beveled mirror. The columns and floor are buff-colored Italian marble, and there are lots of greenery and a lush and dramatic arrangement of fresh flowers. The room is warm and cosmopolitan, and the delightful tea runs $15.

The Palm Court at **The Plaza,** Fifth Ave. at 59th St. (tel. 759-3000), is legendary for its foliage and for violinist Sandu Marcu and pianist Sasha Aloni, who have been serenading guests from what could be termed time immemorial. Native New Yorkers, not impressed by much, fondly remember being taken to tea at the Plaza as the first grown-up activity of their childhoods and await the day when they can initiate the next generation. The decor has been spruced up and the bygone tattered charm has been replaced by a little dazzle—a few Ivana Trump–esque touches: The space is now punctuated by gold columns. Live palms cast flattering shadows, and the tea is $18, served from 3:45 to 6pm.

The Pierre, Fifth Ave. at 61st St. (tel. 838-8000), serves tea from 3 to 5:30pm in its elegant rotunda, where guests lounge on silk settees surrounded by dramatic frescoes of ladies and gentlemen strolling in gardens and languishing outdoors. As the menu points out, "the romantic setting is enhanced by celestial blue skies, marble pillars and ornate candelabras." The price for all this atmosphere, not to mention the tea, scones, sandwiches, and pastries, is $16.

LATE-NIGHT/24-HOUR

BRASSERIE, 100 East 53rd St., between Park and Lexington Aves. in the Seagram Building. Tel. 751-4840.
   Cuisine: ALSATIAN FRENCH. **Reservations:** Recommended.
$ **Prices:** Appetizers $4.50–$7.95; main courses $9.50–$19.75; prix-fixe dinner $19.93. AE, CB, DC, MC, V.
   Open: Daily 24 hrs. Breakfast, 6–11am. Lunch, 11am–5pm. Dinner, 5–10pm. Supper, 10pm–6am. **Bus:** Any Lexington Ave. bus.

It's always open, it's always fun, and the food does not disappoint here at one of Midtown's most popular informal restaurants. The decor is brightly French Provincial, the menu a combination of French and Alsatian dishes, plus some French-American hybrids, like fromage burgers. Le déjeuner, le dîner, and le souper menus feature the likes of omelet Lorraine, choucroûte à l'alsacienne (a house specialty), and onion soup. Complete dinners are also available, with a changing menu that features duck, fish, and steak items for around $20, served with hors d'oeuvres or soup, vegetables, dessert, and beverage. Lunch, with main courses like quiche of the day and eggs Benedict, goes from about $9.95 to

$17.95. The late supper is perfect after an evening's entertainment, and the Brasserie is also the scene of many a "power" breakfast.

THE LOST DINER, 357 West St., north of Houston St. Tel. 691-4332. Tel. 691-4332.

Cuisine: AMERICAN DINER. **Reservations:** Not accepted.

$ Prices: Appetizers $2.95–$5.50; main courses $4.50–$10.95. MC, V.

Open: Mon–Thurs 5am–11pm; Fri–Sat 24 hrs.

You'll undoubtedly get lost trying to find this place on foot, so hail a cab and join the hungry crowds who keep it hopping at all hours, especially on weekends. The Lost Diner embraces the traditions of American roadside culture: a vintage setting, reasonable prices, quick service, and a classic diner menu enhanced by some contemporary culinary creativity. Meatloaf with mashed potatoes, firehouse chili, panfried chicken, and seafood fritters with roasted-pepper mayonnaise are all popular. Breakfast is served all day; try the cream-cheese omelets. Apple pies, cakes, and cobblers are all freshly baked.

PICNIC FARE & WHERE TO EAT IT

When the weather is fair, New York is picnic country. The parks, the plazas, and the atriums around town are all fine places for holding an impromptu picnic. If you're attending one of the free entertainments in Central Park (perhaps the New York Philharmonic or the New York Shakespeare Festival), a picnic is essential. And you need never look far to find provisions.

Starting with the most exalted picnic fare, there's lofty **Fraser Morris** at 1264 Third Ave., between 72nd and 73rd Sts. (tel. 288-2727), where an epicurean's basket of caviar, foie gras, cheese, fruit, pâté, and whatever could easily cost between $400 and $500, although you can, of course, put together a gourmet meal for less. But for more realistic fare, consider the appetizing stores discussed in Chapter 9 under "Gourmet Food Stores." All of them dispense incredible selections of imported cheese, breads, smoked fish, sausages, baked goods, homemade salads, and spreads—all of it mouth-watering and well priced. **Fairway,** 2127 Broadway, at 74th St. (tel. 595-1888), has delectable picnic possibilities in the rear, and some of the freshest and most beautiful produce up front—at just about the lowest prices for food of this caliber.

A specialty gourmet shop with an Italian theme, **Piatti Pronti,** 34 W. 56th St. (tel. 315-4800), also at 34 W. 46th St. (tel. 575-4820), and 8 Maiden Lane downtown (tel. 233-1500), is the place to pick up wonderful gourmet sandwiches, Italian sandwiches and cold dishes, unusual pizzas, and pastas for elegant picnicking.

You'll see the name **Burke & Burke** at various outlets around town, including one at 2 E. 23rd St. (tel. 505-2020); it offers wonderful muffins, croissants, and striking salads, sandwiches, and desserts. Trust **Zaro's Bread Basket,** too, which specializes in bakery items, for sandwiches, topped baked potatoes, and more, all moderately priced. There are branches at the South Street Seaport, Grand Central Station, Penn Station, Port Authority, and elsewhere.

Most of the major supermarkets—such as **Food Emporium, D'Agostino,** and **Gristede's,** found all over town—have deli counters that could well be called delicacy counters, where you can arrange the elements of quite a gracious meal. And year round on Wednesday, Friday, and Saturday, weather permitting, you can pop over to the farmer's market at **Union Square** (14th to 17th Sts. near Park Avenue South) to pick up homemade pies, cakes and muffins, bagels, breads, preserves, fresh-off-the-farm fruits and vegetables, and even an occasional New York State wine.

But wherever you are you'll find good food to go. Delis are on almost every corner, as are Korean groceries with their amazing salad-buffet bars, often with quite an extensive selection of hot and cold dishes and salad fixings. And the price is right.

Remember that, with one or two exceptions, you can purchase a bottle of wine only at a licensed liquor store and never on Sunday, but beer is available in any grocery store.

CHAPTER 7

WHAT TO SEE & DO IN NEW YORK

New York tourists generally fall into one of two categories. The first are the compulsive sightseers who feel that if they don't get to the top of the World Trade Center, visit the United Nations, have a meal in Chinatown, and take the boat to the Statue of Liberty, they might as well have stayed home. The second are the lazy ones who like to know that the World Trade Center is there if they really want it, but are perfectly happy just walking around the city, absorbing the sights, sounds, and sensations as they find them.

Both have a point: The major sights of New York are exciting and important, and you should see as many of them as you comfortably can. But you should also allow yourself plenty of time to let New York sink in by osmosis: to rummage through Village antiques stores or watch lovers stroll through Central Park or sip a martini at a cocktail lounge in the sky as the city shimmers below. A holiday in New York, I think, ought to be made up of equal parts of doing and dreaming—with enough leisure for both.

But fitting everything in can be quite complicated, especially if you're here for just a short time. So have a look at the following listings of the city's attractions, decide what you want to see, and get started. After you've seen the main sights, you may also want to make some walking tours covering historical and architectural highlights of the city (see Chapter 8). Note that you'll be doing plenty of walking, so be sure to wear comfortable shoes. You should also carry with you bus and subway maps, available on the buses and at subway stations, also at the New York Convention and Visitors Bureau at 2 Columbus Circle.

SUGGESTED ITINERARIES

IF YOU HAVE ONE DAY

Get up early and take the ferry to the Statue of Liberty and Ellis Island before the crowds get too heavy. If you visit both places, you will have spent most of the day. Repair to Chinatown for the late afternoon and early evening.

IF YOU HAVE 2 DAYS

Day 1 Spend Day 1 as outlined above.
Day 2 Visit the Metropolitan Museum of Art in the morning, then spend the afternoon and early evening downtown at the South Street Seaport.

IF YOU HAVE 3 DAYS

Days 1–2 Spend Days 1–2 as discussed above.
Day 3 Visit the Empire State Building, Rockefeller Center, Radio City Music Hall, and the Museum of Modern Art. Spend the late afternoon and early evening wandering around Greenwich Village and SoHo.

IF YOU HAVE 4 DAYS

Days 1–3 Spend Days 1–3 as discussed above.
Day 4 Visit the Observation Deck at the World Trade Center, tour downtown Manhattan, and relax in the afternoon on the Circle Line boat trip around Manhattan.

IF YOU HAVE 5 DAYS

Days 1–4 Spend Days 1–4 as discussed above.
Day 5 Spend the morning at the United Nations and, depending on the weather, the afternoon in Central Park or shopping New York's major department stores—Saks Fifth Avenue, Bloomingdale's, Lord & Taylor, Macy's, and A&S.

1. THE TOP ATTRACTIONS

DOWNTOWN

THE STATUE OF LIBERTY.
    The Statue of Liberty is one sight in New York that no one, not even the most blasé, should miss. You'll enjoy your visit more if you come early on a weekday, since the crowds get thick in the afternoon and particularly on weekends and holidays. (Tel. for general information, 363-3200; for the ferry, 269-5755.)
    Every schoolchild, of course, knows the story of the statue: of

how it was given to the United States by the people of France in 1886 to commemorate the alliance of the two countries during the American Revolution. Its construction became the ruling passion of French sculptor Auguste Bartholdi, who raised funds in France and then designed the monument (Alexandre Gustave Eiffel, who built a rather famous tower in France, did the supporting framework); and the people of the United States, reluctant to match the 1-million-franc contribution of the French people, had to be prodded into it by an intensive campaign led by the *New York World*'s Joseph Pulitzer. Finally, the money was raised, and now it seems as if the statue has always been there, so magnificently does it blend into its site in Upper Bay, so splendidly does it typify the ideals and dreams on which the nation was built. Stepping from her chains, Liberty, a tablet commemorating the date of July 4, 1776, in her left hand, the torch of freedom held high in her right, has become the symbol of a new life to thousands of immigrants and exiles from all over.

When you actually get to the statue, the statistics—the figure is 152 feet high, the pedestal another 150 feet, the arm 42 feet long, the head large enough for a couple of people to stand in—become an awesome reality. The 21-foot-high bronze doors through which you enter the statue recount, in bas-relief panels, the history of Lady Liberty's construction and her restoration, a massive 2½-year, almost $70-million project that was completed in time for the gala centenni-

 ## FROMMER'S FAVORITE NEW YORK EXPERIENCES

A Morning or Afternoon in Central Park   Row on a surprisingly rural lake, ride a bike, sail a model boat, visit the zoo, hear the street musicians and the sound of birds, and watch the incredible people parade.

Late Afternoon and Early Evening at the South Street Seaport   Soak up the ocean breezes, board the old ships, shop at a bevy of intriguing stores, dine, and maybe even take a cruise around New York Harbor. There are often free concerts on the pier in early evening.

English Tea   Try Danal, 90 E. 10th St., or Little Nell's Tea Room, 343 E. 85th St., for a proper English tea in enchanting surroundings.

A Visit to Ellis Island   An incredibly moving journey back to the early years of the century when over 12 million immigrants passed through this portal to the new world.

The Metropolitan Museum of Art by Night.   On Friday or Saturday night the museum stays open late. Leisurely browse through the galleries, then dine at the museum's own restaurant, where there is usually music.

al celebration on July 4, 1986. Although the statue still looks on the outside as it always did, major changes were made in the landscaping of Liberty Island; in the American Museum of Immigration at the base (a new museum space holds the stunning "Liberty Exhibit"); and in the entrance to and the interior of the statue, which has been opened up to expose the "bones" of Eiffel's original structure and create an amazing indoor space. The former flame (it was also replaced in the restoration) is mounted in the center of the lobby floor. There's an elevator to the top of the pedestal, and from there, a 12-story (146-step) circular stairway to the crown's viewing platform. All in all, this is an unforgettable experience of what many consider to be America's greatest piece of monumental sculpture.

Open: Daily 9am to 5pm (subject to change, so call first); admission to the statue is free, though donations are gratefully accepted.

BY SUBWAY Take the **1 train** to South Ferry, and head for the Castle Clinton National Monument in Battery Park and the Statue of Liberty ferry.

Departures: Ferries leave every half hour from 9:15am to 3:30pm every day. They will deposit you, in about 20 minutes, on Liberty Island, a short distance from the statue. A stop at Ellis Island (see below) is included in the fare.

Prices: Fares are $6 for adults, $5 for seniors, $3 for children 3 to 17, free under 3.

BY CAR & FERRY An alternate way to reach the Statue of Liberty is now available to those driving to New York via the New Jersey Turnpike and from New York through the Holland Tunnel. In both cases take Exit 14B to Liberty State Park (parking and park admission are free). The advantage here is that lines are generally shorter and parking is free. Incidentally, Liberty State Park is the scene of frequent concerts and events.

Departures: Circle Line ferries depart every half hour from 9:30am to 3:30pm daily (except November 27 to early spring) for the Statue.

Prices: Fares are $6 for adults, $5 for seniors, $3 for children 3 to 17, free for children under 3, the same as from Battery Park.

ELLIS ISLAND.

One of New York's newest—and most moving—sights, opened in the fall of 1990, is the restored Ellis Island, a few hundred yards north of the Statue of Liberty. Ellis Island was the portal through which more than 12 million immigrants entered the United States between 1892 and 1954. More than 100 million living Americans—40% of the nation's population—trace their roots to an ancestor who came through Ellis Island. Focal point of the restoration is the Ellis Island Immigration Museum, which does a masterful job of telling the immigrant's story in a series of innovative displays that feature historic artifacts and photos, interactive devices and taped reminiscences of the immigrants themselves. Don't miss the superb documentary film shown free throughout the day. Also powerful is the American Immigrant Wall of Honor, which includes the names of nearly 200,000 American immigrants who have been commemorated by their descendants. Overlooking both the Statue of Liberty and the Manhattan skyline, it is the longest wall of names in the world.

Circle Line Tours runs daily ferries to Ellis Island both from Battery Park and from Liberty State Park at frequent intervals. (For details, see "The Statue of Liberty" above.)

SOUTH STREET SEAPORT & THE SOUTH STREET SEA-PORT MUSEUM.

To see what a very practical group of dreamers and visionaries are doing to commemorate the old days of South Street, visit the South Street Seaport Museum (tel. 669-9400). The museum is the 11-block South Street Seaport that stretches from Piers 15 and 16 all the way over to Fulton Street. Stroll out on the piers to see the magnificent ships of the museum's collection, or better still, take a museum walking tour to discover the history of the ships and the people of the old port. Museum admission of $6 for adults, $5 for senior citizens, and $3 for children allows you to visit museum galleries on Water and John streets; see museum films; board the original lightship *Ambrose,* which guarded the approach to the Port of New York for more than two decades; and climb aboard the *Peking,* a barque that is longer than a football field, with four masts 17 stories high! Your ticket also allows you to join the basic guided tour of the ships and the historic district, plus a tour behind the scenes of the restoration of the great ship *Wavertree* (built in 1885) and a tour of the unrestored district.

If you'd like to get out on the water yourself, that's also possible. In spring, summer, and early fall, you can take 1½-hour **cruises** aboard the modern-day sidewheeler *Andrew Fletcher,* modeled after the paddle boats that once made regular day excursions up the Hudson. The three-decked *Fletcher* holds 400 passengers, cruises New York's Harbor Park, and affords a close-up view of the Statue of Liberty. Tickets cost $12 for adults, $7 for museum members, and $6 for children 12 and under. For more information about daily cruises and group rates or charters, call 233-4800. Even more fun for those who like to sail is a cruise aboard the 100-year-old schooner *Pioneer.* Its specific destination depends on winds and tides; passengers are limited to 40, and those who wish to do so are invited to help sail the vessel. For a two-hour sail, the cost is $15 for adults, $12 for seniors, $11 for students with valid ID, and $7 for children 12 and under. For more information, call 669-9417.

Another museum attraction is **Bowne & Co., Stationers,** at 211 Water St., a re-creation of a 19th-century stationery shop whose antique letterpresses are used daily. Bowne sells fine paper products, many printed in the shop itself. Other museum stores include the **Edmund M. Blunt Book & Chart Store** (nautical books and materials); the **Museum Shop** (museum merchandise); **Staple & Fancy Goods** (antique gifts and decorative items); and the **Container Store** at Pier 16, in season (children's toys and accessories).

There's always plenty of activity going on at the South Street Seaport Museum, including concerts, films, readings, nautical events, classes, workshops, and special events.

The museum's ships and piers and its architectural focal point, the 1811 countinghouses called **Schermerhorn Row,** are part and parcel of the South Street Seaport area; it may remind you of Boston's Fanueil Hall Marketplace and Baltimore's Harborplace. It's great fun to shop at dozens of specialty shops, eat from exotic food stalls or at fancy restaurants, or just enjoy the street life; there are always street musicians and entertainers performing.

The **Fulton Fish Market building,** once the site of the Fulton Fish Market (which now operates weeknights from midnight to 8am right next door), is devoted exclusively to food—provisions on the first floor, fine restaurants and international "fast-food" menus from all over the world on the upper floors. Some of my favorite shops in this area include **Brookstone** for one-of-a-kind gadgets; **Captain Hook's** for nifty marine antiques; **Caswell-Massey** for George Washington's favorite cologne, Sarah Bernhardt's cucumber cream, and other authentic old-time apothecary items.

Be sure to visit **Pier 17,** a huge three-story pavilion that juts out into the East River, housing more restaurants, bars, clothing stores, and food and specialty shops. There's another fast-food court here, and while the food is not exciting, it's fun to pick up a drink or a snack and take it out to the second-floor balcony to enjoy the tangy sea air and the splendid views of the river and the Brooklyn Bridge. From the third floor you get good views of the Statue of Liberty. As for the shopping here, it's pricey but very entertaining. My favorites are: **The Sharper Image,** the catalog store to end all catalog stores, where there's always a line waiting to try out such wonderful adult playthings as electronic massage tables, talking scales, or indoor rowing machines; and **A2Z,** which also has nifty gadgets, like a solar-powered baseball cap with a built-in brow fan!

THE STATEN ISLAND FERRY.

The cost is 50¢ round trip (25¢ each way) for an enthralling, hour-long excursion into the world's biggest harbor. Ferries run every half hour. Most of the Staten Island commuters will be sitting inside reading their papers, but do join the sightseers out on the deck, where you can view the busy harbor traffic. You'll pass close to the Statue of Liberty. When the boat arrives at St. George, Staten Island, debark, walk through the terminal, and catch the next boat going back to Manhattan. This is really the best part of the trip, for now you can catch sight of the fabled New York skyline looming up there ahead of you. If you have time, try a ferry ride at night, when the skyline is even more dazzling. (For directions, see "The Statue of Liberty," above.)

MIDTOWN

CIRCLE LINE SIGHTSEEING CRUISES, with departures from Pier 83, at the foot of West 43rd St. and Twelfth Ave. Tel. 563-3200.

The Circle Line sightseeing boat makes a 3-hour around-the-island tour of Manhattan, and it is one of the most popular attractions in town—and one of the best. The trip will give you an unusual perspective on Manhattan; the buildings that you've already seen at close range suddenly look quite different when viewed from the sea. Your orbit around the island begins at Pier 83, at the foot of West 42nd Street; takes you down into Upper Bay past the Statue of Liberty and Ellis Island; then continues up along the East River, as the Brooklyn Bridge, the Manhattan Bridge, and the former Brooklyn Navy Yard come into view. Up you go along the East River you'll view the splendor of the United Nations from the sea, and farther along, Gracie Mansion, the home of the mayor. The East River merges into the Harlem River at Hell Gate, then on northward through Spuyten Duyvil and exits into the Hudson River. The giant lacework of the George Washington Bridge emerges now, and you go down the Hudson, joining slews of tiny pleasure craft, work boats, perhaps even an oil tanker or freighter coming down from the upper Hudson. To your left is Riverside Park. You'll spot Grant's Tomb as you come down along 122nd Street. As you approach Midtown, the docks of the great shipping companies come into view. When your sightseeing yacht docks, you may be lucky enough to see a slew of tugs nudge a beauty like the *QE II* into its berth!

The sightseeing boat comes equipped with a refreshment stand and a narrator who is likely to tell some very ancient jokes; but you will emerge rested, cool, and well-informed about New York. *Parent's note:* Children about 8 and over love this trip, but young ones can get awfully wriggly; remember, it takes 3 hours, and you can't get off!

Prices: $16 adults; $8 children under 12. Prices subject to change. **Departures:** Summer trips scheduled daily every 45 minutes, from 9:30am to 4:30pm, less frequently at other times of year (season runs from late March to December 31). Harbor Lights cruises are held every night at 7pm from May 2 to September 7. On weekends only, cruises are held March 21 to May 1 and September 8 to December 27. **Bus:** 42nd St. (no. 106), 49th St., or 34th St. westbound crosstown buses all stop within a few feet of the ticket booth.

THE EMPIRE STATE BUILDING, Fifth Ave. and 34th St. Tel. 736-3100.

No visitor should leave New York without a visit to the top of the Empire State Building. You'll have plenty of company; over 2½ million visitors a year, from all over the world, make the pilgrimage to the world's once-highest building: At 1,454 feet above sea level, 102 stories high, this sleek, modernistic monument typifies the skyscraper city in its boldness, daring, and dominance. The real excitement starts when you reach the 86th-floor **Observatory:** from the outdoor promenade deck, it's a 360-degree view, and if the day is clear, you can see as far as 80 miles into the distance. But the big show lies below you: Manhattan, an island of steel and concrete and glass rising out of the sea, looking from this height like a Lilliputian landscape. For a view from an even higher vantage, you can go up another 16 stories, to the 102nd floor and its spaceship environment. After dark, the city becomes a fantasy of sparkling lights and stars against a panoramic background of darkness.

Admission: $3.50 adults; $1.75 children.

Open: Daily 9:30am–midnight. Tickets sold until 11:20pm. **Subway:** B, D, or F train to 34th St.

While you're here, stop in at the **Guinness World Record Exhibit Hall** on the concourse level (right next to the Observatory ticket office) to see who and what broke all the records. This multimedia display is great fun for kids and adults alike. **Open:** Daily 9am to 10pm; admission is $5.50 for adults, and $3.50 for children 5 to 12 (tel. 947-2335).

MUSEUM OF MODERN ART, 11 West 53rd St. Tel. 708-9480 for information on current exhibitions and film programs.

The Museum of Modern Art (MOMA) has been controversial since it opened in 1929. The Modern's early shows—of fur-lined teacups, Dadaesque landscapes of the mind, cubism, and abstractions—were considered shocking by the staid art establishment of the time; now there are some who declare MOMA to be too old hat! Whichever side you're on, MOMA is a great, lively, wonderfully exciting museum that takes all of modern art and design as its province—and that includes photography, film, prints, illustrated books, furniture, and architecture, as well as paintings and sculpture. It presents the world's most comprehensive survey of 20th-century art.

Of course you must see the Picassos, Chagalls, Kandinskys, Mondrians, and Matisses on permanent display, as well as the Rodin and Calder and Moore and Maillols in the splendid outdoor Abby Aldrich Rockefeller Sculpture Garden. Film buffs practically make the museum's theaters a second home; it's the place to catch an early Garbo classic, a Flaherty masterpiece, your favorite Bogart flick, recent films you might have missed at the box office, as well as the work of new filmmakers. Because there is usually a heavy demand for movie tickets, get there as early as possible to commandeer a reservation. Summer garden is a popular series of free musical evenings held in the Sculpture Garden during July and August.

Overlooking the Sculpture Garden are two restaurants: the **Garden Café,** a cafeteria for the public, and the **Members Dining Room,** which is open to the public, space permitting.

Admission (including entrance to movie): $7.50 adults; $4.50 students with valid ID and senior citizens; members and children under 16 accompanied by an adult free. Thursday 6 to 9pm, it's "Pay What You Wish."

Open: Mon–Tues and Fri–Sun 11am–6pm; Thurs 11am–9pm. **Closed:** Wed. **Subway:** E or F train to Fifth Ave.

RADIO CITY MUSIC HALL, Avenue of the Americas at 50th St. Tel. 247-4777 for computerized information on events.

The world's biggest theater is, of course, the famed Radio City Music Hall Entertainment Center. Restored to its 1930s art deco elegance, the 5,875-seat theater is an architectural wonder, and its shows—concerts, spectacular presentations, and special events (rarely movies)—run the gamut from family entertainment like The Magnificent Christmas Spectacular starring the Rockettes (America's most famous chorus girls) to pop acts such as Aretha Franklin and Engelbert Humperdinck—and even the Moscow Circus!

Tickets, priced according to the attraction, are available at the box office or can be charged through any **Ticketmaster** outlet (tel. 307-7171). Even if you don't see a show at Radio City, take a guided tour viewing the grand foyer, the orchestra, back and below stage, and the Wurlitzer.

Tours: Hour-long tours usually given daily 10:15am–4:45pm for $7. **Subway:** B, D, F, or Q to 47–50 Sts.

ROCKEFELLER CENTER, 47th St. to 52nd St., west of Fifth Ave.

It's noted as one of the architectural marvels of New York—and of the United States—a high-water mark of urban design. Although it is one of the busiest, most heavily trafficked areas in the city, this 24-acre, 19-skyscraper complex gives the feeling of old-world gentility and beauty, thanks to its masterful use of open space. You'll appreciate this as you approach the Center from the best vantage point, the Channel Gardens, which begin between 49th and 50th streets, across Fifth Avenue from St. Patrick's Cathedral and Saks Fifth Avenue. Depending on the season, the gardens will be abloom with chrysanthemums, lilies, roses, or tropical plants, and you'll see scores of people stopping to sit on the benches and maybe munch a lunchtime sandwich. On either side of the walk is an array of shops and services. Continue down the promenade to the central sunken plaza, the focal point of the complex. In winter, the plaza is an ice-skating rink, a Breughel canvas in the heart of the city; in summer, it's an open-air restaurant. Directly behind the plaza is the massive statue of *Prometheus* by Paul Manship, with its fountain in back; behind that the RCA Building soars skyward.

Subway: B, D, F, or Q to 47–50th Sts.

THE UNITED NATIONS, on the East River, bounded by 42nd St. on the south and 48th St. on the north. Tel. 963-7713.

At the United Nations, world history happens every day. An international enclave on the East River, it is headquarters for almost 6,000 men and women from all over the world who carry on the work of the Secretariat and the General Assembly.

Just *being* at the United Nations has an excitement about it that exists nowhere else. You could have a lovely visit just walking around, observing the sculptures and artworks donated by the member nations (in the garden, for example, a massive sculpture of a Soviet worker beats a sword into a plowshare, shopping in the downstairs stores (more about these later), and observing the lively international crowd; but do take time to attend one of the General Assembly or other meetings and/or to take a guided tour. The guided tours, a wonderful introduction to the history and activities of the U.N., give you a chance to explore the varied collections of art and sculpture. There are also tours for non-English-speaking guests. For information, phone 963-7713.

Free tickets to the meetings are given out in the lobby of the General Assembly building just before they start, on a first-come, first-served basis. To find out in advance what meetings will be held, phone 963-1234 after 9:30am on the day you wish to attend. Once you gain admission, you can plug in your earphones and listen to the debates—sometimes quite lively—in English or French or Chinese or Spanish or Russian or Arabic—the official languages of the U.N.

You could easily browse away a few hours downstairs at the United Nations. My favorite spot here is the **Gift Center,** where beautiful and tasteful handcrafts from many of the member nations are sold. On one visit, for example, I found pewterware from Norway, beautifully painted nesting dolls from the Soviet Union, silk scarves from India, brassware from Iran, and carved figures from Nigeria. The collection of ethnic dolls is enough to win the heart of any little girl on your list. Stamp buffs should stop in at the **United Nations Postal Administration Sales Counter,** the only spot on the globe (besides the United Nations offices in Geneva and Vienna) where you can mail cards and letters bearing U.N. postage stamps.

If you arrive early enough, have lunch at the United Nations in the **Delegates Dining Room.** It's open to the public Monday to Friday between 11:30am and 1:30pm. You may get to see a few of the delegates, and the view of the East River and the United Nations gardens is one of the best in town. Call 963-7625 for reservations.

Tours: Guided tours begin about every half hour, from 9:15am–4:45pm; they cost $6.50 adults, $4.50 seniors, $4.50 college and high school students, $3.50 for children grades 1–9 (children under 5 are not permitted on tours). **Bus:** M104, 42nd St. crosstown bus, M15 uptown.

LINCOLN CENTER/UPPER WEST SIDE

LINCOLN CENTER FOR THE PERFORMING ARTS, 70 Lincoln Center Plaza. Tel. 875-5350, or 769-7020 for information on tours of the Metropolitan Opera House.

Whether or not you see any performances at Lincoln Center (more details in Chapter 10), take a tour of this impressive complex of theaters and concert halls. Just to see the art and sculpture on the grounds is an experience in itself: Alexander Calder's *Le Guichet* in front of the Library and Museum of Performing Arts; Richard Lippold's *Orpheus and Apollo* in Avery Fisher Hall; Henry Moore's gigantic *Reclining Figure* in the reflecting pool in front of the Vivian Beaumont Theater; and Marc Chagall's lilting paintings for the Metropolitan Opera House. The buildings themselves—the Metropolitan Opera House, the New York State Theater, the Vivian Beaumont Theater, Avery Fisher Hall, Alice Tully Hall, The Juilliard School, the Walter Reade Theater, and the New York Public Library for the Performing Arts—have been both criticized and praised: Take a look and reach your own conclusions. You'll probably see all the buildings and may even get to watch rehearsals of the New York City Ballet or the New York City Opera Company. But if you have your heart set on seeing the interiors of the theaters, do not come on a Saturday afternoon; that's matinée time, and the doors are closed to tour takers.

Tours: Hour-long tours daily 10am–5pm; cost is $7.50 adults, $4.25 children, $6.50 senior citizens and students. Tours of Metropolitan Opera House alone held Sept–June. **Subway:** 1 or 9 to 66th St.

THE AMERICAN MUSEUM OF NATURAL HISTORY, Central Park West at 79th St. Tel. 769-5100.

One of the great scientific museums of the world, the American

PARENTS

TODAY YOUR CHILDR

A Special Idea for You and You

Museum brings the natural history of humans and animals to vivid life for visitors of all ages. Added to such perennial crowd-pleasing (and kid-pleasing) exhibitions as the Hall of Minerals and Gems, the Hall of African Peoples, the Hall of Reptiles and Amphibians, and the Hall of Ocean Life (with its 94-foot whale suspended from the ceiling) is the exciting Arthur Ross Hall of Meteorites, whose centerpiece is the largest meteorite ever retrieved. The new Barosaurus exhibit—not to be missed—is the largest free-standing dinosaur display in the world. Another winner is the Hall of Asian Peoples, which explores the complex cultures of the Asian continent. Children over five will enjoy the learning games in the Discovery Room. You could spend days—no, weeks—here, enjoying ethnological and anthropological collections, seeing the dioramas of animals in their natural habitats, and watching the dance, music, and crafts programs shown live at the Leonhardt People Center. And you won't want to miss seeing the exciting films shown daily in the Naturemax Theater on New York's largest screen. Admission is $5 adults, $2.50 children (tel. 769-5650).

Admission: Suggested admission $5 adults; $2.50 children.

Open: Mon–Thurs and Sun 10am–5:45pm; Fri–Sat 10am–8:45pm. **Closed:** Christmas and Thanksgiving. **Subway:** C to 81st St.

THE UPPER EAST SIDE

FRICK COLLECTION, 1 East 70th St., at Fifth Ave. Tel. 288-0700.

One of the most beautiful small museums in the world, this former home of industrialist magnate Henry C. Frick is filled with treasures: Rembrandts, Turners, Vermeers, El Grecos, French furniture, Chinese vases, and Limoges enamels. Its central courtyard, with greenery and fountains, is an oasis in the city. Concerts and lectures are held here from October through May. Phone for details.

Admission: $3 adults; $1.50 students and senior citizens. Children under 10 not admitted, and those under 16 must be accompanied by an adult.

Open: Tues–Sat 10am–6pm; Sun and minor holidays 1–6pm. **Closed:** Mon and major hols. **Subway:** 6 to 68th St. **Bus:** M1 and M4 southbound on Fifth Ave., northbound on Madison Ave.

GUGGENHEIM MUSEUM, 1071 Fifth Ave., near 89th St. Tel. 423-3500.

Completely restored and expanded with the addition of a 10-story tower, Frank Lloyd Wright's 1959 creation, considered to be one of the greatest buildings of the 20th century, has been reopened after a two-year hiatus: Wright's landmark building is now more exciting and dramatic than ever. From the outside, it looks something like a gigantic wedding cake tilted to one side; on the inside, it's a superb showcase for art—a large, spiral ramp on which you walk downward, viewing art set in bays along the curved walls. Many exciting shows—like the major 1992 exhibit "Beyond Zero: The Avant-Garde in Russia 1915–1932"—complement Solomon Guggenheim's collection of 20th-century art, which focuses mainly on abstract expressionist and nonobjective masters. The Justin K. Thannhauser Wing permanently displays such impressionists and post-impressionists as Picasso, Degas, and Cézanne. A full-service café run by Dean & Deluca and based on Wright's original design, offers refreshments.

The Guggenheim Museum has also expanded downtown: the Guggenheim Museum SoHo is located in a 19th-century landmark building at 575 Broadway (tel. 423-3500), in the SoHo Cast-Iron Historic District.

Admission: For adults, $7 Guggenheim Museum, $5 Guggenheim Museum SoHo, $10 both locations. For students and senior citizens, $4 Guggenheim Museum, $3 Guggenheim Museum SoHo, $6 both locations. Children under 12 free with adult.

Open: Guggenheim Museum Fifth Ave., Fri–Wed 10am–8pm. Guggenheim Museum SoHo, Sun, Mon, and Wed 11am–6pm; Thurs, Fri, and Sat 11am–10pm.

METROPOLITAN MUSEUM OF ART, Fifth Ave. at 82nd St. Tel. 535-7710 for recorded information, 879-5512 for news of concerts and lectures.

Whether you're interested in Egyptian artifacts or Roman armor or Chinese porcelain or Renaissance or impressionist painting, the Metropolitan is the place. You could spend weeks studying the collection of European and American paintings, a masterful group of Raphaels, Titians, El Grecos, Rembrandts, Picassos, Pollocks, and Braques—enough to make your head swim. You'll surely want to visit the spectacular wing devoted to the art of Africa, the Pacific Islands, and Pre-Columbian and Native America. You must not miss the American wing, which has brought some of Central Park indoors in a glass-enclosed, 70-foot-tall garden that leads to three floors of American paintings, furniture, sculpture, silver, glass, textiles, and decorative arts. Also high on your agenda should be the splendid 19th-century European Painting Galleries, with particular emphasis on the impressionist and post-impressionist painters and a large collection of Rodin sculptures. If your interest is 20th-century art, visit the Lila Acheson Wallace Wing; during the summer, its roof garden is a showplace for large-scale sculpture. The Chinese Scholars garden court and the superb Asian collection are a must. The 32 dramatic Egyptian galleries, including the incredible Temple of Dendur, are considered a triumph of art and scholarship, one of the most distinguished collections of its kind anywhere. The exhibit is absorbing for everyone, and the kids, especially, will love the mummy cases! The kids—and grownups, too—will also be enthralled by the new Arms and Armor galleries, displaying an encyclopedic collection of the art of the armorer, swordsman, and gunmaker, from the 5th to the 19th century. There is a particularly large collection of Japanese arms and armor, as well as works from Europe, America, the Near East, and elsewhere in Asia.

Admission (including same-day admission to The Cloisters, detailed in Section 2): Suggested charge $6 adults; $3 students and seniors.

Open: Sun and Tues–Thurs 9:30am–5:15pm; Fri–Sat 9:30am–8:45pm. The Metropolitan now stays open until 8:45pm on Friday and Saturday night, when the museum restaurant is open for cocktails and/or dinner. Visitors can dine leisurely (and very reasonably), then browse through the museum's collection or special exhibitions. **Closed:** New Year's Day, Thanksgiving, and Christmas. **Bus:** Any southbound Fifth Ave. or northbound Madison Ave. bus.

WHITNEY MUSEUM OF AMERICAN ART, 945 Madison Ave., at 75th St. Tel. 570-3600.

What many consider the very best collection of 20th-century

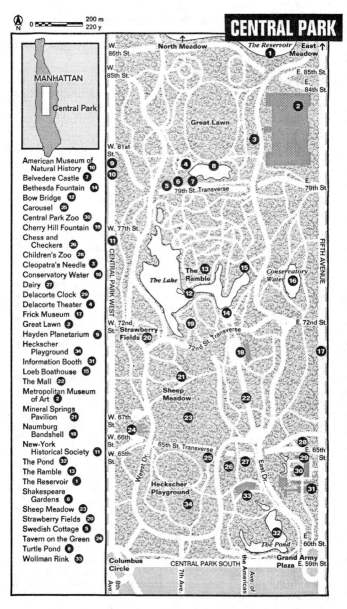

0 — 200 m
0 — 220 y
N

MANHATTAN

Central Park

American Museum of Natural History ⑩
Belvedere Castle ⑦
Bethesda Fountain ⑭
Bow Bridge ⑫
Carousel ㉕
Central Park Zoo ㉚
Cherry Hill Fountain ⑲
Chess and Checkers ㉖
Children's Zoo ㉘
Cleopatra's Needle ③
Conservatory Water ⑯
Dairy ㉗
Delacorte Clock ㉙
Delacorte Theater ④
Frick Museum ⑰
Great Lawn ②
Hayden Planetarium ⑨
Heckscher Playground ㉞
Information Booth ㉛
Loeb Boathouse ⑮
The Mall ㉒
Metropolitan Museum of Art ②
Mineral Springs Pavilion ㉑
Naumburg Bandshell ⑱
New-York Historical Society ⑪
The Pond ㉜
The Ramble ⑬
The Reservoir ①
Shakespeare Gardens ⑥
Sheep Meadow ㉓
Strawberry Fields ⑳
Swedish Cottage ⑤
Tavern on the Green ㉔
Turtle Pond ⑧
Wollman Rink ㉝

North Meadow
The Reservoir ①
East Meadow
W. 86th St.
W. 85th St.
E. 85th St.
E. 84th St.
②
Great Lawn ②
③
W. 81st St.
⑨
④ ⑧
⑩
⑥ ⑦
⑤
79th St. Transverse
E. 79th St.
W. 77th St.
⑪
⑬ ⑮
The Ramble
Conservatory Water ⑯
The Lake
⑫
⑭
W. 72nd St.
Strawberry Fields
⑲
E. 72nd St.
⑳
72nd St. Transverse
⑱
⑰
CENTRAL PARK WEST
FIFTH AVENUE
㉑
Sheep Meadow
㉒
㉓
W. 67th St.
㉔
W. 66th St.
65th St. Transverse
㉘
W. 65th St.
㉙
㉕
㉗
㉖
㉚
West Dr.
East Dr.
㉛
Heckscher Playground
㉝
㉞
㉜
The Pond
Columbus Circle
CENTRAL PARK SOUTH
Grand Army Plaza E. 59th St.
E. 60th St.
8th Ave.
7th Ave.
Ave. of the Americas

American art is housed in Marcel Breuer's superb modernistic building, an inverted wedding cake to which you gain entrance by crossing a bridge. Founded by Gertrude Vanderbilt Whitney, the museum opened in the Village in 1931 and is now in its third home. At least two major exhibitions are on view at all times, including selections from the permanent collection by such artists as Alexander Calder, Edward Hopper, Jasper Johns, Roy Lichtenstein, Reginald Marsh, Louise Nevelson, and Georgia O'Keeffe.

Sarabeth's at the Whitney offers lunch and an afternoon light tea service daily, and brunch on weekends.

Note: The Whitney's Midtown branch, at the world headquarters of **Philip Morris,** Park Avenue and 42nd Street, across from Grand Central Terminal, features a sculpture court and garden, with an adjacent gallery for changing exhibitions. The sculpture court is open Monday to Saturday from 7:30am–9:30pm, Sunday and holidays 11am–7pm; gallery is open Monday to Saturday from 11am–6pm, Thursday to 7:30pm. Admission is free (tel. 878-2550).

Admission (including programs in the New American Film and Video Series): $5 adults; $3 senior citizens and college students with valid ID; children under 12 with an adult free. Thurs free.

Open: Wed 11am–6pm; Thurs 1–8pm; Fri–Sun 11am–6pm. **Closed:** National holidays. **Bus:** Any southbound Fifth Ave. or northbound Madison Ave. bus.

CENTRAL PARK, between Central Park West and Fifth Ave., from Central Park South (59th St.) to 110th St. Tel. 360-8111, 360-1333 for recorded information.

What Tivoli is to Copenhagen and Chapultec is to Mexico City, Central Park is to New York: the great public playground. A magnificent garden in the midst of the concrete canyons, it offers city-jaded New Yorkers a breath of the country, a chance to wander along bosky landscapes, climb rocks, listen to the song of birds, and stare at the sky. It also gives them the chance to stare at one another: Frederick Law Olmsted and Calvert Vaux's 19th-century greensward is one of the most popular places in town. The park offers many recreational and cultural outlets. During the summer, there's the **New York Shakespeare Festival,** plus concerts by the Metropolitan Opera, the New York Philharmonic, and many others—most of them free. The Department of Recreation also sponsors many interesting events in the park, from free tennis lessons for kids to Hula-Hoop contests! So many things go on in the park, in fact, that daily reports are given via a recorded tape, on the telephone.

There's always something going on at **The Dairy** (tel. 794-6564), a beautiful and historic restoration of one of Olmsted and Vaux's original park buildings, open Tuesday through Sunday from 11am to 5pm except Friday, 1 to 5pm. Free concerts are held every Saturday and Sunday at noon during the summer, followed by a walk/talk series; there are frequent exhibits; and walking tours led by the N.Y.C. Urban Park Rangers begin here every weekend.

With or without kids, don't miss taking a rowboat out on **Conservatory Lake** (north of 72nd Street), an unexpectedly rural spot for New York. (You can rent boats just north of the 72nd Street transverse on the east side of the lake.) And when you've finished, join the throngs strolling around the beautiful **Bethesda Fountain** area, which is really the focal point of the park. The setting—with the fountain, the lake, and the towers of New York in the background—is one of the most romantic in the city.

A particularly romantic way to see Central Park is in a **horse-drawn carriage** ($34 for a 20-minute ride; pick up a carriage on 59th Street). The energetic can join the local jogging set or rent a horse from the **Claremont Riding Academy,** 175 W. 89th St. (tel. 724-5100; about $30 an hour; you must be experienced in English riding at walk, trot, and canter) and trot through miles of lovely bridle paths. Or you can rent a bike from the **bicycle concession** near the boathouse on the east side of the lake just north of the 72nd Street and join the throngs of New Yorkers—families, kids, and singles looking for other singles—who've discovered the joy of life on wheels. During the summer, the park is closed to traffic from 10am to 3pm and again from 7 to 10pm on weekdays, as well as all day on the weekends, so bikers, riders, and kids reign supreme. Tennis buffs can also find a home in Central Park; the courts at 93rd Street are insanely popular. **Tennis permits** cost $50 for adults, $20 for senior citizens, and $10 for juniors, and they entitle you to an hour of play every day. Good news for short-term visitors: Single-play tickets, good for an hour, are available for $5 and can be purchased right at the courts. There are also several bubbled courts that stay open during the winter. For information on permits and what courts are open, phone the **Permit Office,** 830 Fifth Ave. (tel. 360-8133). Skaters can enjoy the ice in winter or roller-skating in summer at the **Wollman Rink** (tel. 517-4800); enter the park at 59th Street. Just to the north on the other side of the northbound Park Drive at about 64th Street is the **Carousel** (open daily from St. Patrick's Day to Thanksgiving, and only on weekends the rest of the year). More sedentary types can enjoy browsing through the **book-stalls** (New York's modest answer to the Left Bank quais of Paris) along the outer wall of the park, at Fifth Avenue and 60th Street. (There are also some great little kiosks serving all sorts of international snacks.)

A living memorial to John Lennon grows in Central Park, in a hilly, 2½-acre area across the street from the Dakota Apartments, Central Park West and 72nd Street, where Lennon was slain in 1980. Five years after the event, his widow, Yoko Ono, who donated $1 million to the project, joined in an opening ceremony for **Strawberry Fields** with an array of international diplomats, many of whose countries had sent gifts to this "International Garden of Peace." There are river birches from the Soviet Union, maples from Canada, cedars from Israel, daffodils from Holland, and dogwoods from the late Princess Grace of Monaco. Most poignant, perhaps, is Italy's gift, a black-and-white mosaic starburst with the word "Imagine" inscribed in its center. For those who remember John Lennon, this is a very special bit of New York.

2. MORE ATTRACTIONS

The possibilities are endless. I haven't attempted to cover everything in New York, since this is a guidebook and not an encyclopedia. Listed below are some major and minor sights of the city, chosen either for their importance or their special, if offbeat, charm.

ARCHITECTURAL HIGHLIGHTS

AT&T BUILDING, 550 Madison Ave., between 55th and 56th Sts.

Designed by Philip Johnson and John Burgee, the former AT&T corporate headquarters (now leased to Sony) was hailed as the first major office structure in the post-modern style when it opened in 1983. The facade is pink granite, the inside walls are marble. Its distinctive top resembles a notched piece of 18th-century Chippendale furniture. A loggia affording public seating and an arcade of retail stores surround the building.

CHRYSLER BUILDING, 405 Lexington Ave., at 42nd St.

One of the best examples of the art deco period in New York, the Chrysler Building was completed in 1930 and was the world's tallest building for a year. Its lobby is considered one of the city's most splendid art deco interiors. Its stainless-steel tower has brick designs that recall automobile hubcaps.

FORD FOUNDATION, 320 East 43rd St., just east of Second Ave. Tel. 573-5000.

The Ford Foundation building, designed by Kevin Roche, is considered one of the rare modern architectural masterpieces of New York, a structure built with humanistic concerns for its employees and environment. It is especially notable for its splendid indoor garden—a glorious, 12-story, 160-foot-high hothouse. The former architecture critic of the *New York Times*, Ada Louise Huxtable, called the building "a splendid, shimmering Crystal Palace" and its garden "probably one of the most romantic environments ever devised by corporate man." Don't miss a quiet few moments here.

Open: Garden, Mon–Fri 9am–5pm.

GRAND CENTRAL TERMINAL, 42nd St. at Park Ave.

A symbol of the power of New York City, Grand Central Terminal is a magnificent beaux arts structure built in 1913. Its architectural focus is the main concourse, one of the great interiors of New York City.

WOOLWORTH BUILDING, 233 Broadway, at Park Place in the Financial District.

Until the coming of the Empire State Building, this was the world's tallest—60 stories, pretty good for 1913. It's a lovely, lacy, Gothic froufrou. Walk in to see the lobby with its walls of golden marble.

ART GALLERIES

Art is "hot" in New York City. At last official count, there were something like 560 art galleries in town—and the number keeps growing, almost weekly. New York now is the acknowledged center of the international art scene, and collecting is at an all-time high. For art-happy New Yorkers, gallery-going is a favorite pastime, and the uptown scene of the action is still 57th Street and up Madison Avenue into the East 70s and 80s. Also, many prestigious East Side galleries have relocated to SoHo. Saturday, is the big browsing, shopping day. If your interest in art is more than casual, come join the crowd.

Since there is no admission fee to galleries (unless there is a special charity benefit), you can come and go as you please. Where you go will be determined by what you're interested in: the moderns, the traditionalists, or the Old Masters. The quickest way to find out who's showing where is to consult the art pages in the Entertainment Section of Sunday's *New York Times*. The following are some of the big names among the galleries showing the moderns: **Holly Solomon,** 724 Fifth Ave.; **Marlborough,** 40 W. 57th St.; **André Emmerich,** 41 E. 57th St.; **Spanierman,** 50 E. 78th St.; **Tibor de Nagy,** 41 W. 57th St.; **Saidenberg,** 1018 Madison Ave.; **Cordier & Ekstrom,** 417 E. 75th St.; **Forum,** 745 Fifth Ave. at 57th St.; **Terry Dintenfass,** 50 W. 57th St.; and **Pace,** 32 E. 57th St.

Should your taste run more to the Impressionists and French masters, relax at **Hammer Galleries,** 33 E. 57th St., or **Wally Findlay Galleries,** 17 E. 57th St. (which also shows contemporary Europeans and Americans). **Hirschl & Adler,** 21 E. 70th St., specializes in American paintings from the 18th century to the present, as well as French and European paintings from the early 19th to the early 20th century (during August, open by appointment only). Old Masters? Get out your checkbook and head for the hallowed and haughty temples of **Wildenstein,** 19 E. 64th St. (where you could also pick up an impressionist, post-impressionist, or 20th-century master). **Knoedler & Co.,** 19 E. 70th St., is noted for contemporary American and European paintings and sculpture.

CEMETERIES

Should you want to pay your respects to some famous New Yorkers, you can visit these four famous cemeteries.

MANHATTAN

TRINITY CHURCH, 74 Trinity Place. Tel. 602-0787.

The churchyard that surrounds the historic church on three sides contains the graves of some noted parishioners—among them, Alexander Hamilton, Robert Fulton, and Albert Gallatin.

Open: Daily 9am–5pm. **Subway:** 4 or 5 to Wall St.

TRINITY CHURCH CEMETERY, 770 Riverside Drive, at 153rd to 155th Sts. Tel. 368-1600.

This is the largest cemetery in Manhattan. You'll spot names of historic New York families, among them the Astors, the Van Burens, and the Schermerhorns. Clement C. Moore, the author of the poem "'Twas the Night Before Christmas," is also buried here.

Open: Daily 9am–5pm. **Subway:** 1 to 157th St.

BROOKLYN

GREENWOOD CEMETERY, Fifth Ave. and 25th St. Tel. 718/783-8776.

Some half-a-million people are interred here: Famous names include De Witt Clinton, Horace Greeley, Samuel F. B. Morse, and Rev. Henry Ward Beecher.

Open: Daily 8am–4pm. **Subway:** R to 25th St.

BRONX

WOODLAWN CEMETERY, E. 233rd St. and Webster Ave. Tel. 920-0500.

This enormous park dates back to 1863. It contains the mausoleums of such tycoons as Jay Gould, F. W. Woolworth, and O. H. P. Belmont. Famous literary, journalists, and entertainment figures buried here include Herman Melville, Joseph Pulitzer, Charles Scribner, George M. Cohan, and Duke Ellington. An ongoing schedule of free events takes place on a monthly basis— concerts, tours musical theater and the like. Call for information.

Open: Daily 9am–4:30pm. **Subway:** 4 to Woodlawn.

CHURCHES & SYNAGOGUES

ST. PATRICK'S CATHEDRAL, Fifth Ave. at 50th St. Tel. 753-2261.

"St. Pat's" is New York's foremost Roman Catholic cathedral and the seat of the Archdiocese of New York. Designed by James Renwick and built in 1879, it is a majestic structure, one of the finest Gothic churches in the United States.

Admission: Free.

Open: Daily 7am–8pm. **Bus:** Fifth Ave. southbound, Madison Ave. northbound.

MARBLE COLLEGIATE CHURCH, Fifth Ave. at 29th St. Tel. 686-2770.

The church that Norman Vincent Peale made famous, this is the city's oldest Dutch Reformed church. Its elegant facade is made entirely of marble.

Admission: Free.

Open: Services at 10:30am in summer, 11:15am in fall and winter. **Bus:** Fifth Ave. southbound. **Subway:** 6 to 28th St. and Park Ave., or R and N to 28th St. and Broadway.

TRINITY CHURCH, Broadway at Wall St. Tel. 602-0800.

Consecrated in 1846, and the church of such famous people as Alexander Hamilton and Robert Fulton, Trinity Church is still a vital center for the downtown community. Featured are tours, organ recitals, and museum.

Admission: Free. $2 suggested donation to recitals.

Open: Mon–Fri 7am–6pm; Sat–Sun 8am–4pm. **Subway:** 4 or 5 to Wall St.; N or R to Rector St.

ST. PAUL'S CHAPEL, Broadway at Fulton and Vesey Sts. Tel. 602-0874.

The oldest public building in continual use in Manhattan, St. Paul's dates back to 1776; George Washington's pew is still here. There are noontime concerts and exhibits.

Admission: Free. $2 suggested donation to concerts.

Open: Mon–Sat 7am–4pm; Sun 7am–3:30pm. **Subway:** 4 or 5 to Fulton St.

CENTRAL SYNAGOGUE, 123 East 55th St., at Lexington Ave. Tel. 838-5122.

This New York City and National Historic Landmark, built in 1872, is perhaps the finest example of Moorish Revival architecture in New York.

Admission: Free.

Open: Services (Reform Jewish) Friday night and Saturday, other visits by appointment. **Bus:** Lexington Ave. southbound, Third Ave. northbound. **Subway:** 4, 5, or 6 to 59th St. or 6 to 51st St.

TEMPLE EMANU-EL, Fifth Ave. and 65th St. Tel. 744-1400.

The city's most famous synagogue—its congregations have always included New York's most prominent and wealthy Jewish families—Temple Emanu-El is the largest Reform synagogue in the world. Its magnificent building is largely Romanesque in design, with Byzantine and Gothic elements.

Admission: Free.
Open: Services daily at 5:30pm, Friday at 5:15, and Saturday at 10:30am. **Bus:** Fifth Ave. southbound, Madison Ave. northbound.

CONGREGATION SHEARITH ISRAEL [THE SPANISH AND PORTUGUESE SYNAGOGUE], 2 West 70th St. Tel. 873-0300.

This Orthodox Sephardic synagogue, dating back to 1654, was erected by the oldest Jewish congregation in North America. It was founded by descendants of Spanish and Portuguese Jews persecuted by the Inquisition who had found refuge first in Brazil, later in New York. Louis Comfort Tiffany designed the windows of this landmark structure.
Open: Services every morning and evening. Call the synagogue office for a schedule. Tours by appointment. **Bus:** M10. **Subway:** C to 72nd St.

ST. PETER'S LUTHERAN CHURCH, Lexington Ave. at 54th St. Tel. 935-2200.

This modern church, part of Citicorp Center, boasts the Louise Nevelson chapel, the External Pomodoro Cross, and three art galleries.
Admission: Free.
Open: The church is noted for its Jazz Vespers, held Sunday at 5pm. Traditional masses are held Sunday at 8:45am, and sung mass at 11am Sunday. **Bus:** Lexington Ave. southbound, Third Ave. northbound. **Subway:** 6 to 51st St.

CATHEDRAL CHURCH OF ST. JOHN THE DIVINE, 1047 Amsterdam Ave. at 112th St. Tel. 316-7540.

The largest Gothic cathedral in the world, St. John's is still not finished—and construction began in 1892! One of the major cultural and spiritual forces of New York, the cathedral is known for presenting outstanding musical events and important speakers. The free New Year's Eve concert at St. John's draws thousands of New Yorkers—so, too, does its annual "Blessing of the Animals."
Admission: Suggested donation, $2.
Open: Daily 7am–5pm. **Tours:** Tues–Sat 11am; Sun 12:45pm. **Bus:** Broadway. **Subway:** 1 or 9 to 110th St.

RIVERSIDE CHURCH, 490 Riverside Drive at 120th St. Tel. 222-5900.

Built in 1930 and funded by John D. Rockefeller, Jr., Riverside Church was modeled on the Cathedral at Chartres. Noted for its commitment to major social issues, it attracts a diverse, interracial, and cosmopolitan group of congregants. Be sure to visit the Laura Spelman Rockefeller Carillon, the world's largest, with 74 bells; its observation platform affords a splendid view of the city.
Admission: Free.
Open: Services: Sundays at 10:45, with carillon recitals before and after. Summer organ recitals are held Tuesdays at 7pm in July ($7). **Bus:** Riverside Drive M4 or M5.

HISTORIC BUILDINGS & MONUMENTS

CITY HALL, City Hall Park, Broadway and Park Row. Tel. 566-8681.

Head for City Hall and the mayor will be out to greet you if you're an astronaut, a prime minister, or a beauty queen, but you may not get to see him if you're just an ordinary mortal. You can, however, see the splendid place in which he works, a 19th-century Federal building considered to be one of New York's prime architectural treasures. Walk up the majestic marble staircase to the Governor's Room, a museum with historic furniture (the desk George Washington used as president is here) and Trumbull portraits of Washington, Alexander Hamilton, and others.

A lot of history was made at City Hall Park out front, which, in the early days of New York, was a kind of village square: Political riots, hangings, police wars, and one of the first readings, in 1776, of the Declaration of Independence to a group of New York revolutionaries, all took place here.

Admission: Free.

Open: Mon–Fri 10am–3:30pm. Groups of more than five by appointment only. **Subway:** 4, 5, or 6 to Brooklyn Bridge/City Hall/Centre St.

MORRIS-JUMEL MANSION, in Roger Morris Park, 1765 Jumel Terrace, at West 160th St., just east of St. Nicholas Ave. Tel. 923-8008.

One of New York's most important landmarks, built in 1765 by Roger Morris, the Georgian mansion was headquarters for Gen. George Washington in 1776. It is Manhattan's oldest remaining residence. Aaron Burr was married here in 1833. For elegance and sweep of historical significance, no house in New York outshines this.

Admission: $3 adults; $1 students and senior citizens; children under 12 with adult free.

Open: Tues–Sun 10am–4pm. **Subway:** A to 125th St., switch to B to 163rd St.

OLD MERCHANT'S HOUSE, 29 East 4th St. Tel. 777-1089.

Miraculously saved from demolition, this splendid example of a 19th-century wealthy New York home is once again open for visitors. The Tredwell family lived in this house from 1835 to 1933, and its restoration has remained faithful to the original design. Household furnishings, glass, and china are still as they were a century ago.

Admission: $3 adults; $2 senior citizens and students; children under 12 free with an adult.

Open: Sun 1–4pm; call to find out about special events. Also open Mon–Fri, by appointment, for groups and for private tours. **Closed:** Aug. **Subway:** 6 to Astor Place. N or R to 8th St.

THEODORE ROOSEVELT BIRTHPLACE, 28 East 20th St. Tel. 260-1616.

Teddy Roosevelt, the 26th president, was born here in 1858 and lived here until he was 15 years old. Five rooms of this reconstructed Victorian brownstone, now a National Historic Site, have been restored to look as they did during Teddy's boyhood. The house also contains a museum of Roosevelt memorabilia.

Admission: $1 adults; children under 17 and seniors free.

Open: Wed–Sun 9am–5pm. **Closed:** Federal holidays. **Subway:** 6 to 23rd St., N or R to Broadway and 23rd St.

VIETNAM VETERANS MEMORIAL, Vietnam Veterans Plaza, next to 55 Water St.

Sixteen feet high and 66 feet long, this new memorial not far from the South Street Seaport contains excerpts from news dispatches, letters, diaries, and personal and public observations on the war.

LIBRARIES

NEW YORK PUBLIC LIBRARY, Fifth Ave. at 42nd St. Tel. 930-0800.

One of the finest examples of beaux arts architecture in the country, the majestic New York Public Library is a true "people's palace." Outside, office workers, shoppers, strollers, and street musicians frequent the broad stone steps presided over by two majestic lions. Inside, you'll find classical grandeur, modern technology, and changing exhibits. Behind the library, newly restored Bryant Park is a great place for sunbathing and people-watching. Restrooms have baby-changing tables.

Tours: Free tours given Tues–Sat 11am and 2pm.
Open: Collections are open at varying hours; phone for details.
Subway: 4, 5, or 6 to 42nd St.

THE NEW YORK PUBLIC LIBRARY FOR THE PERFORMING ARTS, at Lincoln Center, 40 Lincoln Center Plaza, at 65th St. Tel. 870-1600 or 870-1630 for information during open hours.

A branch of the New York Public Library at Lincoln Center, the Library for the Performing Arts is an entry unto itself and one of the liveliest places in town. Everything is dedicated to the performing arts here, and you can do a lot more than just borrow a book. You can sit in a comfortable chair and listen to a recording of an opera or a musical (while studying the score at the same time); see excellent exhibits; catch concerts, plays, and dance performances (more details in Chapter 10); and take the children to free story hours, puppet shows, concerts, dance presentations, and films in the Heckscher Oval.

Admission: Free.
Open: Days and hours vary, call for details. **Subway:** 1 to 66th St.

PIERPONT MORGAN LIBRARY, 29 East 36th St., near Madison Ave. Tel. 685-0610.

An architectural gem, built of perfectly fitted marble by McKim, Mead, and White in 1906, this magnificent palazzo is known not only for its outstanding collections of master drawings, rare books (including the Gutenberg Bible), medieval manuscripts, and historical documents, but also for its medieval and Renaissance artworks and for J. P. Morgan's private library, maintained just as he left it. In 1991 the Library annexed the historic brownstone of J. P. Morgan, Jr., and constructed a glass-enclosed garden court for visitors.

Admission: $5 adults; $3 seniors and students.
Open: Tues–Sat 10:30am–5pm; Sun 1–5pm. **Subway:** 6 to 33rd. St.

MUSEUMS & GALLERIES

DOWNTOWN

THE NEW YORK CITY FIRE MUSEUM, 278 Spring St., between Varick and Hudson Sts. Tel. 691-1303.

This combined collection of the old Fire Department Museum and the Firefighting Museum of The Home Insurance Company makes up one of the most comprehensive assemblages of firefighting memorabilia anywhere, with items dating from 1765 to the present.

Admission: Suggested donation $3 adults; 50¢ children.

Open: Tues–Sat 10am–4pm. **Closed:** Holidays. **Subway:** C, E, 1, 2, or 3 to Houston St.

THE POLICE ACADEMY MUSEUM, 235 East 20th St., between Second and Third Aves. Tel. 477-9753.

You've heard about "New York's Finest"—now see their collection of police memorabilia, one of the largest in the world.

Admission: Free.

Open: Mon–Fri 9am–3pm, but call in advance to make sure they are open on the day you wish to visit. **Subway:** 6 to 23 St., N or R to 14th St.

FORBES MAGAZINE GALLERIES, 62 Fifth Ave., at 12th St. Tel. 206-5548.

Kids will be intrigued by the permanent exhibit of 12,000 toy soldiers, 500 toy boats, and 300 trophies. Adults can admire the Imperial Easter Eggs created by Carl Fabergé, jeweler to the czar, and the rotating exhibits of historical paintings and presidential papers.

Admission: Free.

Open: Tues–Wed and Fri–Sat 10am–4pm. **Closed:** Major hols. **Subway:** 4, 5, 6, or R to Union Square.

MIDTOWN

THE AT&T INFOQUEST CENTER, 550 Madison Ave. at 56th St. Tel. 605-5555.

Meet the hottest robot in town, Gor-don, at this interactive exhibit on communications and technology. You ride the glass elevator up and work your way down InfoQuest's multilevel exhibit of high-tech entertainment. An Access Card, which you personalize on a touch-screen computer, becomes your key to unlocking the mysteries of the Information Age. The center's 40 interactive exhibits are devoted to Photonics, Microelectronics, and Computer Software. All this, plus two robots! There's also a handicapped-accessible gift shop.

Admission: Free.

Open: Tues 10:30am–9pm; Wed–Sun 10am–6pm. Visitors must arrive 30 minutes before closing. **Subway:** E or F to 53rd St., 4, 5, or 6 to 59th St. **Bus:** M1, M2, M3, M4.

INTERNATIONAL CENTER OF PHOTOGRAPHY MID-TOWN, 1133 Ave. of the Americas, at 43rd St. Tel. 768-4680.

Twice the size of its parent gallery, the International Center of Photography Midtown features exhibits, lectures, and a unique photography bookstore.

Admission: $3.50 adults; $2 students and senior citizens.

Open: Tues, 11am–8pm; Wed–Sun 11am–6pm. **Subway:** B, D, F, or Q to 42nd St.

THE *INTREPID* SEA-AIR-SPACE MUSEUM, at Pier 86, Hudson River and the foot of West 46th St. Tel. 245-2533 or 245-0072.

One of New York's most popular attractions, the aircraft carrier *Intrepid,* a salty veteran of World War II and Vietnam, has been converted into a fascinating floating museum of naval history and technology.

Admission: $7 adults; $6 seniors; $4 children 7–12; under 6 free.

Open: Summer: Daily 10am–4pm. Winter: Wed–Sun 10am–5pm, with last admission at 4pm. **Bus:** 42 (42nd St.) or 50 (49th St.) to Twelfth Ave.

JAPAN SOCIETY, 333 East 47th St. Tel. 832-1155.

This stunning example of contemporary Japanese architecture, with its beautiful gallery, extensive library, the Lila Acheson Wallace Auditorium, and outdoor garden, is headquarters of the Japan Society. Contemporary and traditional performing arts, lectures, and special exhibits are held year round. There are regular series of contemporary and classic Japanese films as well. Call for a program schedule.

Admission: $6.50 admission to films; $2.50 suggested donation for gallery.

Open: Tues–Sun 11am–5pm during exhibitions. **Subway:** 6 to 51st St.

MUSEUM OF TELEVISION AND RADIO, 25 West 52nd St. Tel. 621-6800.

Want to catch up on the Ed Sullivan shows of the 1950s or the Jack Benny broadcasts of the 1930s? You can watch Uncle Milty cavort, hear FDR's campaign speeches, and lots more at this enormously popular museum. Its collection includes just about everything that's ever gone out on the airwaves, yours to watch or hear at your own private console. Selected programs are also presented on large exhibit screens.

Admission: Suggested donation $5 adults; $4 students; $3 senior citizens and children under 13.

Open: Tues, Wed, Sat, and Sun noon–6pm; Thurs noon–8pm; Fri noon–9pm (private viewings close at 6pm, screenings at 9pm). **Subway:** B, D, F, or Q to 47–50 Sts.

THE UPPER EAST SIDE

THE ASIA SOCIETY GALLERIES, 725 Park Ave., at 70th St. Tel. 288-6400.

A splendid building houses one of the most well known private collections of Asian art in the world, the Mr. and Mrs. John D. Rockefeller III collections of sculpture, ceramics, and paintings from India, Southeast Asia, China, Korea, and Japan. In addition, changing exhibitions of the greatest art of Asia, both traditional and contemporary, are shown. Outstanding cultural and performing art events are also presented each season.

Admission: $2 adults; $1 seniors and students with ID; children under 12 free.

Open: Tues–Sat 11am–6pm; Fri 6–8pm; Sun noon–5pm. **Subway:** 6 to 68th St.

COOPER-HEWITT, National Museum of Design, Smithsonian Institution, 2 East 91st St., at Fifth Ave. Tel. 860-6868.

The Cooper-Hewitt is an exquisite gem of a museum, housed in the restored Neo-Georgian Andrew Carnegie mansion. Its holdings are acknowledged to have the world's finest collection of design and decorative arts, including everything from porcelain, embroideries, furniture, drawings, and prints, to birdcages, pressed flowers, and Valentines. There are changing exhibitions.

Admission: $3 adults; $1.50 senior citizens and students. Free Tues after 5pm.

Open: Tues 10am–9pm; Wed–Sun 10am–5pm; Sun noon–5pm. **Closed:** Major hols. **Subway:** 4, 5, or 6 to 86th St. **Buses:** Fifth Ave. or Madison Ave. northbound buses.

THE INTERNATIONAL CENTER OF PHOTOGRAPHY, 1130 Fifth Ave. at 94th St. Tel. 860-1777.

Housed in a superb Georgian building, this is the city's only museum devoted to photography, offering a great variety of changing exhibitions, workshops, and educational programs.

Admission: $3.50 adults; $2 students and senior citizens.

Open: Tues noon–8pm; Wed–Fri noon–5pm; Sat–Sun 11am–6pm. **Subway:** 6 to 96th St.

MUSEUM OF THE CITY OF NEW YORK, 1220 Fifth Ave., at 103rd St. Tel. 534-1672.

For a capsule look at New York history, this is the place—especially before beginning your historical tour of downtown Manhattan. Special and permanent exhibits trace the city's history from Native American days to the present, through costumes, photographs, prints, ship models, fire engines, maps, furnishings, theatrical memorabilia, and toys. "The Big Apple," an exciting film exhibition, tells the story of the city from 1624 to today. Programs for both children and adults, including concerts, lectures, and panel discussions, are presented throughout the year; many are free, while others involve a nominal fee.

A special note: The museum has long been known for its outstanding walking tours, which explore various city neighborhoods in depth, focusing on architecture and social history. The cost is $15; call for a free brochure and information.

Admission: Free, but suggested donation $5 adults; $3 children, senior citizens, and students; $8 for families.

Open: Wed–Sat 10am–5pm; Tues 10am–2pm (for preregistered school group tours only); Sun 1–5pm. **Closed:** Mon and all legal hols. **Bus:** Fifth Ave. southbound or Madison Ave. northbound.

UPPER WEST SIDE

THE AMERICAN MUSEUM—HAYDEN PLANETARIUM, 81st St. at Central Park West. Tel. 769-5900 for general information; 769-5920 for Sky Show information; 769-5921 for Laser Show information.

This is one of the most exciting shows in town—for children, for adults, for anyone who ponders the mystery of the stars and of the great drama of outer space. Through the magic of the Zeiss VI star projector and hundreds of special effects, audiences can be shown the wonders of the night sky and be taken to other worlds and even beyond. Show topics range from black holes to the search for life beyond our galaxy. Sky shows, included in the price of admission, are given every day except Thanksgiving and Christmas. Dazzling light shows are performed to popular rock music on Friday and Saturday evenings. On Saturday mornings, there are often special programs for children and preschoolers.

Admission: $5 those 13 and over; $3.75 students and senior citizens with I.D.; $2.50 children. **Laser shows:** $7.

Open: Oct–Sun, Mon–Fri 12:30–4:45pm; Sat 10am–5:45pm; Sun noon–4:45pm; July–Sept Mon–Fri 12:30–4:45pm, Sat–Sun noon–4:45pm. **Subway:** C or B to 81st St., 1 or 9 to 79th St.

THE NEW-YORK HISTORICAL SOCIETY, 170 Central Park West, at 77th St. Tel. 873-3400.

Of special interest at New York's oldest museum is the collection of 19th-century landscapes by artists of the Hudson River School, including Asher B. Durand, Frederic Church, and John Kensett. Genre paintings and 18th- and 19th-century portraiture by such notable artists as Gilbert Stuart, Benjamin West, and Charles Willson Peale are also in the collection. In addition to numerous special exhibitions each year, permanent installations are devoted to the original watercolors of John James Audubon; American silver; and the stained glass lamps of Louis Comfort Tiffany.

Admission: $4.50 adults; $3 seniors and students; $1 children under 12.

Open: Tues, Wed, Fri, and Sun 11am–5pm; Thurs 11am–8pm. **Closed:** National hols. **Subway:** C or B to 81st St., 1 or 9 to 79th St.

THE MUSEUM OF AMERICAN FOLK ART, 2 Lincoln Square at Columbus Ave., between 65th and 66th Sts. Tel. 977-7298.

Until it settles into its permanent home on West 53rd Street late in 1995, the Museum of American Folk Art is temporarily ensconced in handsome galleries across the street from Lincoln Center. On display are some of the outstanding pieces from its permanent collection of some 3,000 objects—quilts, toys, furniture, pottery, paintings, sculpture, decorative ornaments, and a giant Indian chief weathervane at its central point. Next door is an engaging shop with many handmade objects in the folk tradition.

Admission: Free.

Open: Tues–Sun 11:30am–7:30pm. **Closed:** Mon and legal hols. **Subway:** 1 or 9 to 66th St. **Bus:** M104, M7.

WASHINGTON HEIGHTS

THE CLOISTERS, in Fort Tryon Park. Tel. 923-3700.

This is one of the high points of New York, artistically and geographically. The Cloisters is a bit of medieval Europe transplanted to a cliff overlooking the Hudson. The Metropolitan Museum of Art, of which this is the medieval branch, brought intact from Europe a 12th-century chapter house, parts of five cloisters from medieval monasteries, a Romanesque chapel, and a 12th-century Spanish apse. Smaller treasures include rare tapestries like the 15th-century *Hunt of the Unicorn,* paintings, frescoes, stained glass, precious metalwork. All this is set in tranquil gardens overlooking the Hudson; note the herb garden in the Bonnefont Cloister and the garden in the Trie Cloister, planted with flora depicted in the Unicorn tapestries. Recorded concerts of medieval music are played over speakers at 12:45 and 3:15pm every day. Since this extraordinary collection is one of the most popular in the city, especially in fine weather, try to schedule your visit during the week, rather than on a crowded Saturday or Sunday afternoon.

Admission (including same-day admission to Metropolitan Museum of Art): Suggested admission $6 adults; $3 students and seniors.

Open: March–Oct, Tues–Sun 9:30am–5:15pm. Nov–Feb, Tues–Sun 9:30am–4:45pm. **Closed:** Monday, Thanksgiving, Christmas Day, and New Year's Day. **Bus:** No. 4 bus up Madison Ave., marked "Fort Tryon Park—The Cloisters" takes about an hour and a half from midtown. **Subway:** A to 190th St. (Overlook Terrace), then about a five-minute walk.

NEIGHBORHOODS

CHINATOWN & LITTLE ITALY.

Chinatown and Little Italy are all about street life, sometimes strident and overwhelming but always vibrating with an energy unmistakably their own. Although there are few architectural landmarks and most housing is tenement style, these tiny neighborhoods offer a real glimpse of New York's cultural diversity at its lively best. Little Italy bustles with animated cafés and restaurants, and every August it is transformed into a carnival-like atmosphere with lights and banners for the festival of San Gennero. In Chinatown, shopkeepers hawk their produce from open-fronted stores along Canal Street each day, while behind them lies a warren of streets and alleyways filled with restaurants and shops.

Located south of Canal Street, Chinatown centers on Mott and Pell streets. On the north side of Canal Street is Little Italy, just east of Broadway; the heart of this enclave is Mulberry Street.

SOHO.

Until the late 1840s what we now call SoHo (a fractured acronym for *So*uth of *Ho*uston Street) was a quiet residential quarter of the northern edge of town. Around 1850, a commercial building boom (petering out finally in the 1990s) totally transformed the place into a neighborhood of swank retail stores and loft buildings for light manufacturing. All this activity coincided with the development of cast iron as a building material. Columns, arches, pediments, brackets, keystones, and everything else that once had to be carved in stone could now be mass-produced at lower cost in iron. The result was a commercial building spree that gave free rein to the opulent architectural styles of the day.

After the spree came long generations of neglect. But by the late 1960s the area began attracting impoverished artists. By the early 1970s the real estate boom was on. Today the area is literally lined with rarified boutiques, avant-garde galleries, and trendy restaurants. SoHo lofts now appear in the pages of *Architectural Digest*.

Centered around West Broadway and Spring and Greene streets between Houston and Canal streets (just west of Little Italy), SoHo is home to the world's largest collection of cast-iron commercial architecture and is one of New York's most vital artists' colonies.

OUTDOOR ART & PLAZAS

Not all the green space in New York is found in the city's parks. A new trend in the past few years has been for builders to include atriums and courtyards on the ground floors of new buildings, many of them rich with flowers, plantings, trees, waterfalls, art galleries, and exhibits. They're all free and all fine places for sightseers, shoppers, and local office workers to have a rest, have a bite, and watch the passing parade. Here are some to look for as you wend your way around town. **The Market at Citicorp,** 53rd and 54th Sts., between Third and Lexington Aves.: Three levels of entertaining shops and restaurants surround a graceful central café area, the scene of numerous free entertainments and concerts; adjoining it is St. Peter's Church, with its Louise Nevelson sculptures. . . . **Chem-Court,** 277 Park Ave., at 47th St.: A handsome greenhouse in the center of town, featuring flowers, trees, pools, and sculpture . . . **IBM Garden Plaza,** 56th St. at Madison Ave.: Visit the New York Botanical Garden shop and the IBM Gallery of Science and Art, then relax at tables and chairs amid the tall bamboo trees. Free concerts are held on Wednesday at 12:30pm . . . **Trump Tower,** 56th St. and Fifth Ave.: An indoor street paved with pink marble and bronze leads to five stories of pricey shops and restaurants. Crowned by a transparent skylight in a bronze frame, the atrium is graced by terraced walkways, hanging gardens, and a spectacular 80-foot waterfall that cascades into a series of pools on the garden level. . . . **Crystal Pavilion,** 50th St. at Third Ave., one of New York's most glamorous arcades: Neon flashing lights and disco music set the tone for this ultramodern space. . . . **Olympic Towers Arcade,** 51st St. and Fifth Ave.: A more tranquil oasis, with a reflecting waterfall, 291 street benches and chairs, and a Japanese restaurant. . . . **The Center of Fifth,** at Fifth Ave. and 47th St., has a nice little courtyard on its lower level, with a marble floor, greenery, fountains, benches, and small tables—perfect for resting your feet during a busy day. . . . **AT&T,** Madison Ave. between 55th and 56th Sts.: Philip Johnson's handsome public arcade recalls the grand spaces of ancient Rome. Included are art, sculpture, shops, cafés, and the InfoQuest Center, an interactive technology information center. . . . **Whitney Museum** at Phillip Morris, Park Ave. at 42nd St.: The museum features an indoor garden with ficus trees and flowers, a gallery and sculpture court, and free tours and entertainment.

PARKS & GARDENS

BROOKLYN BOTANIC GARDEN, 1000 Washington Ave., at Eastern Pkwy. Tel. 718/622-4433.

Next door to the Brooklyn Museum and a major destination in its own right, the Brooklyn Botanic Garden is a glorious 52 acres worth of flowers, trees, and exotic plants. If you are in town in May, make a pilgrimage here to see the flowering of the cherry trees; they are even more beautiful than the ones in Washington, D.C. (Phone the garden to check on blossoming time.) The Japanese mood also prevails in the traditional Japanese Garden, considered one of the finest outside of Japan. Other special treats include the Cranford Rose Garden, the Fragrance Garden for the Blind, and the Shakespeare Garden. You can browse through the greenhouses with their exotic tropical, desert, and temperate plants and be convinced that you are light-years away from Brooklyn. The Bonsai Museum houses the most outstanding collection in the western world, and the Trail of Evolution offers a unique look at 3½ billion years of plant life.

Admission: General admission free, but on Sat–Sun and holidays 25¢ admission to the Japanese Hill-and-Pond Garden; admission to the splendid Conservatory is $2.

Open: Hours change with seasons, so call for exact times. Summer, Tues–Fri 8am–6pm; Sat–Sun 10am–6pm. **Subway:** 2 or 3 to Eastern Pkwy.

NEW YORK BOTANICAL GARDEN, Bronx Park. Tel. 220-8700.

Greenhouses, gardens, seasonal plantings, and an air of peace and quiet make this the place for a lovely respite from city tensions. See the NYBG Forest, largely unchanged since the days of the Native Americans in Manhattan, and the magnificent collections of rhododendron, daffodils, azaleas, and chrysanthemums. Restored to its turn-of-the-century elegance is the 90-foot doomed landmark Enid A. Haupt Conservatory (covering an acre of plants under glass and similar to London's Royal Botanic Gardens at Kew), with its palms, tropical rain-forest plantings, waterfall, desert areas, and seasonal floral displays—all in eleven distinct environments.

Stop in at the gift shop for unusual objets d'art and plants, then have lunch at the Tulip Tree Café on Museum Mall or romantic Snuff Mill Café, on a terrace overlooking the Bronx River, which looks positively rural at this point.

Admission: Grounds; contribution required. Conservatory, $3 adults; $2 senior citizens, children, and students; free Sat 10am-noon.

Open: Apr–Oct, Tues–Sun 10am–6pm. Nov–Mar, 10am–4pm. Conservatory 10am–4pm, with last admission at 3pm. Visitors can reserve a seat on the Garden Shuttle minibus from Manhattan; for schedules and reservations, call 220-8700. **Train:** Metro North's Harlem line (20 minutes from Grand Central) to Botanical Garden Station. **Subway:** D, C, or 4 to Bedford Park Station; then walk eight blocks east. **Directions:** The garden is on Southern Blvd., south of Mosholu Pkwy. and half a mile north of Fordham Rd. and the Bronx Zoo. Parking is $4.

ZOOS

BRONX ZOO, Bronx River Pkwy. and Fordham Rd. Tel. 367-1010.

For many years, the Bronx Zoo, one of the biggest (265 acres with 3,600 animals) and the best zoos in the world, has been a prime visitor's magnet, and now it's better than ever. Traditional zoo cages have been replaced with naturalistic habitats. African Market, a plaza area, links **Baboon Reserve,** featuring gelada baboons and ibex, with the **African Plains,** where lions, gazelles, giraffes, and zebras can be seen. **Wild Asia** offers a guided 20-minute safari via monorail (the Bengali Express) through 38 densely forested acres where elephants, tigers, and other animals roam free ($1.50). **Jungleworld,** another segment of Wild Asia, recreates a Southeast Asian rain forest, mangrove swamp, and scrub forest (50¢ admission Wed; free other days). **Himalayan Highlands Habitat** features snow leopards, the world's most beautiful and elusive cats, along with cunning red pandas, white-naped cranes, and tragopans. Don't miss the architecturally exciting exhibits in the **World of Birds,** complete with waterfalls and thunderstorms, in which visitors walk through a rain forest and into jungles while birds swoop around their heads.

A big one for kids! Take the moppets to the world-famous **Children's Zoo** (open Apr–Oct), where they can climb on a spider's web, try on a turtle's shell, and crawl through a prairie dog tunnel ($1.50). They'll also love a ride in **Skyfari,** a four-seater cable car ($1.50).

Admission: $5.75 adults; $2 children and seniors; children under 2 free. Wed, by donation.

Open: Mon–Fri 10am–4:30 or 5pm, depending on time of year. Sat–Sun 10am–4:30 or 5:30pm. **Bus** (most convenient): Liberty Line Express Bus service from midtown Manhattan. Phone 652-8400 weekdays 9am–5pm for schedules and timetable; fare is $3.50.
Train: From midtown Manhattan via Metro North; phone 532-4900. **Subway:** 2 to Pelham Pkwy., walk west to Bronxdale entrance. **Car:** Take Exit 6 off Bronx River Pkwy. Parking is $5.

THE CENTRAL PARK ZOO, near the park entrance at Fifth Ave. and East 64th St. Tel. 861-6030.

After a $35-million renovation, the Central Park Zoo emerged as one of the most endearing small zoos anywhere. The joyful 5½-acre "animal garden" is state of the art, designed to make both its inhabitants and its visitors very happy. A beautifully landscaped Central Garden and **Sea Lion Pool** is flanked on three sides by a glass-roofed colonnade (no need to stay away if it rains), which leads to three polar ecological areas. Inside the skylighted octagonal building called the **Tropic Zone** is a misty rain forest inhabited by the likes of red-bellied piranhas, caiman, and a python or two here and there. The **Temperate Territory** is open to the skies and provides realistic outdoor habitats for, among others, Asian red pandas and North American river otters. Most fun of all is the **Polar Circle,** an indoor-outdoor environment, glass walls of which provide views of frolicking penguins and polar bears both above and below water. The cafeteria and gift shop are both great fun.

Admission: $2.50 adults; $1.25 seniors; 50¢ children 3–12; toddlers free.

Open: Mon–Fri 10am–4:30pm winter, 5pm summer; Sun 10:30am–5:30pm.

IN BROOKLYN & QUEENS

THE BROOKLYN MUSEUM, 200 Eastern Pkwy. Tel. 718/638-5000.

One of the best reasons for leaving Manhattan is to see the Brooklyn Museum, among the best museums in the country. It has superb collections of Egyptian, Asian, American, and European art, as well as a fine primitive collection, 28 period rooms, and Japanese and Korean galleries. The Frieda Schiff Warburg Sculpture Garden is a repository for some of the architectural relics of the city (bits and pieces of the old Steeplechase Amusement Park in Coney Island and the Pennsylvania Station that was torn down to make way for the new Madison Square Garden), as well as the scene of changing exhibits.

Don't miss a visit to the museum shop, with its wonderful handcrafts from Mexico, Japan, South America, and Scandinavia—all of it authentic, beautifully made, and well priced. The kids can stock up here on slews of inexpensive presents to bring their friends back home. Brunch and lunch are available at reasonable prices at the Museum Café.

Admission: Suggested contribution $4 adults; $2 students with valid ID; $1.50 seniors; free for children under 12 accompanied by an adult.

Open: Wed–Sun 10am–5pm. **Closed:** Thanksgiving, Christmas Day, and New Year's Day. **Subway:** 2 or 3 to Eastern Pkwy.

QUEENS

AMERICAN MUSEUM OF THE MOVING IMAGE, 35th Ave. at 36th St., Astoria. Tel. 718/784-0077.

Opened in the fall of 1988 on the site of the East Coast facility of Paramount Pictures in the 1920s, this is the first museum in the United States dedicated exclusively to film, television, and video. Through exhibitions, screenings, and collections, visitors explore the art, history, technique, and technology of the moving image media and their influence on 20th-century American life.

Admission: $5 adults; $4 senior citizens; $2.50 children and students with valid ID.

Open: Tues–Fri noon–4pm; Sat–Sun noon–6pm. **Subway:** R or G to Steinway St., Astoria.

3. COOL FOR KIDS

For kids worn out by too much sightseeing, an hour or so in **Central Park** is the perfect antidote. There's so much for them to do here, however, that you may want to schedule it for an entire morning or afternoon. First, everybody must see the wonderfully renovated **Central Park Zoo;** really small children will also enjoy the Central Park **Children's Zoo.** Then take them for a ride on the **Carousel,** opposite 75th Street in the center of the park. The whole family will enjoy rowboating on the picturesque lake: Boats can be rented at Loeb Boathouse (near the 72nd Street and Fifth Avenue entrance), cost $7 for a minimum of one hour, and require a $20 deposit. Or let the kids sail their model boats at **Conservatory Water** near 72nd Street and Fifth, join the local youngsters flying kites, or work off some excess energy at any of the inspired **Adventure Playgrounds** (there are at least nine of them in the park; two locations are at 86th Street and Central Park West and 67th Street and Fifth Avenue). Summer Saturdays between 11am and noon, they can listen to stories at the charming **Hans Christian Andersen statue,** near the model boathouse. Check in, too, at **The Belvedere,** a castle at 79th Street, south of the Great Lawn, which has frequent exhibits and special programs for parents and children (tel. 772-0210).

BROOKLYN CHILDREN'S MUSEUM, 145 Brooklyn Ave., at St. Mark's Ave. Tel. 718/735-4400.

This is one museum that children will want to visit again and again; here they can touch and play with the exhibits. BCM has focused on "interactive play or learning" since its opening in 1899 as the world's first children's museum. The semiunderground structure is a high-tech, learning/looking/growing environment, with its own greenhouse, running-water stream, boneyard, workshops, and library.

Admission: Suggested contribution $3 adults; $1 children.

Open: Wed–Fri 2–5pm; Sat–Sun and school holidays noon–5pm. **Closed:** Mon–Tues. **Subway:** 3 to Kingston Ave.

THE CHILDREN'S MUSEUM OF MANHATTAN, in the Tisch Building, 212 West 83rd St., between Broadway and Amsterdam Ave. Tel. 721-1234.

The $6.4-million Children's Museum of Manhattan is such a magical, mind-boggling place for kids ages 2 to 12 that there is only one problem about bringing them here: They may not want to leave and see the rest of New York! One of the most technologically and conceptually sophisticated children's museums in the world, the museum's theme is self-discovery, which it fosters through a series of brilliant interactive exhibits and activity centers. At the Time-Warner Center for Media, the Performing Arts, and Early Childhood Education, children can learn animation techniques and produce their own videotapes; they can also work as engineers, writers, newscasters, and camera operators in a full-size television studio and control room. Performances by children's theater groups, dancers, musicians, puppeteers, and storytellers are held every weekend. Participatory creative arts workshops are offered throughout the year.

Admission: $4.

Open: Wed–Mon 1–5pm; Sat–Sun 10am–5pm. **Closed:** Tues, Thanksgiving, Christmas Day, and New Year's Day. **Subway:** 1 or 9 to 86th St.

OTHER ATTRACTIONS FOR KIDS

The following attractions of special interest to children have already been described in this chapter.

American Museum—Hayden Planetarium (see p. 206). Kids love the sky and laser shows.

American Museum of Natural History (see p. 192). There are hours of absorbing interest here for the kids. Those over 5 will enjoy the learning games in the Discovery Room.

AT&T Infoquest Center (see p. 204). An 8-foot-tall robotic host welcomes kids to a fascinating display of interactive scientific exhibits. The center is open daily; call 605-5555 for information.

The Bronx Zoo (see p. 210). Simply the best. Really small children will adore the Children's Zoo (open April through October), which allows them to experience what it feels like to be a particular animal. They can even ride a real camel.

Central Park Zoo (see p. 211). Another must. Small, beautiful, and enchanting, it's for kids of all ages.

Ellis Island (see p. 187). A marvelous history lesson for older children.

Empire State Building (see p. 189). Youngsters love the view from the top.

Forbes Magazine Galleries (see p. 204). Youngsters will admire the display of 12,000 toy soldiers, 500 toy boats, and 300 trophies.

Intrepid Sea-Air-Space Museum (see p. 204). Kids of all ages find this one exciting.

Lincoln Center (see p. 192). Older children will enjoy the backstage tours.

Metropolitan Museum of Art (see p. 194). The mummies in the Egyptian galleries and the "Arms and Armor" exhibit are all-time kid-pleasers.

Museum of the City of New York (see p. 206). New York history comes to life here. There are many special shows for children, including puppet shows.

Museum of Television and Radio (see p. 205). Here's a chance to catch the old shows.

The **New York City Fire Museum** (see p. 203). Guaranteed to fascinate anyone who dreams of growing up to be a firefighter.

The **New York Public Library for the Performing Arts** (see p. 203). Free story hours, puppet shows, concerts, dance presentations, films, and more are presented in the Hecksher Oval.

The **Statue of Liberty** (see p. 184). A must. Kids are enthralled by the whole experience, from the ferryboat ride and the first sight of the Lady, up to the 12-story climb to the viewing platform in the crown (parents, be warned).

---

4. SPECIAL-INTEREST SIGHTSEEING

FOR LITERARY BUFFS   New York City is full of hallowed spots for literary buffs. There's the **Chelsea Hotel** (222 W. 23rd St.), for example, where Thomas Wolfe wrote *You Can't Go Home Again,* Arthur Miller penned *After the Fall,* and William Burroughs worked on *Naked Lunch.* Dylan Thomas and Brendan Behan are among the many who found solace and inspiration here. Thomas's favorite drinking spot, by the way, was the **White Horse Tavern** in Greenwich Village (corner of Hudson and 11th Sts.), where such American literary lights as Norman Mailer, Louis Auchincloss, and Calder Willingham were once regulars.

The Village, of course, has long been home to scores of writers and other assorted Bohemians. In the 1920s and 1930s, **137 Bleecker Street** was the site of the old Liberal Club, a hotbed for anarchists and free-thinkers of all stripes. Among these were John Reed, who wrote *Ten Days That Shook the World,* and whose story was told in the film *Reds.* Next door, in what is still the **Provincetown Playhouse,** George Cram Cook and his wife, Susan Glaspell, founded the Provincetown Players; in tow they had a promising young playwright named Eugene O'Neill and a young actress from Maine named Edna St. Vincent Millay. On Commerce Street in the Village is the still active **Cherry Lane Theater,** which Edna St. Vincent Millay founded. "Vincent," one of the most authentic of the Village Bohemians, made her home at **75½ Bedford Street,** still known as the "narrowest house in the Village."

In another part of the Village, at Fifth Avenue and Waverly Place, is Washington Square. Project yourself back into the world of the 19th-century New York aristocracy as you study the elegant Greek Revival houses of **Washington Square North.** Henry James's novel *Washington Square* took place here, and James, Edith Wharton, William Dean Howells, John Dos Passos, and painter Edward Hopper have all lived on this block at one time or another. Poet e. e. cummings lived on Patchin Place.

In Midtown, the **Algonquin Hotel** (49 W. 44th St.) is something of a literary shrine, for it was here that the celebrated wits of the Round Table—Robert Benchley, James Thurber, H. L. Mencken, and Dorothy Parker—traded their *bon mots*. Of course, the Algonquin is not far from the offices of ***The New Yorker*** (25 W. 43rd St.), where many of their pieces were published over the years.

Uptown on the East Side, the **Poetry Center of the YM-YMHA,** (part of the Tisch Center for the Arts) 92nd St. and Lexington Ave., is the place where Dylan Thomas, W. H. Auden, and T. S. Eliot enthralled admiring crowds.

5. ORGANIZED TOURS

MANHATTAN NEIGHBORHOOD TROLLEY There's a new, easy way to get around lower Manhattan these days—take the trolley! Actually a 30-seat, comfortably air-conditioned bus painted to look like a red-and-green trolley, the kind that plied New York's streets in the early 1900s, it makes a narrated 1-hour sightseeing tour of lower Manhattan weekends from 1 to 6pm every hour on the hour. Passengers can get off at any of the eight stops—South Street Seaport, the Battery, the World Trade Center, the World Financial Center, City Hall, Chinatown, Little Italy, and the Lower East Side—and reboard at any time, at no extra charge. It's a great way to work in a variety of attractions in one day; you could break up your sightseeing with an hour or two of shopping for bargains on the Lower East Side's Orchard Street, or have lunch at a trattoria in Little Italy, to suggest just a few possibilities. Fare is $5 for adults, $4 for seniors and those under 12. Tours begin at the South Street Seaport, on South Street on the corner of Fulton in front of Sloppy Louie's restaurant. For details, call 677-7268.

SINGER'S BROOKLYN According to the U.S. Census Bureau, one out of seven families in the United States has roots in Brooklyn. Perhaps this is what makes Lou Singer's tours so popular. Singer, a self-taught historian who must know more about Brooklyn than anybody, conducts absorbing tours focusing on Revolutionary, Dutch, ethnic, and architectural Brooklyn, via bus or private car. You'll see the private parlors of restored Victorian brownstones, the masterful last landscape by Louis Comfort Tiffany, Stanford White's *Prison Ship Martyrs' Monument,* and much more. Unusual lunch stops are arranged. Singer, who has taught at Brooklyn College, will arrange special trips to ethnic neighborhoods and elsewhere for special interests. (Often entire families, spanning several generations, come to the city just to take such a trip in search of their roots.) Evening tours, which always start with a sunset view of the city from the Promenade in Brooklyn Heights, usually wind up with dinner and dancing at one of the lively Russian nightclubs in Brighton Beach. The "Hollywood in Brooklyn" tour visits film locales (for *Prizzi's Honor, Moonstruck, Brighton Beach Memoirs,* and more); the home of Mary Pickford; and the original site of the Vitagraph studios, where the film industry was born.

Singer offers some 16 different adventures; all are eminently worthwhile and enjoyable excursions. For individuals, costs should run about $25 per person, plus food (group rates are also available). Phone **Lou Singer** at 718/875-9084 after 7pm.

A WHOLESALE SHOPPING TOUR So you'd like to shop the

wholesale houses of New York's Garment District but don't know how to go about it? Sara Gardner of **Fashion Update** (tel. 718/377-8873) will take you by the hand and arrange a highly personalized tour to designers' showrooms, where you can save from 50% to 90% off retail prices, on men's, women's, and children's clothing; bridal attire; furs; leather; cosmetics; shoes; and accessories. Cost of the tour is $50. Group rates are available also.

WALKING TOURS A number of individuals and organizations offer exemplary walking tours around the streets of New York. Contact any of the following when you're in town to check schedules and make reservations. For news of specific tours being held each week, consult the "Other Events" listing section of *New York* magazine.

Adventure on a Shoestring (tel. 265-2663) offers members of this 30-year-old organization a variety of unusual excursions—perhaps a visit to a Broadway rehearsal or a Japanese Tea Ceremony. If you're in the city for an extended stay, it's worthwhile to pay the $40 membership fee and join. However, even if you're not a member, you can still participate in their walking tours held year round, rain or shine, for a fee of just $5. Excursions have taken visitors to historic Gramercy Park; to Coney Island; and to the Ironbound section of Newark, N.J., to visit a lively Portuguese community. Tours are usually accompanied by ethnic eating adventures. Phone or write Howard Goldberg, Shoestring, 300 W. 53rd St., New York, NY 10019.

City Walks (tel. 989-2456) are offered three weekends a month by John Wilson, a 36-year-resident of New York and a former lecturer for the Municipal Art Society, who leads small groups on informal, "homey," tours of Greenwich Village, Midtown, downtown, the Lower East Side, sometimes to Harlem. Two-hour tours cost $12.

Lower East Side Tenement Museum Tours (tel. 431-0233) covers the Lower East Side, the place the immigrants most often went *after* they left Ellis Island. In honor of these "urban pioneers," a dedicated group is preserving an 1863 tenement and offering an exciting program of walking tours, dramas, "urban explorations," children's programs, and exhibitions from their storefront galleries. Two or three tours are held every Sunday afternoon at noon. These include "Peddlar's Pack," the Jewish heritage tour, traces the life of a real immigrant family with a costumed actor as the guide; stops are made at the *Daily Forward* Building, the Educational Alliance, and a yeshiva. "The Streets Where We Lived," led by a Columbia University professor, is a multiethnic tour examining past and present on the Lower East Side, Chinatown, and Little Italy. An "African-American Heritage Tour" provides a fascinating look at the vibrant free African-American community of 19th-century New York, including stops at the Cooper Union, St. Mark's Church, and the home of abolitionist Isaac Hooper. All tours begin at the museum headquarters at 97 Orchard St.; last 90 minutes to two hours; and cost $12 for adults, $10 for seniors, and $6 for students.

The 92nd Street Y (tel. 996-1100), one of the city's leading cultural institutions, offers a series of Sunday walking tours that are a bit different. "Tour and Tea at the Waldorf," for example, is a behind-the-scenes exploration of the Waldorf-Astoria Hotel, followed by an authentic English afternoon tea. Other topics include

"Jewish Williamsburg," "Edith Wharton's New York," "The Chelsea Hotel," "Manhattan's New Mosque," and even a "Moonlit Walk in Central Park," a stroll at dusk with a naturalist. Tours vary from about $15 to $25 and should be reserved in advance by calling the number above; call them also for a brochure, or write to the 92nd Street Y, 1395 Lexington Ave., New York, NY 10128.

Sidewalks of New York (tel. 517-0201) offers a large number of unusual walking tours every weekend. Favorite topics include "All in the Family," a Mafia walking tour of Little Italy; "A Writer's Walk Through Greenwich Village"; "The Lively and Mysterious East" (the East Village); and "Beverly Hills East," past the homes of famous movie stars who live near the Waldorf-Astoria. Most tours cost $10. For a calendar, write to P.O. Box 1660, Cathedral Station, New York, NY 10025.

Urban Explorations (tel. 718/721-5254), the creation of Patricia Olmstead, has a roster of engaging tours in which Ms. Olmstead combines her extensive knowledge of architecture, history, and landscaping, revealing the city as a "museum" in itself, full of such treasures as landmark architecture and multiethnic neighborhoods. Favorite tours include "Chinatown" (focusing on history and architecture), the food of Chinatown (followed by a dim sum luncheon), Islamic architecture and the 96th Street Mosque, and a visit to the New York flower market. Tours, which run 2½ to 3 hours, are intimate since groups are limited to 10 to 15 people; the cost is $15.

Wild Food Tours (tel. 718/291-6825) has some of the most unusual and enjoyable walking tours, taking place not on the city streets but in its parks, with "Wildman" Steven Brill, a naturalist-ecologist-author-artist who is a self-made authority on the wild edible fruits, vegetables, roots, nuts, seeds, and mushrooms that grow in New York City's parks, backyards, and vacant lots. Although it's illegal (and dangerous) to forage on your own, it's absolutely legal and safe when you do so on one of Wildman's tours, because he supervises very carefully. Brill's commentaries are highly informative and enjoyable, interspersed with cooking information, folklore, and "plenty of bad jokes." Four-hour fieldwalks are held in parks throughout the New York Metropolitan area every Saturday and Sunday from March through December. Central Park is the locale about once every three weeks. Reservations must be made in advance by phoning the number above; or write to **"Wildman" Steve Brill,** 143-25 84 Drive, Apt. 6-C, Jamaica, NY 11435 for a free yearly schedule of field walks, his Forager's Field Botany Course, and "Wildman's mushroom course." The tour is $10, or whatever you can afford. No smoking on walks.

6. SPORTS & RECREATION

SPORTS

BASEBALL   New York baseball fans are incurable fanatics who root for either the **New York Mets** or the **New York Yankees.** The Mets play at Shea Stadium in Queens from April through October. For ticket information, phone 718/507-8449. The New York Yankees, a.k.a. the Bronx Bombers, play at Yankee Stadium; call 293-6000.

BASKETBALL The local basketball season runs from November through April. Madison Square Garden is the home of the **New York Knickerbockers (the Knicks)** (tel. 563-3800). Just a short bus trip from Manhattan is the Brendan Byrne Arena at the Meadowlands Sports Complex in East Rutherford, N.J., home of the **New Jersey Nets** (tel. 201/935-8888).

FOOTBALL Both New York teams now play in New Jersey! The **New York Jets** and the **New York Giants** play from September through December at Giants Stadium in the Meadowlands Sports Complex (tel. 201/935-8222). The best way to get to see a game is to know someone who's holding a season ticket; almost all the seats are sold out.

HORSE RACING New Yorkers love the races. They bet on them constantly at numbers of Off Track Betting parlors (OTBs) throughout the city. But, of course, it's much more enjoyable to get out to the track. Consider these: **Aqueduct Racetrack** in Jamaica, Queens (tel. 718/641-4700), which presents thoroughbred racing from mid-October through May; **Belmont Park** in Elmont, on the Queens/Nassau County border (tel. 718/641-4700), where thoroughbred racing goes on from May through July and September through October. Then there's **Meadowland Racetrack** in East Rutherford, N.J. (tel. 201/935-8500), which offers thoroughbred racing September through mid-December and trotters late December through August. There's trotters racing all year long at **Yonkers Raceway in Yonkers,** N.Y. (tel. 914/698-5200).

The tracks are easily reachable by buses from the Port Authority Bus Terminal; the A train goes to Aqueduct.

ICE HOCKEY The **Rangers** and the **Islanders** are the two home teams making all the ruckus. Home base for the Rangers is Madison Square Garden (tel. 563-8136); the Islanders are at the Nassau Coliseum, Hempstead Turnpike, Uniondale, N.Y. (tel. 516/587-9222), not difficult to get to by the Long Island Rail Road.

RECREATION

In addition to **Central Park** (see Section 1 of this chapter), New Yorkers also have **Riverside Park,** a lovely stretch on the Upper West Side, which contains the 79th Street Boat Basin and the Soldiers and Sailors Monument at 89th Street and Riverside Drive. **Carl Schurz Park,** which lies between the East River and East End Avenue in the upper 80s is another popular spot; at its northern end is Gracie Mansion, the residence of the mayor of New York. (Schurz, incidentally, was a German revolutionary who became a close friend and advisor of Abraham Lincoln.)

BICYCLING The best place in the city to bike is Central Park. Bikes can be rented at the **Loeb Boathouse,** Park Drive North at 72nd St. (tel. 861-4137) and at **West Side Bicycle Store,** 231 W. 96th St. (tel. 663-7531), just a few blocks from the entrance to the park on the West Side. **Metro Bicycles,** 1311 Lexington Ave, at the corner of 88th St. (tel. 427-4450), is convenient to the park on the East Side; and **Midtown Bicycles,** 360 W. 47th St., at the corner of Ninth Ave., caters to the Midtown hotel crowd.

HORSEBACK RIDING Claremont Riding Academy, 175 W. 89th St. (tel. 724-5100), will rent you a horse for about $30 an hour; you must be experienced in English riding, walk, trot, and canter. If not, take a lesson; they have expert instructors.

RUNNING   All of the parks are popular places to run. Several of the luxury hotels now provide personal trainers who will run with you if you feel uneasy venturing out into the streets and parks on your own. The **New York Road Runners Club,** 6 E. 89th St. (tel. 860-4455), is the place to contact concerning group runs and races. They are the sponsors of the annual New York City Marathon, held each November.

SWIMMING   Several city hotels now have pools (see Chapter 5). In summer, join the crowds at New York's best public beach, **Jones Beach,** out on Long Island. Excursion trains of the Long Island Rail Road will take you there and back for around $10.

TENNIS   Central Park's tennis courts at 93rd Street welcome visitors; you can purchase tickets for single play, good any hour, for $4. For information, phone the **Permit Office** at 360-8133.

CHAPTER 8

STROLLING AROUND NEW YORK CITY

1. DOWNTOWN & THE FINANCIAL DISTRICT

2. GREENWICH VILLAGE

3. UPPER WEST SIDE

To me, one of the most fascinating free activities in New York is a simple walk through several of Manhattan's fabled neighborhoods, soaking up the architecture, learning a bit about the history, absorbing the sights and sounds.

The financial district with its winding, narrow streets is New York's oldest area. Greenwich Village offers picturesque variety. And don't neglect the Upper East Side with its elegant ambiance, or the lively, trendy Upper West Side.

Put on a pair of comfortable shoes and take off.

WALKING TOUR 1 — Downtown & the Financial District

Start: Broadway and Wall Street.
Finish: South Street Seaport.
Time: About 2 hours.
Best Time: Weekdays, when the New York Stock Exchange is open.

If you are interested in history—or money or architecture or the sea—you will have to visit downtown Manhattan. Haunted with ghosts of the city's past, booming with the construction and commerce of the present, an area rich in classic architecture and sleek, new futuristic office buildings, ringed by the sea that made its wealth possible, this oldest area of the city is so richly textured that you could spend days here.

More than anything else, New York is a marketplace, today the greatest on earth. It has always been a marketplace. It was settled, back in 1626, not as a haven for political or religious freedom but as a fur-trading post. Peter Minuit technically "bought" the island from Native Americans for $24 worth of baubles. The fledgling revolutionary government of the United States of America established its capital and inaugurated its first president here. And through the years its ideal deep-water harbor attracted the commerce of many nations. The temples of finance and commerce grew up along the water's edge, and this is where they still are. A modest stock exchange had already been set up—under a buttonwood tree in 1792—but it was not until the New York financiers had been able to underwrite the

Civil War that Wall Street took its place as the financial power of the nation—and, indirectly, of much of the world. Residential New York grew up and moved north, but the citadel of money and power remains. And this is where you begin your downtown tour.

Take subway line 4, 5, or 6 to the Wall Street station at Broadway and Wall Street. Upon emerging from the station, you'll spot:

1. Trinity Church, a graceful English Gothic beauty that was built by Richard Upjohn and completed in 1846. This designated National Landmark was once the tallest building in Lower Manhattan. In its tranquil churchyard lie buried a few parishioners who once lived in this area: Robert Fulton, Alexander Hamilton, and other early leading Americans. You can visit both church and churchyard weekdays from 7am to 6pm, weekends to 4pm. Guided tours are given daily at 2pm. The Trinity Museum is open daily.

After paying your respects to these early New Yorkers, proceed down Wall Street (there really was once a wall here made of tree trunks by the Dutch settlers to protect their city from the wilderness) and stop at the corner of Wall and Nassau streets, at the:

2. Federal Hall National Memorial. This place is full of ghosts: It was on this site that John Peter Zenger won the case that established the right of freedom of the press, and it was here that General Washington took the oath of office as the first president, in 1789. A statue of Washington commemorates the event. The first American Congress met here and adopted the Bill of Rights. First a Customs House, later a Sub-Treasury, now a museum of the Colonial and Early Federal periods, it is considered perhaps the finest example of Greek Revival architecture in the city. It is open Monday to Friday from 9am to 5pm.

Double back along Wall Street and on the other side at the corner of Broad you'll see the:

3. New York Stock Exchange. If Federal Hall is the shrine to history on Wall Street, the New York Stock Exchange, corner of Wall and Broad streets, is the temple to the gods of money. Appropriately, the building is done in "Renaissance-temple" architecture. Inside, in the Great Hall of the Exchange, the member brokers, acting for clients all over the world, buy and sell millions of dollars' worth of securities in an atmosphere that, to the uninitiated, looks like pandemonium. To understand the subtle inner workings of the whole scheme, go to the two-tiered Visitors' Gallery, entrance at 20 Broad St. (tel. 656-5167), open Monday to Friday from 9:10am to 3:30pm (closed on major holidays); the activities are described by automatic narration in four languages. Only a certain number of tickets are given out each day, so it's wise to get your tickets as early as possible. For more information and reservations for groups of 10 or more, phone 656-5168. The Exchange is the second most popular tourist attraction in New York.

Continue back to Broadway and turn right. Walk north a few blocks and turn right on Liberty Street, where you'll find the:

4. Federal Reserve Bank of New York at 33 Liberty St. Modeled after a Renaissance palace, this formidable building contains the world's largest known accumulation of monetary

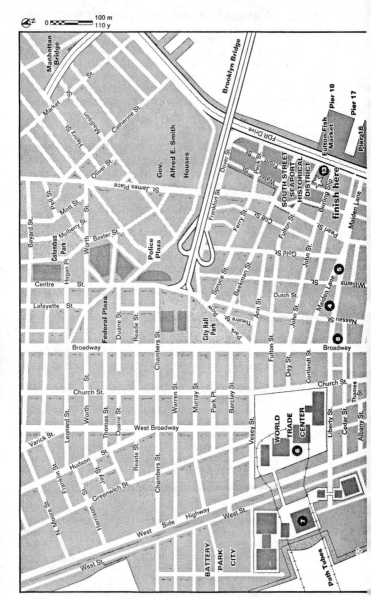

gold. Take a guided tour through the gold vault and view an exhibit on cash processing, which includes many examples of old currency and coins. Tours are given at 10:30 and 11:30am and 1:30 and 2:30pm during banking days, and reservations must be made at least one week in advance. Family groups may include children. (Large groups should make reservations several months in advance.) You may write to the Public Information Department at the bank (the Zip code is 10045), or phone 720-6130 to request a reservation.

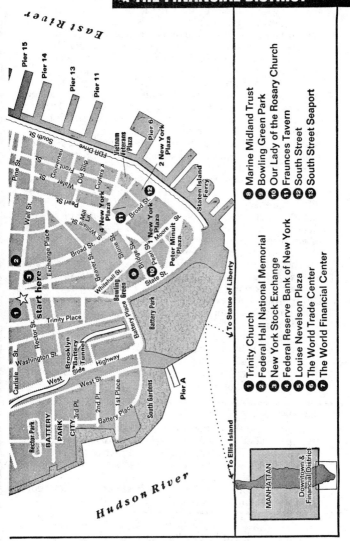

WALKING TOUR — DOWNTOWN & THE FINANCIAL DISTRICT

① Trinity Church
② Federal Hall National Memorial
③ New York Stock Exchange
④ Federal Reserve Bank of New York
⑤ Louise Nevelson Plaza
⑥ The World Trade Center
⑦ The World Financial Center
⑧ Marine Midland Trust
⑨ Bowling Green Park
⑩ Our Lady of the Rosary Church
⑪ Fraunces Tavern
⑫ South Street
⑬ South Street Seaport

Continue east on Liberty Street to:

5. Louise Nevelson Plaza, where William Street, Liberty Street, and Maiden Lane meet at a tiny vestpocket park fitted out with trees, benches, and seven vertical sculptures by Nevelson called *Shadows and Flags.*

Head back to Broadway now and continue walking west one block for the highlight of your downtown excursion:

6. The World Trade Center. A less-than-a-minute ride will take you zooming to the top of the world's almost-tallest building.

Here, at the glass-enclosed Observation Deck on the 107th floor of the **South Tower (Tower Two)**—more than a quarter mile in the sky—you'll see perhaps the most spectacular view on earth. Below you is all of New York, its bridges, its monuments, the maze of streets below, the rivers and their toy ships, and, on a clear day, a view that extends 50 miles in all directions. At dusk, when the lights are just beginning to come up on the darkening city, it is particularly enchanting. If you also go up to the promenade on the roof above the 110th floor, you'll be on the highest outdoor observation platform in the world. Since anywhere from 6,000 to 9,000 people visit the Observation Deck on fine summer and holiday weekends, try to plan your visit for a weekday, when there will be only a few thousand. It's open from 9:30am to 11:30pm daily, with an admission charge of $4 for adults, $2.25 for seniors, $2 for children 6 to 12, and free for those under 6 (tel. 435-7377).

Now come down to earth and inspect some of the monumental art at the World Trade Center, including a gigantic **Joan Miró tapestry** (considered one of his masterworks), hung against a 50-foot-high marble wall in the mezzanine of 2 World Trade Center; Alexander Calder's **World Trade Center Stabile,** resembling three giant sails, at Church and Vesey streets; and Louise Nevelson's sculpture **Sky-Gate New York,** which hangs in the mezzanine of 1 World Trade Center. You can also have a peek at the changing exhibits at the **United States Customs House** or stop in at the free visitors' gallery of the **Commodity Exchange,** on the ninth floor of 4 World Trade Center, to watch some fast and furious financial trading (open weekdays from 9:30am to 3pm).

If you're planning to see a Broadway or Off-Broadway show at night, stop in at the branch of **TKTS** on the mezzanine level of 2 World Trade Center for half-price day-of-performance tickets. Hours are Monday to Friday from 11am to 5:30pm and Saturday from 11am to 3:30pm.

REFUELING STOPS For the same glorious views you've seen from the Observation Deck, go to the Hors D'Oeuvrerie section of the stunning **Windows on the World Restaurant,** perched above Tower One, the North Tower of the WTC (see Chapter 6). Or, stop for refreshment back on the ground at the **Market Dining Rooms & Bar,** built on the site of the old Washington Market, or at the **Big Kitchen** with its various food stalls and modestly priced food for every taste.

A block west of the World Trade Center, across the North Pedestrian Bridge to Battery Park City is:
7. **The World Financial Center,** whose four soaring granite-and-glass towers designed by architect Cesar Pelli house corporate headquarters for many international financial firms. When you cross the bridge, you'll find yourself in the splendid indoor **Winter Garden,** a crystal palace atrium with a 120-foot vaulted glass ceiling, a magnificent marble-and-granite staircase, live palm trees, changing art exhibits, and glorious views out to the Hudson, the Statue of Liberty, and lower New York Harbor.

It's one of New York's great indoor spaces. There are dozens of shops and services here, and a handful of restaurants and outdoor cafés, including the luxurious **Hudson River Club.** You may choose to make your refueling stop here. It's quite likely there will be some form of free entertainment going on in good weather, everything from sunset dancing to live bands to puppet shows for the kids. Ogle the splendid boats in the yacht harbor at the North and South coves. You could then stroll along the **Hudson River Esplanade,** admiring the waterfront views and the parks and sculptures and flower gardens that make Battery Park City, which was built on 92 acres of landfill from the World Trade Center, one of the most graceful residential/commercial areas in New York. You can follow the esplanade all the way around to the tip of the island, until you arrive at Battery Park. From here, you can take a ferry to the Statue of Liberty and Ellis Island (see Chapter 7 for details). (If you're coming to the World Trade Center or World Financial Center from midtown, take the 1, R, or N train to the World Trade Center; or the A, C, or E train to Chambers Street/World Trade Center. Cross West Street to the bridge.) For more information on activities and events at the Winter Garden, phone 945-0505.

Alternatively, if you've decided to skip the World Financial Center on this particular excursion, return to Broadway after visiting the World Trade Center and proceed south. You'll see the:

8. Marine Midland Trust building at 140 Broadway, with Isamu Noguchi's enormous rectangular cube precariously balanced on one corner in front of it. This is one of the few new buildings in the area that has made any attempt at public art or sculpture.

Continue down Broadway to:

9. Bowling Green Park. Where the Dutch burghers actually used to bowl is ahead of you (it has been restored to look the way it did a century ago with London plane trees, wooden benches, and old-time lamp posts), and so is the massive neoclassic former **Customs House,** with its imposing sculptures of Asia, America, Africa, and Europe, done by Daniel Chester French of Lincoln Memorial fame. Inside, in the Rotunda Room, are Reginald Marsh's famed WPA murals.

Bear left, following the other side of the street from Bowling Green and Battery Park, until you come to the building at 7 State Street:

10. Our Lady of the Rosary Church, one of the few remaining examples of early Federal architecture in New York. Built by John McCoomb as a private town house in 1800, Watson House is noted for the colonnade that curves with the line of the street. As Our Lady of the Rosary Church, it is the shrine of Saint Elizabeth Seton.

Right behind State Street is Pearl Street, which you should follow west to the corner of Broad Street to see one of New York's most famous historical houses:

REFUELING STOP   11. Fraunces Tavern. Built in 1719, Fraunces Tavern became part of American history when George Washington bade farewell to his officers in the Long Room here on December 4, 1783, after the American Revolution. It is now owned and maintained by the Sons of the Revolution in the State of New York as a museum with permanent and changing exhibits of the Revolutionary War and 18th-century American history and culture. You might catch the museum's audiovisual presentation of the early history of New York City or attend some of their lectures and concerts (open Monday to Friday from 10am to 4pm; adults $2.50, seniors, students, and children under 12 with adult, $1; tel. 425-1778 for information). On the ground floor is the oldest continuously operated restaurant in America (tel. 269-0144), where the food is excellent, and you could have a lovely lunch (or breakfast or dinner) in the company of illustrious ghosts. Open weekdays only.

Now make your way to the waterfront on Broad Street and begin walking up:

12. South Street, once dotted with ship chandlers' stores and other establishments having to do with sailing and the sea. Those who mourn the old days on the waterfront have mixed emotions about the steel-and-glass monsters, but there is no denying that some are handsome. If you're interested in architecture, have a look yourself at the soaring columns of **2 New York Plaza** or **55 Water Street,** which I find the most impressive building here. Next to it is the moving **Vietnam Veterans Memorial.** I especially like the plaza at 55 Water Street on its northern side that overlooks the highway. Here you can join the local office workers eating lunch at the chairs and tables outside or just sit and watch the tugs and the whirlybirds and the harbor traffic, catch the marvelous ocean breezes, and dream a little bit about the vanished days of the tall ships, the giant clippers that came from all over the world to drop anchor at the port of New York, arching their bowsprits across South Street. Continue walking until you reach the:

13. South Street Seaport, which you can explore now (see details in Chapter 7) or save for a later day.

To get back to Midtown, walk west from the South Street Seaport on Fulton Street and make connections to all major subway lines.

WALKING TOUR 2 — Greenwich Village

Start: Sixth Avenue and Waverly Place, near the West 4th Street subway station.
Finish: Same as start.
Time: Approximately 1 hour and 10 minutes.

The original Greenwich Village, the separate town that once lay beyond the boundaries of New York, is located in the region between Greenwich Avenue and the Hudson River, bounded on the south by West Houston Street. That Greenwich Village was one of the earliest settlements on Manhattan, a bucolic hamlet until the 1820s. Its

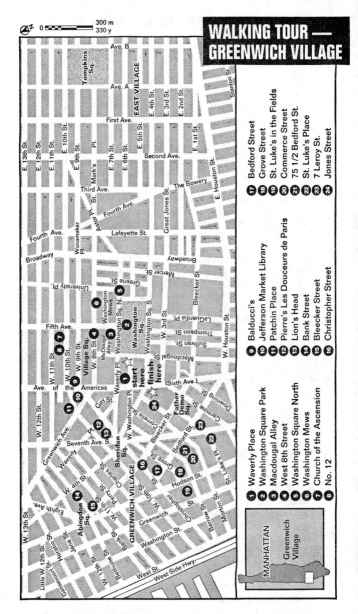

WALKING TOUR — GREENWICH VILLAGE

① Waverly Place
② Washington Square Park
③ Macdougal Alley
④ West 8th Street
⑤ Washington Square North
⑥ Washington Mews
⑦ Church of the Ascension
⑧ No. 12

⑨ Balducci's
⑩ Jefferson Market Library
⑪ Patchin Place
⑫ Pierre's Les Douceurs de Paris
⑬ Lion's Head
⑭ Bank Street
⑮ Bleecker Street
⑯ Christopher Street

⑰ Bedford Street
⑱ Grove Street
⑲ St. Luke's in the Fields
⑳ Commerce Street
㉑ 75 1/2 Bedford St.
㉒ St. Luke's Place
㉓ 7 Leroy St.
㉔ Jones Street

MANHATTAN
Greenwich Village

sudden prosperity was largely a function of the poor quality of the
drinking water in the neighboring city of New York. In those days
epidemics of typhoid and smallpox were almost annual affairs. As
soon as the new season's plague struck New York, everyone who
could afford to decamped immediately to healthful semirural and
nearby Greenwich.

Greenwich possessed its own bewildering network of built-up

streets well before burgeoning New York City engulfed it. They still exist, and even native New Yorkers can get lost in the Village, at least without a map.

This tour starts at Sixth Avenue and Waverly Place, an intersection located one block south of 8th Street and quite near the uptown exits from the Washington Square–West 4th Street subway stop. Proceed east from Sixth Avenue toward Washington Square Park on:

1. **Waverly Place,** a typical Village street lined with well-used brick town houses from the early 19th century, as well as buildings of more recent vintage. At the end of one block you arrive at Macdougal Street and:

2. **Washington Square Park.** In 1789 the park was designated a pauper's burial ground. But by 1826 fashion was on the march. The paupers were unceremoniously removed and the former graveyard became a parade ground. Soon fine Greek Revival houses began to appear along the southern boundary. All of these have disappeared, victims of time and the encroaching building programs of New York University's campus.

   Now make a short detour. Turn to your left (north) and head away from Washington Square Park up Macdougal Street. After a few steps you'll see:

3. **Macdougal Alley** on your right. This little street, lined with former carriage houses, is typical of the sort of small enclave that makes the Village such an appealing place to live. You might stroll up to the end of Macdougal Street (the Alley is private) and have a look at:

4. **West 8th Street** while you're here. It's a wilderness of shoe stores, clothing stores, poster shops, and copy centers. It's hard to believe that its mutilated buildings were ever aristocratic private houses.

   Now return to Washington Square, turn left (east) and walk along:

5. **Washington Square North.** Collectively known as The Row, the brick houses that still stand on the park's northern boundary give a vivid idea of what the whole square once looked like. They enjoyed their day (in the 1830s) as the homes of New York's elite. Henry James and Edith Wharton both lived and worked at **1 Washington Square North.** Today many of these old mansions are only facades masking new apartments inside, but a few have survived almost intact. Note the double house at **no. 20,** built in 1828 as a freestanding suburban mansion for one George P. Rogers. The very air on this block is redolent with the gentility of the past. You can almost imagine the clip-clop of horses and the creak of carriage springs as ladies lift their skirts while climbing out to make their calls. At Fifth Avenue, turn left (uptown). On the east side of the avenue you'll see:

6. **Washington Mews,** another alley lined with former carriage houses that are now converted to residences. Although the original town houses along this stretch of Fifth were long ago replaced with apartment houses, the Mews preserves a dignified residential air.

   Three blocks north of Washington Square at 10th Street is the:

7. **Church of the Ascension,** a pleasant old place set back from

the street behind an antique iron fence. It's been here since 1841, although the interior dates from a renovation in the 1880s by the celebrated McKim, Mead, and White! Turn left off Fifth Avenue onto West 10th Street, one of the nicest blocks in the Village, lined with fine city houses. Note:

8. No. 12, a particularly capacious old manse once owned by Bruce Price, the architect of Tuxedo Park and the father of etiquette expert Emily Post.

At the end of the block you'll reach the corner of Sixth Avenue. Turn left on Sixth and down the block is:

9. Balducci's, the famous Italian gourmet emporium.

Across Sixth is the:

10. Jefferson Market Library. This exuberant Victorian castle, dating from the 1870s, was once considered one of the half dozen most beautiful buildings in the United States. Subsequent generations considered it a horror. Concerned Villagers saved it from demolition in the late 1960s after it had stood vacant for over 20 years. When built, it was part of an innovative multiple-use complex that included a jail, a market, a courthouse, and a prison.

Across 10th Street from the Jefferson Library is another little enclave of the sort that so typifies Greenwich Village. Called:

11. Patchin Place, it contains but ten modest brick houses facing one another across a leafy cul-de-sac. Theodore Dreiser, Jane Bowles, and e. e. cummings were among Patchin Place's illustrious residents in the days when the Village was America's "Bohemia."

Now continue walking west on 10th Street away from Sixth Avenue, across Greenwich Avenue, and keep walking west on 10th Street. The modest-looking tenements that line the street contain apartments as pricey as those on the elegant block between Fifth and Sixth. Why? Because they're on West 10th Street, a premium New York address. Continue straight across the intersection of 10th Street and Waverly Place. Walk down Waverly one block, make a right at Christopher Street, and take a break at:

REFUELING STOP   12. Pierre's Les Douceurs de Paris, 170 Waverly Place (tel. 929-7194), on the left side of Christopher Park as you approach Seventh Avenue. It's a true Parisian bistro, offering classic food at moderate prices. On Tuesday and Wednesday the specialty is couscous. There are a few sidewalk tables. On the right side of the park is the **13. Lion's Head,** 59 Christopher St. (tel. 929-0670), a popular village tavern with an imaginative menu and brick walls lined with covers of books by its many literary patrons.

To the west is Seventh Avenue South. Cross the avenue and go just a few steps to the intersection of West 10th and West 4th streets (one of those conceptually bizarre intersections for which the Village is famous). Then turn right and start walking northwest up West 4th. Now you're getting into the real Greenwich Village. The next couple of intersecting streets— Charles, Perry, West 11th, and Bank—are filled with old brick houses, shady trees, a smattering of better shops and galleries, and a great feeling of calm. Note the brick house at the corner of West 11th and West 4th. It must have looked just as it does now for over 100 years, which is no mean feat in New York.

Turn left (west) when you reach:

14. Bank Street, where during a particularly virulent smallpox epidemic in the 1820s, so many New York banking institutions set up temporary offices on this street that the Village of Greenwich named it after them. Note the ancient wisteria growing on no. 60. This is the sort of tenement house that invaded the Village as it became less fashionable in the latter part of the 19th century. Today even the tenements have an appealing patina of age. Many fine old Greek Revival houses remain on this block of Bank, making it one of the Village's nicest. At the end of the block, at Abington Square, turn left onto:

15. Bleecker Street. This is a street of antiques shops, occasional boutiques, interesting bookstores, cracked sidewalks, and some blowsy-looking modernish buildings. The narrow tree-lined side streets, however, are absolutely delightful. Continue south on Bleecker for five blocks to:

16. Christopher Street and turn right (west toward the Hudson). Ahead in the distance you can see New Jersey across the river. On the street around you you'll see gay New York in full flower, as Christopher Street is more or less its spiritual center.

Stay on Christopher one short block to:

17. Bedford Street and turn left (south). At the end of the block, on the corner of Grove Street, is a nest of particularly picturesque wooden houses. No. 17 Grove Street, on the corner of Bedford and Grove, was built by a Village sash-maker in the 1820s. It sags wonderfully and evokes the past quite vividly. No. 100 Bedford St., in midblock, is a Grimm's fairy-tale concoction of stucco, timbers, and crazy angles called Twin Peaks. At the end of the block, make a right on Grove Street in the direction of the Hudson. The road makes a dogleg turn just a few steps from Bedford. Right at the angle of the turn you'll see a little gate set into a brick wall. Although it's private beyond, you can step up to the gate and look over it into:

18. Grove Court. Built for blue-collar tenants about 1830 and originally called Mixed Ale Alley, this tree-shaded enclave of little brick houses is the sort of Village spot many New Yorkers would kill to live in. After you've admired the Federal houses here, continue another half block to the end of Grove at Hudson Street. The old church across Hudson is:

19. St. Luke's in the Fields, built in the 1820s when so much of this part of the Village was going up. The original St. Luke's was destroyed by fire, but the restoration preserves its rural look, despite the enormous Victorian-era warehouses looming behind it. As you leave Grove Street, turn left (south) on Hudson for one block to Barrow Street, and turn left again. The first corner you'll come to is called:

20. Commerce Street. The intersection sports an interesting pair of identical houses, no. 39 and no. 41 Commerce St., which were built in the 1830s and "modernized" in the 1870s with matching mansard roofs. Turn right off Barrow into tiny Commerce Street. This crooked little thoroughfare used to be called Cherry Lane until the big smallpox scare of 1822 sent so many businesses up here from New York that the name was changed. When you reach the end of the block, you'll be back on Bedford Street. Turn right (south) again and then look to your right for:

21. **No. 75½ Bedford St.** This 9½-foot-wide house holds the distinction of being the narrowest house in Greenwich Village, as well as the one-time residence of poet Edna St. Vincent Millay. Keep walking south on Bedford for two blocks to Seventh Avenue to:

22. **St. Luke's Place,** where you should turn right. Although the south side of St. Luke's Place is occupied by a modern playground, the north side preserves a terrific old row of houses from the 1850s. No. 6 St. Luke's Place was the residence of a former mayor of New York, the popular James J. ("Gentleman Jimmy") Walker. Although a crook and a scoundrel, Walker managed to epitomize the glamour of the 1920s. Incredibly enough, he is remembered quite fondly to this day.

    Return to Seventh Avenue and continue straight across it on the line of St. Luke's Place. Once across Seventh you'll note that St. Luke's becomes Leroy Street. Stay on Leroy, past the continuation of Bedford Street for one block to the corner of Bleecker Street. Just before this intersection, note:

23. **No. 7 Leroy St.,** a nearly perfect circa 1810 house, complete with alley entrance and original dormers. When you get to Bleecker, note the local shops, then turn left for two very short blocks to:

24. **Jones Street.** Turn right onto Jones and take a quick look at no. 17 to see what usually happens to old houses like the one at no. 7 Leroy. A pity, no? At the end of the block, you'll be back on West 4th Street. Turn right for another short block and presto, here you are again back on Sixth Avenue, a mere two blocks south of Waverly Place, where the tour began.

WALKING TOUR 3 — Upper West Side

Start: Lincoln Center for the Performing Arts.
Finish: Northeast corner of 73rd and Broadway.
Time: 2 to 4 hours, depending on stops.
Best Times: Tuesday to Sunday, when museums are open.

Begin your tour at:

1. **Lincoln Center for the Performing Arts,** Broadway to Amsterdam Avenue, from 62nd to 66th streets. An energetic revitalization of the Upper West Side really began full force with the completion of the city's controversial multicultural facility at Lincoln Center; some criticize the architecture as too conservative, others fault it for being too daring. The complex includes Avery Fisher Hall, formerly Philharmonic Hall (1962); the New York State Theater (1964); the Vivian Beaumont Theater (1965); the Library and Museum of the Performing Arts (1965); the Metropolitan Opera House (1966); and across 65th Street, Alice Tully Hall, the Juilliard School of Music (1968), and the Walter Reade Theater (1991). Three of the buildings face the central

plaza—the Metropolitan Opera House in the middle, Avery Fisher Hall to the right, and the New York State Theater to the left. The plaza itself is dominated by a handsome fountain and, on summer evenings, by café tables that spill out from Avery Fisher Hall. (See Chapter 7 for details on tours.)

Looking east across the plaza, notice the rooftop replica of:

2. The Statue of Liberty, 43 W. 64th St. Her torch is gone and her spiral staircase is now closed permanently, but this 1902 lady is an exact duplicate of her larger, more famous counterpart.

In front of the plaza, in an island where Broadway and Columbus Avenue meet, is the tiny:

3. Dante Park. The bronze statue of the Italian poet Dante Alighieri was erected here in 1921 to commemorate the 600th anniversary of his death. He holds a copy of *The Divine Comedy,* in good company with the artistic offerings of Lincoln Center.

Cross Broadway and walk north to the:

4. Museum of American Folk Art, 2 Lincoln Square. (See Chapter 7 for details.) The museum also has a charming shop filled with such treasures as ceramics, mobiles, toys, doll houses, and miniature Pennsylvania Dutch blanket chests—all handmade, naturally.

Recrossing (west) Broadway at 66th Street, you'll pass:

5. Tucker Park. A bronze bust honors Richard Tucker, the operatic tenor who, during his 21-year career with the Metropolitan Opera, sang almost 500 performances.

A branch of:

6. Tower Records, 1965 Broadway at 66th St., contains two neon-lit floors of records, tapes, CDs, and videos, both domestic and imported, at discount prices.

Cross Broadway again and head east on 67th Street toward Central Park. The block between Columbus Avenue and the park is a delightful enclave of older buildings designed originally as artists' studios. Concealed behind their facades are double-height studio spaces.

7. The Atelier, no. 33, dates from 1902 and has a handsome stone-arched facade.

8. No. 15 is notable for its Gothic Revival lobby resembling a chapel. And finally, the:

9. Hotel des Artistes, No. 1, is one of New York's treasures. Completed in 1918, this splendid building actually shows balconied artists' spaces behind its buoyant Elizabethan facade. A list of past residents reads like a who's who of entertainment and the arts: Noël Coward, Norman Rockwell, Isadora Duncan, and Edna Ferber, among others. Just across Central Park West and slightly into the park, trees strung with tiny lights identify:

10. Tavern on the Green, 67th Street near Central Park West, one of the most romantic dining/dancing spots in town. (See Chapter 6 for details.)

11. Central Park, 59th to 110th streets, Fifth Avenue to Central Park West, a splendid 840 acres of landscaped lakes, hills, meadows, footpaths, bridges, bridle paths, secluded glens, a bird sanctuary, two skating rinks, a first-rate zoo, multiple recreational facilities, and an impressive collection of sculpture. The park was designated a National Historic Landmark in 1965. It remains one of the most successful landscaped areas anywhere.

At the southwest corner of Central Park West and 70th Street is:

12. The Spanish and Portuguese Synagogue, Congregation Shearith Israel, 8 W. 70th St. This is the fifth home of the oldest Jewish congregation in the United States—Spanish and Portuguese refugees from the Inquisition in Brazil who built their first house of worship in 1730. After four successive moves uptown, this Classic Revival building was erected in 1897.

Continuing north you reach the:

13. Majestic Apartments, 115 Central Park West, 71st to 72nd streets. Built in 1930, this is a fine example of the art deco style of the late 1920s and '30s. One of four twin-towered apartment houses that enliven the Central Park skyline, the attractive, much-imitated brickwork was designed by French sculptor René Chanbellan. Continuing north, you'll come to:

14. The Dakota Apartments, 1 W. 72nd St., northwest corner of Central Park West. Legend has it that this building got its name for its location in what was in 1884 the boondocks of Manhattan, so remote from the city center that it might as well have been in Dakota. It was designed by Henry J. Hardenbergh (also architect of the Plaza Hotel) in German Renaissance style, part fortress (it's surrounded by a dry moat), part château, with dormers, gables, arches, balconies, finials, and ornate stonework. Despite its status then and now as one of New York's most exclusive apartment houses, the Dakota has a moody atmosphere—it was the setting for the film *Rosemary's Baby* and the site of the tragic 1980 murder of former rock star and Beatle John Lennon, in whose memory his widow, Yoko Ono, has created the touching memorial directly across the street:

15. Strawberry Fields, Central Park at 72nd Street (See "Central Park" in Chapter 7 for details.)

After you've paid your respects, cross Central Park West, walk to 73rd Street, and turn left, noticing the ornamental iron gate and dry moat of the Dakota. Clark and Hardenbergh joined forces in another project after the Dakota, the development of what is now the:

16. Central Park West–West 73rd–74th Street Historic District, animated by a series of rental row houses in polychrome, a departure from the relentless rows of brownstones that lined the city streets during the 1870s and '80s. Note especially nos. 15A–19 and 41–65, built between 1882 and 1885.

Continue west to:

REFUELING STOPS Columbus Avenue, which from 72nd to 81st streets is dotted with good eating places in a range of prices. **17. Ruppert's** (72nd and 73rd streets) and the **18. Museum Café** (77th Street) are well-established and popular bets for leisurely lunches and dinners (they can get crowded, so best arrive at off hours). More casual is the branch of **19. Pizzeria Uno** at 81st Street.

As a diversion from sightseeing, explore some of the shops along Columbus Avenue. Kenar (no. 303), French Connection (no. 304), and Express Ltd. (no. 321) sell women's fashions; the jewelry at Ylang-Ylang (no. 324) is funky and off-beat. Putumayo (no. 339) specializes in interesting ethnic clothing and accessories. At Mythology Unlimited (no. 370) you'll find everything from art supplies to antique toys. The Hero's Journey (no. 489, between 83rd and 84th streets, necessitates a small detour) is a serene emporium oriented to inner development, with a wide selection of metaphysical books, New Age music, natural crystals, crystal jewelry, and the like.

Along Columbus Avenue to Central Park West, from 77th to 81st streets is the spectacular:

20. American Museum of Natural History, which houses one of the world's most important scientific collections and is among the most frequently visited museums in town. The original entrance is on the 77th Street side, a massive Romanesque Revival edifice in pink Vermont granite built from 1892 to 1899, with a carriage entrance, arcaded porch, towers and turrets, and a grand staircase. The Central Park West facade is dominated by an equestrian statue of Theodore Roosevelt sculpted by J. E. Frazer in 1939. (See Chapter 7 for details.)

Though overshadowed by the Natural History Museum, the:

21. New-York Historical Society, 170 Central Park West, on the southwest corner of 77th Street, is a pleasing, understated classical palace begun in 1908, with wings added in 1938; it's a major research venue for students of American history. (See Chapter 7.) Walk north, rounding the corner at 81st Street to the:

22. Hayden Planetarium, 81st Street and Central Park West, where "cosmic laser concerts" are featured along with other heavenly explorations. The building is a 1935 adjunct to the American Museum of Natural History. Before heading west, glance at the:

23. Beresford, 211 Central Park West, on the northwest corner of 81st, built in 1929 during Central Park West's glory days. It's a luxury apartment house by a baroque tower that gives it a decidedly romantic aura, not easy for a structure as large as this.

Walking west on 81st Street to Broadway, you'll pass the typical turn-of-the-century residential brownstones that characterize the side streets of the Upper West Side. At Broadway the foot-weary can hop a 7 or 104 bus north to visit the:

24. Cathedral of St. John the Divine (Amsterdam Avenue and 112th Street) and/or **25. The Riverside Church** (Riverside Drive and 122nd Street).

The hardy can continue south along:

26. Broadway, the main thoroughfare of the Upper West Side and the only major artery that runs on the diagonal in New York's grid system of streets. Seedy though it may be in parts, it's a monumental avenue edged by monumental buildings and centered by wide grassy malls. At the southwest corner of 81st Street is:

27. Shakespeare and Co. Booksellers, a great place to browse. And just south is:

28. Zabar's, 2245 Broadway, between 80th and 81st streets. New York would be unimaginable without the gourmet food emporium whose variety of temptations defies categorizing. Known throughout the city, frequented by the cognoscenti in all boroughs, Zabar's is a landmark, an institution, an absolute must for anyone interested in the New York food lover's state of mind. Continue south to:

29. The First Baptist Church, Broadway at 79th Street, an austere Romanesque Revival structure dating from 1891, with curious asymmetrical twin towers.

The entire block, Broadway to West End Avenue, and West 79th to West 78th streets, is taken up by the:

30. Apthorp Apartments, a dignified luxury building that still retains its old-world elegance. Built for William Waldorf Astor in 1908, the limestone structure surrounds a central courtyard with fountain beyond high vaulted passageways. Except for ground-floor shops on Broadway, the building remains intact and original. It is named for Charles Apthorpe, who bought the land in 1763. It remained in the family until 1879, when Astor purchased it. Walk west on 77th Street to:

31. West End Avenue, until the early 20th century, a "millionaire's row" of stylish town houses. The wealthy moved a block west when Riverside Drive opened, but after World War I a plethora of apartment houses were built to lure tenants back.

Continue west down the hill to:

32. Riverside Park, designed in 1875 by Central Park architect Frederick Law Olmsted and completed 15 years later. A flight of steps to the left leads to a tunnel that in turn takes you down more steps, along a path, and through a rotunda to the:

33. 79th Street Boat Basin, an unexpected and delightful marina where many New Yorkers tie up or live permanently on their houseboats.

Return to Riverside Park and relax on a bench for a few minutes before taking the curved stairway at the basketball court up to Riverside Drive. Head east on 76th Street to:

34. No. 252 W. 76th St. and view it from the opposite side to appreciate the recently restored and quite splendid eclectic Classical facade.

Turn right at Broadway. On the east side, near 75th Street is the:

35. Beacon Theater, 2124 Broadway. No matter what's playing, don't miss the magnificent art deco interior, a designated city landmark. Walk around the theater to the:

36. Berkeley Garage, 201 W. 75th St., a wonderful 1890 Romanesque Revival building that once housed the stables of the New York Cab Company. The three arches provided a broad entrance for horses and carriages in the 1880s and '90s. Return to the west side of Broadway and continue south to one of New York's architectural masterpieces, the French beaux arts:

37. Ansonia Hotel, 2109 Broadway, on the northwest corner of 73rd Street. Now a bit frayed (a restoration is in progress), the Ansonia was a grande dame among apartment hotels when it opened in 1904. Opulent and richly ornamental, it meant to imitate the French resort hotels along the Riviera. Over the years the Ansonia became the bastion of the music profession: Among its illustrious tenants were Enrico Caruso, Ezio Pinza, Lily Pons, Igor Stravinsky, Arturo Toscanini, and Yehudi Menuhin. The building is striking for its mansard roof and rounded towers.

If you're hungry, continue north on Broadway and between 81st and 82nd streets you'll find:

REFUELING STOP 38. Teacher's Too, 2271 Broadway (tel. 362-4900), a block north of Zabar's. This ever-popular neighborhood spot offers wonderful American food and a few Thai dishes at reasonable prices—fish selections are especially good. Sidewalk tables in good weather.

Returning to the intersection of Broadway and West 72nd Street, the:

39. Subway Station Entrance is one of the few remaining art nouveau structures of its kind, dating from 1904, when the underground railway was first built. The intersection is divided into Verdi Square to the north and Sherman Square to the south.

40. Verdi Square honors the Italian operatic composer, whose statue in marble stands on a granite pedestal above four life-size figures of his characters from *Aida, Falstaff, Otello,* and *La Forza del Destino.*

Dominating the north side of Verdi Square is the former:

41. Central Savings Bank building (now the Apple Bank for Savings), 2100 Broadway, at the northeast corner of 73rd Street. This massive Palladian palace gives an impression of financial security—obviously the intention of its builders. The wrought-iron window grilles and lanterns (by Samuel Yellin) embellish the facade, while two lions flanking a large clock decorate the 73rd Street entrance.

CHAPTER 9

SHOPPING A TO Z

Quite a lot of people come to New York for only one reason: to go shopping. For them, the greatest show in town begins right on Fifth Avenue. One woman I know flies in regularly from Detroit, checks into her hotel, grabs a cab, and heads immediately for Saks. "Then," she says, "I know I'm in New York."

What my friend senses, of course, is that New York is one of the great fashion capitals of the world, a city where *Women's Wear Daily* sits on the best coffee tables, where the fashion business provides a living, a *raison d'être*, or, at the very least, a subject of conversation for thousands of people. As a result of this high-keyed fashion consciousness, the New York woman, regardless of her income, is one of the best, most individually dressed women in the world. Close at hand she has the great department and specialty stores like Lord & Taylor, Saks Fifth Avenue, Bergdorf Goodman, Galeries Lafayette, Bloomingdale's, A&S, and Macy's. She also has hundreds of small boutiques and shops where she can buy anything from a Paris ball gown whose price tag runs into or even over four figures to a Mickey Mouse T-shirt for $12. She can suit her flights of fancy with a pair of fine Italian boots, a silk sari from India, a peasant dress from Guatemala, or the latest from a trendy Japanese designer. She can also rummage through old capes and costumes in the Village. It's a wide-open, exciting scene, and one that any woman (or man, for that matter, since men's boutiques are proliferating almost as widely as women's) with an ounce of fashion curiosity will find absorbing.

Note: New York City has a hefty **sales tax** of 8.25%.

INSIDE INFORMATION In any one month, there are 100 to 150 sales in the private showrooms of New York's designers and manufacturers. Not only samples, but overstocks and cancellations—in women's, men's, and children's clothing; accessories; furs; furniture; and household goods. And if you were an insider in these businesses, you'd know, via the grapevine, when and where those sales, which are never advertised, were being held. Well, now you can get inside information, thanks to two publications sold by subscription to thousands of avid New York shoppers who wouldn't dream of paying retail, not when they can realize spectacular savings—anywhere from 50% to 90% on top brand-name and designer labels. Thanks to the recession, most merchandise is now being sold below wholesale. If you'd like to join in the fun and buy, say, a $700 man's designer suit from Italy for $200, or a woman's $2,000 mink coat for $895, or a $350 leather bomber jacket for $60, or a child's $50 outfit from $5 to $10, here's how you do it.

Fashion Update, which comes out quarterly, costs $54 a year, with single copies $20. A hotline phone number is provided to subscribers for late-breaking sales. Publisher Sara Gardner also leads highly enjoyable personalized three-hour shopping tours for $50. Bridal and mother-of-the-bride shopping is one of her specialties: She reports a source of customized bridal gowns, where a $2,000 gown can be copied for $700. Phone 718/377-8873 or write Fashion Update, 1274 49th St., Suite 209, Brooklyn, NY 11219.

The other sales-and-bargain guide is **The S&B Report,** which is published monthly. It costs $49 for a yearly subscription, or $8.60 for single copies; get one or both by phoning 212/679-5400, or tollfree 800/283-MART out-of-state or writing *The S&B Report,* 112 E. 36th St., 4th floor, New York, NY 10016. Elyse Lazar, the publisher, advises that the most spectacular bargains are often in costume jewelry and accessories. "Stores mark these up as much as 400%," she says.

Lazar also has a new publication called *Kid's Report,* which covers children's showroom sales, factory outlets, discounters, and mail-order companies. It also covers free educational, cultural, and recreational services for children in New York. The cost is $29 a year for six issues.

ANTIQUES

AMERICA HURRAH ANTIQUES, third floor of 766 Madison Ave., at 66th Street. Tel. 535-1930.

Hung up on patchwork quilts? America Hurrah Antiques has a superb collection of antique American quilts, most made between 1830 and 1930 in New York and Pennsylvania (many are Amish) at prices averaging $800 to $3,000. They are familiar with European bed sizes and can advise Europeans precisely which quilts will be suitable. Also beautiful are folk art and Americana, such as antique Native American art, hooked rugs, paintings, pottery, handmade antique weathervanes, baskets, and country accessories.

ANNEX ANTIQUES FAIR AND FLEA MARKET, Sixth Ave., between 24th and 27th Sts. Tel. 243-5343.

This is a favorite weekend activity for New York's antique hunters. Prices here are lower than those in the stores, and there's something for everyone, most of it of fairly modern vintage: glass, pottery, china, jewelry, furniture, you-name-it. Over 300 vendors offer their wares. **Open:** Sat–Sun 9am–5pm.

THE MANHATTAN ARTS & ANTIQUE CENTER, 1050 Second Ave., at 56th Street. Tel. 355-4400.

The Manhattan Arts & Antique Center is a handsome enclosed mall where over 100 antiques dealers have gathered their wares. The range goes from country furniture to rare Chinese porcelains, from African masks to temple hangings from Tibet. Collect a print or a Persian carpet, a music box or an old master, depending on what the budget will bear. **Open:** Mon–Sat 10:30am–6pm; Sun noon–6pm.

PLACE DES ANTIQUAIRES, 125 East 57th St. Tel. 758-2900.

This combination art-and-antiques center represents some of the most prestigious American and international dealers. While you're eyeing the collectors' items or some inexpensive baubles, you can also enjoy exhibits, presentations, and seminars; it's like a small museum unto itself. A free lecture series is held September through June, on Wednesday at 2pm: Call for information. Café à 'la Place is there to provide sophisticated refreshment. **Open:** Mon–Sat 11am–6pm.

SOHO ANTIQUES FAIR AND FLEA MARKET, corner of Broadway and Grand St. Tel. 682-2000.

New York's newest outdoor antiques and collectibles market is located in the heart of the vibrant SoHo gallery and shopping scene. Over 100 vendors offer American and European antiques, furniture, fine and decorative objects, vintage clothing, silver, china, glassware, jewelry, coins, original paintings, American Indian artifacts, folk art, and memorabilia. **Open:** Sat–Sun 9am–5pm.

AUCTIONS

Scores of New Yorkers have become auction addicts. When they need to furnish an apartment, buy a painting, or get a high chair for the baby, they wouldn't consider buying anything new or price-tagged. For them, the game is in the bidding, the adventure in seeing who gets what. You can visit New York auction houses and bid for anything from sewing machines to silverware, from lamps to lorgnettes, from baubles to museum-quality collectibles.

When you're out for big game (or just spectator sport), the most exciting place is **Sotheby's,** 1334 York Ave., at 72nd St. (tel. 606-7000), where the cognoscenti vie for Rembrandts, pedigreed furniture, decorative arts, and precious jewelry. Many items, however, are not exorbitant, so don't be afraid to participate, especially at the frequent "Arcade Auctions," which feature sales of "affordable antiques." Illustrated catalogs with estimated values are published for each auction. Sotheby's is really like a wonderful museum with an intimacy that museums can never achieve, in that prospective bidders are allowed to touch and handle the objects for sale in the pre-auction showings. Before a sale of antique books, scholars get to study; before a sale of rare violins, musicians may be allowed to try out the Stradivarius! For 24-hour auction and exhibition information, phone 606-7245. Admission is free, and no tickets are required, except for prestigious evening sales. To get these, you should write or call at least six weeks in advance of the sale: You may not get a seat in the main salesroom, but you will get either standing room or a seat in another salesroom with a video monitor. **Open:** Mon–Sat 10am–5pm; Sun 1–5pm.

Christie's, 502 Park Ave. (tel. 546-1000), and its lower-priced annex **Christie's East,** 219 E. 67th St. (tel. 606-0400), are New York branches of the famous British firm. Auctions are held in all fields of collecting, with items ranging from several hundred dollars to $82.5 million! Several exhibitions and auctions are held each week from September to July.

Phillips, 406 E. 79th St. (tel. 570-4830), is another prestigious London firm. They specialize in jewelry, paintings, prints, coins, silver, watches, and more. **Open:** Mon–Fri 9am–5pm; some auctions held Sat.

Regularly scheduled auctions of antique American, English and continental furniture, decorations, paintings and sculpture, books and prints, as well as estate jewelry, are held at **William Doyle Galleries,** 175 E. 87th St. (tel. 427-2730). Doyle is a specialist in estates, and anything from these estates that might not be worthy of being auctioned finds its way to the **Tag Sale** store next door; this is a great source for anything from pewter tankards at $15 to a Regency style secretary/bookcase for $700. The stock changes daily, so it's always fun to stop by. **Open:** Mon–Fri 8:30am–5pm; Sat 10am–5pm; Sun noon–5pm. (tel. 410-9285).

One of the oldest American-owned auction houses in the United

States is **Tepper Galleries,** 110 E. 25th St. (tel. 677-5300), which primarily handles estate sales of antiques, fine reproductions, paintings, decorations, and accessories. Specialized auctions of artwork, jewelry, and collectibles also are held. Auctions are scheduled every two weeks through the year. Phone for schedules. **Lubin Galleries,** 30 W. 26th St. (tel. 924-3777), is always a good source for both antiques and reproductions of antique furniture, paintings, silver, Oriental rugs, jewelry, and the like; they run estate-auction sales every two weeks. Call for days and times of viewing and auctions.

For news of upcoming auctions each week, check the Antiques pages of the Friday and Sunday *New York Times.*

BRIDAL WEAR

KLEINFELD, Fifth Ave. and 82nd St., Bay Ridge section of Brooklyn. Tel. 718/833-1100.

Planning a wedding? Prospective brides come from all over the country—and from other countries, too—just to buy their gowns at Kleinfeld, known for almost half a century for its in-depth collection, wonderfully personalized service, and very fair prices (the average gown goes from $1,000 to $1,500 these days). In addition to designer bridal gowns, it also has bridesmaids' dresses, mother-of-the-bride ensembles, and other special-occasion gowns. Appointments are a must. Complimentary transportation from the Westbury Hotel in Manhattan is available by reservation.

CRAFTS

FIVE EGGS, 436 W. Broadway, in SoHo. Tel. 226-1606.

Japanese stores are plentiful in New York, but this one leads the way in taste. Working on the theory that there is "nothing too ordinary to be wrapped beautifully," they have five eggs wrapped in straw and a book called *How to Wrap Five Eggs.* Japanese matchbooks start at $3, but furniture may go up into the hundreds. In between are furoshiki scarves, designer T's, miniature Zen gardens, handsome cotton robes, vintage kimonos, and more.

THE MAD MONK, 500 Ave. of the Americas, at 12th St. Tel. 242-6678.

Those who love handmade ceramics—at very reasonable prices—should make tracks to the Village and the Mad Monk. The genial Carl Monk, who presides over the store, shows the work of over 75 upstate and New England potters; their handsome teapots, casseroles, ornamental mirrors, jars, pitchers, planters, and the like, range mostly from $6 to $75, although very special pieces may go much higher. Also sold at reasonable prices (discounts of 20%) is a fine collection of books on East-West philosophy. **Closed:** Sun–Mon.

DEPARTMENT & SPECIALTY STORES

A&S, tel. 594-8500, and A&S Plaza, Sixth Ave. at 33rd St. Tel. 465-0500.

A&S and A&S Plaza are the most exciting new developments in New York retailing in years. A&S is the famed Brooklyn emporium Abraham & Straus, which opened a Manhattan store just a few years ago (on the site of the late, lamented Gimbel's). A&S Plaza, a handsome nine-floor atrium courtyard, surrounds it on three sides. It is most attractive, with its white marble floors, pink-and-green walls, and four glass elevators that kids will love to ride. All told, there are about 60 shops here, most in a moderate price range, and a vast, internationally minded food court called **A Taste of New York,** the largest of its kind in the city, with attractive food dispensaries and seemingly acres of seating.

Be sure to stop in at the **Visitor Center** on level 7, or phone them at 465-0600; they will give you specific information on seeing the city, even make restaurant reservations, car service calls, or help you get theater tickets. You may be able to catch one of the free entertainments that A&S Plaza offers several times a month.

BERGDORF GOODMAN, 754 Fifth Ave., at 57th St. Tel. 753-7300.

The ultimate in fine clothing and accessories, Bergdorf's in-depth collection of designer merchandise features such top names as Chanel, Georgio Armani, Claude Montana, Ralph Lauren, and Calvin Klein, for starters. There's an outstanding gift collection on the seventh floor. Across the street at 745 Fifth Avenue is Bergdorf's "The Ultimate Store for Gentlemen," with everything from the most daring Italian designers to traditional clothing and formal wear. And an amazing assortment of ties.

BLOOMINGDALE'S, 1000 Third Ave., at 59th St., main entrance on Lexington Ave. Tel. 355-5900.

Bloomie's, as it is affectionately known to the chic sophisticates who practically make it a second home, has the latest in everything from fashions for juniors to designer clothing to the trendiest housewares and even a marvelous bakery-gourmet department. Its haute designer rooms on the fifth floor are outstanding, as are the frequent themed shows, when the entire store salutes the art, culture, and fashion of an exotic country.

GALERIES LAFAYETTE, 4–10 East 57th St. Tel. 355-0022.

Next door to Tiffany's, in the space once occupied by Bonwit Teller, the first American branch of Paris's famed Galeries Lafayette has opened its doors. From the sleek modern lines of the building, to the sleek modern lines of the women's fashions here, the look is very much French contemporary. Yves Saint Laurent, Nathalie Rykiel, Jean-Charles de Castelbajac are some of the featured designers from an almost exclusively French roster, both traditional names and striking young talents. Prices: Anywhere from $50 to $2,000.

HENRI BENDEL, 712 Fifth Ave., at 56th St. Tel. 247-1100.

In its very French-inspired new building, Bendel continues to offer its outstanding collections, everything from such top international designers as Karl Lagerfeld, Claude Montana, and Carolina Herrera to outstanding new stars shown in its New Creators boutique. Its tabletop and gifts for the home shop is outstanding, and its cosmetics department sometimes draws lines six deep on Saturdays, especially for its exclusive line of Mac cosmetics from Canada, much favored by fashion models. Women's clothing only.

LORD & TAYLOR, Fifth Ave. at 39th St. Tel. 391-3344.

Lord & Taylor, 156 years old, boasts a shimmering street floor, the swinging Young New Yorker shop, top American designers, beautiful antique furniture, and lovely things for the whole family. Its windows are one of the joys of the New York Christmas season.

MACY'S, 151 West 34th St., at Herald Square. Tel. 563-3894.

The world's biggest store, Macy's has it all. Selections in every department are vast and always of good quality. You can shop here for anything from children's hats to haute couture. Be sure to visit "The Cellar," a veritable street of shops for cookware, gadgets, gifts and souvenirs, plus a pastry shop and a candy shop.

POLO/RALPH LAUREN, 867 Madison Ave., at the corner of 72nd St. Tel. 606-2100.

Ralph Lauren's clothing and furnishings have always looked as if they were intended for the English gentry; now his showcase store looks for all the world like an English country place, complete to the family portraits on the wall, the working fireplaces, the Persian rugs and treasured antiques, and a grand baronial staircase. Polo/Ralph Lauren is a multimillion-dollar renovation of New York's 1895 Rhinelander mansion, and it's as much worth seeing as a living museum as for the merchandise it sells. The mood ranges from clublike for men's furnishings to more romantic for the areas selling women's clothing to country charm for the home-furnishings section, which contains a series of exquisitely accessorized model rooms. Service and quality are superior, and the prices match.

SAKS FIFTH AVENUE, 611 Fifth Ave., at 50th St. Tel. 753-4000.

Saks Fifth Avenue—it's a name long synonymous with fashion elegance. Here you can browse and shop for the likes of Louis Vuitton luggage, Revillon furs, or the top French and American designers in their own boutiques. Twice a year, in January and June, Saks runs storewide clearances, and everyone in town shows up for the bargains.

DISCOUNT SHOPPING

Here are some of the special secrets of New York shopping: how to pick up a dress for $55, a mink coat for $1,000, or a great pair of pants for $30—or where to get designers' originals for one-third the price in the salons.

DISCOUNT RETAIL STORES

BOLTON'S, 1191 Third Ave., near 69th St. Tel. 628-7553.

Current top-brand fashions at about one-third off department store prices—that's what you'll find at Bolton's. Fresh selections arrive three times a week and include a fashionable mix of famous-label dresses, suits, coats, contemporary casuals, and accessories. Dresses range from about $50 to over $100.

Bolton's also has many other locations around Manhattan, including shops at 1180 Madison Ave. (near 86th St.); 225 E. 57th St., and 4 E. 34th St. (near the Empire State Building). Check the phone book for other listings.

BURLINGTON COAT FACTORY, 45 Park Place, off West Broadway. Tel. 571-2631.

If you can't find a coat at Burlington, it's unlikely you can find one anywhere. This is the largest retailer of coats in the United States, and each of its 175 stores (coast to coast, and Florida to Alaska), has something like 15,000 coats in stock at any one time—woolens, leather, suedes, shearlings, rainwear, fur, fake fur, you name it—everything from leading brand names to top European and American designers. And it's all at prices of 25% to 60% less than those in the regular stores. As if that weren't enough, Burlington also has a complete menswear department (4,000 men's suits, a Large Men's shop, and more), an attractive women's sportswear department (with good selections in career clothing), and a big children's department for youngsters ranging from kindergarten to college age. Decor is pipe rack, dressing rooms are community style, but the savings are worth writing home about. Take the 1, 2, or 3 to Chambers Street.

CENTURY 21, 22 Cortlandt St., near the World Trade Center. Tel. 227-9092.

It's worth a trip downtown to the financial district to pay a visit to Century 21, which may be New York's most spectacular discount department store, with everything from toys to TVs and designer wear for women, men, and children at prices that are often 30% to 50% off the regular tabs. I've seen Jones New York pants, Christian Dior beachwear, Jack Mulqueen silk dresses, and Vittorio Ricci shoes. The biggest bargains are in women's lingerie and shoes, but everything is well priced here, including electronic games, small appliances, and men's sport shoes. There are, alas, no dressing rooms. **Open:** Mon–Fri 7:45am–7pm; Sat 10am–6:30pm.

DAFFY'S, 111 Fifth Ave., at 18th St. Tel. 529-4477.

"Clothing bargains for millionaires" is the philosophy behind Daffy's, an exuberant three-level store that features stylish togs for women (and, to a lesser extent, for men and children, too). Daffy's buyers shop both Seventh Avenue and the European designers for terrific values and pass them on to the customers on everything from designers to name brand clothing, plus bags and shoes. Savings range from 40% to 80% below regular retail prices. There's a smaller version of Daffy's uptown at 335 Madison Ave., corner of 43rd St. (tel. 557-4422), with less space and a slightly crowded feeling, but still those same terrific bargains. **Open** (both Daffy's): Mon–Fri 10am–9pm; Sat 10am–9pm, to 6pm uptown; Sun 11am–6pm.

S&W FAMOUS DESIGNERS APPAREL, at Seventh Ave. and 26th St. Tel. 924-6656.

Call S&W Famous Designers Apparel "off Seventh Avenue," if you will. It features name brands from the Seventh Avenue houses, at discounted—but still expensive—prices. There are actually four stores in the complex. At 165–167 W. 26th St., the upper level shows top-designer suits, dresses, and sportswear; the lower level is the clearance section. Around the corner at 283 Seventh Ave., you'll find shoes, handbags, jewelry, and accessories; 287 Seventh Ave. has designer coats in suedes, wools, and leather, and an extensive selection of raincoats as well as petite coats and medium-priced sportswear. **Open:** Mon–Wed 10am–6:30pm; Thurs 10am–8pm; Fri 10am–3pm; Sun 10am–6pm.

SYMS, 42 Trinity Place. Tel. 797-1199.

Well worth a special trip downtown, Syms is a vast store whose decor is about as dazzling as that of an airline hangar (its walls are totally black). But never mind: Its merchandise, for both men and women, is very good, and the prices are well below what you'd find in regular stores. Designer clothes sell for about one-third off regular prices, with a progressive markdown policy. Syms specializes in clothing, but they also discount handbags (wonderful buys here), shoes, luggage, linens, and more. **Open:** Tues–Wed 8am–6:30pm; Thurs–Fri 8am–8pm; Sun 11:30am–5:30pm. **Subway:** Take the 1, N, or R trains to the Rector Street station.

ALMOST WHOLESALE ON SEVENTH AVENUE

Gaining access to New York's famed wholesale houses, unless you have a connection, is not so easy. But I've discovered something even better: shopping at the showrooms of the jobbers and exporters who are the middlemen of Seventh Avenue. Besides carrying a vast array of merchandise from many manufacturers, they welcome retail customers, provide fitting rooms (nonexistent in wholesale houses), courteous service (you are usually not allowed to browse), and exceptional merchandise at prices 20% to 50% or 60% off what you would have to pay retail. Usually, it's cash only and no returns.

ABE J. GELLER, 9th floor, 141 West 36th St., between Broadway and Seventh Ave. Tel. 736-8077.

Start your Seventh Avenue expedition at Abe J. Geller. You'll be dazzled by racks and racks of stunning clothes, all with name brand labels still in them! Management claims that prices are 40% to 60% lower than they are in the fancy stores, but even so they're not inexpensive. **Open:** Mon–Fri 9am–5pm; Sat 9am–3pm.

MS., MISS OR MRS., 3rd floor, 462 Seventh Ave., at 35th St. Tel. 736-0557.

You may have to wait a little while to be waited on here, but it will be worth every minute. MMM represents some 200 of the top-name manufacturers on Seventh Avenue, in sportswear, coats (all-wool, imported tweed, novelty, raincoats), and an extensive selection of designer dresses and cocktail/evening dresses, averaging $150 to $400. Their markup is very low, so your savings are phenomenal (30% to 50%—and more at the time of seasonal closeouts). *Note:* They ask that you phone them first and tell them you read about them in this book. Located diagonally opposite Macy's. **Open:** Mon–Fri 9am–5:30pm; Sat 9am–4pm. **Closed:** July–Aug.

CONSIGNMENT SHOPS

To find out where some of the city's smartest women pick up designer clothing at a mere fraction of their original prices, join them at New York's consignment shops. Designer or upscale merchandise, in excellent condition, is left here for resale. You'd be amazed at what can turn up at these places. And the prices are painless.

DEBUT II, 136 West 83rd St., between Columbus and Amsterdam Aves. Tel. 875-8809.

The only consignment shop on the West Side, Debut II has both new and gently worn merchandise, with a full line of sportswear, formal gowns, and maternity wear. I spotted a magnificent bridal gown here for a mere $150 and an $850 Yves Saint Laurent outfit for $110. Shoes, handbags, accessories, and more. **Open:** Mon–Wed and Fri 11am–6:30pm; Thurs until 7:30pm, Sat until 6pm.

DESIGNERS RESALE, 324 East 81st St., between Second and First Aves. Tel. 734-3639.

Beautiful dresses, outerwear, accessories, jewelry, and many selections for petite women are available here. **Open:** Mon–Wed and Fri 11am–7pm; Thurs until 8pm; Sat 10am–6pm.

ENCORE RESALE DRESS SHOP, 1132 Madison Ave., at 84th St. Tel. 879-2850.

Two floors of good finds are here, including clothing, furs, new merchandise, handbags, and accessories. **Open:** Mon–Sat 10:30am–6pm; Thurs until 7pm.

MICHAEL'S, 2nd floor, 1041 Madison Ave., 2nd at 79th St. Tel. 737-7273.

Some of the city's wealthiest women leave their glamorous clothing here: The top name designers are well represented. **Open:** Sun–Wed and Fri–Sat. 9:30–6pm; Thurs until 8pm. **Closed:** Sat in Summer.

CLOSEOUTS

Where, under one roof, might you find $250 watches for $55, $30 sneakers for $7.95, a $90 set of cookware for $30, a $20 name-brand perfume for $2.95, or a $2 lip gloss for 29¢? These are the kinds of bargains New Yorkers are crazy about, and you will be, too, once you discover the stores of either **Odd-Job Trading Company** or **The Pushcart, Job Lot Trading Company.** Both of these companies do an amazing business in brand-name goods acquired at auctions and closeouts or as overruns. Stock changes constantly, but it's always worthwhile to see what they have in camping and sporting goods, hardware, pet supplies, kitchenware and china, toys, linens, stationery, and party goods—to name just a few categories. At these stores, the crowds are apt to be fierce, especially during lunch hours. Odd-Job has huge stores: one at 7 E. 40th St., another at 66 W. 48th St., a third at 149 W. 32nd St. The Pushcart has its original store, downtown at 140 Church St. in the City Hall area, in an atmosphere re-creating the old-time pushcarts of the Lower East Side; another one downtown at 80 Nassau St.; and an uptown store at 1633 Broadway, at 50th Street. For the Church Street Pushcart, take the IND or IRT subway to Chambers Street.

SOMETHING FOR THE MEN

With the price of men's suits rising astronomically, many of the better-heeled men in town have left their usual haberdashers and are now shopping the outlet stores. There are many such stores advertised, but not all deliver first quality: Some simply buy last year's or unpopular styles. The ones mentioned here carry fine clothing and prices about 30% to 40% lower than elsewhere. Most levy a slight charge for alterations. The decor in some places may be pipe rack, but service is usually good—and you can't beat the prices. Already listed above, **Syms,** in the financial district at 42 Trinity Place, is very popular for menswear, carrying shoes as well as apparel and accessories.

DOLLAR BILLS, 99 East 42nd St., next to Grand Central Station. Tel. 867-0212.

It looks like nothing much from the outside, but inside there are surprises! Dollar Bills buys directly from Italian designers and sells top-name, avant-garde men's suits for 40% to 50% of what they would go for in the fancy stores. Shipments vary from day to day, so it's a matter of luck as to what you'll find. Women's designer knits are also available.

GILCREST CLOTHES CO., 3rd floor, 900 Broadway, near 20th St. Tel. 254-8933.

Top designer labels from Europe and the United States are represented here—Perry Ellis, Ralph Lauren, and Felix Ungaro are a few. Tuxedos are stocked, too. Discounts are substantial. **Open:** Mon–Fri 7:30am–5pm, Sat 8:30am–4pm; Sun 10am–4pm. **Closed:** Sat–Sun in summer.

HARRY ROTHMAN'S, 200 Park Ave. South (17th St. at Union Square). Tel. 777-7400.

★ Harry Rothman's buys from top manufacturers, puts its own label on the merchandise, and sells prestigious clothing for 20% to 50% off regular retail prices. This is the high end of the menswear line, the same kind of clothing you find at Barney's or Saks Fifth Avenue—but at much more comfortable prices. A full line of menswear—from suits to socks, shirts, ties, and outerwear—is available.

L. S. MEN'S CLOTHING, 19 West 44th St., room 403. Tel. 575-0933.

This is a small family operation that's been in business for over 40 years. Their traditional woolen suits are sold at discounts of 45% to 65% off comparable prices of $385 to $950; and they have many contemporary fashions and sportswear, as well as tuxedos for sale.

MOE GINSBURG, 162 Fifth Ave., at the corner of 21st St. Tel. 242-3482.

Four floors of men's clothing, furnishings, and shoes are well priced at Moe Ginsburg, and that includes European contemporary and American collections.

NBO MENSWEAR, 1965 Broadway, near 67th St. Tel. 595-1550.

NBO, in a handsome store one block from Lincoln Center, offers a top-flight selection of designer menswear at very good prices. They also have an excellent shoe selection. **Open:** Mon–Sat 10am–9pm; Sun noon–5pm.

PARK KENNY/ROYAL FASHION, 920 Broadway, third floor, at the corner of 21st St. Tel. 477-1948.

There are lots of good buys here: A recent sale advertised super worsted suits at $225 each, custom fabrics sports jackets at $130, and fine worsted slacks at $30 to $55. Shirts, ties, raincoats, and casual wear are always at very good prices.

SAINT LAURIE, LTD., 897 Broadway, at 20th St. Tel. 473-0100.

Saint Laurie has been manufacturing classic men's clothing since 1913, and it is sold at some of the finest stores in the country. Their exclusive Avery Lucas menswear collection is attracting much media attention. And they also offer a newly designed collection of women's classic apparel. Prices at the factory-outlet store are about one-third less than in the regular stores. Visitors are invited to take self-guided tours of the workrooms on three different floors.

LOWER EAST SIDE SHOPPING

There's nothing like shopping to whet the appetite—and tire the feet—so while you're shopping here, have a rest and enjoy a dairy meal at **Ratner's,** 138 Delancey St., where the pastries are mind-boggling, or sample the legendary corned beef and hot pastrami at **Katz's Delicatessen,** 205 E. Houston St. (Ratner's, a New York tradition since 1905, serves from breakfast to after-theater.) It would be unthinkable to come home from the Lower East Side without "a little something for later"—perhaps a knish or a kugel from **Yonah Schimmel's Knishery,** 137 E. Houston St. (The same family has owned the knishery for over 94 years, bakes 12 varieties of knishes daily in a 103-year-old brick oven, and has a yogurt culture that has been ongoing for over 84 years!) Or pick up some lox or caviar or pistachio nuts from famed **Russ & Daughters,** 179 E. Houston St., continuously owned and operated by the Russ family since 1914. Taste, shop, enjoy!

You could spend a week shopping the Lower East Side, and I could write a book just telling you about the bargains here, in these narrow, tenemented streets where New York's immigrant Jewish colony once flourished. Many of the shopkeepers live uptown or in the wealthy suburbs now, and so do most of the customers. But they still keep coming down here for marvelous bargains in just about everything. I'll simply point you in the direction of a few of my favorites and let you take it from there. Bring plenty of cash, wear good walking shoes, and be prepared for sometimes inconvenient or nonexistent fitting rooms (although this situation has improved of late) and usually a strict no-return policy. Try to come during the week, since most places are closed late Friday and all day Saturday, and when they open again on Sunday, it's total insanity.

Subway: F or Q, M, or J train to Delancey and Essex streets, or D (Sixth Ave. line) to Grand St.; about 20 minutes from Midtown Manhattan.

Clothing for Children

RICE & BRESKIN, 323 Grand St. Tel. 925-5515.
This is a good place to stock up on name-brand children's clothing—brands like Healthtex, Carter's, and Renzo Rothschild. The range goes from layettes (in which they are a specialist) to toddlers to size 14. Discount is 20% off already low prices.

Clothing for Men

G&G INTERNATIONAL, 53 Orchard St. Tel. 431-4530.
Again, top names—Adolpho and Geoffrey Beene, Bill Blass, Harvé Benard, and more—are offered here at good discounts.

PAN AM MEN'S WEAR, 50 Orchard St. Tel. 925-7032.
Discounts are substantial on such top names as Polo by Ralph Lauren, Charles Jourdan, Perry Ellis, and many Italian designers.

Linens & Home Furnishings

EZRA COHEN, 307 Grand St. Tel. 925-7800.
This is a great place for buys in designer linens, towels, bed-spreads, and more.

HARRIS LEVY, 278 Grand St. Tel. 226-3102.
A direct importer of fine bed and table linens for over 98 years, Harris Levy also features a complete bath shop, closet and kitchen accessories, and a custom boutique.

Clothing for Women

BREAKAWAY DESIGNER FASHIONS AND FURS, 125 Orchard St. Tel. 475-6660.
Name-brand sportswear, designer duds, and magnificent furs at solid discounts can be found here.

FISHKIN KNITWEAR CO., 314 and 316 Grand St. Tel. 225-6538.
This old-time favorite has wonderful discounts on such designers at Adrienne Vittadini and Regina Porter—plus some of the best deals anywhere on top-level cashmere sweaters.

FORMAN'S APPAREL, 82, 94, and 78 Orchard St. Tel. 228-2500.
Prestigious designer labels, good discounts, and a store to suit your size—what more could the bargain shopper ask for? Regular-sized women should try Forman's Designer Apparel at 82 Orchard; petite women, 5'4" and under, will find a whole store of fashion for them at Forman's Petites, 94 Orchard; and larger women, who often have problems finding stylish clothes, have a source for designer-label sportswear, dresses, and suits at Forman's Plus, 78 Orchard.

SHULIE'S, 175 Orchard St. Tel. 473-2480.
You've heard of the designer Tahari? Well, come meet his sister, Shulie. Her prices on her famous brother's clothing are very relaxing, and the discounts are deep—you'll pay about half of what you would uptown. She also carries well-known designer shoes at greatly discounted prices.

Women's Lingerie

D & A MERCHANDISE COMPANY, 22 Orchard St. Tel. 925-4766.
These long-time merchants have all kinds of lingerie and underwear for everybody in the family (catalogs at $2 will be sent on request).

GOLDMAN & COHEN, 55 Orchard St. Tel. 966-0737.
This place discounts at least 20% on fine-quality women's lingerie and loungewear; you'll want to stock up when you see the prices!

MENDEL WEISS, 91 Orchard St. Tel. 925-6815.
The shop is nothing fancy to look at, but they do have couturier underwear at unfancy prices. *Women's Day* magazine has called it "one of the best mail-order houses in America."

Gloves

BERNARD KRIEGER, 216 Grand St. Tel. 226-4927.
Leather gloves, mostly imported from Italy, are a real bargain here, and so are ski gloves, wools, and suedes, for both men and

women. They also carry some attractive women's hats, designer scarves, and a good line of Lycra tops and bottoms.

Handbags

FINE & KLEIN, 119 Orchard St. Tel. 674-6720.

Top name and designer bags are sold on three floors; discounts are around 35%.

Shoes

LACE UP SHOE SHOP, 110 Orchard St. Tel. 475-8040.

Current styles and colors of top designer footwear—Anne Klein, Charles Jourdan, Arshe, Yves Saint Laurent, Joan & David, Evan Picone, and more—at very good prices. They also carry the largest selection of both men's and women's Mephisto walking, biking, hiking, and casual footwear in the northeast.

ORCHARD BOOTERY, 75 Orchard St. Tel. 966-0688.

Look for the top designer names here—Bruno Meli, André Assous, Charles David, Drosana, Peter Kaiser, and Martinez Valero—and more, discounted at least 30%.

GOURMET FOOD STORES

Allow me to introduce you to the word "appetizing," which is not an adjective but a New York noun (or state of mind) that means salty smoked fish and pickled herring and lusty breads and fragrant coffee beans and heady pâtés and delicate cheeses—and much more. New York has at least four appetizing emporiums to which the faithful make pilgrimages from near and very far. Each is gigantic, is mind-boggling in its variety of offerings, and purveys food (including gourmet takeout) of superb quality. Make tracks to the following: In SoHo, **Dean & Deluca,** 584 Broadway, corner Prince St. (tel. 431-1691); in Greenwich Village, **Balducci's,** 426 Ave. of the Americas, at 9th St. (tel. 673-2600); on the Upper East Side, **Grace's Marketplace,** 1237 Third Ave., at 71st St. (tel. 737-0600); and on the Upper West Side, **Zabar's,** 2245 Broadway, at 80th St. (tel. 787-2000), which also has a mezzanine full of housewares and gourmet kitchen gadgets at the best prices in town.

HERBAL COSMETICS & SOAPS

THE BODY SHOP, at A&S Plaza, 901 Ave. of the Americas at 33rd St. Tel. 268-7427.

Cruelty-free cosmetics—that's an idea whose time has come. Here's a company that refuses to test ingredients or final products on animals; is committed to protecting the environment; uses natural-based, close-to-source ingredients whenever possible; and sells its customers straightforward products in inexpensive packaging and encourages them to come back for refills. Body Shop's free catalog is well worth your attention: Phone toll free 800/541-2535 to order one.

Other branches of The Body Shop are at 16 Fulton St. downtown (tel. 480-9876); 485 Madison Ave., at 52nd St. (tel. 832-0812); 733 Lexington Ave., at 61st St. (tel. 755-7851); and 2159 Broadway, at 76th St. (tel. 721-2947).

CAMBRIDGE CHEMISTS, 21 East 65th St. Tel. 734-5678.

This is the kind of place that makes visiting Europeans feel right at home. Here you can buy pure and natural products by Cyclax of London (the only U.S. agent for these beauty products used by Queen Elizabeth), Floris, Penhaligons, G. F. Trumper, Taylor of Old Bond Street, Phyto Products from France (which has a unique sun-protectant cream for the hair), and a variety of other European toiletries, cosmetics, and treatment preparations. Although a listing of their clients might read like a page out of the Social Register, everyone is treated with old-fashioned courtesy. A wooden shaving bowl, a natural clove pomander in a bed of potpourri, a perfume vaporizer, or a crystal atomizer are a few unique gift possibilities here.

CASWELL-MASSEY, 518 Lexington Ave., at 48th St. Tel. 755-2254.

The oldest chemists and perfumers in the United States, Caswell-Massey, in business for 235 years, still carries the same colognes that were favorites with George and Martha Washington and the Marquis de Lafayette! Pick and choose from the largest collection of imported soaps in the world, imported shaving equipment, pomanders, potpourri, and cough drops and lozenges from England and France. A wondrous nostalgic place full of things you can't get elsewhere. For a copy of their fanciful catalog phone toll free 800/326-0500.

Other stores are located at the South Street Seaport (tel. 608-5401) and the World Financial Center (tel. 945-2630).

ORIGINS, 402 West Broadway. Tel. 219-1764.

If the idea of Plant Spirits/Splashing Waters or Sensory Therapy Inhalations or Honey Elixirs appeals to you, visit this sparkling, environmentally sensitive store in the heart of SoHo. An alternative-cosmetic company concerned with both inner and outer beauty and well-being, Origins happily marries nature and science in its products. It uses recycled materials whenever possible and is committed to no animal testing and using no animal-derived materials: its brushes, for example, are handmade of Japanese palm-plant bristles, with birch handles. They also feature such easy-on-the environment items as handmade floral stationery, leather-looking handbags made of natural rubber, and T-shirts made of 100%-natural unbleached cotton.

IRISH IMPORTS

THE IRISH SECRET, 155 Spring St., in SoHo. Tel. 334-6711.

People expect Irish import stores to be filled with traditional items such as Aran wool fishermen's sweaters, tweed jackets and walking hats, cashmere and mohair capes and coats, and the like. Well, this store has them in plentiful supply, but it also has a "secret"—some highly fashionable clothing, including ladies linen dresses and skirts, men's silk and linen jackets, brightly colored Irish linen men's shirts, and much more—by fashionable Dublin designers. Irish writer's T-shirts—take your pick of George Bernard Shaw, William Butler Yeats, James Joyce, or Samuel Beckett—are just $19.95.

JEWELRY

New York is the diamond center of the country, and if you're convinced that diamonds (or even pearls) are a girl's best friend, you should have a look at some of the town's outstanding jewelry shops. A stroll along 47th Street, between Fifth and Sixth avenues, where diamonds are being traded on street corners, polished in workrooms, and sold in a number of small jewelry stores, puts you right in the heart of the jewelry world. To catch the Village jewelry scene, walk on West 4th Street between Sixth and Seventh avenues; here and elsewhere in the Village you'll find any number of small shops selling avant-garde rings, pins, and brooches.

CARTIER, 2 East 52nd St., at Fifth Ave. Tel. 753-0111.
You can find old Cartier designs of the 1920s and 1930s as well as today's classic jewelry, plus Paris-designed watches, jewelry, and small leather goods at "young prices" in the Cartier Boutique. There's also a branch of Cartier at Trump Tower, 725 Fifth Ave. at 56th St. (tel. 308-0843).

TIFFANY & CO., 727 Fifth Ave., at 57th St. Tel. 755-8000.
Beside the splendors of its emerald brooches and diamond necklaces and the like, Tiffany also has inexpensive gift items, and an affordably priced collection of sterling silver jewelry. It's *the* place for wedding gifts.

KILIMS

BEYOND THE BOSPHORUS, 79 Sullivan St., between Spring and Broome Sts. Tel. 219-8257.
One-of-a-kind kilims, handmade flatwoven Turkish rugs and pillows that are between 50 to 100 years old can be found at this cozy little shop on the western fringes of SoHo. Proprietor Ismail Basbagi travels home to Turkey frequently to purchase the rugs, and since there is no middleman involved and since he has them cleaned and repaired in Turkey, he is able to offer them at remarkably good prices, starting at $30 for pillows. Kilims look great as wall hangings, runners, or room-size rugs, and wear practically forever. Special sales are held in January and July, when everything comes down about 30%. Mr. Basbagi will ship rugs and pillows anywhere in the country. **Open:** Tues–Sun noon–6pm (also open "by chance or by appointment"). **Closed:** Sun in summer.

MUSIC

HMV (His Majesty's Voice), Lexington Ave. at 86th St. Tel. 348-0800.
This East Side store, said to be the largest in the United States (40,000 square feet), has a permanent stage where performers showcase their recordings. Both this store and the only-slightly-smaller West Side address, aim to make shopping very pleasant, with audio and visual disc jockeys, and listening booths. Prices on its vast stock are competitive with the other mega-retailer, Tower Records (see below). Their West Side store is at Broadway at 72nd St. (tel. 721-5900).

TOWER RECORDS & VIDEO, 692 Broadway, at East 4th St. Tel. 505-1500.
A "happening" since it first opened—a place where people go to

be seen as much as to buy recordings—Tower still continues strong. As many as 6,000 people are said to pack the aisles on Saturday and Sunday. Tower stocks half a million recordings (in all configurations) in every conceivable category, sells many of them at discount prices, and also shows videos on 17 screens.

Its Sales Annex, which carries over 200,000 items in closeout, overstock, and out-of-print merchandise, is located nearby at 920 Lafayette St. Also nearby, at 383 Lafayette St. (tel. 505-1166) is Tower Video and Bookstore. In the Lincoln Center area, at 1961 Broadway, at 66th St. (tel. 799-2500), there's another huge and exciting Tower Records, and at 1977 Broadway you'll find another Tower Video (tel. 496-2500). **Open:** Daily 9am–midnight.

TOYS

F.A.O. SCHWARZ, 767 Fifth Ave. at 58th St. Tel. 644-9400.

If you have children with you, your first stop should be America's most famous toy store, a kid's wonderland, with everything from a talking tree to a 28-foot-high clock tower that sings birthday greetings. In addition to a vast array of toys, including life-sized plush lions and giraffes and a gas-powered children's car, they also have a children's clothing boutique and a hair salon. **Open:** Mon–Wed and Fri–Sat 10am–6pm; Thurs until 8pm; Sun noon–6pm.

PENNYWHISTLE TOYS, 448 Columbus Ave., between 80th and 81st Sts. Tel. 873-9090.

This eclectic toy store is filled with wonderful things, all of them preselected by the store's savvy buyers. They carry a vast array of wooden toys, puzzles, games, educational toys that challenge a child's imagination, and arts and crafts—many of the items imported from Italy, England, and Sweden. They also have dress-up costumes, outdoor games, and the best in infant-care products. Because they're in the midst of the artsy Columbus Avenue shopping area, they tend to carry things not found in ordinary stores. And the service is out-of-the-ordinary, too—very helpful and friendly; their large, neighborhood clientele is on a first-name basis.

Open: Mon–Wed and Fri–Sat 10am–6 or 7pm; Thurs until 8pm; Sun 11am–6pm. There are two other Penny Whistle stores in town: on the East Side at 1238 Madison Ave., at 91st St. (tel. 369-3868), and in SoHo at 132 Spring St. (tel. 925-2088).

WHIMSY

THE LAST WOUNDUP, 1595 Second Ave., at 83rd St. Tel. 288-7585.

You won't believe this incredible collection of windup toys and music boxes. Amid a scene of happy Victorian clutter, modern and antique toys range from fire-spitting apes for $3 to a tin duck pedaling a bicycle for $40. Wonderful operatic music boxes are $75. This shop is irresistible for kids of all ages. **Open:** Mon–Wed 10am–6pm; Thurs–Sat 10am–9pm; Sun noon–6pm.

STAR MAGIC, 275 Amsterdam Ave., corner of 73rd St. Tel. 769-2020.

This is a magical place for anyone tuned in to either inner or outer space. These "space-age gifts of science and spirit" feature everything from telescopes, globes, robots, holograms, and space shuttle models to healing crystals, pyramids, crystal jewelry, and "celestial music." There's also a Star Magic downtown at 734 Broadway (tel. 228-7500), and at 1256 Lexington Ave. (tel. 988-0100).

THINK BIG!, 390 West Broadway. Tel. 925-7300.

New York's wittiest sculpture gallery, Think Big!, in SoHo, has affordable collectibles for everyone: how about a 5-foot-tall toothbrush (use it as a towel rack), a 6-foot-long pencil, or a 2-foot-high single galosh that makes a nifty umbrella holder? Prices begin around $10 and go way up. Call for a catalog; they will ship anywhere. **Open:** Mon–Sat 11am–7pm; Sun noon–6pm.

CHAPTER 10

NEW YORK NIGHTS

1. **THE PERFORMING ARTS**
2. **THE CLUB & MUSIC SCENE**
3. **THE BAR SCENE**
4. **MORE ENTERTAINMENT**

New York City is, of course, the entertainment capital of the nation, and here you will catch not only Broadway theater and New York opera but also outstanding musical, dance, and theater groups from all over the world—everything from the Moscow Circus to the Comédie Française.

New York's many beautiful parks are also sites for an extraordinary array of musical and operatic performances, plays, festivals, poetry readings, and much more. Of course, almost all of these outdoor events are in the summer. Call 360-1333 to get the **Parks Department's** recorded message giving all free events in the parks and in the rest of the city.

TICKET-BUYING MADE SIMPLE Want to know what's playing in New York in theater, dance, and music? Talk to a computer. **NYC/On Stage,** a service of the Theater Development Fund, sponsored by the American Express Card, enables callers to find out what's playing, when, and how to buy tickets. Press a series of buttons refining your query into ever-narrowing categories. Eventually, you'll be able to make your selection and charge your tickets "by American Express or any other means." The toll-free out-of-state number is 800-STAGE NY. The New York State number is 212/768-1818. Both numbers are in service 24 hours every day.

Be sure to pay a visit to the **Music & Dance Booth,** in Bryant Park, on 42nd Street just east of Sixth Avenue (behind the New York Public Library). Half-price day-of-performance tickets for music and dance concerts (including those at Lincoln Center, Carnegie Hall, 92nd Street Y, and City Center) are available there. Advance full-price tickets are also on sale for many events. The box office is open Tuesday, Thursday, and Friday from noon to 2pm and from 3 to 7pm; Wednesday and Saturday, from 11am to 2pm and 3 to 7pm; and Sunday from noon to 6pm. Tickets for Monday performances may be purchased on Sunday. Call 382-2323 for information about ticket availability.

See below, under "Theater," for information on how to get theater tickets.

1. THE PERFORMING ARTS

OPERA

METROPOLITAN OPERA COMPANY, Lincoln Center, 64th St. and Broadway. Tel. 362-6000.

One of the most prestigious opera companies in the world, the 110-year-old Metropolitan continues to enthrall opera buffs. The season usually runs from late September to mid-April. Even though most of its seats are taken by subscribers, there's a good chance you can get tickets for a single performance. The best way to do so is to phone the box office directly and ask to be put on the mailing list for a brochure. This will include a "single sales" calendar and inform you of the earliest dates when mail and phone orders will be accepted. You should, of course, mail or phone in your order as early as possible.

Failing all else, go to the Metropolitan box office or a ticket broker as soon as you arrive in town. Unless it's a *very* popular production with very popular singers, you should be able to get a seat. The only way to really save money is to stand: Standees' places go on sale on Saturday at 10am for all performances Saturday through Friday. Be sure to bring opera glasses—the house is very large. **Prices:** Orchestra tickets $55–$100 Mon–Thurs; $60–$117 Fri–Sat. Family Circle tickets $20 Mon–Thurs; $21 Fri–Sat. Standees' places $9 in Family Circle; $13 in the orchestra.

THE NEW YORK CITY OPERA, in the New York State Theater, Lincoln Center. Tel. 870-5570.

Now in its 48th year, the New York City Opera also has a superb company and is better than ever these days. The season begins early in July and runs through mid-November (there is no winter season). Write to the company at 20 Lincoln Center, New York, NY 10023, for a brochure. Mail-order three or four weeks in advance will usually do the trick. Otherwise, try the box office or a ticket broker. You can also buy tickets through Ticketmaster, which will tell you if there are tickets in your price range (tel. 307-7171). **Prices:** Tickets $10–$68.

AMATO OPERA THEATER, 319 Bowery, at the corner of 2nd St. Tel. 228-8200.

A New York standby for over 40 years now, the Amato Opera Theater gives full productions of the classic repertory—Verdi, Puccini, Mozart, Rossini, and Donizetti—as well as rarely performed operas. Scores of its "graduates" have gone on to sing at the Metropolitan and the New York City Opera. Tickets can be reserved by calling the box office up until a day before curtain time. Performances are usually given weekends from September to May. **Prices:** Tickets $16.

CLASSICAL MUSIC

NEW YORK PHILHARMONIC, Avery Fisher Hall at Lincoln Center, 65th St. and Broadway. Tel. 875-5030.

One of the treasures of New York and of the world of music, the New York Philharmonic is the oldest symphonic orchestra in the United States and one of the oldest in the world. In September of 1992, it began its 151st season under the new leadership of Kurt Masur, Music Director. It is considered an orchestra of virtuoso players. During the subscription season, September to June, you should have no trouble getting a ticket at the box office. Or, you may write to the following address for a New York Philharmonic concert calendar: New York Philharmonic, Avery Fisher Hall, 10 Lincoln Center, New York, NY 10023-6973.

In the summer, you may be able to get to hear the Philharmonic in a series of free concerts held in the city's parks in July and August: See local papers for exact listings. These concerts are *popular!* The one given in Central Park on July 5, 1986, under the baton of Zubin Mehta, attracted no less than 800,000 people! Come early and bring a blanket and a picnic supper.

MUSIC IN THE MUSEUMS

What could be lovelier than hearing a major concert artist give a free Sunday-afternoon recital in the splendid setting of the **Frick Collection?** Phone them at 288-0700 for details on getting tickets. Concerts are held September through May. You can also listen to live concerts or recorded music on certain Sundays in the medieval splendors of **The Cloisters** (part of the Metropolitan Museum of Art, but located uptown in Fort Tryon Park; call 923-3700 for ticket information).

These are only two of the many fine musical offerings in New York's major museums. Check the papers for news of frequent concerts, too, at the **Metropolitan Museum of Art,** the **Museum of the City of New York,** and the **New-York Historical Society,** among others.

MUSIC IN THE PARKS & PUBLIC PLACES

During the summer, there is free music in the parks and other public places almost every night, from the **Summerstage** performing arts series in the Central Park Bandshell to concerts at **Damrosch Park** in Lincoln Center, the **Riverside Park Rotunda,** and **Washington Square Park;** also look for the **New York Philharmonic and Metropolitan Opera in the Park.** The **South Street Seaport** is the home of frequent free concerts, and **Summergarden,** in the Museum of Modern Art Sculpture Garden, is a particular delight. Downtown, frequent concerts are held on the Plaza of the **World Financial Center.** For timely listings, see the *New York Times,* or *New York* magazine, *The New Yorker,* and *The Village Voice.* All of these are available at newsstands throughout the city.

DANCE COMPANIES

New York's dance offerings are among the greatest in the world. Its leading ballet companies perform at Lincoln Center: The **New York City Ballet** at the New York State Theater and the **American Ballet Theater** at the Metropolitan Opera House. City Center is home to the exciting **Joffrey Ballet;** the **Alvin Ailey American Dance Theater;** and the **Merce Cunningham, Martha Graham,** and **Paul Taylor** companies. The Lincoln Center halls, City Center, and the Joyce Theater (a major dance venue located in Chelsea) frequently play host to visiting U.S. companies as well as to those from overseas for short seasons, as does Carnegie Hall, the Paramount at Madison Square Garden, and the Brooklyn Academy of Music.

MAJOR CONCERT HALLS & ALL-PURPOSE AUDITORIUMS

LINCOLN CENTER FOR THE PERFORMING ARTS, 670 Lincoln Center Plaza. Tel. 875-5400.

New York's most important center for music, dance, and opera is, of course, Lincoln Center. **Avery Fisher Hall** is the home of the New York Philharmonic; the **Metropolitan Opera House** of the Metropolitan Opera Company and American ballet theater; the **New York State Theater** of the New York City Opera Company and New York City Ballet. All of the houses, including the smaller **Alice Tully Hall,** host preeminent performing groups from all over the world. Lincoln Center Theater makes its home at the **Vivian Beaumont Theater** and the **Mitzi E. Newhouse Theater.** Lincoln Center Out-of-Doors presents a free, summer-long festival of music and dance by groups from around the world—everything from Latin music to jazz to a Marathon Rockabilly Jamboree and a Mardi Gras Carnival and parade. Lincoln Center Plaza, Damrosch Park, and Guggenheim Bandshell are also the scenes of delightful free summer presentations. And the fountain plaza is surely one of New York's most glamorous meeting places (remember it from the movie *Moonstruck?*).

Also check out what's being offered by the Juilliard School (tel. 769-7406).

To find out what's happening at Lincoln Center, check local papers when you arrive. To get a two-months calendar of information in advance, send a stamped (52¢) self-addressed envelope to Lincoln Center Calendar, 70 Lincoln Center Plaza, New York, NY 10023.

For information on guided tours of Lincoln Center, see Chapter 7.

CARNEGIE HALL, 57th St. at Seventh Ave. Tel. 247-7800.

On May 5, 1891, Peter Ilyich Tchaikovsky rose to the podium to conduct the first concert at the hall that would become known as a symbol of musical excellence all over the world. Caruso and Paderewski, Heifetz and Horowitz, Casals and Bernstein, Benny Goodman and the Beatles—they are all part of the legend. Miraculously saved from the wrecker's ball in 1960 and extensively restored in 1986 in time for its gala centennial celebration, Carnegie Hall continues to present world-renowned orchestras, chamber groups, and recitals. The gilded, red-plush auditorium, with its splendid acoustics, is perhaps the best in the city. Intimate concerts are presented in its jewel-box-like Weill Recital Hall.

Tours of this National Historical Landmark are given September through July, on Monday, Tuesday, and Thursday at 11:30, 2 and 3pm. Tickets are $6 adults; $5 seniors and students; $3 children. For information, call 247-7800.

The new **Carnegie Hall Museum,** 154 W. 57th St., second floor, is open daily from 11am to 4:30pm and half an hour before a concert and during intermission. Admission is free. For information, call 903-9629.

Single concert admissions are usually available at the box office, or in advance by phoning 247-7800. Prices vary with events.

TOWN HALL, 123 West 43rd St. Tel. 840-2824.

Built by suffragettes 70 years ago as a public forum that would enlighten women on the social and political issues of the day, Town Hall has been a platform for the great speakers of the times—from

Winston Churchill to William Butler Yeats. Because of its superb acoustics and intimate sight lines, the hall also became a stage for legendary concert performances from Heifetz to Billie Holiday. With the revitalization of the Times Square area and the building's major renovation in 1984, Town Hall is once again one of the city's preeminent cultural facilities. It produces a full season of films, music, concerts, and dramatic readings, and is now in the second year of a provocative 10-year New York cultural festival, "Century of Change." Tickets for many events are quite modest, from $10 up.

CITY CENTER THEATER, 131 West 55th St. Tel. 581-7907.

Built originally as a Masonic temple in 1923 but taken over by the city under the reign of Fiorello La Guardia as a "cultural center for all New Yorkers," City Center is one of New York's largest, most inviting, and beloved theaters. It is now recognized as the country's premier performance home for dance and is host to many of the nation's leading dance troupes, including the Alvin Ailey American Dance Theater; Dance Theatre of Harlem; and the Martha Graham, Merce Cunningham, Joffrey Ballet, and Paul Taylor companies. International dance and other performing companies are frequent guests. Ticket prices vary by artist.

THE PARAMOUNT, Madison Square Garden, Seventh Ave., between 33rd and 31st Sts. Tel. 465-6741.

The 5,600-seat replacement of the old Felt Forum is a stunner. *The* place for top popular artists—Cher, Barry Manilow, Bill Cosby, and Patti La Belle have all appeared here—and other major attractions.

RADIO CITY MUSIC HALL, 1260 Ave. of the Americas, at 50th St. Tel. 247-4777.

The world's biggest theater and perhaps its most famous, Radio City Music Hall is still alive and well, restored to its 1930s art deco splendor. Movies are not usually shown here, but the Rockettes are still around, and there's a huge variety of entertainment—you might catch Aretha Franklin or Diana Ross or the Moiseyev Dance Company. Christmas and Easter see major holiday spectaculars for family audiences.

For tickets, the price of which varies with the event, apply to the box office or call Ticketmaster (tel. 212/307-7171) and charge with a major credit card. The number listed above provides a computerized information source of current and future events.

THE TISCH CENTER FOR THE ARTS, at the 92nd Street Y, 92nd St. and Lexington Ave. Tel. 996-1100.

The Upper East Side is home to one of New York's leading performing arts centers: the Tisch Center for the Arts, at the 92nd Street Y. The New York Chamber Symphony, under the direction of Gerard Schwarz, performs here more than two dozen times per season. You can also hear such renowned chamber ensembles as the Tokyo and String Quartets, as well as solo recitals performed by the likes of Shlomo Mintz, Julian Bream, Richard Stoltzman, and Paula Robeson. Concerts are given September through June. **Prices:** Tickets $12.50–$35.

Note: Tisch Center is also the home of the Unterberg Poetry Center, where outstanding writers read from their own works on most Monday nights, September through May. Arthur Miller, Susan

Sontag, Umberto Ecco, and Philip Roth are among those scheduled for the current season.

BEACON THEATER, 2124 Broadway, at 74th St. Tel. 496-7070.

One of the city's most splendid movie palaces when it was built in 1928, the Beacon became a city landmark in 1978. It is noted for its splendid art deco lobby and an eclectic mix of other architectural styles. Now it is a favorite venue for contemporary popular music performances, theater, revival films, and opening night premieres of new movies. Ticket prices vary with events.

THE BROOKLYN ACADEMY OF MUSIC, 30 Lafayette St., Brooklyn. Tel. 718/636-4100.

This is the oldest performing arts center in the United States. Its opulent Opera House and Playhouse, and the smaller experimental theater, the Leqercq Space, are home to the famed Next Wave Festival. The complex is also an active center for dance, opera, children's programs, and theater. Music is well represented through the concerts of the resident Brooklyn Philharmonic Orchestra. A fourth theater—the BAM Majestic Theater—is a refurbished 1905 vaudeville house that has been retained in a state of suspended ruin and is home to theater, music, and dance. It is located one-and-a-half blocks from BAM's main building at 651 Fulton St. Most events are held between September and June. **Prices:** Tickets from $10.

THEATER

Many people come to New York for only one reason—to take in as much theater as possible. Indeed, the very name "Broadway" has become synonymous with the American theater, and whether you're a "tired businessperson" or an ardent avant-gardist, you will want to attend a few plays while you're in New York. But you will have two problems: first, getting seats; second, getting seats that you can afford. There are seven general tips for dealing with this sticky wicket.

TIPS FOR PLAYING THE BROADWAY THEATER TICKET GAME

1. Write ahead for tickets. As soon as you know you are coming to New York—even if it's months ahead of the date—write to the theater box offices for the tickets you want. This is especially important for hit musicals, often sold out months in advance. (To find out what will be playing, consult the Sunday "Arts & Leisure" section of the *New York Times,* which is sold everywhere.) That way, you will be assured of a seat at box-office prices. If you wait until you get into town, you will probably have to resort to a ticket broker's services (they have branches in almost every hotel in the city), and then you must pay a commission on every seat. And you will have a hard time getting seats for the hits.

2. Pick the previews. As out-of-town tryouts for new Broadway shows have gotten too expensive and complicated, in the last few years the trend has been to substitute these with New York "previews." So you can often realize considerable savings on a preview ticket, even for musicals. There will be some changes in the productions before opening night, of course, when the shows are "set," and you are taking a chance since you have no reviews to guide you. But if it's a play that's been imported after a long and

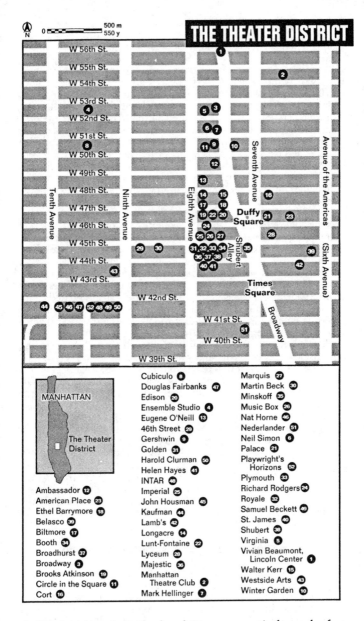

THE THEATER DISTRICT

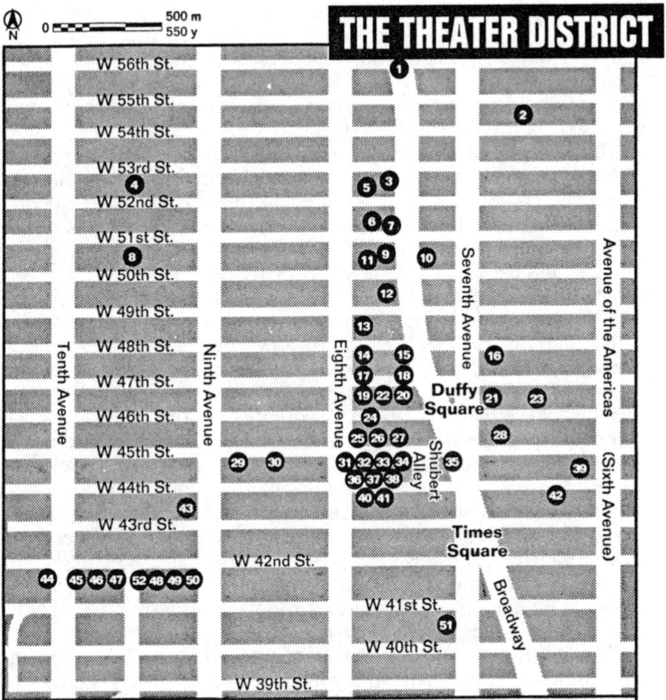

N
0
500 m
550 y
W 56th St.
W 55th St.
W 54th St.
W 53rd St.
W 52nd St.
W 51st St.
W 50th St.
W 49th St.
W 48th St.
W 47th St.
W 46th St.
W 45th St.
W 44th St.
W 43rd St.
W 42nd St.
W 41st St.
W 40th St.
W 39th St.
Tenth Avenue
Ninth Avenue
Eighth Avenue
Seventh Avenue
Avenue of the Americas (Sixth Avenue)
Duffy Square
Shubert Alley
Times Square
Broadway

MANHATTAN
The Theater District

Ambassador ⑫
American Place ㉓
Ethel Barrymore ⑱
Belasco ㊴
Biltmore ⑰
Booth ㉞
Broadhurst ㊲
Broadway ③
Brooks Atkinson ⑲
Circle in the Square ⑪
Cort ⑯
Cubiculo ⑧
Douglas Fairbanks ㊼
Edison ⑳
Ensemble Studio ④
Eugene O'Neill ⑬
46th Street ㉙
Gershwin ⑨
Golden ㉛
Harold Clurman ㊿
Helen Hayes ㊶
INTAR ㊽
Imperial ㉕
John Housman ㊺
Kaufman ㊹
Lamb's ㊷
Longacre ⑭
Lunt-Fontaine ㉒
Lyceum ㉘
Majestic ㊱
Manhattan Theatre Club ②
Mark Hellinger ⑦
Marquis ㉗
Martin Beck ㉚
Minskoff ㉟
Music Box ㉖
Nat Horne ㊻
Nederlander (51)
Neil Simon ⑥
Palace ㉑
Playwright's Horizons (52)
Plymouth ㉝
Richard Rodgers ㉔
Royale ㉜
Samuel Beckett ㊾
St. James ㊵
Shubert ㊳
Virginia ⑤
Vivian Beaumont, Lincoln Center ①
Walter Kerr ⑮
Westside Arts ㊸
Winter Garden ⑩

well-reviewed run in England, or has top stars, or is the work of an important playwright, you're not risking too much. So be your own critic. Preview dates are listed along with the regular ads in the *New York Times*, *New York* magazine, and *The New Yorker*.

3. Join the long line over at TKTS. At its Times Square Theater Center outlet at Broadway and 47th Street (tel. 354-5800), half-price theater tickets are made available for the day of performance only from 3 to 8pm on Monday to Saturday for evening shows, from 10am to 2pm on Wednesday and Saturday for matinees, and from noon to closing for Sunday matinee and evening shows. Downtown at its Lower Manhattan Theater Center on the mezzanine of Two World Trade Center, tickets are available the day of performance for evening shows on Monday to Friday from 11am to 5pm and Saturday from 11am to 1pm, while tickets for Wednesday, Saturday, and Sunday matinees are sold the day before the performance. Naturally, these tickets are for shows that haven't sold out, so don't expect to get the "hottest" tickets this way. There is a $2 service charge, and cash and traveler's checks are accepted.

4. Take the "twofers." When a show is not completely sold every night—perhaps it's at the end of its run or in previews—it often goes on "twofers." This means that, by presenting a slip at the box office, you can buy two seats for the price of one, on certain nights of the week. You're running little risk here, since any show lasting long enough to go on "twofers" has some merit; you will probably not, however, see the original cast. "Twofers" are available at most hotel desks, at restaurant cashier's booths, and at the offices of the Visitors and Convention Bureau, 2 Columbus Circle.

5. Take advantage of standing room. If nothing you want to see is available at TKTS, and you've just got to see the biggest hit in town, your best strategy is to present yourself at the box office (or phone in advance) to see if standing room is available. Some 18 theaters on Broadway sell standing-room spaces (around $12) when their house is completely sold out; sometimes they will sell these tickets in advance. The view may be slightly obstructed in some areas, but usually it is excellent, and you can't beat the price.

6. Go to a ticket broker. If you are willing to pay full price and a little bit more, you'll find the best seats in the house are usually commandeered by them, and they will certainly get you into something. You can often get a ticket for a nonmusical by just going to the box office a day or two before the performance.

7. Call to purchase tickets by credit card. Tickets for many productions can be ordered via phone 24 hours a day, 7 days a week, through **Tele-charge,** 239-6200. **Ticketmaster** (tel. 307-7171) also has ticket service locations at Pennsylvania Station; at Tower Records, Broadway and 66th St.; and at 59th Street Video, 1071 First Ave. It handles tickets for some of the Broadway shows, plus major sporting and music events. Also try **NYC/On Stage** mentioned under "Ticket-buying Made Simple" earlier in this chapter.

OFF-BROADWAY & OFF-OFF-BROADWAY

New York theatergoers have been going "off-Broadway" for well over 50 years now, ever since the **Provincetown Playhouse** set up shop on Macdougal Street to show the works of a young playwright named Eugene O'Neill. Off-Broadway went into high gear, however, in the 1950s and 1960s, the golden years of **Circle in the Square, Theater de Lys,** and the **Cherry Lane Theater.** It was at places like these that the late Geraldine Page rose to stardom, that Edward Albee tried out his first works, and that names like Ionesco and Beckett and Bertolt Brecht and Kurt Weill (his *Threepenny Opera* ran here for seven years) became household words. The longest-running show, on Broadway or off, Tom Jones and Harvey Schmidt's *The Fantasticks,* has run for over 31 years!

The brightest news in the Off-Broadway scene in many a year has been the creation of 42nd Street Theater Row: The transformation of the once-seedy block between Ninth and Tenth avenues into a sparkling new theater neighborhood, complete with nine theaters— including the **Harold Clurman Theater, Playwright's Horizon, Judith Anderson Theater, Samuel Beckett Theater, INTAR Mainstage Theater,** and **Douglas Fairbanks, Jr. Theater**—at least three cabarets, and half a dozen restaurants. A lot of creative work goes on in these houses, and there is often a real attempt made to keep prices down; for example, Playwright's Horizon, which runs a subscription series in its main theater, also houses **Don Scardino's New Theater Wing** upstairs. It presents unproduced plays by both aspiring and established writers, for fixed runs, and sells tickets for around $5! For information, phone 279-2400 after 1pm. Elsewhere around town, the **Manhattan Theater Club** mounts productions by new playwrights, usually at City Center, and **La Mama E.T.C.** on the Lower East Side is a longtime home of the avant-garde. The tiny **National Improvisational Theater,** 233 Eighth Ave. (tel. 243-7224) packs a mighty wallop with fast-paced evenings of totally improvised comedy, drama, and music. Its "Interplay" group performs on Monday night, its "Split-Second" company on other weeknights. Call for information.

Off-Broadway can still afford to be more daring than Broadway theater, mainly because there is much less financial risk involved in mounting a production. The houses are much smaller than the Broadway houses (they are often converted factories, or church basements, or cellars); and the actors and technicians receive much less than a Broadway wage scale. This freedom sometimes leads to great artistic successes, to brilliant revivals of the classics, and sometimes to the merely inept and mediocre (there is, however, no shortage of the latter on Broadway, either). Occasionally, plays that open here to great success go on to Broadway.

It is usually much easier to get a ticket to an Off-Broadway production than to a Broadway one. Check the listings in the *New York Times, New York* magazine, or *The New Yorker,* phone the theater, and pick up your reservation about an hour before curtain time. Many Off-Broadway playhouses will honor student ID cards.

Also check with theater schools, such as Actors Studio and the Juilliard School.

NEW YORK TRADITIONS

THE NEW YORK SHAKESPEARE FESTIVAL, performing in the Delacorte Theater, in Central Park. Tel. (Public Theater) 598-7100.

The Shakespeare Festival can be counted on all summer long for high-quality productions of the Bard and other entertainments in a delightful outdoor setting in Central Park. To get tickets for the free performances (every night except Monday from late June to early September), you must join the line outside the Delacorte Theater by mid-afternoon to receive a coupon (one per person) that may be redeemed for two tickets at 6:15pm. Seats are reserved, and you can be seated between 7:15 and 7:30. The Delacorte can be approached from either 81st Street and Central Park West or 79th Street and Fifth Avenue. **Prices:** Tickets free.

THE NEW YORK SHAKESPEARE FESTIVAL AT THE JO-SEPH PAPP PUBLIC THEATER, 425 Lafayette St., at Astor Place. Tel. 598-7150.

During the winter, the Shakespeare Festival runs the Joseph Papp Public Theater in Greenwich Village and lets new playwrights have their fling. At this writing, there were some five theaters and a cinema under the Public's roof; the complex presents one of the most vital and compelling theatrical experiments in New York today. It was at the Public that *Hair, A Chorus Line,* and *For Colored Girls* got their start. Tickets are $25 to $35; Quicktix are sold on the day of the performance at 6pm for evening performances, at 1pm for matinees. Film tickets are $7. The box office is open Tuesday to Sunday from 1 to 8pm, Monday until 6pm.

2. THE CLUB & MUSIC SCENE

In general, you should know that, barring Miami Beach or Las Vegas, New York is the "latest" town in the country. Bars and lounges can stay open and serve liquor until 4am every morning. Informality is the mode of dress—come-as-you-will—allowed everywhere, except in the top rooms, where coats and ties are de rigueur for the men. (A few places do bar jeans and sneakers.) Nowadays, women solo or in tandem can count on being welcomed everywhere. Drinks average around $6 in the fancier places, somewhat less elsewhere. Even in the neighborhood pubs, the days of the $1 glass of beer are no more: Plan to spend $4 and up.

How much will it all cost? Here, the latitude is enormous, and the choice is yours. You could easily spend $100 or more (for a couple, plus tips) as you dine, dance, and watch the big names in entertainment. Or you can go pub crawling with the natives and spend lots less. *Tips:* Many places have lower prices or no covers or minimums during the week; weekend prices soar everywhere. Also, a drink or two at the bar, plus a cover charge, can often be your price of admission to some of the best entertainment in town. Note that I've given charges only where they seem to be fixed; in the changeable nightclub scene, however, most covers and admissions will vary with the performer, the time of year, and the state of business. Except in the neighborhood pubs and the bars, reservations are imperative; for the major clubs, it might be wise to phone a day in advance.

New York clubs come and go with alarming frequency. Sometimes they change their entertainment format or decide to open only on certain days of the week. It's always wise to check local papers when you come and call in advance.

Note: The legal drinking age in New York has been raised to 21. Some clubs admit 18-year-olds but will not serve them alcohol; others will not admit them at all. Some clubs require double proof of age, other clubs look the other way. Good luck.

NIGHTCLUBS & CABARET

Other cities may have discos, rock clubs, and pubs, but none have cabarets to match New York's. Most of today's variety stars got their first break in New York cabarets in the 1960s. Today, talented young performers as well as major stars still strut their dreams in these beloved vestiges of vaudeville.

THE BALLROOM, 253 West 28th St. Tel. 244-3005.

Legends and luminaries like Peggy Lee, Eartha Kitt, Blossom Dearie, Karen Akers, and Charles Pierce have all called The Ballroom home. Its cabaret area also showcases revues like last year's ingenious "Casino Paradise," a "cabaret opera" by Pulitzer Prize–winning composer William Bolcom, featuring sets by renowned artist Larry Rivers. The restaurant here is quite special, featuring the oldest tapas bar on these shores, with some 50 traditional appetizers for the tasting. Come for lunch from noon to 3pm on Tuesday to Friday and you can feast on an open tapas buffet for $18.50. In the evening, there's continental cuisine and a classical guitarist, too, on Tuesday to Sunday. Sunday buffet brunch ($22.50) is served from noon, with special shows in the cabaret throughout the afternoon and early evening. **Admission:** $15 cover and two-drink minimum.

BLUE ANGEL THEATRE, 323 West 44th St. Tel. 262-3333.

Featuring the Off-Broadway show *Pageant*, a spoof on beauty pageants, the Blue Angel offers a five-course dinner/theater package. **Admission:** $32.50–$35; optional prix-fixe dinner $21. Reduced parking rate available across the street.

CAFÉ FEENJON, 40 West 8th St. Tel. 979-8686.

There's a slightly different accent at a favorite Middle Eastern oasis in those Greenwich Village sands—it could be Greek, Hebrew, or Arabic. Shows get under way around 9pm on Tuesday to Sunday. There is belly dancing on every Saturday night and on an occasional Friday night also. The Middle Eastern and American food is good, and the crowd lively. **Admission:** $2–$10 cover; $2–$8 minimum.

CAFÉ SOCIETY, 915 Broadway, at 21st St. Tel. 529-8282.

Follow the alluring red lights into the soaring, sophisticated space at Café Society, which offers swing on Monday and Tuesday, celebrity impersonators on Thursday, 1980s dance music on Friday and Saturday, and revues and surprises in between. Northern Italian food, too, is offered. **Admission:** Mon, Tues, Thurs $5 cover; Fri and Sat $10 cover.

DON'T TELL MAMA, 343 West 46th St. Tel. 757-0788.

If you're lucky, you may wander into the piano room at Don't Tell Mama and catch Liza Minnelli, Michael Feinstein, or your favorite Broadway musical star casually crooning show tunes. In the back room, Don't Tell Mama presents incredibly diverse cabaret acts, from jazz combos to gospel groups to female impersonators, seven nights a week. There are also singing waiters and an open mike singalong nightly at the piano bar. **Admission:** Cabaret room, $6–$15 plus two-drink minimum. Piano bar, two-drink minimum at table.

DUPLEX, 61 Christopher St. Tel. 255-5438.

Be a star at this three-level "entertainment complex," where the entire staff performs. Downstairs in the Piano Bar, patrons and staff sing along nightly from 9pm to 4am (no cover). Upstairs features the

Game Room with pool table, jukebox, and New York's oldest continuing cabaret, with shows nightly. There's standup comedy every Wednesday at 8pm, with the "Stars of Tomorrow" contest Friday at 11:30pm. **Admission:** Cabaret, $5–$12 cover plus two-drink minimum.

EIGHTY-EIGHTS, 228 West 10th St. Tel. 924-0088.

Cabaret fixture Erv Raible, who opened the original Duplex, has created one of the city's most attractive cabaret rooms in shades of lilac with chrome accents. Downstairs, friendly regulars surround the sunken piano and sing show tunes; upstairs, a diminutive stage hosts a parade of performers, from *Cats*' Betty Buckley to rising star Billy Stritch. Eighty-Eights serves light bar fare until very late, and its Sunday brunch has become a popular hangout for Village theater gypsies (dancers). **Admission:** Cover upstairs varies from $10–$12.50; two-drink minimum on both levels.

IBIS, 327 West 44th St. Tel. 262-1111.

The old days of the ethnic Greek and Middle Eastern nightclubs in the 20s on Eighth and Ninth avenues are long gone, but there's a glamorous Middle Eastern club right in Midtown. With columns of Egyptian statues, hieroglyphic wall murals, and mummies' tombs, IBIS transports you "back to the days of Cleopatra." Try to concentrate on your hummus and moussaka as you admire the belly dancers and the whirling dervish. A seven-piece Egyptian band provides the right romantic rhythms. Jackets required. **Admission:** $10 cover, two-drink minimum.

JUDY'S, 49 West 44th St. Tel. 764-8930.

With a lively front-room piano bar and a romantic cabaret area in back, Judy's has a wonderfully intimate supper club feeling. Chanteuse Barbara Lea, singer-songwriter Arthur Siegel, and voice-and-piano partners Judy Kreston and David Lahm all frequent Judy's small stage. Judy's also serves good Italian and continental fare for lunch on weekdays from noon to 5pm. Dinner is served on Monday to Saturday from 5:30pm until midnight, and you can order a late supper from 10pm until midnight. The shows take place nightly at 9 and 11pm. **Admission:** Cabaret shows, $6–$10 cover; $10 minimum.

RAINBOW & STARS, on the 65th floor of the RCA Building, 30 Rockefeller Plaza. Tel. 632-5000.

This jewel box of a club is perhaps the most elegant and intimate cabaret/supper club in New York, a cousin to the famed Rainbow Room for dining and dancing. Not only can you gaze at such stars as Tony Bennett or Hildegarde, Helen Schneider or Maureen McGovern, Rosemary Clooney or Robert Merrill, but you can also gaze at the stars outside: The view overlooks Central Park, with sightings up the Hudson and as far as lower Connecticut. Curved walls display fiberoptic stars and form private nooks for two. Elegant dinners and late suppers recall the supper club days of the 1930s with caviar and lobster and strawberries Romanoff; what could be more romantic? The evening of dining and show begins at 7pm for a 9 o'clock performance and at 10:30pm for supper and show at 11:15pm. Jackets and ties—and reservations—are required. **Admission:** $35 per person.

S.O.B., 204 Varick St. Tel. 243-4940.

A club with an international reputation, S.O.B. (Sounds of Brazil and Beyond) lures huge crowds to its cavernous space for the best in authentic Brazilian food and music. The throbbing sambas of Brazil alternate with African, Latin, Caribbean, and "World Music." The crowd ranges from the blue jeans set to the black tie set—there's something for everybody here.

Come to S.O.B.'s Mango Tree Café for lunch (Monday to Friday from noon to 3pm) or dinner (dinner entrees run $6.95 to $13.95) and sample some of the regional cuisines of Brazil and the Caribbean, partake of some of the national Brazilian drinks like caipirinhas or batidas, and enjoy one of the most unique evenings north of Rio. It's always best to call for dinner reservations and for information. Happy Hours are Monday to Friday from 5 to 8pm. **Admission:** $5–$15 cover, depending on performer; special group rates are available, and all major credit cards are accepted.

STEVE MCGRAW'S, 158 West 72nd St. Tel. 595-7400.

Steve McGraw's is not only the best cabaret/supper club on the Upper West Side; it's one of the best in town. *Forever Plaid*, which has received unanimous rave reviews, is the current long-run offering. Forever Plaid is the name of a mythical 1950s male quartet, cut off in a bus accident on the way to their debut concert 26 years ago and miraculously returned to life and the stage. The result is a tender, nostalgic, hilarious sendup of the music and humor of the 1950s, with everything from four-part harmony pop tunes to the story of Perry Como's golden cardigan and a three-minute, no-holds-barred version of the Ed Sullivan show. It's a knockout. There's entertainment upstairs, and good continental fare both upstairs and downstairs. Performances are Tuesday to Friday at 8pm; Saturday at 7:30 and 10:30pm; Sunday at 3 and 7:30pm. Reservations are essential, as it often sells out. **Admission:** $30 Tues, Wed, Thurs, and Sun; $35 Fri and Sat. Dinner package: $27, including tax and tip (or just order à la carte from the menu); dinner-and-show package: $57 or $62.

THEATRE EAST, 211 East 60th St. Tel. 838-9090.

This perennial favorite changes with each new Broadway season, and it's always hilarious. Proving once again that no play is spoof-proof, *Forbidden Broadway*'s raucous 10th anniversary edition declares war on classics from *Evita* to *Fiddler*; scores with dead-on spoofs of Streisand, Madonna, and Patti Lupone; and still does not Miz a single chance to lampoon *Les Misérables*. This show shoots from the lip and aims for the stars. Drinks and desserts are available during the show. Performances are Tuesday to Friday at 8:30pm, Wednesday at 2:30pm, Saturday at 7 and 10pm, and Sunday at 3:30pm. **Admission:** All tickets $35. Reservations essential.

TOP OF THE GATE AND THE VILLAGE GATE THEATRE, 160 Bleecker St. at Thompson St. Tel. 475-5120.

Cabaret musicals are offered at Top of the Gate and the Village Gate Theatre, both parts of a fascinating complex now in its 33rd year as a Village favorite. Showcase comics and singers appear every Friday and Saturday after 10pm. **Admission:** Varies, depending on featured artists or production.

FOLK & ROCK

THE BITTER END, 147 Bleecker St. Tel. 673-7030.

★ This legendary club still continues its quarter-of-a-century tradition of showcasing up-and-coming talent. Some of the greatest names in the music business have started here: Bob Dylan, Joni Mitchell, Stevie Wonder, Linda Ronstadt, and Billy Joel. (Comics like Lily Tomlin, Woody Allen, Billy Crystal, and George Carlin are Bitter End alumni, too.) Currently, the club showcases up-and-coming singer-songwriters; Tracy Chapman performed here before she became a worldwide sensation. **Admission:** $5.

BOND STREET CAFE, 6 Bond St. Tel. 979-6565.

Not a café at all, this intimate rock club showcases up-and-coming local bands with names like Mars Needs Women and Squirrels from Hell. **Admission:** $5.

BOTTOM LINE, 15 West 4th St. Tel. 228-6300.

Although it's considered the preeminent rock club in the city—some say in the country—the huge, always-packed Bottom Line does not limit its acts strictly to rock. You might catch folk singers, jazz artists (of the stature of Chick Corea), even classical performers. The crowd is young, the food ordinary. No one under 21 admitted; double proof of age is required. **Admission:** $15, no minimum.

CHINA CLUB, 2130 Broadway, at 75th St. Tel. 877-1166.

You never know who'll show up—onstage or off—at this legendary record-biz hangout. David Bowie shocked the house by jumping on stage a while ago; Bruce Willis made a recent appearance in the audience. Lesser mortals (mostly up-and-coming bands) perform nightly. **Admission:** $10 Tues–Sun, $15 Mon.

CONTINENTAL, 25 Third Ave., at St. Mark's Place. Tel. 529-6924.

A huge fiberglass pterodactyl still hovers over the roof here, the lone holdout from the kitschy old Continental Divide. Now the club has dropped "Divide" from its name, installed a snazzy art deco sign, and stripped the decor down to East Village black. The expanded stage means there's room for bigger acts, from local favorites the Lunachicks to the legendary Fleshtones to punk pioneers the Dictators; the crowd and the decibel level vary depending on the bill, which features anything from punk to country to jazz to blues. **Admission:** $2 cover Fri and Sat; no minimum.

THE DAN LYNCH BAR, 221 Second Ave., at 14th St. Tel. 677-0911.

Dan Lynch's has just celebrated its 11th anniversary. It's popular with a young and friendly crowd. The music, usually blues, but occasionally rock and roll, is loud, and the drinks—you must buy two—are cheap. On weekends, you might hear a hot local favorite such as Frankie Paris and friends, who rock the house monthly. Music nightly and an open jam Saturday and Sunday at 4pm. **Admission:** $5 Fri–Sat.

THE EAGLE TAVERN, 355 West 14th St. Tel. 924-0275.

★ Despite its location near the Ninth Avenue wholesale meat-packing district, the Eagle Tavern draws lovers of Irish folk music from all over town. Every Monday there's an Irish "seisiun," in which people bring their own instruments and join in a big houseparty; on Tuesday it's American folk music; on Thursday it's Bluegrass. Friday is for Irish folk and traditional music, Saturday for rock 'n roll. Closed Sunday. The atmosphere is blue-collar bar, the crowd casual. **Admission:** Free Mon–Tues; $5 Thurs and Sat; $7 Fri.

HARD ROCK CAFE, 221 West 57th St. Tel. 459-9320.

If you like to listen to high-energy, high-volume rock music while you eat, then be sure to dine at the very popular Hard Rock Café. Jammed with rock memorabilia (Elvis Presley's suit, Jimi Hendrix's guitar), the café serves a menu that ranges from $6.95 hamburgers to steaks that go up to about $18. There's a soda fountain with good desserts, too. **Open:** Sun–Thurs 11:30am–2am (kitchen until 12:45am); Fri–Sat 11:30pm–4am (kitchen until 2:45am). They do not take reservations, and the line to get in can be quite long—but it does move quickly. **Admission:** No admission, no cover. Must order an entree at the tables.

KENNY'S CASTAWAYS, 157 Bleecker St. Tel. 473-9870.

Kenny's Castaways is one of the hottest spots on the street, with a long bar, two levels, a back room devoted exclusively to music and a comfortable, music-art atmosphere. It's a showcase for musicians, featuring the full range of American rock and roll. More than a few of its groups—like the Smithereens—have secured record deals. A great place to catch new acts before you have to pay concert prices to see them. Open noon to 4am. **Admission:** Varies with act.

KNITTING FACTORY, 47 East Houston St. (between Mott and Mulberry St.). Tel. 219-3055.

For something completely different, unpack your favorite all-black outfit and head down to the Knitting Factory, a dark, unpretentious performance space. Downtown New York institutions like Lydia Lunch, John Zorn, and Arto Lindsay all make regular appearances, in an atmosphere so laid-back you may think you're in your own living room. **Admission:** $5–$15 (includes one drink).

THE MARQUEE, 547 West 21st St. Tel. 249-8870.

An offshoot of London's famous club, the Marquee showcases anything from alternative acts like OMD to stalwart old rockers like KISS. One caveat: When crowded, the airless, boxlike room can become a sauna. **Admission:** Ticket prices vary from $12.50–$25, depending on act.

MISSION, 531 East 5th St. Tel. 254-2610.

Nitzer Ebb, Bauhaus, Skinny Puppy, and Sisters of Mercy—if these names mean anything to you, troop to the rather dicey block that houses this dark "alternative rock" bar, the only one in the city to feature gothic, industrial, techno, and psychedelic music exclusively. **Admission:** $5.

THE RITZ, 254 West 54th St. Tel. 956-3731.

British, Australian, and alternative American bands often play the Ritz, whose stage overlooks both standing room and reserved seating areas. At crowded concerts, you can escape to one of the quiet upstairs bars and enjoy the show on closed-circuit TV. **Admission:** Tickets $12.50–$21.

SPEAKEASY, 107 Macdougal St. Tel. 598-9670.

In the still-folksy heart of the Village, Speakeasy offers "a little bit of folk and jazz, a little blues and rock 'n roll" seven nights a week. Special events might include three women's bands playing in "New Music Seminars," a guest appearance with Speakeasy veteran David

Massengill, or the annual "Bob Dylan Imitator's Contest." Open mike night is Monday.

TOMMY MAKEM'S IRISH PAVILION, 130 East 57th St. Tel. 759-9040.

⭐ Not only is the music good at Irish Pavilion, but the Irish coffee is so good it must have been made by the little people themselves. Music is featured Tuesday to Saturday. It's usually Irish, but sometimes American folk. **Admission:** No cover or minimum.

TRAMPS, 45 West 21st St. Tel. 727-7788.

Tramps, a spacious loft, showcases eclectic, fearless (as in they'll do anything) rock, zydeco, and blues lineups seven nights a week. When the Cajun-influenced zydeco bands do their thing, there's no keeping the audience off the dance floor. Reggae bands often alternate with zydeco, keeping the Caribbean beat throbbing. Tramps now serves Cajun Creole cuisine (entrées $8–$13.50). Tramps is open for lunch on Monday to Friday from 11:30am to 3pm. **Admission:** $5–$15.

WETLANDS, 161 Hudson St. Tel. 966-4225.

With its authentic 1960s posters, "natural snacks," black lights, and a crowd that favors tie-dyed tops and bell-bottoms, Wetlands looks like a cleaned-up version of a 1960s love-in. There's even an old psychedelic-painted VW van at the club's entrance. The bulletin board bespeaks worthy causes—ecological concerns, animal rights, and such. Some of the music is from the 1960s, but there are also reggae bands, blues singers, jangle-guitar groups, and comeback bands like New Riders of the Purple Sage. Monday night, the club becomes Soul Kitchen, an enormously popular place to dance to funk, house, and disco. **Admission:** $6–$15.

COMEDY CLUBS

CAROLINE'S, 1626 Broadway, at 50th St. Tel. 757-4100.

Forget the old image of smoky, claustrophobic comedy clubs. New York's Queen of Comedy, Caroline Hirsch, has created a soaring, sophisticated venue that feels more like a luxurious lounge than a performance room. Headliners include the hottest names in comedy, from Rita Rudner to Gilbert Gottfried to Jeff Altman. For a comedy club, Caroline's also offers a very serious Italian menu, with delicious antipasta, Caesar salad, and lasagne bolognese. **Admission:** Cover varies from $12.50–$15, depending on headliner; two-drink minimum.

CATCH A RISING STAR, 1487 First Ave., between 77th and 78th Sts. Tel. 794-1906.

⭐ You can always catch bright new comedy and musical talent, and sometimes a visit by such established stars as Rodney Dangerfield, Kevin Meaney, Jerry Seinfeld, David Brenner, Dennis Miller, or Robin Williams, who might drop by when they are preparing for a TV special or a live appearance. Call for reservations. **Admission:** Sun–Thurs $8 cover, two-drink minimum; Fri and Sat $12 cover, two-drink minimum. Drinks start at $3.

THE COMEDY CELLAR AT THE OLIVE TREE, 117 Macdougal St. Tel. 254-3630.

Top TV comics from Letterman, HBO, and MTV create a night

laughathon. Great comics, great food, great fun. A full menu (light American and Mediterranean fare) is available. Call for reservations. **Admission:** Sun–Thurs $5 cover. Fri and Sat $10 cover, $9 drink minimum.

DANGERFIELD'S, 1118 First Ave., near 61st St. Tel. 593-1650.

You can see some of the best of the standup comics perform at comic Rodney Dangerfield's popular East Side club. Many are veterans of Letterman and Rodney's own HBO specials. Five-act shows are presented every night. **Admission:** Sun–Thurs $12.50 cover, $7 minimum. Fri and Sat $15 cover, $7 minimum. Special $5 Kinney parking for club patrons.

INTERPLAY, at National Improvisational Theater, 233 Eighth Ave., between 21st and 22nd Sts. Tel. 243-7224.

No two shows here are ever the same. Using no scripts, props, or costumes, Interplay's talented music and comedy performers create a new show every time, based solely on the suggestions of the audience. Great fun. **Admission:** $15.

MOSTLY MAGIC, 55 Carmine St. Tel. 924-1472.

Manhattan's only magic/comedy club, Mostly Magic is as mirthful as ever after "twelve years of outrageousness, magic, and tomfoolery." Comedy/magic performances are given on Tuesday, Wednesday, and Thursday at 9pm; Friday and Saturday at 9 and 11pm; with children's matinee Saturday at 2pm. (Carmine Street is in the West Village, between Sixth and Seventh avenues, just north of Hudson Street.) Dinner is served Tuesday to Saturday from 6pm to 12am (entrees $8.95–$13.95). **Admission:** Tues–Thurs $10 cover, $8 minimum; Fri and Sat $15 cover, $8 minimum. Children's Magic Matinee: $10 (light lunch available).

NEW YORK COMEDY CLUB, 915 Second Ave. Tel. 888-1696.

The owners of this new club swear that they aren't joking about their "Wal-Mart approach" to comedy, meaning "low overhead and top quality." The modest, wood-paneled room certainly attests to their thrift, and the acts really do include the city's top names. Recent guests include Damon Wayans from "In Living Color" and "Tonight Show" veterans Randy Credico and Bob Shaw. Wednesday at 9pm, Bob "In-Your-Face" Golub—who appeared in the film *Goodfellas*—earns his moniker in a one-man show dealing with "the truth and real-life issues." Sunday offers improvisational comedy with the Improv-ables. **Admission:** $5 weeknights; $10 weekends—two-drink minimum.

THE N.Y. COMIC STRIP, INC., 1568 Second Ave., near 81st St. Tel. 861-9386.

At the Comic Strip, you might occasionally see Eddie Murphy, who was discovered here. Others discovered here include Joe Piscopo, Jerry Seinfeld, and Dennis Wolfberg. Scores of others, from Robin Williams to Steven Wright, stop in to do "a few minutes," joining the regulars. **Admission:** Cover varies. Two-drink minimum (drinks run $4.25–$4.50).

THE ORIGINAL IMPROVISATION, 358 West 44th St. Tel. 765-8268.

⭐ "Now," in the words of proprietor Silver Friedman, "celebrating 29 years of love, truth, and laughter." The Original Improv could easily be dubbed the cradle of comedy from Pryor to Piscopo. Danny Aiello, Richard Lewis, and Jay Leno all started here; so did Lily Tomlin, Bette Midler, Robert Klein, and Rodney Dangerfield. The Improv showcases the hottest new talent of the '90s. **Admission:** Mon–Tues $8 minimum, $8 cover; Wed–Thurs and Sun $9 minimum, $11 cover; Fri, Sat, and hol eves $9 minimum, $12 cover.

STAND UP NEW YORK, 236 West 78th St., at Broadway. Tel. 595-0850.

⭐ This is the West Side's premier standup comedy club, with the best television comedians. Surprise drop-in guests often include Steven Wright, Jonathan Solomon, and Elayne Boosler. Dinner and snacks are available. **Admission:** Sun–Thurs $7; Fri–Sat $12—two-drink minimum.

COUNTRY MUSIC

THE LONE STAR ROADHOUSE, 240 West 52nd St. Tel. 245-2950.

Country music clubs come and go in New York, but this one holdout still exists. Yes, they still serve Lone Star beer, celebrate Texas Independence Day, and have a full Texas-American menu—try the chili, Texas ribs, and BBQ. The club's facade recalls the buses that country bands travel in. Up on the big stage, you might catch acts like Dr. John, Leon Russell, or Buckwheat Zydeco, plus other big names of country and western music, as well as blues and rock artists like The Band. Live music is presented every night of the week. **Admission:** $7–$15 is average, although you may pay more or less depending on which band is playing; two-drink minimum or dinner during the show.

JAZZ & BLUES

Jazz went through some lean years in New York, but now it's back, bigger and better than ever. So big has the jazz revival become, in fact, that a **Jazzline** (tel. 718/465-7500 to find out who's playing where) has been established and is flourishing mightily. On the club scene, much of the action is downtown.

Most jazz clubs charge $10 to $15 covers and/or a one- or two-drink minimum, but it all depends on the performer. And with the jazz renaissance in full swing, new clubs are opening all the time. Check the listings in the magazines (*The New Yorker* has the best), also in *The Village Voice*. It's best to make reservations, and check the credit-card policy of the club.

B. SMITH'S ROOFTOP CAFE, 771 Eighth Ave. Tel. 247-2222.

To her ultrapopular Midtown restaurant, Barbara Smith recently added a glass-enclosed, plant-filled upstairs room where musicians like Eddie Palmieri and Will Downing entertain a well-dressed, mostly local crowd. Entertainment is on Friday and Saturday; showtimes vary. **Admission:** $10 or $20, depending on artist; $10 minimum.

BIRDLAND, 2745 Broadway, at 105th St. Tel. 749-2228.

Birdland houses eclectic jazz and great dining. Its high ceilings, enormous windows, and inviting atmosphere make it an exceptionally warm place to enjoy cool tunes seven nights a week. Sets are Sunday to Thursday at 9 and 11pm and Friday and Saturday at 9 and 10:30pm and midnight. **Admission:** Sun–Thurs, no cover, but $10 minimum at the tables, $5 minimum at the bar. Fri–Sat, cover $10–$20, depending on who is performing, and $10–$20 minimum.

BLUE NOTE, 131 West 3rd St., near Sixth Ave. Tel. 475-8592.

A throwback to the elegant New York nightspots of the past, Blue Note is a posh jazz bistro featuring top-name performers on a nightly basis, like Ray Charles, Nancy Wilson, Dizzy Gillespie, Wynton Marsalis, and George Benson. Show times are at 9 and 11:30pm during the week, with sometimes a third show at 1:30am on Friday and Saturday. There is a late-night jam session every Tuesday through Saturday, after the last set, until 4am, and a Jazz Brunch every Saturday and Sunday from 2 to 6pm. Dinner is served from 7pm to midnight, entrees running from $7.95 to $23.95. **Admission:** Varies, depending on performer; $5-drink minimum.

BLUE WILLOW CAFE, 644 Broadway, at Bleecker St. Tel. 673-6480.

This self-styled "oasis of civilization in a sea of madness," has vintage marble walls, wrought-iron ceilings, and antique mahogany furniture. Jazz duos and soloists perform Wednesday, Thursday and Saturday from 9pm on, and at Sunday brunch, from noon on. **Admission:** Free, no cover.

BRADLEY'S, 70 University Place, at 11th St. Tel. 228-6440.

Modern jazz piano and bass duos are the usual fare at Bradley's. **Admission:** $10–$15 cover, $8 minimum.

CAJUN, 129 Eighth Ave., at 16th St. Tel. 691-6174.

In the mood for terrific Dixieland bands and Bourbon Street blues? Head over to Cajun any Monday to Thursday (8 to 11pm), Friday and Saturday (9pm to midnight), or for the Sunday champagne jazz brunch, which is served from noon to 4pm (for $9.95, it's one of the best treats in town). Dine on inexpensive Cajun/Creole food or have drinks at the bar. **Admission:** Free, no minimum.

CALIBAN, 360 Third Ave., at 26th St. Tel. 689-5155.

This intimate and dimly lit venue offers live jazz Thursday, Friday, and Saturday nights. The decor is exposed-brick walls and high ceilings, the food is barbecue. Music begins at 9pm Thursday, 10pm Friday and Saturday. You can dine until 11pm and drink well into the night. **Admission:** No cover, $10 minimum at tables until midnight.

CHICAGO B.L.U.E.S., 73 Eighth Ave., near 14th St. Tel. 255-7373.

In a sort of educational exchange, this blues bar brings in the greats direct from Chicago—they even have an official airline—where many say the form was born. Notables like The Kinsey Report, Eddie Burke, and Delta Blue number among recent performers here. **Admission:** Varies from no cover to $10, depending on act. No minimum.

FAT TUESDAY'S, downstairs at Tuesday's Restaurant, 190 Third Ave., at 17th St. Tel. 533-7902.

This one was a winner from the day it opened. The plush mirrored rooms with intimate seating feature the best of avant-garde and mainstream artists (Michel LeGrand, Michel Camilo, and Dizzy Gillespie, among others); food is available from upstairs. Saturday and Sunday feature a jazz brunch at $9.95, including champagne. **Admission:** $12.50–$15 cover, $7.50 minimum.

GREENE STREET, 101 Greene St., near Prince St. Tel. 925-2415.

✪ SoHo's big jazz venue is Greene Street, a truck warehouse turned nightclub and a very successful one at that. Mainstream jazz instrumentalists appear in a stunning supper club environment, and the classic American cuisine is excellent (entrees run about $17 to $26 à la carte). There's also live entertainment at Sunday brunch, noon to 4pm, except Memorial Day through Labor Day, when Greene Street is closed on Sunday. **Admission:** Mon–Fri $3 cover; Sat and Sun $5.

J'S, 2581 Broadway, 2nd floor, between 97th and 98th Sts. Tel. 666-3600.

Uptown west, try J's, a window-lined, airy jazzroom that also dishes up some creative continental American grill cuisine. J's attracts top-drawer acts like Dick Hyman and Victor Jones; the entertainment starts around 8:30pm Sunday to Thursday, 9pm on Friday and Saturday; the kitchen is open from 7pm nightly. **Admission:** $12 minimum at tables, $7 at the bar.

KNICKERBOCKER BAR AND GRILL, 33 University Place, at 9th St. Tel. 228-8490.

The Knickerbocker is a cozy spot to catch some of the greats. It's known for its commendable, medium-priced kitchen, famous for its T-bone steaks for 2 for $35. **Admission:** Wed–Sun from 9:45pm; $2–$3.50 cover charge.

MANNY'S CAR WASH, 1558 Third Ave., between 87th and 88th Sts. Tel. 369-BLUES.

What can be said of a Chicago-style blues bar that serves a drink called a Woo Woo (cranberry juice, triple sec, and vodka)? There is music every night of the week. It starts at 9:15pm and runs pretty continuously, except on Sunday when things get under way at 8:45pm. The sandwich menu features—believe it or not—World Famous White Castle Hamburgers. They're 75¢ each or 3 for $2. On "Windy City Wednesday" (every Wednesday, that is), you can eat one for 50¢. On Tuesday, anyone wearing a Manny's T-shirt or hat (which you can purchase at Manny's) gets in free. On Thursday, nationally known and Grammy-winning musicians play. On Sunday, it's Manny's World Famous Blues Jam. **Admission:** Mon, free for women, $3 for men; Tues–Wed $3–$5 cover (free with Manny's T-shirt or hat); Thurs $5–$10 cover; Fri and Sat $5 cover; Sun no cover. No minimum ever.

MICHAEL'S PUB, 211 East 55th St. Tel. 758-2272.

This English-pub style place that everybody seems to like has an eclectic entertainment policy—everybody from Vic Damone to Woody Allen's New Orleans Funeral & Ragtime Band occasionally checking in on a Monday night when the comedian is in town. **Admission:** Cover and minimum depend on the act.

SWEET BASIL JAZZ RESTAURANT, 88 Seventh Ave. South, at Bleecker St. Tel. 242-1785.

Highly rated among Village jazz clubs, Sweet Basil is strong on talent. It consistently features top names in traditional and contemporary jazz, as well as very good American cuisine with some Thai touches; shows are from 10pm nightly. A special treat is the weekend jazz brunch, with the music of the Eddie Chamblee Quartet on Saturday from 2 to 6pm, and the legendary trumpeter Doc Cheatham's Quartet on Sunday from 3 to 7pm. **Admission:** No music charge at brunch; $15 music charge at evening performances; $6 minimum at all times.

THE VILLAGE GATE, 160 Bleecker St., at Thompson St. Tel. 475-5120.

The Village Gate is known for a variety of entertainment, from the Village Gate theater downstairs to the Top of the Gate (see "Nightclubs & Cabaret" above). The Terrace Bar, on the main floor in between is a nightly hot spot where top-name jazz trios and quartets start at 10pm. Off-Broadway musicals are usually playing in one or both of the theater spaces, and are often followed by such jazz performers as Dr. John and Dizzy Gillespie. There is listening as well as dancing when the "Salsa Meets Jazz" series takes place on Monday nights, with name Latin bands and jazz soloists such as Wynton Marsalis. **Admission:** Terrace Bar free nightly, two-drink minimum weekends after 10pm. On other evenings and in other spaces there may or may not be a drink minimum or cover, depending on who is performing.

THE VILLAGE VANGUARD, 178 Seventh Ave. South, just below 11th St. Tel. 255-4037.

Called the "most famous jazz club in the world," the Village Vanguard has been around since the 1930s with some of the best jazz there is. Big names (like Wynton and Branford Marsalis and Illinois Jacquet) and newcomers alike appear every night starting at 9:30pm; The Vanguard Seventeen Piece Jazz Orchestra plays every Monday night. There's no food but a friendly crowd. **Admission:** Sun-Thurs $12 cover, $7.50 minimum; Fri and Sat $15 cover, $7.50 minimum.

VISIONES, 125 Macdougal St. Tel. 673-5576.

Like, this hot club grooves on the same vibe as those old Village jazz clubs where cats caught the coolest jazz. And you're just as likely to hear stars of the future now as you may have been back then. In this small (it seats 74), black, white, and gray room, jazz masters take their "left of center" projects; sidemen from national touring bands take the stage as leaders; and talented newcomers get to strut their stuff. In fact, luminaries like New York Voices, Ralph Moore, Bob Belden, Robin Eubanks, and Joe Lovano all got their start here. On weekend afternoons, legendary trumpeter Eddie Henderson takes over as Visiones "director of jam sessions" and heats up the joint even more. **Admission:** Covers vary from $5-$10; no cover for jam sessions.

WEST END GATE, 2911 Broadway at 113th St. Tel. 662-8830.

You can mix with the Columbia kids and other enthusiastic music buffs at this reincarnation of the old West End Café. Newly renovated, with a glittering interior, this is still an informal place that features various musical combos, jazz, rock, and comedy, from 9pm nightly. On Sundays, from noon to 4pm, fall through spring, there is a Klezmer Brunch featuring Jewish folk music. Lunch and dinner are served daily, with an affordable, eclectic international menu. **Admission:** Cover depends on event; $8 for Klezmer music.

ZINNO, 126 West 13th St. Tel. 924-5182.

Along with wonderful Italian cuisine, Zinno dishes up top-drawer local jazz acts seven nights a week in an intimate, charming room. **Admission:** No cover or minimum.

DANCE CLUBS & DISCOS

You should know a few things before you start out: First, nobody who is anybody arrives until very late (from 10pm on); secondly, clubs do not admit all comers (it all depends on the whim of the management); and third, note that the door fee can be very high, up to $25 per person. While clubs come and go with alarming rapidity, and many are too specialized, faddy, or ephemeral to bear listing here (see papers like *Paper*, and *The New York Press* for information on these), the following, in all likelihood, will still be doing business when you come.

ADAM'S APPLE, 1117 First Ave., near 61st St. Tel. 371-8650.

Adam's Apple is very large, with two dining rooms, a bar area, and three dance floors, making it one of the area's most popular dance clubs.

AU BAR, 41 East 58th St. Tel. 308-9455.

The decidedly more "uptown" Au Bar looks like a whimsically decorated country mansion's library. Indeed, proprietor (and ex-Xenon owner) Howard Stein hired two young Britons to furnish his club with heirlooms and antiques. A supper club, Au Bar offers simple, sophisticated dinner and breakfast fare (entrées range from $10 to $25). A DJ entertains the Beautiful People on a small dance floor, and reservations are a must. **Admission:** $10 Sun–Wed; $15 Thurs–Sat.

BAJA, 246A Columbus Ave., between 71st and 72nd Sts. Tel. 724-8890.

A smart crowd of young Upper West Siders do a lot of socializing and networking here. There is occasionally live entertainment, and there is a DJ and disco dancing every night. **Admission:** $10 Fri–Sat; prices vary Wed–Thurs by event.

THE COPACABANA, 10 East 60th St. Tel. 755-6010.

Remember the Copa, New York's legendary glamour nightclub of the 1940s? It reopened at the same old stand a few years back, and now it's disco and Latin entertainment that brings in the crowds on Tuesday, Friday, and Saturday. There's a free buffet between 6 and 8pm on Tuesday and Saturday. **Admission:** Tues free 6–7pm, $5 women and $10 men after 7pm; Fri $5 6–9pm, $10 women, $15 men after 9pm; Sat $10 women, $15 men.

COUNTRY CLUB, 210 East 86th St. Tel. 879-8400.

With a black-and-white-checkerboard dance floor and a "singin' 'n' swinging'" orchestra, this romantic retro room "reintroduces nostalgia to New York," recalling grand old clubs like the El Morocco. Sweeping trompe-l'oeil murals depict fairways, palm trees, and a swimming pool; for a moneyed old Palm Beach ambiance, navy-and-white-striped canvas billows from the ceiling. Chef David Page's menu even draws 1940s favorites through a time warp, with goat-cheese fondue, macaroni with house-smoked salmon in horseradish cream, and beef tenderloin with mashed red potatoes among my favorites. In a neighborhood not known for imaginative nightspots, Country Club makes an unusual and welcome addition. Dancing is from 10pm nightly. **Admission:** $10 cover for nondiners weeknights, $15 weekends.

FLAMINGO EAST, 219 Second Ave. Tel. 533-2860.

Don't let the staff's icy attitude frighten you away from this East Village hotspot. The sleek retromodern restaurant and cozy nightclub make it worth staying. In the wide banquettes and booths, you can enjoy Asian-influenced cuisine from spring rolls to shrimp and fried rice. Afterward, dance off delicious desserts—like walnut brownie à la mode—upstairs, where Flamingo's DJs spin a wild mix of '70s, '80s, and '90s music. **Admission:** No cover or minimum.

LAURA BELLE, 120 West 43rd St., between Sixth Ave. and Broadway. Tel. 819-1000.

Put on your party clothes (a jacket is required for men, which is meant to set the tone) and get set to enter one of the 1930s-style supper clubs that are springing up around the city. The crowd ranges in age from the 20s set to people in their 60s. You can arrive from 8:30 on and have a sumptuous continental dinner from 9pm to 2am (expensive: entrees $17–$25). Or arrive stylishly late anytime from 10pm on and dance, drink, and perhaps have a snack à la carte from the dinner menu. Tables and banquettes ring the dance floors, and diners may also sit in the balcony and enjoy an overview of the grand, amphitheater-shaped room with its 40-foot ceiling, faceted columns, limestone-frescoed walls, antique sconces, chandeliers, theatrical lights, and, of course, all the people who decorate the place with panache. Open Wednesday to Saturday. **Admission:** $10 after 10pm. No minimum.

LIMELIGHT, 660 Sixth Ave., at 20th St. Tel. 807-7850.

A still-popular place to dance to rock music is this nightclub created out of a mid-19th-century city landmark church (it was deconsecrated some years back). Dancing takes place in the main sanctuary, and you can look down upon the goings-on from the choir loft above. There are four bars, a library, and many cozy nooks for sitting and talking. Crowds line up to gain access to this cavernous place (it can hold 2,500 people), but the lines move quickly. Limelight also hosts occasional live acts; call for schedule. **Admission:** $10 Sun–Thurs; $15 Fri–Sat.

NELL'S, 224 West 14th St. Tel. 675-1567.

When it opened in 1987, Nell's broke the mold with live jazz and Victorian furnishings; although no longer original, the club still feels refreshing and quite distinctive. Sundays and Thursdays continue to draw hordes, so expect to wait; you'll have an easier time getting in Fridays and Saturdays, but you'll also miss the "A" crowd. There's light supper upstairs from 10pm, entertainment from 11:30, and dancing downstairs all night. **Admission:** $6 Sun–Thurs; $12 Fri and Sat.

PALLADIUM, 126 East 14th St. Tel. 473-7171.

If you really miss the old days, then visit Palladium. Although no longer the glamour spot it once was, the club is still an architectural marvel and continues to draw crowds. Within an old movie palace, Japanese architect Arata Isoazaki has placed a cubic, metallic grid that rises less than halfway to the roof of the seven-story building; and within this gigantic frame are rooms featuring stunning works by contemporary artists, intimate areas for socializing, and several bars, including one that re-creates the atmosphere of a Depression-era speakeasy. And then, of course, there's the dance floor, composed of lights set in glass blocks, and twin banks of 25 video screens each, which are raised and lowered from above. Palladium is so huge that no one who can pay the cover—usually $20 on weekends but cheaper if you have a pass—is turned away. **Admission:** $20.

ROSELAND, 239 West 52nd St. Tel. 247-0200.

For those hankering after a nice old-fashioned ballroom fling, there's half-century-old Roseland, with a dance floor approximately the size of the Gobi Desert and a huge restaurant as well. Roseland also showcases rock singers and bands on occasional weekends (The Pet Shop Boys and the Sugarcubes were recent notable acts). Open Thursday and Sunday 2:30 to 11pm; closed Tuesday, Wednesday, Friday, and Saturday, except for special events. **Admission:** Thurs $6; Sun $10. At special events cover varies depending on performer, call for information.

ROXY, 515 West 18th St., at Tenth Ave. Tel. 645-5156.

This roller-rink boasts "New York's largest dance floor" in an 18,000-square-foot main room. Once you get your bearings, dance to some of the city's hottest DJs, or take a break in the glass-enclosed balcony bar overlooking all the action. Occasional live performances; call for schedules. Roller-skating to disco music is Tuesday and Wednesday. Dance Club is Friday and Saturday. **Admission:** $8–$15.

SOUND FACTORY, 530 West 27th St. Tel. 643-0728.

On Friday and Saturday, everyone who's anyone downtown eventually lands at Sound Factory—usually *after* 3am, when the nonstop action seems almost surreal. A big black room with a massive sound system, Sound Factory has also become one of Madonna's hangouts, and rumor has it the club plays her new records long before the public ever hears them. Watch in awe as the mainly gay crowd "Vogues" or "Bus Stops" to powerhouse DJs like Junior Vasquez and Frankie Knuckles. No alcohol is served, but fruit juice and water are available; dress ranges from T-shirts and jeans to very elaborate drag. **Admission:** $20.

SOUND FACTORY BAR, 12 West 21st St. Tel. 206-7770.

More a club than a bar, this fresh Chelsea hotspot sometimes shares DJs, like Frankie Knuckles, with its namesake nightclub (see above). Small and dark, Sound Factory Bar changes hours, covers, and crowds depending on the night of the week; call first to check the evening's program, which could run the gamut from techno to industrial noise. **Admission:** $5 Mon–Fri; $10 Sat and Sun.

SUPPER CLUB, 240 West 47th St. Tel. 921-1940.

Reviews have been mixed about this dazzling dancing-and-dining spot. Critics praise the striking cobalt-and-gold decor that transforms the cavernous, columned space into an elegant *boîte*. The uneven food and spotty service, however, have drawn darts. Skipping dinner to enjoy high-profile acts like Melba Moore seems a sensible compromise. **Admission:** Cover $10 Mon–Fri; $15 Sat and Sun.

TATOU, 151 East 50th St., near Third Ave. Tel. 753-1144.
An opera house in the 1930s, then the club Versailles (where Edith Piaf, Judy Garland, and others sang the night away), Tatou has resurrected the bygone glamour, even to the grand chandelier and imposing bronze Amazons beside the rococo stage. To be assured a place amongst all this glitter (painstakingly tarnished for effect), dine at Tatou (reserve days in advance), and segue onto the floor when the dancing gets under way—at around 11pm, when dinner service is over. Then, doors are selectively opened to those who arrive for disco dancing, until 4am.

Dinner, with live jazz, is from 6 to 11pm (average check about $45, sans wine). Late supper is 11pm to 1am. There are shows Monday through Wednesday at 11pm. Monday nights's Variety Showcase presents rhythm and blues, Gospel, and country. Tuesday's Star Cabaret has one dazzling performer—perhaps Nell Campbell of Nell's (see above), Christopher Mason, or Phoebe Legere. Wednesday's lineup varies. Lunch is served weekdays noon to 3pm. Jacket and tie required. **Admission:** $10 Mon–Thurs; $15 Fri and Sat.

TRIXIES, 307 West 47th St. Tel. 582-5480.
Anything goes—literally—at Trixie's, where a "typical" week might feature "Fondue Muumuu Mondays," impromptu talent shows, and dance contests. Not the most intimate meeting spot, Trixie's themes and decor change constantly; food is "funky and eclectic;" dancing is "when people feel like it and we can move the furniture." **Admission:** No cover ($10 food minimum at tables).

3. THE BAR SCENE

'Tis pleasant in the cool of evening to drop into a warm and atmospheric public house and slake the thirst with a brew, a drop of the grape, or a belt of the grain. Below is a sampling of some favorite watering holes around town. (A number have been reviewed as restaurants in Chapter 6.) At most places, mixed drinks cost at least $6; for wines by the glass, expect to pay $4 to $6, or more.

DOWNTOWN MANHATTAN

NORTH STAR PUB, 93 South St., at the South Street Seaport. Tel. 509-6757.
More than just traditional English brews, food, and atmosphere prevail at the jolly North Star Pub. There's usually a zany celebration of some sort taking place: A recent one, for example, was a "British Forgive George Washington" bash! Their major celebrations are St. George's Day (April 23) and Boxing Day

(December 26); others occur "as the spirit (or spirits) move us." For anyone who's counting, they boast a 60-plus collection of single malt scotches.

LOWER BROADWAY

ACME BAR AND GRILL, 9 Great Jones St. Tel. 420-1934.

Any noise on quiet Great Jones Street is likely to come from Acme Bar and Grill, where solid Southern food is served in what looks like a converted garage, albeit a stylish one. After your hush puppies and collard greens, head downstairs for jams—of the musical variety. Under Acme, Acme's funky underground bar, hosts live music acts nightly.

AMSTERDAM'S GRAND BAR & ROTISSERIE CORP., 454 Broadway at Grand St. Tel. 925-6166.

Amsterdam's, in the heart of SoHo's gallery district, draws a quiet, party crowd. There's usually a long wait for restaurant seating, but it's easy to get to the 30-foot bar, active every night.

BAYAMO, 704 Broadway. Tel. 475-5151.

Pulsatingly popular Bayamo, named for a Cuban town where many Chinese and Cubans intermarried, offers an upscale version of Chino-Latino fare, plus a bar scene that hops all week.

CARAMBA II, 684 Broadway, at Great Jones St. Tel. 420-9817.

Caramba II offers the same Mexican food, ridiculous margaritas, and young-crowd, high-decibel atmosphere that have made its uptown counterparts so popular.

GONZALES Y GONZALES, 625 Broadway, between Houston and Bleecker Sts. Tel. 473-8787.

Come fiesta time, the crowds also gather here for Mexican food—and music from both sides of the border—in an atmosphere of frenetic fun. Slightly outré live acts like Downtown diva Phoebe Legere and the Rio Funk Band perform nightly for a friendly crowd. The decor (wild colors, oversized sombreros, and peppers) adds to the ambiance. There is dancing, yes, and cover, no.

TIME CAFE, 380 Lafayette St. Tel. 533-7608.

Expert people-watchers gather to see and be seen in this strikingly simple space, with whitewashed walls and a single blown-up black-and-white mural photograph. Times Café bills itself as an environment-conscious restaurant; its moderately priced menu serves some organic dishes, and its bright store annex sells ecologically sound products. An outdoor café is open in warm weather.

SOHO

I TRE MERLI, 463 West Broadway. Tel. 254-8699.

The most glamorous of the wine bars? That's I Tre Merli, a SoHo outpost of Italian chic. I Tre Merli means "the three blackbirds," and it's the brand name of the wine imported from northern Italy by the owners. It's served here, along with about 25 other wines by the glass; the cuisine is of Genoa in the region of Liguria. A very popular spot for a fashionable crowd in the late evening.

SOHO KITCHEN AND BAR, 103 Greene St. Tel. 925-1866.

SoHo has several wine bars where dedicated oenophiles may

while away the evening, and this is the biggest. State-of-the-art preservation technology allows this bistro to offer an astonishing number of wines by the glass, more than 100 different types. Part of the Greene Street complex, its entrance is just down the street from the main door.

GREENWICH VILLAGE

THE LION'S HEAD, 59 Christopher St., just off Sheridan Square. Tel. 929-0670.

The Lion's Head attracts young writers, newspaper people (it's columnist Pete Hamill's favorite pump), and TV news personalities like Linda Ellerbee and Chauncey Howell. Doors stay open until 4am.

WHITE HORSE TAVERN, 567 Hudson St. at the corner of 11th St. Tel. 243-9260.

Bookish types touring the Village will want to knock back an "arf 'n arf" at the White Horse Tavern, where Dylan Thomas dwelt and allegedly drank himself to death, and where such American literary lights as Norman Mailer and Louis Auchincloss used to be regulars in the back room. A large and comfortable outdoor café offering light foods is open during the warm weather, usually from May 1 through early fall.

GRAMERCY PARK AREA & EAST VILLAGE

CAFE IGUANA, 235 Park Ave. South at 19th St. Tel. 529-4771.

A brass iguana over the door beckons you inside, and if it's Happy Hour (4pm to 7pm, seven days a week), you can fix yourself tacos at the free taco bar and order a margarita for $4 ($6 at other times), or a margarita with an extra shot of tequila, otherwise known as an Iguanarita for $5 ($7 at other times). A crystal iguana over the bar is named Ava, in honor of Ava Gardner, who was in *Night of the Iguana,* from whence the theme derives. They serve Mexican pizza (what will they think of next?)—peppers and spice, sausage, and onions, rolled in a large taco and smothered with cheese ($7.95). There is no dancing, but there is a DJ nightly. A photographer will snap your picture with Ava, in case the folks at home want to know if you made any new friends in the big city.

PETE'S TAVERN, 129 East 18th St. at Irving Place. Tel. 473-7676.

Pete's Tavern, the oldest original bar in New York City, a 128-year-old shrine, was a favorite haunt of O. Henry (who lived across the street). It was commemorated by the author in one of his stories.

SUGAR REEF, 93 Second Ave., between Fifth and Sixth Sts. Tel. 477-8427.

Caribbean food and drink are "hot" in New York right now, so to see what that scene is all about, calypso over to the East Village, to Sugar Reef. Dine on sizzling hot Caribbean food, cooled by the sounds of calypso, merengue, and reggae. At the bar, sip a long, cool, rum something while you munch on conch fritters or shrimp-and-coconut fritters or the like. The bar, by the way, is a "beach-style" affair, its base made of multicolored steel drums; other decor includes native art, plus plastic plants, bananas, and birds.

MIDTOWN & THE THEATER DISTRICT

B. SMITH'S, 771 Eighth Ave., at 47th St. Tel. 247-2222.

Cover girl–turned–restaurateur Barbara Smith attracts a stunning, stylish, multiethnic crowd to the bar of B. Smith's Restaurant. Lots of show-business folk gather here.

THE BLUE BAR, at the Algonquin Hotel, 59 West 44th St. Tel. 840-6800.

Although recently ensconced in slightly larger quarters, this may be the most petite, chummy lounge in Manhattan—you'll surely be privy to every conversation. Here, too, you'll find celebrities, often itinerant actors or authors from Britain.

CAFE NICOLE, at the Novotel Hotel, 226 West 52nd St. Tel. 765-4989.

If you'd like to combine a spectacular view with a view of celebrities, then try Café Nicole, which is blessed with a commanding view east and downtown on Broadway from its seventh-floor, glass-enclosed lounge; for city watching, it's hard to beat the outdoor terrace, open in warm weather. A pianist performs six nights a week, and the cuisine (American with a European slant) at breakfast, lunch, brunch, and dinner is excellent here, too.

CLARKE'S BAR, 915 Third Ave., at 55th St. Tel. 759-1650.

✪ Only the noncognoscenti persist in calling Clarke's— incorrectly—P. J. Clarke's. This is truly a landmark and one that began its life as a workingman's saloon—and still looks the part. Now tout le monde turns up there. (Jackie Onassis likes the burgers.) The time to go is late (well after midnight), in time to catch the celebrity flow. Incidentally, sequences for that classic film *The Lost Weekend*, starring Ray Milland, were filmed here.

THE GOLD ROOM, in the Helmsley Palace Hotel, 455 Madison Ave., at 50th St. Tel. 888-7000.

The Gold Room is perhaps the most splendid cocktail lounge in New York. Designed by Stanford White, the two-story room with vaulted ceilng has decorative panels based on the 15th-century Luca della Robbia panels in the cathedral of Florence, and demilunette paintings and stained-glass windows by artist John La Farge. And the drinks and hors d'oeuvres, brought round from 5pm to 1am nightly aren't bad, either. You can have tea, too, in The Gold Room from 2 to 5:30 every afternoon.

HARRY'S NEW YORK BAR, in the New York Helmsley Hotel, 212 East 42nd St. Tel. 490-8900.

Harry's, a convivial spot for a drink, is madly popular during the 5 to 7pm Happy Hour, when they offer a free selection of hors d'oeuvres—shrimp, hot appetizers, and the like—with drinks.

PEACOCK ALLEY, in the Waldorf-Astoria Hotel, Park Ave. at 50th St. Tel. 872-4895.

★ Nostalgia reigns in Peacock Alley, a posh watering spot in the Waldorf-Astoria. Cole Porter's splendid Louis XVI–style Steinway piano is played nightly and at the fabulous Sunday brunch, by leading pop/jazz pianists. Gourmet-inspired French Provincial fare adds to the enjoyment.

SAMPLINGS BAR, at the Holiday Inn Crowne Plaza, Broadway at 49th St. Tel. 977-4000, ext. 6820.

Samplings, at the Holiday Inn Crowne Plaza, offers a stunning view of the Broadway scene; the multitiered room offers drinks and a moderately priced grazing-style menu of light tavern fare.

SARDI'S, 234 West 44th St. Tel. 221-8440.

Almost all visitors to the Big Apple find themselves at a Broadway theater on at least one evening. The most obvious suggestion for a nightcap is Sardi's, a landmark institution in the area. A contingent of authentic Broadway personalities sometimes still arrives after the last curtain, around 11:30pm, and the supreme vantage point for checking all comings and goings is the bar, just inside the entrance. Continental cuisine is also available daily from noon until 1am.

UPPER EAST SIDE

ELAINE'S, 1703 Second Ave. between 88th and 89th Sts. Tel. 534-8103.

Elaine's is an old-timer, famous for its celebrity clientele—the people at the next table could easily be Joan Rivers, Woody Allen, or one of that crowd.

T.G.I. FRIDAY'S, 1152 First Ave., at 63rd St. Tel. 832-8512.

New York's singles bar scene is not quite the thing it once was, but some of the denizens of First Avenue in the 60s, where it all started, are still very popular. Friday's, perhaps the first of the bunch, has low lighting, a crowded bar, semioutdoor seating, good drinks, and some of the most solid food around, from about $6.95 to $16.

JIM MCMULLEN'S, 1341 Third Ave., at 76th St. Tel. 861-4700.

Another place to catch the celebrity scene is Jim McMullen's. Jim, a former model, has a huge crowd of buddies who hang out at the enormous bar in this art deco restaurant. It's always a party. The food is very good, too.

NEAR LINCOLN CENTER

THE GINGER MAN, 51 West 64th St. Tel. 874-5100.

A charming watering hole with period-piece fixtures, this is an oldtime favorite, owned by Michael and Patrick O'Neal.

THE SALOON, 1920 Broadway, at 64th St. Tel. 874-1500.

This huge restaurant with a bar and, in summer, a sidewalk café has enjoyable food, good drinks, and roller-skating waiters to serve them all.

THE UPPER WEST SIDE

BAHAMA MAMA, 2628 Broadway, at 100th St. Tel. 866-7660.

Uptown, the mood's always upbeat at Bahama Mama. Bask in this brashly colorful oasis and sample some of the island rums imported from such far-flung locales as Brazil and Jamaica. Then chow down on the restaurant's hot island food.

THE FIREHOUSE, 522 Columbus Ave. at 85th St. Tel. 362-3004 or 787-FIRE.

Firehouse paraphernalia adorns the walls and also refers to the spiciness of the inexpensive food, particularly the Buffalo Chicken Wings and the European Pan Pizzas with exotic toppings, which the mixed crowd (mainly 25 to 35) often doesn't wait for a table to enjoy. The cheap beers attract rowdy softball teams who come to celebrate after a game, and on Thursday, Friday, and Saturday nights the management turns the CD jukebox way up.

BIMINI TWIST, 345 Amsterdam Ave., at 76th St. Tel. 362-1260.

The house drink, Bimini Twist, is made with cranberry juice, pineapple juice, Triple Sec, and lemon, lime, and orange slices, and is $4.75. The decor might be called Hemingway-esque—fishing tackle, fishing photos, and a tarpaulin over the bar. (Hemingway, who had a home in Bimini, you may remember, was an avid fisherman.) The food is American bistro fare. The lights are low, the bar crowd lively, and you can play backgammon. Many people tend to pop in after concerts at The Beacon Theater (74th and Broadway). Open until midnight.

HI-LIFE BAR AND GRILL, 477 Amsterdam Ave. Tel. 787-7199.

Miami Beach—circa 1962—meets Manhattan at this clever, kitschy restaurant and watering hole that's always packed, especially in summer, when tables and crowds occupy the sidewalk. **Admission:** No cover, no minimum.

LUCY'S RESTAURANT, 503 Columbus Ave., near 85th St. Tel. 787-3009.

Surfers and other assorted beach bums might want to stop by Lucy's for a Shark Attack. For $6 you get vodka, lemonade, and grenadine "garnished with a shark." This is just one of the beachy concoctions the bartender mixes up, and by the time you've had a few, you will probably feel right at home with the California theme—surfer murals, surfboards, surfer photographs, lots of aqua. The crowd is 24 to 30 and ethnically mixed, the bar almost always packed, the mood upbeat and friendly, and the decibel level often high. It's open until 4am, there's Mexican food in back, and you can tote home a choice of eight different Lucy's T-shirts and 10 different-colored hats.

PERFECT TOMMMY'S, 511 Amsterdam Ave. Tel. 787-7474.

No, that's not a typo in the name. That's just the Perfect Tommmy's attitude—relaxed, irreverent, and slightly off-center. A young crowd of loud students and professionals have made this the Upper West Side's new mixing-and-meeting mecca. The interior is just basic black and neon; the real attractions are the raucous hordes and equally boisterous bartenders. **Admission:** No cover or minimum.

COCKTAILS WITH A VIEW

CITY LIGHTS BAR, and the adjoining Hors d'Oeuvrerie restaurant at Windows on the World, atop the World Trade Center. Tel. 938-1111.

The most romantic spot in town for drinks and music? That could well be the City Lights Bar and the adjoining Hors d'Oeuvrerie restaurant at Windows on the World. There's piano music from 4:30 to 7:30pm; then a three-piece combo from 7:30pm until closing, either for dancing or listening; with marvelous international hors d'oeuvres for nibbling and a billion city lights for backdrop. (There's a no-jeans dress code.) On Sunday it's tea dancing from 4pm on. **Prices:** $3.50 cover after 7:30pm.

RAINBOW PROMENADE, on the 65th floor of 30 Rockefeller Plaza. Tel. 632-5000, or 632-5100.

In a class by itself is the Rainbow Promenade, just outside the fabulous, recently restored Rainbow Room, and around the bend from Rainbow and Stars, the complex's intimate nightclub. A sophisticated crowd will be drinking champagne by the glass, or 1930s style cocktails, or grazing on precious "little meals." Open until 1am Monday to Saturday, 11pm on Sunday, and for Sunday brunch from 11:30am until 2:30pm. It's also great for a theatrical after-theater stop. No reservations required.

TOP OF THE TOWER, at the top of the Beekman Tower, 3 Mitchell Place, First Ave. near 49th St. Tel. 355-7300.

Top of the Tower has breathtaking views along with songs and music at the piano. The entertainment is from 9pm to 1am Tuesday to Saturday. **Prices:** No cover.

THE VIEW, on the 48th and 49th floors of the Marriott Marquis Hotel, 1535 Broadway at 45th St. Tel. 398-1900.

If the room is spinning before you've even had your first drink, it's likely you're at The View, New York's only revolving restaurant and lounge. Relax and watch as the city lights seem to spin around you; it takes about 60 minutes for the room to make one complete rotation. In The View Lounge, open nightly, there's live entertainment and dancing Friday and Saturday from 10pm to 2am. No T-shirts or sneakers allowed. (For information on The View Restaurant, see Chapter 6.) **Price:** $5 cover during entertainment.

4. MORE ENTERTAINMENT

TELEVISION Tickets to a limited number of television shows filmed or taped in New York are free and are often available at the offices of the **Visitors and Convention Bureau,** 2 Columbus Circle; pick them up as early in the morning as possible.

But for the most important shows, advance planning is necessary. For "Late Night with David Letterman," for example, send a postcard to Letterman, NBC-TV, 30 Rockefeller Plaza, New York,

NY 10112. Lotteries are held every four months. Or try your luck at getting standby tickets, often distributed Tuesday to Friday at 8:15am at the studio. Write to NBC, as well, for the Phil Donahue show, two to five months in advance. Securing tickets for NBC's "Saturday Night Live" is an art: Send a postcard in August of the year before your trip; lottery winners get tickets, either to the regular show or to the dress rehearsals. Standby tickets are distributed at ABC-TV, Columbus Avenue and 67th Street, weekdays at 8am for "Live with Regis and Kathie Lee"; or send a postcard to "Live" Tickets, Ansonia Station, P.O. Box 777, New York, NY 10023-0777, at least eight months in advance. For the Geraldo Rivera show, send a stamped, self-addressed envelope to "Geraldo" Tickets, 524 West 57th St., New York, NY 10019, six weeks before your trip.

You will be well entertained and educated by taking the 55-minute **NBC Studio Tour** of its television and radio facilities. In summer, tours leave from 30 Rockefeller Plaza every 15 minutes from 9:30am to 4pm (early arrival is advised) every day; admission is $7.75. Children under 6 are not admitted. Phone 664-4000 for information.

CINEMA   New York provides endless opportunities for dedicated film buffs. In addition to scores of first-run movie houses, there are any number of alternative movie houses and screening rooms all around town. While admission to first-run theaters in New York is now $7 and $7.50, alternative theaters usually charge somewhat less. Revivals, documentary films, and avant-garde works are shown regularly at **Theatre 80,** 80 St. Marks (tel. 254-7400); **Film Forum,** 209 W. Houston St. (tel. 727-8110); the **Millennium Film Workshop,** 66 E. Fourth St. (tel. 673-0090); and the **Anthology Film Archives,** 32 Second Ave., near Second St. (tel. 505-5181). Everybody's favorite "revival house" is the **Museum of Modern Art,** 11 W. 53rd St. (tel. 708-9490), where films are included in the price of admission; here's your chance to catch up with Myrna Loy or Norma Shearer or the early Marx Brothers. Films are also free for museum-goers at the **Whitney Museum of American Art,** Madison Ave. and 75th St. (tel. 570-0537), long known for its "New American Film Series," featuring works by creative newcomers. Vintage films can be seen (for a fee) at the Summer Film Festival, at the **Metropolitan Museum of Art,** Fifth Ave. at 82nd St. (tel. 570-3717). **The Film Society of Lincoln Center** has a splendid new art theater: The Walter Reade Theater, 70 Lincoln Center Plaza, 165 W. 66th St. (tel. 875-5610), showing many outstanding works by international filmmakers.

Want more? **Columbia University,** Broadway and 116th St. (tel. 854-3574), obliges with free films on Tuesday and Thursday nights at 9pm in summer at Lewisohn Hall on campus. The **French Institute/Alliance Française (FIAF),** 22 E. 60th St. (tel. 355-6100), screens French films with English subtitles most Wednesdays (four showings) at its splendid performing arts center, Florence Gould Hall, 55 E. 59th St. (For performing arts events, call Gould Hall box office, 355-6160; for general information about the programs at FIAF, including photographic exhibitions and lectures, call the main number, 355-6100.)

Then there's the **Joseph Papp Public Theater,** 425 Lafayette St. (tel. 598-7150), which, in addition to featuring live theater, screens very special films most days of the week. And you can catch films by renowned Japanese filmmakers from September to June at the **Japan**

Society, 333 E. 47th St. (tel. 752-3015). Free films are presented at branches of the **New York Public Library;** in the midtown area, **Donnell Library Center,** 20 W. 53rd St. (tel. 621-0618) is the name to remember.

To find out where the movies, first-run and revival, are playing, consult the local papers or *New York Magazine* or *The New Yorker,* both of which give capsule reviews. If you like playing with a touch-tone phone, call 777-FILM, a free call that provides computerized movie information.

INDEX

GENERAL INFORMATION

SIGHTS & ATTRACTIONS

ACCOMMODATIONS

Key to Abbreviations: *B* = Budget; *E* = Expensive; *M* = Moderate; *VE* = Very expensive; * = Author's favorite; $ = Super-value choice.

RESTAURANTS

BY CUISINE

Key to Abbreviations: *B* = Budget; *E* = Expensive; *M* = Moderate; *VE* = Very expensive; *** = Author's favorite; *$* = Super-value choice.

Please Send Me the Books Checked Below

FROMMER'S COMPREHENSIVE GUIDES
(Guides listing facilities from budget to deluxe, with emphasis on the medium-priced)

	Retail Price	Code		Retail Price	Code
☐ Acapulco/Ixtapa/Taxco 1993–94	$15.00	C120	☐ Jamaica/Barbados 1993–94	$15.00	C105
☐ Alaska 1990–91	$15.00	C001	☐ Japan 1992–93	$19.00	C020
☐ Arizona 1993–94	$18.00	C101	☐ Morocco 1992–93	$18.00	C021
☐ Australia 1992–93	$18.00	C002	☐ Nepal 1992–93	$18.00	C038
☐ Austria 1993–94	$19.00	C119	☐ New England 1993	$17.00	C114
☐ Austria/Hungary 1991–92	$15.00	C003	☐ New Mexico 1993–94	$15.00	C117
☐ Belgium/Holland/ Luxembourg 1993–94	$18.00	C106	☐ New York State 1992– 93	$19.00	C025
☐ Bermuda/Bahamas 1992–93	$17.00	C005	☐ Northwest 1991–92	$17.00	C026
			☐ Portugal 1992–93	$16.00	C027
☐ Brazil, 3rd Edition	$20.00	C111	☐ Puerto Rico 1993–94	$15.00	C103
☐ California 1993	$18.00	C112	☐ Puerto Vallarta/ Manzanillo/ Guadalajara 1992–93	$14.00	C028
☐ Canada 1992–93	$18.00	C009			
☐ Caribbean 1993	$18.00	C102			
☐ Carolinas/Georgia 1992–93	$17.00	C034	☐ Scandinavia 1993–94	$19.00	C118
			☐ Scotland 1992–93	$16.00	C040
☐ Colorado 1993–94	$16.00	C100	☐ Skiing Europe 1989– 90	$15.00	C030
☐ Cruises 1993–94	$19.00	C107			
☐ DE/MD/PA & NJ Shore 1992–93	$19.00	C012	☐ South Pacific 1992–93	$20.00	C031
			☐ Spain 1993–94	$19.00	C115
☐ Egypt 1990–91	$15.00	C013	☐ Switzerland/ Liechtenstein 1992–93	$19.00	C032
☐ England 1993	$18.00	C109			
☐ Florida 1993	$18.00	C104	☐ Thailand 1992–93	$20.00	C033
☐ France 1992–93	$20.00	C017	☐ U.S.A. 1993–94	$19.00	C116
☐ Germany 1993	$19.00	C108	☐ Virgin Islands 1992–93	$13.00	C036
☐ Italy 1993	$19.00	C113	☐ Virginia 1992–93	$14.00	C037
			☐ Yucatán 1993–94	$18.00	C110

FROMMER'S $-A-DAY GUIDES
(Guides to low-cost tourist accommodations and facilities)

	Retail Price	Code		Retail Price	Code
☐ Australia on $45 1993–94	$18.00	D102	☐ Israel on $45 1993–94	$18.00	D101
			☐ Mexico on $50 1993	$19.00	D105
☐ Costa Rica/ Guatemala/Belize on $35 1993–94	$17.00	D108	☐ New York on $70 1992–93	$16.00	D016
			☐ New Zealand on $45 1993–94	$18.00	D103
☐ Eastern Europe on $25 1991–92	$17.00	D005			
			☐ Scotland/Wales on $50 1992–93	$18.00	D019
☐ England on $60 1993	$18.00	D107			
☐ Europe on $45 1993	$19.00	D106	☐ South America on $40 1993–94	$19.00	D109
☐ Greece on $45 1993– 94	$19.00	D100			
			☐ Turkey on $40 1992– 93	$22.00	D023
☐ Hawaii on $75 1993	$19.00	D104			
☐ India on $40 1992–93	$20.00	D010	☐ Washington, D.C. on $40 1992–93	$17.00	D024
☐ Ireland on $40 1992– 93	$17.00	D011			

FROMMER'S CITY $-A-DAY GUIDES
(Pocket-size guides with an emphasis on low-cost tourist accommodations and facilities)

	Retail Price	Code		Retail Price	Code
☐ Berlin on $40 1992–93	$12.00	D002	☐ Madrid on $50 1992– 93	$13.00	D014
☐ Copenhagen on $50 1992–93	$12.00	D003			
			☐ Paris on $45 1992–93	$12.00	D018
☐ London on $45 1992– 93	$12.00	D013	☐ Stockholm on $50 1992–93	$13.00	D022

FROMMER'S TOURING GUIDES
(Color-illustrated guides that include walking tours, cultural and historic sights, and practical information)

	Retail Price	Code		Retail Price	Code
☐ Amsterdam	$11.00	T001	☐ New York	$11.00	T008
☐ Barcelona	$14.00	T015	☐ Rome	$11.00	T010
☐ Brazil	$11.00	T003	☐ Scotland	$10.00	T011
☐ Florence	$ 9.00	T005	☐ Sicily	$15.00	T017
☐ Hong Kong/Singapore/ Macau	$11.00	T006	☐ Thailand	$13.00	T012
			☐ Tokyo	$15.00	T016
☐ Kenya	$14.00	T018	☐ Venice	$ 9.00	T014
☐ London	$13.00	T007			

FROMMER'S FAMILY GUIDES

	Retail Price	Code		Retail Price	Code
☐ California with Kids	$17.00	F001	☐ San Francisco with Kids	$17.00	F004
☐ Los Angeles with Kids	$17.00	F002			
☐ New York City with Kids	$18.00	F003	☐ Washington, D.C. with Kids	$17.00	F005

FROMMER'S CITY GUIDES
(Pocket-size guides to sightseeing and tourist accommodations and facilities in all price ranges)

	Retail Price	Code		Retail Price	Code
☐ Amsterdam 1993–94	$13.00	S110	☐ Minneapolis/St. Paul, 3rd Edition	$13.00	S119
☐ Athens, 9th Edition	$13.00	S114	☐ Montréal/Québec City 1993–94	$13.00	S125
☐ Atlanta 1993–94	$13.00	S112			
☐ Atlantic City/Cape May 1991–92	$ 9.00	S004	☐ New Orleans 1993–94	$13.00	S103
☐ Bangkok 1992–93	$13.00	S005	☐ New York 1993	$13.00	S120
☐ Barcelona/Majorca/ Minorca/Ibiza 1993–94	$13.00	S115	☐ Orlando 1993	$13.00	S101
			☐ Paris 1993–94	$13.00	S109
☐ Berlin 1993–94	$13.00	S116	☐ Philadelphia 1993–94	$13.00	S113
☐ Boston 1993–94	$13.00	S117	☐ Rio 1991–92	$ 9.00	S029
☐ Cancún/Cozumel/ Yucatán 1991–92	$ 9.00	S010	☐ Rome 1993–94	$13.00	S111
			☐ Salt Lake City 1991– 92	$ 9.00	S031
☐ Chicago 1993–94	$13.00	S122	☐ San Diego 1993–94	$13.00	S107
☐ Denver/Boulder/ Colorado Springs 1990–91	$ 8.00	S012	☐ San Francisco 1993	$13.00	S104
			☐ Santa Fe/Taos/ Albuquerque 1993–94	$13.00	S108
☐ Dublin 1993–94	$13.00	S128	☐ Seattle/Portland 1992– 93	$12.00	S035
☐ Hawaii 1992	$12.00	S014			
☐ Hong Kong 1992–93	$12.00	S015	☐ St. Louis/Kansas City 1993–94	$13.00	S127
☐ Honolulu/Oahu 1993	$13.00	S106	☐ Sydney 1993–94	$13.00	S129
☐ Las Vegas 1993–94	$13.00	S121	☐ Tampa/St. Petersburg 1993–94	$13.00	S105
☐ Lisbon/Madrid/Costa del Sol 1991–92	$ 9.00	S017			
☐ London 1993	$13.00	S100	☐ Tokyo 1992–93	$13.00	S039
☐ Los Angeles 1993–94	$13.00	S123	☐ Toronto 1993–94	$13.00	S126
☐ Madrid/Costa del Sol 1993–94	$13.00	S124	☐ Vancouver/Victoria 1990–91	$ 8.00	S041
☐ Mexico City/Acapulco 1991–92	$ 9.00	S020	☐ Washington, D.C. 1993	$13.00	S102
☐ Miami 1993–94	$13.00	S118			